Don't wait.
Get a test date **now!**
Register at
takethegre.com

And you can retake the test about every **30 days**.

MONTH
30

Plus, you can save because the test **costs less**.

$

DISCARDED BY
MACPHÁIDÍN LIBRARY

Start **preparing** now.
Get official
GRE Top Test Tips
FREE!

For graduate school. For business school. For your future.

D0218455

Listening. Learning. Leading.®

2014 EDITION

BEST
GRADUATE
SCHOOLS

Business • Education
Engineering • Health & Medicine • Law
Social Sciences • Sciences

HOW TO ORDER: Additional copies of *U.S.News & World Report*'s *Best Graduate Schools 2014* are available for purchase at *www.usnews.com/grad2014* or by calling (800) 836-6397. To order custom reprints, please call (877) 652-5295 or E-mail *usnews@wrightsmedia.com*. For permission to republish articles, data, or other content from this book, E-mail *permissions@usnews.com*.

CONTENTS

Mykel Green, an engineering student at Georgia Tech

Kaleigh LaRiche, in teacher ed at the University of Akron

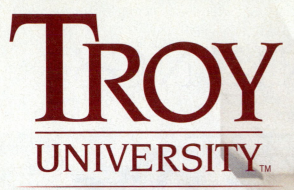

THE RANKINGS

University of Pennsylvania Law School, No. 7

@ USNEWS.COM / EDUCATION

Prospective graduate students researching their options will find the **U.S. News** *website (home of the* **Best Graduate Schools** *and* **Best Colleges** *rankings) full of tips on everything from choosing the right school to landing the most generous scholarships. Here's a sampling:*

Morse Code Blog
usnews.com/morsecode

Go inside the rankings with Director of Data Research Bob Morse, the mastermind behind them. Morse explains how we rank graduate programs and keeps you up to date on all the commentary and controversy, such as reactions to our new rankings of online degree programs and the new, more detailed way law schools report graduates' employment statistics.

M.B.A. Admissions Blog
usnews.com/mbaadmissions

Get admissions advice from blogger Stacy Blackman, a business school specialist with degrees from Wharton and Kellogg and coauthor of *The MBA Application Roadmap: The Essential Guide to Getting into a Top Business School*. Learn how to master M.B.A. essays, prepare for interviews, and pay for business school.

Online Education
usnews.com/online

Want to get that M.B.A. without spending time in the classroom? See our new rankings of the best online degree programs in business, education, engineering, computer information technology, and nursing. And read time-management and funding tips from students who have completed online degree programs.

Law Admissions Blog
usnews.com/lawadmissions

Get the lowdown on admissions from blogger Shawn P. O'Connor, an attorney who is an honors grad of Harvard Law School and Harvard Business School and is founder and CEO of Stratus Prep, a New York City-based test prep and admissions counseling firm. Learn how to do your best on the LSAT, determine the value of a dual J.D./M.B.A., and examine potential career paths.

World's Best Universities
usnews.com/worldsbest

Compare schools across borders—and see how U.S. institutions stack up—with our rankings of the top 400 universities worldwide, as well as global rankings by subject area (arts and humanities, engineering and technology, life sciences, natural sciences, and social sciences) and geographic location (Asia and Latin America).

Paying for Graduate School
usnews.com/payforgrad

Find tips and tools for financing your education, including the latest guidance on scholarships, grants, and loans. Read about your borrowing options, including interest-free loans and loan forgiveness, and repayment assistance programs for people who work in public service, nonprofits, or underserved areas.

U.S. News Graduate School Compass
usnews.com/gradcompass

Gain access to the *U.S. News* Graduate School Compass, a wealth of searchable data with tools and an expanded directory of programs. (To get a 25 percent discount, subscribe at *www.usnews.com/compassdiscount*.) Curious how much you could make coming out of law school? Which medical residency programs are most popular? Check the Graduate School Compass.

A Sharp New Focus on Job Skills

Postgraduate programs are getting a lot more practical. BY CHRISTOPER J. GEARON

Back when he was mulling an advanced degree in microbiology, Kyle Mak of Thousand Oaks, Calif., got some advice from his older brother, who had preceded him on that path: Think *really* hard before investing 10 years of your life only to come out buried in debt. So Mak, 26, chose a more direct and less costly route. Last May, he earned a two-year professional science master's degree in bioscience from California's Keck Graduate Institute, part of the Claremont Colleges consortium. Then Mak hit the ground running—straight into a job as a supply chain manager at biotech giant Amgen, which manufactures medicines, making nearly $90,000.

The professional science master's, or PSM, got its start in 1997 as a way to better (and more rapidly) equip students with much-needed skills in the science, technology, engineering, and math (STEM) fields. A decade and a half later, nearly 300 PSM programs are offered by KGI and 128 other institutions, including Pennsylvania State University, Creighton University in Omaha, Neb., Cornell University in Ithaca, N.Y., and the University of Florida. The degree combines intensive study in science or math with courses in management, policy, or law and emphasizes writing, project management, and other industry-sought skills. Because internships and capstone projects guided by mentors in industry are a key part of the curriculum, companies "use these programs to screen prospective employees," notes James Sterling, KGI's vice president for academic affairs. "Students are getting great jobs with this."

Shorter and less of a drain

Tuition runs between $10,000 and $40,000 annually; with scholarships, Mak's two-year degree totaled $40,000, which he was able to manage without borrowing. Grads fetch salaries equivalent to what a master's in science would get, says Sterling, "but they are on a trajectory to leadership, and their salaries are increasing substantially and quickly."

The recent rise of the PSM degree reflects a new reality in postgraduate education: Recession-wary students have become significantly more pragmatic. With traditional programs still skewed toward producing future academics, prospective students aren't buying in as they once did; after years of growth, new enrollment in graduate programs dropped in 2011 for the second consecutive year.

"We're seeing people asking some very hard questions about value," says Debra Stewart, president of the Council of Graduate Schools. They are scrutinizing offer packages, calculating the debt levels they would have to assume, and weighing costs against potential earnings. And they "are looking for something different than in-depth scholarship," says Kathleen Scott Gibson, assistant dean of the graduate school and College of Arts and Sciences

Meredith Aronson chose Georgetown's professional studies master's in sports industry management.

at Indiana's Valparaiso University. "They are looking for skills."

An advanced degree that delivers on that score is more important in many fields than ever. At one time, a grad degree was an "inconsequential afterthought to the B.A.," says Anthony Carnevale, director of Georgetown University's Center on Education and the Workforce. "Today, it's become the engine on the train." Between 2010 and 2020, about 2.6 million new and replacement jobs are expected to require an advanced degree. That's an increase of about 22 percent and 20 percent for jobs requiring a master's and doctorate, respectively.

The problem is, says Carnevale, that "there is a disconnect" between what graduate schools tend to produce—the next generation of academics, steeped in research and toiling largely in isolation—and what employers seek. In a December report, the American Chemical Society concluded that "current educational opportunities for graduate students, viewed on balance as a system, do not provide sufficient preparation for their careers after graduate school."

Yes, people with Ph.D. degrees can "provide leadership to drive scientific discovery, inspire inspiration, and solve challenges," says Ron Townsend, executive vice president of global laboratory operations for Battelle Memorial Institute, which manages several federal national laboratories and hires thousands of people with grad degrees. But they generally lack key people skills needed for immediate success on the job. "You're preparing to be a monk" at a time when employers want people adept at collaboration, teamwork, and project management, and who know how to communicate and problem-solve, Carnevale says. To that wish list, Townsend would add the ability to explain technical topics to non-techies and to think and act like an entrepreneur.

To be sure, professional schools in law, business, and education have made skill-building through field experience much more of a priority in recent years. Now, the rest of the ivory tower is awakening to the need. "The world is changing, and deans of graduate schools are looking at career development," says Patrick Osmer, dean of Ohio State University's graduate school. "Now the focus has to be on jobs, which is okay."

Engineering programs like those at Georgia Tech, the University of Cincinnati, and Massachusetts Institute of Technology, for example, are offering graduate students co-op and other experiential learning opportunities (story, Page 42). Short of getting a two-year M.B.A., many would-be business magnates are opting for a master's of entrepreneurship that's focused tightly on the ins and outs of launching a start-up and entails producing a real product and business plan. Some 70 such programs are offered now, up from 25 in 2003-04, according to the business school accrediting body. The University of Michigan's new entrepreneurship curriculum, a joint venture between the business and engineering schools, should really boost his "potential for success," predicts Steven Sherman, 23, who entered the 12-month program with

"We're seeing people asking some very hard questions about value."

a bachelor's in chemical engineering and a master's in energy systems engineering. As part of his coursework, he's launching two businesses: a solar leasing outfit that takes high upfront costs out of residential solar energy and a firm selling a home energy monitor to cost-minded consumers.

Meanwhile, schools from State U. to the Ivy League are launching programs similar to the professional science master's in all sorts of other disciplines. "Professional master's programs are one of the fastest-growing areas of education," Osmer says. The hallmarks, as with the professional science master's programs, include strategically using professionals as adjunct faculty (as well as on-the-ground industry contacts), an emphasis on internships (often paid), and capstone projects. Because these tracks may be shorter than traditional programs, they often come with lower price tags.

"The program allowed me to get in the kind of job I have now more quickly," says Meredith Aronson, 24, of the master's in professional studies in sports industry management she completed in December at Georgetown University after weighing similar offerings at New York University and Columbia. Aronson, of Arlington, Va., now works for the President's Council on Fitness, Sports & Nutrition's President's Challenge program; she started there as an intern while still in school. Georgetown's program is one of eight professional master's degrees introduced over the past six years within Georgetown's School of Continuing Studies (SCS). The 16-month curriculum exposed Aronson to adjunct faculty working for such organizations as the U.S. Olympic Committee, the State Department's SportsUnited program, the National Basketball Association, and the Washington Nationals baseball franchise. Coursework included sports marketing, ethics, and sports finance, and a capstone project on addressing obesity and physical inactivity in young people with school-based solutions.

"You've got 10 people who have worked in the industry who you can potentially use as references," says Walter Rankin, interim dean of Georgetown's SCS, whose other offerings include professional master's degrees in journalism, public relations, corporate communications, technology management, and real estate. Rankin notes that the $27,000 price tag is slightly more than half of the traditional Georgetown master's.

All of Valparaiso's master's programs take "a hands-on, practical approach," says Gibson. Valpo's 18-month master's in arts and entertainment administration, for example, is intended to provide artists or performers with marketing and business skills and people with a business background a foundation in the arts. Every program requires an internship or practicum. Most grad students get a grounding in career opportunities outside of academia, how to use an E-portfolio in the job search, and job-hunting etiquette.

Ph.D. candidates, too, are being given much more exposure to the real world. Keck Graduate Institute uses the professional science master's as a platform for candidates pursuing its Ph.D. in the applied life sciences, and offers a separate skills-focused postdoc professional master's degree. Some universities are infusing experiential learning into their Ph.D. programs. At the University of Tennessee-Knoxville, energy science and engineering Ph.D. student Melissa Allen, 46, is studying how to take global climate, weather, and air-quality data and model the impact on communities for planning purposes. At the same time, she is applying that knowledge as an intern at Oak Ridge National Laboratory, getting practice in collaboration, communication, project management, and delivering outcomes on budget. And whereas many Ph.D. students huddle only occasionally with a dissertation advisor, "I have four mentors," she says. Engineering doctoral students at Purdue University get a shot at a program that supports them in coming up with a business plan and commercializing their research. The University of California-Davis offers science and engineering Ph.D. students and postdocs the option of coursework and a certificate in business development.

Beyond workplace skills, experts say, grad students need much better career guidance. A Council of Graduate Schools commission issued a report last April revealing that just one third of students felt they had entered grad school understanding their career options. Most end up relying on faculty for career advice, but faculty members typically are not well-versed in paths outside academia. The report recommended beefing up career counseling services; connecting students with alumni; and adding opportunities to engage with professionals in industry and government. The report was "a wake-up call" says Debasish Dutta, graduate college dean at the University of Illinois at Urbana-Champaign. "Universities need to prepare graduate students for the full spectrum of careers in the economy."

More help mapping the paths

Some universities are ahead of the curve. Michigan State, for example, has hired a career services officer specifically to assist graduate students with landing nonacademic positions—to help English doctoral students find spots in company communications departments, say, and historians get work in a preservation society. A robust "career services" website allows students to conduct job searches, perform career self-assessments, and build an E-portfolio. The school also brings industry scientists to campus for career chats. Meanwhile, Ph.D. candidates who do want to teach can take a yearlong prep course in the art of managing and inspiring a class. Princeton is stressing counseling focused on developing professional skills; connecting students to alumni; bringing employers to campus for panel discussions, networking, and job fairs; and workshops on résumé writing, job search strategies, negotiation, personal branding, and career transitions.

In another practical step, some schools are slashing the time to a Ph.D. Stanford University, for example, recently encouraged its humanities departments to

make doctoral degrees achievable in five years. At the University of Colorado-Boulder, the Ph.D. program in English is being reworked to reduce the time to degree from as many as nine years to five. "Our goal is to move them through," says William Kuskin, chair of the English department. A new four-year German studies doctorate that Boulder plans to introduce will aim specifically at putting grads into global business, diplomacy, and arts jobs as well as education positions. "Germany is one of Colorado's largest international trading partners," says John Stevenson, dean of the graduate school. "This is fertile ground."

To a growing number of people seeking postgraduate education, the most practical route of all is not even a graduate degree. After getting laid off as a banker several years ago, Ian Karakas of Bradenton, Fla., sat for the Graduate Management Admission Test, but decided he "really didn't see the payoff" in getting an M.B.A. Karakas, 49, decided it would be a far better financial move to enroll in a 10-month $4,300 certificate program in medical coding and billing at Manatee Technical Institute. He now works at an orthopedic practice, making a third more than his previous pay, and next plans to get an associate's degree in health information management, where the average salary now runs about $65,000. "For the first time in my life, I feel like I have a decent career path," he says. Of the 1 million certificates awarded annually by community colleges and other career and technical training providers to recognize mastery of specific job skills, notes Carnevale, 15 percent go to people who have at least a bachelor's degree. ●

Instead of a Ph.D., Kyle Mak pursued a two-year professional bioscience master's at Keck Graduate Institute and immediately landed a job at Amgen.

///////////////

Check out the complete *U.S. News* rankings of graduate programs, and find out everything you need to know about applying to schools and financing an advanced degree, at **www.usnews.com/grad.**

The Virtual Path

Hundreds of colleges and universities now offer grad degrees online. BY KELSEY SHEEHY

Graduate school was always part of the puzzle for Jefferson Macias, 36, a supply chain manager for Intel in Tucson, Ariz., when he started planning his move. But finding an M.B.A. program that meshed with his roles as a manager, husband, and father meant thinking outside of the brick-and-mortar box. While a part-time master's program would allow him to keep working—a priority for Macias—it also limited his options to schools near home. A traditional part-time program also would mean spending nights and weekends in a classroom instead of with his wife and two kids, Jackson and then-newborn daughter Rowan. So Macias somewhat skeptically started looking into an online M.B.A. "I wasn't entirely sold on it," he says. But he started noticing many well-known schools "coming onto the scene, and that's what started to really get me interested." Macias signed on to start Washington State University's online M.B.A. program in the fall of 2010 and graduated in December 2012.

Hundreds of colleges and universities now offer graduate programs entirely or partly online, including such established public and private institutions as the University of Southern California, New York's Columbia University, and Arizona State and Pennsylvania State universities. Each of those schools earned high marks for one or more of its graduate programs in the new *U.S. News* rankings

Students can benefit at work and at school by turning classroom theory into workplace results.

of the best online degree programs in business, computer information technology, education, engineering, and nursing (Page 98). Washington State University came in first among the online M.B.A. options. For-profit schools such as the University of Phoenix, DeVry University, and the American Public University System also factor into the mix of choices. In some cases, students can earn a degree without setting foot on a physical campus; others blend virtual instruction with in-person residencies that can range from a weekend seminar to several weeks abroad. The program Macias enrolled in at

WSU can be completed entirely online, but starting this summer, students also will have the option to participate in a 10-day international trip to visit businesses in China and Switzerland, for example.

Choosing the best path—public or private, for-profit or nonprofit, blended or 100 percent online—requires a lot of thought and research, and prospective students should consider a variety of factors before settling on a program. Chief among them, experts say: accreditation.

"I learned that it was essentially the gold standard of business education," says Macias of the stamp of approval by AACSB International–The Association to Advance Collegiate Schools of Business. "It really focused me in on a few key programs." While business students may be able to move up the ranks with an M.B.A. from an unaccredited school, employers may be wary of the merits of the degree. Professions that require state licensure, such as nursing, teaching, or counseling, often do not recognize degrees from programs that lack accreditation.

No business programs at the country's for-profit schools have AACSB accreditation currently, but they may be backed by another credentialing body, such as the Accreditation Council for Business Schools and Programs. Students considering a master's in nursing should look for a program accredited by either the Commission on Collegiate Nursing Education or the National League for Nursing Accrediting Commission. Accrediting bodies for disciplines such as education or engineering can vary by speciality.

Most colleges will tout the program's accreditation on their website, but students should do some legwork to ensure the credentials are legitimate. Some institutions list credentials from accrediting bodies that either don't exist or aren't seen as authoritative, warns Anne Johnson, director of Campus Progress, an advocacy group that promotes progressive policies on issues from healthcare to college affordability. Students can verify the accreditation of any graduate school on their radar using The College Navigator tool on the Department of Education's website (*nces.ed.gov/collegenavigator*).

Using this tool, students can also see graduation, retention, and student loan default rates for any given institution—which can tell them a lot about the quality of a program. Dismal completion rates, for instance, might clue students into subpar academic support services, and a high loan default rate can be a tipoff to poor financial aid counseling. Low employment rates after graduation may hint at an even larger issue—that the school is a "diploma mill," churning out graduates with degrees that carry little weight with employers because of low-quality curricula or lack of legitimate accreditation. Students should look for online programs that have 24-hour-a-day tech support, live tutoring, a digital library, and career services.

Academic reputation was a key consideration for Felipe Millon, 26, who earned an M.B.A. from Duke University's Fuqua School of Business, No. 11 in the *U.S. News* ranking of traditional business schools. Millon, then a strategy engineer at Lockheed Martin and now a manager with McMaster-Carr, an industrial supply company in Los Angeles, was "fairly certain" he wanted a full-time program, "so I was looking at your traditional top 20 schools," he says. But a coworker suggested he check out Duke's Cross Continent M.B.A. program, a hybrid of online courses and six two-week residencies in places such as Shanghai and Dubai aimed at honing students' global business skills.

"For me, it was a perfect combination," Millon says of his 20-month Fuqua stint. "It was a program that was designed for working professionals, with a very good global aspect to it." That global experience, which includes developing the networking skills required to collaborate with classmates in different time zones and hemispheres, can come in especially handy for students working (or hoping to work) for an international corporation.

As is true with traditional part-time graduate programs, people who pursue an online degree can often benefit both at work and in school by turning a classroom theory into workplace results. Licensed nurses pursuing a master's in their field can quickly see how well new patient care techniques work in practice, and business students studying new supply chain management and finance concepts can test them out almost immediately.

"I was able to take the learnings from a specific course, and immediately turn that into a competitive advantage at work," says Macias about his statistics class. "Other teams were asking me to do regression analysis and help with regression testing statistics," he recalls. "Once I was able to show them

what I was doing, I became instantly a much more valuable commodity." In fact, Macias was promoted in November 2012, a month before collecting his degree. "I was already a manager within the supply chain, but I really wanted to be a business architect," he says. Getting an M.B.A. "made me much more attractive to take a chance on for a higher-level position."

You don't need to work for a multinational corporation to benefit from the online degree format. Dalene Erickson, a daycare provider, earned her master's in early childhood education from the University of North Dakota without leaving her home (and her business) in Maryland. "It was online or nothing," says Erickson, 47, whose coursework started paying off right away. As word spread of her educational pursuits, the daycare operation's

waiting list lengthened.

While the parents of Erickson's charges seem indifferent to whether she earned her master's online or on campus, some employers are still leery of the quality of online degree programs. But that perception is gradually changing as more marquee names venture into the online learning arena, experts say. Macias says his own employer had no issue with his online degree, as long as it was from an accredited program. "I don't feel like in 15 years it's going to be as big of a deal as it may have been five years ago, or even is today," Macias says. That assumes, of course, that today's graduates go on to become the proof of the programs' value. ●

Plotting Your Payment Strategy

Potential sources of financial support range from your boss to Uncle Sam. BY MICHAEL MORELLA

Five years ago, when he was thinking about pursuing a Ph.D., Damien Frierson knew what he wanted to study—social work—and where he wanted to study it—Howard University in Washington, D.C.—but not where he would get the money. He'd already accumulated some debt from earning a bachelor's and two master's degrees and didn't want more. He also faced giving up the $72,000 he earned annually from his work as a program officer for the Corporation for National and Community Service in Washington and as a remote online instructor of African-American studies for Temple University in Philadelphia.

He sent in his application anyway and discovered something every prospective grad student should know: By applying very early (about three months before the deadline) he put himself on the radar of the social work school, which contacted him about applying separately for a generous fellowship. For three years, the award covered the full cost of Fri-

erson's tuition and provided a biweekly stipend totaling $18,000 a year for 15 hours per week of research, teaching, or other work. Frierson, 33, expects to graduate in 2014, and is covering the rest of the tab with his earnings as an assistant director of a domestic violence program in Philadelphia. "You really need to put funding somewhere at the forefront," he says. To do so, consider these smart strategies:

Get your boss to pay

Many companies looking to boost their collective skill set without hiring will sponsor all or part of an employee's graduate schooling through tuition reimbursement. Last year, 58 percent of the 550 employers responding to a survey by the Society for Human Resource Management offered some form of financial assistance for grad school. Most firms require that the coursework have some connection to the employee's job role—tax courses for an accountant, say, or computer science training for someone working in IT. And some companies require that the person work at the firm for a certain period after school or pay back part of the tuition. Up to $5,250 of such tuition assistance qualifies as a tax-free benefit.

Absent a formal tuition remission program, employees can often earn assistance if they demonstrate to the boss how a course of study could add value, says Peter Cappelli, director of the Center for Human Resources at the University of Pennsylvania's Wharton School. And many universities offer reimbursement programs for their own workers. For instance, full-time Duke University employees who meet certain requirements can receive up to $5,250 per year in

Howard student Damien Frierson, with coworker Rayna Gray, supports his Ph.D. studies by helping direct a domestic violence program in Philadelphia.

BRETT ZIEGLER FOR *USN&WR*

Cover up to 100% of graduate school costs.

HEALTH PROFESSIONS LOAN | LAW LOAN | MBA LOAN | GRADUATE LOAN

DISCOVER® | STUDENT LOANS

The cost of higher education shouldn't stand in the way of your success.
We're ready to help.

- Fixed or variable interest rates
- Zero fees
- 24/7 customer service

Learn More   **1-877-728-3030** 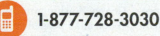 **DiscoverStudentLoans.com**

Please visit DiscoverStudentLoans.com for current terms and conditions.

Discover Student Loans are made by Discover Bank
©2013 Discover Bank, Member FDIC

tuition reimbursement to take classes at Duke or another accredited institution in North Carolina, as long as the course material relates to their work.

Secure a scholarship

Graduate programs typically award scholarships and fellowships based on merit. "It's going to vary from school to school and where that particular student sits in that applicant pool," says Joseph Russo, former director of student financial strategies at the University of Notre Dame in Indiana. At many schools, aid is given out by academic departments or the specific graduate school instead of a central financial aid office, so you may have to do some digging. "You might find information at the school's website, but don't trust that it is up to date or captures all of the potential opportunities," says Robert Schmansky, a financial planner in Detroit. A graduate admissions official or someone affiliated with your desired program can help you sort

59 Zero in on faculty who might take you on as an assistant.

through the options. Experts advise applying for funds as early as possible to ensure access to the full pot.

A number of private and public organizations also offer money for graduate school, though these fellowships are typically highly competitive. The Truman Scholarship Foundation, for instance, annually awards up to $30,000 to each of about 60 prospective grad students looking at public service fields from among an applicant pool of more than 600. Both Cornell (*www.gradschool.cornell.edu/fellowships*) and the University of California–Los Angeles (*www.gdnet.ucla.edu/asis/grapes/search.asp*) provide comprehensive online databases of awards across a range of fields.

Work for the school

Research and teaching assistantships generally cover at least part of tuition and pay a periodic stipend in exchange for research or classroom instruction. Like scholarships, assistantships are often presented by individual departments. Being proactive is key; once you know a specific topic you want to study, zero in on relevant programs and faculty members in the

field who might be willing to take you on as an assistant. Doctoral students typically have a better shot than master's candidates, since they're presumably considering a professorial career.

Borrow smart

Chances are you'll need to borrow at least part of the tab. To be eligible for federal loans, the first step is to file a Free Application for Federal Student Aid (FAFSA). Low-income students—which many grad students are once they're independent of their parents—might qualify for Perkins loans, which award up to $8,000 annually (to a maximum, including undergrad amounts, of $60,000) and have a 5 percent interest rate. Stafford loans pay out up to $20,500 a year. The loans carry a 6.8 percent interest rate and a 1 percent fee, and a lifetime maximum of $138,500. Currently, all graduate Stafford loans are unsubsidized, so interest accrues during the entire time that the borrowers are enrolled, though payments aren't required until six months after graduation. For the rest, grad PLUS loans are available (at 7.9 percent interest plus 4 percent in fees), as are private loans. Private lender Sallie Mae has just dropped its fixed loan rates for grad students so they range from 5.75 to 8.875 percent, with no fees, from a top rate of 12.875 percent; its variable rates have dropped, too.

Potential borrowers can get a sense of the total loan tab—and perhaps size it up against an expected starting salary—using a student loan calculator, like those available at FinAid.org and StudentAid.ed.gov. Certain state, federal, and school-sponsored repayment programs also offer adjusted rates or loan forgiveness for qualifying graduates pursuing careers in the nonprofit or public interest sectors and certain in-demand fields such as teaching and primary care.

Take your credit

Grad students will also want to see if they qualify for the federal Lifetime Learning Tax Credit, which allows individuals to subtract up to $2,000 annually from their tax bill. The credit applies to 20 percent of tuition and other required education expenses up to $10,000, and is available to single filers whose modified adjusted gross income is $62,000 or less, or to married people whose adjusted gross income falls at or under $124,000.

Bottom line: If you need funds, you have to be creative, says Geri Rypkema, director of the Office of Graduate Student Assistantships and Fellowships at George Washington University in Washington, D.C. "Look at all possible sources," she advises, "because sometimes you have to put it together." ●

Puzzled about how you'll ever pay for grad school? Check out the wealth of advice on getting in and funding your studies, plus the latest rankings of top graduate programs, at **www.usnews.com/grad.**

About the *U.S. News* Rankings

Objective measures are important, as are the opinions of peers and recruiters

BY ROBERT J. MORSE AND SAMUEL FLANIGAN

Each year, *U.S. News* ranks professional school programs in business, education, engineering, law, and medicine. The rankings are based on two types of data: expert opinions about program excellence and statistical indicators that measure the quality of a school's faculty, research, and students. The data come from surveys of administrators at more than 1,250 programs and over 13,000 academics and professionals, conducted during the fall of 2012 and early 2013.

As you research course offerings and weigh schools' intangible attributes, the information in these pages can help you compare concrete factors such as faculty-student ratio and placement success upon graduation. It's important that you use the rankings to supplement—not substitute for—careful thought and your own inquiries. In each of the five major disciplines, the ranking tables show approximately the top half of the schools that were eligible to be ranked; longer lists and more complete data can be found at *www. usnews.com/grad*. Detailed information about the methodologies used in each discipline can be found there, too, as well as with each ranking in these pages.

Stanford Graduate School of Business, tied at No. 1

Beyond the five disciplines ranked annually, we also periodically rank programs in the sciences, social sciences, humanities, the health arena, and many other areas based solely on the ratings of academic experts. This year, new peer surveys were conducted and new rankings published for Ph.D. programs in economics, English, history, political science, psychology, and sociology. For the first time, the new Ph.D. rankings were based on the results of the two latest surveys, in 2008 and 2012. Rankings of programs in the health fields and Ph.D. programs in the sciences are based on earlier surveys; the date of each of those rankings appears on the list. Full rankings for these categories, plus Web-exclusive rankings of schools of public affairs and public policy, fine arts, and library and information studies, can be found at *www.usnews.com/grad*.

To gather the peer assessment data, we asked deans, program directors, and senior faculty to judge the academic quality of programs in their field on a scale of 1 (marginal) to 5 (outstanding). In business, education, engineering, law, and medicine, we also surveyed professionals who hire new graduates. Statistical indicators used in these disciplines fall into two categories: inputs, or measures of the qualities that students and faculty bring to the educational experience, and outputs, measures of graduates' achievements linked to their degrees. As inputs, for example, we use the appropriate admission test scores for each discipline: the LSAT, GMAT, MCAT, or GRE. In computing the full-time and part-time M.B.A. rankings, we have introduced GRE scores of students entering in the fall of 2012 as a ranking factor, while retaining GMAT scores; this allowed us to take into account the admissions test scores of the entire class. In education and engineering, we incorporated both the new GRE scores (on a 130-170 scale) and the old GRE scores as ranking variables; only the new GRE scores are displayed in the ranking tables.

Different output measures are available for different fields. In business, for example, we use starting salaries and the ability of new M.B.A.'s to find jobs upon graduation or three months later. In law, we look at employment rates and state bar exam passage rates. This year we changed the way we computed placement rates for 2011 J.D. grads employed at graduation and nine months later because more detailed statistics about the types of positions new attorneys land is now reported to the American Bar Association and *U.S. News* (related story, Page 73).

How schools are scored

To arrive at a school's rank, we examined the data for each quality indicator. We then standardized the value of each indicator about its mean. The weights applied to the indicators, which are discussed in the methodology explanations that appear with the tables, reflect our judgment about their relative importance, as determined in consultation with experts in each field. The final scores were rescaled so that the highest-scoring school was assigned 100; the other schools' scores were recalculated as a percentage of that top score. The scores were then rounded to the nearest whole number, and schools were placed in descending order.

Every school's performance is presented relative to those with which it is compared. A school with an overall score of 100 did not necessarily top out on every indicator; it accumulated the highest composite score. A school's rank reflects the number of schools that sit above it; if three schools are tied at 1, the next school will be ranked 4, not 2. Tied schools are listed alphabetically. ●

Working on a project at top-ranked Stanford

BUSINESS

Overhauling the Dated M.B.A.

Comparing B-schools? You'll explore a landscape in the throes of change. BY MARGARET LOFTUS

After working for five years in California at an unfulfilling job as a musical supervisor for film trailers, Nick Martin, 30, decided to tap into his analytical side at Texas Christian University's Neeley School of Business in Fort Worth. As part of his studies, he works in digital marketing and advertising as an intern for Smith & Nephew, a medical technology company, and is being recruited for a position with the firm after he graduates this spring. With a background in film, getting hired by Smith & Nephew was a long shot, he says. But his employers were impressed by how well he managed a market opportunity analysis students did for the company on a wound care product. Such on-the-ground experience is key to a revamped curriculum at TCU aimed at making students more appealing to employers. "I was looking for a way to gracefully pivot out of my current situation," Martin says. "I think I found the right answer."

That should be music to the ears of administrators at Neeley and elsewhere who are scrambling to find new ways to sharpen graduates' edge in a leaner, meaner business world. In some cases, change has been sweeping. In 2006, Yale School of Management replaced core classes such as finance and marketing with interdisciplinary courses based on the "organizational perspectives" of different parties; students now explore the concerns of the investor, say, and the customer. The University of Pennsylvania's Wharton School rolled out a whole new plan last fall that allows students greater leeway to customize their studies within six "pathways," including Managing the Global Enterprise and Understanding and Serving Customers.

Arizona State's new curriculum is letting Tim Blankenship specialize early, before a summer internship.

Northwestern University's Kellogg School of Management will infuse its entire curriculum with four themes that cut across the traditional disciplines like accounting and marketing: innovation and entrepreneurship; private enterprise/public policy interface; markets and customers; and "architectures of collaboration."

Most institutions, like Neeley, are taking smaller steps that are "evolutionary, not revolutionary," says Bob Sullivan, dean of the Rady School of Management at the University of California–San Diego and chair-elect of the accrediting body AACSB International–The Association to Advance Collegiate Schools of Business. They are working within their existing curricula to allow students opportunities to specialize earlier, expanding offerings on the hot topics of entrepreneurship and innovation, and integrating experiential learning as well as more (and more sophisticated) ways to get a global perspective.

"The external environment is calling on us to step up," says Sarah Fisher Gardial, dean of the University of Iowa's Henry B. Tippie College of Business and president of the MBA Roundtable, a nonprofit group of B-schools focused on curricular innovation. People who are seeking postgraduate work in business "now have an exponentially expanding number of ways to get it" that don't necessarily include a traditional M.B.A., she notes, from the new crop of professional master's degrees (story, Page 8) to certificate programs and online courses.

Battling a drop in applications

Schools are responding to new pressures to compete among themselves, too. Applications were down at nearly two thirds of the country's full-time M.B.A. programs last year, according to a study last fall by the Graduate Management Admission Council. Indiana University's Kelley School of Business and Columbia Business School reported declines in applications of 21 percent and 19 percent, respectively, for example. "The increasingly competitive nature of the M.B.A. landscape mandates that you are always on the leading edge," says Stacey Whitecotton, associate dean for M.B.A. programs at Arizona State University's W.P. Carey School of Business.

W.P. Carey has used a university-wide switch from trimesters to quarters to get students focused early on their areas of interest. The new curriculum, which debuted last fall, still relies on core courses such as accounting, finance, and marketing as a foundation in the first two quarters. But it now integrates more electives into the third and fourth quarters, so students can go after greater depth in their chosen areas before showing up for a summer internship.

"[Intel] doesn't want to teach a new batch of interns how to calculate equations," says Tim Blan-kenship, 26, a first-year financial markets and management student at W.P. Carey who will report there as an intern in finance this May. By taking Valuation Techniques and Investment Strategies in the third and fourth quarters, he says, he'll "hopefully make a splash and receive an offer."

Courses in entrepreneurship are becoming *de rigueur* in the elective mix. Of the 94 percent of programs that reported having made changes to their elective offerings since 2009 in an MBA Roundtable study last year, more than half have added an elective in the creative thinking needed by business startups (and increasingly valued by large employers, too.) Entrepreneurship and innovation were wish list items that Raj Echambadi heard again

Applications fell at nearly two thirds of full-time M.B.A. programs last year.

and again when he polled employers and alumni of the University of Illinois at Urbana-Champaign as part of a quest to reposition the school's executive M.B.A. program in Chicago, a 20-month, part-time curriculum for professionals with at least seven years of supervisory experience. It was clear to Echambadi, a professor of business administration and academic director of executive programs at the school, that all sorts of companies are hungry for entrepreneurial leaders who can manage their businesses as if they are agile upstarts.

As a result, UIUC introduced several core courses last fall that are being integrated as well into the full-time M.B.A. program. These include entrepreneurship and corporate renewal, in which teams develop business plans for new ventures and compete for seed grants from the university, and strategic innovation management, where students analyze innovation success stories across industries and countries, from Cirque du Soleil to Netflix to LG Electronics.

The fresh lineup hooked Airies Davis, 41, a senior technical trainer for Monster Worldwide who sought to pursue a sideline interest: developing a nonprofit academy to teach underserved kids about etiquette and character. "That sexy word of innova-

Wharton students on a mountaineering trek to Alaska, to gain confidence in their leadership abilities

tion is what drew me to the program," she says. "I had the idea, but I didn't have the business acumen. The entrepreneurship course is forcing me to create a business plan."

Her classmate Scott Rylko, 39, a vice president of a foodservice equipment and supplies manufacturer, says the most valuable takeaway so far has been instruction on the importance of "disruptive innovation" in setting a course for businesses, as digital photography and online periodicals have done for publishing, for example. "Instead of waiting for someone else to disrupt your business through technology," he says, the goal is to figure out how to disrupt yourself. While he has yet to put the theory to the test in his job, understanding it has inspired a reevaluation of his company's product line in light of a recent merger.

Real consulting gigs

Unlike working executive M.B.A. students, full-time candidates traditionally haven't had the advantage of immediately applying what they learn in the classroom. That's changing rapidly as programs build in consulting projects and other experiential learning. "It gives the companies the opportunities to view [potential employees] not in synthetic decisionmaking environments, but real decisionmaking environments," says the Rady School's Sullivan. Each year, Tippie students form teams from across business specialties to consult for companies in different industries. Students have helped Goodwill of the Heartland move into the baked goods business, for instance, and worked with Stihl to analyze a lithium ion versus a gas engine for its power tools. Five years ago, the University at Buffalo School of Management introduced the Corporate Champions program, in which teams of first-semester students draw on their communication, statistics, and organizational behavior classes to conduct a survey project for a local company over the course of the semester. One year, teams analyzed data from a regional supermarket chain to determine the extent to which the corporate culture had penetrated individual stores.

Some B-schools are borrowing a page from the corporate book to build skills through outdoor experiences. In Wharton's Leadership Ventures program, students take seven- to 10-day wilder-

Need more flexibility in your studies? Besides the *U.S. News* rankings of top graduate business programs, you can check out the best part-time and online M.B.A. options at **www.usnews.com/bizschools.**

ness trips, like mountaineering in Alaska or trekking in South America's Atacama Desert. Instructors teach basic survival skills, but leave most of the decisionmaking to the expeditioners, with the goal of instilling confidence in their ability to lead.

At the same time, educators are realizing that a simple field trip is not the answer to understanding global business. "Early on, we all thought if we sent our students abroad for a couple weeks that would create a global mindset. That alone will not do it," argues Gardial.

At TCU, for example, students who wanted a global perspective used to get a 10-day trip to Munich and London. Now, everyone takes a new first-semester course on global business and can choose from several electives such as international marketing, international finance, and a global supply chain course, plus five additional 10-day trips (Cape Town, South Africa and China's Pearl River Delta among them), in the second and third semester. Teams of students at the University of Michigan's Ross School of Business, who immerse themselves for seven weeks in projects at companies, can do so abroad. One team traveled to Santiago, Chile, to help LAN Airlines improve passengers' deplaning experience. At UIUC, second-semester students take the new Global Business Horizons and Sustainability course, where Prof. Madhu Viswanathan discusses his research on subsistence markets such as India and asks students to role

Entrepreneurship is becoming *de rigueur* in the elective mix.

play as, say, the head of a large Indian family who lives on $15 a month. The theme of operating in resource-constrained environments stretches into the second year's global experience, in which students do consulting stints with a local corporation, like Motorola or Wrigley, and travel abroad to present their projects.

Educators agree that there's no end to change in sight. "The next five years will be the biggest time of change in education that we're ever seen," says Kellogg Dean Sally Blount, who thinks getting an M.B.A. online for little or no money will become a reality in the near future. Says Echambadi: "The world was very different 10 years ago, but reasonably predictable, like chess." Now, he says, the game is more like poker. ●

A Welcome Hike in Hiring

Many good opportunities for M.B.A.'s lie off the beaten track. BY KATHERINE HOBSON

Here's some good news for prospective M.B.A.'s: Ninety-two percent of 2012 grads surveyed by the Graduate Management Admission Council had a job three months after graduation, a track record 6 percentage points better than that of the class before them. And 77 percent of those new hires said their salary met or exceeded their expectations.

The pickup in hiring is leading many recent grads off the traditionally well-worn paths into finance and consulting. "Career outcomes for M.B.A.'s are far more diverse than they were five years ago," says Nunzio Quacquarelli, managing director of the higher education research firm Quacquarelli Symonds, whose latest TopMBA.com Jobs and Salary Report gives a snapshot of what's going on at 3,305 employers around the world. Among the industries projected to see double-digit growth in M.B.A. hiring this year: information technology and computer services, energy, and pharmaceuticals and healthcare.

Student interest is shifting, too, says Michelle Chevalier, director of the Graduate Business Career Center at the University of Minnesota's Carlson School of Management. Many of today's graduates are seeking—and finding—work with start-ups, nonprofits, and companies whose products and services "benefit the world in some way," she says. And the entrepreneurial ranks are expanding at B-schools across the country. "I an-

On the international front, the demand for M.B.A.'s in Asia will grow by 26 percent in 2013 alone.

ticipate doing this full time" after graduation, says Dan Wolchonok, 29, who has focused on entrepreneurship at the Yale School of Management and who, while still a student last year, won funding from the school's entrepreneurial institute to start PrepWork, a software-based service that acts as a personal research assistant. On the international front, the most recent QS report projects that the demand for M.B.A.'s in Asia will grow by 26 percent in 2013 alone. India now has more reported openings for new M.B.A. grads than this country does, says Quacquarelli.

To be sure, there is still interest—and plenty of hiring going on—in some of the more traditional fields, too. TopMBA.com projects 9 percent growth in demand in consulting and professional services for 2012-13, and 22 percent in electronics and high tech. People interested in financial services still face a bit of a challenge; QS estimates only 3 percent growth there. "Financial and regulatory uncertainty have caused banks to be very cautious about hiring," says Lisa Feldman, executive director of M.B.A. Career Management at the Haas School of Business at the University of California-Berkeley.

When financial services companies do hire, they often pull directly from their summer internship programs, which means the hunt for a job really begins in the first year of an M.B.A. program. Banks "want to make sure that people really understand the culture," says Ron Peracchio, senior director of the Career Development Office at the Massachusetts Institute of Technology's Sloan School of Management. "If [students] don't get an internship in the summer, there aren't a lot of opportunities unless they have banking experience."

Other industries also like to hire from their intern pool, even if not to the same extent as banking. "I'd say that over 50 percent of my friends have jobs from the summer or have good relationships with their summer employer," says Grace Chang Mazza, 29, who is studying marketing at the University of Pennsylvania's Wharton School and interned for consumer goods giant Unilever last summer. She went into the job believing it could serve as an entry point, and indeed will work there after getting her M.B.A. this spring. ●

Reflect™ by GMAC

Get where you want to go by knowing who you are.

DISCOVER AND IMPROVE YOUR PERSONAL AND PROFESSIONAL QUALITIES AND PLAN FOR SUCCESS—ON THE JOB, IN SCHOOL, IN LIFE.

LIKE A CAREER COACH, THE REFLECT™ PERSONAL INSIGHT TOOL HELPS YOU:

- Understand yourself and how others perceive you
- Build the very qualities corporate recruiters and graduate admissions directors look for, and
- Create a personalized plan to reach your goals

THE REFLECT ADVANTAGE GIVES YOU:

- Personalized tips, videos, and articles based on your score
- Action items that help you improve your strengths and identify opportunities for improvement
- Customizable work plan and career benchmarking tools
- Three years of access to your report and its resource library for US$99.99

Get started today at **gmac.com/reflect**

Schools of Business

THE TOP SCHOOLS

Rank	School	Overall score	'12 Peer assessment score (5.0=highest)	Recruiter assessment score (5.0=highest)	'12 full-time average undergrad GPA	'12 full-time average GMAT score	'12 full-time acceptance rate	'12 average starting salary and bonus	'12 graduates employed at graduation	Employed 3 months after graduation	'12 out-of-state tuition and fees	'12 total full-time enrollment
1.	Harvard University (MA)	100	4.8	4.5	3.67	724	11.5%	$142,501	77.4%	89.3%	$63,288	1,824
1.	Stanford University (CA)	100	4.8	4.6	3.69	729	7.1%	$140,459	71.3%	87.8%	$57,300	803
3.	University of Pennsylvania (Wharton)	99	4.8	4.6	3.60	718	20.0%	$138,302	79.7%	91.7%	$62,034	1,685
4.	Massachusetts Institute of Technology (Sloan)	97	4.7	4.4	3.53	710	15.6%	$139,035	84.5%	94.4%	$58,200	816
4.	Northwestern University (Kellogg) (IL)	97	4.7	4.4	3.69	708	22.9%	$134,001	76.9%	91.7%	$56,775	1,161
6.	University of Chicago (Booth)	96	4.7	4.4	3.52	720	23.0%	$135,653	84.1%	92.3%	$56,931	1,161
7.	University of California–Berkeley (Haas)	93	4.6	4.1	3.61	715	13.8%	$133,786	74.4%	92.7%	$56,275	490
8.	Columbia University (NY)	91	4.5	4.2	3.50	715	20.8%	$134,868	77.0%	91.6%	$60,896	1,274
9.	Dartmouth College (Tuck) (NH)	90	4.3	4.0	3.49	717	20.4%	$138,713	85.8%	92.9%	$60,510	549
10.	New York University (Stern)	87	4.2	3.9	3.51	720	15.7%	$133,919	79.5%	90.5%	$55,154	780
11.	Duke University (Fuqua) (NC)	86	4.3	4.0	3.42	690	27.5%	$136,461	86.5%	91.7%	$54,922	874
12.	University of Virginia (Darden)	85	4.2	3.9	3.45	703	26.6%	$131,906	81.5%	90.9%	$53,900	637
13.	Yale University (CT)	84	4.2	4.1	3.55	717	21.3%	$121,631	66.5%	85.5%	$56,530	494
14.	University of California–Los Angeles (Anderson)	82	4.1	3.8	3.56	704	22.6%	$121,864	71.9%	86.5%	$54,530	737
14.	University of Michigan–Ann Arbor (Ross)	82	4.3	3.9	3.40	703	40.6%	$134,360	74.3%	81.4%	$55,194	992
16.	Cornell University (Johnson) (NY)	80	4.1	3.9	3.29	694	27.6%	$127,368	82.0%	89.8%	$56,811	568
17.	University of Texas–Austin (McCombs)	79	4.0	3.8	3.40	692	28.6%	$123,177	80.7%	92.5%	$49,532	504
18.	Emory University (Goizueta) (GA)	76	3.8	3.4	3.38	677	34.2%	$124,066	86.1%	96.0%	$45,114	338
19.	Carnegie Mellon University (Tepper) (PA)	75	3.9	3.6	3.26	693	26.7%	$128,101	75.7%	89.7%	$55,800	418
20.	U. of North Carolina–Chapel Hill (Kenan-Flagler)	74	3.9	3.8	3.34	692	42.6%	$118,195	72.2%	84.3%	$52,074	580
21.	Washington University in St. Louis (Olin)	71	3.7	3.3	3.43	698	34.1%	$106,009	79.0%	96.0%	$48,900	279
22.	Indiana University–Bloomington (Kelley)	70	3.8	3.6	3.33	664	38.5%	$108,807	76.1%	89.4%	$45,544	398
23.	University of Minnesota–Twin Cities (Carlson)	69	3.6	2.8	3.40	692	43.4%	$118,986	83.6%	90.9%	$49,034	206
23.	University of Washington (Foster)	69	3.4	3.4	3.37	670	43.4%	$110,768	80.6%	96.8%	$40,170	230
25.	Georgetown University (McDonough) (DC)	68	3.7	3.3	3.32	683	49.4%	$114,744	67.9%	88.8%	$51,925	506
26.	University of Southern California (Marshall)	67	3.9	3.2	3.34	690	29.5%	$109,841	66.3%	77.3%	$54,754	431
27.	Georgia Institute of Technology	66	3.4	3.2	3.38	678	38.1%	$101,612	77.8%	93.7%	$38,626	131
27.	Ohio State University (Fisher)	66	3.6	3.0	3.38	668	31.8%	$102,162	60.2%	97.1%	$45,667	229

BRETT ZIEGLER FOR *USN&WR*

No. 4
Northwestern

More at **www.usnews.com/grad**

ACHIEVE ON YOUR TERMS.

With Kelley Direct's flexible MBA program, you're the one who decides how to get where you want to go. Our renowned faculty and programs offer you what you need, without putting your life on hold. Learn more at kelley.iu.edu/onlineMBA.

THE TOP SCHOOLS

Rank	School	Overall score	Peer assessment score (5.0=highest)	Recruiter assessment score (5.0=highest)	'12 full-time average undergrad GPA	'12 full-time average GMAT score	'12 full-time acceptance rate	'12 average starting salary and bonus	'12 graduates employed at graduation	Employed 3 months after graduation	'12 out-of-state tuition and fees	'12 total full-time enrollment
27.	University of Notre Dame (Mendoza) (IN)	66	3.6	3.3	3.26	687	35.2%	$111,255	75.1%	87.3%	$44,110	314
30.	Arizona State University (Carey)	65	3.5	3.0	3.40	676	36.0%	$100,984	78.8%	89.4%	$38,066	142
30.	Brigham Young University (Marriott) (UT)	65	3.2	3.0	3.50	672	54.2%	$108,227	81.5%	91.9%	$21,900	325
30.	Rice University (Jones) (TX)	65	3.4	2.9	3.40	673	27.0%	$108,587	77.1%	93.8%	$48,903	231
30.	Vanderbilt University (Owen) (TN)	65	3.6	3.2	3.37	682	37.1%	$108,889	71.1%	87.2%	$45,404	336
34.	University of Wisconsin–Madison	64	3.6	3.0	3.32	675	24.0%	$105,614	69.9%	85.8%	$27,789	203
35.	Texas A&M University–College Station (Mays)	63	3.3	3.1	3.40	649	25.1%	$104,723	73.5%	93.9%	$34,849	132
36.	University of Florida (Hough)	61	3.4	2.9	3.46	695	21.2%	$78,102	63.9%	86.9%	$30,983	116
37.	University of Maryland–College Park (Smith)	60	3.5	3.0	3.30	656	43.7%	$101,604	58.5%	88.1%	$47,448	230
37.	University of Rochester (Simon) (NY)	60	3.3	2.7	3.45	680	34.3%	$95,046	65.0%	92.0%	$49,012	267
37.	University of Texas–Dallas	60	2.9	3.8	3.50	669	25.7%	$82,564	50.0%	89.6%	$28,218	112
40.	Boston College (Carroll)	58	3.3	2.8	3.41	666	34.8%	$102,423	58.0%	85.2%	$38,566	195
40.	Boston University	58	3.2	2.8	3.35	680	32.6%	$101,204	66.1%	86.6%	$42,934	297
40.	University of California–Davis	58	3.3	2.6	3.30	680	19.1%	$98,592	63.4%	92.7%	$48,692	100
43.	Michigan State University (Broad)	57	3.3	3.0	3.30	641	40.8%	$96,579	75.9%	89.2%	$41,511	180
44.	Purdue University–West Lafayette (Krannert) (IN)	56	3.4	3.1	3.23	643	44.8%	$97,293	70.8%	83.1%	$43,697	241
44.	University of Arizona (Eller)	56	3.4	3.0	3.28	634	54.8%	$93,836	67.6%	88.2%	$40,533	99
44.	University of Iowa (Tippie)	56	3.2	2.6	3.35	665	42.0%	$87,026	72.9%	89.6%	$36,045	129
47.	University of Illinois–Urbana-Champaign	55	3.6	3.0	3.20	650	31.9%	$94,331	70.7%	83.7%	$34,236	237
47.	Wake Forest University (Babcock) (NC)	55	3.2	2.9	3.25	648	53.6%	$100,897	75.9%	83.3%	$41,132	123
49.	Pennsylvania State Univ.–University Park (Smeal)	54	3.4	3.2	3.23	643	29.5%	$91,563	54.4%	80.0%	$35,968	159
49.	University of California–Irvine (Merage)	54	3.3	2.4	3.35	657	33.4%	$80,809	69.4%	93.5%	$46,584	215
51.	University of Massachusetts–Amherst (Isenberg)	53	2.9	2.7	3.40	655	24.9%	$86,491	55.0%	95.0%	$9,937	65
52.	Case Western Reserve Univ. (Weatherhead) (OH)	52	3.3	2.9	3.30	631	24.3%	$83,953	63.5%	85.7%	$45,640	122
52.	Southern Methodist University (Cox) (TX)	52	3.1	3.0	3.40	639	49.5%	$95,296	52.3%	76.2%	$46,708	216
52.	University of Georgia (Terry)	52	3.3	2.8	3.21	637	39.2%	$91,830	65.8%	86.8%	$31,822	93
52.	University of Missouri (Trulaske)	52	2.8	3.1	3.50	658	43.2%	$61,846	79.7%	84.4%	$27,737	195
56.	Babson College (Olin) (MA)	51	3.3	2.9	3.23	618	72.8%	$93,064	55.2%	87.7%	$91,180**	408
56.	George Washington University (DC)	51	3.2	2.9	3.29	632	49.8%	$89,508	55.7%	85.2%	$1,420*	239
58.	Temple University (Fox) (PA)	50	2.9	2.1	3.42	643	33.7%	$87,297	74.4%	97.7%	$36,821	90
58.	University of Alabama (Manderson)	50	2.7	2.6	3.55	642	39.1%	$69,002	77.3%	90.7%	$25,780	166
58.	University of Connecticut	50	2.8	2.4	3.48	654	48.8%	$83,330	62.5%	90.0%	$32,158	91
61.	Louisiana State University–Baton Rouge (Ourso)	49	2.9	2.7	3.42	632	35.8%	$62,329	74.6%	90.5%	$54,920**	93
61.	Northeastern University (MA)	49	2.9	2.8	3.27	643	28.4%	$73,042	59.0%	95.1%	$1,345*	219
61.	Rutgers, the State U. of N.J.–New Brunswick & Newark	49	2.8	2.5	3.31	643	44.3%	$92,635	60.0%	93.3%	$41,347	244
61.	University of Pittsburgh (Katz)	49	3.2	2.8	3.24	608	34.7%	$80,752	69.3%	88.0%	$57,716**	171
61.	University of Utah (Eccles)	49	2.9	2.7	3.43	615	54.2%	$72,465	75.5%	92.0%	$78,000**	139
66.	University of Arkansas–Fayetteville (Walton)	48	3.0	2.6	3.20	631	46.7%	$60,750	90.5%	95.2%	$36,603	71
67.	Tulane University (Freeman) (LA)	47	3.1	2.7	3.24	629	82.9%	$79,356	54.9%	86.3%	$51,291	169
67.	University of Oklahoma (Price)	47	2.8	2.9	3.49	616	72.6%	$75,780	63.6%	79.5%	$652*	107
67.	University of Tennessee–Knoxville	47	3.0	2.4	3.40	608	69.7%	$78,957	65.2%	89.9%	$65,355**	149
70.	Baylor University (Hankamer) (TX)	46	2.9	2.8	3.31	628	39.2%	$67,282	65.7%	82.9%	$34,116	100
70.	College of William and Mary (Mason) (VA)	46	2.9	3.0	3.30	610	58.2%	$79,969	56.9%	83.1%	$40,390	206
70.	Iowa State University	46	2.6	2.6	3.55	603	50.0%	$64,602	77.3%	95.5%	$22,410	57

SPECIALTIES

PROGRAMS RANKED BEST BY BUSINESS SCHOOL DEANS AND M.B.A. PROGRAM DIRECTORS

ACCOUNTING

1. **University of Texas–Austin** (McCombs)
2. **University of Pennsylvania** (Wharton)
3. **University of Illinois–Urbana-Champaign**
4. **University of Chicago** (Booth)
5. **University of Michigan–Ann Arbor** (Ross)
6. **Stanford University** (CA)
7. **Brigham Young University** (Marriott) (UT)
8. **University of Southern California** (Marshall)
9. **New York University** (Stern)
9. **University of North Carolina–Chapel Hill** (Kenan-Flagler)
11. **University of Notre Dame** (Mendoza) (IN)
12. **Northwestern University** (Kellogg) (IL)
13. **Indiana University–Bloomington** (Kelley)
14. **Gonzaga University** (WA)
15. **Columbia University** (NY)
16. **Michigan State University** (Broad)
16. **Ohio State University** (Fisher)

ENTREPRENEURSHIP

1. **Babson College** (Olin) (MA)
2. **Stanford University** (CA)
3. **Massachusetts Institute of Technology** (Sloan)
4. **Harvard University** (MA)
4. **University of Pennsylvania** (Wharton)
6. **University of California–Berkeley** (Haas)
7. **University of Michigan–Ann Arbor** (Ross)
7. **University of Texas–Austin** (McCombs)

*Tuition is reported on a per-credit-hour basis. **Total program tuition
Sources: *U.S. News* and the schools. Assessment data collected by Ipsos Public Affairs.

SPECIALTIES

9. **University of Southern California** (Marshall)
10. **Indiana University–Bloomington** (Kelley)
11. **University of Arizona** (Eller)
12. **University of Virginia** (Darden)
13. **Santa Clara University** (Leavey) (CA)
14. **University of Chicago** (Booth)

EXECUTIVE MBA

1. **University of Pennsylvania** (Wharton)
2. **University of Chicago** (Booth)
3. **Northwestern University** (Kellogg) (IL)
4. **Columbia University** (NY)
4. **Duke University** (Fuqua) (NC)
6. **New York University** (Stern)
7. **University of California–Los Angeles** (Anderson)
8. **University of Michigan–Ann Arbor** (Ross)
9. **University of North Carolina–Chapel Hill** (Kenan-Flagler)
10. **University of California–Berkeley** (Haas)
11. **University of Southern California** (Marshall)
12. **University of Virginia** (Darden)
13. **Stanford University** (CA)

FINANCE

1. **University of Pennsylvania** (Wharton)
2. **University of Chicago** (Booth)
3. **New York University** (Stern)
4. **Columbia University** (NY)
4. **Stanford University** (CA)
6. **Massachusetts Institute of Technology** (Sloan)
7. **Harvard University** (MA)
8. **University of California–Berkeley** (Haas)
9. **Northwestern University** (Kellogg) (IL)
10. **University of California–Los Angeles** (Anderson)
11. **University of Michigan–Ann Arbor** (Ross)
12. **Boston College** (Carroll)
12. **Duke University** (Fuqua) (NC)
14. **University of Texas–Austin** (McCombs)
15. **Fordham University** (NY)
16. **Carnegie Mellon University** (Tepper) (PA)
16. **University of Rochester** (Simon) (NY)

INFORMATION SYSTEMS

1. **Massachusetts Institute of Technology** (Sloan)
2. **Carnegie Mellon University** (Tepper) (PA)
3. **University of Texas–Austin** (McCombs)
4. **University of Arizona** (Eller)

4. **University of Minnesota–Twin Cities** (Carlson)
6. **University of Pennsylvania** (Wharton)
7. **University of Maryland–College Park** (Smith)
8. **Georgia State University** (Robinson)
8. **Stanford University** (CA)
10. **New York University** (Stern)

INTERNATIONAL

1. **Thunderbird School of Global Management** (AZ)
2. **University of Pennsylvania** (Wharton)
3. **University of South Carolina** (Moore)
4. **University of Michigan–Ann Arbor** (Ross)
5. **New York University** (Stern)
6. **Columbia University** (NY)
7. **University of Southern California** (Marshall)
8. **Harvard University** (MA)
9. **University of California–Berkeley** (Haas)
10. **Duke University** (Fuqua) (NC)
11. **Stanford University** (CA)
12. **Georgetown University** (McDonough) (DC)
13. **St. Louis University** (Cook)

MANAGEMENT

1. **Harvard University** (MA)
2. **Stanford University** (CA)
3. **University of Pennsylvania** (Wharton)
4. **University of Virginia** (Darden)
5. **Northwestern University** (Kellogg) (IL)
6. **University of Michigan–Ann Arbor** (Ross)
7. **University of California–Berkeley** (Haas)
8. **Dartmouth College** (Tuck) (NH)
9. **Columbia University** (NY)
10. **Duke University** (Fuqua) (NC)
11. **University of Chicago** (Booth)
12. **University of North Carolina–Chapel Hill** (Kenan-Flagler)

MARKETING

1. **Northwestern University** (Kellogg) (IL)
2. **University of Pennsylvania** (Wharton)
3. **Stanford University** (CA)
4. **Duke University** (Fuqua) (NC)
5. **Harvard University** (MA)
6. **University of Chicago** (Booth)
7. **Columbia University** (NY)
8. **University of Michigan–Ann Arbor** (Ross)
9. **University of California–Berkeley** (Haas)
10. **New York University** (Stern)
11. **University of Texas–Austin** (McCombs)
12. **University of California–Los Angeles** (Anderson)

SPECIALTIES

NONPROFIT
1. **Yale University** (CT)
2. **Stanford University** (CA)
3. **Harvard University** (MA)
4. **University of California–Berkeley** (Haas)
5. **Northwestern University** (Kellogg) (IL)

PRODUCTION/OPERATIONS
1. **Massachusetts Institute of Technology** (Sloan)

2. **Carnegie Mellon University** (Tepper) (PA)
2. **University of Pennsylvania** (Wharton)
4. **Stanford University** (CA)
5. **University of Michigan–Ann Arbor** (Ross)
6. **Northwestern University** (Kellogg) (IL)
7. **Purdue University–West Lafayette** (Krannert) (IN)
8. **Columbia University** (NY)

9. **Harvard University** (MA)
10. **Indiana University–Bloomington** (Kelley)
11. **University of Texas–Austin** (McCombs)

SUPPLY CHAIN/LOGISTICS
1. **Massachusetts Institute of Technology** (Sloan)
2. **Michigan State University** (Broad)
3. **Pennsylvania State University–University Park** (Smeal)
4. **Ohio State University** (Fisher)

4. **Stanford University** (CA)
6. **Arizona State University** (Carey)
6. **Carnegie Mellon University** (Tepper) (PA)
8. **University of Pennsylvania** (Wharton)
9. **Purdue University–West Lafayette** (Krannert) (IN)
9. **University of Michigan–Ann Arbor** (Ross)
11. **University of Tennessee–Knoxville**
12. **Northwestern University** (Kellogg) (IL)

METHODOLOGY

The 448 master's programs in business accredited by the Association to Advance Collegiate Schools of Business were surveyed; 380 responded, with 140 providing the data needed to calculate rankings based on a weighted average of eight indicators:

Quality assessment: Two separate surveys were conducted in fall 2012. Business school deans and directors of accredited M.B.A. programs were asked to rate overall academic quality of the master's programs at each school on a scale from marginal (1) to outstanding (5); 43 percent

responded, and the average score is weighted by .25 in the overall ranking model. Corporate recruiters and company contacts who hired M.B.A. graduates from previously ranked programs also were asked to rate the programs; 16 percent responded. The two most recent years' recruiter surveys were averaged and are weighted by .15 in the overall model.
Placement success (weighted by .35): Measured by average starting salary and bonus (40 percent of this measure) and employment rates for full-time M.B.A. program 2012 graduates, computed at graduation (20 percent) and

three months later (40 percent). To calculate M.B.A. placement rates, those not seeking jobs and those for whom the school has no information are excluded. Salary is based on the number of graduates reporting data. Signing bonus is weighted by the proportion of graduates reporting their salaries who received a bonus, since not everyone with a base salary received a signing bonus.
Student selectivity (.25): The strength of full-time students entering in the fall of 2012 was measured by the average GMAT and GRE scores (65 percent), average undergraduate GPA (30

percent), and the proportion of applicants accepted by the school (5 percent).
Overall rank: Data were standardized about their means, and standardized scores were weighted, totaled, and rescaled so that the top school received 100; others received their percentage of the top score.
Specialty rankings: These rankings are based solely on ratings by educators at peer schools. Business school deans and M.B.A. program heads were asked to nominate up to 10 programs for excellence in each specialty. Those receiving the most nominations are listed.

Part-Time M.B.A. Schools

Part-time business programs play a vital role for working people who can't go to school full time because of family or financial reasons. The *U.S. News* part-time M.B.A. ranking is based on five factors: average peer assessment score (50 percent of the overall score); average GMAT score and GRE scores of part-time M.B.A. students entering in the fall of 2012 (15 percent); average undergraduate GPA (5 percent); work experience (15 percent); and the percentage of the fall 2012 M.B.A. enrollment that is part time (15 percent). The aver-

age peer assessment score is calculated from a fall 2012 survey that asked business school deans and M.B.A. program directors at each of the nation's 325 part-time M.B.A. programs to rate the other part-time programs on a 5-point scale, from marginal (1) to outstanding (5); 45 percent responded. To be eligible for the part-time ranking, a program needed to be accredited by the Association to Advance Collegiate Schools of Business and have at least 20 students enrolled part time in the fall of 2012; 282 programs met those criteria.

THE TOP SCHOOLS

Rank School	Overall score	Peer assessment score (5.0=highest)	'12 part-time average GMAT score	'12 part-time acceptance rate	'12 total part-time enrollment
1. University of California–Berkeley (Haas)	100	4.5	692	39.7%	803
2. University of Chicago (Booth)	97	4.6	681	N/A	1,473
3. Northwestern University (Kellogg) (IL)	95	4.6	667	N/A	813
4. New York University (Stern)	94	4.4	671	61.7%	2,031
5. University of California–Los Angeles (Anderson)	89	4.2	685	65.7%	867
6. University of Michigan–Ann Arbor (Ross)	84	4.3	648	85.0%	366
7. University of Texas–Austin (McCombs)	76	4.1	643	73.1%	199
8. Ohio State University (Fisher)	75	3.7	621	56.9%	318
9. Carnegie Mellon University (Tepper) (PA)	74	4.0	646	76.5%	172
9. Indiana University–Bloomington (Kelley)	74	3.9	631	57.1%	302
11. Georgetown University (McDonough) (DC)	73	3.7	665	52.0%	377
11. University of Minnesota–Twin Cities (Carlson)	73	3.6	607	87.5%	1,342
11. University of Southern California (Marshall)	73	3.9	602	78.1%	729

Note: The data listed for acceptance rate and enrollment are for informational purposes only and are not used in the computation of the part-time M.B.A. program rankings. N/A=Data were not provided by the school.
Sources: *U.S. News* and the schools. Assessment data collected by Ipsos Public Affairs.

Rank	School	Overall score	Peer assessment score (5.0=highest)	'12 part-time average GMAT score	'12 part-time acceptance rate	'12 total part-time enrollment
14.	Emory University (Goizueta) (GA)	72	3.8	645	72.4%	258
15.	University of Washington (Foster)	71	3.6	638	71.8%	305
16.	Washington University in St. Louis (Olin)	69	3.8	587	86.5%	357
17.	Georgia State University (Robinson)	68	3.3	611	63.8%	880
17.	Rice University (Jones) (TX)	68	3.6	615	74.5%	311
19.	University of California–Davis	66	3.4	576	79.3%	400
19.	University of South Carolina (Moore)	66	3.2	599	70.7%	416
19.	University of Wisconsin–Madison	66	3.7	593	85.3%	149
22.	Arizona State University (Carey)	65	3.4	574	74.1%	366
22.	University of Massachusetts–Amherst (Isenberg)	65	3.0	572	80.3%	1,179
24.	Georgia Institute of Technology	63	3.4	601	81.6%	415
24.	Santa Clara University (Leavey) (CA)	63	3.1	611	73.2%	758
24.	University of Florida (Hough)	63	3.4	580	65.8%	370
24.	University of Maryland–College Park (Smith)	63	3.5	579	82.9%	819
28.	University of Iowa (Tippie)	62	3.2	568	91.4%	768
28.	Wake Forest University (Babcock) (NC)	62	3.3	582	94.9%	250
30.	Case Western Reserve University (Weatherhead) (OH)	61	3.4	585	38.8%	167
31.	Boston University	60	3.2	606	82.8%	707
31.	Southern Methodist University (Cox) (TX)	60	3.4	591	66.7%	344
31.	University of California–Irvine (Merage)	60	3.5	570	77.3%	422
34.	Colorado State University	59	2.7	540	85.4%	35
34.	Lehigh University (PA)	59	2.7	620	88.5%	219
34.	University of Nebraska–Lincoln	59	3.1	610	59.4%	77
34.	Virginia Tech (Pamplin)	59	3.1	609	89.2%	150
38.	Bentley University (McCallum) (MA)	58	3.0	585	85.8%	327
38.	Boston College (Carroll)	58	3.4	590	90.1%	407
38.	St. Louis University (Cook)	58	3.0	577	66.1%	251
38.	University of Colorado–Boulder (Leeds)	58	3.2	615	83.6%	96

THE TOP PART-TIME PROGRAMS

Rank	School	Overall score	Peer assessment score (5.0=highest)	'12 part-time average GMAT score	'12 part-time acceptance rate	'12 total part-time enrollment
38.	University of Texas–Dallas	58	3.1	654	47.9%	681
43.	Clemson University (SC)	57	2.9	578	95.1%	214
43.	Kennesaw State University (Coles) (GA)	57	2.6	590	37.7%	275
43.	Loyola University Chicago	57	2.9	581	60.0%	701
46.	Babson College (Olin) (MA)	56	3.4	569	98.6%	421
46.	Miami University (Farmer) (OH)	56	2.7	567	49.4%	68
46.	Temple University (Fox) (PA)	56	3.0	596	60.8%	364
46.	University of Arizona (Eller)	56	3.4	513	93.8%	150
50.	Creighton University (NE)	55	2.8	522	92.3%	160
50.	DePaul University (Kellstadt) (IL)	55	3.0	598	69.7%	2,003
50.	Marquette University (WI)	55	3.0	577	55.4%	346
50.	Pepperdine University (Graziadio) (CA)	55	3.1	531	89.4%	648
50.	Purdue University–West Lafayette (Krannert) (IN)	55	3.5	595	91.4%	130
50.	University of Connecticut	55	2.8	576	74.9%	1,094
50.	University of North Carolina–Charlotte (Belk)	55	2.8	585	69.4%	305
50.	Villanova University (PA)	55	2.8	623	70.2%	134
58.	Loyola Marymount University (CA)	54	2.9	582	47.8%	242
58.	University of San Diego	54	2.9	616	78.1%	150
60.	George Washington University (DC)	53	3.1	579	79.3%	409
60.	Seattle University (Albers)	53	2.8	585	64.6%	584
60.	University of Arkansas–Fayetteville (Walton)	53	3.0	579	72.9%	118
60.	University of Rochester (Simon) (NY)	53	3.3	558	100.0%	229
64.	University of Pittsburgh (Katz)	52	3.2	539	89.9%	571
64.	University of Richmond (Robins) (VA)	52	2.7	604	83.3%	113
64.	University of Utah (Eccles)	52	3.0	570	69.7%	330
67.	Butler University (IN)	51	2.6	580	81.2%	196
67.	Claremont Graduate School (Drucker) (CA)	51	3.4	528	100.0%	39
69.	College of William and Mary (Mason) (VA)	50	3.1	593	86.5%	180
69.	Elon University (Love) (NC)	50	2.5	563	73.7%	137
69.	Rutgers, the State U. of N.J.–New Brunswick and Newark	50	2.8	579	83.7%	1,013
69.	University of Delaware (Lerner)	50	2.6	561	97.4%	249
73.	CUNY Bernard M. Baruch College (Zicklin)	49	2.8	578	56.3%	1,198
73.	Gonzaga University (WA)	49	2.9	569	64.6%	276
73.	North Carolina State University (Jenkins)	49	2.8	577	89.7%	254
73.	University of Alabama–Birmingham	49	2.7	552	86.6%	365
73.	University of Houston (Bauer) (TX)	49	2.8	588	65.0%	615
73.	University of Michigan–Dearborn	49	2.4	577	50.8%	193

BRETT ZIEGLER FOR *USN&WR*

In class at Wharton

Class at the University of Texas-Austin, ranked No. 4

EDUCATION

Wanted: 100,000 STEM Teachers

There's a sharper focus on producing crack science and math pros. BY CHRISTOPHER J. GEARON

Biologist Kaleigh LaRiche spent most of her first two years after college working in wildlife education at the Akron, Ohio, zoo. Today, she's a first-year science teacher in a Cleveland middle school. Plenty of new teachers "have their moments when they are scared or terrified," says LaRiche, who earns her master's in education from the University of Akron this spring. In fact, research has shown that 3 in 5 new teachers don't feel adequately prepared for what they find in the classroom, a major reason nearly a third (and up to 50 percent in city schools) leave the profession within five years. "I was able to bypass that feeling," she says.

LaRiche thanks the Woodrow Wilson Teaching Fellowship for her confidence. The two-year master's program recruits accomplished science, technology,

engineering, and math (STEM) college graduates, as well as career changers like LaRiche, and puts them through their paces in preparation to work in high-need schools. It is one of several model programs leading the charge to fulfill President Obama's call for 100,000 highly qualified STEM teachers over the next decade, and to get them ready for the much-anticipated new K-12 math and science standards. With only 26 percent of U.S. 12th graders now deemed proficient in math, most states have adopted more rigorous new Common Core Standards for what kids should master at each level. These guidelines stress depth over breadth; a separate effort, the Next Generation Science Standards, emphasizes questioning and discovery rather than rote memorization.

"We need teachers who can think like a scientist and impart the scientific inquiry method," says Linda Darling-Hammond, a Stanford University education professor and the force behind a Stanford master's program that places STEM degree holders in classrooms. "A lot of people didn't learn science that way."

The Wilson Fellowship (*www.wwteachingfellowship.org*) operates by partnering with several graduate schools of education in Ohio, Indiana, Michi-

Former wildlife educator Kaleigh LaRiche now teaches middle-school science in Cleveland.

gan, and New Jersey, including the University of Indianapolis, Ball State University, the University of Michigan, Wayne State University, and Montclair State University. Almost from the start, fellows are immersed for the school year in local K-12 classrooms. LaRiche's four-day-a-week internship at a Canton, Ohio, middle school provided a $30,000 stipend and two mentors to show her the ropes. Coursework included classes in the biology department and on problem- and project-based learning.

Now in her last year at the university, LaRiche is a licensed teacher at Cleveland's Harvard Avenue Community School. When covering renewable and non-renewable energy in her 6th grade science class, she breaks students into groups and has them examine which renewable energy alterative would work best for a fictitious town and why. "They are not used to learning this way," she says. "They are used to a teacher lecturing, taking notes, doing worksheets and labs." The goal is to make clear that science is a process.

Such innovations reflect the latest thinking about what is needed to put better science and math teachers—all kinds of teachers, in fact—into classrooms: an emphasis on subject content knowledge, abundant field experience, and high-caliber candidates, as outlined in a 2010 National Research Council report. Additionally, teacher-prep programs are creating subject-specific methods courses—so a biology candidate can study how best to teach biology, say—that provide training in problem-solving and project-based instruction, skills teachers will need (and model for their students) to meet the game-changing new standards.

"Woodrow Wilson really opened us to innovation and thinking creatively," says Jennifer Drake, dean of the college of arts and sciences at the University of Indianapolis, one of the fellowship's partners. UIndy therefore has embedded intensive hands-on practice in all of its teacher-prep programs, is moving to require elementary-ed candidates to take more math and science courses, and has deepened cross-pollination between the arts and sciences and education schools. "That's a struggle on some campuses," says Kathy Moran, dean of UIndy's ed school.

But it's a necessary one, experts say. Teachers "must have a deep mastery of the content so they know what expert thinking is," as well as " 'pedagogical content knowledge,'" wrote noted physicist and 2001 Nobel Prize winner Carl Wieman in a recent National Academy of Sciences article on improving science education. "This is an understanding of how students learn the particular content, and the challenges and opportunities for facilitation of learning at a topic-specific level."

"In math, there is always a right answer, but there are always different ways to get there," says Christopher Lewine, a third-year teacher in Redwood City, Calif. So instead of moving to the next problem when a correct answer is given to an algebraic problem, Lewine's class at Everest Public High School is just getting started. Rather than lecturing, he prompts students to discuss and defend how they solved the problem, discovering different approaches from one another. He learned this technique while getting his master's in the yearlong practice-heavy Stanford Teacher Education Program.

Fresh out of Yale with an economics degree in 2009, Lewine earned his sea legs observing and teaching in a five-week middle school math summer program, then was placed at Everest 20 hours a week while getting schooled at Stanford in how

Look for a program that puts you on the front lines from the outset.

best to teach the principles of high school math, hold kids' attention, facilitate group work, and keep all students engaged regardless of their ability. With his master's and a preliminary California secondary teaching credential in hand, he was hired by Everest and now teaches algebra and AP statistics.

Strong support, total immersion

Above all else, experts agree, people who want to teach should look for master's programs that place them on the front lines from the outset. Though the pace of innovation has picked up, teacher-prep programs vary widely in quality, and far too many still prepare teachers in a bubble, disconnected from the realities of the classroom, says Arthur Levine, president of the Woodrow Wilson National Fellowship Foundation and author of "Educating School Teachers," a milestone 2006 report highly critical of the low standards and performance of many of America's education schools in preparing teachers.

You want "strong support in a total immersion program," preferably one that partners with K-12 schools and provides teacher-mentors, says Charles Coble, codirector of an Association of Public and Land-Grant Universities initiative to overhaul teacher training. That effort, the Science & Math Teacher Imperative, has sparked a move toward these sorts of best practices at 132 public and flagship universities and 13 university systems, which together produce more than 40 percent of the nation's math and

science teachers. "We're putting [student] teachers directly into the schools and wrapping the university education around [the clinical experience]," says Thomas James, provost and dean of Teachers College at Columbia University.

Tapping the medical model

Some of the new master's options aimed at scientists and mathematicians have been conceived as "teaching residencies" and are modeled on the clinical training medical residents get. Kevin Perry, 36, was in fact headed for a career in surgery when he decided he'd rather teach middle-school biology in New York City instead. He gets his teaching certification in middle- and high-school science this summer after a year in New York University's Clinically Rich Integrated Science Program (CRISP).

"On the second day of the program, we were put in the classroom," Perry says. After several weeks observing during a summer session last July, he was paired with a biology teacher in September to observe and then begin co-teaching at East Side Community School in Manhattan. Each week, Perry and fellow teaching residents are led by NYU and K-12 school faculty in instructional "rounds" in which they discuss what works and what doesn't. He also takes courses in science, teaching methods, literacy and language acquisition, and data and assessment. Perry receives $30,000 in scholarships from NYU's Steinhart school and New York State, along with a $20,000 living stipend. Similar residencies are offered by the University of Pennsylvania, University

of Delaware, and Georgia State University, among many others.

How can current teachers beef up their STEM bona fides and get set for the coming standards? Part-time and online options are springing up to meet their needs. Central Texas high school teachers, for example, can check out the University of Texas-Austin's master's in STEM education-engineering (MASEE) program. Offered jointly by the schools of engineering and education, MASEE preps teachers in the emerging field of conveying secondary math and science principles through engineering. The three-year program—offered in nine-week sessions over three summers plus four semesters of online work—is a twist on the university's storied UTeach program for undergraduates, now in 34 universities nationwide, which recruits and trains STEM majors to be teachers. The University of Maryland has created a teacher-oriented master's of education in middle-school mathematics.

"This truly has made me a better teacher," says Germantown, Md., algebra teacher Adam Ritchie, 29, who finished the Maryland evening and summer program in December. "I was able to apply [coursework] right off the bat in the classroom." Besides studies that encouraged exploratory and inquiry-based learning and gave him the know-how to better challenge all kids regardless of ability, Ritchie took algebra, geometry, and statistics, and now feels much more ready for the Common Core in math, which gets rolled out in county middle schools next year. The other welcome payoff: a 20 percent bump in salary. ●

Sizzling Spots in K-12

Demand in a number of teaching specialties is heating up. BY RETT FISHER

Big changes in education, driven by changing curriculum standards, demographics, and diagnoses of kids with special needs, are creating opportunities for graduates with the right skill sets. Josh Fernandez is one new teacher who has capitalized on these changes. In 2008, Fernandez, a communications grad of East Carolina University, began working as a paraprofessional at Maryland's Gaithersburg High School, helping a paraplegic student with his day-to-day activities. Realizing that he'd found his calling, Fernandez pursued a master's in special education part time at the Johns Hopkins University School of Education. After graduating in June of 2012, he was immediately hired by his high school to teach special ed.

Around the country, many districts are adding staff in response to the burgeoning number of students diagnosed with special needs; the Bureau of Labor Statistics projects hires will grow 17 percent between 2010 and 2020. The increasing prevalence of autism (affecting 1 in 88 children in 2008 versus 1 in 150 in 2000, reports the Centers for Disease Control and Prevention) and attention deficit hyperactivity disorder (9 percent of 5 to 17 year olds in the CDC's latest survey, up two points since the late '90s) have contributed to the sudden surge. Special ed is such a "critical need area at all levels," says Jeffrey Martinez, director of the department of recruitment and staffing for Montgomery County Public Schools, where Fernandez teaches, that the district offers to pick up a substantial portion of the costs for tuition, books, and fees for employees pursuing a master's at Johns Hopkins who agree to work in the school system for two years.

Demographic shifts are fueling hiring in another hot area: English as a second language. According to the Pew Research Center, a record 23.9 percent of children in pre-K through 12th grade were Hispanic in 2011. This trend will only continue: By 2050, Hispanics will represent 38 percent of all school-age children. Jeff Edmundson, director of master's degree programs in the department of education studies at the University of Oregon, says having a "bilingual endorsement," too, is better yet—meaning the teacher is also proficient in the language of the students being taught.

Meanwhile, the U.S. effort to stay globally competitive is creating an urgent push to get scientists and mathematicians into the classroom. In 2012, President Obama challenged schools to "recruit 100,000 math and science teachers within the next 10 years" to help bring student performance up to snuff. While the challenge of finding qualified teachers has "been going on forever," it is even greater now, says Steve Head, director of education portfolios and career services at the University of Wisconsin-Madison School of Education. That's because new Common Core standards, adopted by almost all states and the District of Columbia, establish more rigorous uniform national learning goals for students in math,

 and a second movement is afoot to boost science standards. The College Board is also overhauling the way Advanced Placement science is taught.

Job candidates must now be "able

Many districts are adding staff in response to the burgeoning number of students with special needs.

to teach at the level that our students are going to be assessed at," explains Laurie deBettencourt, associate dean of educator preparation programs at Hopkins's School of Education. Several school districts deBettencourt works with have teamed up with universities to provide financial incentives to students with backgrounds in math and science who agree to get their master's and certification to teach K-12. Anecdotally, the incentives seem to be working, she says. Many grads who before would have moved into other careers or higher education positions are opting instead to teach in grade school or high school. ●

Schools of Education

THE TOP SCHOOLS

Rank	School	Overall score	Peer assessment score (5.0=highest)	Superintendent assessment score (5.0=highest)	'12 mean GRE scores (verbal/ quantitative)[1]	'12 doctoral acceptance rate	'12 doctoral students/ faculty[2]	Doctorals granted/ faculty 2011-12	'12 funded research (in millions)	'12 funded research/faculty member (in thousands)	'12 total graduate education enrollment
1.	Vanderbilt University (Peabody) (TN)	100	4.6	4.7	162/158	5.5%	2.6	0.6	$40.6	$455.9	808
2.	Johns Hopkins University (MD)	98	3.8	4.8	164/152	24.1%	0.3	0.0	$43.3	$849.8	1,404
3.	Harvard University (MA)	97	4.4	4.8	163/158	6.2%	4.7	0.7	$31.1	$598.1	945
4.	University of Texas–Austin	94	4.1	4.3	159/152	19.4%	4.5	0.9	$60.9	$438.4	1,225
5.	Stanford University (CA)	93	4.7	4.9	161/156	6.4%	3.9	0.5	$21.0	$437.2	380
6.	Teachers College, Columbia University (NY)	90	4.4	4.7	158/153	19.3%	5.3	1.6	$47.5	$322.9	5,034
7.	University of Pennsylvania	88	4.1	4.2	162/156	6.3%	1.9	0.3	$30.4	$468.0	1,222
8.	University of California–Los Angeles	87	4.2	4.5	158/152	29.0%	9.1	1.8	$31.3	$696.2	795
8.	University of Oregon	87	3.5	3.8	159/152	17.1%	3.6	0.7	$34.8	$965.8	677
10.	University of Wisconsin–Madison	85	4.3	4.5	157/153	29.1%	4.2	1.1	$35.5	$358.4	1,010
11.	University of Michigan–Ann Arbor	83	4.4	4.3	157/154	21.5%	5.1	0.5	$22.0	$467.2	473
12.	University of California–Berkeley	81	4.3	4.4	159/152	16.9%	8.3	1.2	$16.1	$502.6	344
12.	University of Washington	81	4.0	4.0	155/152	38.3%	5.2	1.3	$39.4	$729.5	971
14.	Northwestern University (IL)	80	3.9	4.5	161/153	8.9%	2.1	0.2	$12.5	$403.1	378
15.	Michigan State University	78	4.3	4.2	156/151	37.1%	5.2	0.6	$32.3	$301.8	2,051
16.	Ohio State University	77	3.9	4.3	156/153	34.0%	2.0	0.4	$40.5	$235.2	1,161
17.	New York University (Steinhardt)	75	4.0	4.2	161/153	8.2%	3.0	0.8	$23.9	$178.1	3,451
17.	University of Southern California (Rossier)	75	3.9	4.2	161/154	16.4%	7.6	5.6	$19.0	$704.1	1,993
19.	Boston College (Lynch)	72	3.7	4.3	160/156	6.0%	3.4	1.0	$13.3	$238.2	861
19.	Indiana University–Bloomington	72	3.9	4.3	156/151	31.6%	3.4	0.8	$24.0	$244.9	919
19.	University of Illinois–Urbana-Champaign	72	4.1	4.2	156/157	38.1%	3.9	0.9	$14.0	$177.0	936
22.	University of Kansas	71	3.8	4.0	152/150	67.9%	4.0	0.8	$36.8	$471.9	962
22.	University of Virginia (Curry)	71	4.1	4.3	157/154	22.2%	3.1	0.7	$14.7	$209.7	949
24.	Arizona State University	69	3.6	3.6	160/149	28.6%	2.8	1.3	$31.7	$348.0	2,462
24.	Utah State University	69	3.0	3.3	155/156	24.9%	1.0	0.3	$42.8	$321.9	1,010
26.	University of Minnesota–Twin Cities	68	3.8	3.9	N/A / N/A	41.4%	5.2	0.9	$33.0	$259.6	1,880
27.	University of Maryland–College Park	65	3.9	4.1	157/152	23.1%	4.1	1.1	$12.6	$126.8	986
28.	Pennsylvania State University–University Park	63	3.8	4.1	N/A / N/A	41.5%	4.0	0.8	$16.1	$136.8	1,138
28.	University of Colorado–Boulder	63	3.7	3.9	159/151	16.3%	2.6	0.4	$6.4	$211.8	354
28.	University of Connecticut (Neag)	63	3.7	4.2	156/153	39.3%	3.2	0.8	$13.4	$216.1	796
28.	Virginia Commonwealth University	63	3.1	3.7	158/150	40.5%	1.4	0.5	$17.2	$358.3	1,075
32.	College of William and Mary (VA)	61	3.4	4.5	157/155	48.2%	2.3	0.6	$7.0	$183.6	398
32.	Purdue University–West Lafayette (IN)	61	3.5	4.0	151/150	42.0%	2.4	0.6	$12.7	$191.7	523
32.	University of Illinois–Chicago	61	3.5	4.3	153/148	56.4%	3.1	0.6	$13.8	$306.6	691
32.	University of Iowa	61	3.6	4.0	155/150	48.8%	4.5	0.9	$14.7	$186.5	693
32.	University of Pittsburgh	61	3.6	3.8	149/144	46.9%	4.5	0.8	$22.2	$397.0	1,047
37.	University of California–Irvine	60	3.3	3.8	162/156	13.0%	3.5	0.7	$4.2	$198.9	229
37.	University of Delaware	60	3.2	3.6	160/156	41.9%	3.3	0.9	$16.5	$459.2	363
37.	University of North Carolina–Chapel Hill	60	3.9	4.2	156/149	45.7%	4.8	0.6	$7.6	$179.8	522
40.	Syracuse University (NY)	59	3.4	4.3	157/153	44.1%	2.6	0.4	$8.6	$143.6	678
40.	University of California–Santa Barbara (Gevirtz)	59	3.4	4.5	154/151	14.7%	6.3	1.3	$3.5	$97.5	344
40.	University of Florida	59	3.6	4.0	155/147	41.2%	6.6	1.0	$17.9	$251.5	1,268
43.	University of Georgia	58	3.9	4.1	153/148	34.0%	3.4	0.9	$13.5	$73.7	1,857
44.	Florida State University	57	3.4	3.8	N/A / N/A	35.5%	3.4	0.9	$12.8	$170.9	1,069
44.	George Washington University (DC)	57	3.4	4.0	156/152	49.1%	5.3	1.2	$12.7	$259.9	1,699
46.	University of Miami (FL)	56	3.2	3.8	158/152	15.8%	3.4	0.4	$6.3	$196.5	310
47.	Rutgers, the State U. of N. J.–New Brunswick	55	3.4	3.8	156/152	47.1%	2.7	0.5	$8.8	$184.2	1,008
47.	Temple University (PA)	55	3.1	4.1	155/151	61.8%	5.2	0.8	$14.8	$344.9	1,153
47.	Texas A&M University–College Station	55	3.6	4.2	151/148	57.9%	3.9	0.9	$13.3	$126.6	1,289
47.	University at Albany–SUNY	55	3.4	3.7	155/155	26.0%	3.5	0.5	$6.8	$125.8	1,001
51.	Boston University	54	3.4	4.2	153/148	37.3%	3.2	0.7	$2.9	$96.1	576
51.	Lehigh University (PA)	54	2.8	3.7	157/147	15.8%	3.1	1.0	$11.1	$412.6	523
51.	University of Arizona	54	3.6	3.9	154/150	66.2%	4.8	0.6	$10.0	$204.5	716
51.	University of Missouri	54	3.4	3.7	154/146	16.2%	4.7	0.8	$11.4	$123.7	1,498
51.	University of Nebraska–Lincoln	54	3.4	4.1	155/149	43.4%	3.2	0.6	$12.8	$150.5	1,075
51.	University of North Carolina–Greensboro	54	3.2	3.9	155/149	40.5%	2.4	0.6	$13.5	$197.8	925

More at www.usnews.com/grad

Rank	School	Overall score	Peer assessment score (5.0=highest)	Superintendent assessment score (5.0=highest)	'12 mean GRE scores (verbal/quantitative)[1]	'12 doctoral acceptance rate	'12 doctoral students/faculty[2]	Doctorals granted/faculty 2011-12	'12 funded research (in millions)	'12 funded research/faculty member (in thousands)	'12 total graduate education enrollment
51.	University of Tennessee–Knoxville	54	3.3	4.0	156/154	53.3%	1.2	0.4	$11.7	$104.5	640
58.	University of Massachusetts–Amherst	53	3.4	4.0	154/145	44.7%	3.7	0.6	$9.9	$193.7	708
58.	Washington University in St. Louis	53	3.1	3.9	162/158	15.0%	1.0	N/A	$0.0	$0.0	22
60.	Georgia State University	52	3.0	4.1	155/151	39.1%	2.4	0.7	$12.3	$118.3	1,582
60.	University of California–Davis	52	3.4	3.8	155/150	34.1%	5.6	0.9	$6.5	$217.1	429
60.	University of Vermont	52	3.2	3.7	154/148	55.2%	0.7	0.2	$9.8	$256.8	353
63.	George Mason University (VA)	51	3.2	3.8	155/149	54.4%	2.2	0.2	$11.3	$164.0	2,317
63.	University of Kentucky	51	3.2	3.9	157/150	37.1%	3.0	0.5	$10.1	$110.0	818
65.	Fordham University (NY)	50	3.0	4.1	154/153	36.3%	9.0	1.6	$7.0	$219.3	1,165
65.	Marquette University (WI)	50	2.8	4.4	159/151	14.3%	1.4	0.6	$0.1	$6.2	238
65.	Old Dominion University (Darden) (VA)	50	2.8	3.7	152/147	39.5%	1.8	0.6	$33.7	$366.2	1,611
65.	San Diego State University	50	3.1	3.5	153/146	50.0%	0.7	0.3	$16.4	$178.5	1,155
65.	University of Cincinnati	50	3.0	3.5	153/150	26.9%	2.4	0.5	$13.7	$151.0	1,258
65.	University of Hawaii–Manoa	50	2.8	3.3	155/150	44.1%	1.0	0.3	$19.7	$171.2	990
65.	University of Oklahoma (Rainbolt)	50	3.0	4.1	153/148	16.3%	3.2	0.6	$6.6	$97.9	769
65.	University of Utah	50	3.1	3.7	160/151	23.7%	3.5	0.8	$5.0	$97.1	585
65.	University of Wisconsin–Milwaukee	50	3.3	4.1	153/150	25.2%	1.6	0.4	$2.7	$36.7	650
74.	Loyola Marymount University (CA)	49	2.7	4.0	155/152	40.0%	2.0	0.5	$5.6	$175.2	1,402
74.	Oklahoma State University	49	2.9	3.8	153/163	29.6%	2.4	0.8	N/A	N/A	832
74.	University of California–Riverside	49	3.3	3.9	153/152	43.0%	4.8	0.7	$2.3	$113.7	212
74.	University of Louisville (KY)	49	2.8	4.0	N/A / N/A	22.0%	2.0	0.8	$7.7	$113.1	1,143
78.	Auburn University (AL)	48	3.2	4.1	152/144	27.1%	2.4	0.8	$5.1	$62.6	872
79.	North Carolina State University–Raleigh	47	3.1	3.6	N/A / N/A	40.1%	3.0	0.8	$12.7	$165.4	1,457
79.	University at Buffalo–SUNY	47	3.1	3.5	151/149	40.5%	4.5	0.7	$7.7	$151.9	1,085
81.	Ball State University (IN)	46	3.0	3.9	154/148	23.6%	1.7	0.6	$2.9	$35.0	2,728
81.	Brigham Young University–Provo (McKay) (UT)	46	2.8	3.7	158/151	22.1%	1.0	0.2	$1.4	$16.7	345
81.	Southern Illinois University–Carbondale	46	2.8	3.4	144/145	61.4%	2.0	0.5	$20.9	$239.7	929
81.	University of Alabama	46	3.2	4.1	151/149	54.2%	3.7	0.7	$4.3	$44.0	1,087
81.	University of California–Santa Cruz	46	2.8	4.0	158/148	39.5%	1.9	0.1	$2.5	$157.8	93
81.	University of Colorado–Denver	46	3.0	3.8	N/A / N/A	55.6%	1.2	0.5	$5.0	$139.0	1,329
81.	University of South Florida	46	2.9	3.5	160/154	31.5%	3.2	0.6	$11.5	$110.6	1,490
88.	American University (DC)	45	2.7	3.9	154/149*	N/A	N/A	N/A	$3.1	$240.2	205
88.	Kansas State University	45	3.1	3.7	153/147	73.1%	2.4	0.5	$6.0	$145.9	1,058
88.	Washington State University	45	3.0	4.1	153/146	35.8%	2.6	0.5	$2.5	$39.9	674
91.	Clemson University (Moore) (SC)	44	2.9	3.9	152/148	56.4%	1.4	0.3	$4.1	$71.4	504
91.	Illinois State University	44	2.9	3.8	154/148	62.9%	1.0	0.3	$10.4	$90.9	722
91.	Loyola University Chicago	44	3.1	4.0	152/145	27.4%	5.3	1.2	$2.4	$67.3	675
91.	Miami University (OH)	44	3.0	3.8	N/A / N/A	N/A	0.4	0.1	$1.8	$22.8	691
91.	University of Central Florida	44	3.1	3.8	N/A / N/A	48.4%	3.4	0.7	$7.3	$100.9	1,928
91.	University of San Diego	44	3.1	3.6	157/149	45.8%	2.1	0.4	$0.7	$24.5	596
97.	Baylor University (TX)	43	2.9	4.0	152/152	33.3%	1.0	0.2	$0.3	$6.0	229
97.	Hofstra University (NY)	43	2.8	4.1	155/149	50.8%	1.7	0.4	$2.0	$39.7	813
97.	University of South Carolina	43	3.1	3.8	154/153	53.6%	2.2	1.0	$1.0	$15.8	1,103
100.	CUNY–Graduate Center	42	3.0	3.9	159/150	12.4%	12.6	2.1	$0.8	$85.1	92
100.	Louisiana State University–Baton Rouge	42	3.0	3.7	151/146	54.9%	1.7	0.5	$6.5	$86.3	512
100.	Virginia Tech	42	3.0	3.9	N/A / N/A	79.5%	4.4	1.2	$8.9	$194.6	833
103.	Claremont Graduate University (CA)	41	3.2	4.1	152/147	65.3%	12.4	2.0	$1.9	$147.7	471
103.	Iowa State University	41	3.2	3.7	152/144	85.2%	1.6	0.8	$2.9	$71.0	613
103.	Kent State University (OH)	41	2.8	3.8	151/147	27.7%	3.0	0.5	$5.5	$47.8	1,982
103.	Ohio University	41	2.9	3.9	147/152	55.9%	2.8	0.6	$2.1	$43.3	934
103.	University of North Carolina–Charlotte	41	3.0	3.8	N/A / N/A	56.8%	1.4	0.4	$4.2	$46.0	1,681
108.	Northern Arizona University	40	2.8	3.5	152/150	70.3%	1.7	0.6	$5.2	$78.2	2,238
108.	University of Idaho	40	2.7	3.3	N/A / N/A	40.0%	2.1	0.5	$9.7	$262.2	490
108.	University of Maine	40	2.7	3.4	N/A / N/A	63.2%	1.8	0.3	N/A	N/A	458
111.	Howard University (DC)	39	3.0	4.0	N/A / N/A	61.8%	3.6	0.4	$3.7	$115.5	288
111.	Mills College (CA)	39	2.6	3.9	N/A / N/A	73.0%	N/A	0.6	$2.2	$224.5	222
111.	Mississippi State University	39	2.5	3.3	N/A / N/A	23.3%	1.9	0.3	$10.1	$116.2	808
111.	University of Houston (TX)	39	2.8	3.6	153/151	32.4%	5.1	1.3	$2.7	$50.5	768
111.	University of Mississippi	39	2.7	3.7	149/139	38.7%	1.5	0.4	$5.6	$121.9	623
111.	University of South Alabama	39	2.3	3.7	150/157	50.0%	0.4	N/A	$5.2	N/A	409
111.	University of Texas–San Antonio	39	2.8	3.5	149/143	52.9%	1.2	0.3	N/A	N/A	1,660
111.	West Virginia University	39	2.8	3.7	150/146	53.2%	2.0	0.4	$4.7	$66.9	1,249

[1]GRE scores are for doctoral students only, and all those displayed are for exams taken during or after August 2011 using the new 130-170 score scale.
[2]Student/faculty ratio is for all full-time equivalent doctoral students and full-time faculty.
*The school could not break out GRE scores for doctoral students; average scores for all entering students are shown.
N/A=Data were not provided by the school. Sources: U.S. News and the schools. Assessment data collected by Ipsos Public Affairs.

PROGRAMS RANKED BEST BY EDUCATION SCHOOL DEANS

ADMINISTRATION/SUPERVISION

1. Vanderbilt University (Peabody) (TN)
2. University of Wisconsin–Madison
3. Stanford University (CA)
4. Harvard University (MA)
5. Teachers College, Columbia University (NY)
6. Pennsylvania State University–University Park
7. University of Texas–Austin
8. Ohio State University
9. Michigan State University
10. University of Virginia (Curry)
10. University of Washington

COUNSELING/PERSONNEL SERVICES

1. University of Maryland–College Park
2. University of Georgia
3. University of North Carolina–Greensboro
4. University of Minnesota–Twin Cities
4. University of Missouri
4. University of Wisconsin–Madison
7. Ohio State University
8. University of Florida

CURRICULUM/INSTRUCTION

1. University of Wisconsin–Madison
2. Michigan State University
3. Teachers College, Columbia University (NY)
4. Stanford University (CA)
5. University of Illinois–Urbana-Champaign
6. Ohio State University
6. University of Michigan–Ann Arbor
8. Vanderbilt University (Peabody) (TN)
9. University of Georgia

EDUCATION POLICY

1. Stanford University (CA)
2. Harvard University (MA)
3. Vanderbilt University (Peabody) (TN)
4. University of Wisconsin–Madison
5. Teachers College, Columbia University (NY)
6. University of Michigan–Ann Arbor

7. University of California–Berkeley
8. University of Pennsylvania
9. University of California–Los Angeles
10. University of Virginia (Curry)
11. Michigan State University
11. Pennsylvania State University–University Park

EDUCATIONAL PSYCHOLOGY

1. University of Wisconsin–Madison
2. Stanford University (CA)
3. University of Michigan–Ann Arbor
4. University of Maryland–College Park
5. University of Illinois–Urbana-Champaign
6. Vanderbilt University (Peabody) (TN)
7. Michigan State University
8. University of California–Berkeley
9. University of Texas–Austin
10. Pennsylvania State University–University Park
11. University of California–Los Angeles
11. University of Minnesota–Twin Cities

ELEMENTARY EDUCATION

1. Michigan State University
2. Teachers College, Columbia University (NY)
3. University of Wisconsin–Madison
4. Vanderbilt University (Peabody) (TN)
5. University of Georgia
6. University of Michigan–Ann Arbor
7. University of Virginia (Curry)
8. Ohio State University
9. University of Washington
10. University of Illinois–Urbana-Champaign
11. Indiana University–Bloomington

HIGHER EDUCATION ADMINISTRATION

1. University of Michigan–Ann Arbor
2. Michigan State University

3. University of California–Los Angeles
4. Pennsylvania State University–University Park
5. Vanderbilt University (Peabody) (TN)
6. University of Georgia
6. University of Pennsylvania
6. University of Southern California (Rossier)
9. Indiana University–Bloomington
10. Harvard University (MA)
11. University of Maryland–College Park

SECONDARY EDUCATION

1. Michigan State University
2. University of Michigan–Ann Arbor
3. Stanford University (CA)
3. University of Georgia
5. University of Wisconsin–Madison
6. Teachers College, Columbia University (NY)
7. Vanderbilt University (Peabody) (TN)
8. University of Washington
9. University of Virginia (Curry)
10. Ohio State University
11. University of Illinois–Urbana-Champaign

SPECIAL EDUCATION

1. Vanderbilt University (Peabody) (TN)
2. University of Kansas
3. University of Oregon
4. University of Texas–Austin
5. University of Virginia (Curry)
6. University of Florida
7. University of Washington
8. University of Illinois–Urbana-Champaign
9. University of Minnesota–Twin Cities
10. University of Wisconsin–Madison
11. University of Maryland–College Park

VOCATIONAL/TECHNICAL

1. University of Georgia
2. Pennsylvania State University–University Park
3. Ohio State University

Graduate programs at 278 schools granting doctoral degrees were surveyed; 239 responded, and 235 provided data needed to calculate rankings based on 10 measures: **Quality assessment:** Two surveys were conducted in the fall of 2012. Education school deans and deans of graduate studies were asked to rate program quality from marginal (1) to outstanding (5); 43 percent responded. The resulting score is weighted by .25. School superintendents from a sample of districts nationwide were also asked to rate programs; 11 percent responded. The two most recent years' superintendents' surveys were averaged and weighted by .15. **Student selectivity (weighted by .18):** Combines mean verbal and quantitative GRE scores of doctoral students entering in fall 2012 and the acceptance rate of doctoral applicants for 2012-2013 (each accounts for one third of the measure). Where mean GRE scores are not available for doctoral students, mean GRE scores for all entering students may be substituted, if available. Scores for the new and old GRE were converted to a common scale; only new scores are displayed. **Faculty resources (.12):** Resources include the 2012 ratio of full-time-equivalent doctoral students to full-time faculty (37.5 percent); average percentage of full-time faculty holding awards or editorships at selected education journals in 2011 and 2012 (20.8 percent); and ratio of doctoral degrees granted to full-time faculty in the 2011-12 school year (41.7 percent). **Research activity (.30):** This measure uses average total education school research expenditures (50 percent) and average expenditures per full-time faculty member (50 percent). Expenditures refer to separately funded research, public and private, conducted by the school, averaged over fiscal years 2011 and 2012. **Overall rank:** Data were standardized about their means, and standardized scores were weighted, totaled, and rescaled so that the top school received 100; other schools received their percentage of the top score. **Specialty rankings:** These ratings are based solely on nominations by deans and deans of graduate studies, who were asked to choose up to 10 programs for excellence in each specialty. The top ones are listed; more are at *www.usnews.com/grad.*

ENGINEERING

In the Surface Science Instrumentation Lab at Caltech, ranked No. 4

The Field Gets a Facelift

Schools are emphasizing real-world problem solving, not just theory. BY CATHIE GANDEL

Mykel Green planned to become a physician, at least until he spent two undergraduate summers doing research on tissue engineering. The 22-year-old from Augusta, Ga., graduated from Atlanta's Morehouse College in May 2012, and in August began a five-year Ph.D. program in biomedical engineering offered jointly by the Georgia Institute of Technology and the Emory School of Medicine. His focus? Biomaterials and regenerative medicine. Green hopes to develop life-saving therapies for patients who suffer the excruciating bone and joint pain that is a symptom of sickle cell disease, an inherited blood disorder. "I wanted to be a doctor because it's clear that doctors help people," says Green. But he realized that engineering is also a means to improve lives.

"It's blatantly obvious that engineering can make your life better," says T.E. "Ed" Schlesinger, head of the department of electrical and computer engineering at Carnegie Mellon University in Pittsburgh. Think cell phones, medical devices, solar power—and engineered bone. But for years graduate school programs often failed to make that real-world connection apparent. Traditionally, engineering students have been seen as focusing almost exclusively on advanced math, taking notes in large lecture halls, and working in isolated labs on narrow, abstract projects.

"In the past, engineers and engineering schools tended to do their own thing without a lot of intermingling or collaboration with experts in other disciplines," says Paul Westerhoff, associate dean for research and graduate services at the Ira A. Fulton Schools of Engineering at Arizona State University in Tempe.

Many prospective students turned away from the discipline, not seeing a satisfying payoff for the hard slog required to earn an advanced degree. These lean years left the United States lagging behind the rest of the world in innovation and technology. Today, however, graduate schools are revamping their engineering programs to help America regain its competitive edge. These efforts are paying off as almost 47,000 master's degrees were conferred in 2011, up 8 percent over the previous year.

The turnaround has been achieved by schools offering more cross-disciplinary choices in the classroom; collaborations with government, industry, and other universities; and opportunities to gain practical experience solving problems. And institutions are also taking steps to fill the demand for engineers by broadening the pool, attracting more diverse student populations.

Multiple disciplines, dual degrees

Engineering is at the core of so many complex global challenges—in healthcare, medicine, energy, food safety, manufacturing, communications, the environment—that grad programs have realized "the days in which you can solve major problems by applying a single discipline are more or less behind us," says Alec Gallimore, a professor of aerospace engineering and associate dean for research and graduate education in the College of Engineering at the University of Michigan–Ann Arbor. Cross-disciplinary, even multidisciplinary programs, are essential now to train the next generation of engineers, he says.

Mykel Green (left), a biomedical engineering student pursuing his Ph.D., works in a university lab at Georgia Tech.

What this means, notes Schlesinger, is that in addition to taking core classes, one graduate student in electrical and computer engineering, for example, may add public policy, while another might opt for a business course. Students "have freedom to pursue their own interests," he says, and, at the same time, improve their marketability.

Universities have also moved to set up formal multi-disciplinary advanced degrees offered by two or more departments or even, in certain cases, with partnering institutions. Carnegie Mellon offers a master of product development degree, involving its department of mechanical engineering, its Tepper School of Business, and the School of Design. Degree candidates learn to design new products, considering the various elements needed to bring them to fruition: form, function, marketing, and consumer behavior.

At the University of Michigan, the Engineering Sustainable Systems dual degree allows students to get an M.S.E. from the College of Engineering along with an M.S. from the School of Natural Resources and Environment. The goal is to better prepare graduates to create greener manufacturing, water, and energy processes and systems that are also economically sustainable.

Another curricular innovation is the professional science master's degree, which combines academic training with prac-tical education. For example, ASU's Solar Energy Engineering & Commercialization degree lets candidates explore solar energy technologies plus the business and nontechnical aspects of turning them into a viable product. Currently, there are nearly 300 PSM programs offered at 129 institutions, according to the National Professional Science Master's Association (story, Page 8). Some university engineering departments are also training Ph.D. candidates to apply their research skills to the business world, teaching basics like accounting as well as teamwork, communication, and entrepreneurship.

Learning by doing good

Experiential learning has long been a component of undergraduate education "as a way to engage and excite students," says Paul Johnson, dean of ASU's engineering school. Now, he says, grad programs, too, are building in ways for budding engineers to apply classroom theory to real world situations "as the incoming students expect it."

The nonprofit organization Engineers Without Borders-USA, based in Boulder, Colo., but with chapters on more than 180 campuses around the country, is one avenue for this kind of experience. After receiving a request for a specific need from a nongovernmental organization or community, domestic or international, EWB-USA puts the job out for "bid" and awards it to the chapter that seems best able to develop a solution. Lauren McBurnett, 19, who completed an accelerated undergraduate-plus-master's degree at Arizona State University and is now a Ph.D.-track candidate in civil engineering there, led a team sponsored by EWB-USA to Bondo, Kenya, last summer to implement a rainwater collection system they had designed: large in-ground tanks to store rainwater from school roofs.

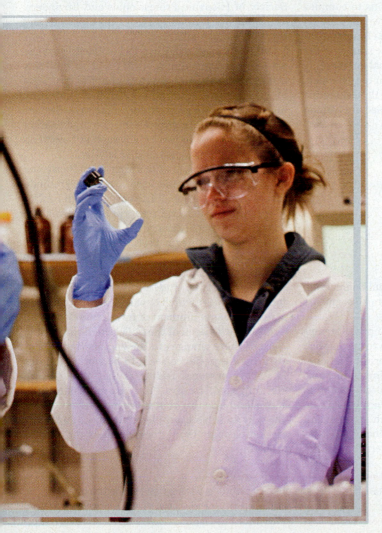

"We really impacted people's lives," says McBurnett, who hopes to get her degree in 2016. "It was hard but I'd go back and do it again." In fact, she is currently working on the design phase of a dam renovation in Bondo to be carried out over the summer.

Out on the factory floor

Major corporations have also helped provide students with real-world experience (and priceless networking opportunities) in partnerships with universities. Rachel Kelley, 29, from Centerville, Tenn., will graduate from the Massachusetts Institute of Technology in the spring of 2013 with a master's in systems engineering from the school of engineering and an M.B.A. from MIT's Sloan School of Management. Kelley is in MIT's Leaders of Global Operations program, which allows students to earn two degrees in two years, including a six-month internship with a sponsoring company, like Amazon, General Motors, and Nike.

Last year, Kelley spent her internship in La Coruña, Spain, at the headquarters of clothing manufacturer Zara, helping the company optimize inventory transfers between its stores. "It was fun working on a real problem that made a difference to their bottom line," she says.

Similarly, engineering students at Georgia Tech can

participate in the Graduate Co-op Internship program, which facilitates semester-long work assignments, full- or part-time, with government research programs or industries related to the student's master's or doctoral thesis.

Encouraging diversity

In a 2012 report, the President's Council of Advisors on Science and Technology noted that the United States must produce 1 million more professionals in the fields of science, technology, engineering, and mathematics over the next decade to regain its global competitiveness. The country will never get there, experts believe, unless more women and underrepresented minorities enroll in graduate programs. Though women make up 50.8 percent of the U.S. population, they only represented 22.6 percent of those earning master's degrees in engineering in 2011. In that same year Hispanics and African-Americans received only 6.3 percent and 4.9 percent of master's degrees, respectively, despite accounting for a combined 30 percent of the U.S. population.

"To get the best solutions to complex engineering challenges, we need to get the best talent," says Gilda Barabino, associate chair for graduate studies in the department of biomedical engineering at Georgia Tech. This can only happen, says Barabino (who in 2012 became the first African-American and second woman

Engineering is at the core of many complex global problems.

to serve as president of the Biomedical Engineering Society), if engineers are pulled from all segments of the population.

In fact, many universities and nonprofit organizations have put in place programs to accomplish this goal. For example, the nonprofit National GEM Consortium, which is working to increase the participation of underrepresented groups in postgraduate engineering and science education, partners with universities, research centers, and corporations to offer master's and doctoral fellowships, coupled with paid summer internships, to Af-

rican-Americans, American Indians, and Hispanic Americans. More information can be found on the Consortium's website, *www.gemfellowship.org*. At MIT, the Xerox Fellowship Program provides financial support for students pursuing advanced degrees, especially women and other traditionally underrepresented groups. Xerox Fellowships are open to second-, third-, and fourth-year School of Engineering graduate students, with a preference for those pursuing Ph.D.s or master's candidates who are likely to enter a Ph.D. program. In addition to full tuition and a stipend for nine months, students are invited to work at one of Xerox's four research centers worldwide during the summer.

Beyond financial aid, underrepresented students desperately need moral support. "It's great to have a nice tossed salad in the classroom," says Gallimore, "but there have to be mechanisms to support these diverse groups." Faculty and peer mentoring programs have sprung up to fill the role. The University of Michigan, for example, is home to graduate chapters of the Society of Minority Engineers and Scientists, the Society of Women Engineers, and the Society of Hispanic Professionals and Engineers. The latter was formed by Tizoc Cruz-Gonzalez and some fellow students.

"Minority candidates can feel isolated," says the 30-year-old from Azusa, Calif., who is half way through a Ph.D. program in mechanical engineering. "I felt we needed a strong Latino organization to support Latino grad students," he says. Besides providing a social environment, the organization offers workshops in basic skills such as how to do research and how to talk to your adviser.

Georgia Tech is also working to increase the number of African-Americans attending graduate school in engineering and science through FACES (Facilitating Academic Careers in Engineering and Science), a National Science Foundation-sponsored effort between Georgia Tech, Morehouse College, Emory University, and Spelman College. The FACES fellowship provides a stipend of $3,000 or $5,000 to Ph.D. students at Georgia Tech that can be used for research or career development expenses such as equipment or travel, says Gary May, Georgia Tech's dean of the College of Engineering.

All of these changes to the engineering graduate school experience seem to be working, notes May. "My personal feeling is that students are more engaged," he says. "They are more hands-on, active, and learning that there may be more than one way to solve a problem." In turn, engineers are increasingly being recognized as the world's problem-solvers. ●

Find out more about engineering programs of interest and check whether a school rises to the top of a certain specialty at **www.usnews.com/engineering.**

More Choices Than Ever

A growing array of career paths awaits future engineers. BY ARLENE WEINTRAUB

Engineering has become an "it" degree, recent grads are discovering, in both traditional tech professions and across the economy. While the unemployment rate for people with bachelor's degrees was 3.9 percent in December 2012, says Mark Regets, a senior analyst at the National Science Foundation, the rate for engineers was 2 percent. And the picture will only get rosier with the aging of the baby boomers. "Half of the engineers in the power industry are going to be retiring in the next five years," says T.E. "Ed" Schlesinger, department head of electrical and computer engineering at Carnegie Mellon University in Pittsburgh.

Civil engineers, for example, are benefiting from a boom in new construction and an urgent need to update the nation's aging infrastructure that has only been exacerbated by recent catastrophic weather events like "super storm" Sandy. "They're looking at gas pipelines, water, waste water, buildings—making sure they all stay safe during those events," says Dan Wittliff, president of the National Society of Professional Engineers in Alexandria, Va. The government's Bureau of Labor Statistics estimates the current crop of some 263,000 civil engineers will grow 19 percent by 2020. "I like taking something when it's in the planning stages and bringing it to life," says Brittani Grant, who, after finishing her master's degree in civil engineering in December at Carnegie Mellon, headed straight into her dream position—staff engineer at Clark Construction in Bethesda, Md., helping build the Smithsonian's National Museum of African American History and Culture in Washington. "There are not many people in their construction career who can say they built a museum that's going to stand for hundreds of years."

Environmental, petroleum, and computer engineers are similarly in demand, both for their part in the infrastructure update and for tackling other high-priority challenges, such as climate change and energy exploration and production technology development. "You hear about smart grids and smart meters—it's the whole idea of bringing information technology to the power industry. This is driving an enormous need for engineers," says Schlesinger. Nuclear and petroleum engineering grads boast the highest median salaries, in the $126,000 to $129,000 range, according to the NSPE's latest salary survey. Despite the disaster at the Fukushima nuclear power plant in Japan after the 2011 earthquake there, enthusiasm for nuclear energy has not noticeably waned in the

United States, says Wittliff, who thinks the number of jobs for nuclear and petroleum engineers will grow in the "15 to 20 percent range over the next 10 years." Computer engineers start at just under $70,000 a year, according to figures from the National Association of Colleges and Employers. Civil engineers average about $55,000, the median for engineers of all types, though grads with a master's degree command about 10 percent more than that, Wittliff says.

Meanwhile, more than half of the 3.7 million people in the country who hold engineering degrees have found a welcome in non-scientific arenas such as investment banking and consulting, prompting many experts to call engineering the new liberal arts degree. "I like technology and working with numbers, but at the same time I'm a people person,"

"Half of the engineers in the power industry are going to be retiring in the next five years."

says Lisa Thompson, who graduated in May 2012 with a master's in biomedical engineering from Washington University in St. Louis and took a job as a consultant with a Chicago company. Thompson's first project involves helping an insurance firm on technology alignment and process improvement. She says her company so values people with technical training who can work collaboratively that it plans to keep adding engineers until they represent 70 percent of the technology consultants. ●

Schools of Engineering

THE TOP SCHOOLS

Rank	School	Overall score	Peer assessment score (5.0=highest)	Recruiter assessment score (5.0=highest)	'12 average quantitative GRE score	'12 acceptance rate	'12 Ph.D. students/ faculty	'12 faculty membership in National Academy of Engineering	'12 engineering school research expenditures (in millions)	'12 research expenditures per faculty member (in thousands)	Ph.Ds granted 2011-2012	'12 total graduate engineering enrollment
1.	Massachusetts Institute of Technology	100	4.9	4.8	164	16.4%	5.5	13.2%	$362.8	$978.0	288	3,163
2.	Stanford University (CA)	95	4.8	4.6	165	18.9%	8.1	17.8%	$193.4	$895.6	307	3,548
3.	University of California–Berkeley	87	4.8	4.6	163	12.4%	5.9	16.2%	$192.5	$802.0	228	1,837
4.	California Institute of Technology	78	4.7	4.5	164	8.0%	6.1	14.1%	$106.9	$1,175.2	62	587
5.	Carnegie Mellon University (PA)	77	4.3	4.2	161	28.8%	5.2	10.5%	$204.4	$848.0	183	2,857
5.	Georgia Institute of Technology	77	4.5	4.3	162	26.0%	4.4	3.7%	$225.1	$452.9	356	4,651
5.	University of Illinois–Urbana-Champaign	77	4.5	4.3	163	27.0%	4.4	3.1%	$236.4	$637.2	297	2,975
8.	Purdue University–West Lafayette (IN)	73	4.2	4.1	162	26.9%	4.9	5.0%	$239.7	$667.7	236	3,070
9.	University of Michigan–Ann Arbor	72	4.4	4.1	164	24.7%	4.3	3.6%	$196.0	$541.5	266	3,184
9.	University of Southern California (Viterbi)	72	3.7	3.8	161	30.7%	5.6	10.7%	$173.7	$998.3	154	4,398
11.	Texas A&M University–College Station (Look)	71	3.8	3.8	161	25.8%	4.5	2.9%	$282.3	$901.9	221	2,918
11.	University of Texas–Austin (Cockrell)	71	4.2	4.0	162	18.7%	4.8	7.5%	$186.2	$618.6	234	2,425
13.	Cornell University (NY)	70	4.3	4.1	164	28.4%	4.6	11.9%	$132.4	$668.8	128	1,768
14.	University of California–San Diego (Jacobs)	68	3.8	3.7	163	22.7%	5.3	11.9%	$163.6	$898.9	150	1,614
15.	Columbia University (Fu Foundation) (NY)	66	3.7	3.7	164	22.7%	4.8	12.1%	$139.1	$933.4	119	2,525
16.	University of California–Los Angeles (Samueli)	65	3.7	3.8	163	25.9%	6.1	15.2%	$93.3	$605.7	152	1,776
17.	Princeton University (NJ)	64	4.2	4.0	163	10.4%	4.0	17.4%	$89.0	$674.1	82	574
18.	University of Wisconsin–Madison	63	3.9	3.9	162	15.6%	4.6	4.0%	$160.2	$708.9	137	1,903
19.	University of Maryland–College Park (Clark)	61	3.7	3.6	162	24.5%	4.2	3.0%	$181.9	$780.6	150	2,254
20.	Northwestern University (McCormick) (IL)	60	4.0	3.8	163	21.7%	4.5	4.3%	$111.6	$620.0	129	1,669
20.	University of California–Santa Barbara	60	3.6	3.6	164	16.7%	4.6	14.7%	$108.6	$816.4	75	760
22.	University of Pennsylvania	59	3.4	3.6	167	23.4%	4.3	7.4%	$107.5	$986.4	57	1,704
23.	Harvard University (MA)	58	3.7	3.9	160	9.8%	5.4	14.5%	$52.0	$693.1	54	404
24.	Virginia Tech	57	3.8	3.7	160	24.8%	3.7	3.3%	$151.4	$457.3	172	2,278
25.	Johns Hopkins University (Whiting) (MD)	54	3.9	3.9	162	27.6%	4.7	2.0%	$78.1	$542.5	95	3,434
25.	Pennsylvania State University–University Park	54	3.7	3.8	162	24.1%	3.1	0.8%	$152.3	$431.5	165	1,863
25.	University of Washington	54	3.6	3.5	162	18.4%	3.8	7.3%	$113.0	$528.0	114	2,030
28.	Duke University (Pratt) (NC)	53	3.6	3.8	162	18.9%	4.2	2.5%	$80.1	$679.2	58	944
29.	North Carolina State University	52	3.4	3.4	163	17.0%	2.6	3.0%	$154.0	$475.4	145	2,918
29.	Ohio State University	52	3.5	3.6	163	18.3%	3.8	2.5%	$116.8	$476.8	137	1,738
29.	University of Minnesota–Twin Cities	52	3.7	3.6	N/A	22.4%	3.8	3.7%	$97.3	$461.2	127	1,920
32.	Rice University (Brown) (TX)	51	3.7	3.7	164	17.1%	4.7	6.8%	$50.4	$442.5	80	716
33.	University of California–Davis	50	3.4	3.7	161	22.3%	4.3	6.6%	$74.2	$414.3	114	1,169
34.	University of Colorado–Boulder	47	3.3	3.4	160	33.0%	4.7	5.3%	$77.6	$513.6	86	1,613
34.	Yale University (CT)	47	3.3	3.6	164	12.0%	4.0	10.4%	$28.2	$564.1	28	217
36.	Vanderbilt University (TN)	46	3.2	3.5	N/A	12.9%	4.5	2.3%	$66.5	$801.1	53	457
37.	University of California–Irvine (Samueli)	45	3.2	3.3	161	16.9%	4.0	3.3%	$85.0	$461.7	112	1,276
38.	Boston University	44	3.0	3.2	162	25.6%	4.0	5.9%	$75.6	$646.5	70	857
38.	Rensselaer Polytechnic Institute (NY)	44	3.5	3.7	163	24.0%	3.5	2.0%	$57.4	$387.8	85	831
38.	University of Florida	44	3.3	3.3	161	43.2%	3.7	0.4%	$65.6	$250.2	207	2,967
38.	University of Rochester (NY)	44	2.7	3.1	160	30.9%	3.7	4.7%	$92.9	$1,056.2	41	547
38.	University of Virginia	44	3.3	3.3	162	16.8%	3.7	3.1%	$71.4	$549.0	84	667
43.	Iowa State University	42	3.1	3.5	159	17.2%	2.4	2.2%	$83.9	$388.5	112	1,013
44.	Arizona State University (Fulton)	41	3.1	3.3	161	55.4%	3.0	1.9%	$75.9	$381.3	121	2,692
45.	Lehigh University (Rossin) (PA)	40	3.1	3.3	163	18.0%	5.4	7.5%	$22.2	$211.3	41	787
45.	University of Notre Dame (IN)	40	3.2	3.4	162	16.7%	4.2	2.6%	$42.4	$365.7	56	501
45.	University of Pittsburgh (Swanson)	40	3.0	3.1	161	30.1%	3.4	0.7%	$86.7	$646.7	56	1,032
48.	Brown University (RI)	39	3.3	3.4	160	21.2%	2.7	6.0%	$23.4	$354.6	25	323
48.	University of Arizona	39	3.1	3.2	166	30.7%	3.2	4.0%	$63.3	$368.2	78	993
48.	Washington University in St. Louis	39	3.1	3.5	163	31.0%	4.2	2.5%	$24.7	$325.0	47	775
51.	Case Western Reserve University (OH)	38	3.1	3.3	162	18.7%	3.4	1.8%	$40.6	$387.1	55	633
51.	Michigan State University	38	3.1	3.4	N/A	12.3%	3.3	1.8%	$53.4	$314.2	68	858
51.	Rutgers, the State Univ. of N. J.–New Brunswick	38	3.1	3.3	161	21.9%	2.2	4.4%	$60.0	$338.8	75	1,004
51.	University of Utah	38	2.8	3.0	161	37.5%	3.1	4.7%	$81.2	$537.7	82	1,073
55.	Dartmouth College (Thayer) (NH)	37	3.0	3.4	163	20.9%	3.0	2.2%	$20.6	$428.6	19	289

More at www.usnews.com/grad

Rank School	Overall score	Peer assessment score (5.0=highest)	Recruiter assessment score (5.0=highest)	'12 average quantitative GRE score	'12 acceptance rate	'12 Ph.D. students/ faculty	'12 faculty membership in National Academy of Engineering	'12 engineering school research expenditures (in millions)	'12 research expenditures per faculty member (in thousands)	Ph.D.s granted 2011-2012	'12 total graduate engineering enrollment
55. University of Delaware	37	2.9	3.0	160	25.3%	4.3	3.8%	$52.8	$393.9	82	862
57. Colorado School of Mines	36	2.8	3.6	158	40.9%	3.1	1.8%	$55.5	$334.3	59	1,343
57. Northeastern University (MA)	36	2.8	3.2	160	44.6%	3.9	2.2%	$37.6	$263.3	47	2,295
57. Polytechnic Institute of New York University (NY)	36	2.6	3.2	160	40.3%	1.3	9.4%	$16.8	$311.9	29	2,114
57. University of Massachusetts–Amherst	36	2.8	3.3	162	25.8%	3.5	0.7%	$53.5	$354.1	71	862
61. University at Buffalo–SUNY	35	2.8	3.0	161	24.3%	3.3	1.4%	$63.5	$444.2	48	1,324
61. University of Iowa	35	2.8	3.1	160	24.8%	3.1	1.1%	$45.9	$534.2	48	418
63. University of Dayton (OH)	34	2.1	2.7	N/A	48.3%	2.1	N/A	$77.9	$1,236.4	15	689
64. Stony Brook University–SUNY	33	2.7	3.0	N/A	36.6%	4.3	2.3%	$31.2	$247.5	54	1,433
65. University of Illinois–Chicago	32	2.7	3.2	159	31.1%	3.6	1.9%	$29.3	$290.0	70	1,078
65. University of Tennessee–Knoxville	32	2.7	3.0	159	27.9%	3.0	0.6%	$59.0	$378.2	61	1,000
67. Auburn University (Ginn) (AL)	31	2.8	3.2	159	54.5%	1.3	1.4%	$60.1	$408.9	65	851
67. Colorado State University	31	2.7	3.0	159	42.4%	1.2	1.0%	$64.0	$615.6	40	660
67. Drexel University (PA)	31	2.8	3.1	159	46.3%	3.5	2.3%	$36.8	$266.9	66	1,128
67. University of California–Riverside (Bourns)	31	2.4	2.9	161	21.3%	4.6	2.2%	$37.8	$455.4	70	534
67. University of Connecticut	31	2.7	3.0	161	29.9%	3.2	1.5%	$42.0	$328.2	56	774
72. Illinois Institute of Technology (Armour)	30	2.7	3.0	159	59.7%	3.0	2.1%	$22.2	$244.4	39	1,450
72. Stevens Institute of Technology (Schaefer) (NJ)	30	2.5	3.1	N/A	70.3%	2.8	1.4%	$28.1	$374.7	34	1,728
72. Tufts University (MA)	30	2.7	3.2	161	37.8%	2.3	2.7%	$21.1	$293.2	31	622
72. University of Central Florida	30	2.4	2.7	N/A	40.9%	3.7	0.8%	$63.6	$513.0	61	1,293
76. Syracuse University (NY)	29	2.7	3.0	162	39.0%	2.7	1.4%	$12.8	$188.9	28	862
76. University of Houston (Cullen) (TX)	29	2.6	2.8	161	43.8%	3.3	4.5%	$25.9	$198.9	52	1,070
76. University of Texas–Dallas (Jonsson)	29	2.4	2.8	N/A	50.7%	2.5	3.1%	$42.9	$354.7	79	1,809
79. Clemson University (SC)	28	2.8	2.9	N/A	37.9%	2.5	N/A	$29.0	$154.0	88	1,317
79. University of North Carolina–Chapel Hill	28	2.8	3.3	157	28.2%	2.1	N/A	$9.0	$280.6	12	129
81. Missouri University of Science & Technology	27	2.7	3.3	158	61.3%	1.9	0.6%	$29.5	$174.6	50	1,050
81. University of Cincinnati	27	2.5	3.0	161	25.4%	2.8	N/A	$25.8	$185.8	67	859
81. University of New Mexico	27	2.4	2.6	164	61.9%	4.2	1.0%	$31.3	$319.2	42	712
81. Washington State University	27	2.6	2.9	159	30.2%	3.8	1.1%	$20.1	$211.2	44	674
85. Mississippi State University (Bagley)	26	2.4	2.6	159	25.2%	2.1	N/A	$50.6	$486.3	45	622
85. Oregon State University	26	2.6	2.9	158	23.0%	2.3	N/A	$34.1	$273.1	46	834
87. University of California–Santa Cruz (Baskin)	25	2.3	2.6	162	26.7%	3.1	1.3%	$35.0	$438.0	35	334
87. University of Missouri	25	2.5	2.8	159	35.5%	2.3	N/A	$32.1	$281.6	41	618
89. Michigan Technological University	24	2.5	3.0	N/A	40.3%	1.9	N/A	$29.0	$196.0	43	823
89. University of Alabama–Huntsville	24	2.3	2.8	157	63.4%	1.5	N/A	$54.1	$676.1	30	763
89. University of Kentucky	24	2.5	2.6	158	40.3%	2.0	0.7%	$45.5	$305.3	46	520
89. University of Nebraska–Lincoln	24	2.4	2.9	161	41.8%	2.0	N/A	$38.0	$234.4	40	599
89. Worcester Polytechnic Institute (MA)	24	2.6	3.1	160	42.7%	1.3	0.9%	$11.5	$107.1	28	1,057
94. George Washington University (DC)	23	2.4	3.0	160	37.2%	1.4	N/A	$14.1	$188.4	53	1,542
94. Kansas State University	23	2.6	2.9	158	30.3%	0.8	N/A	$22.5	$187.2	30	496
94. New Jersey Institute of Technology	23	2.6	2.8	N/A	67.9%	1.1	N/A	$48.6	$392.2	41	1,340

THE SPECIALTIES

PROGRAMS RANKED BEST BY ENGINEERING SCHOOL DEPARTMENT HEADS

Rank School	Average assessment score (5.0=highest)
AEROSPACE	
1. California Institute of Technology	4.6
1. Massachusetts Institute of Technology	4.6
3. Stanford University (CA)	4.5
3. University of Michigan–Ann Arbor	4.5
5. Georgia Institute of Technology	4.4
6. Purdue University–West Lafayette (IN)	4.3
7. University of Illinois–Urbana-Champaign	4.1
8. University of Texas–Austin (Cockrell)	4.0
9. Princeton University (NJ)	3.9

Rank School	Average assessment score (5.0=highest)
9. Texas A&M University–College Station (Look)	3.9
BIOLOGICAL/AGRICULTURAL	
1. Purdue University–West Lafayette (IN)	4.7
2. University of Illinois–Urbana-Champaign	4.6
3. Cornell University (NY)	4.4
3. University of Florida	4.4
5. Texas A&M University–College Station (Look)	4.3
6. Iowa State University	4.2
6. North Carolina State University	4.2

Rank School	Average assessment score (5.0=highest)
8. University of California–Davis	4.1
9. Virginia Tech	4.0
10. University of Nebraska–Lincoln	3.9
BIOMEDICAL	
1. Johns Hopkins University (Whiting) (MD)	4.8
2. Georgia Institute of Technology	4.6
3. University of California–San Diego (Jacobs)	4.5
4. Duke University (Pratt) (NC)	4.4
5. Massachusetts Institute of Technology	4.3

GRE scores displayed are for master's and Ph.D. students and are only for those GRE exams taken during or after August 2011 using the new 130-170 score scale.
N/A=Data were not provided by the school. Sources: *U.S. News*, the schools. Assessment data collected by Ipsos Public Affairs.

THE SPECIALTIES

Rank School	Average assessment score (5.0=highest)
6. Stanford University (CA)	4.1
6. University of Pennsylvania	4.1
6. University of Washington	4.1
9. Rice University (Brown) (TX)	4.0
10. University of California–Berkeley	3.9
10. University of Michigan–Ann Arbor	3.9

CHEMICAL

Rank School	Average assessment score (5.0=highest)
1. Massachusetts Institute of Technology	4.9
2. California Institute of Technology	4.8
3. University of California–Berkeley	4.7
4. Stanford University (CA)	4.6
4. University of Minnesota–Twin Cities	4.6
6. Princeton University (NJ)	4.3
6. University of Texas–Austin (Cockrell)	4.3
6. University of Wisconsin–Madison	4.3
9. University of California–Santa Barbara	4.2
10. Georgia Institute of Technology	4.1

CIVIL

Rank School	Average assessment score (5.0=highest)
1. University of Illinois–Urbana-Champaign	4.8
2. University of California–Berkeley	4.7
3. Stanford University (CA)	4.5
4. Georgia Institute of Technology	4.4
5. University of Texas–Austin (Cockrell)	4.3
6. Purdue University–West Lafayette (IN)	4.2
7. Massachusetts Institute of Technology	4.0
7. University of Michigan–Ann Arbor	4.0
7. Virginia Tech	4.0
10. Carnegie Mellon University (PA)	3.9
10. Cornell University (NY)	3.9

COMPUTER

Rank School	Average assessment score (5.0=highest)
1. Massachusetts Institute of Technology	5.0
2. University of California–Berkeley	4.9
3. Carnegie Mellon University (PA)	4.7
4. University of Illinois–Urbana-Champaign	4.6
5. Cornell University (NY)	4.2
5. Georgia Institute of Technology	4.2

Rank School	Average assessment score (5.0=highest)
5. University of Michigan–Ann Arbor	4.2
5. University of Texas–Austin (Cockrell)	4.2
9. Princeton University (NJ)	4.1
10. Purdue University–West Lafayette (IN)	4.0

ELECTRICAL/ELECTRONIC

Rank School	Average assessment score (5.0=highest)
1. Massachusetts Institute of Technology	4.9
1. Stanford University (CA)	4.9
3. University of California–Berkeley	4.7
3. University of Illinois–Urbana-Champaign	4.7
5. California Institute of Technology	4.5
5. Georgia Institute of Technology	4.5
7. Carnegie Mellon University (PA)	4.3
7. Cornell University (NY)	4.3
7. University of Michigan–Ann Arbor	4.3
10. Purdue University–West Lafayette (IN)	4.2

ENVIRONMENTAL

Rank School	Average assessment score (5.0=highest)
1. University of California–Berkeley	4.6
2. Stanford University (CA)	4.5
3. University of Illinois–Urbana-Champaign	4.4
4. University of Michigan–Ann Arbor	4.1
5. Georgia Institute of Technology	4.0
6. University of Texas–Austin (Cockrell)	3.9
7. Carnegie Mellon University (PA)	3.8
7. Johns Hopkins University (Whiting) (MD)	3.8
9. California Institute of Technology	3.7
9. Massachusetts Institute of Technology	3.7

INDUSTRIAL/MANUFACTURING/SYSTEMS

Rank School	Average assessment score (5.0=highest)
1. Georgia Institute of Technology	4.8
2. University of Michigan–Ann Arbor	4.6
3. Massachusetts Institute of Technology	4.3
3. Northwestern University (McCormick) (IL)	4.3
3. Stanford University (CA)	4.3
3. University of California–Berkeley	4.3
7. Cornell University (NY)	4.1
7. University of Wisconsin–Madison	4.1
7. Virginia Tech	4.1

Rank School	Average assessment score (5.0=highest)
10. Purdue University–West Lafayette (IN)	4.0

MATERIALS

Rank School	Average assessment score (5.0=highest)
1. Massachusetts Institute of Technology	4.7
2. Stanford University (CA)	4.4
2. University of California–Santa Barbara	4.4
4. Northwestern University (McCormick) (IL)	4.3
4. University of Illinois–Urbana-Champaign	4.3
6. University of California–Berkeley	4.2
7. California Institute of Technology	4.0
7. Cornell University (NY)	4.0
9. Georgia Institute of Technology	3.9
9. University of Michigan–Ann Arbor	3.9

MECHANICAL

Rank School	Average assessment score (5.0=highest)
1. Massachusetts Institute of Technology	4.9
1. Stanford University (CA)	4.9
3. California Institute of Technology	4.7
3. University of California–Berkeley	4.7
5. Georgia Institute of Technology	4.6
5. University of Michigan–Ann Arbor	4.6
7. University of Illinois–Urbana-Champaign	4.4
8. Purdue University–West Lafayette (IN)	4.2
9. Cornell University (NY)	4.1
10. Princeton University (NJ)	4.0
10. University of Texas–Austin (Cockrell)	4.0

NUCLEAR

Rank School	Average assessment score (5.0=highest)
1. Massachusetts Institute of Technology	4.9
2. University of Michigan–Ann Arbor	4.7
3. University of Wisconsin–Madison	4.2
4. Texas A&M University–College Station (Look)	4.1
5. North Carolina State University	3.8
6. University of Tennessee–Knoxville	3.7
7. University of California–Berkeley	3.6
8. Pennsylvania State University–University Park	3.5
8. Purdue University–West Lafayette (IN)	3.5
10. Georgia Institute of Technology	3.3
10. University of Illinois–Urbana-Champaign	3.3

METHODOLOGY

Programs at the 199 engineering schools that grant doctoral degrees were surveyed; 193 responded, and 191 were eligible to be included in the rankings based on a weighted average of 10 indicators described below.

Quality assessment: Two separate surveys were conducted in the fall of 2012. In one, engineering school deans and deans of graduate studies at engineering schools were asked to rate program quality from marginal (1) to outstanding (5); 51 percent responded. The resulting score is weighted by .25 in the overall score. Corporate recruiters and company contacts who hire engineers with graduate degrees from previously ranked engineering schools were also asked to rate programs; 16 percent responded. The two most recent years' results were averaged and are weighted by .15.

Student selectivity (weighted by .10): The strength of master's and Ph.D. students entering in fall 2012 was measured by their mean GRE quantitative score (67.5 percent of this measure) and acceptance rate (32.5 percent). Scores for the new and old GRE were converted to a common scale; only new scores are displayed.

Faculty resources (.25): This score is based on the 2012 ratio of full-time doctoral students to full-time faculty (30 percent) and full-time master's students to full-time faculty (15 percent); the proportion of full-time faculty who were members of the National Academy of Engineering in 2012 (30 percent); and the number of engineering doctoral degrees granted in the past school year (25 percent).

Research activity (.25): Based on total externally funded engineering research expenditures (60 percent) and research dollars per full-time tenured and tenure-track engineering faculty member (40 percent). Expenditures refer to separately funded research, public and private, conducted by the school, averaged over fiscal years 2011 and 2012.

Overall rank: Data were standardized about their means, and standardized scores were weighted, totaled, and rescaled so the top-scoring school received 100; others received their percentage of the top score.

Specialty rankings: These rankings are based solely on assessments by department heads in each specialty, who rated other schools on a 5-point scale. The top-rated schools in each specialty appear here. Names of department heads surveyed are from the American Society for Engineering Education.

CHAPTER 4

HEALTH &
MEDICINE

Medical students consult at No. 4 University of Pennsylvania.

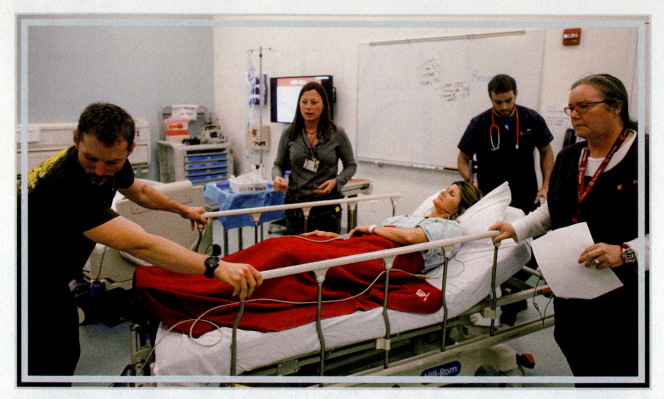

Fitted Out For the Future

Medical and nursing training is undergoing a sea change. BY BETH HOWARD

The patient, a trim middle-aged man named Jack, was undergoing routine surgery when suddenly his heart stopped, and he stopped breathing. The medical team sprang into action, performing CPR and inserting a tube down his throat to force oxygen into his lungs. Thanks to their quick thinking, Jack was stabilized and recovered.

In reality, Jack was never in real danger. A medical mannequin capable of blinking, breathing, and even bleeding, he is a central player in drama after drama at Stanford University School of Medicine's high-tech simulation center. Rare just a decade ago, such simulation centers are part of a transformation taking place in medical education, fueled by calls from the Institute of Medicine and key bodies like the American Medical Association to bring medical training into the 21st century. Practicing on a dummy first has safety benefits, obviously. But even more key, simulations let budding doctors and

nurses practice working seamlessly as members of a team, getting a feel for what it will be like to care for patients alongside anesthesiologists, radiologists, pharmacists, and allied health professionals in an increasingly complex health system. With medical knowledge doubling every eight to 10 years and health reform mandating or strongly encouraging cost-cutting, improved quality of care, and patient empowerment and safety, experts say, the need for new, improved curricula is nothing short of urgent.

"Physicians know that the medical education of the past does not prepare us for the kinds of care we deliver," says Susan Skochelak, group vice president for medical education for the AMA, which is giving $10 million in grants to med schools to boldly shake up their teaching methods and lessons.

High-tech role-playing
It used to be that medical students trained by the motto, "See one, do one, teach one," with real patients

Concerned about finding the money to cover medical school? Start a search for funding possibilities and explore your less pricey options at **www.usnews.com/payformedschool.**

acting as guinea pigs. That was before researchers began compiling data on the dismal safety record of hospitals—a recent nationwide study of surgical errors alone by Johns Hopkins School of Medicine researchers suggests that, each week, foreign objects are left inside patients about 39 times, wrong procedures are performed 20 times, and wrong body sites are operated on 20 times—and taking a cue from the airline industry and its simulated cockpits. Today's wi-fi enabled mannequins, operated by staffers in a control room, do just about anything a real patient does, including responding to the drugs medical students give them.

"It's like 'World of Warcraft,' except instead of killing people, you're working to heal them," says David Gaba, associate dean for immersive and simulation-based learning at Stanford, whose 28,000-square-foot Center for Immersive and Simulation-Based Learning includes four mannequin-equipped rooms, space for actors to role-play visits to the doctor's office, and computer stations where students can practice examining, diagnosing, and treating virtual patients. Using simulation not only builds skills and confidence, Gaba says, but also helps instructors teach more things more quickly. After all, "we can't schedule a real patient to have a cardiac arrest at 10 o'clock on a Tuesday," Gaba says.

In addition to learning, say, the basics of treating an asthma attack, Saima Siddiqi, 24, a second-year student at the Charles E. Schmidt College of Medicine at Florida Atlantic University in Boca Raton, says the lifelike simulation has helped her integrate information from CT scans and MRIs with observation of the patient. "The test results pop up on a screen, and the high-tech aspect can draw your focus," she says. Meanwhile, "the patient's fingers are subtly turning blue or their eyes turn yellow from jaundice, and you have to be watching for that."

Some 86 out of 90 medical schools and all 64 teaching hospitals that responded to a 2011 survey by the Association of American Medical Colleges reported that they now use simulation to train medical students. One of the newest facilities, the 90,000-square-foot Center for Advanced Medical Learning and Simulation at the University of South Florida Health Morsani College of Medicine in Tampa, uses technology and actors to simulate everything from childbirth to combat medicine, even re-creating the sounds and lights of the battlefield.

The technology is a key tool in implementing a second innovation: training all sorts of medical professionals together. The explosion of knowledge over the last half century has led to a highly fragmented healthcare system, where specialization is increasingly narrow—cardiologists become electrophysiology cardiologists, arrhythmia cardiologists, transplant cardiologists. "The Norman Rockwell model of one doctor treating the whole family hasn't been true for decades," even though medical schools still mostly act as though it is, says Molly Cooke, a professor of medicine at the University of California-San Francisco and coauthor of the Carnegie Foundation's 2010 report *Educating Physicians: A Call for Reform of Medical School and Residency.* "The average diabetes patient sees seven different doctors," points out Stephen Klasko, CEO of USF Health. "And they don't talk to each other."

Consequently, medical students should increasingly expect to find themselves in "interprofessional" relationships, training elbow to elbow and coordinating patient care with students in nursing, pharmacy, physical therapy, and other departments.

Battling burnout

About half of medical students show the classic signs: emotional exhaustion, detachment, and a feeling that one's efforts "don't make a difference," says Liselotte Dyrbye, associate professor of medicine at the Mayo Clinic in Rochester, Minn. That's not good, as burnout, in turn, is linked to reduced altruism and unprofessional behavior, such as reporting a physical exam result as normal without actually doing it. "We're Type A personalities," says LaShon Sturgis, a fourth-year student at the Medical College of Georgia in Augusta. "You really have to be encouraged to step back."

To be accredited, medical schools must have some kind of student wellness program. But many are going well beyond a regular aerobics class in their effort to get students to take a break and, yes, have a life. Sturgis says her school has assigned social chairs for each class, operates a wellness center, and urges students to "do what we really enjoy— biking, hiking, reading." Vanderbilt University School of Medicine has formed "fun fitness" athletic groups, offers an anonymous ask-the-psychiatrist online forum, and has divided the student body into four "colleges" for advising purposes that compete annually in a two-day "College Cup" of Iron Chef, trivia, and dance-off contests.

Mayo, Johns Hopkins, and the University of Virginia, among others, have switched to pass/fail grading in the first two years. At Oakland University William Beaumont School of Medicine in Rochester, Mich., which opened its doors in 2011, students meet in mentoring groups with faculty members for an hour every month to discuss such topics as managing stress and conflict and dealing with mistakes. To graduate, fourth-year students at New Jersey Medical School in Newark must complete a podcast-based course intended to ease the transition to residency. One podcast on burnout covers how to combat the physical aspects of stress, change the elements of scheduling that are possible to change, and cultivate self-awareness.

The point, says Chantal Brazeau, an associate professor of psychiatry and family medicine who recorded the podcast, is to master the important skill of balance. ●
—*Katherine Hobson*

At the University of Medicine and Dentistry of New Jersey, learning about patients by observing horses

ened," says Triola.

With health reform putting a premium on patient-centered care, safety is itself much more widespread a medical school topic. Some 62 percent of schools now report teaching students about the urgency of precautions such as infection prevention strategies and using checklists to avoid catastrophe. In one exercise, medical and nursing students at the University of Missouri School of Medicine in Columbia partnered to assess patients' risk of falls—a major safety hazard in hospitals—and created customized fall prevention plans for them.

How best to nurture the connection between physician and real patient? Traditionally, third-year students have spent monthlong rotations in a series of specialty areas, limiting meaningful interactions with the people in the beds. The Harvard Medical School Cambridge Integrated Clerkship turns that model on its head. Instead of these "block rotations," students follow a panel of patients over a six-month period, from diagnosis through hospitalization to discharge and even home visits. The goal: to see the patient not as a disease but as a person. "You really are running a practice, where you have 100 patients you follow any time they interact with the health system, from the emergency department to discharge and through complications down the road," says Christopher Miller, 32, who completed the clerkship in 2009 and is now an anesthesiology resident at Stanford.

"Traditional education is like having a team where the members all practice on their own and only get together for the game," says Klasko. "That makes no sense."

NYU School of Medicine, for example, pairs first-year med students and NYU nursing students to care for a virtual patient and in simulations. "It's important to start early to establish how important teams are, so doctors have the right attitude from the get-go," says Marc Triola, associate dean for educational informatics and assistant professor of medicine. Students are assessed on their ability to work together. Experts expect the team approach to medicine to reap multiple benefits for patients, including fewer errors, shorter hospital stays, and better care overall. "There is good evidence that when a team doesn't perform well, communication and safety are threat-

Bedside manner is getting more emphasis, too, in novel electives like "From Barnyard to Bedside: Improving Nonverbal Communication Skills in Healthcare" at the University of Arizona at Tucson. Class meets at the ranch of neurosurgeon Allan Hamilton, who pioneered the course and also directs the university's simulation center. Students guide, groom, and

Fast Tracking Med School

Primary care doctors can now get a degree in three years. BY ARLENE WEINTRAUB

When Robert Cooper was growing up in Edgewood, Texas, he liked his neighborhood family doctor so much that by the time he got into medical school in 2010, he already knew he wanted to go into primary care. "I used to always go to our family practice physician, so that's what I knew," says

Cooper, 26, who also values "the flexibility of being able to work in a rural area."

It didn't hurt, either, that primary care doctors are so in demand that his medical school is speeding them into the workforce. The program Cooper enrolled in, an accelerated option at Texas Tech University Health Sciences Center School of Medicine

in Lubbock, will allow him to get his medical degree in three years rather than the usual four, provided he commits to primary care. "We have a shortage of physicians, particularly in primary care," says John Prescott, chief academic officer of the Association of American Medical Colleges in Washington, D.C., which

projects the nation will have 45,000 too few primary care doctors by 2020. "This is one step forward in helping to alleviate that. I think we'll see other schools looking closely at this."

The school of medicine at Mercer University in Savannah, Ga., already offers a similar three-year M.D. degree, and Lake Erie Col-

even examine horses as a way to improve their ability to interpret patients' nonverbal cues; as prey animals, horses are exquisitely attuned to humans' touch and behavior. In a similar course at Stanford, one exercise has students helping horses overcome their fear in scary situations like walking past shiny balloons. That theoretically hones students' ability to pick up on signs of fear in their human patients (whether of a flu shot or brain surgery) and show patience and compassion, says Beverley Kane, who runs the course and has spawned others like it across the country. "Unlike our patients, horses will 'tell' us when we have touched them too roughly."

Keeping pace with the science

The imperative to change medical training is becoming ever more urgent as the pace of medical discoveries proceeds at an astonishing rate. Perhaps no breakthrough to date promises to impact medicine's future so profoundly as the sequencing of the human genome completed in 2003. Doctors have already begun practicing medicine differently in some instances, using this tool to personalize care by screening patients for select mutations that put them at greater risk for disease and make them more likely to respond to drugs for cancer and other conditions. "Genomics will become a crucial component in the everyday practice of future physicians," says Dennis Charney, dean at the Icahn School of Medicine at Mount Sinai in New York.

The latest on genomics is taught, of course—at Mount Sinai and Stanford, students actually analyze aspects of their own genome. But more to the point is the need for schools to address the reality that what future physicians learn about cutting-edge medicine is apt to be outdated by the time they finish their residencies. "One thing that will be critical for people coming out of med school in the future is the ability to meaningfully understand 'what don't I know and how can I learn it,'" says Lindsey Henson, vice dean for medical education and student affairs at Florida Atlantic University's medical school.

To cultivate that way of thinking, Florida Atlantic uses "problem-based learning," in which small groups of students grapple with difficult patient cases in their first two years, with a faculty member standing by to help them understand that "you have to figure out what you need to know," she says. The University of Maryland School of Medicine recently approved a new required course, "Foundations of Research and Critical Thinking," whose lecture topics include how to critically evaluate a scientific paper to determine whether it's worth using with patients. "We want to build a thinking mind," says E. Albert Reece, the school's dean. "Those analytic skills will be much more required in the future. In my day, what was required was a very good memory—drug dosages, symptoms, drug interactions, and side effects. In the future, people have devices to provide information rapidly." In fact, students at Stanford and several other medical schools now get iPads upon arrival, which are helpful for taking notes on the spot and for looking up information and accessing patients' electronic medical records later.

Despite all these pockets of innovation, medical schools as a whole still have a way to go to be in step with the trends and technology transforming medicine, argue observers like Eric Topol, chief academic officer of the Scripps Health hospital and clinic system in San Diego and author of the 2012 book *The Creative Destruction of Medicine*. But change is clearly coming, he says. "It's inevitable." ●

Medical **information** **is doubling** every eight to 10 years.

lege of Osteopathic Medicine in Erie, Pa., offers a three-year program for osteopaths who have chosen family medicine and general internal medicine.

How do you cram four years of intense learning into three? At Texas Tech and Mercer, the key is shortening the clinical rotations medical students experience to get trained in other specialties and focusing instead most of their real-world experience on family medicine. "One of the reasons we can do this is a lot of the fourth year is elective—trying to decide what you want to go into, and doing audition rotations around the country," says Steven Berk, dean of the Texas Tech medical school. "The various competencies that are normally covered in the fourth year we cover in eight weeks."

That condensed schedule offers financial rewards, notes Robert Pallay, residency director and chair of family medicine at Mercer. Students "pay one year less of tuition, which saves $40,000 to $50,000," he says. "They get out a year earlier, so rather than making $50,000 as a resident, they [may] end up earning $200,000-plus as a regular doctor." Add in potential state and federal tuition grants that are often offered to students who commit to primary care, and "we figure it comes out to a quarter of million dollars in savings to them," Pallay says. Berk estimates his school's fast-track med students end up only $22,000 in debt vs. $109,000 if they were to choose a conventional four-year program.

That said, accelerated programs can be especially intense, and may not be for everyone. At Texas Tech, fast-trackers sacrifice their summer break after the first year, for example, to attend an eight-week course in preparation for a second-year clerkship in family medicine. Says Cooper, who is now completing his final year: "You really have to buckle down and focus." ●

A Field in Robust Health

The people in primary care are especially in demand. BY KATHERINE HOBSON

Though they may not want to admit it, baby boomers are getting creaky—and a lot of their parents are requiring medical attention, too. And starting in 2014, millions of people who haven't had insurance will gain coverage and feel freer to seek care.

That all adds up to a seller's market for healthcare pros, particularly in the ranks of primary care. Demand is increasing "virtually across the board," says Susan Salka, chief executive of AMN Healthcare, the country's largest healthcare staffing and recruiting company by revenue. "And we are expecting it to become more robust in the next couple of years." Indeed, the Bureau of Labor Statistics predicts net job growth of almost 3 million healthcare jobs in the decade ending in 2020, a 29

Hospitals are leveraging a limited pool of doctors by using nurse practitioners and physican assistants.

percent increase, beating every other group of occupations. Family physicians were the most sought by the employers who used physician search firm (and AMN subsidiary) Merritt Hawkins, according to its most recent annual survey. (Their average salary climbed 6 percent to $189,000.) Internists were in the second spot. Also high on employers' wish lists: hospitalists and psychiatrists.

As healthcare systems reorganize to cut costs and improve care, new physicians increasingly will be employed by a hospital rather than an independent practice. Sixty-three percent of recent Mer-

ritt Hawkins physician searches were for hospitals seeking staff docs, up from just 11 percent in 2004. Within two years, the firm predicts, that figure will hit three quarters. "The amount of opportunities is overwhelming," says Andrew Geha, 30, a third-year family practice resident who recently accepted a job offer from Floyd Valley Hospital in Le Mars, Iowa, and at the peak of his search was getting a phone call and multiple E-mails every day from recruiters. Geha's wife, a nurse practitioner, will be able to work at the same hospital, and a four-day workweek will give him extra time with his two children.

Meantime, hospitals are leveraging a limited pool of physicians by leaning more heavily on nurse practitioners and physician assistants. New RNs fresh out of undergraduate school are now having some trouble landing a job, with older nurses delaying their retirement. But advanced-practice nurses such as NPs and certified nurse-midwives, who must have post-graduate education, remain hot properties, says Peter McMenamin, senior policy fellow at the American Nurses Association. Salaries average 30 to 35 percent higher than those of hospital staff nurses, he says. Maureen O'Keeffe, system vice president of human resources at St. Luke's Health System in Boise, Idaho, which employs about 11,000 people, says the system hired all through the recession and estimates that some 70 advanced practice nurses will be added in 2013, as well as some 300 acute care nurses.

The physician assistant profession will add some 24,700 new jobs between 2010 and 2020, expanding by nearly 30 percent. Duke University's PA program graduated 74 students last August; as of Jan. 1, only five didn't have jobs. "Many physicians are so in need of PAs that if you're talking to [one] they'll say 'Call me, let's talk, I need help,'" says Katherine Pocock, 27, who was weighing several offers early this year as she neared graduation. Pocock chose PA school over med school because she found the prospect of six more years of training (and debt) "daunting." And she thought being a PA would be more lifestyle-friendly. Salaries aren't bad, either. According to the American Academy of Physician Assistants, full-time PAs commanded median pay of almost $91,000 in 2010; those working in specialty settings like orthopedics or dermatology can earn more. ●

Prestigious

- Ranked in *U.S. News & World Report* among the nation's best graduate programs

- Named by *The Princeton Review* as one of the 296 best business schools in the world, 2005–2013

- Listed as a best value executive MBA program by *Fortune* magazine

Hundreds of companies recruit on campus annually, including Citigroup, The Nielsen Company, Coca-Cola, Raymond James Financial Services and Verizon.

We offer full-time, part-time and executive options in our MBA and M.S. programs. When you're ready to invest in yourself, invest in the best: a degree from the Sykes College of Business at The University of Tampa.

Take the next step!
Visit www.ut.edu/gradinfo
or call (813) 258-7409.

THE UNIVERSITY OF TAMPA

SYKES COLLEGE OF BUSINESS

AACSB ACCREDITED

ACCOUNTING | ENTREPRENEURSHIP | FINANCE | INTERNATIONAL BUSINESS | MARKETING

INNOVATION MANAGEMENT | INFORMATION SYSTEMS MANAGEMENT | NONPROFIT MANAGEMENT

Schools of Medicine

THE TOP SCHOOLS - RESEARCH

Rank School	Overall score	Peer assessment score (5.0=highest)	Assessment score, residency directors (5.0=highest)	'12 average undergrad GPA	'12 average MCAT score	'12 acceptance rate	'12 NIH research grants (in millions)	'12 NIH research grants per faculty member (in thousands)	'12 faculty/ student ratio	'12 out-of-state tuition and fees	'12 total medical school enrollment
1. Harvard University (MA)	100	4.8	4.7	3.88	12.1	3.9%	$1,117.1	$122.3	13.0	$53,496	700
2. Stanford University (CA)	89	4.7	4.6	3.79	11.8	2.8%	$323.5	$374.9	1.9	$48,030	461
3. Johns Hopkins University (MD)	87	4.7	4.7	3.87	11.8	6.2%	$534.2	$195.5	5.7	$45,434	479
4. University of California–San Francisco	86	4.7	4.6	3.77	11.5	3.9%	$498.4	$248.8	3.1	$47,379	648
4. University of Pennsylvania (Perelman)	86	4.6	4.5	3.82	12.3	5.6%	$538.8	$210.0	4.0	$50,746	646
6. Washington University in St. Louis	84	4.5	4.6	3.87	12.3	10.0%	$375.9	$210.8	3.7	$52,020	478
7. Yale University (CT)	83	4.3	4.4	3.79	12.1	6.5%	$359.3	$275.5	3.3	$50,080	397
8. Columbia University (NY)	79	4.3	4.4	3.78	11.9	4.1%	$393.1	$206.3	2.9	$54,855	662
8. Duke University (NC)	79	4.4	4.6	3.79	11.7	5.1%	$319.2	$217.3	3.5	$51,366	425
8. University of Chicago (Pritzker)	79	4.0	4.2	3.83	12.1	4.3%	$255.5	$286.8	2.4	$48,293	377
8. University of Michigan–Ann Arbor	79	4.4	4.6	3.78	11.6	7.9%	$383.0	$204.0	2.8	$47,138	679
12. University of Washington	78	4.3	4.3	3.69	10.4	5.2%	$635.3	$254.0	2.8	$57,318	908
13. University of California–Los Angeles (Geffen)	76	4.1	4.2	3.73	11.3	4.1%	$500.4	$196.1	3.3	$47,029	767
14. Vanderbilt University (TN)	74	4.3	4.4	3.78	11.6	5.5%	$332.2	$138.5	5.4	$46,316	444
15. University of California–San Diego	73	4.1	4.1	3.73	11.0	4.6%	$369.4	$287.4	2.5	$46,736	520
16. Cornell University (Weill) (NY)	72	4.1	4.4	3.78	11.5	5.4%	$297.3	$145.0	5.0	$50,765	409
16. University of Pittsburgh	72	4.1	4.2	3.74	11.7	7.9%	$379.5	$167.8	3.8	$46,629	591
18. Baylor College of Medicine (TX)	67	3.9	4.0	3.83	11.5	6.1%	$262.5	$131.3	2.7	$30,068	751
18. Mount Sinai School of Medicine (NY)	67	3.7	3.9	3.75	11.9	7.3%	$237.0	$190.5	2.2	$46,618	568
18. Northwestern University (Feinberg) (IL)	67	3.9	4.3	3.77	11.4	7.5%	$241.2	$133.1	2.5	$51,490	712
21. New York University	66	3.5	3.9	3.81	11.4	5.8%	$257.4	$218.2	1.8	$49,560	651
22. Emory University (GA)	65	3.9	4.2	3.69	11.5	6.0%	$254.2	$115.8	3.9	$47,764	564
22. University of North Carolina–Chapel Hill	65	4.0	4.1	3.65	10.9	4.8%	$252.3	$176.0	1.8	$43,646	782
22. U. of Texas Southwestern Medical Center	65	4.2	4.1	3.84	11.2	10.3%	$199.9	$92.5	2.3	$30,331	939
25. Case Western Reserve University (OH)	63	3.7	3.8	3.70	11.6	8.8%	$301.4	$127.1	2.8	$53,040	846
26. University of Virginia	62	3.7	4.1	3.80	11.5	13.3%	$117.9	$126.1	1.5	$52,800	614
27. Mayo Medical School (MN)	61	3.7	4.1	3.87	10.8	2.1%	$220.4	$88.7	12.8	$35,960	194
28. University of Iowa (Carver)	59	3.7	3.9	3.74	10.8	8.2%	$138.1	$139.2	1.7	$49,409	588
29. University of Wisconsin–Madison	58	3.6	3.9	3.74	10.4	6.4%	$177.8	$151.8	1.7	$34,815	701
30. Boston University	57	3.4	3.5	3.66	11.2	4.9%	$206.5	$153.6	1.8	$51,548	730
31. Brown University (Alpert) (RI)	56	3.4	3.8	3.68	10.9	3.4%	$124.4	$156.2	1.8	$51,137	452
31. Oregon Health and Science University	56	3.6	3.7	3.66	10.5	4.8%	$226.7	$112.0	3.9	$54,859	522
31. University of Rochester (NY)	56	3.4	3.7	3.74	11.0	5.5%	$142.3	$95.6	3.4	$47,116	435
31. University of Southern California (Keck)	56	3.4	3.8	3.64	11.4	5.3%	$155.8	$111.7	2.0	$52,242	700
35. University of Alabama–Birmingham	55	3.7	3.7	3.76	10.0	9.0%	$144.0	$117.0	1.6	$62,194	747
35. University of Colorado–Denver	55	3.7	3.6	3.74	10.7	5.2%	$206.9	$74.0	4.3	$60,682	644
37. University of Maryland	54	3.3	3.4	3.74	10.5	7.2%	$172.2*	$140.7*	1.8	$53,532	663
38. Dartmouth College (Geisel) (NH)	53	3.5	3.9	3.65	10.9	6.0%	$85.8	$90.1	2.4	$52,406	395
38. Ohio State University	53	3.4	3.5	3.68	11.3	6.6%	$163.2	$84.2	2.2	$34,317	878
38. University of Minnesota	53	3.5	3.7	3.72	10.5	7.4%	$148.5	$88.7	1.7	$53,443	984
38. Yeshiva University (Einstein) (NY)	53	3.4	3.5	3.75	11.0	5.8%	$170.7	$82.7	2.6	$49,435	803
42. University of California–Davis	51	3.3	3.4	3.60	10.3	4.5%	$119.4	$164.7	1.8	$51,896	413
42. University of California–Irvine	51	3.0	3.2	3.68	10.7	4.8%	$140.7	$193.5	1.7	$47,579	423
42. University of Cincinnati	51	3.1	3.3	3.72	10.7	8.0%	$205.2	$126.5	2.4	$48,720	663
45. University of Florida	50	3.2	3.4	3.78	10.7	7.2%	$115.1	$89.7	2.4	$48,697	534
46. University of Massachusetts–Worcester	49	3.1	3.2	3.72	10.7	18.8%	$152.8*	$106.7*	2.8	**	519
46. Wake Forest University (NC)	49	3.2	3.5	3.57	10.7	3.1%	$91.9*	$81.4*	2.3	$44,696	486
48. Georgetown University (DC)	48	3.2	3.6	3.60	10.3	3.4%	$140.2	$65.2	2.7	$50,901	805
48. Indiana University–Indianapolis	48	3.4	3.6	3.70	10.2	13.5%	$119.9*	$62.3*	1.4	$50,587	1,332
48. University of Utah	48	3.3	3.7	3.68	9.8	8.8%	$121.2	$84.4	4.4	$58,610	326
51. Medical College of Wisconsin	47	3.0	3.5	3.76	10.6	6.9%	$102.1	$66.7	1.9	$45,179	810
51. Temple University (PA)	47	2.6	3.0	3.68	10.4	4.9%	$93.9	$183.4	0.6	$54,218	805

More at **www.usnews.com/grad**

THE TOP SCHOOLS - RESEARCH

Rank	School	Overall score	Peer assessment score (5.0=highest)	Assessment score, residency directors (5.0=highest)	'12 average undergrad GPA	'12 average MCAT score	'12 acceptance rate	'12 NIH research grants (in millions)	'12 NIH research grants per faculty member (in thousands)	'12 faculty/ student ratio	'12 out-of-state tuition and fees	'12 total medical school enrollment
51.	Tufts University (MA)	47	3.2	3.6	3.62	10.7	7.0%	$82.7	$52.2	2.0	$55,667	810
51.	University of Miami (Miller) (FL)	47	3.1	3.3	3.72	10.7	5.2%	$131.5	$91.6	1.9	$41,415	753
55.	Uniformed Services University (Hebert) (MD)	44	3.0	3.4	3.54	10.4	10.8%	$50.5	$143.0	0.5	N/A	685
55.	Univ. of Texas Health Science Center–Houston	44	3.0	3.4	3.77	10.4	12.0%	$57.2*	$55.2*	1.1	$29,300	965
57.	George Washington University (DC)	43	2.8	3.3	3.70	10.2	2.1%	$53.6	$59.5	1.3	$51,278	716
57.	Stony Brook University–SUNY	43	2.7	3.0	3.70	10.7	6.9%	$76.0	$111.3	1.3	$56,264	512

THE TOP SCHOOLS - PRIMARY CARE

Rank	School	Overall score	Peer assessment score (5.0=highest)	Assessment score, residency directors (5.0=highest)	Selectivity rank	'12 average undergrad GPA	'12 average MCAT score	'12 acceptance rate	% '10-'12 graduates entering primary care	'12 faculty/ student ratio	'12 out-of-state tuition and fees	'12 total medical school enrollment
1.	University of North Carolina–Chapel Hill	100	3.8	4.1	39	3.65	10.9	4.8%	60.3%	1.8	$43,646	782
2.	University of Washington	99	4.1	4.4	53	3.69	10.4	5.2%	51.0%	2.8	$57,318	908
3.	Oregon Health and Science University	93	3.9	4.0	53	3.66	10.5	4.8%	52.0%	3.9	$54,859	522
4.	University of California–San Francisco	88	3.6	4.4	15	3.77	11.5	3.9%	44.7%	3.1	$47,379	648
5.	University of Colorado–Denver	87	3.8	3.9	33	3.74	10.7	5.2%	46.6%	4.3	$60,682	644
6.	University of Nebraska Medical Center	83	3.1	3.2	51	3.77	10.2	10.9%	65.0%	1.2	$68,579	514
7.	University of Minnesota	81	3.5	3.8	47	3.72	10.5	7.4%	48.5%	1.7	$53,443	984
8.	University of Michigan–Ann Arbor	79	3.3	4.0	13	3.78	11.6	7.9%	43.5%	2.8	$47,138	679

THE TOP SCHOOLS - PRIMARY CARE

Rank	School	Overall score	Peer assessment score (5.0=highest)	Assessment score, residency directors (5.0=highest)	Selectivity rank	'12 average undergrad GPA	'12 average MCAT score	'12 acceptance rate	% '10-'12 graduates entering primary care	'12 faculty/ student ratio	'12 out-of-state tuition and fees	'12 total medical school enrollment
9.	University of Massachusetts–Worcester	77	3.2	3.3	47	3.72	10.7	18.8%	54.4%	2.8	**	519
10.	University of Alabama–Birmingham	76	3.4	3.7	58	3.76	10.0	9.0%	47.0%	1.6	$62,194	747
11.	Michigan State U. (Col. of Osteopathic Medicine)	75	2.7	2.9	106	3.56	9.1	12.8%	79.4%	0.2	$80,536	1,254
11.	University of California–Los Angeles (Geffen)	75	3.2	3.8	23	3.73	11.3	4.1%	45.0%	3.3	$47,029	767
13.	University of Pennsylvania (Perelman)	74	3.2	4.0	3	3.82	12.3	5.6%	37.0%	4.0	$50,746	646
14.	Harvard University (MA)	73	2.9	3.8	2	3.88	12.1	3.9%	44.0%	13.0	$53,496	700
14.	University of Wisconsin–Madison	73	3.4	3.8	47	3.74	10.4	6.4%	41.7%	1.7	$34,815	701
16.	University of Iowa (Carver)	71	3.4	3.8	32	3.74	10.8	8.2%	38.4%	1.7	$49,409	588
16.	University of Rochester (NY)	71	3.3	3.8	25	3.74	11.0	5.5%	39.6%	3.4	$47,116	435
18.	University of Virginia	70	3.1	3.8	15	3.80	11.5	13.3%	40.0%	1.5	$52,800	614
19.	East Carolina University (Brody) (NC)	68	3.1	3.2	104	3.60	9.0	15.3%	54.4%	1.3	$41,380	320
19.	Mayo Medical School (MN)	68	3.1	3.7	21	3.87	10.8	2.1%	39.0%	12.8	$35,960	194
19.	University of California–Davis	68	3.2	3.5	75	3.60	10.3	4.5%	44.8%	1.8	$51,896	413
19.	University of New Mexico	68	3.6	3.4	94	3.65	9.4	12.7%	40.7%	2.3	$49,471	374
19.	Wake Forest University (NC)	68	3.0	3.5	61	3.57	10.7	3.1%	48.0%	2.3	$44,696	486
24.	Baylor College of Medicine (TX)	67	2.8	3.8	9	3.83	11.5	6.1%	42.3%	2.7	$30,068	751
24.	Brown University (Alpert) (RI)	67	2.9	3.5	33	3.68	10.9	3.4%	46.9%	1.8	$51,137	452
24.	Johns Hopkins University (MD)	67	3.0	3.9	5	3.87	11.8	6.2%	34.8%	5.7	$45,434	479
24.	Ohio State University	67	3.1	3.5	25	3.68	11.3	6.6%	42.0%	2.2	$34,317	878
24.	University of Pittsburgh	67	3.1	3.7	15	3.74	11.7	7.9%	38.0%	3.8	$46,629	591
29.	Emory University (GA)	66	3.2	3.6	23	3.69	11.5	6.0%	36.6%	3.9	$47,764	564
29.	University of Utah	66	3.3	3.7	80	3.68	9.8	8.8%	39.2%	4.4	$58,610	326
31.	Dartmouth College (Geisel) (NH)	65	3.1	3.5	39	3.65	10.9	6.0%	41.3%	2.4	$52,406	395
31.	Northwestern University (Feinberg) (IL)	65	2.8	3.7	20	3.77	11.4	7.5%	41.7%	2.5	$51,490	712
31.	University of Missouri	65	3.1	3.3	53	3.77	10.1	9.1%	44.3%	1.5	$54,170	401
31.	University of North Texas Health Science Center	65	2.6	2.7	104	3.57	9.2	19.6%	67.0%	0.5	$31,384	857
31.	U. of Texas Southwestern Medical Center	65	2.8	3.7	19	3.84	11.2	10.3%	41.4%	2.3	$30,331	939
31.	Vanderbilt University (TN)	65	3.0	3.7	12	3.78	11.6	5.5%	36.3%	5.4	$46,316	444
37.	Indiana University–Indianapolis	64	3.3	3.4	64	3.70	10.2	13.5%	39.3%	1.4	$50,587	1,332
37.	University of Kansas Medical Center	64	3.0	3.3	92	3.65	9.5	9.7%	48.4%	1.1	$55,257	765
39.	Boston University	63	2.9	3.5	30	3.66	11.2	4.9%	41.7%	1.8	$51,548	730
39.	Uniformed Services University (Hebert) (MD)	63	3.1	3.6	82	3.54	10.4	10.8%	43.0%	0.5	N/A	685
39.	University of California–San Diego	63	3.1	3.6	28	3.73	11.0	4.6%	36.1%	2.5	$46,736	520
39.	University of Chicago (Pritzker)	63	2.6	3.6	4	3.83	12.1	4.3%	41.0%	2.4	$48,293	377
39.	University of Tennessee Health Science Center	63	2.7	3.0	77	3.68	10.0	16.5%	54.3%	1.2	$66,207	658
44.	Duke University (NC)	62	3.2	3.9	9	3.79	11.7	5.1%	27.0%	3.5	$51,366	425
44.	Eastern Virginia Medical School	62	2.9	2.9	87	3.53	10.2	7.0%	52.0%	0.8	$57,828	529
44.	University of Arizona	62	3.1	3.3	87	3.70	N/A	6.2%	43.7%	1.8	$47,388	475
44.	University of Vermont	62	3.2	3.4	64	3.68	10.1	4.5%	39.0%	1.4	$54,543	446
44.	Washington University in St. Louis	62	3.0	3.7	1	3.87	12.3	10.0%	30.2%	3.7	$52,020	478
49.	Case Western Reserve University (OH)	61	3.0	3.7	22	3.70	11.6	8.8%	34.0%	2.8	$53,040	846
49.	Columbia University (NY)	61	2.8	3.7	7	3.78	11.9	4.1%	35.6%	2.9	$54,855	662
51.	Michigan State U. (College of Human Medicine)	60	3.1	3.2	100	3.56	9.3	5.9%	45.2%	0.8	$60,408	796
51.	Mount Sinai School of Medicine (NY)	60	2.9	3.4	9	3.75	11.9	7.3%	36.4%	2.2	$46,618	568
51.	Yeshiva University (Einstein) (NY)	60	2.8	3.2	25	3.75	11.0	5.8%	42.0%	2.6	$49,435	803
54.	Tufts University (MA)	59	2.7	3.3	56	3.62	10.7	7.0%	45.6%	2.0	$55,667	810
55.	Medical College of Wisconsin	58	3.0	3.5	33	3.76	10.6	6.9%	35.0%	1.9	$45,179	810
55.	University of Oklahoma	58	3.0	3.3	64	3.74	10.0	14.6%	39.4%	1.4	$50,263	658
55.	U. of Texas Health Science Center–San Antonio	58	3.0	3.2	89	3.57	10.1	14.2%	42.0%	1.0	$32,688	889

N/A=Data were not provided by the school. *The medical school's National Institutes of Health grants do not include any grants to affiliated hospitals. **The school does not accept out-of-state students to its M.D. program.
Sources: *U.S. News* and the schools. Peer assessment data collected by Ipsos Public Affairs.

SPECIALTIES

MEDICAL SCHOOL DEANS AND SENIOR FACULTY SELECT THE BEST PROGRAMS

AIDS

1. University of California–San Francisco
2. Johns Hopkins University (MD)
3. Harvard University (MA)
4. Columbia University (NY)
5. University of Washington
6. Duke University (NC)
7. University of Pennsylvania (Perelman)
8. University of Alabama–Birmingham
9. University of California–Los Angeles (Geffen)
9. University of North Carolina–Chapel Hill

DRUG/ALCOHOL ABUSE

1. Yale University (CT)
2. Columbia University (NY)
2. Harvard University (MA)
2. University of California–San Francisco
5. University of Pennsylvania (Perelman)

FAMILY MEDICINE

1. University of Washington

2. University of North Carolina–Chapel Hill
3. University of Colorado–Denver
4. University of California–San Francisco
5. Oregon Health and Science University
6. University of Wisconsin–Madison
7. University of New Mexico
8. Duke University (NC)
8. University of Michigan–Ann Arbor
10. University of Minnesota
10. University of Missouri

GERIATRICS

1. Mount Sinai School of Medicine (NY)
2. Johns Hopkins University (MD)
3. University of California–Los Angeles (Geffen)
4. Duke University (NC)
5. Harvard University (MA)
6. University of California–San Francisco
7. University of Michigan–Ann Arbor
7. Yale University (CT)
9. University of Washington

INTERNAL MEDICINE

1. Johns Hopkins University (MD)
2. University of California–San Francisco
3. Harvard University (MA)
4. University of Pennsylvania (Perelman)
5. Duke University (NC)
6. University of Michigan–Ann Arbor
6. Washington University in St. Louis
8. University of Washington
9. Columbia University (NY)

PEDIATRICS

1. University of Pennsylvania (Perelman)
2. Harvard University (MA)
3. University of Cincinnati
4. Johns Hopkins University (MD)
5. University of Colorado–Denver
6. University of Pittsburgh
7. University of California–San Francisco
8. Baylor College of Medicine (TX)
9. Stanford University (CA)
9. University of Washington

RURAL MEDICINE

1. University of Washington
2. University of New Mexico
3. West Virginia University
4. University of North Dakota
5. University of Minnesota
5. University of North Carolina–Chapel Hill
5. University of Pikeville (KY)
8. University of Colorado–Denver
9. University of Iowa (Carver)
9. University of South Dakota (Sanford)
9. West Virginia School of Osteopathic Medicine

WOMEN'S HEALTH

1. Harvard University (MA)
2. University of California–San Francisco
3. University of Pennsylvania (Perelman)
4. Johns Hopkins University (MD)
4. University of Pittsburgh
6. Columbia University (NY)
7. University of Michigan–Ann Arbor
8. Duke University (NC)

METHODOLOGY

The 126 medical schools fully accredited in 2012 by the Liaison Committee on Medical Education and the 23 schools of osteopathic medicine fully accredited in 2012 by the American Osteopathic Association were surveyed for the rankings of research medical schools and for top schools in primary care; 114 schools provided the data needed to calculate the two separate rankings. The research model is based on a weighted average of eight indicators, and the primary care model is based on seven indicators. Most indicators are the same for both. The research model factors in NIH research activity; the primary care model uses the proportion of graduates entering primary care specialties. **Quality assessment**: Three assessment surveys were conducted in the fall of 2012. In a peer survey, medical and osteopathic school deans, deans of academic affairs, and heads of internal medicine or the directors of admissions were asked to rate program quality on a scale of marginal (1) to

outstanding (5). Respondents were asked to rate research and primary care programs separately. The response rate was 39 percent. A research school's average score is weighted by .20 in the overall model; the average score in the primary care model, by .25. In two surveys, residency program directors were asked to rate programs using the same 5-point scale. One survey dealt with research and was sent to a sample of residency program directors designated by schools as being involved in research. (response rate: 12 percent). The other survey was sent to residency directors designated by schools as being involved in clinical practice (response rate: 16 percent). Residency directors' surveys for the two most recent years were averaged and weighted .20 in the research model and .15 in primary care. Med schools supplied the names of those residency program directors who were sent either of the residency program director surveys plus names from *Graduate Medical*

Education Directory were used. **Research activity** (weighted by .30 in the research model only): Research was measured as the total dollar amount of National Institutes of Health research grants awarded to the medical school and its affiliated hospitals (50 percent of this measure) and the average amount of those grants per full-time medical school science and clinical faculty member (50 percent); both factors were averaged for fiscal years 2011 and 2012. An asterisk indicates schools that reported only NIH research grants to their medical school in 2012. The NIH figures published are for fiscal year 2012 only. **Primary care rate** (.30 in primary care model only): The percentage of medical or osteopathic school graduates entering primary care residencies in the fields of family practice, pediatrics, and internal medicine was averaged over the 2010, 2011 and 2012 graduating classes. **Student selectivity** (.20 in research model, .15 in primary

care model): Based on three measures describing the class entering in fall 2012: mean composite Medical College Admission Test score (65 percent of this measure), mean undergraduate GPA (30 percent), and the acceptance rate (5 percent). **Faculty resources** (.10 in research model, .15 in primary care model): Faculty resources were measured as the ratio of full-time science and clinical faculty to medical or osteopathic students in 2012. **Overall rank:** Indicators were standardized about their means, and standardized scores were weighted, totaled, and rescaled so that the top school received 100; other schools received their percentage of the top school's score. **Specialty rankings:** Based solely on ratings by medical school deans and senior faculty at peer schools, who identified up to 10 schools offering the best programs in each specialty. The top half of programs (by number of nominations) appear.

Schools of Nursing

Institutions or departments ranked best by program directors and faculty

MASTER'S Ranked in 2011

Rank	School	Average assessment score (5.0=highest)
1.	Johns Hopkins University (MD)	4.6
1.	University of Pennsylvania	4.6
1.	University of Washington	4.6
4.	University of California–San Francisco	4.5
4.	University of North Carolina–Chapel Hill	4.5
6.	University of Michigan–Ann Arbor	4.4
7.	Duke University (NC)	4.3
7.	Oregon Health and Science University	4.3
7.	University of Pittsburgh	4.3
7.	Yale University (CT)	4.3
11.	University of Illinois–Chicago	4.2
11.	University of Iowa	4.2
11.	University of Maryland–Baltimore	4.2
11.	U. of North Carolina–Chapel Hill (School of Public Health)	4.2
15.	Case Western Reserve University (OH)	4.1
15.	Indiana Univ.–Purdue Univ.–Indianapolis	4.1
15.	Rush University (IL)	4.1
15.	University of Colorado–Denver	4.1
15.	University of Virginia	4.1
15.	Vanderbilt University (TN)	4.1
21.	Arizona State University	4.0
21.	Boston College	4.0
21.	Columbia University (NY)	4.0
21.	Emory University (GA)	4.0
21.	New York University	4.0
21.	University of Alabama–Birmingham	4.0
21.	University of California–Los Angeles	4.0
21.	University of Kentucky	4.0
21.	University of Minnesota–Twin Cities	4.0
21.	University of Wisconsin–Madison	4.0
21.	University of Texas Health Science Center–Houston	4.0
32.	Ohio State University	3.9
32.	University of Arizona	3.9
32.	University of Rochester (NY)	3.9
32.	University of Texas–Austin	3.9
36.	Georgetown University (DC)	3.8
36.	Michigan State University	3.8
36.	University of Kansas	3.8
36.	University of Nebraska Medical Center	3.8
36.	University of Utah	3.8
36.	University of Wisconsin–Milwaukee	3.8
36.	University of Texas Health Science Center–San Antonio	3.8
36.	Virginia Commonwealth University	3.8
44.	Georgia Health Sciences University	3.7
44.	Marquette University (WI)	3.7
44.	Pennsylvania State University–University Park	3.7
44.	University of Arkansas for Medical Sciences	3.7
44.	University of Florida	3.7
44.	University of Tennessee Health Science Center	3.7
50.	Frontier School of Midwifery and Family Nursing (KY)	3.6
50.	George Washington University (DC)	3.6
50.	Loyola University Chicago	3.6

Rank	School	Average assessment score (5.0=highest)
50.	Medical University of South Carolina	3.6
50.	Purdue University–West Lafayette (IN)	3.6
50.	St. Louis University	3.6
50.	University of Massachusetts–Boston	3.6
50.	University of Missouri	3.6
50.	University of Portland (OR)	3.6
50.	University of San Diego	3.6
50.	University of San Francisco	3.6
50.	Washington State University	3.6
50.	Wayne State University (MI)	3.6
50.	Wesley College (DE)	3.6
64.	Baylor University (TX)	3.5
64.	Catholic University of America (DC)	3.5
64.	Creighton University (NE)	3.5
64.	MGH Institute of Health Professions (MA)	3.5
64.	Texas Tech University Health Sciences Center	3.5
64.	Texas Woman's University	3.5
64.	University of Cincinnati	3.5
64.	University of Louisville (KY)	3.5
64.	University of Massachusetts–Amherst	3.5
64.	University of Missouri–St. Louis	3.5
64.	University of South Florida	3.5
64.	University of Texas–Arlington	3.5
64.	University of the Incarnate Word (TX)	3.5
64.	Univ. of Texas Medical Branch–Galveston	3.5
64.	Villanova University (PA)	3.5
79.	California State University–Los Angeles	3.4
79.	George Mason University (VA)	3.4
79.	Georgia Southern University	3.4
79.	Georgia State University	3.4
79.	Indiana State University	3.4
79.	Pace University (NY)	3.4
79.	Rutgers, the State University of New Jersey–Newark	3.4
79.	Uniformed Services U. of the Health Sciences (MD)	3.4
79.	University at Buffalo–SUNY	3.4
79.	University of Central Florida	3.4
79.	University of Connecticut	3.4
79.	University of Massachusetts–Dartmouth	3.4
79.	University of Massachusetts–Worcester	3.4
79.	University of Miami (FL)	3.4
79.	University of Missouri–Kansas City	3.4
79.	University of New Mexico	3.4
79.	University of North Carolina–Greensboro	3.4
79.	University of Oklahoma Health Sciences Center	3.4
79.	University of Tennessee–Knoxville	3.4
79.	Univ. of South Carolina	3.4

Methodology described on Page 68.

NURSING-ANESTHESIA

MASTER'S Ranked in 2011

Rank	School	Average assessment score (5.0=highest)
1.	U.S. Army Graduate Program in Anesthesia Nursing (TX)	4.0
1.	Virginia Commonwealth University	4.0
3.	Rush University (IL)	3.9
3.	University of Pittsburgh	3.9
5.	Baylor College of Medicine (TX)	3.5
5.	Uniformed Services University of the Health Sciences (MD)	3.5
7.	Albany Medical College (NY)	3.4
7.	Cleveland Clinic Foundation/Case Western Reserve Univ.	3.4
7.	Goldfarb School of Nursing at Barnes-Jewish College	3.4
7.	Wake Forest Univ./Univ. of North Carolina–Greensboro	3.4
11.	Case Western Reserve University (OH)	3.3
11.	Duke University (NC)	3.3
11.	Samuel Merritt University (CA)	3.3
11.	University of Detroit Mercy	3.3
11.	University of Iowa	3.3
11.	University of Pennsylvania	3.3

NURSING-MIDWIFERY

MASTER'S/DOCTORATE Ranked in 2011

Rank	School	Average assessment score (5.0=highest)
1.	Oregon Health and Science University	4.4
2.	University of Pennsylvania	4.3
3.	Vanderbilt University (TN)	4.2
4.	U. of Calif.–San Francisco/San Francisco General Hospital	4.1
5.	University of Illinois–Chicago	4.0
5.	University of New Mexico	4.0
5.	Yale University (CT)	4.0
8.	University of Minnesota–Twin Cities	3.9
8.	University of Utah	3.9
10.	University of Michigan–Ann Arbor	3.8
11.	Columbia University (NY)	3.6
11.	University of Washington	3.6

Note: All schools listed have master's programs; some may not have doctoral programs.

NURSING SPECIALTIES

CLINICAL NURSE SPECIALIST
ADULT/MEDICAL-SURGICAL

1. University of California–San Francisco
1. University of Pennsylvania
3. Indiana Univ.-Purdue Univ.–Indianapolis
4. Rush University (IL)

CLINICAL NURSE SPECIALIST
COMMUNITY/PUBLIC HEALTH

1. Johns Hopkins University (MD)
1. University of Washington
3. University of North Carolina–Chapel Hill (School of Public Health)
4. University of California–San Francisco
4. University of North Carolina–Chapel Hill
6. University of Illinois–Chicago
6. University of Minnesota–Twin Cities

CLINICAL NURSE SPECIALIST
PSYCHIATRIC/MENTAL HEALTH

1. University of California–San Francisco
1. Yale University (CT)
3. University of Pennsylvania
4. Rush University (IL)
4. University of North Carolina–Chapel Hill
6. University of Pittsburgh
7. University of Maryland–Baltimore
8. University of Virginia
9. University of Washington
9. Vanderbilt University (TN)

NURSE PRACTITIONER
ADULT

1. University of Pennsylvania
2. University of California–San Francisco
2. University of Washington
4. Columbia University (NY)
4. University of Michigan–Ann Arbor
6. University of Pittsburgh
7. Rush University (IL)
8. University of Maryland–Baltimore
8. Yale University (CT)
10. Duke University (NC)
10. University of Alabama–Birmingham
12. University of North Carolina–Chapel Hill
13. Johns Hopkins University (MD)
13. New York University
13. Oregon Health and Science University
13. Vanderbilt University (TN)

NURSE PRACTITIONER
FAMILY

1. University of California–San Francisco
2. University of Washington
3. University of Pennsylvania
4. University of Michigan–Ann Arbor
5. Columbia University (NY)
6. Oregon Health and Science University
7. Johns Hopkins University (MD)
7. Yale University (CT)
9. University of Maryland–Baltimore

10. Vanderbilt University (TN)
11. University of North Carolina–Chapel Hill
12. University of Alabama–Birmingham
13. Duke University (NC)
14. Frontier School of Midwifery and Family Nursing (KY)
14. University of Pittsburgh
16. University of Colorado–Denver
16. University of Illinois–Chicago
16. University of Kentucky
19. Georgia Southern University
19. Rush University (IL)
21. Emory University (GA)
21. Ohio State University
21. University of Virginia
24. Boston College
24. University of Texas–Arlington

NURSE PRACTITIONER
GERONTOLOGICAL/GERIATRIC

1. New York University
2. University of Iowa
2. University of Pennsylvania
4. Oregon Health and Science University
5. Case Western Reserve University (OH)
6. University of Arkansas for Medical Sciences
7. Rush University (IL)
8. University of California–San Francisco
8. University of Maryland–Baltimore
10. Duke University (NC)
10. University of North Carolina–Greensboro

NURSE PRACTITIONER
PEDIATRIC

1. University of Pennsylvania
2. Yale University (CT)
3. University of Washington
4. University of Pittsburgh
5. Duke University (NC)
5. Rush University (IL)
5. University of Colorado–Denver
8. University of California–San Francisco
9. Columbia University (NY)
10. University of North Carolina–Chapel Hill
11. Emory University (GA)
12. Johns Hopkins University (MD)
12. University of Iowa
12. University of Michigan–Ann Arbor
15. University of Illinois–Chicago
15. University of Maryland–Baltimore
15. Vanderbilt University (TN)
18. Ohio State University

NURSING SERVICE ADMINISTRATION

1. University of Pennsylvania
2. University of Iowa
3. University of Maryland–Baltimore
3. University of Michigan–Ann Arbor
5. Johns Hopkins University (MD)
6. University of North Carolina–Chapel Hill
7. University of Illinois–Chicago
8. Vanderbilt University (TN)
9. University of Pittsburgh
10. University of Alabama–Birmingham
10. University of Kentucky

ACADEMIC INSIGHTS
YOUR SCHOOL BY THE NUMBERS

Designed for schools, U.S. News Academic Insights provides instant access to a rich historical archive of undergraduate and graduate school rankings data.

Advanced Visualizations
Take complex data and turn it into six easily understandable and exportable views.

Social Media Dashboard
Follow trends and buzz for the past 30 days for your school.

U.S. News School Network
Find your closest competitors based on internal web traffic data.

Peer-Group Analysis
Flexibility to create your own peer groups to compare your intstitution on more than 350 metrics.

Historical Trending
Find out how institutions have performed over time based on more than 350 metrics.

To request a demo visit **AI.USNEWS.COM**   or call **202.955.2121**

Health Disciplines

Schools ranked best by program directors and faculty

AUDIOLOGY

DOCTORATE Ranked in 2012

Rank	School	Average assessment score (5.0=highest)
1.	Vanderbilt University (TN)	4.5
2.	University of Iowa	4.2
3.	University of North Carolina–Chapel Hill	4.0
3.	University of Texas–Dallas	4.0
3.	University of Washington	4.0
3.	Washington University in St. Louis	4.0
7.	University of Florida	3.9
8.	Northwestern University (IL)	3.7
8.	University of Pittsburgh	3.7
10.	Rush University Medical Center (IL)	3.5
10.	University of Kansas	3.5
12.	Ohio State University	3.4
12.	Purdue University–West Lafayette (IN)	3.4
12.	University of Arizona	3.4
12.	University of Memphis	3.4
12.	University of South Florida	3.4
17.	Arizona State University	3.3
17.	Indiana University–Bloomington	3.3
17.	James Madison University (VA)	3.3
17.	University at Buffalo–SUNY	3.3

CLINICAL PSYCHOLOGY

DOCTORATE Ranked in 2012

Rank	School	Average assessment score (5.0=highest)
1.	University of California–Los Angeles	4.5
2.	University of North Carolina–Chapel Hill	4.4
2.	University of Washington	4.4
2.	University of Wisconsin–Madison	4.4
2.	Yale University (CT)	4.4
6.	Duke University (NC)	4.3
6.	University of Illinois–Urbana-Champaign	4.3
6.	University of Kansas (Clinical Child Psychology Program)	4.3
6.	University of Minnesota–Twin Cities	4.3
6.	University of Pennsylvania	4.3
11.	Stony Brook University–SUNY	4.2
11.	University of California–Berkeley	4.2
11.	University of Texas–Austin	4.2
14.	Harvard University (MA)	4.1
14.	Northwestern University (IL)	4.1
14.	Vanderbilt University (TN)	4.1
14.	Washington University in St. Louis	4.1
18.	Emory University (GA)	4.0
18.	Indiana University–Bloomington	4.0
18.	Pennsylvania State University–University Park	4.0
18.	University of Colorado–Boulder	4.0
18.	University of Iowa	4.0
18.	University of Pittsburgh	4.0
18.	University of Southern California	4.0
18.	University of Virginia	4.0

HEALTHCARE MANAGEMENT

MASTER'S Ranked in 2011

Rank	School	Average assessment score (5.0=highest)
1.	University of Michigan–Ann Arbor	4.6
2.	University of Minnesota–Twin Cities	4.4
3.	University of North Carolina–Chapel Hill	4.3
4.	University of Pennsylvania (Wharton)	4.2
5.	University of Alabama–Birmingham	4.1
5.	Virginia Commonwealth University	4.1
7.	Northwestern University (Kellogg) (IL)	4.0
8.	University of Washington	3.9
9.	Rush University (IL)	3.6
9.	St. Louis University	3.6
11.	Boston University	3.5
11.	Johns Hopkins University (MD)	3.5
11.	U.S. Army/Baylor University (TX)	3.5
14.	Columbia University (NY)	3.4
14.	Cornell University (NY)	3.4
14.	Ohio State University	3.4
14.	Trinity University (TX)	3.4
14.	University of California–Los Angeles	3.4
14.	University of Iowa	3.4
14.	Yale University (CT)	3.4
21.	George Washington University (DC)	3.3
21.	New York University	3.3
21.	University of Missouri	3.3

OCCUPATIONAL THERAPY

MASTER'S/DOCTORATE Ranked in 2012

Rank	School	Average assessment score (5.0=highest)
1.	University of Southern California	4.6
2.	Boston University (Sargent)	4.5
2.	Washington University in St. Louis	4.5
4.	University of Illinois–Chicago	4.3
5.	University of Kansas Medical Center	4.0
6.	Colorado State University	3.9
6.	Thomas Jefferson University (PA)	3.9
6.	Tufts Univ.-Boston School of Occupational Therapy	3.9
6.	University of Pittsburgh	3.9
10.	New York University	3.8
10.	University of Florida	3.8
10.	University of North Carolina–Chapel Hill	3.8
13.	Columbia University (NY)	3.7
14.	University of Texas Medical Branch–Galveston	3.6
15.	Creighton University (NE)	3.5
15.	Ohio State University	3.5
15.	Texas Woman's University	3.5
15.	University of Washington	3.5
15.	University of Wisconsin–Madison	3.5
15.	Virginia Commonwealth University	3.5

Note: All schools listed have master's programs; some may not have doctoral programs.

More at www.usnews.com/grad

Earn your Online MBA from a nationally recognized **top-25 best value** – the University of Memphis Fogelman College of Business & Economics. In addition to being affordable, the program is accredited by the AACSB – the gold standard in business school achievement, an honor earned by less than 5% of business schools in the country. The program is designed to meet your specific needs, fit your schedule and ultimately demonstrate your business savvy.

Along with an online program, we offer four other MBA programs:
- Customer-Driven MBA – Corporate sponsorship, waived tuition, $36,000 stipend, and employment upon successful completion
- International MBA – Study abroad, internships and waived tuition for deserving students
- Executive MBA – From classroom to boardroom
- Professional MBA – Flexible program for the working professional

memphis.edu/onlinemba

THE UNIVERSITY OF
MEMPHIS.

Fogelman College
of Business & Economics

PHARMACY

PHARM.D. Ranked in 2012

Rank	School	Average assessment score (5.0=highest)
1.	University of California–San Francisco	4.6
2.	University of North Carolina–Chapel Hill	4.5
3.	University of Minnesota	4.4
4.	University of Texas–Austin	4.3
5.	University of Kentucky	4.2
5.	University of Wisconsin–Madison	4.2
7.	Ohio State University	4.1
7.	Purdue University (IN)	4.1
7.	University of Michigan–Ann Arbor	4.1
10.	University of Arizona	4.0
10.	University of Southern California	4.0
10.	University of Utah	4.0
10.	University of Washington	4.0
14.	University of Florida	3.9
14.	University of Illinois–Chicago	3.9
14.	University of Pittsburgh	3.9
17.	University of Tennessee Health Science Center	3.8
17.	University at Buffalo–SUNY	3.8
17.	University of Iowa	3.8
17.	University of Maryland–Baltimore	3.8

PHYSICAL THERAPY

MASTER'S/DOCTORATE Ranked in 2012

Rank	School	Average assessment score (5.0=highest)
1.	University of Southern California	4.3
2.	University of Delaware	4.2
3.	University of Pittsburgh	4.1
3.	Washington University in St. Louis	4.1
5.	University of Iowa	3.9
5.	US Army-Baylor University (TX)	3.9
7.	Emory University (GA)	3.8
7.	MGH Institute of Health Professions (MA)	3.8
9.	Northwestern University (IL)	3.7
9.	University of Miami (FL)	3.7
9.	University of North Carolina–Chapel Hill	3.7
12.	Marquette University (WI)	3.6
12.	University of Florida	3.6
14.	Arcadia University (PA)	3.5
14.	University of Utah	3.5
16.	Boston University	3.4
16.	Creighton University (NE)	3.4
16.	University of Illinois–Chicago	3.4
19.	Ohio State University	3.3
19.	University of Alabama–Birmingham	3.3
19.	University of Kansas Medical Center	3.3
19.	University of Maryland–Baltimore	3.3
19.	University of Minnesota–Twin Cities	3.3
19.	University of Wisconsin–Madison	3.3
19.	U. of Calif.–San Francisco - San Francisco State U.	3.3
19.	Virginia Commonwealth University	3.3

Note: All schools listed have master's programs; some may not have doctoral programs.

PHYSICIAN ASSISTANT

MASTER'S Ranked in 2011

Rank	School	Average assessment score (5.0=highest)
1.	Duke University (NC)	4.4
2.	University of Iowa	4.3
2.	University of Utah	4.3
4.	Emory University (GA)	4.1
4.	George Washington University (DC)	4.1
6.	Baylor College of Medicine (TX)	4.0
6.	Oregon Health and Science University	4.0
8.	University of Texas Southwestern Medical Center–Dallas	3.9
8.	University of Washington	3.9
8.	Univ. of Medicine and Dentistry of New Jersey–Newark	3.9
11.	Quinnipiac University (CT)	3.8
11.	University of Colorado–Denver	3.8
13.	Interservice Physician Assistant Program (TX)	3.7
13.	Northeastern University (MA)	3.7
13.	Stony Brook University–SUNY	3.7
16.	University of Nebraska Medical Center	3.6
16.	University of Oklahoma	3.6
18.	Philadelphia University	3.5
18.	University of Texas Health Science Center–San Antonio	3.5
18.	Wake Forest University (NC)	3.5
18.	Yale University (CT)	3.5

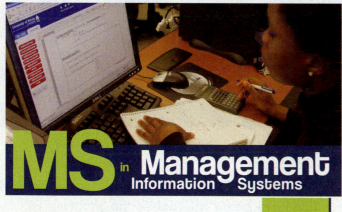

PUBLIC HEALTH

MASTER'S/DOCTORATE Ranked in 2011

Rank	School	Average assessment score (5.0=highest)
1.	Johns Hopkins University (MD)	4.8
2.	University of North Carolina–Chapel Hill	4.6
3.	Harvard University (MA)	4.5
4.	University of Michigan–Ann Arbor	4.3
5.	Columbia University (NY)	4.2
6.	Emory University (GA)	4.1
6.	University of Washington	4.1
8.	University of California–Berkeley	3.8
8.	University of Minnesota–Twin Cities	3.8
10.	University of California–Los Angeles	3.7
11.	Boston University	3.4
11.	University of Pittsburgh	3.4

Note: All schools listed have master's programs; some may not have doctoral programs.

REHABILITATION COUNSELING

MASTER'S/DOCTORATE Ranked in 2011

Rank	School	Average assessment score (5.0=highest)
1.	University of Wisconsin–Madison	4.2
2.	Michigan State University	4.1
2.	University of Iowa	4.1
4.	Pennsylvania State University–University Park	4.0
4.	Southern Illinois University–Carbondale	4.0
6.	University of Arizona	3.8
7.	George Washington University (DC)	3.7
7.	Virginia Commonwealth University	3.7
9.	Illinois Institute of Technology	3.6
9.	San Diego State University	3.6
9.	University of Wisconsin–Stout	3.6
9.	Utah State University	3.6
13.	California State University–Fresno	3.5
13.	East Carolina University (NC)	3.5
13.	University of North Texas	3.5
16.	University of Arkansas–Fayetteville	3.4
17.	Auburn University (AL)	3.3
17.	University of Illinois–Urbana-Champaign	3.3
17.	University of Kentucky	3.3
17.	University of Maryland–College Park	3.3
17.	University of Memphis	3.3
17.	University of Texas–Pan American	3.3

Note: All schools listed have master's programs; some may not have doctoral programs.

SOCIAL WORK

MASTER'S Ranked in 2012

Rank	School	Average assessment score (5.0=highest)
1.	University of Michigan–Ann Arbor	4.4
1.	Washington University in St. Louis	4.4
3.	University of Chicago	4.2
3.	University of Washington	4.2
5.	Columbia University (NY)	4.1
5.	University of North Carolina–Chapel Hill	4.1
7.	University of California–Berkeley	4.0

Rank	School	Average assessment score (5.0=highest)
7.	University of Texas–Austin	4.0
9.	Case Western Reserve University (OH)	3.9
10.	Boston College	3.8
11.	Fordham University (NY)	3.7
11.	University of Pittsburgh	3.7
11.	University of Southern California	3.7
11.	University of Wisconsin–Madison	3.7
11.	Virginia Commonwealth University	3.7
16.	Boston University	3.6
16.	CUNY–Hunter College	3.6
16.	New York University	3.6
16.	Smith College (MA)	3.6
16.	University of California–Los Angeles	3.6
16.	University of Illinois–Urbana-Champaign	3.6
16.	University of Maryland–Baltimore	3.6
16.	University of Pennsylvania	3.6
24.	University at Albany–SUNY	3.5
24.	University of Illinois–Chicago	3.5

SPEECH-LANGUAGE PATHOLOGY

MASTER'S Ranked in 2012

Rank	School	Average assessment score (5.0=highest)
1.	University of Iowa	4.6
2.	University of Wisconsin–Madison	4.5
3.	University of Washington	4.4
3.	Vanderbilt University (TN)	4.4
5.	Northwestern University (IL)	4.3
5.	Purdue University–West Lafayette (IN)	4.3
5.	University of Arizona	4.3
8.	University of Kansas	4.2
8.	University of Pittsburgh	4.2
10.	University of Texas–Austin	4.1
11.	Indiana University	4.0
11.	University of Illinois–Urbana-Champaign	4.0
11.	University of North Carolina–Chapel Hill	4.0
11.	University of Texas–Dallas	4.0
15.	University of Florida	3.9
15.	University of Memphis	3.9
17.	Ohio State University	3.8
17.	University of Maryland–College Park	3.8
17.	University of Minnesota–Twin Cities	3.8
17.	University of Nebraska–Lincoln	3.8
21.	Arizona State University	3.7
21.	Boston University	3.7
21.	Florida State University	3.7
21.	Pennsylvania State University–University Park	3.7

VETERINARY MEDICINE

DOCTOR OF VETERINARY MEDICINE Ranked in 2011

Rank	School	Average assessment score (5.0=highest)
1.	Cornell University (NY)	4.5
2.	University of California–Davis	4.2

VETERINARY MEDICINE

Rank	School	Average assessment score (5.0=highest)
3.	Colorado State University	4.1
3.	North Carolina State University	4.1
5.	Ohio State University	3.8
5.	University of Pennsylvania	3.8

Rank	School	Average assessment score (5.0=highest)
5.	University of Wisconsin–Madison	3.8
8.	Texas A&M University–College Station	3.7
9.	Michigan State University	3.4
9.	University of Georgia	3.4
9.	University of Minnesota–Twin Cities	3.4

METHODOLOGY

The nursing and other health rankings are based solely on the results of peer assessment surveys sent to deans, other administrators, and/or faculty at accredited degree programs or schools in each discipline. Respondents rated the academic quality of programs on a 5-point scale: outstanding (5 points), strong (4), good (3), adequate (2), or marginal (1). They were instructed to select "don't know" if they did not have enough knowledge to rate a program. Only fully accredited programs in good standing during the survey period are ranked. Those with the highest average scores appear.

In the fall of 2011, surveys were conducted for the 2012 rankings of doctor of pharmacy programs accredited by the Accreditation Council for Pharmacy Education (response rate: 39 percent); doctoral programs in clinical psychology accredited by the American Psychological Association (25 percent); graduate programs in occupational therapy accredited by the American Occupational Therapy Association (41 percent); audiology programs and speech-language pathology programs accredited by the American Speech-Language-Hearing Association (55 percent and 31 percent, respectively); physical therapy programs accredited by the Commission on Accreditation in Physical Therapy Education (40 percent); and master of social work programs accredited by the Commission on Accreditation of the Council on Social Work Education (53 percent). Surveys were conducted by research firm Ipsos Public Affairs.

In the fall of 2010, surveys were conducted for 2011 rankings of schools of public health accredited by the Council on Education for Public Health (response rate: 61 percent); healthcare management programs accredited by the Commission on Accreditation of Healthcare Management Education (76 percent); master's programs in nursing accredited by either the Commission on Collegiate Nursing Education or the National League for Nursing Accrediting Commission (33 percent); graduate nurse anesthesia programs accredited by the Council on Accreditation of Nurse Anesthesia Educational Programs of the American Association of Nurse Anesthetists (49 percent); graduate nurse-midwifery programs accredited by the American College of Nurse-Midwives Accreditation Commission for Midwifery Education (59 percent); physician assistant programs accredited by the Accreditation Review Commission on Education for the Physician Assistant (45 percent); rehabilitation counselor education programs accredited by the Commission on Standards and Accreditation: Council on Rehabilitation Education (40 percent); and veterinary schools accredited by the American Veterinary Medical Association (48 percent). The nursing specialty programs are ranked based solely on input from educators at peer nursing institutions, who nominated up to 10 schools for excellence in each area; schools with the most votes are listed. Surveys for the 2011 rankings were conducted by Synovate (now part of Ipsos Public Affairs).

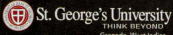

The reading room at
Georgetown University
Law Center, No. 14

LAW

Preparing a Brief on Law School

Before committing three years and $150,000, it's wise to analyze all the arguments

BY MICHAEL MORELLA AND COURTNEY RUBIN

Doing mock trial and debate in high school sparked Abraham Gitterman's interest in law school, but when it came time to apply, he decided to play it slow. After graduating from Penn State University in 2008, he worked for two years in the Washington, D.C., area as a paralegal and as a researcher for a medical education company, saving money and getting a better sense of what he actually wanted to *do* with the law. Gitterman eventually applied to about 10 schools and, after crunching the numbers, chose the University of Maryland's Francis King Carey School of Law in Baltimore. His flexible job schedule and some evening coursework allowed him to keep working, and in-state tuition cut the tab to less than half of some of his options, for a total loan burden of about $50,000. "I put myself in a situation where I wouldn't be owned by this debt," says Gitterman, 27, who was attracted by Maryland's health law program. Knowing early that he wanted to work in that field, he contacted several D.C. firms with health practices during his second year. One offered a summer associate position and, ultimately, a job after graduation this May. "I was very, very strategic," Gitterman says.

Careful planning is the name of the game these days for people considering law school. The job market has changed drastically in recent years; the overall percentage of new grads employed has fallen every year since 2007, with just under two thirds of the class of 2011 finding jobs that require bar passage, according to NALP–the Association for Legal Career Professionals. Fewer than half of those jobs were at law firms, and far more graduates than in past years found positions in smaller or mid-size offices instead of large firms of 100 or more attorneys, which often offer higher pay. Overall, the median starting salary for 2011 grads working full time fell to $60,000, down about 5 percent

from a year earlier. Starting pay at law firms fell even further—to $85,000 from $104,000.

"The equation for people applying to law school these days is very different than it was even five years ago," says Alan Stone, a partner at Milbank, Tweed, Hadley & McCloy in New York. Clients have insisted that law firms cut their costs, which has translated into less recruiting. New technologies and legal services outsourced or performed by temporary attorneys have also made law firms leaner (story, Page 75). "Even if the economy picks up, I think because of these structural changes the sense is they'll need fewer associates," says Mitt Regan, professor of jurisprudence and codirector of the Center for the Study of the Legal Profession at Georgetown University Law Center in Washington, D.C.

While the market does seem to be slowly improving, the Bureau of Labor Statistics forecasts that about 21,900 lawyer jobs will open annually until 2020—even as law schools graduate more than 40,000 students each year. On the other hand, recent application numbers have fallen sharply, and a number of schools have cut the size of their incoming classes. "This is a good time to apply to law school," says Brian Tamanaha, professor of law at Washington University School of Law in St. Louis and author of the 2012 book *Failing Law Schools*. At the moment, though, he cautions, "it's a terrible time to get out."

Given the sobering numbers, experts say that you should begin your law school search by getting a genuine sense of what lawyers do and a clear idea of what you hope to accomplish with a law degree. To help prospective applicants navigate the rest of the process, *U.S. News* pitched six key questions to several dozen professors, attorneys, and law students:

1. Will it be easier to get in this year?

Earning admission is still a competitive process that hinges on an applicant's LSAT score, undergraduate GPA, and other credentials. But over the past two years, the number of law school applicants is down more than 22 percent, from 87,900 to 68,000, according to preliminary data from the nonprofit Law School Admission Council, which administers the LSAT. And early data for fall 2013 suggests the numbers could fall another fifth this year alone: As of early February, applicants were down about 19 percent.

Roughly half of law schools have reduced their incoming class sizes somewhat for fall 2013 in an effort to address the supply/demand mismatch, according to a November survey conducted by Kaplan Test Prep. Still, "for most students, it should be much easier to get in to the law school of their choice than in any year in recent memory," says Frank Wu, chancellor and dean of the University of California Hastings College of the Law. Hastings announced it would enroll about 20 percent fewer

students for fall 2013; as of late January, applications were down some 18 percent from last year.

Fewer applicants overall means that those with lower credentials might have a better shot at getting in at a reach school than they would have otherwise. "Schools will be dipping much deeper into the pool than they would have in the past," Tamanaha says. Financial aid packages could get better, too. Forty-seven percent of law schools increased aid to students for 2012-13, according to the Kaplan survey.

2. Should you work first?

The verdict, from admissions counselors and hiring partners: Work experience can only help. The job doesn't have to be in the legal field to impress admissions with your added depth and maturity, though working as a paralegal or volunteering for a legal nonprofit can give prospective students a reality check (as well as a chunk of savings) before they commit to a law program. And work can enhance your education. Gitterman's time on Capitol Hill during the development of the Affordable Care Act directly informed his health law studies, as did his day-to-day work as a paralegal.

Recruiters, too, tend to look favorably upon a sub-stantial résumé. "Firms like that because they're seeing people with real-world experience who are ready to hit the ground running from day one," says Richard Batchelder, a partner who leads hiring at Ropes & Gray, a firm of 1,069 attorneys in 11 offices across the world. Batchelder notes that about two thirds of the firm's most recent summer associate classes have taken some time off to work before law school.

3. What should you look for in the curriculum?

Partners and other people who hire new attorneys are demanding hands-on experience—grads who not only know the principles of corporate law, but who have actually done project work for local small business owners, for instance. A number of law schools have overhauled their curricula accordingly, expanding clinical courses, beefing up specialized classes on leadership, adding interdisciplinary and joint degree programs, and even offering solo and small firm "incubators," where recent grads thinking of hanging out a shingle can get office space and mentoring. "Necessity has fueled a lot of innovation," says David Meyer, dean of Tulane University Law School in New Orleans.

USC law grad Anna Lee, now clerking for a judge in Texas, with a colleague. She's getting lots of loan repayment assistance.

Students should shop around, experts say, for programs that are strong in experiential opportunities, which could include anything from interning with a local judge or law firm to working with low-income clients through a legal aid society or tackling a simulated bankruptcy case in a classroom workshop. Students at Washington and Lee University School of Law in Lexington, Va., for instance, take an all-experiential third year. Advanced family law students work through mock marriage and divorce proceedings, while prospective government attorneys tackle simulated problems regarding land use or personnel issues. New York University has announced that it will substantially expand its 3L offerings, allowing students to pursue specialized coursework in concentrations like tax and criminal law, as well as study Asian business law in Shanghai or federal regulatory processes in Washington, D.C., for example. And even at the front end, schools like Harvard and Indiana

"For most students, it should be much easier to get in to the law school of their choice... ."

University's Maurer School of Law in Bloomington have constructed first-year courses where, instead of just learning legal theory, students work in teams on simulated problems the way practicing lawyers might.

4. When is it smart to go part time?

If you do, expect to be in class for a few hours on weekday evenings for four straight academic years and usually at least one summer. Going this route while working will almost certainly leave you very little if any time for internships, extracurriculars, and volunteering. And if your goal is to be a lawyer at a big firm, a part-time strategy might actually handicap you, since most large firms prefer to hire entry-level associates who have had a summer post with them or a comparable firm—tough to accomplish when you have a full-time job already. As you consider the possibilities, weigh how good a job a part-time program will do of putting you in front of employers—in its clinical programs and through career services' networking options, say—and the employment data on record for graduates.

But those hoping to earn a J.D. as a way to further a career path, or who really need that steady paycheck, may decide that part time is the only way to go (particularly if it opens up some employer-paid tuition assistance). Evan R. Luce, 31, says his innate frugality, plus the fact that he liked his job as a recruiter for Bayada Home Health Care, helped him choose the part-time program at Temple University's Beasley School of Law in Philadelphia. For his first year of part-time law school, he received $2,000 per semester toward Temple's then $16,000-per-semester tuition. But maintaining a school-work-life balance is a challenge, acknowledges Luce, who left his job and switched to the full-time program for his second year to better manage school and life with a newborn.

In any case, going part time will not necessarily be any cheaper. Consider the case at Georgetown Law: A full-time student's total tuition bill in 2012-13 was $146,505 ($48,835 times three) versus a part-time student's $147,050 ($1,730 per credit hour, with 85 credit hours required to graduate).

5. What will raise the odds of finding a job in the end?

Aspiring law students can get a better sense of their prospects now that the American Bar Association is requiring law schools to report more detailed employment data about graduates—breaking out, for example, how many landed full-time, long-term jobs that require bar admission. The employment statistics, which will also tell you how many graduates found jobs in different-size firms or the public-interest arena and how many positions are funded by the schools themselves, are available on the ABA site (*http://employmentsummary. abaquestionnaire.org*). Such employment data is a significant component of the *U.S. News* Best Law Schools rankings (box, right); we surveyed the schools directly for this information at graduation as well as at nine months out, and display employment rates for various types of positions at *www.usnews. com/lawschools*.

Where you go will matter when it comes to the endgame—not only in terms of a law school's prestige, an important factor particularly for people seeking positions at many large national firms, but also because of the connections institutions have to local clinical and externship opportunities and employers. Indeed, at about 60 percent of all ABA-accredited law schools, at least 2 out of 3 employed 2011 graduates found jobs in the state where they studied. Top-performing students at local or regional law schools are often considered for positions at area law offices alongside those from the most elite institutions. So "do your homework on what market you want to practice in," advises Elizabeth Arias, a partner based in the Raleigh, N.C., office of 500-attorney firm Womble Carlyle Sandridge & Rice.

Once you're in school, get set to do some serious résumé polishing. "Those who do best in the job market are those who find a kind of niche and begin preparing for it early," says Deborah Merritt, professor of law at Ohio State University's Moritz College of Law. So in addition to hands-on training and work experience, developing skills like financial literacy, getting some project management experience, and adding specialized legal training—through a certificate in environmental or business law, say—can be deal-clinchers in the eyes of employers.

Networking, too, can be an essential step in establishing a career path. Students should "be thinking really carefully about forming those connections while they're in law school," suggests Liza Hirsch, 29, who graduated from Northeastern University School of Law in Boston in 2011. Her time as a care coordinator with the Massachusetts Department of Public Health, helping low-income families get access to health and other community services, inspired her to go to law school. There, she participated in six co-ops and experiential clinics, including working on behalf of low-income residents on eviction matters, clerking for a judge, and representing young people in juvenile delinquency proceedings. Contacts from one of her co-op placements helped her develop a proposal for a post-graduate fellowship advocating for better healthcare and affordable housing for low-income families, which earned her two years of foundation funding.

In the cash-strapped public-interest sector, candidates who tend to stand out have experience working with real clients, as well as clear track records of public service and a commitment to a particular issue before and during law school. "Show that this is not a passing interest," advises David Stern, executive director of Equal Justice Works, a nonprofit that funds public-interest law fellowships.

6. How can you cut costs and minimize debt?

Most students borrow to pay at least part of the tab, but advisers say keeping the debt load to a minimum—and in line with a reasonable salary projection—should be a priority. Public law school graduates who borrow average about $75,700 in loans, while private law grads borrow nearly $125,000, according to the most recent ABA statistics. Student loan calculators, such as the one at FinAid.org, can help you get a sense of the monthly payments, including interest, and what salary would be required to pay the money back over certain time periods. If scholarship offers don't meet your expectations, experts point out that this is an opportune time to try to negotiate.

Prospective students should also explore schools' loan repayment assistance programs, as well as those offered by the federal government and certain states. The federal "pay as you earn" repayment program, for instance, allows low-earning graduates who qualify to cap monthly payments at 10 percent of their discretionary income, and will forgive any remaining debt after 20 years of payments. Those who work in certain public-interest jobs might qualify for total loan forgiveness after 10 years of employment and on-time payments. More than 100 law schools offer their own version of loan repayment assistance programs, or LRAPs, according to Equal Justice Works. The University of Virginia's School of Law, for example, will cover 100 percent of the payment amount for public-interest workers making $55,000 or less annually. Yale and the University of Michigan will cover the full amount for someone who goes into any law-related job that pays under $50,000.

Federal income-based repayment and her own school's LRAP have helped Anna Lee manage the $175,000 she borrowed to attend the University of Southern California's Gould School of Law. After graduation last year, Lee, 29, took a job clerking for a judge in Austin, where she earns about $57,000. With the repayment assistance, Lee trimmed her monthly loan bill from $1,200 to about $270. Later this year she will take a job working on federal banking regulation in Washington, D.C., where she will still be eligible for reduced payments and can have the remainder of her loan balance forgiven after 10 years of public legal work. Doing a careful cost-benefit analysis from the start has made a huge difference to her future, Lee says. She thinks the investment will be a good one. ●

Making Sense of Law Schools' Jobs Data

BY ROBERT J. MORSE

There's a very strong case to be made for knowing when you apply to law school what kind of jobs are available afterward, given the ongoing debate about whether a J.D. degree is worth the heavy cost. As a result of new American Bar Association rules, a great deal more information can be had about the many types of positions law students take after they graduate. Each year, the schools report to the ABA how many of their most recent grads had jobs lined up by nine months after graduation; the new standards require them to go into a lot more detail, noting, for example, whether each graduate's employment was long term (defined as lasting at least a year) or shorter term, was full time or part time, and whether it required passage of a bar exam. U.S. News collected these same statistics when we surveyed the schools for our annual rankings, along with the same data on those members of the class who were employed at graduation.

For this year's ranking (Page 76), U.S. News incorporated this richer data into our computation of the employment measure for the class of 2011 at graduation and nine months later. Placement success was calculated by assigning various weights to the number of grads employed in different types of post-J.D. jobs. Full weight was given for graduates who had a full-time job lasting at least a year where bar passage was required or a J.D. degree was an advantage. Less weight went to full-time, long-term jobs that were professional or non-professional and did not require bar passage, to pursuit of an additional advanced degree, and to positions whose start dates were deferred. The lowest weight applied to jobs categorized as both part-time and short-term. These weighted figures were used in the ranking formula only and are not published; employment stats displayed in the tables reflect actual rates for the full-weight jobs: full-time, long-term, and where a J.D. and bar passage are necessary or advantageous. Actual rates for the other types of positions appear in the profiles of each school's latest graduating class at www.usnews.com/lawschools. Check back every now and then, as we occasionally add content to the website when we obtain additional data we think useful (whether on job placement, GPA, test scores, or other factors) or learn information that changes the data. ●

For more on the rankings from Bob Morse, director of data research at U.S.News, follow his Morse Code blog at **www.usnews.com/morsecode.** Get tips on applying at **www.usnews.com/lawschools.**

A Law Prof Counsels Caution

The decision to get a J.D. degree shouldn't be made lightly. BY MICHAEL MORELLA

For a legal scholar and law professor, Paul Campos is surprisingly bearish on law school. In 2011, the University of Colorado prof started the blog "Inside the Law School Scam," anonymously at first, to explore what he sees as the increasingly "risky gamble" of getting a J.D. degree, given the costs and job and salary prospects. Campos's new book, *Don't Go To Law School (Unless): A Law Professor's Inside Guide to Maximizing Opportunity and Minimizing Risk*, helps prospective students make informed decisions. He recently shared some of his thoughts with *U.S. News.* Excerpts:

What's your assessment of the big picture?
The mismatch between the cost of law school and the value of a law degree has been growing for quite a long time. I think in the long term the market for attorneys appears likely to get more constricted. It'll be more and more difficult to make a living as an attorney.

So how should aspiring attorneys approach the decision?
Saying, "I want to be a lawyer" is way too vague. The applicant [should have] genuine exposure to the kind of thing that the applicant hopes to do. And then the second thing you need to do is to look very, very carefully at the probability that you will be able to do that thing, and how much it will cost you to put yourself in

If you're taking on $120,000 of debt to get a $60,000-a-year job, that's deeply problematic.

that position. Take a very critical look at the employment statistics for schools that you're considering, and demand whatever level of detail you need to evaluate whether it's a realistic career aspiration. The other key part of the equation, of course, is cost. I think applicants need to be very aggressive in negotiating cost with law schools. Applications are way down, so that should forearm people in terms of going in there with a hard-nosed negotiating attitude. The advertised tuition price ought to be considered as the starting point of a negotiation.

It's not necessarily the case that just because you can go to a really good law school that that choice is going to make

sense for you, given what your alternatives are. What is my opportunity cost? What is it costing me to go? What am I going to be foregoing?

How important is a school's prestige?
There's definitely a way to think about it, which is how much value is going to be added by going to X instead of Y given what I want to do and what it will cost me to go to X instead of Y. Let's say a person has the choice of Stanford at sticker or [the University of California] Hastings with a full-ride scholarship. Maybe to the extent that somebody's interested in a public interest career, [Hastings] might be a good call. It has to be an individual calculation.

What should applicants be looking for in the employment information that schools report?
They should demand recent graduate class outcomes for schools they're considering. And do some research in regard to what has actually happened to people five and 10 years out. Most states now have searchable bar licensing databases [of individual attorneys and contact information]. Call up a few people, E-mail a few people.

How much debt is too much?
A good rule of thumb is people should be hesitant to take on more educational debt than their probable first-year salary. If you're taking on $120,000 of debt to get a $60,000-a-year job, that's deeply problematic. And you have to be very realistic. Because a $60,000-a-year job is a good outcome for the average law graduate at present.

So who *should* go to law school?
Somebody who should go to law school for sure? Let's say somebody who wants to be a district attorney and who has a 3.9 GPA and a 173 LSAT and gets a free ride to [the University of] Minnesota and whose mother is the DA in Rochester. That person? Great idea. You have a good basis for thinking that you really want to do the kind of work that you're going to law school in order to do; you can go to law school at a very, very reasonable price; and you have connections that make it very realistic for you to be able to get into that line of work.

Don't go to law school as a default option that you just sort of wander into, which, unfortunately, a lot of people do. If you're going to spend $150,000 or $200,000, it had better be for a good enough reason in regard to your likely career outcome. And at the vast majority of law schools right now for the vast majority of students, it doesn't make sense to spend that kind of money. That's a hard truth, but that's the way it is. ●

A Temporary Solution

Tough times boost contract work and legal outsourcing. BY CHRISTOPHER J. GEARON

Eye-popping salaries for first-year associates at big law firms were the norm when Regina Brooks, 29, enrolled at Howard University's law school in 2005. "I thought I'd have a law firm job for four to five years then go in-house and make the kind of money to live a comfortable lifestyle," says Brooks, who got laid off from that law firm job in 2009, a year after graduation. That's when Vikram Arneja, 32, a mergers and acquisitions associate, started at New York Law School, having noticed that attorneys were "very instrumental" in debt, equity, and foreign exchange deals. "We didn't understand the full picture that was unfolding," he says now.

Today, both find themselves in unexpected places. Brooks, of Merrillville, Ind., is doing temporary work for Robert Half Legal, a large Menlo Park, Calif.-based legal staffing firm. Arneja is now in Chicago, serving as a manager of corporate and litigation services at Mindcrest Inc., a legal process outsourcing (LPO) firm, where he had interned as a student. Mindcrest helps companies and big law firms reduce the cost of document review and other basic legal needs. Harnessing technology and cheaper domestic and foreign lawyers, LPOs have become a rising force as law firm clients and corporations have begun demanding a break from pricey billable hours. Firms like Mindcrest boast saving clients as much as 70 percent on legal support work, says Arneja. The LPO industry's revenues are projected to double between 2011 and 2014, according to consulting firm Deloitte.

"You're seeing movement" in both LPO and temp positions, says Mark Medice, senior director of the Thomson Reuters Peer Monitor service, which tracks the legal industry. Brooks, who estimates that she makes "the same as a mid-level associate at a small or medium firm," does document review, oversees other contract attorneys, helps manage projects, and deals with clients. "I've had only one week of downtime since last September," she says. Contract work "has become much more of an accepted norm," says Charles Volkert, executive director of Robert Half Legal. On average, members of the Class of 2011 who pursued legal temp work made $52,000, says James Leipold, executive director of NALP-the Association for Legal Career Professionals.

"We grew from 300-plus lawyers three years ago to 550 to 600 now," says Ganesh Natarajan, Mindcrest's CEO. Besides Chicago, the firm has U.S. offices in Los Angeles, New York, and Salt Lake City. Arneja scopes out client projects, develops a workflow process, manages attorney teams, and provides legal research and drafting services.

As for the bigger picture, there's no beating around the bush: The job market for young attorneys remains a tough one. Medice notes that industry revenue growth in 2012 was a paltry 0.5 percent, and "2013 looks about the same." Only about 10 percent of the employed grads in the class of 2011 landed at a big firm with 251 or more attorneys, about half the number in 2009. Just 49 percent went into private practice, and 43 percent of those to firms with 2 to 10 lawyers, says Leipold. The migration from big to

Only about 10 percent of the employed grads in the class of 2011 landed at a big firm.

small (and temp and outsourced) law is a big reason why average starting salaries in private practice fell sharply—from $130,000 to $85,000—between 2009 and 2011. Half of all new attorneys made less than $60,000 in 2011.

Arneja and Brooks both think their detours will put them in good standing to someday work at law firms or in other legal positions. Indeed, says Volkert, lawyers with five-plus years of experience, business development skills, and client contacts in hot areas such as litigation, general business, and healthcare law are actually in demand. ●

Schools of Law

Rank School	Overall score	Peer assessment score (5.0=highest)	Assessment score by lawyers/ judges (5.0=highest)	'12 undergrad GPA 25th-75th percentile	'12 LSAT score 25th-75th percentile	'12 acceptance rate	'12 student/ faculty ratio	'11 grads employed at graduation[2]	Employed 9 months after graduation[2]	School's bar passage rate in jurisdiction	Jurisdiction's overall bar passage rate
1. Yale University (CT)	100	4.8	4.7	3.84-3.98	170-176	8%	7.9	90.7%	91.2%	96.3%/NY	77%
2. Harvard University (MA)	95	4.8	4.8	3.77-3.95	170-175	16%	11.4	90.9%	93.7%	97.5%/NY	77%
2. Stanford University (CA)	95	4.8	4.7	3.76-3.96	168-173	10%	7.6	93.2%	95.8%	88.5%/CA	67%
4. Columbia University (NY)	92	4.6	4.6	3.58-3.82	170-174	18%	8.0	93.2%	95.4%	96.2%/NY	77%
4. University of Chicago	92	4.6	4.7	3.65-3.96	167-173	20%	7.5	90.6%	95.1%	96.4%/IL	89%
6. New York University	89	4.4	4.6	3.54-3.84	169-173	28%	9.0	93.1%	93.8%	95.5%/NY	77%
7. University of Pennsylvania	85	4.3	4.6	3.55-3.94	164-171	16%	10.3	83.6%	91.2%	94.2%/NY	77%
7. University of Virginia	85	4.4	4.6	3.53-3.93	164-171	15%	10.9	97.3%	96.0%	91.8%/VA	79%
9. University of California–Berkeley	83	4.4	4.4	3.68-3.91	163-170	12%	11.6	72.6%	82.6%	86.8%/CA	67%
9. University of Michigan–Ann Arbor	83	4.4	4.7	3.57-3.83	166-170	24%	12.8	70.7%	85.8%	94.8%/NY	77%
11. Duke University (NC)	81	4.2	4.5	3.58-3.85	166-170	19%	9.1	72.9%	87.4%	95.4%/NY	77%
12. Northwestern University (IL)	79	4.1	4.4	3.38-3.84	164-171	24%	8.2	77.4%	84.7%	93.9%/IL	89%
13. Cornell University (NY)	76	4.2	4.5	3.54-3.77	166-169	29%	9.4	69.7%	76.1%	91.3%/NY	77%
14. Georgetown University (DC)	75	4.1	4.5	3.43-3.82	165-170	28%	11.0	63.7%	71.1%	92.6%/NY	77%
15. University of Texas–Austin	74	4.1	4.3	3.52-3.82	163-169	27%	11.5	62.0%	76.7%	94.2%/TX	86%
15. Vanderbilt University (TN)	74	3.8	4.2	3.43-3.85	163-170	30%	13.1	65.2%	76.3%	95.9%/TN	77%
17. University of California–Los Angeles	70	3.9	4.1	3.58-3.89	164-169	24%	10.9	45.9%	64.8%	84.7%/CA	67%
18. University of Southern California (Gould)	68	3.6	4.1	3.51-3.8	165-168	29%	11.7	54.6%	69.6%	91.3%/CA	67%
19. University of Minnesota–Twin Cities	67	3.5	4.0	3.36-3.89	158-168	23%	10.9	64.0%	66.3%	97.2%/MN	93%
19. Washington University in St. Louis	67	3.6	4.0	3.34-3.78	160-168	29%	10.4	52.7%	66.6%	98.4%/MO	93%
21. George Washington University (DC)	66	3.4	3.9	3.32-3.77	161-168	30%	15.4	81.7%	88.0%	93.9%/NY	77%
21. University of Alabama	66	3.0	3.7	3.31-3.94	158-167	25%	10.1	66.5%	87.8%	93.6%/AL	77%
23. Emory University (GA)	65	3.5	3.9	3.35-3.82	161-166	31%	10.8	52.4%	76.0%	93.2%/GA	85%
23. University of Notre Dame (IN)	65	3.4	4.0	3.43-3.8	161-167	24%	9.3	48.9%	66.8%	88.6%/NY	77%
25. Indiana University–Bloomington (Maurer)	64	3.3	4.0	3.39-3.88	156-166	46%	11.6	62.1%	73.3%	92.6%/IN	83%
26. University of Iowa	62	3.3	3.7	3.46-3.8	158-164	49%	10.8	48.6%	72.7%	90.3%/IA	90%
26. Washington and Lee University (VA)	62	3.3	4.0	3.4-3.73	159-165	30%	10.2	27.9%	63.6%	95.7%/VA	79%
28. University of Washington	61	3.1	3.9	3.5-3.82	162-166	22%	9.3	54.9%	62.6%	87.4%/WA	67%
29. Arizona State University (O'Connor)	60	3.0	3.5	3.3-3.82	161-165	34%	10.2	50.2%	72.1%	85.8%/AZ	76%
29. Boston University	60	3.4	3.8	3.52-3.83	162-167	30%	12.7	44.0%	57.5%	94.8%/MA	87%
31. Boston College	59	3.3	3.7	3.4-3.71	161-166	29%	12.6	51.9%	72.3%	96.2%/MA	87%
31. University of North Carolina–Chapel Hill	59	3.5	4.0	3.33-3.69	160-164	28%	13.0	46.6%	78.1%	89.8%/NC	80%
33. Col. of William and Mary (Marshall-Wythe) (VA)	58	3.2	4.0	3.45-3.84	161-166	32%	14.1	45.6%	68.1%	85.0%/VA	79%
33. University of Georgia	58	3.1	3.6	3.33-3.82	158-165	31%	11.8	56.8%	66.5%	91.6%/GA	85%
33. University of Wisconsin–Madison	58	3.4	3.7	3.33-3.72	157-164	37%	10.9	46.5%	70.1%	99.6%/WI	88%
36. Ohio State University (Moritz)	57	3.2	3.5	3.43-3.79	158-164	47%	11.7	43.7%	71.0%	93.8%/OH	86%
36. Wake Forest University (NC)	57	3.1	3.8	3.4-3.75	159-165	42%	10.6	39.9%	65.2%	90.7%/NC	80%
38. Fordham University (NY)	56	3.2	3.6	3.34-3.68	162-166	32%	13.7	43.9%	60.3%	89.5%/NY	77%
38. University of Arizona (Rogers)	56	3.0	3.6	3.28-3.79	159-162	40%	10.5	49.4%	79.1%	85.1%/AZ	76%
38. University of California–Davis	56	3.4	3.7	3.38-3.71	160-165	36%	10.6	34.9%	60.5%	75.0%/CA	67%
41. George Mason University (VA)	55	2.7	3.4	3.27-3.79	158-164	28%	14.4	49.4%	78.2%	90.6%/VA	79%
41. University of Maryland (Carey)	55	3.0	3.1	3.32-3.77	151-164	27%	11.9	57.6%	62.3%	88.1%/MD	81%
41. University of Utah (Quinney)	55	2.9	3.4	3.32-3.8	156-162	35%	8.6	47.8%	74.6%	90.4%/UT	88%
44. Brigham Young University (Clark) (UT)	54	2.9	3.5	3.4-3.81	158-165	29%	15.1	45.3%	58.0%	98.6%/UT	88%
44. University of Colorado–Boulder	54	3.1	3.3	3.35-3.79	159-166	34%	9.7	33.5%	64.2%	93.5%/CO	86%
46. University of Florida (Levin)	53	3.1	3.9	3.33-3.73	160-164	33%	13.4	35.0%	64.8%	92.0%/FL	80%
47. University of Illinois–Urbana-Champaign	52	3.1	3.7	3.23-3.74	158-165	43%	12.3	36.3%	56.3%	92.4%/IL	89%
48. Florida State University	50	2.9	2.7	3.29-3.73	157-162	33%	12.7	23.3%	78.9%	88.3%/FL	80%
48. Southern Methodist University (Dedman) (TX)	50	2.5	3.3	3.3-3.81	157-164	34%	15.4	43.0%	69.5%	87.1%/TX	86%
48. Tulane University (LA)	50	3.0	3.6	3.23-3.63	156-163	48%	13.3	36.5%	64.7%	77.0%/LA	70%

[1]Law school declined to fill out the *U.S. News* statistical survey. [2]Represents the percentage of all graduates who had a full-time job lasting at least a year for which bar passage was required or a J.D. degree was an advantage. These employment rates are part of the data on placement success used to determine a school's ranking. N/A=Data were not provided by the school. University of California–Irvine, University of La Verne, and University of Massachusetts–Dartmouth were not ranked because as of January 2013, they were only provisionally approved by the American Bar Association. Three other law schools—Pontifical Catholic University and Inter American University in Puerto Rico, and the University of Puerto Rico—did not provide sufficient data to be ranked. The state bar examination pass rates for first-time test-takers in summer 2011 and winter 2011 were provided by the National Conference of Bar Examiners. Numbers with * are from the fall 2011 entering class or school year and 2011 graduating class as reported to the American Bar Association or to *U.S. News*. Sources: *U.S. News* and the schools. Assessment data collected by Ipsos Public Affairs.

More at **www.usnews.com/grad**

CHOOSE HOUSTON LAW

STUDY LAW IN THE ENERGY CAPITAL OF THE WORLD

As the global demand for energy increases and U.S. oil and gas production soars, the market demands lawyers skilled in analyzing regulatory and legal issues involving fuels, energy production, exploration, climate change, renewables, environment, and natural resources. The University of Houston Law Center offers outstanding J.D. and LL.M. programs with a focus on energy and environmental law. That's only fitting given that we are located in the energy capital of the world and the two fields are inextricably intertwined. UH Law Center is ranked as one of the top two law schools in the country in offering energy-specific courses, especially those in oil and gas, and its faculty is internationally recognized for energy law and related fields. Consider these additional factors:

- UH Law Center is the leading law school in the nation's fourth-largest city.

- UH Intellectual Property Law and Health Law programs are consistently ranked in Top 10 nationally by U.S. News & World Report.

- UH Law Center is ranked 29th in 2013 by the National Law Journal among "Go to" law schools based on the percent of graduates hired by the top 250 law firms in U.S.

There is a lot to like about our school. To find out more, visit **www.law.uh.edu**.

UNIVERSITY of HOUSTON | LAW CENTER

THE TOP SCHOOLS

Rank	School	Overall score	Peer assessment score (5.0=highest)	Assessment score by lawyers/judges (5.0=highest)	'12 undergrad GPA 25th-75th percentile	'12 LSAT score 25th-75th percentile	'12 acceptance rate	'12 student/faculty ratio	'11 grads employed at graduation[2]	Employed 9 months after graduation[2]	School's bar passage rate in jurisdiction	Jurisdiction's overall bar passage rate
48.	University of California (Hastings)	50	3.2	3.8	3.29-3.75	158-165	30%	17.3	26.0%	51.6%	78.6%/CA	67%
48.	University of Houston (TX)	50	2.6	3.0	3.23-3.7	159-163	30%	11.5	58.0%	75.8%	92.0%/TX	86%
53.	University of Richmond (Williams) (VA)	49	2.3	3.2	3.21-3.6	158-163	21%	11.4	38.0%	77.1%	83.6%/VA	79%
54.	Baylor University (TX)	48	2.3	3.5	3.23-3.72	158-163	21%	13.6	30.6%	73.2%	95.1%/TX	86%
54.	Georgia State University	48	2.5	2.9	3.19-3.6	156-161	27%	10.9	64.5%	77.4%	94.2%/GA	85%
56.	American University (Washington) (DC)	47	3.0	3.3	3.18-3.58	156-162	33%	11.0	36.4%	47.8%	76.8%/NY	77%
56.	Temple University (Beasley) (PA)	47	2.7	3.0	3.17-3.64	158-163	41%	12.2	37.6%	65.5%	91.2%/PA	85%
58.	University of Connecticut	46	2.8	2.9	3.25-3.66	157-162	36%	11.6	31.3%	60.9%	90.7%/CT	82%
58.	University of Kentucky	46	2.5	3.3	3.25-3.73	155-161	51%	14.6	49.6%	81.5%	94.8%/KY	86%
58.	Yeshiva University (Cardozo) (NY)	46	2.8	3.3	3.3-3.67	158-165	37%	15.0	28.4%	55.8%	88.1%/NY	77%
61.	Pepperdine University (CA)	45	2.6	3.2	3.34-3.74	156-164	43%	13.3	26.6%	51.1%	86.6%/CA	67%
61.	University of Nebraska–Lincoln	45	2.4	3.1	3.31-3.83	155-161	51%	11.5	43.1%	76.2%	88.3%/NE	83%
61.	University of Tennessee–Knoxville	45	2.6	3.1	3.3-3.75	156-161	37%	13.8	34.9%	67.1%	80.5%/TN	77%
64.	Pennsylvania State University (Dickinson)	44	2.3	3.2	3.23-3.73	156-160	42%	9.3	24.6%	49.2%	87.6%/PA	85%
64.	Seton Hall University (NJ)	44	2.4	3.0	3.23-3.72	154-161	52%	14.5	48.1%	72.0%	88.5%/NJ	84%
64.	University of Denver (Sturm)	44	2.7	2.9	3.18-3.64	155-161	46%	9.8	32.8%	56.8%	88.0%/CO	86%
64.	University of New Mexico	44	2.5	2.8	3.09-3.7	152-158	32%	9.9	22.3%	69.9%	85.3%/NM	88%
68.	Case Western Reserve University (OH)	43	2.7	3.3	3.1-3.6	156-161	54%	11.7	35.3%	55.2%	81.8%/OH	86%
68.	Illinois Institute of Technology (Chicago-Kent)	43	2.5	3.0	3.09-3.62	154-161	50%	11.0	28.6%	56.6%	97.2%/IL	89%
68.	Loyola Marymount University (CA)	43	2.7	2.9	3.29-3.65	157-162	38%	15.2	22.6%	46.9%	82.5%/CA	67%
68.	University of Arkansas–Fayetteville	43	2.3	3.1	3.25-3.74	153-158	37%	14.1	38.8%	76.7%	82.6%/AR	84%
68.	University of Louisville (Brandeis) (KY)	43	2.2	3.0	3.17-3.68	155-159	45%	13.1	57.0%	86.6%	89.5%/KY	86%
68.	University of Nevada–Las Vegas	43	2.4	2.6	3.23-3.7	156-161	28%	14.0	52.3%	71.1%	82.7%/NV	76%
68.	University of Oklahoma	43	2.4	3.0	3.1-3.58	155-161	38%	13.5	41.7%	73.6%	88.7%/OK	88%
68.	University of San Diego	43	2.7	3.0	3.28-3.63	157-162	44%	16.1	37.1%	55.7%	73.6%/CA	67%
76.	Louisiana State Univ.–Baton Rouge (Hebert)	42	2.3	3.3	3.09-3.6	153-160	45%	20.3	27.3%	84.7%	86.9%/LA	70%
76.	Loyola University Chicago	42	2.5	3.2	3.12-3.57	156-160	43%	13.7	33.1%	60.6%	88.8%/IL	89%
76.	University of Miami (FL)	42	2.8	3.2	3.14-3.57	155-159	55%	13.0	31.2%	61.0%	83.1%/FL	80%
76.	University of Missouri	42	2.5	2.9	3.1-3.74	152-159	56%	12.9	38.3%	73.8%	97.5%/MO	93%
80.	Brooklyn Law School (NY)	41	2.6	3.1	3.08-3.5	158-164	37%	15.3	N/A	54.3%	89.6%/NY	77%
80.	Catholic Univ. of America (Columbus) (DC)	41	2.4	3.0	3.06-3.52	153-159	36%	10.9	37.5%	66.7%	77.6%/MD	81%
80.	Lewis & Clark College (Northwestern) (OR)	41	2.5	3.2	3.24-3.65	156-162	55%	10.9	27.5%	53.6%	82.1%/OR	78%
80.	Michigan State University	41	2.3	3.0	3.24-3.72	152-160	32%	13.5	N/A	60.1%	88.5%/MI	82%
80.	University of Cincinnati	41	2.5	2.7	3.2-3.73	156-161	59%	10.7	36.7%	67.5%	92.0%/OH	86%
80.	University of Hawaii–Manoa (Richardson)	41	2.5	2.5	3.04-3.59	154-160	29%	9.5	50.5%	72.3%	74.4%/HI	83%
86.	Northeastern University (MA)	40	2.4	2.9	3.27-3.67	154-163	39%	15.0	N/A	55.2%	91.2%/MA	87%
86.	Rutgers, the State U. of New Jersey–Newark	40	2.5	3.0	2.99-3.47	155-160	37%	15.3	46.4%	62.9%	80.2%/NJ	84%
86.	SUNY Buffalo Law School	40	2.4	2.9	3.19-3.67	152-158	44%	12.8	36.3%	62.0%	83.5%/NY	77%
86.	University of Kansas	40	2.6	3.2	3.22-3.71	154-159	54%	12.7	26.2%	61.9%	91.7%/KS	89%
86.	University of Tulsa (OK)	40	2.0	2.8	3.05-3.61	153-158	36%	11.7	32.5%	72.5%	86.6%/OK	88%
91.	Rutgers, the State U. of New Jersey–Camden	39	2.4	2.9	3.02-3.58	153-160	39%	12.1	55.0%	65.3%	81.5%/NJ	84%
91.	University of Pittsburgh	39	2.7	2.9	3.09-3.6	155-160	50%	14.6	24.1%	68.0%	83.5%/PA	85%
91.	West Virginia University	39	2.1	2.8	3.14-3.65	152-158	54%	10.2	52.8%	79.2%	78.9%/WV	83%
94.	Marquette University (WI)	38	2.4	3.0	3.15-3.56	153-158	62%	15.5	34.3%	64.8%	100.0%/WI	88%
94.	University of Oregon	38	2.8	3.2	3.09-3.63	155-160	53%	15.1	22.4%	49.4%	80.0%/OR	78%
96.	Santa Clara University (CA)	37	2.6	3.0	3-3.45	156-160	52%	11.9	38.5%	51.4%	77.1%/CA	67%
96.	Syracuse University (NY)	37	2.3	3.0	3.12-3.46	152-156	47%	12.4	36.8%	60.6%	81.8%/NY	77%
98.	Indiana University–Indianapolis[1]	36	2.5	2.9	3.19-3.68*	152-159*	49%*	16.8*	N/A	63.1%*	N/A	N/A
98.	St. John's University (NY)	36	2.2	2.8	3.12-3.66	153-161	48%	16.5	30.8%	55.1%	84.6%/NY	77%
98.	University of South Carolina	36	2.3	3.0	3.01-3.58	154-159	50%	15.1	29.3%	59.5%	82.9%/SC	77%
98.	Villanova University (PA)	36	2.3	3.2	3.29-3.69	155-161	62%	18.7	27.4%	59.9%	91.9%/PA	85%
102.	Seattle University	35	2.4	3.0	3.07-3.54	154-159	51%	12.0	N/A	49.5%	76.0%/WA	67%
102.	St. Louis University	35	2.0	3.1	3.23-3.7	151-159	59%	13.9	32.0%	67.6%	88.2%/MO	93%
102.	University of Mississippi	35	2.2	2.8	3.07-3.67	151-157	36%	15.2	33.8%	62.3%	84.1%/MS	82%
105.	Florida International University	34	1.6	1.9	3.14-3.76	151-157	22%	12.8	N/A	67.6%	89.3%/FL	80%
105.	Mercer University (George) (GA)	34	2.1	2.8	3.18-3.6	149-156	53%	14.2	29.8%	67.7%	77.4%/GA	85%
105.	Texas Tech University	34	1.9	2.6	3.24-3.68	152-158	48%	16.3	29.0%	73.0%	90.7%/TX	86%
105.	Wayne State University (MI)	34	2.1	2.7	3.1-3.6	153-160	53%	13.3	24.1%	56.2%	79.3%/MI	82%
109.	DePaul University (IL)	33	2.3	3.0	3.07-3.56	153-160	54%	14.1	16.0%	51.4%	92.6%/IL	89%
109.	Drake University (IA)	33	1.9	2.9	3.03-3.58	152-159	66%	13.2	27.1%	71.6%	91.6%/IA	90%

Rank	School	Overall score	Peer assessment score (5.0=highest)	Assessment score by lawyers/judges (5.0=highest)	'12 undergrad GPA 25th-75th percentile	'12 LSAT score 25th-75th percentile	'12 acceptance rate	'12 student/faculty ratio	'11 grads employed at graduation[2]	Employed 9 months after graduation[2]	School's bar passage rate in jurisdiction	Jurisdiction's overall bar passage rate
109.	Stetson University (FL)	33	2.1	2.5	3.02-3.52	152-157	43%	15.5	N/A	65.5%	87.4%/FL	80%
109.	University of Missouri–Kansas City	33	2.2	2.8	3-3.57	149-156	58%	13.8	N/A	71.4%	97.1%/MO	93%
113.	Gonzaga University (WA)	32	2.2	2.8	3-3.58	152-157	63%	15.5	N/A	63.8%	70.4%/WA	67%
113.	Hofstra University (Deane) (NY)	32	2.3	3.1	2.95-3.59	153-159	49%	15.0	N/A	47.5%	79.4%/NY	77%
113.	Samford University (Cumberland) (AL)	32	1.7	2.9	3.09-3.57	151-158	41%	16.4	33.8%	73.6%	92.5%/AL	77%
113.	University of Arkansas–Little Rock (Bowen)	32	2.2	2.7	2.86-3.46	149-156	44%	17.9	N/A	74.0%	82.9%/AR	84%
113.	University of Montana	32	2.0	2.4	3.01-3.66	152-158	58%	16.0	43.5%	68.2%	88.4%/MT	91%
113.	University of Wyoming	32	2.1	2.6	3.15-3.58	149-156	46%	11.1	36.5%	66.2%	56.9%/WY	62%
119.	Cleveland State Univ. (Cleveland-Marshall)	31	1.9	2.4	2.92-3.59	151-157	45%	12.2	27.0%	64.9%	82.4%/OH	86%
119.	Creighton University (NE)	31	2.0	2.9	2.92-3.5	150-156	68%	14.5	32.7%	69.3%	83.6%/IA	90%
119.	University of Akron (OH)	31	1.9	2.4	3.01-3.64	151-156	50%	12.1	21.6%	72.4%	91.1%/OH	86%
119.	Univ. of New Hampshire School of Law (NH)	31	1.9	2.6	2.92-3.59	151-159	59%	16.5	29.3%	55.1%	82.6%/NH	81%
119.	Vermont Law School	31	2.3	2.9	3-3.51	149-158	83%	15.9	20.7%	55.7%	74.2%/VT	71%
124.	University of St. Thomas (MN)	30	1.9	2.4	3.13-3.67	152-160	67%	13.5	17.2%	59.7%	92.4%/MN	93%
124.	University of the Pacific (McGeorge) (CA)	30	2.0	2.6	2.97-3.56	152-159	49%	13.7	N/A	46.9%	67.8%/CA	67%
126.	Campbell University (NC)	29	1.4	2.5	2.98-3.55	152-157	53%	17.7	31.6%	79.7%	92.1%/NC	80%
126.	Chapman University (CA)	29	1.8	2.0	3.2-3.6	154-160	42%	10.2	23.2%	48.0%	78.2%/CA	67%
126.	Drexel University (Mack) (PA)	29	2.0	2.5	3.02-3.6	154-159	39%	14.9	30.5%	50.4%	86.9%/PA	85%
126.	Hamline University (MN)	29	1.9	2.2	3.09-3.61	148-156	61%	15.7	31.7%	69.3%	89.2%/MN	93%
126.	Howard University (DC)	29	2.2	2.8	2.99-3.49	150-155	33%	17.9	48.4%	58.0%	49.3%/MD	81%
126.	Loyola University New Orleans	29	2.1	3.0	2.97-3.46	150-155	67%	15.7	35.1%	59.3%	66.3%/LA	70%
132.	Albany Law School (NY)	28	2.0	2.6	3.02-3.55	149-155	69%	12.9	28.0%	55.9%	78.6%/NY	77%
132.	CUNY	28	2.1	2.5	2.96-3.55	154-159	25%	9.7	N/A	41.4%	69.5%/NY	77%
134.	Pace University (NY)	27	1.9	2.4	3.08-3.58	150-156	45%	12.9	N/A	49.1%	75.5%/NY	77%
134.	Quinnipiac University (CT)	27	2.0	2.1	3.13-3.66	153-158	50%	12.2	18.0%	45.1%	80.6%/CT	82%
134.	University of Baltimore	27	2.0	2.2	2.83-3.41	149-156	61%	14.9	52.7%	63.1%	84.4%/MD	81%
134.	University of Idaho	27	2.1	2.6	2.94-3.52	149-156	65%	15.3	N/A	59.8%	86.2%/ID	85%
134.	University of Maine	27	2.2	2.7	3.1-3.53	152-157	56%	14.2	23.3%	50.0%	71.0%/ME	73%
134.	William Mitchell College of Law (MN)	27	1.8	2.3	3.11-3.57	150-158	76%	18.9	N/A	54.3%	93.7%/MN	93%
140.	Southern Illinois University–Carbondale	26	1.8	2.9	2.65-3.43	149-155	57%	12.8	22.7%	68.2%	88.1%/IL	89%
140.	St. Mary's University (TX)	26	1.6	2.5	2.76-3.41	151-155	53%	21.1	N/A	83.1%	86.3%/TX	86%
140.	University of North Dakota	26	1.9	2.5	3.04-3.58	145-153	44%	18.1	N/A	61.7%	80.5%/ND	85%
140.	Washburn University (KS)	26	1.9	2.6	2.93-3.51	150-156	59%	10.4	N/A	55.6%	83.5%/KS	89%
144.	Duquesne University (PA)	25	1.8	2.7	3.13-3.58	150-155	60%	16.9	26.8%	57.6%	81.8%/PA	85%
144.	South Texas College of Law	25	1.6	2.3	2.89-3.4	151-156	53%	20.2	N/A	73.9%	87.3%/TX	86%
144.	Suffolk University (MA)	25	2.0	3.0	2.98-3.48	146-155	74%	18.1	N/A	48.6%	86.8%/MA	87%
144.	University of Memphis (Humphreys)	25	1.8	2.3	3.04-3.54	152-157	35%	17.5	27.9%	63.6%	93.3%/TN	77%
144.	University of San Francisco	25	2.1	2.4	2.98-3.51	153-159	44%	16.7	10.8%	41.9%	72.1%/CA	67%

Other Schools to Consider

SECOND TIER

(Schools are not ranked, but listed alphabetically.)

The rest of the country's law schools should be considered broadly similar in quality. To be included in the ranking, a law school had to be accredited and fully approved by the American Bar Association and draw most of its students from the United States.

Remember as you weigh your options that you should look not only at a law school's position in the ranking, but also at its many other key characteristics, tangible and intangible: location, price, course offerings, and faculty expertise, to name a few, as well as your prospects of being offered a job upon graduation (story, Page 73). More information on all of the law schools is available in the directory at the back of the book, as well as at www.usnews.com/lawschools.

School	Peer assessment score (5.0=highest)	Assessment score by lawyers/judges (5.0=highest)	'12 undergrad GPA 25th-75th percentile	'12 LSAT score 25th-75th percentile	'12 acceptance rate	'12 student/faculty ratio	'11 grads employed at graduation[2]	Employed 9 months after graduation[2]	School's bar passage rate in jurisdiction	Jurisdiction's overall bar passage rate
Appalachian School of Law (VA)	1.3	1.5	2.73-3.51	143-149	71%	18.0	N/A	38.0%	61.9%/VA	79%
Atlanta's John Marshall Law School	1.4	1.5	2.6-3.27	148-153	52%	11.2	25.0%	51.5%	73.0%/GA	85%

SECOND TIER

School	Peer assessment score (5.0=highest)	Assessment score by lawyers/judges (5.0=highest)	'12 undergrad GPA 25th–75th percentile	'12 LSAT score 25th–75th percentile	'12 acceptance rate	'12 student/ faculty ratio	'11 grads employed at graduation[2]	Employed 9 months after graduation[2]	School's bar passage rate in jurisdiction	Jurisdiction's overall bar passage rate
Ave Maria School of Law (FL)	1.1	1.6	2.81-3.48	144-153	57%	17.6	N/A	44.3%	45.5%/FL	80%
Barry University[1] (FL)	1.2	1.4	2.55-3.26*	147-152*	58%*	15.5*	N/A	47.8%*	N/A	N/A
California Western School of Law	1.6	2.0	2.89-3.45	148-155	68%	16.9	N/A	42.1%	78.6%/CA	67%
Capital University (OH)	1.6	2.1	2.91-3.4	147-153	70%	13.8	N/A	48.0%	80.5%/OH	86%
Charleston School of Law (SC)	1.4	2.3	2.94-3.43	149-154	59%	16.4	N/A	59.6%	74.3%/SC	77%
Charlotte School of Law (NC)	1.2	1.9	2.65-3.32	142-150	76%	19.3	14.4%	38.1%	77.9%/NC	80%
Elon University (NC)	1.7	2.5	2.8-3.48	150-158	56%	15.4	19.2%	58.6%	81.7%/NC	80%
Faulkner University (Jones) (AL)	1.3	2.1	2.69-3.34	145-150	62%	17.5	N/A	66.3%	90.1%/AL	77%
Florida A&M University[1]	1.3	2.0	2.81-3.34*	145-151*	38%*	20.5*	N/A	38.2%*	N/A	N/A
Florida Coastal School of Law	1.3	1.6	2.85-3.34	143-151	74%	19.9	N/A	41.0%	76.0%/FL	80%
Golden Gate University (CA)	1.7	1.8	2.79-3.37	148-154	71%	16.3	N/A	29.8%	62.1%/CA	67%
John Marshall Law School (IL)	1.7	2.5	2.88-3.39	148-154	63%	16.4	18.7%	56.1%	83.3%/IL	89%
Liberty University (VA)	1.2	1.8	2.78-3.63	148-155	48%	12.7	N/A	54.4%	50.0%/VA	79%
Mississippi College	1.6	1.9	3.06-3.57	146-152	66%	17.3	34.5%	82.4%	80.4%/MS	82%
New England Law Boston (MA)	1.6	2.2	2.74-3.4	145-153	89%	25.5	N/A	44.5%	94.0%/MA	87%
New York Law School	1.9	2.2	2.83-3.4	149-154	54%	20.9	N/A	47.0%	80.3%/NY	77%
North Carolina Central University	1.5	2.1	2.91-3.47	143-151	34%	14.3	N/A	58.2%	73.8%/NC	80%
Northern Illinois University	1.7	2.5	2.8-3.39	147-153	59%	16.3	28.9%	59.8%	86.7%/IL	89%
Northern Kentucky University (Chase)	1.6	2.2	2.87-3.4	149-155	70%	14.3	N/A	57.5%	79.2%/KY	86%
Nova Southeastern University (Broad) (FL)	1.6	2.3	2.91-3.37	147-153	51%	16.3	15.6%	67.2%	86.6%/FL	80%
Ohio Northern University (Pettit)	1.6	2.4	2.81-3.45	145-154	51%	12.3	N/A	58.8%	90.7%/OH	86%
Oklahoma City University	1.6	2.2	2.89-3.49	147-153	69%	18.4	N/A	74.4%	89.0%/OK	88%
Phoenix School of Law	1.1	1.6	2.55-3.3	141-150	85%	19.8	N/A	55.0%	67.3%/AZ	76%
Regent University (VA)	1.2	1.9	2.97-3.61	151-159	48%	15.9	N/A	56.8%	75.4%/VA	79%
Roger Williams University (RI)	1.7	2.0	2.96-3.56	147-156	79%	19.6	N/A	57.0%	80.4%/MA	87%
Southern University Law Center (LA)	1.4	1.9	2.57-3.15	143-148	59%	15.0	N/A	49.7%	58.8%/LA	70%
Southwestern Law School (CA)	2.0	2.0	3.03-3.5	151-155	43%	14.6	25.2%	52.3%	60.7%/CA	67%
St. Thomas University (FL)	1.4	1.8	2.77-3.26	146-150	63%	15.8	N/A	54.8%	75.1%/FL	80%
Texas Southern University (Marshall)	1.5	2.0	2.84-3.4	144-148	35%	14.5	9.8%	57.7%	68.5%/TX	86%
Texas Wesleyan University	1.7	1.8	2.84-3.33	149-155	53%	16.7	16.1%	53.8%	87.4%/TX	86%
Thomas Jefferson School of Law (CA)	1.4	2.0	2.69-3.2	146-151	73%	20.1	9.7%	32.2%	36.6%/CA	67%
Thomas M. Cooley Law School (MI)	1.2	1.8	2.57-3.36	142-151	74%	19.6	N/A	43.8%	84.1%/MI	82%
Touro College (Fuchsberg) (NY)	1.6	1.9	2.87-3.35	146-150	64%	16.5	N/A	63.8%	82.0%/NY	77%
University of Dayton (OH)	1.8	2.3	2.84-3.37	146-152	69%	14.3	16.4%	60.8%	71.6%/OH	86%
University of Detroit Mercy	1.4	1.7	2.79-3.33	146-157	48%	17.2	N/A	47.4%	67.1%/MI	82%
University of South Dakota	1.8	2.4	3.01-3.67	146-153	66%	14.4	41.8%	45.5%	90.0%/SD	94%
University of the District of Columbia (Clarke)	1.4	1.8	2.66-3.27	148-153	27%	12.9	N/A	35.9%	59.3%/MD	81%
University of Toledo (OH)	1.9	2.3	2.97-3.54	149-154	46%	12.1	32.2%	47.8%	85.1%/OH	86%
Valparaiso University (IN)	1.8	2.7	2.94-3.48	145-152	76%	14.4	N/A	49.2%	76.2%/IN	83%
Western New England University (MA)	1.5	1.7	2.83-3.42	147-152	74%	12.6	N/A	45.1%	73.2%/MA	87%
Western State Col. of Law at Argosy U. (CA)	1.2	1.5	2.85-3.34	149-155	54%	25.6	N/A	38.9%	78.2%/CA	67%
Whittier College (CA)	1.3	1.6	2.7-3.22	148-153	67%	20.8	N/A	23.6%	55.4%/CA	67%
Widener University (DE)	1.8	2.4	2.86-3.42	148-153	57%	12.9	18.1%	55.9%	85.5%/PA	85%
Willamette University (Collins) (OR)	2.0	2.8	2.79-3.42	151-156	63%	13.1	N/A	48.8%	72.6%/OR	78%

THE SPECIALTIES

PROGRAMS RANKED BEST BY FACULTY WHO TEACH IN THE FIELD

CLINICAL TRAINING
1. Georgetown University (DC)
2. American University (Washington) (DC)
3. New York University
4. CUNY
5. University of Maryland (Carey)
6. University of Michigan–Ann Arbor
7. Yale University (CT)
8. Stanford University (CA)
9. Washington University in St. Louis
10. University of the District of Columbia (Clarke)
11. University of New Mexico
12. Harvard University (MA)
13. Northwestern University (IL)
13. University of California–Berkeley
15. University of Denver (Sturm)

DISPUTE RESOLUTION
1. Pepperdine University (CA)
2. Harvard University (MA)
3. University of Missouri
4. Hamline University (MN)
4. Ohio State University (Moritz)
6. Yeshiva University (Cardozo) (NY)
7. University of Oregon

THE SPECIALTIES

ENVIRONMENTAL LAW
1. Vermont Law School
2. Lewis & Clark College (Northwestern) (OR)
3. Pace University (NY)
3. University of California–Berkeley
5. University of Colorado–Boulder
6. Tulane University (LA)
6. University of Maryland (Carey)
8. University of Oregon
9. Georgetown University (DC)
10. Duke University (NC)
10. New York University
12. George Washington University (DC)
12. University of Florida (Levin)
12. University of Utah (Quinney)

HEALTH LAW
1. St. Louis University
2. Boston University
3. Georgia State University
4. University of Maryland (Carey)
5. Case Western Reserve University (OH)

6. Seton Hall University (NJ)
7. Loyola University Chicago
8. University of Houston (TX)
9. Georgetown University (DC)

INTELLECTUAL PROPERTY LAW
1. University of California–Berkeley
2. Stanford University (CA)
3. Santa Clara University (CA)
4. George Washington University (DC)
5. Yeshiva University (Cardozo) (NY)
6. New York University
7. University of Houston (TX)
8. American University (Washington) (DC)
8. University of New Hampshire School of Law (NH)
10. Boston University
11. Illinois Institute of Technology (Chicago-Kent)
12. John Marshall Law School (IL)
13. Columbia University (NY)
14. Georgetown University (DC)

INTERNATIONAL LAW
1. New York University
2. Harvard University (MA)
3. Georgetown University (DC)
4. Columbia University (NY)
5. American University (Washington) (DC)
5. University of California–Berkeley
7. George Washington University (DC)
8. Yale University (CT)
9. University of Michigan–Ann Arbor
10. Duke University (NC)
10. University of California–Los Angeles

LEGAL WRITING
1. Seattle University
2. John Marshall Law School (IL)
3. Mercer University (George) (GA)
3. University of Nevada–Las Vegas
5. Arizona State University (O'Connor)

5. Stetson University (FL)
5. Suffolk University (MA)
5. Temple University (Beasley) (PA)
5. University of Oregon

TAX LAW
1. New York University
2. Georgetown University (DC)
3. University of Florida (Levin)
4. Northwestern University (IL)
5. University of Miami (FL)
5. University of Southern California (Gould)
7. Boston University
7. Loyola Marymount University (CA)
7. University of Virginia

TRIAL ADVOCACY
1. Stetson University (FL)
2. Temple University (Beasley) (PA)
3. Baylor University (TX)
4. Northwestern University (IL)
5. Illinois Institute of Technology (Chicago-Kent)

METHODOLOGY

Our annual rankings of 194 accredited law schools are based on a weighted average of 12 factors, described below. A law school official at each school that responded to the *U.S. News* statistical survey—in many cases the dean—verified the data for accuracy.

Quality assessment: Quality was measured by two separate surveys conducted in the fall of 2012. The dean and three faculty members at each school were asked to rate schools from marginal (1) to outstanding (5); 63 percent voted. Their average rating for a school is weighted by .25 in the overall ranking. Lawyers and judges also rated schools; 9 percent responded. The two most recent years' surveys of lawyers and judges were averaged and are weighted by .15.

Selectivity (weighted at .25): This measure combines the following

fall 2012 data for all full-time and part-time entering J.D. students: median LSAT scores (50 percent of this indicator), median undergrad GPA (40 percent), and the acceptance rate (10 percent).

Placement success (.20): Success is determined by calculating employment rates for 2011 grads at graduation (20 percent) and nine months after (70 percent) as well as their bar passage rate (10 percent). For ranking purposes only, the placement measure was calculated by assigning various weights to the number of grads employed in 22 different types and durations of jobs as defined by the American Bar Association. Full weight was given for graduates who had a full-time job lasting at least a year for which bar passage was required or a J.D. degree was an advantage; the least weight

applied to jobs categorized as part-time and short-term. (Employment rates published in the tables reflect only the full-weight job categories; employment rates for the other types of jobs can be found at *www.usnews.com/grad*.) The bar passage indicator is the ratio of a school's pass rate in the cited jurisdiction to the overall state rate for first-time test-takers in summer and winter 2011. The jurisdiction is the state where the largest number of 2011 grads first took the test. Note: For a more detailed explanation of how the employment rates were calculated and how employment data is now being published by *U.S. News*, see Page 73.

Faculty resources (.15): Resources are based on average fiscal year 2011 and 2012 expenditures per student for instruction, library, and

supporting services (65 percent) and on all other items, including financial aid (10 percent); 2012 student/teacher ratio (20 percent); and total number of volumes and titles in the library (5 percent).

Overall rank: Scores on each indicator were standardized about their means. Then scores were weighted, totaled, and rescaled so that the top school received 100 and other schools received a percentage of the top score.

Specialty rankings: Results are based solely on votes by faculty teaching in the particular field listed in the Association of American Law Schools' *2010-2011 Directory of Law Teachers* or by directors of clinical and legal writing programs; each named up to 15 schools. Those with the most votes were ranked. Half of schools receiving a statistically significant number of votes appear.

Best Part-Time J.D. Programs

Part-time law programs play a vital role in legal education: The American Bar Association's latest data reveal that in the fall of 2010, some 21,800, or about 15 percent of all the 147,525 U.S. law students, were enrolled part time. For many working adults, it's the only way to afford a law degree and still meet other commitments. Fewer than half of the country's law schools offer part-time programs, which generally take four years to complete. Below, *U.S. News* presents the top half of accredited law schools offering part-time programs. The ranking is based on four factors as described in the methodology below: reputation among deans and faculty at peer schools, LSAT scores and undergraduate GPAs of students entering in fall 2012, and the breadth of each school's part-time program.

THE TOP SCHOOLS

Rank School	Overall score	Peer assessment score (5.0=highest)	'12 part-time LSAT score 25th-75th percentile	'12 part-time acceptance rate	'12 part-time enrollment
1. Georgetown University (DC)	100	4.1	163-170	4.9%	243
2. George Washington University (DC)	85	3.5	160-168	17.9%	322
3. Fordham University (NY)	82	3.5	160-165	18.2%	221
4. George Mason University (VA)	67	2.8	160-165	7.8%	194
5. University of Connecticut	66	2.9	155-161	18.0%	118
6. Loyola Marymount University (CA)	62	2.7	155-162	5.1%	227
6. Loyola University Chicago	62	2.8	151-157	25.6%	107
6. University of Maryland (Carey)	62	2.8	149-163	23.1%	195
9. Lewis & Clark College (Northwestern) (OR)	61	2.7	153-161	46.7%	267
10. American University (Washington) (DC)	58	3.0	153-159	29.2%	307
10. University of San Diego	58	2.8	156-162	22.2%	100
12. Temple University (Beasley) (PA)	57	2.8	156-162	29.2%	173
12. University of Denver (Sturm)	57	2.9	153-159	39.5%	148
12. Yeshiva University (Cardozo) (NY)	57	2.8	157-160	37.5%	107
15. Southern Methodist University (Dedman) (TX)	56	2.7	157-161	25.4%	295
16. Georgia State University	52	2.5	154-160	27.8%	185
16. University of Houston (TX)	52	2.7	157-162	12.6%	143
18. Catholic University of America (Columbus) (DC)	49	2.4	153-159	30.0%	211
18. Marquette University (WI)	49	2.5	153-157	23.8%	131
20. Seattle University	47	2.7	152-158	54.0%	199
21. Brooklyn Law School (NY)	46	2.7	156-160	19.3%	262
21. Illinois Institute of Technology (Chicago-Kent)	46	2.7	149-155	28.0%	161
21. Rutgers, the State Univ. of New Jersey–Newark	46	2.5	154-160	23.9%	205
24. Seton Hall University (NJ)	45	2.5	148-154	24.1%	246
24. University of Nevada–Las Vegas	45	2.5	151-158	28.3%	130
26. University of Baltimore	41	2.1	149-155	48.9%	360
26. University of Louisville (Brandeis) (KY)	41	2.1	147-156	23.4%	28
26. University of the Pacific (McGeorge) (CA)	41	2.3	150-156	38.5%	227
29. Hofstra University (Deane) (NY)	40	2.4	151-158	19.1%	34
29. University of Hawaii–Manoa (Richardson)	40	2.4	151-160	32.4%	82
31. DePaul University (IL)	39	2.4	151-156	36.0%	142
31. New York Law School	39	2.0	149-153	41.2%	411
31. Suffolk University (MA)	39	2.4	144-154	72.3%	559
34. Southwestern Law School (CA)	38	2.4	150-154	41.7%	395
34. St. John's University (NY)	38	2.3	150-158	24.1%	147
36. Pace University (NY)	37	1.9	148-159	23.9%	115
36. Wayne State University (MI)	37	2.2	151-158	45.7%	156
36. Widener University (DE)	37	2.0	147-153	44.3%	362
39. Santa Clara University (CA)	36	2.6	155-160	47.9%	187
40. Hamline University (MN)	35	2.0	145-157	62.3%	158
40. Stetson University (FL)	35	2.1	150-156	39.3%	226
40. University of San Francisco	35	2.3	152-156	29.1%	118
40. William Mitchell College of Law (MN)	35	2.0	146-157	41.7%	300

METHODOLOGY

The ranking of 82 part-time law programs is based on a weighted average of four measures of quality. For a school's program to be eligible for the part-time ranking, it had to have reported at least 20 part-time students enrolled in the fall of 2012 and supplied data on fall 2012 applications and acceptances to its part-time program. **Quality assessment** (weighted by .50): In the fall of 2012, deans and three faculty members at each school were asked to rate programs from marginal (1) to outstanding (5); 51 percent responded, and scores for each school were averaged. **Selectivity** (weighted by .275): For part-time students entering in 2012, this measure combines median LSAT scores (81.8 percent of this indicator) and undergraduate GPAs (18.2 percent). **Part-time focus** (weighted by .225): An index was created from data reported by the schools about their 2012 part-time J.D. programs. Factors used in the creation of this index include the size of part-time first-year sections; the size of part-time first-year small sections; and the number of positions filled by part-time students in seminars, simulation courses, faculty-supervised clinical courses, field placements, law journals, interschool skills competitions, and independent study. Schools received credit for reporting data and additional credit for surpassing a threshold value in the various factors used. **Overall rank:** Schools' scores on each indicator were standardized, weighted, totaled, and rescaled so that the top school received 100 and other schools received a percentage of the top score.

Note: The data listed for acceptance rate and enrollment are for informational purposes only and are not used in the computation of the part-time J.D. program ranking. Only part-time J.D. programs ranked in the top half appear. Sources: *U.S. News* and the schools. Assessment data collected by Ipsos Public Affairs.

More at **www.usnews.com/grad**

THE REST OF THE RANKINGS

Playing the carillon at Berkeley, a top school in several rankings categories

Social Sciences & Humanities

Ph.D. programs ranked best by department chairs and senior faculty

CRIMINOLOGY

Ranked in 2009

Rank	School	Average assessment score (5.0=highest)
1.	University of Maryland–College Park	4.7
2.	University at Albany–SUNY	4.4
3.	University of Cincinnati	4.1
4.	University of Missouri–St. Louis	3.8
5.	Pennsylvania State University–University Park	3.7
5.	University of California–Irvine	3.7
7.	Florida State University	3.5
7.	Michigan State University	3.5
7.	Rutgers, the State University of New Jersey–Newark	3.5
10.	CUNY–John Jay College	3.3
11.	Temple University (PA)	3.2
12.	Arizona State University	3.1
12.	Northeastern University (MA)	3.1
12.	University of Florida	3.1
12.	University of Pennsylvania	3.1

ECONOMICS

Ranked in 2013

Rank	School	Average assessment score (5.0=highest)
1.	Harvard University (MA)	5.0
1.	Massachusetts Institute of Technology	5.0
1.	Princeton University (NJ)	5.0
1.	University of Chicago	5.0
5.	Stanford University (CA)	4.9
5.	University of California–Berkeley	4.9
7.	Northwestern University (IL)	4.8
7.	Yale University (CT)	4.8
9.	University of Pennsylvania	4.5
10.	Columbia University (NY)	4.4
11.	New York University	4.3
11.	University of Minnesota–Twin Cities	4.3
13.	University of Michigan–Ann Arbor	4.2
13.	University of Wisconsin–Madison	4.2
15.	California Institute of Technology	4.1
15.	University of California–Los Angeles	4.1
15.	University of California–San Diego	4.1
18.	Cornell University (NY)	3.9
19.	Brown University (RI)	3.8
19.	Carnegie Mellon University (Tepper) (PA)	3.8
19.	Duke University (NC)	3.8
22.	University of Maryland–College Park	3.7
22.	University of Rochester (NY)	3.7
24.	Boston University	3.6
24.	Johns Hopkins University (MD)	3.6
26.	University of Texas–Austin	3.5
27.	Ohio State University	3.4
27.	Pennsylvania State University–University Park	3.4
27.	Washington University in St. Louis	3.4
30.	Michigan State University	3.3
30.	University of Virginia	3.3
32.	Boston College	3.2
32.	University of California–Davis	3.2

Rank	School	Average assessment score (5.0=highest)
32.	University of Illinois–Urbana-Champaign	3.2
32.	University of North Carolina–Chapel Hill	3.2
36.	Arizona State University	3.1
36.	University of Arizona	3.1
36.	University of Pittsburgh	3.1
36.	Vanderbilt University (TN)	3.1
40.	University of Iowa (Tippie)	3.0
40.	University of Washington	3.0
42.	Indiana University–Bloomington	2.9
42.	Purdue University–West Lafayette (Krannert) (IN)	2.9
42.	Texas A&M University–College Station	2.9
42.	University of California–Santa Barbara	2.9
46.	Georgetown University (DC)	2.8
46.	University of California–Irvine	2.8
48.	North Carolina State University–Raleigh	2.7
48.	Rice University (TX)	2.7
48.	Rutgers, the State U. of New Jersey–New Brunswick	2.7
48.	University of Florida	2.7
48.	University of Southern California	2.7

ECONOMICS SPECIALTIES

DEVELOPMENT ECONOMICS
1. Harvard University (MA)
2. Massachusetts Institute of Technology
3. Princeton University (NJ)
3. Yale University (CT)
5. University of California–Berkeley

ECONOMETRICS
1. Massachusetts Institute of Technology
1. Yale University (CT)
3. Princeton University (NJ)
4. University of California–San Diego
5. Harvard University (MA)
6. Northwestern University (IL)
6. University of California–Berkeley

INDUSTRIAL ORGANIZATION
1. Stanford University (CA)
2. Harvard University (MA)
2. Northwestern University (IL)
4. Yale University (CT)
5. University of Chicago
6. Massachusetts Institute of Technology
6. University of California–Berkeley

INTERNATIONAL ECONOMICS
1. Harvard University (MA)
2. Princeton University (NJ)
3. Columbia University (NY)
4. University of California–Berkeley
5. Massachusetts Institute of Technology

LABOR ECONOMICS
1. Harvard University (MA)
1. Princeton University (NJ)
3. Massachusetts Institute of Technology
4. University of California–Berkeley
5. University of Chicago

MACROECONOMICS
1. Harvard University (MA)
2. Massachusetts Institute of Technology
3. Princeton University (NJ)
4. New York University
5. University of Minnesota–Twin Cities
6. University of Chicago
6. University of Pennsylvania

MICROECONOMICS
1. Stanford University (CA)
2. Massachusetts Institute of Technology
3. Harvard University (MA)
4. Yale University (CT)
5. Northwestern University (IL)
5. Princeton University (NJ)
7. University of Chicago

PUBLIC FINANCE
1. University of California–Berkeley
2. Harvard University (MA)
2. Massachusetts Institute of Technology
4. Stanford University (CA)
5. University of Michigan–Ann Arbor

More at www.usnews.com/grad

Find the right school for you with the
U.S. News Graduate School
Compass

ENGLISH

Ranked in 2013

Rank	School	Average assessment score (5.0=highest)
1.	University of California–Berkeley	4.9
2.	Harvard University (MA)	4.8
2.	Stanford University (CA)	4.8
4.	Columbia University (NY)	4.7
4.	Princeton University (NJ)	4.7
4.	University of Pennsylvania	4.7
4.	Yale University (CT)	4.7
8.	Cornell University (NY)	4.6
8.	University of Chicago	4.6
10.	Duke University (NC)	4.4
10.	University of California–Los Angeles	4.4
10.	University of Virginia	4.4
13.	Johns Hopkins University (MD)	4.3
13.	University of Michigan–Ann Arbor	4.3
15.	Brown University (RI)	4.2
15.	University of North Carolina–Chapel Hill	4.2
17.	Rutgers, the State U. of New Jersey–New Brunswick	4.1
17.	University of Texas–Austin	4.1
17.	University of Wisconsin–Madison	4.1
20.	New York University	4.0
20.	Northwestern University (IL)	4.0
22.	CUNY Graduate School and University Center	3.9
22.	Indiana University–Bloomington	3.9
22.	University of California–Irvine	3.9

Rank	School	Average assessment score (5.0=highest)
22.	University of Illinois–Urbana-Champaign	3.9
26.	Emory University (GA)	3.7
26.	Ohio State University	3.7
26.	Pennsylvania State University–University Park	3.7
26.	University of California–Davis	3.7
26.	University of California–Santa Barbara	3.7
26.	Vanderbilt University (TN)	3.7
32.	University of Iowa	3.6
32.	University of Maryland–College Park	3.6
32.	University of Washington	3.6
32.	Washington University in St. Louis	3.6
36.	Rice University (TX)	3.5
36.	University of Minnesota–Twin Cities	3.5
36.	University of Southern California	3.5
39.	Carnegie Mellon University (PA)	3.4
39.	University of California–San Diego	3.4
39.	University of California–Santa Cruz	3.4
39.	University of Notre Dame (IN)	3.4
39.	University of Pittsburgh	3.4
44.	Boston University	3.3
44.	Brandeis University (MA)	3.3
44.	Claremont Graduate University (CA)	3.3
44.	University at Buffalo–SUNY	3.3
44.	University of California–Riverside	3.3
44.	University of Illinois–Chicago	3.3

ENGLISH SPECIALTIES

AFRICAN-AMERICAN LITERATURE
1. Harvard University (MA)
2. Yale University (CT)
3. Princeton University (NJ)
4. Duke University (NC)
4. University of California–Berkeley
4. Vanderbilt University (TN)

AMERICAN LITERATURE AFTER 1865
1. University of California–Berkeley
2. University of Chicago
3. Stanford University (CA)
4. Columbia University (NY)
4. Harvard University (MA)
4. University of Pennsylvania
4. University of Virginia
4. Yale University (CT)

AMERICAN LITERATURE BEFORE 1865
1. University of California–Berkeley
2. Harvard University (MA)
2. University of Pennsylvania
2. Yale University (CT)
5. University of Virginia

18TH THROUGH 20TH CENTURY BRITISH LITERATURE
1. University of California–Berkeley
2. Harvard University (MA)
2. University of Pennsylvania
2. University of Virginia
5. Stanford University (CA)
6. Columbia University (NY)
6. University of California–Los Angeles
6. Yale University (CT)

GENDER AND LITERATURE
1. University of California–Berkeley
2. Duke University (NC)
3. University of Michigan–Ann Arbor
4. Princeton University (NJ)
4. Stanford University (CA)

LITERARY CRITICISM AND THEORY
1. Duke University (NC)
2. University of California–Berkeley
3. Cornell University (NY)
3. University of California–Irvine
5. Stanford University (CA)
6. Johns Hopkins University (MD)

MEDIEVAL/RENAISSANCE LITERATURE
1. Harvard University (MA)
2. University of California–Berkeley
3. University of Pennsylvania
3. Yale University (CT)
5. Stanford University (CA)
6. University of Notre Dame (IN)

HISTORY

Ranked in 2013

Rank	School	Average assessment score (5.0=highest)
1.	Princeton University (NJ)	4.8
1.	University of California–Berkeley	4.8
1.	Yale University (CT)	4.8
4.	Harvard University (MA)	4.7
4.	Stanford University (CA)	4.7
4.	University of Chicago	4.7
7.	Columbia University (NY)	4.6
7.	University of Michigan–Ann Arbor	4.6
9.	University of California–Los Angeles	4.5
9.	University of Pennsylvania	4.5
11.	Cornell University (NY)	4.4
11.	Johns Hopkins University (MD)	4.4
11.	University of North Carolina–Chapel Hill	4.4
14.	Duke University (NC)	4.3
14.	Northwestern University (IL)	4.3
14.	University of Wisconsin–Madison	4.3
17.	University of Texas–Austin	4.2
18.	Brown University (RI)	4.1

HISTORY

Rank	School	Average assessment score (5.0=highest)
18.	New York University	4.1
20.	Rutgers, the State U. of New Jersey–New Brunswick	4.0
20.	University of Illinois–Urbana-Champaign	4.0
20.	University of Virginia (Corcoran)	4.0
23.	Indiana University–Bloomington	3.9
24.	Ohio State University	3.8
24.	University of Minnesota–Twin Cities	3.8
24.	Vanderbilt University (TN)	3.8
27.	Emory University (GA)	3.7
27.	Massachusetts Institute of Technology	3.7
27.	University of California–Davis	3.7
30.	CUNY Graduate School and University Center	3.6
30.	Georgetown University (DC)	3.6
30.	Rice University (TX)	3.6
30.	University of California–San Diego	3.6
30.	University of Washington	3.6
30.	Washington University in St. Louis	3.6

HISTORY SPECIALTIES

AFRICAN HISTORY
1. University of Wisconsin–Madison
2. University of Michigan–Ann Arbor
3. Michigan State University
4. Northwestern University (IL)
4. University of California–Los Angeles

AFRICAN-AMERICAN HISTORY
1. Yale University (CT)
2. Duke University (NC)
3. University of Michigan–Ann Arbor
4. Harvard University (MA)
5. Columbia University (NY)
6. Princeton University (NJ)
6. University of North Carolina–Chapel Hill

ASIAN HISTORY
1. Harvard University (MA)
1. University of California–Berkeley
3. Yale University (CT)
4. Princeton University (NJ)
4. Stanford University (CA)
4. University of California–Los Angeles

CULTURAL HISTORY
1. University of California–Berkeley
2. University of Michigan–Ann Arbor
3. Yale University (CT)
4. Princeton University (NJ)
5. Columbia University (NY)

EUROPEAN HISTORY
1. University of California–Berkeley
1. Yale University (CT)
3. Harvard University (MA)
3. University of Michigan–Ann Arbor
5. University of Chicago
6. Columbia University (NY)
7. Princeton University (NJ)

LATIN AMERICAN HISTORY
1. University of Texas–Austin
2. Yale University (CT)
3. University of Wisconsin–Madison
4. Duke University (NC)
5. University of California–Los Angeles
6. University of Chicago
6. University of Michigan–Ann Arbor

MODERN U.S. HISTORY
1. Yale University (CT)
2. Harvard University (MA)
2. University of California–Berkeley
4. Columbia University (NY)
4. Princeton University (NJ)
6. University of Michigan–Ann Arbor
6. University of Wisconsin–Madison
8. University of Pennsylvania

U.S. COLONIAL HISTORY
1. Harvard University (MA)
2. University of Pennsylvania
3. College of William and Mary (Tyler) (VA)
4. Yale University (CT)
5. University of Virginia (Corcoran)
6. Johns Hopkins University (MD)
7. University of Michigan–Ann Arbor

WOMEN'S HISTORY
1. Rutgers, the State U. of New Jersey–New Brunswick
2. University of Wisconsin–Madison
3. University of Michigan–Ann Arbor
4. University of Pennsylvania
4. Yale University (CT)
6. New York University
7. University of California–Santa Barbara
7. University of Minnesota–Twin Cities

POLITICAL SCIENCE
Ranked in 2013

Rank	School	Average assessment score (5.0=highest)
1.	Harvard University (MA)	4.9
2.	Princeton University (NJ)	4.8
2.	Stanford University (CA)	4.8
4.	University of Michigan–Ann Arbor	4.7
4.	Yale University (CT)	4.7
6.	University of California–Berkeley	4.6
7.	Columbia University (NY)	4.4
8.	Massachusetts Institute of Technology	4.3
8.	University of California–San Diego	4.3
10.	Duke University (NC)	4.2
10.	University of California–Los Angeles	4.2
12.	University of Chicago	4.1
13.	University of North Carolina–Chapel Hill	4.0
13.	Washington University in St. Louis	4.0
15.	New York University	3.9
15.	Ohio State University	3.9
15.	University of Rochester (NY)	3.9
15.	University of Wisconsin–Madison	3.9
19.	Cornell University (NY)	3.8
19.	University of Minnesota–Twin Cities	3.8
21.	Northwestern University (IL)	3.6
21.	University of Texas–Austin	3.6
23.	University of California–Davis	3.5
23.	University of Illinois–Urbana-Champaign	3.5
25.	Emory University (GA)	3.4
25.	Indiana University–Bloomington	3.4
25.	Texas A&M University–College Station	3.4
28.	Pennsylvania State University–University Park	3.3
28.	University of Maryland–College Park	3.3
28.	University of Pennsylvania	3.3
28.	University of Washington	3.3
32.	Michigan State University	3.2
32.	Rice University (TX)	3.2
32.	Stony Brook University–SUNY	3.2
32.	University of Iowa	3.2
36.	George Washington University (DC)	3.1
36.	University of Notre Dame (IN)	3.1
36.	University of Virginia	3.1
36.	Vanderbilt University (TN)	3.1
40.	Florida State University	3.0
40.	Georgetown University (DC)	3.0
40.	Johns Hopkins University (MD)	3.0
40.	University of California–Irvine	3.0
40.	University of Pittsburgh	3.0

POLITICAL SCIENCE SPECIALTIES

AMERICAN POLITICS
1. Harvard University (MA)
2. Stanford University (CA)
3. University of Michigan–Ann Arbor
4. Princeton University (NJ)
5. University of California–Berkeley
6. Yale University (CT)
7. Duke University (NC)
8. University of California–Los Angeles
9. Columbia University (NY)

COMPARATIVE POLITICS
1. Harvard University (MA)
2. Stanford University (CA)
3. Princeton University (NJ)
3. University of California–Berkeley
5. Columbia University (NY)
6. Yale University (CT)
7. University of Michigan–Ann Arbor
8. University of California–Los Angeles
9. Duke University (NC)

INTERNATIONAL POLITICS
1. Harvard University (MA)
2. Stanford University (CA)
3. Princeton University (NJ)

4. Columbia University (NY)
5. University of California–San Diego
6. University of Michigan–Ann Arbor
7. New York University
8. Ohio State University
8. Yale University (CT)

POLITICAL METHODOLOGY
1. Harvard University (MA)
2. Stanford University (CA)
3. New York University
3. University of Michigan–Ann Arbor
5. Washington University in St. Louis

6. Princeton University (NJ)
7. University of Rochester (NY)
8. University of California–Berkeley

POLITICAL THEORY
1. Princeton University (NJ)
2. Harvard University (MA)
3. University of Chicago
4. Yale University (CT)
5. Johns Hopkins University (MD)
6. University of California–Berkeley
7. Duke University (NC)
8. Northwestern University (IL)

PSYCHOLOGY

Ranked in 2013

Rank	School	Average assessment score (5.0=highest)
1.	Stanford University (CA)	4.8
2.	University of California–Berkeley	4.7
2.	University of California–Los Angeles	4.7
4.	Harvard University (MA)	4.6
4.	University of Michigan–Ann Arbor	4.6
4.	Yale University (CT)	4.6
7.	Princeton University (NJ)	4.5
7.	University of Illinois–Urbana-Champaign	4.5
9.	Massachusetts Institute of Technology	4.4
9.	University of Minnesota–Twin Cities	4.4
9.	University of Wisconsin–Madison	4.4
12.	University of North Carolina–Chapel Hill	4.3
12.	University of Pennsylvania	4.3
14.	Columbia University (NY)	4.2
14.	Cornell University (NY)	4.2
14.	Northwestern University (IL)	4.2
14.	University of California–San Diego	4.2
14.	University of Texas–Austin	4.2
14.	University of Washington	4.2
14.	Washington University in St. Louis	4.2
21.	Carnegie Mellon University (PA)	4.1
21.	Duke University (NC)	4.1
21.	Ohio State University	4.1
21.	University of California–Davis	4.1
21.	University of Chicago	4.1
26.	Brown University (RI)	4.0
26.	Indiana University–Bloomington	4.0
26.	Johns Hopkins University (MD)	4.0
26.	University of Virginia	4.0
30.	New York University	3.9
30.	Pennsylvania State University–University Park	3.9
30.	University of California–Irvine	3.9
30.	University of Colorado–Boulder	3.9
30.	University of Iowa	3.9
30.	University of Oregon	3.9
30.	University of Pittsburgh	3.9
30.	Vanderbilt University (TN)	3.9
38.	Arizona State University	3.8
38.	Emory University (GA)	3.8
40.	University of Arizona	3.7
40.	University of California–Santa Barbara	3.7
40.	University of Florida	3.7

Rank	School	Average assessment score (5.0=highest)
40.	University of Kansas	3.7
40.	University of Maryland–College Park	3.7
40.	University of Southern California	3.7
46.	Boston University	3.6
46.	Dartmouth College (NH)	3.6
46.	Michigan State University	3.6
46.	Purdue University–West Lafayette (IN)	3.6
46.	Stony Brook University–SUNY	3.6
46.	University of Massachusetts–Amherst	3.6
52.	Oregon Health and Science University	3.5
52.	San Diego State Univ. - Univ. of California–San Diego	3.5
52.	Temple University (PA)	3.5
52.	University of Connecticut	3.5
52.	University of Georgia	3.5
52.	University of Miami (FL)	3.5
52.	University of Missouri	3.5
52.	University of Rochester (NY)	3.5
60.	Florida State University	3.4
60.	Rutgers, the State U. of New Jersey–New Brunswick	3.4
60.	University of Illinois–Chicago	3.4
63.	Georgia Institute of Technology	3.3
63.	Teachers College, Columbia University (NY)	3.3
63.	University at Buffalo–SUNY	3.3
63.	University of California–Riverside	3.3
67.	Binghamton University–SUNY	3.2
67.	Boston College	3.2
67.	Brandeis University (MA)	3.2
67.	Rice University (TX)	3.2
67.	Rutgers, the State University of New Jersey–Newark	3.2
67.	Texas A&M University–College Station	3.2
67.	Tufts University (MA)	3.2
67.	University of Delaware	3.2
67.	University of Notre Dame (IN)	3.2
67.	University of Utah	3.2
67.	Virginia Tech	3.2

PSYCHOLOGY SPECIALTIES

BEHAVIORAL NEUROSCIENCE
1. University of California–San Diego
2. Massachusetts Institute of Technology
3. University of Michigan–Ann Arbor
4. Harvard University (MA)
4. University of California–Los Angeles
6. Duke University (NC)
7. Johns Hopkins University (MD)
7. University of California–Berkeley

COGNITIVE PSYCHOLOGY
1. Stanford University (CA)
2. Harvard University (MA)
3. University of California–San Diego
3. University of Illinois–Urbana-Champaign
5. Carnegie Mellon University (PA)
5. University of Michigan–Ann Arbor
5. Yale University (CT)

DEVELOPMENTAL PSYCHOLOGY
1. University of Minnesota–Twin Cities

2. University of Michigan–Ann Arbor
3. Stanford University (CA)
4. Harvard University (MA)
5. Pennsylvania State University–University Park
5. University of California–Berkeley
5. University of California–Los Angeles
5. University of North Carolina–Chapel Hill
5. University of Virginia
5. University of Wisconsin–Madison

INDUSTRIAL AND ORGANIZATIONAL PSYCHOLOGY
1. Michigan State University
1. University of Minnesota–Twin Cities

SOCIAL PSYCHOLOGY
1. Ohio State University
1. University of Michigan–Ann Arbor
3. Harvard University (MA)
3. Princeton University (NJ)
3. Stanford University (CA)
3. University of California–Los Angeles
3. Yale University (CT)

SOCIOLOGY

Ranked in 2013

Rank	School	Average assessment score (5.0=highest)
1.	Princeton University (NJ)	4.7
1.	University of California–Berkeley	4.7
1.	University of Wisconsin–Madison	4.7
4.	Stanford University (CA)	4.6
4.	University of Michigan–Ann Arbor	4.6
6.	Harvard University (MA)	4.5
6.	University of Chicago	4.5
6.	University of North Carolina–Chapel Hill	4.5
9.	University of California–Los Angeles	4.4
10.	Northwestern University (IL)	4.3
10.	University of Pennsylvania	4.3
12.	Columbia University (NY)	4.2
12.	Indiana University–Bloomington	4.2
14.	Duke University (NC)	4.1
14.	University of Texas–Austin	4.1
16.	New York University	4.0
17.	Cornell University (NY)	3.9
17.	Ohio State University	3.9
17.	Pennsylvania State University–University Park	3.9
20.	University of Arizona	3.8
20.	University of Minnesota–Twin Cities	3.8
20.	University of Washington	3.8
20.	Yale University (CT)	3.8
24.	University of Maryland–College Park	3.7
25.	Brown University (RI)	3.6

Rank	School	Average assessment score (5.0=highest)
25.	University of California–Irvine	3.6
27.	Johns Hopkins University (MD)	3.5
28.	CUNY Graduate School and University Center	3.4
28.	Rutgers, the State U. of New Jersey–New Brunswick	3.4
28.	University at Albany–SUNY	3.4
31.	University of California–Davis	3.3
31.	University of California–Santa Barbara	3.3
31.	University of Massachusetts–Amherst	3.3
31.	Vanderbilt University (TN)	3.3
35.	Emory University (GA)	3.2
35.	University of California–San Diego	3.2
35.	University of Iowa	3.2
35.	University of Virginia	3.2
39.	Florida State University	3.1
39.	University of Illinois–Chicago	3.1
39.	University of Southern California	3.1

SOCIOLOGY SPECIALTIES

ECONOMIC SOCIOLOGY

1. Stanford University (CA)
2. Princeton University (NJ)
2. University of California–Berkeley
2. University of Wisconsin–Madison
5. Harvard University (MA)

HISTORICAL SOCIOLOGY

1. Harvard University (MA)
1. University of California–Berkeley

SEX AND GENDER

1. University of California–Santa Barbara
2. University of California–Berkeley
2. University of Wisconsin–Madison
4. Stanford University (CA)

SOCIOLOGY SPECIALTIES

SOCIAL PSYCHOLOGY
1. Stanford University (CA)
2. Indiana University–Bloomington
3. University of Iowa

SOCIAL STRATIFICATION
1. University of Wisconsin–Madison

2. Stanford University (CA)
3. University of California–Los Angeles
3. University of Michigan–Ann Arbor
5. University of California–Berkeley

SOCIOLOGY OF CULTURE
1. Princeton University (NJ)
2. University of California–Berkeley

3. Northwestern University (IL)

SOCIOLOGY OF POPULATION
1. University of Michigan–Ann Arbor
2. University of Wisconsin–Madison
3. University of North Carolina–Chapel Hill

4. University of Pennsylvania
4. University of Texas–Austin
6. Pennsylvania State University–University Park
7. Princeton University (NJ)
7. University of California–Los Angeles

METHODOLOGY

Rankings of doctoral programs in the social sciences and humanities are based solely on the results of peer assessment surveys sent to academics in each discipline. Each school offering a doctoral program was sent two surveys (with the exception of criminology, where each school received four). The questionnaires asked respondents to rate the academic quality of the program at each institution on a 5-point scale: outstanding (5), strong (4), good (3), adequate (2), or marginal (1). Individuals who were unfamiliar with a particular school's programs were asked to select "don't know." Scores for each school were determined by computing a trimmed mean (eliminating the two highest and two lowest responses) of the ratings of all respondents who rated that school for the last two surveys; average scores were then sorted in descending order.

Surveys were conducted in the fall of 2012 by Ipsos Public Affairs, except in the field of criminology, conducted in 2008. Questionnaires were sent to department heads and directors of graduate studies (or, alternatively, a senior faculty member who teaches graduate students) at schools that had granted a total of five or more doctorates in each discipline during the five-year period from 2005 through 2009, as indicated by the 2010 Survey of Earned Doctorates. The American Association of Doctoral Programs in Criminology and Criminal Justice provided the list of criminology programs. The surveys asked about Ph.D. programs in criminology (response rate: 90 percent), economics (25 percent), English (21 percent), history (19 percent), political science (30 percent), psychology (16 percent), and sociology (31 percent). Except in criminology, survey results from fall 2008 and fall 2012 were averaged to compute the scores.

In psychology, a school was listed once on the survey even if it grants a doctoral degree in psychology in multiple departments. Programs in clinical psychology are ranked separately in the health professions section. Specialty rankings are based solely on nominations by department heads and directors of graduate studies at peer schools from the list of schools surveyed. They named up to 10 programs in each area. Those with the most votes appear.

The Sciences

Ph.D. programs ranked best by deans and department chairs

BIOLOGICAL SCIENCES

Ranked in 2010

Listed schools may have multiple programs.

Rank	School	Average assessment score (5.0=highest)
1.	Stanford University (CA)	4.9
2.	Harvard University (MA)	4.8
2.	Massachusetts Institute of Technology	4.8
2.	University of California–Berkeley	4.8
5.	California Institute of Technology	4.7
5.	Johns Hopkins University (MD)	4.7
7.	Princeton University (NJ)	4.5
7.	Scripps Research Institute (CA)	4.5
7.	University of California–San Francisco	4.5
7.	Yale University (CT)	4.5
11.	Cornell University (NY)	4.4
11.	Washington University in St. Louis	4.4
13.	Duke University (NC)	4.3
13.	University of Chicago	4.3
15.	Columbia University (NY)	4.2
15.	Rockefeller University (NY)	4.2
15.	University of California–San Diego	4.2
15.	University of Washington	4.2
15.	University of Wisconsin–Madison	4.2
20.	University of California–Davis	4.1
20.	University of Michigan–Ann Arbor	4.1
20.	University of Pennsylvania	4.1
20.	University of Texas Southwestern Medical Center–Dallas	4.1
24.	University of California–Los Angeles	4.0
24.	University of North Carolina–Chapel Hill	4.0
26.	Baylor College of Medicine (TX)	3.9
26.	Cornell University (Weill) (NY)	3.9
26.	Northwestern University (IL)	3.9
26.	University of Texas–Austin	3.9
30.	University of Colorado–Boulder	3.8
30.	University of Illinois–Urbana-Champaign	3.8
32.	University of Minnesota–Twin Cities	3.7
32.	Vanderbilt University (TN)	3.7
34.	Brown University (RI)	3.6
34.	Case Western Reserve University (OH)	3.6
34.	Dartmouth College (NH)	3.6
34.	Emory University (GA)	3.6
34.	Indiana University–Bloomington	3.6
34.	University of Alabama–Birmingham	3.6
34.	University of Arizona	3.6
34.	University of California–Irvine	3.6
42.	Mayo Medical School (MN)	3.5
42.	Mount Sinai School of Medicine (NY)	3.5
42.	Pennsylvania State University–University Park	3.5
42.	Rice University (TX)	3.5
46.	Carnegie Mellon University (PA)	3.4
46.	Michigan State University	3.4
46.	Ohio State University	3.4
46.	University of California–Santa Barbara	3.4
46.	University of Florida	3.4
46.	University of Georgia	3.4

Rank	School	Average assessment score (5.0=highest)
46.	University of Massachusetts Medical Center–Worcester	3.4
46.	University of Pittsburgh	3.4
46.	University of Southern California	3.4
46.	University of Virginia	3.4
56.	Arizona State University	3.3
56.	Brandeis University (MA)	3.3
56.	Georgia Institute of Technology	3.3
56.	New York University	3.3
56.	Purdue University–West Lafayette (IN)	3.3
56.	Tufts University (MA)	3.3
56.	University of California–Riverside	3.3
56.	University of California–Santa Cruz	3.3
56.	University of Iowa	3.3
56.	University of Maryland–College Park	3.3
56.	University of Oregon	3.3
56.	University of Utah	3.3

BIOLOGICAL SCIENCES SPECIALTIES

BIOCHEMISTRY/BIOPHYSICS/ STRUCTURAL BIOLOGY

1. Harvard University (MA)
2. Stanford University (CA)
3. Massachusetts Inst. of Technology
4. Yale University (CT)
5. Univ. of California–San Francisco
6. Johns Hopkins University (MD)
6. University of California–Berkeley
8. California Inst. of Technology
9. Rockefeller University (NY)
9. Scripps Research Institute (CA)

CELL BIOLOGY

1. Harvard University (MA)
2. Stanford University (CA)
3. Yale University (CT)
4. Johns Hopkins University (MD)
4. University of California–Berkeley
4. Univ. of California–San Francisco
7. Massachusetts Inst. of Technology
8. Rockefeller University (NY)
9. Washington University in St. Louis
10. University of Texas Southwestern Medical Center–Dallas

ECOLOGY/EVOLUTIONARY BIOLOGY

1. University of California–Berkeley
2. Harvard University (MA)
3. University of California–Davis
4. University of Chicago
5. Stanford University (CA)
6. Cornell University (NY)
6. University of Texas–Austin
6. Yale University (CT)
9. Princeton University (NJ)
9. University of Arizona

GENETICS/GENOMICS/ BIOINFORMATICS

1. Stanford University (CA)
2. Massachusetts Inst. of Technology
3. Harvard University (MA)
4. University of California–Berkeley
5. University of Washington
5. Washington University in St. Louis
7. Johns Hopkins University (MD)
8. Univ. of California–San Francisco
8. Yale University (CT)
10. Princeton University (NJ)

IMMUNOLOGY/INFECTIOUS DISEASE

1. Harvard University (MA)
2. Univ. of California–San Francisco
3. Stanford University (CA)
3. Yale University (CT)
5. Johns Hopkins University (MD)
5. Washington University in St. Louis
7. Duke University (NC)
7. University of Pennsylvania
9. University of Texas Southwestern Medical Center–Dallas

MICROBIOLOGY

1. Harvard University (MA)
2. Stanford University (CA)
3. University of Wisconsin– Madison
4. Johns Hopkins University (MD)
4. Univ. of California–San Francisco
4. Washington University in St. Louis
7. Massachusetts Inst. of Technology
7. University of California–Berkeley
7. Yale University (CT)

More at www.usnews.com/grad

MOLECULAR BIOLOGY

1. Harvard University (MA)
2. Massachusetts Inst. of Technology
2. Stanford University (CA)
4. Johns Hopkins University (MD)
4. University of California–Berkeley
6. Univ. of California–San Francisco
7. Yale University (CT)
8. California Inst. of Technology
9. Rockefeller University (NY)
10. Princeton University (NJ)
10. University of Texas Southwestern Medical Center–Dallas

NEUROSCIENCE/NEUROBIOLOGY

1. Harvard University (MA)
2. Stanford University (CA)
3. Univ. of California–San Francisco
4. Johns Hopkins University (MD)
5. Massachusetts Inst. of Technology
6. Yale University (CT)
7. Columbia University (NY)
7. University of California–San Diego
9. University of California–Berkeley
10. Rockefeller University (NY)
10. Washington University in St. Louis

CHEMISTRY

Ranked in 2010

Rank	School	Average assessment score (5.0=highest)
1.	California Institute of Technology	5.0
1.	Massachusetts Institute of Technology	5.0
1.	University of California–Berkeley	5.0
4.	Harvard University (MA)	4.8
4.	Stanford University (CA)	4.8
6.	University of Illinois–Urbana-Champaign	4.6
7.	Northwestern University (IL)	4.5
7.	Scripps Research Institute (CA)	4.5
7.	University of Wisconsin–Madison	4.5
10.	Columbia University (NY)	4.4
10.	Cornell University (NY)	4.4
12.	University of Texas–Austin	4.3
13.	University of Chicago	4.2
13.	University of North Carolina–Chapel Hill	4.2
13.	Yale University (CT)	4.2
16.	Princeton University (NJ)	4.1
16.	University of California–Los Angeles	4.1
16.	University of Michigan–Ann Arbor	4.1
19.	Texas A&M University–College Station	4.0
19.	University of Pennsylvania	4.0
21.	Johns Hopkins University (MD)	3.9
21.	Pennsylvania State University–University Park	3.9
21.	Purdue University–West Lafayette (IN)	3.9
21.	University of California–San Diego	3.9
21.	University of Minnesota–Twin Cities	3.9
26.	Georgia Institute of Technology	3.8
26.	Indiana University–Bloomington	3.8
26.	Ohio State University	3.8
26.	University of California–Irvine	3.8
26.	University of Colorado–Boulder	3.8
26.	University of Washington	3.8
32.	University of California–San Francisco	3.7
33.	Rice University (TX)	3.6
33.	University of California–Santa Barbara	3.6
33.	Washington University in St. Louis	3.6
36.	University of Florida	3.5
36.	University of Utah	3.5
38.	Emory University (GA)	3.4
38.	Iowa State University	3.4
38.	Michigan State University	3.4
38.	University of Arizona	3.4
38.	University of California–Davis	3.4
38.	University of Maryland–College Park	3.4
38.	University of Pittsburgh	3.4
45.	Boston College	3.3

Rank	School	Average assessment score (5.0=highest)
45.	Colorado State University	3.3
45.	Duke University (NC)	3.3
45.	University of Virginia	3.3
49.	Carnegie Mellon University (PA)	3.2
49.	Stony Brook University–SUNY	3.2
49.	University of Rochester (NY)	3.2
49.	Vanderbilt University (TN)	3.2

CHEMISTRY SPECIALTIES

ANALYTICAL

1. Univ. of North Carolina–Chapel Hill
2. Purdue Univ.–West Lafayette (IN)
3. Indiana University–Bloomington
4. University of Illinois–Urbana-Champaign
5. University of Texas–Austin
6. University of Arizona
7. University of Michigan–Ann Arbor
8. University of Florida
8. University of Washington
8. University of Wisconsin–Madison

BIOCHEMISTRY

1. Harvard University (MA)
2. University of California–Berkeley
3. Univ. of California–San Francisco
4. Scripps Research Institute (CA)
5. University of Wisconsin–Madison
6. Massachusetts Inst. of Technology
7. Stanford University (CA)
8. California Inst. of Technology
9. Yale University (CT)
10. University of California–San Diego

INORGANIC

1. Massachusetts Inst. of Technology
2. California Inst. of Technology
3. University of California–Berkeley
4. Northwestern University (IL)
5. University of Illinois–Urbana-Champaign
6. Texas A&M Univ.–College Station
7. Stanford University (CA)
8. Univ. of North Carolina–Chapel Hill
9. University of Wisconsin–Madison
10. Harvard University (MA)

ORGANIC

1. Harvard University (MA)
2. University of California–Berkeley
3. Scripps Research Institute (CA)
4. Stanford University (CA)
5. Massachusetts Inst. of Technology
6. California Inst. of Technology
7. University of Illinois–Urbana-Champaign
8. Columbia University (NY)
8. University of Wisconsin–Madison
10. University of Pennsylvania

PHYSICAL

1. University of California–Berkeley
2. Massachusetts Inst. of Technology
3. California Inst. of Technology
4. Stanford University (CA)
5. Harvard University (MA)
6. University of Chicago
7. University of Wisconsin–Madison
8. University of Colorado–Boulder
9. Northwestern University (IL)
10. University of Illinois–Urbana-Champaign

THEORETICAL

1. University of California–Berkeley
2. University of Chicago
3. California Inst. of Technology
3. Northwestern University (IL)
5. Massachusetts Inst. of Technology
6. Columbia University (NY)
7. Harvard University (MA)
8. Yale University (CT)
9. University of Wisconsin–Madison
10. University of Texas–Austin

COMPUTER SCIENCE

Ranked in 2010

Rank	School	Average assessment score (5.0=highest)
1.	Carnegie Mellon University (PA)	5.0
1.	Massachusetts Institute of Technology	5.0
1.	Stanford University (CA)	5.0
1.	University of California–Berkeley	5.0
5.	Cornell University (NY)	4.6
5.	University of Illinois–Urbana-Champaign	4.6
7.	University of Washington	4.5
8.	Princeton University (NJ)	4.4
8.	University of Texas–Austin	4.4
10.	Georgia Institute of Technology	4.3
11.	California Institute of Technology	4.2
11.	University of Wisconsin–Madison	4.2

COMPUTER SCIENCE

Ranked in 2010

Rank	School	Average assessment score (5.0=highest)
13.	University of Michigan–Ann Arbor	4.1
14.	University of California–Los Angeles	4.0
14.	University of California–San Diego	4.0
14.	University of Maryland–College Park	4.0
17.	Columbia University (NY)	3.9
17.	Harvard University (MA)	3.9
17.	University of Pennsylvania	3.9
20.	Brown University (RI)	3.7
20.	Purdue University–West Lafayette (IN)	3.7
20.	Rice University (TX)	3.7
20.	University of Massachusetts–Amherst	3.7
20.	University of North Carolina–Chapel Hill	3.7
20.	University of Southern California	3.7
20.	Yale University (CT)	3.7
27.	Duke University (NC)	3.6
28.	Johns Hopkins University (MD)	3.4
28.	New York University	3.4
28.	Ohio State University	3.4
28.	Pennsylvania State University–University Park	3.4
28.	Rutgers, the State University of New Jersey–New Brunswick	3.4
28.	University of California–Irvine	3.4
28.	University of Virginia	3.4
35.	Northwestern University (IL)	3.3
35.	University of California–Santa Barbara	3.3
35.	University of Chicago	3.3
35.	University of Minnesota–Twin Cities	3.3

COMPUTER SCIENCE SPECIALTIES

ARTIFICIAL INTELLIGENCE

1. Massachusetts Inst. of Technology
2. Carnegie Mellon University (PA)
3. Stanford University (CA)
4. University of California–Berkeley
5. University of Texas–Austin
6. University of Washington
7. Georgia Institute of Technology
8. University of Illinois–Urbana-Champaign
8. University of Massachusetts–Amherst
10. University of Pennsylvania

PROGRAMMING LANGUAGE

1. Carnegie Mellon University (PA)
2. Stanford University (CA)
2. University of California–Berkeley
4. Massachusetts Inst. of Technology
5. University of Texas–Austin
6. Cornell University (NY)
7. Princeton University (NJ)
8. University of Pennsylvania
9. University of Illinois–Urbana-Champaign
10. University of Wisconsin–Madison

SYSTEMS

1. University of California–Berkeley
2. Massachusetts Inst. of Technology
3. Carnegie Mellon University (PA)
4. Stanford University (CA)
5. University of Washington
6. University of Illinois–Urbana-Champaign
7. University of Wisconsin–Madison
8. University of Texas–Austin
9. Georgia Institute of Technology
10. Cornell University (NY)

THEORY

1. Massachusetts Inst. of Technology
2. University of California–Berkeley
3. Cornell University (NY)
4. Princeton University (NJ)
5. Carnegie Mellon University (PA)
6. Stanford University (CA)
7. Georgia Institute of Technology
8. University of Washington
9. Harvard University (MA)
10. University of Texas–Austin

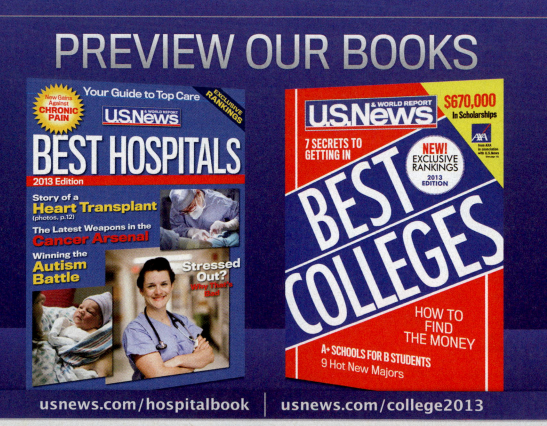

EARTH SCIENCES

Ranked in 2010

Rank	School	Average assessment score (5.0=highest)
1.	California Institute of Technology	4.9
1.	Massachusetts Institute of Technology	4.9
3.	University of California–Berkeley	4.7
4.	Stanford University (CA)	4.6
5.	Columbia University (NY)	4.5
6.	Pennsylvania State University–University Park	4.4
7.	University of Arizona	4.3
8.	Harvard University (MA)	4.2
9.	Princeton University (NJ)	4.1
9.	University of Michigan–Ann Arbor	4.1
9.	University of Texas–Austin	4.1
12.	Yale University (CT)	4.0
13.	Cornell University (NY)	3.9
13.	University of California–Santa Cruz	3.9
13.	University of Washington	3.9
13.	University of Wisconsin–Madison	3.9
17.	Arizona State University	3.8
17.	Brown University (RI)	3.8
17.	University of California–Davis	3.8
17.	University of California–Los Angeles	3.8
17.	University of California–San Diego	3.8
17.	University of Chicago	3.8
23.	University of California–Santa Barbara	3.7
23.	University of Colorado–Boulder	3.7
25.	Colorado School of Mines	3.6
25.	Rice University (TX)	3.6
25.	University of Southern California	3.6

EARTH SCIENCES SPECIALTIES

ENVIRONMENTAL SCIENCES
1. Columbia University (NY)
1. Pennsylvania State Univ.–Univ. Park
3. Stanford University (CA)
3. University of California–Berkeley
5. Duke University (NC)
5. University of Colorado–Boulder

GEOCHEMISTRY
1. California Inst. of Technology
2. Massachusetts Inst. of Technology
3. Pennsylvania State Univ.–Univ. Park
4. University of Michigan–Ann Arbor
5. Columbia University (NY)
5. University of California–Berkeley
7. Univ. of Maryland–College Park
8. University of Wisconsin–Madison
9. Stanford University (CA)
10. University of Arizona
10. University of California–Los Angeles
10. Yale University (CT)

GEOLOGY
1. University of Arizona
1. University of Michigan–Ann Arbor
3. Pennsylvania State Univ.–Univ. Park
3. University of Texas–Austin
5. Stanford University (CA)
6. California Inst. of Technology

7. Massachusetts Inst. of Technology
8. University of Wisconsin–Madison
9. University of California–Berkeley
10. Harvard University (MA)
10. University of Washington

GEOPHYSICS AND SEISMOLOGY
1. California Inst. of Technology
2. Massachusetts Inst. of Technology
3. Stanford University (CA)
4. University of California–Berkeley
5. Columbia University (NY)
6. University of Texas–Austin
7. Harvard University (MA)
7. Princeton University (NJ)
9. University of Southern California
10. University of Washington

PALEONTOLOGY
1. Yale University (CT)
2. University of Chicago
3. University of California–Berkeley
4. Harvard University (MA)
5. University of Michigan–Ann Arbor
6. University of Cincinnati
7. University of Kansas
8. Pennsylvania State Univ.–Univ. Park
9. Ohio State University
9. Virginia Tech

MATHEMATICS

Ranked in 2010

Rank	School	Average assessment score (5.0=highest)
1.	Massachusetts Institute of Technology	5.0
2.	Harvard University (MA)	4.9
2.	Princeton University (NJ)	4.9
2.	Stanford University (CA)	4.9
2.	University of California–Berkeley	4.9
6.	University of Chicago	4.8
7.	California Institute of Technology	4.6
8.	University of California–Los Angeles	4.5
8.	University of Michigan–Ann Arbor	4.5
10.	Columbia University (NY)	4.4
10.	New York University	4.4
10.	Yale University (CT)	4.4
13.	Cornell University (NY)	4.3
14.	Brown University (RI)	4.2
14.	University of Texas–Austin	4.2
16.	Northwestern University (IL)	4.1
16.	University of Wisconsin–Madison	4.1
18.	University of Minnesota–Twin Cities	4.0
18.	University of Pennsylvania	4.0
20.	Rutgers, the State University of New Jersey–New Brunswick	3.9
20.	University of California–San Diego	3.9
20.	University of Illinois–Urbana-Champaign	3.9
20.	University of Maryland–College Park	3.9
24.	Duke University (NC)	3.8
24.	Johns Hopkins University (MD)	3.8
24.	Stony Brook University–SUNY	3.8
27.	Pennsylvania State University–University Park	3.7
27.	Purdue University–West Lafayette (IN)	3.7
27.	University of Washington	3.7
30.	Georgia Institute of Technology	3.6
30.	Indiana University–Bloomington	3.6
30.	Ohio State University	3.6
30.	Rice University (TX)	3.6
30.	University of North Carolina–Chapel Hill	3.6
30.	University of Utah	3.6
36.	Carnegie Mellon University (PA)	3.5
36.	CUNY Graduate School and University Center	3.5
36.	University of California–Davis	3.5
36.	University of Illinois–Chicago	3.5
40.	Brandeis University (MA)	3.4
40.	Texas A&M University–College Station	3.4
40.	Washington University in St. Louis	3.4
43.	Michigan State University	3.3
43.	University of Arizona	3.3
43.	University of California–Irvine	3.3

MATHEMATICS SPECIALTIES

ALGEBRA/NUMBER THEORY/ALGEBRAIC GEOMETRY

1. Harvard University (MA)
2. Princeton University (NJ)
3. University of California–Berkeley
4. University of Chicago
5. Massachusetts Inst. of Technology
6. University of Michigan–Ann Arbor
7. Stanford University (CA)
8. Columbia University (NY)
9. University of California–Los Angeles
10. Yale University (CT)

ANALYSIS

1. Princeton University (NJ)
2. University of California–Berkeley
3. University of California–Los Angeles
4. University of Chicago
5. New York University
6. Massachusetts Inst. of Technology
7. Stanford University (CA)
8. University of Michigan–Ann Arbor
9. Harvard University (MA)
10. University of Wisconsin–Madison

APPLIED MATH

1. New York University
2. University of California–Los Angeles
3. Massachusetts Inst. of Technology
4. California Inst. of Technology
5. Brown University (RI)
6. University of Minnesota–Twin Cities
7. Princeton University (NJ)
8. University of California–Berkeley
9. Stanford University (CA)
9. University of Texas–Austin

DISCRETE MATHEMATICS AND COMBINATIONS

1. Massachusetts Inst. of Technology
2. University of California–Berkeley
3. Princeton University (NJ)
4. Rutgers, the State University of New Jersey–New Brunswick
4. University of Michigan–Ann Arbor
6. University of California–Los Angeles
6. University of California–San Diego
8. Georgia Institute of Technology
9. University of Minnesota–Twin Cities
10. Carnegie Mellon University (PA)

GEOMETRY

1. Harvard University (MA)
2. University of California–Berkeley
3. Princeton University (NJ)
4. Massachusetts Inst. of Technology
5. Stanford University (CA)
6. Columbia University (NY)
6. Stony Brook University–SUNY
8. University of Chicago
9. University of Michigan–Ann Arbor
10. New York University

LOGIC

1. University of California–Berkeley
2. University of California–Los Angeles
3. Carnegie Mellon University (PA)
3. Univ. of Illinois–Urbana-Champaign
5. Cornell University (NY)
5. University of Wisconsin–Madison
7. University of Chicago
8. University of Notre Dame (IN)
9. Rutgers, the State University of New Jersey–New Brunswick

TOPOLOGY

1. University of California–Berkeley
2. Harvard University (MA)
3. Princeton University (NJ)
4. Massachusetts Inst. of Technology
5. Stanford University (CA)
6. University of Chicago
7. Columbia University (NY)
8. University of Texas–Austin
9. University of Michigan–Ann Arbor
10. Cornell University (NY)

PHYSICS

Ranked in 2010

Rank	School	Average assessment score (5.0=highest)
1.	California Instututute of Technology	4.9
1.	Harvard University (MA)	4.9
1.	Massachusetts Instututute of Technology	4.9
1.	Stanford University (CA)	4.9
5.	Princeton University (NJ)	4.8
5.	University of California–Berkeley	4.8
7.	Cornell University (NY)	4.6
7.	University of Chicago	4.6
9.	University of Illinois–Urbana-Champaign	4.5
10.	University of California–Santa Barbara	4.4
11.	Columbia University (NY)	4.2
11.	University of Michigan–Ann Arbor	4.2
11.	Yale University (CT)	4.2
14.	University of California–San Diego	4.1
14.	University of Maryland–College Park	4.1
14.	University of Texas–Austin	4.1
17.	University of Pennsylvania	4.0
17.	University of Wisconsin–Madison	4.0
19.	Johns Hopkins University (MD)	3.9
19.	University of California–Los Angeles	3.9
19.	University of Colorado–Boulder	3.9
19.	University of Washington	3.9
23.	Ohio State University	3.7
23.	Pennsylvania State University–University Park	3.7
23.	Stony Brook University–SUNY	3.7
26.	Rice University (TX)	3.6
26.	Rutgers, the State University of New Jersey–New Brunswick	3.6
26.	University of California–Davis	3.6
26.	University of Minnesota–Twin Cities	3.6
30.	Brown University (RI)	3.5

PHYSICS

Ranked in 2010

Rank	School	Average assessment score (5.0=highest)
30.	Carnegie Mellon University (PA)	3.5
30.	Duke University (NC)	3.5
30.	Georgia Institute of Technology	3.5
30.	Northwestern University (IL)	3.5
30.	University of California–Irvine	3.5
36.	Michigan State University	3.4
36.	University of Arizona	3.4
36.	University of Florida	3.4
36.	University of North Carolina–Chapel Hill	3.4
40.	Boston University	3.3
40.	Indiana University–Bloomington	3.3
40.	New York University	3.3
40.	Purdue University–West Lafayette (IN)	3.3
40.	Texas A&M University–College Station	3.3
40.	University of California–Santa Cruz	3.3
40.	University of Virginia	3.3
40.	Washington University in St. Louis	3.3

PHYSICS SPECIALTIES

ATOMIC/MOLECULAR/OPTICAL
1. Massachusetts Inst. of Technology
1. University of Colorado–Boulder
3. Harvard University (MA)
4. Stanford University (CA)
5. California Inst. of Technology
6. University of Rochester (NY)
7. University of Arizona
7. Univ. of Maryland–College Park
9. Rice University (TX)
9. University of California–Berkeley

CONDENSED MATTER
1. Massachusetts Inst. of Technology
2. Univ. of Illinois–Urbana-Champaign
3. Univ. of California–Santa Barbara
4. Stanford University (CA)
5. Harvard University (MA)
6. University of California–Berkeley
7. Cornell University (NY)
8. Princeton University (NJ)
9. University of Chicago
10. California Inst. of Technology
10. Univ. of Maryland–College Park

COSMOLOGY/RELATIVITY/GRAVITY
1. Princeton University (NJ)
2. California Inst. of Technology
3. Harvard University (MA)
4. Stanford University (CA)
5. University of California–Berkeley
5. University of Chicago
7. Massachusetts Inst. of Technology
8. University of Texas–Austin
9. Univ. of California–Santa Barbara
10. Pennsylvania State University–University Park

ELEMENTARY PARTICLES/FIELDS/STRING THEORY
1. Stanford University (CA)
2. University of California–Berkeley
3. Harvard University (MA)
3. Princeton University (NJ)
5. California Inst. of Technology
6. Massachusetts Inst. of Technology
7. University of Chicago
8. Univ. of California–Santa Barbara
9. Cornell University (NY)
10. Columbia University (NY)

NUCLEAR
1. Michigan State University
2. Massachusetts Inst. of Technology
3. University of Washington
4. Stony Brook University–SUNY
5. Indiana University–Bloomington
5. Yale University (CT)
7. California Inst. of Technology
8. Duke University (NC)
8. University of California–Berkeley
10. Columbia University (NY)
10. Univ. of Illinois–Urbana-Champaign

PLASMA
1. Princeton University (NJ)
2. Massachusetts Inst. of Technology
2. University of Wisconsin–Madison
4. University of California–Los Angeles
5. University of California–San Diego
5. University of Texas–Austin
7. Univ. of Maryland–College Park

QUANTUM
1. Massachusetts Inst. of Technology
2. Harvard University (MA)
3. California Inst. of Technology
4. Stanford University (CA)
5. Univ. of California–Santa Barbara
5. University of Colorado–Boulder
7. Princeton University (NJ)
8. Univ. of Illinois–Urbana-Champaign
9. Univ. of Maryland–College Park
10. University of California–Berkeley

STATISTICS

Ranked in 2010

Rank	School	Average assessment score (5.0=highest)
1.	Stanford University (CA)	4.9
2.	University of California–Berkeley	4.7
3.	Harvard University* (MA)	4.6
3.	University of Washington*	4.6
5.	Johns Hopkins University* (MD)	4.4
6.	Harvard University (MA)	4.3
6.	University of Chicago	4.3
6.	University of Washington	4.3
9.	Carnegie Mellon University (PA)	4.1
10.	Duke University (NC)	4.0
10.	University of North Carolina–Chapel Hill*	4.0
12.	North Carolina State University	3.9
12.	Texas A&M University–College Station	3.9
12.	University of Michigan–Ann Arbor*	3.9
12.	University of Pennsylvania	3.9
12.	University of Wisconsin–Madison	3.9
17.	University of California–Berkeley*	3.8
17.	University of Michigan–Ann Arbor	3.8
17.	University of Minnesota–Twin Cities	3.8
20.	Iowa State University	3.7
20.	Pennsylvania State University	3.7
22.	Columbia University (NY)	3.6
22.	Cornell University (NY)	3.6
22.	Purdue University–West Lafayette (IN)	3.6
22.	University of Minnesota–Twin Cities*	3.6
22.	University of North Carolina–Chapel Hill	3.6

*Denotes a department of biostatistics

METHODOLOGY

Rankings of doctoral programs in the sciences are based on the results of surveys sent to academics in biological sciences, chemistry, computer science, earth sciences, mathematics, physics, and statistics during the fall of 2009. The individuals rated the quality of the program at each institution from marginal (1) to outstanding (5).

Individuals who were unfamiliar with a particular school's programs were asked to select "don't know." The schools with the highest average scores were sorted in descending order and appear here.

All doctoral surveys were conducted by Synovate, now part of Ipsos Public Affairs. The universe surveyed in biological sciences, chemistry, computer science, earth sciences, mathematics, and physics consisted of schools that awarded at least five doctoral degrees in 2003 through 2008, according to the National Science Foundation report "Science and Engineering Doctorate Awards." The American Statistical Association provided *U.S. News* with eligible programs for statistics. In biological sciences, graduate programs may be offered in a university's medical school or college of arts and sciences. In statistics, programs may be offered through a biostatistics or statistics department.

Questionnaires were sent to the department heads and directors of graduate studies at each program in each discipline. Response rates were as follows: for biological sciences, 15 percent; chemistry, 25 percent; computer science, 46 percent; earth sciences, 29 percent; mathematics, 34 percent; physics, 31 percent; and statistics, 67 percent.

Specialty rankings are based solely on nominations by department heads and directors of graduate studies at peer schools. These respondents ranked up to 10 programs in each area. Those with the most votes appear here.

Best Online Options

For our rankings of online graduate degree programs in business, engineering, education, nursing, and computer information technology, *U.S. News* started by surveying more than 3,000 master's programs at regionally accredited colleges. Only programs with classes entirely online were ranked, based on their success at promoting student engagement, the training and credentials of their faculty, the selectivity of their admissions processes, and the services and technologies available to distance learners. The business and engineering rankings also incorporated opinions of deans and other academics at peer distance education programs. Although the results in each discipline rely on some varying criteria, individual ranking factors common to all include retention and graduation rates, student indebtedness at graduation, the average undergraduate grade point averages of new entrants, proportion of faculty members with terminal degrees and who are tenured or tenure-track, and support services like career placement assistance and academic advising accessible to students remotely. In total, 576 programs were ranked. The top programs in each of the five disciplines are listed below; apparent ties in the overall score are due to rounding. To read the detailed methodologies and see the complete rankings, visit *usnews.com/online*.

BUSINESS

Rank	School	Overall score	'12 total enrollment	'12–'13 tuition[1]	Entrance test required	'12 average undergrad GPA	'12 acceptance rate	'12 full-time faculty with terminal degree	'12 retention rate	24/7 tech support	Smart phone app.
1.	Washington State University	73.0	114	$750	GMAT	3.4	51%	100%	100%	Yes	Yes
2.	Arizona State University	72.6	520	$1,052[2]	GMAT or GRE	3.2	60%	90%	100%	Yes	Yes
3.	Indiana University–Bloomington	72.3	682	$1,145	GMAT or GRE	3.3	76%	96%	99%	No	Yes
4.	University of Florida	70.2	309	$975[2]	GMAT or GRE	3.3	70%	100%	N/A	No	Yes
5.	California State University–Fullerton	68.2	49	$679	GMAT or GRE	3.0	57%	100%	89%	Yes	Yes
6.	Central Michigan University	66.3	137	$600	GMAT	2.9	44%	86%	89%	No	Yes
7.	Auburn University (AL)	66.3	263	$750	GMAT	3.3	88%	98%	89%	No	No
8.	University of Connecticut	65.9	247	$680	GMAT	3.5	91%	82%	N/A	No	No
9.	University of Texas–Dallas	65.8	1,053	$1,200	GMAT or GRE	3.3	45%	59%	100%	Yes	Yes
10.	University of Tennessee–Martin	65.6	35	N/A	GMAT	3.2	42%	100%	100%	No	No
11.	Arkansas State University–Jonesboro	64.9	41	$452	GMAT or GRE	3.4	91%	100%	90%	No	Yes
12.	Clarkson University (NY)	64.6	59	$1,259	GMAT or GRE	3.0	76%	94%	70%	Yes	Yes
13.	Marist College (NY)	64.5	181	$720	GMAT	3.4	42%	100%	80%	No	Yes
14.	Worcester Polytechnic Institute (MA)	64.5	120	$1,239	GMAT or GRE	3.3	42%	82%	94%	No	Yes
15.	Georgia College & State University	63.2	57	$700[2]	GMAT or GRE	3.1	39%	100%	100%	Yes	No
16.	University of Illinois–Springfield	63.1	176	$338	GMAT or GRE	3.2	74%	89%	76%	No	Yes
17.	University of Nebraska–Lincoln	63.1	257	$539	GMAT	3.4	64%	100%	86%	No	Yes
18.	St. Joseph's University (PA)	62.6	398	$892	GMAT or GRE	3.2	77%	83%	77%	Yes	No
19.	Pennsylvania State University–World Campus	62.5	747	$1,077[2]	GMAT or GRE	3.4	80%	88%	87%	No	No
20.	University of North Texas	62.5	92	$642	GMAT	3.3	100%	100%	90%	No	Yes
21.	University of Michigan–Dearborn	62.3	206	$1,158[2]	GMAT or GRE	3.2	49%	100%	93%	No	Yes
22.	University of Massachusetts–Amherst	60.9	927	$750[2]	GMAT or GRE	3.2	89%	92%	86%	Yes	No
23.	University of San Diego (CA)	60.7	92	$1,280[2]	None	3.0	75%	100%	91%	Yes	Yes
24.	Quinnipiac University (CT)	60.3	361	$895	GMAT or GRE	3.3	84%	92%	82%	No	Yes
25.	Thunderbird Global Management (AZ)	60.1	160	$1,335	GMAT or GRE	N/A	64%	90%	94%	No	Yes
26.	SUNY–Oswego (NY)	59.1	14	$763	GMAT or GRE	3.2	93%	100%	N/A	No	No
27.	Rutgers–New Brunswick and Newark	59.0	31	$1,528	None	3.2	79%	71%	90%	Yes	Yes
28.	Temple University (PA)	58.9	40	$1,458[2]	None	2.7	48%	79%	88%	Yes	Yes
29.	West Virginia University (WV)	58.8	65	$763	GMAT	3.2	71%	100%	94%	Yes	No
30.	Syracuse University (NY)	58.3	331	$1,249	GMAT	3.0	85%	85%	88%	No	Yes

COMPUTER INFORMATION TECHNOLOGY

Rank	School	Overall score	'12 total enrollment	'12–'13 tuition[1]	Entrance test required	'12 average undergrad GPA	'12 acceptance rate	'12 full-time faculty with terminal degree	'12 retention rate	24/7 tech support	Smart phone app.
1.	University of Southern California	68.8	109	$1,569	GRE	3.5	22%	94%	90%	No	Yes
2.	Sam Houston State University (TX)	68.6	45	$237	GRE	3.2	100%	100%	100%	Yes	Yes
3.	Virginia Tech	65.6	403	$1,246[2]	None	3.3	73%	100%	92%	Yes	No
4.	University of Bridgeport (CT)	64.2	N/A	$700	None	N/A	N/A	100%	85%	No	No
5.	Pennsylvania State University–World Campus	63.3	284	$825[2]	GRE	3.4	63%	66%	77%	No	No
6.	University of West Georgia	62.0	30	$377[2]	None	2.7	58%	100%	N/A	No	Yes
7.	Auburn University (AL)	60.3	25	$674	GRE	3.6	50%	100%	100%	No	Yes
8.	Columbia University (NY)	58.3	N/A	$1,578	GRE	N/A	N/A	100%	99%	Yes	Yes

N/A=Data were not provided by the school.
1. Tuition is reported on a per-credit-hour basis for full-time students, unless otherwise noted. Credit requirements may vary.
2. Part-time per credit tuition

More at **www.usnews.com/grad**

COMPUTER INFORMATION TECHNOLOGY

Rank	School	Overall score	'12 total enrollment	'12-'13 tuition[1]	Entrance test required	'12 average undergad GPA	'12 acceptance rate	'12 full-time faculty with terminal degree	'12 retention rate	24/7 tech support	Smart phone app.
9.	North Carolina State University–Raleigh	58.1	58	$726	GRE	3.7	54%	100%	95%	No	No
10.	Hofstra University (NY)	57.0	24	$1,080	GRE	3.4	74%	100%	64%	No	No

EDUCATION

Rank	School	Overall score	'12 total enrollment	'12-'13 tuition[1]	Entrance test required	'12 average undergad GPA	'12 acceptance rate	'12 full-time faculty with terminal degree	'12 retention rate	24/7 tech support	Smart phone app.
1.	St. John's University (NY)	70.0	41	$1,050	None	3.4	78%	100%	87%	Yes	Yes
2.	Auburn University (AL)	68.8	139	$437	GRE	3.0	54%	100%	73%	No	Yes
3.	South Dakota State University	68.5	61	$383	None	3.5	81%	100%	98%	No	Yes
4.	Northern Illinois University	68.0	91	$637	GRE	3.2	97%	100%	88%	No	Yes
5.	University of South Carolina	67.6	391	$1,008	GRE	3.3	88%	91%	95%	No	Yes
6.	University of Scranton (PA)	66.6	1,008	$465	None	3.3	96%	90%	85%	Yes	Yes
7.	George Washington University (DC)	65.8	385	$618	GRE	3.2	74%	100%	81%	Yes	No
8.	University of Nebraska–Kearney	65.1	896	$393	None	3.4	93%	91%	N/A	Yes	Yes
9.	University of Northern Colorado	64.4	283	$495	GRE	3.6	77%	100%	75%	No	Yes
10.	Eastern Kentucky University	64.1	60	$350	GRE	3.6	N/A	100%	N/A	Yes	No
11.	Graceland University (IA)	64.1	125	$450	None	3.3	N/A	100%	N/A	Yes	Yes
12.	Central Michigan University	63.1	388	$477	None	3.1	83%	100%	85%	No	Yes
13.	University of North Texas	61.2	50	$569	GRE	3.1	42%	100%	86%	Yes	No
14.	Indiana University–Bloomington	61.0	87	$397	GRE	3.4	98%	100%	93%	Yes	No
15.	Wright State University (OH)	60.1	132	$961	GRE	3.2	84%	100%	100%	No	Yes
16.	Campbellsville University (KY)	59.9	191	$1,140[2]	GRE	3.5	N/A	60%	N/A	Yes	Yes
17.	North Carolina State University–Raleigh	59.8	390	N/A	GRE	3.2	100%	100%	N/A	No	No
18.	University of Florida	59.0	310	$483[2]	GRE	3.5	54%	100%	N/A	No	No
19.	Roosevelt University (IL)	58.4	36	$795[2]	None	3.4	100%	100%	83%	No	No
20.	Arkansas State University–Jonesboro	58.4	3,664	$230	None	3.3	76%	86%	97%	Yes	Yes
21.	Georgia Southern University	57.6	584	$400	GRE	3.2	98%	95%	80%	Yes	Yes
22.	Valley City State University (ND)	57.5	222	$258	None	3.4	86%	93%	77%	Yes	No
23.	Michigan State University	57.0	806	$683	None	3.5	90%	96%	76%	Yes	No
24.	California State University–Fullerton	56.7	118	N/A	None	N/A	75%	100%	98%	Yes	No
25.	Pennsylvania State University–World Campus	56.6	250	$736[2]	GRE	3.5	70%	92%	81%	No	No
26.	West Virginia University	56.0	1,065	$1,108	GRE	3.0	78%	93%	99%	No	No
27.	Webster University (MO)	55.7	183	$555	None	3.0	N/A	88%	62%	No	No
28.	Georgia State University	55.5	157	$385	GRE	3.3	82%	100%	81%	No	No
29.	Gardner-Webb University (NC)	55.3	N/A	$355	None	N/A	N/A	100%	N/A	Yes	No
30.	New School (NY)	55.2	N/A	$1,250	None	3.5	58%	100%	100%	Yes	Yes

ENGINEERING

Rank	School	Overall score	'12 total enrollment	'12-'13 tuition[1]	Entrance test required	'12 average undergad GPA	'12 acceptance rate	'12 full-time faculty with terminal degree	'12 retention rate	24/7 tech support	Smart phone app.
1.	University of Southern California	72.8	842	$1,569	GRE	3.4	34%	95%	86%	No	Yes
2.	Pennsylvania State University–World Campus	66.9	436	$930[2]	None	3.3	92%	93%	86%	No	No
3.	Columbia University (NY)	63.2	N/A	$1,578	GRE	N/A	N/A	100%	99%	Yes	Yes
4.	Purdue University–West Lafayette (IN)	63.0	537	$1,111	None	3.5	69%	100%	85%	No	No
5.	University of Michigan–Ann Arbor	62.6	458	$1,469[2]	None	3.6	62%	100%	95%	No	No
6.	Auburn University (AL)	59.0	91	$750	GRE	3.3	65%	100%	67%	No	Yes
7.	North Carolina State University	58.7	536	$726	None	3.3	60%	100%	95%	No	No
8.	University of Wisconsin–Madison	58.6	N/A	$1,575	None	N/A	N/A	100%	95%	Yes	Yes
9.	Polytechnic Institute of New York University	57.8	137	$1,304	GRE	N/A	N/A	100%	88%	Yes	Yes
10.	California State University–Fullerton	57.8	97	$679	None	3.1	70%	100%	86%	No	Yes

NURSING

Rank	School	Overall score	'12 total enrollment	'12-'13 tuition[1]	Entrance test required	'12 average undergad GPA	'12 acceptance rate	'12 full-time faculty with terminal degree	'12 retention rate	24/7 tech support	Smart phone app.
1.	Ferris State University (MI)	75.0	87	$728	None	3.3	53%	60%	83%	Yes	No
2.	Lamar University (TX)	74.5	53	N/A	None	3.0	100%	100%	99%	Yes	No
3.	University of Michigan–Flint	74.4	12	N/A	None	3.9	11%	83%	8%	No	No
4.	Clarkson College (NE)	74.2	369	$487	None	3.5	54%	100%	89%	Yes	Yes
5.	Graceland University (MO)	73.4	450	$625	None	3.6	79%	73%	89%	Yes	Yes
6.	Loyola University New Orleans (LA)	72.4	N/A	$780	None	3.4	86%	100%	86%	Yes	Yes
7.	Duquesne University (PA)	72.1	118	$991	None	3.5	74%	93%	97%	Yes	Yes
8.	Stony Brook University–SUNY (NY)	71.8	391	$695	None	3.5	34%	90%	93%	Yes	No
9.	University of Pittsburgh (PA)	71.7	58	$1,069	None	3.5	74%	100%	95%	Yes	Yes
10.	East Carolina University (NC)	71.1	606	$777	GRE	3.4	57%	67%	90%	Yes	Yes

N/A=Data were not provided by the school.
1. Tuition is reported on a per-credit-hour basis for full-time students, unless otherwise noted. Credit requirements may vary.
2. Part-time per-credit tuition

Find the right school for you with the
U.S. News College
Compass

Build Your Plan Online

Start Now at USNewsUniversityDirectory.com/Build

Connect
with more than
1,900 top colleges
and universities

Target
your search to the
schools that best
meet your needs

Access
the latest education
news from *U.S. News
& World Report*

Discover
how to get more
financial aid with our
free, expert guide

Get Free Assistance
With Your School Search:

855-237-2180

The digital magazine from the editors of U.S.News & World Report.

U.S.News & WORLD REPORT Weekly

Become a political insider–get U.S.News Weekly today!

- ➤ The latest political news, insight, and analysis

- ➤ Exclusive Q&As with leading policymakers

- ➤ Hot gossip from Washington Whispers

- ➤ Commentary by Editor-in-Chief Mort Zuckerman

- ➤ Videos, quizzes, and polls

- ➤ News You Can Use, from Best Colleges to Best Cars

Get the U.S. News Weekly on your desktop by going to usnews.com/subscribe

DIRECTORY OF
GRADUATE
SCHOOLS

Schools are listed alphabetically by state within each
discipline; data are accurate as of late February 2013.
A key to the terminology used in the directory can be
found at the beginning of each area of study.

BUSINESS

The business directory lists all 448 U.S. schools offering master's programs in business accredited by AACSB International–the Association to Advance Collegiate Schools of Business, as of August 2012. Most offer the M.B.A. degree; a few offer the master of business. Three hundred and eighty schools responded to the *U.S. News* survey conducted in the fall of 2012 and early 2013. Schools that did not respond to the survey have abbreviated entries.

KEY TO THE TERMINOLOGY

1. A school whose name is footnoted with the numeral 1 did not return the *U.S. News* statistical survey; limited data appear in its entry.

N/A. Not available from the school or not applicable.

E-mail. The address of the admissions office. If instead of an E-mail address a website is given in this field, the website will automatically present an E-mail screen programmed to reach the admissions office.

Application deadline. For fall 2014 enrollment. "Rolling" means there is no application deadline; the school acts on applications as they are received. "Varies" means deadlines vary according to department or whether applicants are U.S. citizens or foreign nationals.

Tuition. For the 2012-13 academic year or for the cost of the total graduate business degree program, if specified. Includes required annual student fees.

Credit hour. The cost per credit hour for the 2012-13 academic year.

Room/board/expenses. For the 2012-13 academic year.

College-funded aid and international student aid. "Yes" means the school provides its own financial aid to students.

Average indebtedness. Computed for 2012 graduates who incurred business school debt.

Enrollment. Full-time and part-time program totals are for fall 2012.

Minorities. For fall 2012, percentage of students who are black or African-American, Asian, American Indian or Alaskan Native, Native Hawaiian or other Pacific Islander, Hispanic/Latino, or two or more races. The minority percentage was reported by each school.

Acceptance rate. Percentage of applicants to the full-time program who were accepted for fall 2012.

Average Graduate Management Admission Test (GMAT) score. Calculated

separately for full-time and part-time students who entered in fall 2012.

Average undergraduate grade point average (1.0 to 4.0). For full-time program applicants who entered in fall 2012.

Average age of entrants. Calculated for full-time students who entered in fall 2012.

Average months of work experience. Calculated only for full-time program students who entered in fall 2012. Refers to post-baccalaureate work experience only.

TOEFL requirement. "Yes" means that students from non-English-speaking countries must submit scores for the Test of English as a Foreign Language.

Minimum TOEFL score. The lowest score on the paper TOEFL accepted for admission. (The computer-administered TOEFL is graded on a different scale.)

Most popular departments. Based on highest student demand in the 2012-13 academic year.

Mean starting base salary for 2012 graduates. Calculated only for graduates who were full-time students, had accepted full-time job offers, and reported salary data. Excludes employer-sponsored students, signing bonuses of any kind, and other forms of guaranteed compensation, such as stock options.

Employment locations. For the 2012 graduating class; calculated only for full-time students who had accepted job offers. Abbreviations: **Intl.,** international; **N.E.,** Northeast (Conn., Maine, Mass., N.H., N.J., N.Y., R.I., Vt.); **M.A.,** Middle Atlantic (Del., D.C., Md., Pa., Va., W.Va.); **S.,** South (Ala., Ark., Fla., Ga., Ky., La., Miss., N.C., S.C., Tenn.); **M.W.,** Midwest (Ill., Ind., Iowa, Kan., Mich., Minn., Mo., Neb., N.D., Ohio, S.D., Wis.); **S.W.,** Southwest (Ariz., Colo., N.M., Okla., Texas); **W.,** West (Alaska, Calif., Hawaii, Idaho, Mont., Nev., Ore., Utah, Wash., Wyo.).

ALABAMA

Auburn University
415 W. Magnolia, Suite 503
Auburn, AL 36849-5240
http://www.business.
auburn.edu/mba
Public
Admissions: (334) 844-4060
E-mail: mbadmis@auburn.edu
Financial aid: (334) 844-4367
Application deadline: 02/01
In-state tuition: full time: $14,640;
part time: $750/credit hour
Out-of-state tuition: full time:
$30,372
Room/board/expenses: $16,258
College-funded aid: Yes
International student aid: Yes
**Average student indebtedness at
graduation:** $8,500
Full-time enrollment: 39
men: 59%; women: 41%;
minorities:5%; international: 36%
Part-time enrollment: 240
men: N/A; women: N/A;
minorities: N/A; international: N/A
Acceptance rate (full time): 46%
Average GMAT (full time): 635
Average GMAT (part time): 565
Average GPA (full time): 3.36
**Average age of entrants to full-time
program:** 24
**Average months of prior work
experience (full time):** 39
TOEFL requirement: Yes
Minimum TOEFL score: 550
Most popular departments: finance,
manufacturing and technology
management, marketing, management information systems,
operations management
**Mean starting base salary for 2012
full-time graduates:** $57,169
Employment location for 2012 class:
Intl. 5%; N.E. 9%; M.A. 5%; S.
77%; M.W. N/A; S.W. N/A; W. 5%

Auburn University–Montgomery
7300 University Drive
Montgomery, AL 36117
http://www.aum.edu
Public
Admissions: (334) 244-3623
E-mail: tpeters7@aum.edu
Financial aid: (334) 244-3571
Application deadline: rolling
In-state tuition: full time: $308/
credit hour; part time: $308/
credit hour
Out-of-state tuition: full time: $924/
credit hour
Room/board/expenses: N/A
College-funded aid: Yes
International student aid: Yes
Full-time enrollment: 63
men: 52%; women: 48%;
minorities:83%; international: 30%
Part-time enrollment: 74
men: 53%; women: 47%;
minorities:53%; international: 7%
Acceptance rate (full time): 93%
Average GMAT (full time): 500
**Average age of entrants to full-time
program:** 26
TOEFL requirement: Yes
Minimum TOEFL score: 500
Most popular departments: economics, finance, general management, marketing, management
information systems

Jacksonville State University[1]
700 Pelham Road N
Jacksonville, AL 36265
http://www.jsu.edu/depart/ccba/
Public
Admissions: (256) 782-5329
E-mail: graduate@jsu.edu
Financial aid: (256) 782-5006
Tuition: N/A
Room/board/expenses: N/A
Enrollment: N/A

Samford University (Brock)
800 Lakeshore Drive
Birmingham, AL 35229
http://www.samford.edu/mba
Private
Admissions: (205) 726-2931
E-mail: lcharper@samford.edu
Financial aid: (205) 726-2905
Application deadline: 08/01
Tuition: full time: N/A; part time:
$688/credit hour
Room/board/expenses: $15,500
College-funded aid: Yes
International student aid: No
Full-time enrollment: N/A
men: N/A; women: N/A;
minorities:N/A; international: N/A
Part-time enrollment: 97
men: 69%; women: 31%;
minorities:11%; international: 20%
Average GMAT (part time): 545
TOEFL requirement: Yes
Minimum TOEFL score: N/A

University of Alabama–Birmingham
1530 Third Avenue S, BEC 203
Birmingham, AL 35294-4460
http://www.business.uab.edu
Public
Admissions: (205) 934-8817
E-mail: cmanning@uab.edu
Financial aid: (205) 934-8223
Application deadline: rolling
In-state tuition: full time: N/A; part
time: $367/credit hour
Out-of-state tuition: full time: N/A
Room/board/expenses: N/A
College-funded aid: Yes
International student aid: No
Full-time enrollment: N/A
men: N/A; women: N/A;
minorities:N/A; international: N/A
Part-time enrollment: 365
men: 59%; women: 41%;
minorities:30%; international: 6%
Average GMAT (part time): 552
TOEFL requirement: Yes
Minimum TOEFL score: N/A

University of Alabama–Huntsville
BAB 202
Huntsville, AL 35899
http://cba.uah.edu
Public
Admissions: (256) 824-6681
E-mail: gradbiz@uah.edu
Financial aid: (256) 824-6241
Application deadline: rolling
In-state tuition: full time: $8,535;
part time: $6,193
Out-of-state tuition: full time:
$20,435
Room/board/expenses: $10,650
College-funded aid: Yes
International student aid: Yes

Average student indebtedness at graduation: $15,197
Full-time enrollment: 51
men: 57%; women: 43%;
minorities:18%; international: 24%
Part-time enrollment: 140
men: 47%; women: 53%;
minorities:14%; international: 3%
Acceptance rate (full time): 86%
Average GMAT (full time): 534
Average GMAT (part time): 535
Average GPA (full time): 3.33
Average age of entrants to full-time program: 27
Average months of prior work experience (full time): 36
TOEFL requirement: Yes
Minimum TOEFL score: 550
Most popular departments: accounting, human resources management, marketing, supply chain management, other

University of Alabama (Manderson)
Box 870223
Tuscaloosa, AL 35487
http://www.cba.ua.edu/~mba
Public
Admissions: (888) 863-2622
E-mail: mba@cba.ua.edu
Financial aid: (205) 348-6517
Application deadline: 04/15
In-state tuition: full time: $12,030; part time: N/A
Out-of-state tuition: full time: $25,780
Room/board/expenses: N/A
College-funded aid: Yes
International student aid: Yes
Full-time enrollment: 166
men: 72%; women: 28%;
minorities:16%; international: 11%
Part-time enrollment: N/A
men: N/A; women: N/A;
minorities:N/A; international: N/A
Acceptance rate (full time): 39%
Average GMAT (full time): 642
Average GPA (full time): 3.55
Average age of entrants to full-time program: 24
Average months of prior work experience (full time): 16
TOEFL requirement: Yes
Minimum TOEFL score: 550
Most popular departments: finance, general management, management information systems, supply chain management, statistics and operations research
Mean starting base salary for 2012 full-time graduates: $65,849

University of Montevallo
Morgan Hall 201, Station 6540
Montevallo, AL 35115
http://www.montevallo.edu/grad/
Public
Admissions: (205) 665-6350
E-mail: graduate@montevallo.edu
Financial aid: (205) 665-6050
Application deadline: rolling
In-state tuition: full time: $319/credit hour; part time: $319/credit hour
Out-of-state tuition: full time: $638/credit hour
Room/board/expenses: N/A
College-funded aid: Yes
Full-time enrollment: N/A
men: N/A; women: N/A;
minorities:N/A; international: N/A
Part-time enrollment: 47
men: N/A; women: N/A;
minorities:N/A; international: N/A
TOEFL requirement: Yes
Minimum TOEFL score: 525
Most popular departments: general management

University of South Alabama (Mitchell)[1]
307 N. University Boulevard
Mobile, AL 36688
http://mcob.southalabama.edu/
Public
Admissions: (251) 460-6494
E-mail: dstearns@usouthal.edu
Financial aid: (251) 460-6619
Tuition: N/A
Room/board/expenses: N/A
Enrollment: N/A

ALASKA

University of Alaska–Anchorage[1]
3211 Providence Drive
Anchorage, AK 99508
http://www.cbpp.alaska.edu
Public
Admissions: (907) 786-1480
E-mail: ayenrol@uaa.alaska.edu
Financial aid: (907) 786-1586
Tuition: N/A
Room/board/expenses: N/A
Enrollment: N/A

University of Alaska–Fairbanks
PO Box 756080
Fairbanks, AK 99775-6080
http://www.uaf.edu/index.html
Public
Admissions: (800) 478-1823
E-mail: admissions@uaf.edu
Financial aid: (888) 474-7256
Application deadline: 06/01
In-state tuition: full time: $383/credit hour; part time: $383/credit hour
Out-of-state tuition: full time: $783/credit hour
Room/board/expenses: $11,310
College-funded aid: Yes
International student aid: Yes
Average student indebtedness at graduation: $17,291
Full-time enrollment: 26
men: 38%; women: 62%;
minorities:23%; international: 12%
Part-time enrollment: 38
men: 34%; women: 66%;
minorities:24%; international: 0%
Acceptance rate (full time): 63%
Average GMAT (full time): 497
Average GMAT (part time): 450
Average age of entrants to full-time program: 28
TOEFL requirement: Yes
Minimum TOEFL score: 550

ARIZONA

Arizona State University (Carey)
PO Box 874906
Tempe, AZ 85287-4906
http://wpcareymba.asu.edu
Public
Admissions: (480) 965-3332
E-mail: wpcareymba@asu.edu
Financial aid: (480) 965-6890
Application deadline: 06/30
In-state tuition: full time: $23,518; part time: $25,768
Out-of-state tuition: full time: $38,066
Room/board/expenses: $18,408
College-funded aid: Yes
International student aid: Yes
Average student indebtedness at graduation: $59,706
Full-time enrollment: 142
men: 79%; women: 21%;
minorities:14%; international: 35%
Part-time enrollment: 366
men: 74%; women: 26%;
minorities:20%; international: 7%
Acceptance rate (full time): 36%
Average GMAT (full time): 676

Average GMAT (part time): 574
Average GPA (full time): 3.40
Average age of entrants to full-time program: 27
Average months of prior work experience (full time): 62
TOEFL requirement: Yes
Minimum TOEFL score: 550
Most popular departments: finance, general management, leadership, marketing, supply chain management
Mean starting base salary for 2012 full-time graduates: $92,556
Employment location for 2012 class: Intl. 0%; N.E. 7%; M.A. 2%; S. 14%; M.W. 7%; S.W. 39%; W. 32%

Northern Arizona University (Franke)
PO Box 15066
Flagstaff, AZ 86011-5066
http://www.franke.nau.edu/mba
Public
Admissions: (928) 523-7342
E-mail: mba@nau.edu
Financial aid: (928) 523-4951
Application deadline: rolling
In-state tuition: total program: $16,578 (full-time); part time: N/A
Out-of-state tuition: total program: $27,672 (full-time)
Room/board/expenses: $19,105
College-funded aid: Yes
International student aid: Yes
Full-time enrollment: 31
men: 65%; women: 35%;
minorities:23%; international: 13%
Part-time enrollment: N/A
men: N/A; women: N/A;
minorities:N/A; international: N/A
Acceptance rate (full time): 88%
Average GMAT (full time): 531
Average GPA (full time): 3.40
Average age of entrants to full-time program: 24
Average months of prior work experience (full time): 32
TOEFL requirement: Yes
Minimum TOEFL score: 550

Thunderbird School of Global Management
1 Global Place
Glendale, AZ 85306-6000
http://www.thunderbird.edu
Private
Admissions: (602) 978-7100
E-mail: admissions@thunderbird.edu
Financial aid: (602) 978-7130
Application deadline: 05/10
Tuition: full time: $44,040; part time: N/A
Room/board/expenses: $5,265
College-funded aid: Yes
International student aid: Yes
Average student indebtedness at graduation: $88,195
Full-time enrollment: 380
men: 73%; women: 27%;
minorities:7%; international: 56%
Part-time enrollment: N/A
men: N/A; women: N/A;
minorities:N/A; international: N/A
Acceptance rate (full time): 78%
Average GMAT (full time): 602
Average GPA (full time): 3.30
Average age of entrants to full-time program: 28
Average months of prior work experience (full time): 53
TOEFL requirement: Yes
Minimum TOEFL score: 600
Most popular departments: entrepreneurship, finance, general management, international business, marketing
Mean starting base salary for 2012 full-time graduates: $83,034
Employment location for 2012 class: Intl. 13%; N.E. 13%; M.A. 4%; S. 3%; M.W. 5%; S.W. 34%; W. 27%

University of Arizona (Eller)
McClelland Hall, Room 417
Tucson, AZ 85721-0108
http://ellermba.arizona.edu
Public
Admissions: (520) 621-6227
E-mail: mba_admissions@eller.arizona.edu
Financial aid: N/A
Application deadline: rolling
In-state tuition: full time: $20,622; part time: $20,000
Out-of-state tuition: full time: $36,033
Room/board/expenses: $13,200
College-funded aid: Yes
International student aid: Yes
Average student indebtedness at graduation: $50,831
Full-time enrollment: 99
men: 75%; women: 25%;
minorities:11%; international: 31%
Part-time enrollment: 150
men: 64%; women: 36%;
minorities:35%; international: 5%
Acceptance rate (full time): 55%
Average GMAT (full time): 634
Average GMAT (part time): 513
Average GPA (full time): 3.28
Average age of entrants to full-time program: 27
Average months of prior work experience (full time): 53
TOEFL requirement: Yes
Minimum TOEFL score: 600
Most popular departments: entrepreneurship, finance, general management, marketing, management information systems
Mean starting base salary for 2012 full-time graduates: $86,388
Employment location for 2012 class: Intl. 3%; N.E. 13%; M.A. 3%; S. 7%; M.W. 0%; S.W. 53%; W. 20%

ARKANSAS

Arkansas State University–Jonesboro
PO Box 970
State University, AR 72467
http://www2.astate.edu/business/
Public
Admissions: (870) 972-3029
E-mail: gradsch@astate.edu
Financial aid: (870) 972-2310
Application deadline: 06/15
In-state tuition: full time: $5,994; part time: $277/credit hour
Out-of-state tuition: full time: $10,134
Room/board/expenses: $13,274
College-funded aid: Yes
International student aid: Yes
Average student indebtedness at graduation: $33,200
Full-time enrollment: 90
men: 59%; women: 41%;
minorities:2%; international: 76%
Part-time enrollment: 129
men: 55%; women: 45%;
minorities:7%; international: 32%
Acceptance rate (full time): 72%
Average GMAT (full time): 545
Average GMAT (part time): 520
Average GPA (full time): 3.50
Average age of entrants to full-time program: 26
Average months of prior work experience (full time): 12
TOEFL requirement: Yes
Minimum TOEFL score: 550
Most popular departments: accounting, finance, health care administration, international business, supply chain management
Mean starting base salary for 2012 full-time graduates: $56,350
Employment location for 2012 class: Intl. 13%; N.E. 7%; M.A. 0%; S. 40%; M.W. 27%; S.W. 13%; W. 0%

Henderson State University[1]
1100 Henderson Street, Box 7801
Arkadelphia, AR 71999-0001
http://www.hsu.edu/dept/bus/mba.html
Public
Admissions: (870) 230-5126
E-mail: grad@hsu.edu
Financial aid: (870) 230-5148
Tuition: N/A
Room/board/expenses: N/A
Enrollment: N/A

Southern Arkansas University
100 E. University
Magnolia, AR 71753
http://web.saumag.edu/graduate/programs/mba/
Public
Admissions: (870) 235-4167
E-mail: mamayo@saumag.edu
Financial aid: N/A
Application deadline: rolling
In-state tuition: full time: $244/credit hour; part time: $244/credit hour
Out-of-state tuition: full time: $356/credit hour
Room/board/expenses: N/A
College-funded aid: Yes
International student aid: Yes
Full-time enrollment: 65
men: 51%; women: 49%;
minorities:22%; international: 12%
Part-time enrollment: 7
men: 71%; women: 29%;
minorities:0%; international: 0%
Acceptance rate (full time): 93%
Average GMAT (full time): 438
Average GMAT (part time): 426
Average GPA (full time): 3.21
Average age of entrants to full-time program: 31
TOEFL requirement: Yes
Minimum TOEFL score: 550

University of Arkansas–Fayetteville (Walton)
310 Williard J. Walker Hall
Fayetteville, AR 72701
http://gsb.uark.edu
Public
Admissions: (479) 575-2851
E-mail: gsb@walton.uark.edu
Financial aid: (479) 575-3806
Application deadline: 04/01
In-state tuition: full time: $15,447; part time: $15,048
Out-of-state tuition: full time: $36,543
Room/board/expenses: $17,542
College-funded aid: Yes
International student aid: Yes
Full-time enrollment: 71
men: 63%; women: 37%;
minorities:11%; international: 31%
Part-time enrollment: 118
men: 72%; women: 28%;
minorities:8%; international: 3%
Acceptance rate (full time): 47%
Average GMAT (full time): 631
Average GMAT (part time): 579
Average GPA (full time): 3.20
Average age of entrants to full-time program: 25
Average months of prior work experience (full time): 32
TOEFL requirement: Yes
Minimum TOEFL score: 550
Most popular departments: entrepreneurship, finance, marketing, non-profit management, supply chain management
Mean starting base salary for 2012 full-time graduates: $60,750
Employment location for 2012 class: Intl. 0%; N.E. 0%; M.A. 0%; S. 94%; M.W. 6%; S.W. 0%; W. 0%

University of Arkansas–Little Rock

2801 S. University Avenue
Little Rock, AR 72204
http://cba.ualr.edu
Public
Admissions: (501) 569-3356
E-mail: rmmoore@ualr.edu
Financial aid: (501) 569-3035
Application deadline: rolling
In-state tuition: full time: $280/credit hour; part time: $280/credit hour
Out-of-state tuition: full time: $620/credit hour
Room/board/expenses: $12,363
College-funded aid: Yes
International student aid: Yes
Average student indebtedness at graduation: $49,948
Full-time enrollment: 39
men: 56%; women: 44%;
minorities:44%; international: 26%
Part-time enrollment: 103
men: 67%; women: 33%;
minorities:28%; international: 5%
Acceptance rate (full time): 79%
Average GMAT (full time): 565
Average GMAT (part time): 549
Average age of entrants to full-time program: 27
TOEFL requirement: Yes
Minimum TOEFL score: 550
Employment location for 2012 class: Intl. N/A; N.E. N/A; M.A. N/A; S. 100%; M.W. N/A; S.W. N/A; W. N/A

University of Central Arkansas

201 Donaghey
Conway, AR 72035
http://www.uca.edu/divisions/academic/mba
Public
Admissions: (501) 450-5316
E-mail: mrubach@uca.edu
Financial aid: (501) 450-3140
Application deadline: 07/15
In-state tuition: full time: $183/credit hour; part time: $183/credit hour
Out-of-state tuition: full time: $367/credit hour
Room/board/expenses: N/A
College-funded aid: Yes
International student aid: No
Full-time enrollment: 21
men: 86%; women: 14%;
minorities:10%; international: 33%
Part-time enrollment: 27
men: 63%; women: 37%;
minorities:7%; international: 0%
Acceptance rate (full time): 100%
Average GMAT (full time): 542
Average GMAT (part time): 520
Average GPA (full time): 3.25
Average age of entrants to full-time program: 23
TOEFL requirement: Yes
Minimum TOEFL score: 550

CALIFORNIA

California Polytechnic State University–San Luis Obispo (Orfalea)

1 Grand Avenue
San Luis Obispo, CA 93407
http://www.cob.calpoly.edu/gradprograms/
Public
Admissions: (805) 756-2311
E-mail: admissions@calpoly.edu
Financial aid: (805) 756-2927
Application deadline: 07/01
In-state tuition: full time: $12,906; part time: N/A
Out-of-state tuition: full time: $20,346
Room/board/expenses: $15,837

College-funded aid: Yes
International student aid: No
Full-time enrollment: 38
men: 66%; women: 34%;
minorities:N/A; international: 3%
Part-time enrollment: N/A
men: N/A; women: N/A;
minorities:N/A; international: N/A
Acceptance rate (full time): 30%
Average GMAT (full time): 610
Average GPA (full time): 3.30
Average months of prior work experience (full time): 24
TOEFL requirement: Yes
Minimum TOEFL score: 550
Most popular departments: accounting, general management, manufacturing and technology management, tax, other

California State Polytechnic University–Pomona

3801 W. Temple Avenue
Pomona, CA 91768
http://www.csupomona.edu/~mba
Public
Admissions: (909) 869-3210
E-mail: admissions@csupomona.edu
Financial aid: (909) 869-3700
Application deadline: 08/01
In-state tuition: full time: $11,464; part time: $6,604
Out-of-state tuition: full time: $17,416
Room/board/expenses: $14,171
College-funded aid: Yes
International student aid: Yes
Full-time enrollment: N/A
men: N/A; women: N/A;
minorities:N/A; international: N/A
Part-time enrollment: 115
men: 55%; women: 45%;
minorities:54%; international: 12%
Average GMAT (part time): 508
TOEFL requirement: Yes
Minimum TOEFL score: 580

California State University–Bakersfield[1]

9001 Stockdale Highway
Bakersfield, CA 93311-1099
http://www.csub.edu/BPA
Public
Admissions: (661) 664-3036
E-mail: hmontalvo@csubak.edu
Financial aid: (661) 664-3016
Tuition: N/A
Room/board/expenses: N/A
Enrollment: N/A

California State University–Chico[1]

Tehama Hall 301
Chico, CA 95929-0001
http://www.csuchico.edu/MBA
Public
Admissions: (530) 898-6880
E-mail: graduatestudies@csuchico.edu
Financial aid: (530) 898-6451
Tuition: N/A
Room/board/expenses: N/A
Enrollment: N/A

California State University–East Bay

25800 Carlos Bee Boulevard
Hayward, CA 94542
http://www.csueastbay.edu
Public
Admissions: (510) 885-2784
E-mail: admissions@csueastbay.edu
Financial aid: (510) 885-2784
Application deadline: rolling

In-state tuition: full time: $12,873; part time: $7,563
Out-of-state tuition: full time: $18,825
Room/board/expenses: $15,000
College-funded aid: Yes
International student aid: No
Average student indebtedness at graduation: $3,970
Full-time enrollment: N/A
men: N/A; women: N/A;
minorities:N/A; international: N/A
Part-time enrollment: 222
men: 53%; women: 47%;
minorities:36%; international: 44%
Average GMAT (part time): 514
TOEFL requirement: Yes
Minimum TOEFL score: 550
Most popular departments: finance, human resources management, marketing, operations management, organizational behavior

California State University–Fresno (Craig)

5245 N. Backer Avenue
Fresno, CA 93740-8001
http://www.craig.csufresno.edu/mba
Public
Admissions: (559) 278-2107
E-mail: mbainfo@csufresno.edu
Financial aid: (559) 278-2183
Application deadline: rolling
In-state tuition: full time: N/A; part time: N/A
Out-of-state tuition: full time: N/A
Room/board/expenses: N/A
College-funded aid: Yes
International student aid: Yes
Full-time enrollment: N/A
men: N/A; women: N/A;
minorities:N/A; international: N/A
Part-time enrollment: 102
men: 65%; women: 35%;
minorities:40%; international: 10%
Average GMAT (part time): 600
TOEFL requirement: Yes
Minimum TOEFL score: 550

California State University–Fullerton (Mihaylo)

PO Box 6848
Fullerton, CA 92834-6848
http://business.fullerton.edu
Public
Admissions: (657) 278-4035
E-mail: mba@fullerton.edu
Financial aid: (657) 278-3125
Application deadline: 04/01
In-state tuition: full time: $12,020; part time: $6,140
Out-of-state tuition: full time: $18,716
Room/board/expenses: $18,332
College-funded aid: Yes
International student aid: Yes
Full-time enrollment: 40
men: 48%; women: 53%;
minorities:28%; international: 50%
Part-time enrollment: 317
men: 60%; women: 40%;
minorities:42%; international: 19%
Acceptance rate (full time): 45%
Average GMAT (full time): 558
Average GMAT (part time): 519
Average GPA (full time): 3.21
Average age of entrants to full-time program: 24
TOEFL requirement: Yes
Minimum TOEFL score: 570
Most popular departments: accounting, entrepreneurship, finance, general management, marketing

California State University–Long Beach

1250 Bellflower Boulevard
Long Beach, CA 90840-8501
http://www.csulb.edu/colleges/cba/mba
Public
Admissions: (562) 985-8627
E-mail: mba@csulb.edu
Financial aid: (562) 985-4141
Application deadline: rolling
In-state tuition: full time: N/A; part time: N/A
Out-of-state tuition: full time: N/A
Room/board/expenses: N/A
College-funded aid: Yes
International student aid: Yes
Full-time enrollment: 55
men: 65%; women: 35%;
minorities:73%; international: 42%
Part-time enrollment: 102
men: 58%; women: 42%;
minorities:55%; international: 6%
Acceptance rate (full time): 31%
Average GMAT (full time): 563
Average GMAT (part time): 555
Average GPA (full time): 3.24
Average age of entrants to full-time program: 27
TOEFL requirement: Yes
Minimum TOEFL score: 550

California State University–Los Angeles

5151 State University Drive
Los Angeles, CA 90032-8120
http://mbacbe@exchange.calstatela.edu
Public
Admissions: (323) 343-2800
E-mail: ehsieh@calstatela.edu
Financial aid: (323) 343-6260
Application deadline: rolling
In-state tuition: full time: $380/credit hour; part time: N/A
Out-of-state tuition: full time: $628/credit hour
Room/board/expenses: N/A
College-funded aid: Yes
International student aid: Yes
Full-time enrollment: 91
men: 51%; women: 49%;
minorities:N/A; international: N/A
Part-time enrollment: N/A
men: N/A; women: N/A;
minorities:N/A; international: N/A
Average GMAT (full time): 551
TOEFL requirement: Yes
Minimum TOEFL score: 550
Most popular departments: accounting, finance, general management, marketing, tax

California State University–Northridge

18111 Nordhoff Street
Northridge, CA 91330-8380
http://www.csun.edu/mba/
Public
Admissions: (818) 677-2467
E-mail: MBA@csun.edu
Financial aid: N/A
Application deadline: 05/01
In-state tuition: full time: $16,092; part time: $9,666
Out-of-state tuition: full time: $25,020
Room/board/expenses: $19,466
College-funded aid: Yes
International student aid: Yes
Full-time enrollment: N/A
men: N/A; women: N/A;
minorities:N/A; international: N/A
Part-time enrollment: 169
men: 65%; women: 35%;
minorities:34%; international: 8%
Average GMAT (part time): 580

TOEFL requirement: Yes
Minimum TOEFL score: 550

California State University–Sacramento

6000 J Street
Sacramento, CA 95819-6088
http://www.csus.edu/cbagrad
Public
Admissions: (916) 278-6772
E-mail: cbagrad@csus.edu
Financial aid: (916) 278-6554
Application deadline: 11/13
In-state tuition: full time: N/A; part time: $5,396
Out-of-state tuition: full time: N/A
Room/board/expenses: N/A
College-funded aid: No
International student aid: No
Full-time enrollment: N/A
men: N/A; women: N/A;
minorities:N/A; international: N/A
Part-time enrollment: 147
men: 58%; women: 42%;
minorities:32%; international: 5%
Average GMAT (part time): 564
TOEFL requirement: Yes
Minimum TOEFL score: 550

California State University–San Bernardino

5500 University Parkway
San Bernardino, CA 92407
http://www.cpba.csusb.edu/mba_program/welcome
Public
Admissions: (909) 537-5703
E-mail: mbaprogram@csusb.edu
Financial aid: (909) 537-5227
Application deadline: 07/15
In-state tuition: full time: $8,451; part time: $5,361
Out-of-state tuition: full time: $17,379
Room/board/expenses: $26,000
College-funded aid: Yes
International student aid: Yes
Average student indebtedness at graduation: $37,015
Full-time enrollment: 160
men: 61%; women: 39%;
minorities:36%; international: 33%
Part-time enrollment: 44
men: 61%; women: 39%;
minorities:43%; international: 27%
Acceptance rate (full time): 47%
Average GMAT (full time): 539
Average GMAT (part time): 550
Average GPA (full time): 3.29
Average age of entrants to full-time program: 29
TOEFL requirement: Yes
Minimum TOEFL score: 550
Mean starting base salary for 2012 full-time graduates: $62,000
Employment location for 2012 class: Intl. 0%; N.E. 0%; M.A. 0%; S. 0%; M.W. 0%; S.W. 0%; W. 100%

California State University–Stanislaus[1]

1 University Circle
Turlock, CA 95382
http://www.csustan.edu/Grad
Public
Admissions: (209) 667-3129
E-mail: graduate_school@csustan.edu
Financial aid: (209) 667-3336
Tuition: N/A
Room/board/expenses: N/A
Enrollment: N/A

Chapman University (Argyros)

1 University Drive
Orange, CA 92866
http://www.chapman.edu/argyros
Private
Admissions: (714) 997-6596
E-mail: mba@chapman.edu
Financial aid: (714) 997-6741
Application deadline: 11/01
Tuition: full time: $1,300/credit hour; part time: $1,300/credit hour
Room/board/expenses: $20,100
College-funded aid: Yes
International student aid: Yes
Average student indebtedness at graduation: $42,776
Full-time enrollment: 59
men: 63%; women: 37%;
minorities:22%; international: 34%
Part-time enrollment: 146
men: 56%; women: 44%;
minorities:36%; international: 18%
Acceptance rate (full time): 46%
Average GMAT (full time): 615
Average GMAT (part time): 520
Average GPA (full time): 3.34
Average age of entrants to full-time program: 25
Average months of prior work experience (full time): 36
TOEFL requirement: Yes
Minimum TOEFL score: 600
Most popular departments: entrepreneurship, finance, international business, marketing
Mean starting base salary for 2012 full-time graduates: $63,864
Employment location for 2012 class: Intl. 7%; N.E. N/A; M.A. N/A; S. N/A; M.W. N/A; S.W. N/A; W. 93%

Claremont Graduate University (Drucker)

1021 N. Dartmouth Avenue
Claremont, CA 91711-6184
http://www.drucker.cgu.edu
Private
Admissions: (800) 944-4312
E-mail: drucker@cgu.edu
Financial aid: (909) 621-8337
Application deadline: rolling
Tuition: full time: $1,636/credit hour; part time: $1,636/credit hour
Room/board/expenses: $14,000
College-funded aid: Yes
International student aid: Yes
Average student indebtedness at graduation: $45,515
Full-time enrollment: 84
men: 67%; women: 33%;
minorities:29%; international: 42%
Part-time enrollment: 39
men: 56%; women: 44%;
minorities:49%; international: 8%
Acceptance rate (full time): 61%
Average GMAT (full time): 614
Average GMAT (part time): 528
Average GPA (full time): 3.29
Average age of entrants to full-time program: 27
Average months of prior work experience (full time): 33
TOEFL requirement: Yes
Minimum TOEFL score: 550
Most popular departments: general management, international business, leadership, marketing, other
Mean starting base salary for 2012 full-time graduates: $56,000
Employment location for 2012 class: Intl. 6%; N.E. N/A; M.A. N/A; S. N/A; M.W. 6%; S.W. N/A; W. 89%

Loyola Marymount University

1 LMU Drive, MS 8387
Los Angeles, CA 90045-2659
http://mba.lmu.edu
Private
Admissions: (310) 338-2848
E-mail: mbapc@lmu.edu
Financial aid: (310) 338-2753
Application deadline: rolling
Tuition: full time: N/A; part time: $1,184/credit hour
Room/board/expenses: $29,226
College-funded aid: Yes
International student aid: Yes
Full-time enrollment: N/A
men: N/A; women: N/A;
minorities:N/A; international: N/A
Part-time enrollment: 242
men: 66%; women: 34%;
minorities:36%; international: 14%
Average GMAT (part time): 582
TOEFL requirement: Yes
Minimum TOEFL score: 600
Most popular departments: entrepreneurship, finance, general management, marketing, management information systems

Monterey Institute of International Studies (Fisher)[1]

460 Pierce Street
Monterey, CA 93940
http://fisher.miis.edu
Private
Admissions: (831) 647-4123
E-mail: mba@miis.edu
Financial aid: (831) 647-4119
Tuition: N/A
Room/board/expenses: N/A
Enrollment: N/A

Naval Postgraduate School[1]

555 Dyer Road
Monterey, CA 93943
http://www.nps.navy.mil/gsbpp/
Public
Admissions: (831) 656-1062
E-mail: sgdooley@nps.edu
Financial aid: N/A
Tuition: N/A
Room/board/expenses: N/A
Enrollment: N/A

Pepperdine University (Graziadio)

24255 Pacific Coast Highway
Malibu, CA 90263-4100
http://www.bschool.pepperdine.edu
Private
Admissions: (310) 568-5535
E-mail: gsbmadm@pepperdine.edu
Financial aid: (310) 568-5530
Application deadline: 05/01
Tuition: full time: $42,360; part time: $1,476/credit hour
Room/board/expenses: $25,100
College-funded aid: Yes
International student aid: Yes
Average student indebtedness at graduation: $85,672
Full-time enrollment: 217
men: 58%; women: 42%;
minorities:17%; international: 34%
Part-time enrollment: 648
men: 58%; women: 42%;
minorities:30%; international: 3%
Acceptance rate (full time): 66%
Average GMAT (full time): 633
Average GMAT (part time): 531
Average GPA (full time): 3.21
Average age of entrants to full-time program: 27
Average months of prior work experience (full time): 51

San Diego State University

5500 Campanile Drive
San Diego, CA 92182-8228
http://www.sdsu.edu/business
Public
Admissions: (619) 594-6336
E-mail: admissions@sdsu.edu
Financial aid: (619) 594-6323
Application deadline: 03/01
In-state tuition: full time: $15,134; part time: $8,352
Out-of-state tuition: full time: $24,062
Room/board/expenses: $12,091
College-funded aid: Yes
International student aid: Yes
Average student indebtedness at graduation: $18,320
Full-time enrollment: 309
men: 56%; women: 44%;
minorities:26%; international: 26%
Part-time enrollment: 288
men: 57%; women: 43%;
minorities:30%; international: 4%
Acceptance rate (full time): 62%
Average GMAT (full time): 591
Average GMAT (part time): 595
Average GPA (full time): 3.27
Average age of entrants to full-time program: 25
Average months of prior work experience (full time): 45
TOEFL requirement: Yes
Minimum TOEFL score: 550
Most popular departments: accounting, finance, general management, marketing, sports business
Mean starting base salary for 2012 full-time graduates: $70,622
Employment location for 2012 class: Intl. N/A; N.E. N/A; M.A. N/A; S. N/A; M.W. 100%; S.W. N/A; W. N/A

San Francisco State University

835 Market Street, Suite 550
San Francisco, CA 94103
http://mba.sfsu.edu
Public
Admissions: (415) 817-4300
E-mail: mba@sfsu.edu
Financial aid: (415) 338-1581
Application deadline: 04/01
In-state tuition: full time: $16,202; part time: $9,322
Out-of-state tuition: full time: $25,130
Room/board/expenses: $22,500
College-funded aid: Yes
International student aid: Yes
Average student indebtedness at graduation: $20,000
Full-time enrollment: 189
men: 44%; women: 56%;
minorities:22%; international: 40%
Part-time enrollment: 143
men: 47%; women: 53%;
minorities:25%; international: 25%
Acceptance rate (full time): 41%
Average GMAT (full time): 570
Average GMAT (part time): 570
Average GPA (full time): 3.42
Average age of entrants to full-time program: 28
Average months of prior work experience (full time): 56

TOEFL requirement: Yes
Minimum TOEFL score: 600
Most popular departments: entrepreneurship, finance, general management, leadership, marketing
Mean starting base salary for 2012 full-time graduates: $72,815
Employment location for 2012 class: Intl. 7%; N.E. 1%; M.A. 1%; S. 3%; M.W. 3%; S.W. 4%; W. 79%

San Jose State University (Lucas)

1 Washington Square
San Jose, CA 95192-0162
http://www.sjsu.edu/lucasschool
Public
Admissions: (408) 924-3420
E-mail: lucas-school@sjsu.edu
Financial aid: (408) 283-7500
Application deadline: 05/01
In-state tuition: full time: $12,927; part time: $8,571
Out-of-state tuition: full time: $19,623
Room/board/expenses: N/A
College-funded aid: Yes
International student aid: No
Full-time enrollment: 62
men: 58%; women: 42%;
minorities:N/A; international: N/A
Part-time enrollment: 97
men: 71%; women: 29%;
minorities:N/A; international: N/A
Acceptance rate (full time): 47%
Average GMAT (full time): 542
Average GMAT (part time): 563
Average GPA (full time): 3.18
Average age of entrants to full-time program: 27
TOEFL requirement: Yes
Minimum TOEFL score: 550

Santa Clara University (Leavey)

Lucas Hall
Santa Clara, CA 95053
http://www.scu.edu/business
Private
Admissions: (408) 554-4539
E-mail: mbaadmissions@scu.edu
Financial aid: (408) 554-4505
Application deadline: 06/10
Tuition: full time: N/A; part time: $888/credit hour
Room/board/expenses: $19,069
College-funded aid: Yes
International student aid: No
Full-time enrollment: N/A
men: N/A; women: N/A;
minorities:N/A; international: N/A
Part-time enrollment: 758
men: 62%; women: 38%;
minorities:36%; international: 22%
Average GMAT (part time): 611
TOEFL requirement: Yes
Minimum TOEFL score: 600
Most popular departments: entrepreneurship, finance, leadership, manufacturing and technology management, marketing

Sonoma State University

1801 E. Cotati Avenue
Rohnert Park, CA 94928
http://www.sonoma.edu/ar/
Private
Admissions: (707) 664-2778
E-mail: rosanna.kelley@sonoma.edu
Financial aid: (707) 664-2389
Application deadline: 03/30
Tuition: full time: N/A; part time: $8,380
Room/board/expenses: N/A
College-funded aid: Yes
International student aid: Yes
Full-time enrollment: N/A
men: N/A; women: N/A;
minorities:N/A; international: N/A
Part-time enrollment: 58
men: 59%; women: 41%;
minorities:19%; international: 2%
Average GMAT (part time): 565
TOEFL requirement: Yes
Minimum TOEFL score: 550

Stanford University

655 Knight Way
Stanford, CA 94305-7298
http://www.gsb.stanford.edu/mba
Private
Admissions: (650) 723-2766
E-mail: mba.admissions@gsb.stanford.edu
Financial aid: (650) 723-3282
Application deadline: N/A
Tuition: full time: $57,300; part time: N/A
Room/board/expenses: $33,231
College-funded aid: Yes
International student aid: Yes
Average student indebtedness at graduation: $84,553
Full-time enrollment: 803
men: 65%; women: 35%;
minorities:24%; international: 31%
Part-time enrollment: N/A
men: N/A; women: N/A;
minorities:N/A; international: N/A
Acceptance rate (full time): 7%
Average GMAT (full time): 729
Average GPA (full time): 3.69
Average months of prior work experience (full time): 50
TOEFL requirement: Yes
Minimum TOEFL score: 600
Most popular departments: entrepreneurship, finance, general management, leadership, organizational behavior
Mean starting base salary for 2012 full-time graduates: $129,652
Employment location for 2012 class: Intl. 14%; N.E. 19%; M.A. 1%; S. 0%; M.W. 1%; S.W. 3%; W. 60%

University of California–Berkeley (Haas)

545 Student Services Building
Berkeley, CA 94720-1900
http://mba.haas.berkeley.edu
Public
Admissions: (510) 642-1405
E-mail: mbaadm@haas.berkeley.edu
Financial aid: (510) 643-0183
Application deadline: 03/12
In-state tuition: full time: $53,728; part time: $2,657/credit hour
Out-of-state tuition: full time: $56,275
Room/board/expenses: $23,542
College-funded aid: Yes
International student aid: Yes
Average student indebtedness at graduation: $63,652
Full-time enrollment: 490
men: 69%; women: 31%;
minorities:25%; international: 37%
Part-time enrollment: 803
men: 74%; women: 26%;
minorities:25%; international: 40%
Acceptance rate (full time): 14%
Average GMAT (full time): 715
Average GMAT (part time): 692
Average GPA (full time): 3.61
Average age of entrants to full-time program: 29
Average months of prior work experience (full time): 64
TOEFL requirement: Yes
Minimum TOEFL score: 570
Most popular departments: consulting, entrepreneurship, finance, leadership, marketing
Mean starting base salary for 2012 full-time graduates: $116,045
Employment location for 2012 class: Intl. 21%; N.E. 3%; M.A. 1%; S. 0%; M.W. 1%; S.W. 1%; W. 71%

University of California–Davis
1 Shields Avenue
Davis, CA 95616-8609
http://gsm.ucdavis.edu
Public
Admissions: (530) 752-7658
E-mail: admissions@gsm.ucdavis.edu
Financial aid: (530) 752-7658
Application deadline: 06/14
In-state tuition: full time: $36,447; total program: $75,600 (part-time)
Out-of-state tuition: full time: $48,692
Room/board/expenses: $20,051
College-funded aid: Yes
International student aid: Yes
Average student indebtedness at graduation: $62,145
Full-time enrollment: 100
men: 65%; women: 35%; minorities:23%; international: 30%
Part-time enrollment: 400
men: 68%; women: 32%; minorities:46%; international: 9%
Acceptance rate (full time): 19%
Average GMAT (full time): 680
Average GMAT (part time): 576
Average GPA (full time): 3.30
Average age of entrants to full-time program: 28
Average months of prior work experience (full time): 60
TOEFL requirement: Yes
Minimum TOEFL score: 600
Most popular departments: entrepreneurship, finance, general management, organizational behavior, technology
Mean starting base salary for 2012 full-time graduates: $91,569
Employment location for 2012 class: Intl. 3%; N.E. 0%; M.A. 3%; S. 3%; M.W. 3%; S.W. 0%; W. 89%

University of California–Irvine (Merage)
SB 350
Irvine, CA 92697-3125
http://www.merage.uci.edu
Public
Admissions: (949) 824-4622
E-mail: mba@merage.uci.edu
Financial aid: (949) 824-7967
Application deadline: 04/01
In-state tuition: full time: $37,945; part time: $31,011
Out-of-state tuition: full time: $46,584
Room/board/expenses: $26,302
College-funded aid: Yes
International student aid: Yes
Average student indebtedness at graduation: $42,466
Full-time enrollment: 215
men: 65%; women: 35%; minorities:24%; international: 43%
Part-time enrollment: 422
men: 67%; women: 33%; minorities:47%; international: 7%
Acceptance rate (full time): 33%
Average GMAT (full time): 657
Average GMAT (part time): 570
Average GPA (full time): 3.35
Average age of entrants to full-time program: 28
Average months of prior work experience (full time): 60
TOEFL requirement: Yes
Minimum TOEFL score: 600
Most popular departments: finance, marketing, management information systems, operations management, organizational behavior
Mean starting base salary for 2012 full-time graduates: $76,736
Employment location for 2012 class: Intl. 5%; N.E. 2%; M.A. 0%; S. 0%; M.W. 2%; S.W. 5%; W. 86%

University of California–Los Angeles (Anderson)
110 Westwood Plaza, Box 951481
Los Angeles, CA 90095-1481
http://www.anderson.ucla.edu
Public
Admissions: (310) 825-6944
E-mail: mba.admissions@anderson.ucla.edu
Financial aid: (310) 825-2746
Application deadline: 04/17
In-state tuition: full time: $48,243; part time: $37,590
Out-of-state tuition: full time: $54,530
Room/board/expenses: $23,512
College-funded aid: Yes
International student aid: Yes
Average student indebtedness at graduation: $71,995
Full-time enrollment: 737
men: 69%; women: 31%; minorities:27%; international: 32%
Part-time enrollment: 867
men: 73%; women: 27%; minorities:37%; international: 14%
Acceptance rate (full time): 23%
Average GMAT (full time): 704
Average GMAT (part time): 685
Average GPA (full time): 3.56
Average age of entrants to full-time program: 29
Average months of prior work experience (full time): 70
TOEFL requirement: Yes
Minimum TOEFL score: 560
Most popular departments: consulting, entrepreneurship, finance, marketing, technology
Mean starting base salary for 2012 full-time graduates: $105,556
Employment location for 2012 class: Intl. 12%; N.E. 6%; M.A. 1%; S. 1%; M.W. 3%; S.W. 1%; W. 77%

University of California–Riverside (Anderson)
900 University Avenue
Riverside, CA 92521-0203
http://www.agsm.ucr.edu/mba/
Public
Admissions: (951) 827-6200
E-mail: mba@ucr.edu
Financial aid: (951) 827-3878
Application deadline: 09/01
In-state tuition: full time: $37,495; part time: $20,461
Out-of-state tuition: full time: $49,740
Room/board/expenses: $15,045
College-funded aid: Yes
International student aid: Yes
Average student indebtedness at graduation: $50,531
Full-time enrollment: 184
men: 51%; women: 49%; minorities:26%; international: 74%
Part-time enrollment: 1
men: 100%; women: 0%; minorities:0%; international: 0%
Acceptance rate (full time): 54%
Average GMAT (full time): 578
Average GPA (full time): 3.38
Average age of entrants to full-time program: 24
Average months of prior work experience (full time): 18
TOEFL requirement: Yes
Minimum TOEFL score: 550
Most popular departments: e-commerce, finance, marketing, operations management, supply chain management
Mean starting base salary for 2012 full-time graduates: $49,403
Employment location for 2012 class: Intl. 38%; N.E. 3%; M.A. 0%; S. 3%; M.W. 0%; S.W. 3%; W. 53%

University of California–San Diego
9500 Gilman Drive #0553
San Diego, CA
http://www.rady.ucsd.edu/mba/
Public
Admissions: (858) 534-0864
E-mail: mbaadmissions@ucsd.edu
Financial aid: N/A
Application deadline: rolling
In-state tuition: full time: $41,783; part time: $1,065/credit hour
Out-of-state tuition: full time: $46,672
Room/board/expenses: N/A
College-funded aid: Yes
International student aid: Yes
Full-time enrollment: 54
men: 59%; women: 41%; minorities:22%; international: 46%
Part-time enrollment: 38
men: 66%; women: 34%; minorities:32%; international: 5%
Acceptance rate (full time): 37%
Average GMAT (full time): 680
Average GMAT (part time): 615
Average GPA (full time): 3.21
Average age of entrants to full-time program: 29
Average months of prior work experience (full time): 53
TOEFL requirement: Yes
Minimum TOEFL score: 550
Most popular departments: entrepreneurship, finance, marketing, operations management, technology
Mean starting base salary for 2012 full-time graduates: $76,014
Employment location for 2012 class: Intl. 6%; N.E. 0%; M.A. 0%; S. 0%; M.W. 0%; S.W. 0%; W. 94%

University of San Diego
5998 Alcala Park
San Diego, CA 92110-2492
http://www.sandiego.edu/mba
Private
Admissions: (619) 260-4860
E-mail: mba@sandiego.edu
Financial aid: (619) 260-4514
Application deadline: 05/15
Tuition: full time: $1,280/credit hour; part time: $1,280/credit hour
Room/board/expenses: $21,560
College-funded aid: Yes
International student aid: Yes
Full-time enrollment: 39
men: 74%; women: 26%; minorities:15%; international: 33%
Part-time enrollment: 150
men: 68%; women: 32%; minorities:17%; international: 6%
Acceptance rate (full time): 56%
Average GMAT (full time): 626
Average GMAT (part time): 616
Average GPA (full time): 3.25
Average age of entrants to full-time program: 27
Average months of prior work experience (full time): 45
TOEFL requirement: Yes
Minimum TOEFL score: 580
Most popular departments: finance, international business, marketing, supply chain management, other
Mean starting base salary for 2012 full-time graduates: $78,289
Employment location for 2012 class: Intl. 6%; N.E. N/A; M.A. N/A; S. N/A; M.W. N/A; S.W. N/A; W. 94%

University of San Francisco (Masagung)
2130 Fulton Street
San Francisco, CA 94117-1080
http://www.usfca.edu/management/graduate/
Private
Admissions: (415) 422-2221
E-mail: management@usfca.edu
Financial aid: (415) 422-2020
Application deadline: N/A
Tuition: full time: $1,235/credit hour; part time: $1,235/credit hour
Room/board/expenses: N/A
College-funded aid: Yes
International student aid: Yes
Average student indebtedness at graduation: $70,845
Full-time enrollment: 117
men: 54%; women: 46%; minorities:10%; international: 21%
Part-time enrollment: 139
men: 58%; women: 42%; minorities:20%; international: 7%
Acceptance rate (full time): 49%
Average GMAT (full time): 588
Average GMAT (part time): 569
Average GPA (full time): 3.10
Average age of entrants to full-time program: 27
Average months of prior work experience (full time): 48
TOEFL requirement: Yes
Minimum TOEFL score: 600
Most popular departments: entrepreneurship, finance, international business, marketing
Mean starting base salary for 2012 full-time graduates: $69,353
Employment location for 2012 class: Intl. 6%; N.E. N/A; M.A. 6%; S. N/A; M.W. N/A; S.W. N/A; W. 88%

University of Southern California (Marshall)
University Park
Los Angeles, CA 90089-1421
http://www.marshall.usc.edu
Private
Admissions: (213) 740-7846
E-mail: marshallmba@marshall.usc.edu
Financial aid: (213) 740-1111
Application deadline: 03/15
Tuition: full time: $48,515; part time: $1,511/credit hour
Room/board/expenses: $19,072
College-funded aid: Yes
International student aid: Yes
Full-time enrollment: 431
men: 70%; women: 30%; minorities:38%; international: 19%
Part-time enrollment: 729
men: 72%; women: 28%; minorities:48%; international: 2%
Acceptance rate (full time): 30%
Average GMAT (full time): 690
Average GMAT (part time): 602
Average GPA (full time): 3.34
Average age of entrants to full-time program: 27
Average months of prior work experience (full time): 58
TOEFL requirement: Yes
Minimum TOEFL score: 600
Most popular departments: entrepreneurship, finance, international business, marketing, other
Mean starting base salary for 2012 full-time graduates: $97,022
Employment location for 2012 class: Intl. 5%; N.E. 8%; M.A. 1%; S. 3%; M.W. 5%; S.W. 1%; W. 76%

University of the Pacific (Eberhardt)
3601 Pacific Avenue
Stockton, CA 95211
http://www.pacific.edu/mba
Private
Admissions: (209) 946-2629
E-mail: mba@pacific.edu
Financial aid: (209) 946-2421
Application deadline: 03/01
Tuition: total program: $61,591 (full-time); part time: N/A
Room/board/expenses: $23,308
College-funded aid: Yes
International student aid: Yes
Full-time enrollment: 41
men: 51%; women: 49%; minorities:37%; international: 29%
Part-time enrollment: N/A
men: N/A; women: N/A; minorities:N/A; international: N/A
Acceptance rate (full time): 57%
Average GMAT (full time): 593
Average GPA (full time): 3.37
Average age of entrants to full-time program: 24
Average months of prior work experience (full time): 12
TOEFL requirement: Yes
Minimum TOEFL score: 550
Most popular departments: entrepreneurship, finance, health care administration, marketing, sports business
Mean starting base salary for 2012 full-time graduates: $66,675
Employment location for 2012 class: Intl. 8%; N.E. N/A; M.A. N/A; S. N/A; M.W. N/A; S.W. N/A; W. 92%

COLORADO

Colorado State University
110 Rockwell Hall West
Fort Collins, CO 80523-1270
http://www.csumba.com
Public
Admissions: (970) 491-3704
E-mail: gradadmissions@business.colostate.edu
Financial aid: (970) 491-6321
Application deadline: 07/15
In-state tuition: full time: N/A; part time: $795/credit hour
Out-of-state tuition: full time: N/A
Room/board/expenses: N/A
College-funded aid: Yes
International student aid: Yes
Full-time enrollment: N/A
men: N/A; women: N/A; minorities:N/A; international: N/A
Part-time enrollment: 35
men: 66%; women: 34%; minorities:14%; international: 14%
Average GMAT (part time): 540
TOEFL requirement: Yes
Minimum TOEFL score: 565
Most popular departments: accounting, finance, marketing, other

Colorado State University–Pueblo
2200 Bonforte Boulevard
Pueblo, CO 81001
http://hsb.colostate-pueblo.edu
Public
Admissions: (719) 549-2461
E-mail: info@colostate-pueblo.edu
Financial aid: N/A
Application deadline: rolling
In-state tuition: full time: $235/credit hour; part time: $235/credit hour
Out-of-state tuition: full time: $699/credit hour
Room/board/expenses: N/A
College-funded aid: Yes
International student aid: Yes

More at www.usnews.com/grad

Full-time enrollment: 49
men: 80%; women: 20%; minorities:N/A; international: N/A
Part-time enrollment: 19
men: 47%; women: 53%; minorities:N/A; international: N/A
TOEFL requirement: Yes
Minimum TOEFL score: 550

University of Colorado–Boulder (Leeds)

995 Regent Drive 419 UCB
Boulder, CO 80309
http://leeds.colorado.edu/mba
Public
Admissions: (303) 492-8397
E-mail: leedsmba@Colorado.edu
Financial aid: (303) 492-8223
Application deadline: 04/01
In-state tuition: full time: $16,718; total program: $48,000 (part-time)
Out-of-state tuition: full time: $31,334
Room/board/expenses: $18,692
College-funded aid: Yes
International student aid: Yes
Average student indebtedness at graduation: $26,517
Full-time enrollment: 186
men: 72%; women: 28%; minorities:8%; international: 21%
Part-time enrollment: 96
men: 77%; women: 23%; minorities:7%; international: 6%
Acceptance rate (full time): 62%
Average GMAT (full time): 623
Average GMAT (part time): 615
Average GPA (full time): 3.32
Average age of entrants to full-time program: 29
Average months of prior work experience (full time): 58
TOEFL requirement: Yes
Minimum TOEFL score: 600
Mean starting base salary for 2012 full-time graduates: $76,750
Employment location for 2012 class: Intl. 0%; N.E. 3%; M.A. 0%; S. 2%; M.W. 2%; S.W. 90%; W. 3%

University of Colorado–Colorado Springs

1420 Austin Bluffs Parkway
Colorado Springs, CO 80918
http://www.uccs.edu/mba
Public
Admissions: (719) 255-3408
E-mail: mba@uccs.edu
Financial aid: (719) 255-3460
Application deadline: 06/01
In-state tuition: full time: N/A; part time: $615/credit hour
Out-of-state tuition: full time: N/A
Room/board/expenses: N/A
College-funded aid: Yes
International student aid: No
Full-time enrollment: N/A
men: N/A; women: N/A; minorities:N/A; international: N/A
Part-time enrollment: 235
men: N/A; women: N/A; minorities:N/A; international: N/A
Average GMAT (part time): 572
TOEFL requirement: Yes
Minimum TOEFL score: 550
Most popular departments: accounting, finance, general management, international business, marketing

University of Colorado–Denver

Campus Box 165, PO Box 173364
Denver, CO 80217-3364
http://www.ucdenver.edu/business/
Public
Admissions: (303) 315-8200
E-mail: grad.business@ucdenver.edu
Financial aid: (303) 556-2886
Application deadline: rolling
In-state tuition: full time: N/A; part time: N/A
Out-of-state tuition: full time: N/A
Room/board/expenses: N/A
College-funded aid: Yes
International student aid: Yes
Full-time enrollment: N/A
men: N/A; women: N/A; minorities:N/A; international: N/A
Part-time enrollment: 735
men: 61%; women: 39%; minorities:13%; international: 4%
Average GMAT (part time): 580
TOEFL requirement: Yes
Minimum TOEFL score: 560

University of Denver (Daniels)

2101 S. University Boulevard
Denver, CO 80208
http://www.daniels.du.edu/
Private
Admissions: (303) 871-3416
E-mail: daniels@du.edu
Financial aid: (303) 871-3416
Application deadline: rolling
Tuition: full time: $43,290; part time: $40,356
Room/board/expenses: $15,200
College-funded aid: Yes
International student aid: Yes
Full-time enrollment: 178
men: 59%; women: 41%; minorities:7%; international: 31%
Part-time enrollment: 159
men: 67%; women: 33%; minorities:16%; international: 2%
Acceptance rate (full time): 75%
Average GMAT (full time): 607
Average GMAT (part time): 573
Average GPA (full time): 3.26
Average age of entrants to full-time program: 25
Average months of prior work experience (full time): 49
TOEFL requirement: Yes
Minimum TOEFL score: 570
Most popular departments: accounting, entrepreneurship, general management, international business, marketing
Mean starting base salary for 2012 full-time graduates: $61,609
Employment location for 2012 class: Intl. 0%; N.E. 3%; M.A. 0%; S. 0%; M.W. 3%; S.W. 85%; W. 9%

University of Northern Colorado (Monfort)[1]

800 17th Street
Greeley, CO 80639
http://mcb.unco.edu
Public
Admissions: N/A
Financial aid: N/A
Tuition: N/A
Room/board/expenses: N/A
Enrollment: N/A

CONNECTICUT

Fairfield University (Dolan)

1073 N. Benson Road
Fairfield, CT 06824
http://www.fairfield.edu/dsb/dsb_grad_1.html
Private
Admissions: (203) 254-4000
E-mail: dsbgrad@fairfield.edu
Financial aid: (203) 254-4125
Application deadline: rolling
Tuition: full time: $780/credit hour; part time: $780/credit hour
Room/board/expenses: N/A
College-funded aid: Yes
International student aid: Yes
Full-time enrollment: 84
men: 58%; women: 42%; minorities:38%; international: 37%
Part-time enrollment: 69
men: 64%; women: 36%; minorities:49%; international: 3%
Acceptance rate (full time): 49%
Average GMAT (full time): 531
Average GMAT (part time): 531
Average GPA (full time): 3.45
Average age of entrants to full-time program: 23
TOEFL requirement: Yes
Minimum TOEFL score: 550
Most popular departments: accounting, finance, general management, human resources management, marketing

Quinnipiac University

275 Mount Carmel Avenue
Hamden, CT 06518
http://www.quinnipiac.edu/
Private
Admissions: (800) 462-1944
E-mail: graduate@quinnipiac.edu
Financial aid: (203) 582-8384
Application deadline: rolling
Tuition: full time: $895/credit hour; part time: $895/credit hour
Room/board/expenses: $19,196
College-funded aid: Yes
International student aid: Yes
Average student indebtedness at graduation: $31,715
Full-time enrollment: 103
men: 48%; women: 52%; minorities:10%; international: 21%
Part-time enrollment: 204
men: 57%; women: 43%; minorities:11%; international: 1%
Acceptance rate (full time): 94%
Average GMAT (full time): 557
Average GMAT (part time): 497
Average GPA (full time): 3.47
Average age of entrants to full-time program: 23
TOEFL requirement: Yes
Minimum TOEFL score: 575
Most popular departments: finance, general management, health care administration, marketing, supply chain management

Sacred Heart University (Welch)

5151 Park Avenue
Fairfield, CT 06825
http://www.sacredheart.edu/johnfwelchcob.cfm
Private
Admissions: (203) 365-7619
E-mail: gradstudies@sacredheart.edu
Financial aid: (203) 371-7980
Application deadline: rolling
Tuition: full time: N/A; part time: $750/credit hour
Room/board/expenses: N/A
College-funded aid: Yes
International student aid: Yes
Full-time enrollment: N/A
men: N/A; women: N/A; minorities:N/A; international: N/A
Part-time enrollment: 198
men: 48%; women: 52%; minorities:19%; international: 3%
Average GMAT (part time): 520
TOEFL requirement: Yes
Minimum TOEFL score: 570

University of Connecticut

2100 Hillside Road, Unit 1041
Storrs, CT 06269-1041
http://www.business.uconn.edu
Public
Admissions: (860) 486-2872
E-mail: uconnmba@business.uconn.edu
Financial aid: (860) 486-2819
Application deadline: 03/01
In-state tuition: full time: $14,950; part time: $680/credit hour
Out-of-state tuition: full time: $32,158
Room/board/expenses: $24,500
College-funded aid: Yes
International student aid: Yes
Average student indebtedness at graduation: $32,742
Full-time enrollment: 91
men: 67%; women: 33%; minorities:12%; international: 49%
Part-time enrollment: 1,094
men: 68%; women: 32%; minorities:17%; international: 1%
Acceptance rate (full time): 49%
Average GMAT (full time): 654
Average GMAT (part time): 576
Average GPA (full time): 3.48
Average age of entrants to full-time program: 29
Average months of prior work experience (full time): 67
TOEFL requirement: Yes
Minimum TOEFL score: 575
Most popular departments: finance, health care administration, marketing, management information systems, real estate
Mean starting base salary for 2012 full-time graduates: $77,536
Employment location for 2012 class: Intl. 6%; N.E. 81%; M.A. 11%; S. 0%; M.W. 0%; S.W. 3%; W. 0%

University of Hartford (Barney)

200 Bloomfield Avenue
West Hartford, CT 06117
http://www.hartford.edu/barney
Private
Admissions: (860) 768-5003
E-mail: spierce@hartford.edu
Financial aid: (860) 768-4900
Application deadline: 08/15
Tuition: full time: $580/credit hour; part time: $580/credit hour
Room/board/expenses: N/A
College-funded aid: Yes
International student aid: Yes
Full-time enrollment: 73
men: N/A; women: N/A; minorities:N/A; international: N/A
Part-time enrollment: 352
men: N/A; women: N/A; minorities:N/A; international: N/A
Acceptance rate (full time): 48%
Average GMAT (full time): 540
Average GMAT (part time): 540
Average GPA (full time): 3.25
Average age of entrants to full-time program: 33
TOEFL requirement: Yes
Minimum TOEFL score: 550
Most popular departments: accounting, finance, general management, international business, marketing

Yale University

Box 208200
New Haven, CT 06520-8200
http://mba.yale.edu
Private
Admissions: (203) 432-5635
E-mail: mba.admissions@yale.edu
Financial aid: (203) 432-5635
Application deadline: N/A
Tuition: full time: $56,530; part time: N/A
Room/board/expenses: $25,640
College-funded aid: Yes
International student aid: Yes
Average student indebtedness at graduation: $95,235
Full-time enrollment: 494
men: 65%; women: 35%; minorities:24%; international: 28%
Part-time enrollment: N/A
men: N/A; women: N/A; minorities:N/A; international: N/A
Acceptance rate (full time): 21%
Average GMAT (full time): 717
Average GPA (full time): 3.55
Average age of entrants to full-time program: 28
Average months of prior work experience (full time): 64
TOEFL requirement: No
Minimum TOEFL score: N/A
Mean starting base salary for 2012 full-time graduates: $104,147
Employment location for 2012 class: Intl. 10%; N.E. 53%; M.A. 9%; S. 4%; M.W. 5%; S.W. 3%; W. 16%

DELAWARE

Delaware State University

1200 DuPont Highway
Dover, DE 19901
http://www.desu.edu/business-administration-mba-program
Public
Admissions: (302) 857-6930
E-mail: ksheth@desu.edu
Financial aid: N/A
Application deadline: rolling
In-state tuition: full time: $417/credit hour; part time: $417/credit hour
Out-of-state tuition: full time: $920/credit hour
Room/board/expenses: $18,472
College-funded aid: Yes
International student aid: Yes
Full-time enrollment: 91
men: 45%; women: 55%; minorities:30%; international: 42%
Part-time enrollment: 11
men: 45%; women: 55%; minorities:45%; international: N/A
Acceptance rate (full time): 68%
Average GMAT (full time): 476
Average age of entrants to full-time program: 26
TOEFL requirement: Yes
Minimum TOEFL score: 550

University of Delaware (Lerner)

103 Alfred Lerner Hall
Newark, DE 19716
http://www.mba.udel.edu
Public
Admissions: (302) 831-2221
E-mail: mbaprogram@udel.edu
Financial aid: (302) 831-8761
Application deadline: rolling
In-state tuition: full time: $15,472; part time: $757/credit hour
Out-of-state tuition: full time: $29,092
Room/board/expenses: $14,408
College-funded aid: Yes
International student aid: Yes
Full-time enrollment: 102
men: 50%; women: 50%; minorities:10%; international: 69%
Part-time enrollment: 249
men: 38%; women: 62%; minorities:21%; international: 4%
Acceptance rate (full time): 39%
Average GMAT (full time): 624
Average GMAT (part time): 561
Average age of entrants to full-time program: 27
Average months of prior work experience (full time): 49
TOEFL requirement: Yes
Minimum TOEFL score: 600

DISTRICT OF COLUMBIA

American University (Kogod)

4400 Massachusetts Avenue NW
Washington, DC 20016
http://www.kogod.american.edu
Private
Admissions: (202) 885-1913
E-mail: kogodgrad@american.edu

Financial aid: (202) 885-1907
Application deadline: rolling
Tuition: full time: $33,444; total program: $71,400 (part-time)
Room/board/expenses: $20,000
College-funded aid: Yes
International student aid: Yes
Full-time enrollment: 94
men: N/A; women: N/A; minorities:N/A; international: N/A
Part-time enrollment: 107
men: N/A; women: N/A; minorities:N/A; international: N/A
Acceptance rate (full time): 42%
Average GMAT (full time): 550
Average GMAT (part time): 545
Average GPA (full time): 3.18
Average age of entrants to full-time program: 28
Average months of prior work experience (full time): 50
TOEFL requirement: Yes
Minimum TOEFL score: N/A
Mean starting base salary for 2012 full-time graduates: $68,540
Employment location for 2012 class: Intl: 8%; N.E. 11%; M.A. 67%; S. 8%; M.W. 3%; S.W. 3%; W. 0%

Georgetown University (McDonough)

Rafik B. Hariri Building
37th and O Streets NW
Washington, DC 20057
http://msb.georgetown.edu
Private
Admissions: (202) 687-4200
E-mail: georgetownmba@georgetown.edu
Financial aid: (202) 687-4547
Application deadline: N/A
Tuition: full time: $51,925; part time: $1,455/credit hour
Room/board/expenses: $27,500
College-funded aid: Yes
International student aid: Yes
Average student indebtedness at graduation: $51,750
Full-time enrollment: 506
men: 70%; women: 30%; minorities:19%; international: 31%
Part-time enrollment: 377
men: 68%; women: 32%; minorities:19%; international: 5%
Acceptance rate (full time): 49%
Average GMAT (full time): 683
Average GMAT (part time): 665
Average GPA (full time): 3.32
Average age of entrants to full-time program: 28
Average months of prior work experience (full time): 61
TOEFL requirement: Yes
Minimum TOEFL score: 600
Most popular departments: consulting, finance, general management, international business, marketing
Mean starting base salary for 2012 full-time graduates: $99,799
Employment location for 2012 class: Intl: 7%; N.E. 34%; M.A. 35%; S. 8%; M.W. 9%; S.W. 2%; W. 7%

George Washington University

2201 G Street NW
Washington, DC 20052
http://business.gwu.edu/grad/mba/
Private
Admissions: (202) 994-1212
E-mail: gwmba@gwu.edu
Financial aid: (202) 994-6822
Application deadline: 03/15
Tuition: full time: $1,420/credit hour; part time: $1,420/credit hour
Room/board/expenses: $28,457
College-funded aid: Yes
International student aid: Yes
Average student indebtedness at graduation: $84,410

Full-time enrollment: 239
men: 64%; women: 36%; minorities:19%; international 32%
Part-time enrollment: 409
men: 55%; women: 45%; minorities:31%; international: 4%
Acceptance rate (full time): 50%
Average GMAT (full time): 632
Average GMAT (part time): 579
Average GPA (full time): 3.29
Average age of entrants to full-time program: 28
Average months of prior work experience (full time): 48
TOEFL requirement: Yes
Minimum TOEFL score: 600
Most popular departments: consulting, general management, international business, non-profit management, public policy
Mean starting base salary for 2012 full-time graduates: $84,208
Employment location for 2012 class: Intl. 12%; N.E. 12%; M.A. 60%; S. 4%; M.W. 5%; S.W. 0%; W. 7%

Howard University

2600 Sixth Street NW, Suite 236
Washington, DC 20059
http://www.bschool.howard.edu
Private
Admissions: (202) 806-1725
E-mail: MBA_bschool@howard.edu
Financial aid: (202) 806-2820
Application deadline: 05/15
Tuition: full time: $32,523; part time: $1,740/credit hour
Room/board/expenses: $25,271
College-funded aid: Yes
International student aid: Yes
Average student indebtedness at graduation: $34,993
Full-time enrollment: 65
men: 42%; women: 58%; minorities:80%; international: 20%
Part-time enrollment: 30
men: 50%; women: 50%; minorities:100%; international: N/A
Acceptance rate (full time): 44%
Average GMAT (full time): 542
Average GPA (full time): 3.05
Average age of entrants to full-time program: 26
Average months of prior work experience (full time): 47
TOEFL requirement: Yes
Minimum TOEFL score: 550
Most popular departments: entrepreneurship, finance, general management, marketing, supply chain management
Mean starting base salary for 2012 full-time graduates: $92,455
Employment location for 2012 class: Intl. N/A; N.E. 39%; M.A. 39%; S. 4%; M.W. 9%; S.W. 4%; W. 4%

FLORIDA

Barry University (Andreas)

11300 N.E. Second Avenue
Miami Shores, FL 33161-6695
http://www.barry.edu/mba
Private
Admissions: (305) 899-3146
E-mail: dfletcher@mail.barry.edu
Financial aid: (305) 899-3673
Application deadline: rolling
Tuition: total program: $33,660 (full-time); $33,660 (part-time)
Room/board/expenses: N/A
College-funded aid: Yes
International student aid: Yes
Full-time enrollment: N/A
men: N/A; women: N/A; minorities:N/A; international: N/A
Part-time enrollment: 107
men: 64%; women: 36%; minorities:38%; international: 42%
Average GMAT (part time): 518
TOEFL requirement: Yes

Minimum TOEFL score: 550
Most popular departments: finance, general management, international business, marketing, sports business

Florida Atlantic University

777 Glades Road
Boca Raton, FL 33431
http://www.business.fau.edu
Public
Admissions: (561) 297-3624
E-mail: graduatecollege@fau.edu
Financial aid: (561) 297-3131
Application deadline: 07/01
In-state tuition: full time: $303/credit hour; part time: $303/credit hour
Out-of-state tuition: full time: $927/credit hour
Room/board/expenses: $27,600
College-funded aid: Yes
International student aid: Yes
Full-time enrollment: 109
men: 61%; women: 39%; minorities:32%; international: 7%
Part-time enrollment: 202
men: 55%; women: 45%; minorities:38%; international: 5%
Average GMAT (part time): 536
TOEFL requirement: Yes
Minimum TOEFL score: 600
Most popular departments: accounting, economics, general management, health care administration, tax

Florida Gulf Coast University (Lutgert)

10501 FGCU Boulevard S
Fort Myers, FL 33965-6565
http://www.fgcu.edu/cob/
Public
Admissions: (239) 590-7988
E-mail: graduate@fgcu.edu
Financial aid: (239) 590-7920
Application deadline: 05/01
In-state tuition: full time: $10,362; part time: N/A
Out-of-state tuition: full time: $33,133
Room/board/expenses: $11,242
College-funded aid: Yes
International student aid: Yes
Full-time enrollment: 50
men: 64%; women: 36%; minorities:14%; international: 10%
Part-time enrollment: 93
men: 42%; women: 58%; minorities:22%; international: 1%
Average GMAT (full time): 528
Average GMAT (part time): 505
Average GPA (full time): 3.19
Average age of entrants to full-time program: 26
TOEFL requirement: Yes
Minimum TOEFL score: 550

Florida International University

1050 S.W. 112 Avenue, CBC 300
Miami, FL 33199-0001
http://business.fiu.edu
Public
Admissions: (305) 348-7398
E-mail: chapman@fiu.edu
Financial aid: (305) 348-7272
Application deadline: rolling
In-state tuition: total program: $34,000 (full-time); $45,000 (part-time)
Out-of-state tuition: total program: $39,000 (full-time)
Room/board/expenses: $18,000
College-funded aid: Yes
International student aid: Yes
Full-time enrollment: 65
men: 62%; women: 38%; minorities:38%; international: 45%

Part-time enrollment: 1,010
men: 50%; women: 50%; minorities:64%; international: 20%
Acceptance rate (full time): 45%
Average GMAT (full time): 568
Average GMAT (part time): 544
Average GPA (full time): 3.36
Average age of entrants to full-time program: 25
Average months of prior work experience (full time): 36
TOEFL requirement: Yes
Minimum TOEFL score: 550
Most popular departments: entrepreneurship, finance, general management, health care administration, international business
Mean starting base salary for 2012 full-time graduates: $49,443

Florida State University

Graduate Programs
233 Rovetta Building
Tallahassee, FL 32306-1110
http://www.cob.fsu.edu/grad
Public
Admissions: (850) 644-6455
E-mail: lbeverly@cob.fsu.edu
Financial aid: (850) 644-5716
Application deadline: rolling
In-state tuition: full time: $750/credit hour; part time: $750/credit hour
Out-of-state tuition: full time: $750/credit hour
Room/board/expenses: $29,250
College-funded aid: Yes
International student aid: Yes
Average student indebtedness at graduation: $24,000
Full-time enrollment: 215
men: 70%; women: 30%; minorities:13%; international: 6%
Part-time enrollment: 109
men: 66%; women: 34%; minorities:17%; international: 2%
Acceptance rate (full time): 58%
Average GMAT (full time): 580
Average GMAT (part time): 580
Average GPA (full time): 3.35
Average age of entrants to full-time program: 25
Average months of prior work experience (full time): 28
TOEFL requirement: Yes
Minimum TOEFL score: 600
Most popular departments: accounting, finance, general management, marketing, real estate

Jacksonville University[1]

2800 University Boulevard N
Jacksonville, FL 32211
http://dcob.ju.edu
Private
Admissions: N/A
Financial aid: N/A
Tuition: N/A
Room/board/expenses: N/A
Enrollment: N/A

Rollins College (Crummer)

1000 Holt Avenue
Winter Park, FL 32789-4499
http://www.rollins.edu/mba/
Private
Admissions: (800) 866-2405
E-mail: jbrito@rollins.edu
Financial aid: (407) 646-2395
Application deadline: rolling
Tuition: full time: $33,000; part time: $1,104/credit hour
Room/board/expenses: $16,000
College-funded aid: Yes
International student aid: Yes

Average student indebtedness at graduation: $59,169
Full-time enrollment: 127
men: 56%; women: 44%; minorities:15%; international: 16%
Part-time enrollment: 124
men: 65%; women: 35%; minorities:27%; international: 1%
Acceptance rate (full time): 37%
Average GMAT (full time): 580
Average GMAT (part time): 537
Average GPA (full time): 3.44
Average age of entrants to full-time program: 23
Average months of prior work experience (full time): 15
TOEFL requirement: Yes
Minimum TOEFL score: 600
Most popular departments: entrepreneurship, finance, general management, international business, marketing
Mean starting base salary for 2012 full-time graduates: $48,253
Employment location for 2012 class: Intl. 5%; N.E. 5%; M.A. 2%; S. 82%; M.W. 0%; S.W. 3%; W. 3%

Stetson University

421 N. Woodland Boulevard, Unit 8398
DeLand, FL 32723
http://www.stetson.edu/mba
Private
Admissions: (386) 822-7100
E-mail: admissions@stetson.edu
Financial aid: (800) 688-7120
Application deadline: 06/30
Tuition: full time: $835/credit hour; part time: $835/credit hour
Room/board/expenses: N/A
College-funded aid: Yes
International student aid: Yes
Full-time enrollment: 98
men: 51%; women: 49%; minorities:16%; international: 12%
Part-time enrollment: 33
men: 55%; women: 45%; minorities:24%; international: 0%
Average GMAT (full time): 563
Average GMAT (part time): 493
Average GPA (full time): 3.42
Average age of entrants to full-time program: 28
TOEFL requirement: Yes
Minimum TOEFL score: 550

University of Central Florida

PO Box 161400
Orlando, FL 32816-1400
http://www.ucfmba.ucf.edu
Public
Admissions: (407) 823-4723
E-mail: graduate@mail.ucf.edu
Financial aid: (407) 823-2827
Application deadline: rolling
In-state tuition: full time: $14,327; part time: $4,408
Out-of-state tuition: full time: $46,478
Room/board/expenses: $14,522
College-funded aid: Yes
International student aid: Yes
Average student indebtedness at graduation: $31,961
Full-time enrollment: 45
men: 56%; women: 44%; minorities:22%; international: 2%
Part-time enrollment: 339
men: 58%; women: 42%; minorities:24%; international: 6%
Acceptance rate (full time): 45%
Average GMAT (full time): 613
Average GMAT (part time): 538
Average GPA (full time): 3.50
Average age of entrants to full-time program: 25
TOEFL requirement: Yes
Minimum TOEFL score: 575
Mean starting base salary for 2012 full-time graduates: $46,700

Employment location for 2012 class:
Intl. 0%; N.E. 0%; M.A. 0%; S.
100%; M.W. 0%; S.W. 0%; W. 0%

University of Florida (Hough)

Hough Hall 310
Gainesville, FL 32611-7152
http://www.floridamba.ufl.edu
Public
Admissions: (352) 392-7992
E-mail: traditionalmba@
warrington.ufl.edu
Financial aid: (352) 392-1275
Application deadline: 01/15
In-state tuition: full time: $12,589;
part time: $22,433
Out-of-state tuition: full time:
$29,983
Room/board/expenses: $15,690
College-funded aid: Yes
International student aid: Yes
Average student indebtedness at
graduation: $30,748
Full-time enrollment: 116
men: 64%; women: 36%;
minorities:10%; international: 13%
Part-time enrollment: 370
men: 72%; women: 28%;
minorities:19%; international: 11%
Acceptance rate (full time): 21%
Average GMAT (full time): 695
Average GMAT (part time): 580
Average GPA (full time): 3.46
Average age of entrants to full-time
program: 27
Average months of prior work
experience (full time): 40
TOEFL requirement: Yes
Minimum TOEFL score: 550
Most popular departments:
consulting, entrepreneurship,
finance, general management,
marketing
Mean starting base salary for 2012
full-time graduates: $73,791
Employment location for 2012 class:
Intl. 0%; N.E. 7%; M.A. 7%; S.
78%; M.W. 7%; S.W. 0%; W. 0%

University of Miami

PO Box 248027
Coral Gables, FL 33124-6520
http://www.bus.miami.edu/grad
Private
Admissions: (305) 284-2510
E-mail: mba@miami.edu
Financial aid: (305) 284-5212
Application deadline: 06/03
Tuition: full time: $1,660/credit
hour; part time: N/A
Room/board/expenses: $20,711
College-funded aid: Yes
International student aid: Yes
Average student indebtedness at
graduation: $58,929
Full-time enrollment: 156
men: 65%; women: 35%;
minorities:19%; international: 42%
Part-time enrollment: N/A
men: N/A; women: N/A;
minorities:N/A; international: N/A
Acceptance rate (full time): 45%
Average GMAT (full time): 630
Average GPA (full time): 3.28
Average age of entrants to full-time
program: 25
Average months of prior work
experience (full time): 18
TOEFL requirement: Yes
Minimum TOEFL score: 587
Most popular departments: finance,
general management, internation-
al business, marketing, statistics
and operations research
Mean starting base salary for 2012
full-time graduates: $62,613
Employment location for 2012 class:
Intl. 6%; N.E. 9%; M.A. 15%; S.
61%; M.W. 3%; S.W. 0%; W. 6%

University of North Florida (Coggin)

1 UNF Drive
Jacksonville, FL 32224-2645
http://www.unf.edu/coggin
Public
Admissions: (904) 620-1360
E-mail: kmartin@unf.edu
Financial aid: (904) 620-5555
Application deadline: 07/01
In-state tuition: full time: $11,593;
part time: $483/credit hour
Out-of-state tuition: full time:
$24,983
Room/board/expenses: $19,900
College-funded aid: Yes
International student aid: Yes
Average student indebtedness at
graduation: $27,554
Full-time enrollment: 113
men: 57%; women: 43%;
minorities:17%; international: 27%
Part-time enrollment: 275
men: 62%; women: 38%;
minorities:13%; international: 1%
Average GMAT (part time): 561
TOEFL requirement: Yes
Minimum TOEFL score: 550
Most popular departments:
accounting, finance, general
management, international
business

University of South Florida

4202 Fowler Avenue
Tampa, FL 33620
http://www.mba.usf.edu
Public
Admissions: (813) 974-3335
E-mail: mba@coba.usf.edu
Financial aid: (813) 974-4700
Application deadline: 07/01
In-state tuition: full time: $467/
credit hour; part time: $467/
credit hour
Out-of-state tuition: full time: $891/
credit hour
Room/board/expenses: $16,500
College-funded aid: Yes
International student aid: Yes
Full-time enrollment: 356
men: 60%; women: 40%;
minorities:10%; international: 38%
Part-time enrollment: 307
men: 60%; women: 40%;
minorities:25%; international: 13%
Acceptance rate (full time): 74%
Average GMAT (full time): 566
Average GMAT (part time): 558
Average GPA (full time): 3.32
Average age of entrants to full-time
program: 26
Average months of prior work
experience (full time): 45
TOEFL requirement: Yes
Minimum TOEFL score: 550
Most popular departments:
entrepreneurship, finance,
general management, marketing,
management information systems
Mean starting base salary for 2012
full-time graduates: $58,894
Employment location for 2012 class:
Intl. N/A; N.E. 21%; M.A. N/A; S.
76%; M.W. N/A; S.W. 3%; W. N/A

University of South Florida–Sarasota-Manatee

8350 N. Tamiami Trail
Sarasota, FL 34243
http://www.usfsm.edu/
academics/cob
Public
Admissions: N/A
Financial aid: N/A
Application deadline: 07/01
In-state tuition: full time: $418/
credit hour; part time: $418/
credit hour
Out-of-state tuition: full time: $842/
credit hour

Room/board/expenses: N/A
College-funded aid: Yes
International student aid: Yes
Average student indebtedness at
graduation: N/A
Full-time enrollment: 6
men: 50%; women: 50%;
minorities:17%; international: 0%
Part-time enrollment: 38
men: 66%; women: 34%;
minorities:24%; international: 0%
Acceptance rate (full time): 10%
Average GMAT (full time): 470
Average GMAT (part time): 504
Average GPA (full time): 3.87
Average age of entrants to full-time
program: 39
Average months of prior work
experience (full time): 27
TOEFL requirement: Yes
Minimum TOEFL score: 550

University of South Florida–St. Petersburg

COB 348, 140 Seventh Avenue S
St. Petersburg, FL 33701
http://www.stpt.usf.edu/cob/
graduate/index.HTM
Public
Admissions: N/A
E-mail: mba@stpt.usf.edu
Financial aid: N/A
Application deadline: rolling
In-state tuition: full time: $460/
credit hour; part time: $460/
credit hour
Out-of-state tuition: full time: $885/
credit hour
Room/board/expenses: N/A
College-funded aid: Yes
International student aid: Yes
Full-time enrollment: 36
men: 47%; women: 53%;
minorities:22%; international: 11%
Part-time enrollment: 117
men: 50%; women: 50%;
minorities:23%; international: 3%
Acceptance rate (full time): 31%
Average GMAT (full time): 580
Average GMAT (part time): 540
Average GPA (full time): 3.50
Average age of entrants to full-time
program: 25
TOEFL requirement: Yes
Minimum TOEFL score: 550

University of Tampa (Sykes)

401 W. Kennedy Boulevard
Tampa, FL 33606-1490
http://grad.ut.edu
Private
Admissions: (813) 257-3642
E-mail: utgrad@ut.edu
Financial aid: (813) 253-6219
Application deadline: rolling
Tuition: full time: $535/credit hour;
part time: $535/credit hour
Room/board/expenses: $18,541
College-funded aid: Yes
International student aid: Yes
Average student indebtedness at
graduation: $26,806
Full-time enrollment: 311
men: 54%; women: 46%;
minorities:11%; international: 38%
Part-time enrollment: 198
men: 55%; women: 45%;
minorities:13%; international: 3%
Acceptance rate (full time): 42%
Average GMAT (full time): 550
Average GMAT (part time): 550
Average GPA (full time): 3.40
Average age of entrants to full-time
program: 25
Average months of prior work
experience (full time): 10
TOEFL requirement: Yes
Minimum TOEFL score: 577
Most popular departments: ac-
counting, economics, finance,
general management, marketing

Mean starting base salary for 2012
full-time graduates: $60,227
Employment location for 2012 class:
Intl. 24%; N.E. 3%; M.A. 9%; S.
56%; M.W. 9%; S.W. 0%; W. 0%

University of West Florida

11000 University Parkway
Pensacola, FL 32514
http://www.uwf.edu
Public
Admissions: (850) 474-2230
E-mail: mba@uwf.edu
Financial aid: (850) 474-2400
Application deadline: rolling
In-state tuition: full time: $353/
credit hour; part time: $353/
credit hour
Out-of-state tuition: full time:
$1,013/credit hour
Room/board/expenses: $13,718
College-funded aid: Yes
International student aid: Yes
Full-time enrollment: 23
men: 48%; women: 52%;
minorities:9%; international: 22%
Part-time enrollment: 110
men: 62%; women: 38%;
minorities:16%; international: 9%
Average GMAT (full time): 503
Average GMAT (part time): 448
Average GPA (full time): 3.12
Average age of entrants to full-time
program: 28
TOEFL requirement: Yes
Minimum TOEFL score: 550
Most popular departments:
accounting, tax, other

GEORGIA

Augusta State University[1]

2500 Walton Way
Augusta, GA 30904-2200
http://hull.aug.edu
Public
Admissions: (706) 737-1565
E-mail: mbainfo@aug.edu
Financial aid: (706) 737-1431
Tuition: N/A
Room/board/expenses: N/A
Enrollment: N/A

Berry College (Campbell)[1]

PO Box 495024
Mount Berry, GA 30149-5024
http://campbell.berry.edu
Private
Admissions: (706) 236-2215
E-mail: admissions@berry.edu
Financial aid: (706) 236-1714
Tuition: N/A
Room/board/expenses: N/A
Enrollment: N/A

Clark Atlanta University

223 James P. Brawley Drive SW
Atlanta, GA 30314
http://www.cau.edu
Private
Admissions: (404) 880-8443
E-mail: pkamos@cau.edu
Financial aid: (404) 880-6265
Application deadline: rolling
Tuition: full time: $792/credit hour;
part time: $792/credit hour
Room/board/expenses: $17,527
College-funded aid: Yes
International student aid: Yes
Full-time enrollment: 69
men: 52%; women: 48%;
minorities:87%; international: 7%
Part-time enrollment: 10
men: 30%; women: 70%;
minorities:90%; international: 10%
Acceptance rate (full time): 98%

Average GMAT (full time): 400
Average GPA (full time): 3.12
Average age of entrants to full-time
program: 24
Average months of prior work
experience (full time): 28
TOEFL requirement: Yes
Minimum TOEFL score: 500
Most popular departments:
accounting, economics,
finance, marketing, supply
chain management
Mean starting base salary for 2012
full-time graduates: $78,842
Employment location for 2012 class:
Intl. 0%; N.E. 17%; M.A. 8%; S.
25%; M.W. 42%; S.W. 8%; W. 0%

Clayton State University[1]

2000 Clayton State Boulevard
Morrow , GA 30260-0285
http://graduate.clayton.edu
Public
Admissions: (678) 466-4113
E-mail: graduate@clayton.edu
Financial aid: (678) 466-4185
Tuition: N/A
Room/board/expenses: N/A
Enrollment: N/A

Columbus State University (Turner)

4225 University Avenue
Columbus, GA 31907
http://cobcs.columbusstate.edu
Public
Admissions: (706) 507-8800
E-mail: lovell_susan@
columbusstate.edu
Financial aid: N/A
Application deadline: 06/30
In-state tuition: full time: $235/
credit hour; part time: $235/
credit hour
Out-of-state tuition: full time: $939/
credit hour
Room/board/expenses: N/A
College-funded aid: Yes
International student aid: Yes
Average student indebtedness at
graduation: $36,196
Full-time enrollment: 20
men: 60%; women: 40%;
minorities:30%; international: 15%
Part-time enrollment: 70
men: 56%; women: 44%;
minorities:31%; international: 6%
Acceptance rate (full time): 59%
Average GMAT (full time): 483
Average GMAT (part time): 477
Average GPA (full time): 3.20
Average age of entrants to full-time
program: 24
TOEFL requirement: Yes
Minimum TOEFL score: 550

Emory University (Goizueta)

1300 Clifton Road NE
Atlanta, GA 30322
http://www.goizueta.emory.edu
Private
Admissions: (404) 727-6311
E-mail: mbaadmissions@
emory.edu
Financial aid: (404) 727-6039
Application deadline: 03/07
Tuition: full time: $45,114; part
time: $1,300/credit hour
Room/board/expenses: $22,288
College-funded aid: Yes
International student aid: Yes
Average student indebtedness at
graduation: $62,716
Full-time enrollment: 338
men: 72%; women: 28%;
minorities:18%; international: 35%
Part-time enrollment: 258
men: 73%; women: 27%;
minorities:29%; international: 12%
Acceptance rate (full time): 34%

Average GMAT (full time): 677
Average GMAT (part time): 645
Average GPA (full time): 3.38
Average age of entrants to full-time program: 29
Average months of prior work experience (full time): 63
TOEFL requirement: Yes
Minimum TOEFL score: 600
Most popular departments: consulting, finance, general management, marketing, organizational behavior
Mean starting base salary for 2012 full-time graduates: $103,453
Employment location for 2012 class: Intl. 0%; N.E. 27%; M.A. 3%; S. 48%; M.W. 10%; S.W. 8%; W. 3%

Georgia College & State University (Bunting)

Campus Box 019
Milledgeville, GA 31061
http://mba.gcsu.edu
Public
Admissions: (478) 445-6283
E-mail: grad-admit@gcsu.edu
Financial aid: (478) 445-5149
Application deadline: 07/01
In-state tuition: full time: $275/credit hour; part time: $275/credit hour
Out-of-state tuition: full time: $997/credit hour
Room/board/expenses: $13,356
College-funded aid: Yes
International student aid: Yes
Average student indebtedness at graduation: $18,424
Full-time enrollment: 5
men: 20%; women: 80%;
minorities:20%; international: 0%
Part-time enrollment: 60
men: 55%; women: 45%;
minorities:22%; international: 0%
Acceptance rate (full time): 54%
Average GMAT (part time): 493
Average GPA (full time): 3.47
Average age of entrants to full-time program: 23
Average months of prior work experience (full time): N/A
TOEFL requirement: Yes
Minimum TOEFL score: 550
Employment location for 2012 class: Intl. N/A; N.E. N/A; M.A. N/A; S. N/A; M.W. 100%; S.W. N/A; W. N/A

Georgia Institute of Technology

800 W. Peachtree Street NW
Atlanta, GA 30332-0520
http://scheller.gatech.edu
Public
Admissions: (404) 894-8722
E-mail: mba@scheller.gatech.edu
Financial aid: (404) 894-4160
Application deadline: 03/15
In-state tuition: full time: $27,664; part time: $941/credit hour
Out-of-state tuition: full time: $38,626
Room/board/expenses: $14,360
College-funded aid: Yes
International student aid: Yes
Average student indebtedness at graduation: $39,294
Full-time enrollment: 131
men: 73%; women: 27%;
minorities:16%; international: 24%
Part-time enrollment: 415
men: 77%; women: 23%;
minorities:26%; international: 6%
Acceptance rate (full time): 38%
Average GMAT (full time): 678
Average GMAT (part time): 601
Average GPA (full time): 3.38
Average age of entrants to full-time program: 28
Average months of prior work experience (full time): 64
TOEFL requirement: Yes

Minimum TOEFL score: 600
Most popular departments: entrepreneurship, marketing, management information systems, operations management, supply chain management
Mean starting base salary for 2012 full-time graduates: $92,138
Employment location for 2012 class: Intl. 0%; N.E. 3%; M.A. 5%; S. 78%; M.W. 5%; S.W. 3%; W. 5%

Georgia Southern University

PO Box 8050
Statesboro, GA 30460-8050
http://coba.georgiasouthern.edu/mba
Public
Admissions: (912) 478-2357
E-mail: mba@georgiasouthern.edu
Financial aid: (912) 478-5413
Application deadline: 07/01
In-state tuition: full time: N/A; part time: $388/credit hour
Out-of-state tuition: full time: N/A
Room/board/expenses: $16,140
College-funded aid: Yes
International student aid: Yes
Full-time enrollment: N/A
men: N/A; women: N/A;
minorities:N/A; international: N/A
Part-time enrollment: 121
men: 60%; women: 40%;
minorities:19%; international: 5%
Average GMAT (part time): 503
TOEFL requirement: Yes
Minimum TOEFL score: 550

Georgia Southwestern State University[1]

800 Georgia Southwestern State University Drive
Americus, GA 31709
http://gsw.edu/SOBA/
Public
Admissions: (229) 931-2725
E-mail: cbishop@canes.gsw.edu
Financial aid: N/A
Tuition: N/A
Room/board/expenses: N/A
Enrollment: N/A

Georgia State University (Robinson)

PO Box 3989
Atlanta, GA 30302-3989
http://robinson.gsu.edu/
Public
Admissions: (404) 413-7167
E-mail: rcbgradadmissions@gsu.edu
Financial aid: (404) 413-2400
Application deadline: 04/01
In-state tuition: total program: $67,000 (full-time); part time: $437/credit hour
Out-of-state tuition: total program: $67,000 (full-time)
Room/board/expenses: $15,208
College-funded aid: Yes
International student aid: Yes
Full-time enrollment: 38
men: 45%; women: 55%;
minorities:39%; international: 34%
Part-time enrollment: 880
men: 60%; women: 40%;
minorities:41%; international: 5%
Acceptance rate (full time): 87%
Average GMAT (full time): 568
Average GMAT (part time): 611
Average GPA (full time): 3.16
Average age of entrants to full-time program: 32
Average months of prior work experience (full time): 69
TOEFL requirement: Yes
Minimum TOEFL score: 610

Most popular departments: finance, general management, health care administration, marketing, organizational behavior

Kennesaw State University (Coles)

MD 3306
Kennesaw, GA 30144-5591
http://www.kennesaw.edu/graduate/admissions
Public
Admissions: (770) 420-4377
E-mail: ksugrad@kennesaw.edu
Financial aid: (770) 423-6525
Application deadline: 07/01
In-state tuition: full time: N/A; part time: $300/credit hour
Out-of-state tuition: full time: N/A
Room/board/expenses: N/A
College-funded aid: Yes
International student aid: Yes
Full-time enrollment: N/A
men: N/A; women: N/A;
minorities:N/A; international: N/A
Part-time enrollment: 275
men: 58%; women: 42%;
minorities:38%; international: 11%
Average GMAT (part time): 590
TOEFL requirement: Yes
Minimum TOEFL score: 550

Mercer University–Atlanta (Stetson)

3001 Mercer University Drive
Atlanta, GA 30341-4155
http://business.mercer.edu
Private
Admissions: (678) 547-6194
E-mail: atlbusadm@mercer.edu
Financial aid: (678) 547-6444
Application deadline: rolling
Tuition: full time: $668/credit hour; part time: $668/credit hour
Room/board/expenses: N/A
College-funded aid: No
International student aid: No
Full-time enrollment: 14
men: 29%; women: 71%;
minorities:29%; international: 29%
Part-time enrollment: 175
men: 44%; women: 56%;
minorities:25%; international: 23%
Acceptance rate (full time): 81%
Average GMAT (full time): 521
Average GMAT (part time): 497
Average GPA (full time): 3.19
Average age of entrants to full-time program: 25
Average months of prior work experience (full time): 18
TOEFL requirement: Yes
Minimum TOEFL score: 550
Most popular departments: accounting, finance, general management, international business, marketing

North Georgia College and State University

82 College Circle
Dahlonega, GA 30597
http://www.northgeorgia.edu/bschool
Public
Admissions: (770) 205-5448
E-mail: mhjordan@northgeorgia.edu
Financial aid: (706) 864-1412
Application deadline: rolling
In-state tuition: full time: N/A; part time: $7,762
Out-of-state tuition: full time: N/A
Room/board/expenses: N/A
College-funded aid: Yes
International student aid: No
Full-time enrollment: N/A
men: N/A; women: N/A;
minorities:N/A; international: N/A
Part-time enrollment: 33
men: 70%; women: 30%;
minorities:3%; international: 0%

Average GMAT (part time): 540
TOEFL requirement: Yes
Minimum TOEFL score: 550

Savannah State University[1]

PO Box 20359
Savannah, GA 31404
http://www.savannahstate.edu
Public
Admissions: N/A
Financial aid: N/A
Tuition: N/A
Room/board/expenses: N/A
Enrollment: N/A

University of Georgia (Terry)

335 Brooks Hall
Athens, GA 30602-6251
http://mba.terry.uga.edu
Public
Admissions: (706) 542-5671
E-mail: terrymba@uga.edu
Financial aid: (706) 542-6147
Application deadline: 03/03
In-state tuition: full time: $14,112; part time: N/A
Out-of-state tuition: full time: $31,822
Room/board/expenses: $16,500
College-funded aid: Yes
International student aid: Yes
Average student indebtedness at graduation: $28,577
Full-time enrollment: 93
men: 72%; women: 28%;
minorities:15%; international: 18%
Part-time enrollment: N/A
men: N/A; women: N/A;
minorities:N/A; international: N/A
Acceptance rate (full time): 39%
Average GMAT (full time): 637
Average GPA (full time): 3.21
Average age of entrants to full-time program: 28
Average months of prior work experience (full time): 46
TOEFL requirement: Yes
Minimum TOEFL score: N/A
Most popular departments: entrepreneurship, finance, marketing, operations management, real estate
Mean starting base salary for 2012 full-time graduates: $81,163
Employment location for 2012 class: Intl. 9%; N.E. 3%; M.A. 15%; S. 64%; M.W. 6%; S.W. 3%; W. 0%

University of West Georgia (Richards)

1601 Maple Street
Carrollton, GA 30118-3000
http://www.westga.edu/rcob/index_9954.php
Public
Admissions: (678) 839-5355
E-mail: hudombon@westga.edu
Financial aid: (678) 839-6421
Application deadline: 07/15
In-state tuition: full time: $7,930; part time: $253/credit hour
Out-of-state tuition: full time: $26,050
Room/board/expenses: $8,482
College-funded aid: Yes
International student aid: Yes
Average student indebtedness at graduation: $18,142
Full-time enrollment: 44
men: 59%; women: 41%;
minorities:20%; international: 23%
Part-time enrollment: 89
men: 48%; women: 52%;
minorities:35%; international: 3%
Acceptance rate (full time): 69%
Average GMAT (full time): 503
Average GMAT (part time): 483

Average GPA (full time): 3.53
Average age of entrants to full-time program: 30
TOEFL requirement: Yes
Minimum TOEFL score: 550

Valdosta State University (Langdale)

1500 N. Patterson Street
Valdosta, GA 31698
http://www.valdosta.edu/coba/grad/
Public
Admissions: (229) 245-2243
E-mail: rcallen@valdosta.edu
Financial aid: (229) 333-5935
Application deadline: rolling
In-state tuition: full time: $223/credit hour; part time: $223/credit hour
Out-of-state tuition: full time: $804/credit hour
Room/board/expenses: N/A
College-funded aid: Yes
International student aid: Yes
Full-time enrollment: 39
men: 51%; women: 49%;
minorities:10%; international: 10%
Part-time enrollment: N/A
men: N/A; women: N/A;
minorities:N/A; international: N/A
TOEFL requirement: Yes
Minimum TOEFL score: 550

HAWAII

University of Hawaii–Manoa (Shidler)

2404 Maile Way
Business Administration C-204
Honolulu, HI 96822
http://www.shidler.hawaii.edu
Public
Admissions: (808) 956-8266
E-mail: mba@hawaii.edu
Financial aid: (808) 956-7251
Application deadline: rolling
In-state tuition: full time: $17,592; part time: $733/credit hour
Out-of-state tuition: full time: $28,152
Room/board/expenses: $15,844
College-funded aid: Yes
International student aid: Yes
Full-time enrollment: 38
men: 74%; women: 26%;
minorities:66%; international: N/A
Part-time enrollment: 98
men: 53%; women: 47%;
minorities:80%; international: 0%
Acceptance rate (full time): 52%
Average GMAT (full time): 634
Average GMAT (part time): 571
Average GPA (full time): 3.30
Average age of entrants to full-time program: 26
Average months of prior work experience (full time): 42
TOEFL requirement: Yes
Minimum TOEFL score: 600
Most popular departments: accounting, entrepreneurship, finance, general management, international business
Mean starting base salary for 2012 full-time graduates: $62,300

IDAHO

Boise State University

1910 University Drive, MBEB4101
Boise, ID 83725-1600
http://cobe.boisestate.edu/graduate
Public
Admissions: (208) 426-3116
E-mail: graduatebusiness@boisestate.edu
Financial aid: (208) 426-1664
Application deadline: 04/15
In-state tuition: full time: $9,092; part time: $312/credit hour

Out-of-state tuition: full time: $20,532
Room/board/expenses: $29,450
College-funded aid: Yes
International student aid: Yes
Average student indebtedness at graduation: $16,898
Full-time enrollment: 71
men: 62%; women: 38%; minorities:20%; international: 20%
Part-time enrollment: 79
men: 65%; women: 35%; minorities:14%; international: 4%
Acceptance rate (full time): 64%
Average GMAT (full time): 563
Average GMAT (part time): 569
Average GPA (full time): 3.39
Average age of entrants to full-time program: 28
Average months of prior work experience (full time): 37
TOEFL requirement: Yes
Minimum TOEFL score: 587
Mean starting base salary for 2012 full-time graduates: $78,700
Employment location for 2012 class: Intl. 25%; N.E. 0%; M.A. 0%; S. 0%; M.W. 0%; S.W. 0%; W. 75%

Idaho State University[1]

921 S. 8th Ave Stop 8020
Pocatello, ID 83209
http://cob.isu.edu
Public
Admissions: (208) 282-2966
E-mail: mba@cob.isu.edu
Financial aid: (208) 282-2756
Tuition: N/A
Room/board/expenses: N/A
Enrollment: N/A

University of Idaho[1]

PO Box 443161
Moscow, ID 83844-3161
http://www.uidaho.edu/cogs
Public
Admissions: (800) 885-4001
E-mail: gadms@uidaho.edu
Financial aid: (208) 885-6326
Tuition: N/A
Room/board/expenses: N/A
Enrollment: N/A

ILLINOIS

Bradley University (Foster)

1501 W. Bradley Avenue
Peoria, IL 61625
http://www.bradley.edu/mba
Private
Admissions: (309) 677-3714
E-mail: mba@bradley.edu
Financial aid: (309) 677-3089
Application deadline: rolling
Tuition: full time: N/A; part time: $740/credit hour
Room/board/expenses: N/A
College-funded aid: Yes
International student aid: Yes
Full-time enrollment: N/A
men: N/A; women: N/A; minorities:N/A; international: N/A
Part-time enrollment: 78
men: 60%; women: 40%; minorities:13%; international: 12%
Average GMAT (part time): 552
TOEFL requirement: Yes
Minimum TOEFL score: 550
Most popular departments: finance, general management, marketing

DePaul University (Kellstadt)

1 E. Jackson Boulevard
Chicago, IL 60604-2287
http://www.kellstadt.depaul.edu/
Private
Admissions: (312) 362-8810
E-mail: kgsb@depaul.edu
Financial aid: (312) 362-8091
Application deadline: 07/01
Tuition: full time: $935/credit hour; part time: $935/credit hour
Room/board/expenses: $15,000
College-funded aid: Yes
International student aid: Yes
Average student indebtedness at graduation: $64,074
Full-time enrollment: 93
men: 57%; women: 43%; minorities:10%; international: 32%
Part-time enrollment: 2,003
men: 55%; women: 45%; minorities:14%; international: 28%
Acceptance rate (full time): 43%
Average GMAT (full time): 625
Average GMAT (part time): 598
Average GPA (full time): 3.14
Average age of entrants to full-time program: 27
Average months of prior work experience (full time): 43
TOEFL requirement: Yes
Minimum TOEFL score: 550
Mean starting base salary for 2012 full-time graduates: $66,877
Employment location for 2012 class: Intl. 3%; N.E. 3%; M.A. 0%; S. 3%; M.W. 91%; S.W. 0%; W. 0%

Eastern Illinois University (Lumpkin)

600 Lincoln Avenue
Charleston, IL 61920-3099
http://www.eiu.edu/mba
Public
Admissions: (217) 581-3028
E-mail: mba@eiu.edu
Financial aid: (217) 581-3714
Application deadline: 08/01
In-state tuition: full time: $279/credit hour; part time: $279/credit hour
Out-of-state tuition: full time: $670/credit hour
Room/board/expenses: $8,820
College-funded aid: Yes
International student aid: Yes
Full-time enrollment: 46
men: 61%; women: 39%; minorities:15%; international: 13%
Part-time enrollment: 24
men: 42%; women: 58%; minorities:8%; international: 0%
Acceptance rate (full time): 90%
Average GMAT (full time): 525
Average GMAT (part time): 524
Average GPA (full time): 3.42
Average age of entrants to full-time program: 24
Average months of prior work experience (full time): 52
TOEFL requirement: Yes
Minimum TOEFL score: 550
Mean starting base salary for 2012 full-time graduates: $47,285
Employment location for 2012 class: Intl. 0%; N.E. 0%; M.A. 10%; S. 0%; M.W. 71%; S.W. 5%; W. 14%

Illinois Institute of Technology (Stuart)

10 W. 35th St.
Chicago, IL 60616
http://www.stuart.iit.edu
Private
Admissions: (312) 567-3020
E-mail: admission@stuart.iit.edu
Financial aid: (312) 567-7219
Application deadline: 07/10
Tuition: full time: $1,540/credit hour; part time: $1,540/credit hour
Room/board/expenses: $9,678
College-funded aid: Yes
International student aid: Yes
Full-time enrollment: 160
men: 56%; women: 44%; minorities:5%; international: 80%
Part-time enrollment: 39
men: 67%; women: 33%; minorities:23%; international: 21%
Acceptance rate (full time): 81%
Average GMAT (full time): 602
Average GMAT (part time): 700
Average GPA (full time): 3.10
Average age of entrants to full-time program: 25
TOEFL requirement: Yes
Minimum TOEFL score: 600
Most popular departments: finance, general management, marketing, public administration, other

Illinois State University

MBA Program, Campus Box 5570
Normal, IL 61790-5570
http://www.mba.ilstu.edu/
Public
Admissions: (309) 438-8388
E-mail: isumba@exchange.cob.ilstu.edu
Financial aid: (309) 438-2231
Application deadline: 07/01
In-state tuition: full time: $384/credit hour; part time: $384/credit hour
Out-of-state tuition: full time: $715/credit hour
Room/board/expenses: $15,029
College-funded aid: Yes
International student aid: Yes
Average student indebtedness at graduation: $23,561
Full-time enrollment: 72
men: 63%; women: 38%; minorities:13%; international: 39%
Part-time enrollment: 107
men: 63%; women: 37%; minorities:7%; international: 7%
Average GMAT (part time): 568
TOEFL requirement: Yes
Minimum TOEFL score: 600
Most popular departments: finance, human resources management, insurance, marketing, organizational behavior

Loyola University Chicago

820 N. Michigan Avenue
Chicago, IL 60611
http://www.luc.edu/quinlan/mba/index.shtml
Private
Admissions: (312) 915-8908
E-mail: quinlangrad@luc.edu
Financial aid: (773) 508-8928
Application deadline: 07/15
Tuition: full time: $1,337/credit hour; part time: $1,337/credit hour
Room/board/expenses: $45,273
College-funded aid: Yes
International student aid: Yes
Full-time enrollment: N/A
men: N/A; women: N/A; minorities:N/A; international: N/A
Part-time enrollment: 701
men: 47%; women: 53%; minorities:16%; international: 25%
Average GMAT (part time): 581
TOEFL requirement: Yes
Minimum TOEFL score: 577
Most popular departments: accounting, finance, general management, human resources management, marketing

Northern Illinois University

Office of MBA Programs
Barsema Hall 203
De Kalb, IL 60115-2897
http://www.cob.niu.edu/mbaprograms
Public
Admissions: (866) 648-6221
E-mail: mba@niu.edu
Financial aid: (815) 753-1395
Application deadline: 07/15
In-state tuition: full time: $39,875; part time: $657/credit hour
Out-of-state tuition: total program: $54,000 (full-time)
Room/board/expenses: N/A
College-funded aid: Yes
International student aid: Yes
Full-time enrollment: 37
men: 78%; women: 22%; minorities:32%; international: 16%
Part-time enrollment: 529
men: 68%; women: 32%; minorities:25%; international: 8%
Acceptance rate (full time): 67%
Average GMAT (full time): 487
Average GMAT (part time): 500
Average GPA (full time): 3.14
Average age of entrants to full-time program: 24
Average months of prior work experience (full time): 48
TOEFL requirement: Yes
Minimum TOEFL score: 550
Most popular departments: entrepreneurship, finance, international business, leadership, marketing
Employment location for 2012 class: Intl. 28%; N.E. N/A; M.A. N/A; S. N/A; M.W. 72%; S.W. N/A; W. N/A

Northwestern University (Kellogg)

2001 Sheridan Road
Evanston, IL 60208-2001
http://www.kellogg.northwestern.edu
Private
Admissions: (847) 491-3308
E-mail: mbaadmissions@kellogg.northwestern.edu
Financial aid: (847) 491-3308
Application deadline: 04/03
Tuition: full time: $56,775; part time: $5,519/credit hour
Room/board/expenses: $27,904
College-funded aid: Yes
International student aid: Yes
Average student indebtedness at graduation: $88,740
Full-time enrollment: 1,161
men: 66%; women: 34%; minorities:22%; international: 38%
Part-time enrollment: 813
men: 68%; women: 32%; minorities:16%; international: 14%
Acceptance rate (full time): 23%
Average GMAT (full time): 708
Average GMAT (part time): 667
Average GPA (full time): 3.69
Average age of entrants to full-time program: 28
Average months of prior work experience (full time): 64
TOEFL requirement: Yes
Minimum TOEFL score: N/A
Most popular departments: entrepreneurship, finance, marketing, organizational behavior, other
Mean starting base salary for 2012 full-time graduates: $116,864
Employment location for 2012 class: Intl. 16%; N.E. 20%; M.A. 3%; S. 3%; M.W. 33%; S.W. 6%; W. 19%

Southern Illinois University–Carbondale

133 Rehn Hall
Carbondale, IL 62901-4625
http://mba.business.siu.edu
Public
Admissions: (618) 453-3030
E-mail: cobgp@business.siu.edu
Financial aid: (618) 453-4334
Application deadline: 06/15
In-state tuition: full time: $432/credit hour; part time: $432/credit hour
Out-of-state tuition: full time: $994/credit hour
Room/board/expenses: N/A
College-funded aid: Yes
International student aid: Yes
Full-time enrollment: 72
men: 57%; women: 43%; minorities:22%; international: 31%
Part-time enrollment: N/A
men: N/A; women: N/A; minorities:N/A; international: N/A
Acceptance rate (full time): 80%
Average GMAT (full time): 594
Average GPA (full time): 3.49
Average age of entrants to full-time program: 27
Average months of prior work experience (full time): 108
TOEFL requirement: Yes
Minimum TOEFL score: 550
Most popular departments: finance, general management, international business, marketing, organizational behavior

Southern Illinois University–Edwardsville

Box 1051
Edwardsville, IL 62026-1051
http://www.siue.edu/business
Public
Admissions: (618) 650-3840
E-mail: mba@siue.edu
Financial aid: (618) 650-3880
Application deadline: rolling
In-state tuition: full time: $271/credit hour; part time: $271/credit hour
Out-of-state tuition: full time: $678/credit hour
Room/board/expenses: $22,500
College-funded aid: Yes
International student aid: Yes
Full-time enrollment: N/A
men: N/A; women: N/A; minorities:N/A; international: N/A
Part-time enrollment: 134
men: 67%; women: 33%; minorities:9%; international: 3%
Average GMAT (part time): 501
TOEFL requirement: Yes
Minimum TOEFL score: 550

University of Chicago (Booth)

5807 S. Woodlawn Avenue
Chicago, IL 60637
http://ChicagoBooth.edu
Private
Admissions: (773) 702-7369
E-mail: admissions@ChicagoBooth.edu
Financial aid: (773) 702-7369
Application deadline: 04/04
Tuition: full time: $56,931; part time: N/A
Room/board/expenses: $25,350
College-funded aid: Yes
International student aid: Yes
Average student indebtedness at graduation: $72,959
Full-time enrollment: 1,161
men: 65%; women: 35%; minorities:23%; international: 32%
Part-time enrollment: 1,473
men: 77%; women: 23%; minorities:26%; international: 15%
Acceptance rate (full time): 23%
Average GMAT (full time): 720
Average GMAT (part time): 681
Average GPA (full time): 3.52
Average age of entrants to full-time program: 28
Average months of prior work experience (full time): 58
TOEFL requirement: Yes
Minimum TOEFL score: 600
Most popular departments: accounting, economics, entrepreneurship, finance, other
Mean starting base salary for 2012 full-time graduates: $115,079
Employment location for 2012 class: Intl. 18%; N.E. 27%; M.A. 4%; S. 4%; M.W. 29%; S.W. 6%; W. 13%

University of Illinois–Chicago (Liautaud)
705 S. Morgan Street
MC077, 110DH
Chicago, IL 60607
http://www.mba.uic.edu/
Public
Admissions: (312) 996-4573
E-mail: mba@uic.edu
Financial aid: (312) 996-3126
Application deadline: 06/15
In-state tuition: full time: $22,812; part time: $16,450
Out-of-state tuition: full time: $34,810
Room/board/expenses: $12,749
College-funded aid: Yes
International student aid: Yes
Full-time enrollment: 133
men: 65%; women: 35%; minorities:22%; international: 26%
Part-time enrollment: 123
men: 67%; women: 33%; minorities:20%; international: 4%
Acceptance rate (full time): 41%
Average GMAT (full time): 564
Average GMAT (part time): 576
Average GPA (full time): 3.28
Average age of entrants to full-time program: 28
Average months of prior work experience (full time): 53
TOEFL requirement: Yes
Minimum TOEFL score: 570
Most popular departments: accounting, entrepreneurship, finance, marketing
Mean starting base salary for 2012 full-time graduates: $71,679
Employment location for 2012 class: Intl. N/A; N.E. N/A; M.A. N/A; S. 6%; M.W. 94%; S.W. N/A; W. N/A

University of Illinois–Springfield
1 University Plaza, MS UHB 4000
Springfield , IL 62703
http://www.uis.edu/admissions
Public
Admissions: (888) 977-4847
E-mail: admissions@uis.edu
Financial aid: N/A
Application deadline: rolling
In-state tuition: full time: N/A; part time: $305/credit hour
Out-of-state tuition: full time: N/A
Room/board/expenses: N/A
College-funded aid: Yes
International student aid: Yes
Full-time enrollment: N/A
men: N/A; women: N/A; minorities:N/A; international: N/A
Part-time enrollment: 146
men: 66%; women: 34%; minorities:12%; international: 8%
Average GMAT (part time): 496
TOEFL requirement: Yes
Minimum TOEFL score: 550

University of Illinois–Urbana-Champaign
515 E. Gregory Drive
3019 BIF, MC 520
Champaign, IL 61820
http://www.mba.illinois.edu
Public
Admissions: (217) 244-7602
E-mail: mba@illinois.edu
Financial aid: (217) 333-0100
Application deadline: 03/15
In-state tuition: full time: $24,236; part time: $26,754
Out-of-state tuition: full time: $34,236
Room/board/expenses: $18,947
College-funded aid: Yes
International student aid: Yes
Average student indebtedness at graduation: $63,718
Full-time enrollment: 237
men: 70%; women: 30%; minorities:20%; international: 43%
Part-time enrollment: N/A
men: N/A; women: N/A; minorities:N/A; international: N/A
Acceptance rate (full time): 32%
Average GMAT (full time): 650
Average GPA (full time): 3.20
Average age of entrants to full-time program: 28
Average months of prior work experience (full time): 60
TOEFL requirement: Yes
Minimum TOEFL score: 550
Most popular departments: consulting, finance, general management, marketing, operations management
Mean starting base salary for 2012 full-time graduates: $87,818
Employment location for 2012 class: Intl. 4%; N.E. 6%; M.A. 1%; S. 6%; M.W. 67%; S.W. 6%; W. 10%

Western Illinois University
1 University Circle
Macomb, IL 61455
http://www.wiu.edu/cbt
Public
Admissions: (309) 298-2442
E-mail: JT-Drea@wiu.edu
Financial aid: (309) 298-2446
Application deadline: rolling
In-state tuition: full time: N/A; part time: N/A
Out-of-state tuition: full time: N/A
Room/board/expenses: N/A
College-funded aid: Yes
International student aid: Yes
Average student indebtedness at graduation: $22,000
Full-time enrollment: 44
men: 61%; women: 39%; minorities:2%; international: 16%
Part-time enrollment: 34
men: 62%; women: 38%; minorities:0%; international: 9%
Acceptance rate (full time): 76%
Average GMAT (full time): 517
Average GMAT (part time): 588
Average GPA (full time): 3.30
Average months of prior work experience (full time): 12
TOEFL requirement: Yes
Minimum TOEFL score: 550
Most popular departments: accounting, finance, general management, international business, supply chain management

INDIANA

Ball State University (Miller)
Whitinger Building,147
Muncie, IN 47306
http://www.bsu.edu/mba/
Public
Admissions: (765) 285-1931
E-mail: mba@bsu.edu
Financial aid: (765) 285-5600
Application deadline: 01/07
In-state tuition: total program: $16,362 (full-time); part time: $388/credit hour
Out-of-state tuition: total program: $26,472 (full-time)
Room/board/expenses: $30,000
College-funded aid: Yes
International student aid: Yes
Average student indebtedness at graduation: $15,357
Full-time enrollment: 65
men: 65%; women: 35%; minorities:6%; international: 23%
Part-time enrollment: 146
men: 67%; women: 33%; minorities:8%; international: 1%
Acceptance rate (full time): 95%
Average GMAT (full time): 529
Average GMAT (part time): 533
Average GPA (full time): 3.25
Average age of entrants to full-time program: 28
Average months of prior work experience (full time): 50
TOEFL requirement: Yes
Minimum TOEFL score: 550
Most popular departments: entrepreneurship, finance, general management, other
Mean starting base salary for 2012 full-time graduates: $49,250
Employment location for 2012 class: Intl. 0%; N.E. 0%; M.A. 0%; S. 22%; M.W. 70%; S.W. 4%; W. 4%

Butler University
4600 Sunset Avenue
Indianapolis, IN 46208-3485
http://www.butlermba.com
Private
Admissions: (317) 940-9842
E-mail: mba@butler.edu
Financial aid: (317) 940-8200
Application deadline: 07/01
Tuition: full time: $674/credit hour; part time: $674/credit hour
Room/board/expenses: $12,060
College-funded aid: No
International student aid: No
Full-time enrollment: N/A
men: N/A; women: N/A; minorities:N/A; international: N/A
Part-time enrollment: 196
men: 70%; women: 30%; minorities:5%; international: 6%
Average GMAT (part time): 580
TOEFL requirement: Yes
Minimum TOEFL score: 550
Most popular departments: finance, international business, leadership, marketing

Indiana State University
MBA Program
800 Sycamore Street
Terre Haute, IN 47809
http://www.indstate.edu/business/mba/
Public
Admissions: (812) 237-2002
E-mail: ISU-Gradstudy@mail.indstate.edu
Financial aid: (812) 237-2215
Application deadline: 07/01
In-state tuition: full time: $366/credit hour; part time: $366/credit hour
Out-of-state tuition: full time: $719/credit hour
Room/board/expenses: N/A
College-funded aid: Yes
International student aid: Yes
Full-time enrollment: 44
men: 61%; women: 39%; minorities:0%; international: 25%
Part-time enrollment: N/A
men: N/A; women: N/A; minorities:N/A; international: N/A
Acceptance rate (full time): 51%
Average GMAT (full time): 500
Average GPA (full time): 3.50
Average age of entrants to full-time program: 29
Average months of prior work experience (full time): 60
TOEFL requirement: Yes
Minimum TOEFL score: 550

Indiana University–Bloomington (Kelley)
1275 E. 10th Street, Suite 2010
Bloomington, IN 47405-1703
http://kelley.iu.edu/mba
Public
Admissions: (812) 855-8006
E-mail: iumba@indiana.edu
Financial aid: (812) 855-8006
Application deadline: 04/15
In-state tuition: full time: $26,562; part time: $700/credit hour
Out-of-state tuition: full time: $45,544
Room/board/expenses: $18,190
College-funded aid: Yes
International student aid: Yes
Average student indebtedness at graduation: $76,685
Full-time enrollment: 398
men: 69%; women: 31%; minorities:18%; international: 37%
Part-time enrollment: 302
men: 76%; women: 24%; minorities:15%; international: 17%
Acceptance rate (full time): 39%
Average GMAT (full time): 664
Average GMAT (part time): 631
Average GPA (full time): 3.33
Average age of entrants to full-time program: 28
Average months of prior work experience (full time): 62
TOEFL requirement: Yes
Minimum TOEFL score: 600
Most popular departments: entrepreneurship, finance, general management, marketing, other
Mean starting base salary for 2012 full-time graduates: $97,489
Employment location for 2012 class: Intl. 8%; N.E. 12%; M.A. 8%; S. 5%; M.W. 54%; S.W. 5%; W. 9%

Indiana University–Kokomo[1]
2300 S. Washington Street
Kokomo, IN 46904-9003
http://www.iuk.edu/academics/majors/business/graduate-programs/mba/index.shtml
Public
Admissions: (765) 455-9275
E-mail: tbutler@iuk.edu
Financial aid: (765) 455-9216
Tuition: N/A
Room/board/expenses: N/A
Enrollment: N/A

Indiana University Northwest
3400 Broadway
Gary, IN 46408-1197
http://www.indiana.edu/~bulletin/iun/grad/busec.html#pro
Public
Admissions: N/A
Financial aid: N/A
Application deadline: rolling
In-state tuition: full time: N/A; part time: $300/credit hour
Out-of-state tuition: full time: N/A
Room/board/expenses: N/A
College-funded aid: Yes
International student aid: No
Full-time enrollment: N/A
men: N/A; women: N/A; minorities:N/A; international: N/A
Part-time enrollment: 106
men: 51%; women: 49%; minorities:44%; international: 0%
Average GMAT (part time): 453
TOEFL requirement: Yes
Minimum TOEFL score: 550

Indiana University-Purdue University-Fort Wayne (Doermer)
2101 E. Coliseum Boulevard
Fort Wayne, IN 46805-1499
http://www.ipfw.edu/mba
Public
Admissions: (260) 481-6498
E-mail: mba@ipfw.edu
Financial aid: (260) 481-6820
Application deadline: rolling
In-state tuition: full time: $600/credit hour; part time: $314/credit hour
Out-of-state tuition: full time: $995/credit hour
Room/board/expenses: N/A
College-funded aid: Yes
International student aid: Yes
Full-time enrollment: 36
men: 83%; women: 17%; minorities:25%; international: 11%
Part-time enrollment: 119
men: 63%; women: 37%; minorities:3%; international: 4%
Acceptance rate (full time): 60%
Average GMAT (part time): 581
Average GPA (full time): 3.20
Average age of entrants to full-time program: 36
TOEFL requirement: Yes
Minimum TOEFL score: 550

Indiana University–South Bend[1]
1700 Mishawaka Avenue
PO Box 7111
South Bend, IN 46634-7111
http://www.iusb.edu/~buse
Public
Admissions: (574) 520-4138
E-mail: gradbus@iusb.edu
Financial aid: (574) 520-4357
Tuition: N/A
Room/board/expenses: N/A
Enrollment: N/A

Indiana University–Southeast
4201 Grant Line Road
New Albany, IN 47150
http://www.ius.edu/graduatebusiness
Public
Admissions: (812) 941-2364
E-mail: iusmba@ius.edu
Financial aid: (812) 941-2246
Application deadline: 07/20
In-state tuition: full time: N/A; part time: $365/credit hour
Out-of-state tuition: full time: N/A
Room/board/expenses: N/A
College-funded aid: Yes
International student aid: Yes
Full-time enrollment: N/A
men: N/A; women: N/A; minorities:N/A; international: N/A
Part-time enrollment: 225
men: 67%; women: 33%; minorities:5%; international: 5%
Average GMAT (part time): 521
TOEFL requirement: Yes
Minimum TOEFL score: 550

Purdue University–West Lafayette (Krannert)
100 S. Grant Street
Rawls Hall, Room 2020
West Lafayette, IN 47907-2076
http://www.krannert.purdue.edu/programs/masters
Public
Admissions: (765) 494-0773
E-mail: krannertmasters@purdue.edu
Financial aid: (765) 494-0998
Application deadline: 05/31
In-state tuition: full time: $23,931; part time: $21,281
Out-of-state tuition: full time: $43,697
Room/board/expenses: $12,873
College-funded aid: Yes
International student aid: Yes
Full-time enrollment: 241
men: 76%; women: 24%; minorities:15%; international: 63%
Part-time enrollment: 130
men: 81%; women: 19%; minorities:42%; international: 26%
Acceptance rate (full time): 45%
Average GMAT (full time): 643
Average GMAT (part time): 595
Average GPA (full time): 3.23

Average age of entrants to full-time program: 28
Average months of prior work experience (full time): 56
TOEFL requirement: Yes
Minimum TOEFL score: 550
Most popular departments: consulting, finance, marketing, operations management, supply chain management
Mean starting base salary for 2012 full-time graduates: $85,897
Employment location for 2012 class: Intl. 15%; N.E. 4%; M.A. 8%; S. 8%; M.W. 50%; S.W. 11%; W. 4%

University of Notre Dame (Mendoza)

276 Mendoza College of Business
Notre Dame, IN 46556
http://business.nd.edu/mba
Private
Admissions: (574) 631-8488
E-mail: mba.business@nd.edu
Financial aid: (574) 631-6436
Application deadline: 04/01
Tuition: full time: $44,110; part time: N/A
Room/board/expenses: $18,100
College-funded aid: Yes
International student aid: Yes
Average student indebtedness at graduation: $57,969
Full-time enrollment: 314
men: 74%; women: 26%;
minorities:16%; international: 20%
Part-time enrollment: N/A
men: N/A; women: N/A;
minorities:N/A; international: N/A
Acceptance rate (full time): 35%
Average GMAT (full time): 687
Average GPA (full time): 3.26
Average age of entrants to full-time program: 27
Average months of prior work experience (full time): 61
TOEFL requirement: Yes
Minimum TOEFL score: 600
Most popular departments: consulting, finance, leadership, marketing, other
Mean starting base salary for 2012 full-time graduates: $98,623
Employment location for 2012 class: Intl. 2%; N.E. 16%; M.A. 6%; S. 9%; M.W. 41%; S.W. 10%; W. 16%

University of Southern Indiana

8600 University Boulevard
Evansville, IN 47712
http://www.usi.edu
Public
Admissions: (812) 465-7015
E-mail: gssr@usi.edu
Financial aid: (812) 464-1767
Application deadline: 07/25
In-state tuition: full time: $294/ credit hour; part time: $581/ credit hour
Out-of-state tuition: full time: $294/ credit hour
Room/board/expenses: N/A
College-funded aid: Yes
International student aid: Yes
Full-time enrollment: N/A
men: N/A; women: N/A;
minorities:N/A; international: N/A
Part-time enrollment: 86
men: 60%; women: 40%;
minorities:3%; international: 8%
Average GMAT (part time): 534
TOEFL requirement: Yes
Minimum TOEFL score: 550

Valparaiso University

Urschel Hall, 1909 Chapel Drive
Valparaiso, IN 46383
http://www.valpo.edu/mba/
Private
Admissions: (219) 465-7952
E-mail: mba@valpo.edu

Financial aid: (219) 464-5015
Application deadline: 06/27
Tuition: full time: $699/credit hour; part time: $699/credit hour
Room/board/expenses: $45,158
College-funded aid: No
International student aid: No
Average student indebtedness at graduation: $45,158
Full-time enrollment: 16
men: 50%; women: 50%;
minorities:6%; international: 19%
Part-time enrollment: 47
men: 64%; women: 36%;
minorities:9%; international: 0%
Acceptance rate (full time): 82%
Average GMAT (full time): 515
Average GMAT (part time): 577
Average GPA (full time): 3.44
Average age of entrants to full-time program: 28
Average months of prior work experience (full time): 60
TOEFL requirement: Yes
Minimum TOEFL score: 575
Mean starting base salary for 2012 full-time graduates: $57,750
Employment location for 2012 class: Intl. 0%; N.E. 50%; M.A. 0%; S. 0%; M.W. 50%; S.W. 0%; W. 0%

IOWA

Drake University

2507 University Avenue
Des Moines, IA 50311
http://www.cbpa.drake.edu
Private
Admissions: (515) 271-2188
E-mail: cbpa.gradprograms@ drake.edu
Financial aid: (515) 271-2905
Application deadline: 07/15
Tuition: full time: $595/credit hour; part time: $595/credit hour
Room/board/expenses: N/A
College-funded aid: No
International student aid: No
Full-time enrollment: N/A
men: N/A; women: N/A;
minorities:N/A; international: N/A
Part-time enrollment: 184
men: 58%; women: 42%;
minorities:10%; international: 6%
Average GMAT (part time): 575
TOEFL requirement: Yes
Minimum TOEFL score: 550
Most popular departments: accounting, finance, leadership, marketing, non-profit management

Iowa State University

1360 Gerdin Business Building
Ames, IA 50011-1350
http://www.business.iastate.edu
Public
Admissions: (515) 294-8118
E-mail: busgrad@iastate.edu
Financial aid: (515) 294-2223
Application deadline: 07/01
In-state tuition: full time: $10,488; part time: $524/credit hour
Out-of-state tuition: full time: $22,410
Room/board/expenses: $15,500
College-funded aid: Yes
International student aid: Yes
Full-time enrollment: 57
men: 65%; women: 35%;
minorities:4%; international: 39%
Part-time enrollment: 79
men: 66%; women: 34%;
minorities:8%; international: 4%
Acceptance rate (full time): 50%
Average GMAT (full time): 603
Average GMAT (part time): 521
Average GPA (full time): 3.55
Average age of entrants to full-time program: 24
TOEFL requirement: Yes
Minimum TOEFL score: 600

Most popular departments: accounting, finance, marketing, supply chain management, technology
Mean starting base salary for 2012 full-time graduates: $63,017
Employment location for 2012 class: Intl. N/A; N.E. 10%; M.A. N/A; S. N/A; M.W. 85%; S.W. 5%; W. N/A

University of Iowa (Tippie)

108 John Pappajohn Business Building, Suite W160
Iowa City, IA 52242-1000
http://tippie.uiowa.edu/mba
Public
Admissions: (319) 335-1039
E-mail: tippiemba@uiowa.edu
Financial aid: (319) 335-1039
Application deadline: 07/30
In-state tuition: full time: $20,383; part time: $600/credit hour
Out-of-state tuition: full time: $36,045
Room/board/expenses: $16,929
College-funded aid: Yes
International student aid: Yes
Average student indebtedness at graduation: $49,056
Full-time enrollment: 129
men: 75%; women: 25%;
minorities:12%; international: 26%
Part-time enrollment: 768
men: 68%; women: 32%;
minorities:9%; international: 6%
Acceptance rate (full time): 42%
Average GMAT (full time): 665
Average GMAT (part time): 568
Average GPA (full time): 3.35
Average age of entrants to full-time program: 28
Average months of prior work experience (full time): 52
TOEFL requirement: Yes
Minimum TOEFL score: 600
Most popular departments: finance, general management, marketing, operations management, portfolio management
Mean starting base salary for 2012 full-time graduates: $80,737
Employment location for 2012 class: Intl. 0%; N.E. 7%; M.A. 0%; S. 9%; M.W. 67%; S.W. 9%; W. 7%

University of Northern Iowa

Curris Business Building 325
Cedar Falls, IA 50614-0123
http://www.cba.uni.edu/mba/
Public
Admissions: (319) 273-6243
E-mail: mba@uni.edu
Financial aid: (319) 273-2700
Application deadline: 05/30
In-state tuition: full time: $10,299; part time: $518/credit hour
Out-of-state tuition: full time: $19,569
Room/board/expenses: $10,000
College-funded aid: Yes
International student aid: No
Full-time enrollment: N/A
men: N/A; women: N/A;
minorities:N/A; international: N/A
Part-time enrollment: 76
men: 64%; women: 36%;
minorities:13%; international: 36%
Average GMAT (part time): 527
TOEFL requirement: Yes
Minimum TOEFL score: 550
Most popular departments: accounting, general management

KANSAS

Emporia State University

1200 Commercial
Campus Box 4059
Emporia, KS 66801-5087
http://emporia.edu/business/ programs/mba
Public
Admissions: (877) 468-6378
E-mail: gradinfo@emporia.edu
Financial aid: (620) 341-5457
Application deadline: rolling
In-state tuition: full time: $277/ credit hour; part time: $277/ credit hour
Out-of-state tuition: full time: $713/ credit hour
Room/board/expenses: N/A
College-funded aid: Yes
International student aid: Yes
Full-time enrollment: 79
men: 48%; women: 52%;
minorities:8%; international: 65%
Part-time enrollment: 39
men: 67%; women: 33%;
minorities:8%; international: 5%
Acceptance rate (full time): 73%
Average GMAT (full time): 558
Average GMAT (part time): 477
Average GPA (full time): 3.28
Average age of entrants to full-time program: 26
TOEFL requirement: Yes
Minimum TOEFL score: 550
Most popular departments: accounting, management information systems, other

Kansas State University

107 Calvin Hall
Manhattan, KS 66506-0501
http://www.cba.ksu.edu/cba/
Public
Admissions: (785) 532-7190
E-mail: flynn@ksu.edu
Financial aid: (785) 532-6420
Application deadline: 02/01
In-state tuition: full time: $12,259; part time: $327/credit hour
Out-of-state tuition: full time: $24,073
Room/board/expenses: $18,000
College-funded aid: Yes
International student aid: Yes
Full-time enrollment: 50
men: 54%; women: 46%;
minorities:4%; international: 40%
Part-time enrollment: 16
men: 31%; women: 69%;
minorities:13%; international: N/A
Acceptance rate (full time): 53%
Average GMAT (full time): 562
Average GMAT (part time): 487
Average GPA (full time): 3.37
Average age of entrants to full-time program: 26
Average months of prior work experience (full time): 54
TOEFL requirement: Yes
Minimum TOEFL score: 550

Pittsburg State University (Kelce)

1701 S. Broadway
Pittsburg, KS 66762
http://www.pittstate.edu/kelce/ graduate.html
Public
Admissions: (620) 235-4222
E-mail: grad@pittstate.edu
Financial aid: (620) 235-4240
Application deadline: 06/02
In-state tuition: full time: $7,422; part time: $261/credit hour
Out-of-state tuition: full time: $15,766
Room/board/expenses: $6,538
College-funded aid: Yes
International student aid: Yes

Full-time enrollment: 102
men: 54%; women: 46%;
minorities:13%; international: 49%
Part-time enrollment: 24
men: 50%; women: 50%;
minorities:21%; international: 50%
Acceptance rate (full time): 67%
Average GMAT (full time): 510
Average GMAT (part time): 500
Average GPA (full time): 3.25
Average age of entrants to full-time program: 26
Average months of prior work experience (full time): 16
TOEFL requirement: Yes
Minimum TOEFL score: 550
Most popular departments: accounting, general management, international business

University of Kansas

1300 Sunnyside Avenue
Lawrence, KS 66045-7585
http://www.mba.ku.edu
Public
Admissions: (785) 864-7556
E-mail: bschoolmba@ku.edu
Financial aid: (785) 864-7596
Application deadline: 06/01
In-state tuition: full time: $330/ credit hour; part time: $330/ credit hour
Out-of-state tuition: full time: $772/ credit hour
Room/board/expenses: $11,500
College-funded aid: Yes
International student aid: Yes
Full-time enrollment: 116
men: 74%; women: 26%;
minorities:15%; international: 21%
Part-time enrollment: 163
men: 69%; women: 31%;
minorities:16%; international: 7%
Acceptance rate (full time): 56%
Average GMAT (full time): 590
Average GMAT (part time): 558
Average GPA (full time): 3.32
Average age of entrants to full-time program: 27
Average months of prior work experience (full time): 29
TOEFL requirement: Yes
Minimum TOEFL score: 570
Most popular departments: finance, general management, marketing
Mean starting base salary for 2012 full-time graduates: $65,353
Employment location for 2012 class: Intl. 0%; N.E. 4%; M.A. 0%; S. 0%; M.W. 83%; S.W. 8%; W. 4%

Washburn University

1700 S.W. College Avenue
Topeka, KS 66621
http://www.washburn.edu/ business
Public
Admissions: (785) 670-1308
E-mail: ba@washburn.edu
Financial aid: N/A
Application deadline: rolling
In-state tuition: full time: N/A; part time: $388/credit hour
Out-of-state tuition: full time: N/A
Room/board/expenses: N/A
College-funded aid: Yes
International student aid: Yes
Full-time enrollment: N/A
men: N/A; women: N/A;
minorities:N/A; international: N/A
Part-time enrollment: 60
men: 57%; women: 43%;
minorities:N/A; international: N/A
Average GMAT (part time): 534
TOEFL requirement: Yes
Minimum TOEFL score: 550

Wichita State University (Barton)

1845 N. Fairmount, Box 48
Wichita, KS 67260-0048
http://www.wichita.edu/mba
Public
Admissions: (316) 978-3230
E-mail: grad.business@
wichita.edu
Financial aid: (316) 978-3430
Application deadline: 07/01
In-state tuition: full time: N/A/credit
hour; part time: $225/credit hour
Out-of-state tuition: full time: N/A/
credit hour
Room/board/expenses: $2,233
College-funded aid: Yes
International student aid: Yes
Full-time enrollment: N/A
men: N/A; women: N/A;
minorities:N/A; international: N/A
Part-time enrollment: 160
men: 75%; women: 25%;
minorities:13%; international: 8%
Average GMAT (part time): 551
TOEFL requirement: Yes
Minimum TOEFL score: 570

KENTUCKY

Bellarmine University (Rubel)[1]

2001 Newburg Road
Louisville, KY 40205-0671
http://www.bellarmine.edu/
business/
Private
Admissions: N/A
E-mail: gradadmissions@
bellarmine.edu
Financial aid: (502) 452-8124
Tuition: N/A
Room/board/expenses: N/A
Enrollment: N/A

Eastern Kentucky University

521 Lancaster Avenue
Richmond, KY 40475
http://www.
cbt.eku.edu/welcome.php
Public
Admissions: (859) 622-1742
E-mail: graduateschool@eku.edu
Financial aid: (859) 622-2361
Application deadline: 09/07
In-state tuition: full time: $440/
credit hour; part time: $440/
credit hour
Out-of-state tuition: full time: $770/
credit hour
Room/board/expenses: N/A
College-funded aid: Yes
International student aid: Yes
Full-time enrollment: 24
men: 58%; women: 42%;
minorities:4%; international: 46%
Part-time enrollment: 35
men: 51%; women: 49%;
minorities:9%; international: 3%
Average GMAT (full time): 480
Average GMAT (part time): 480
Average GPA (full time): 3.13
**Average age of entrants to full-time
program:** 26
TOEFL requirement: Yes
Minimum TOEFL score: 550

Morehead State University[1]

Combs Building 214
Morehead, KY 40351
http://www.
moreheadstate.edu/mba
Public
Admissions: (606) 783-2183
E-mail: msu-mba@
moreheadstate.edu
Financial aid: (606) 783-2011

Tuition: N/A
Room/board/expenses: N/A
Enrollment: N/A

Murray State University[1]

109 Business Building
Murray, KY 42071
http://murraystate.edu/
business.aspx
Public
Admissions: (270) 809-3779
E-mail: kathy.garrison@
murraystate.edu
Financial aid: (270) 809-2546
Tuition: N/A
Room/board/expenses: N/A
Enrollment: N/A

Northern Kentucky University[1]

Suite 401, BEP Center
Highland Heights, KY 41099
http://www.nku.edu/~mbusiness
Public
Admissions: (859) 572-6336
E-mail: mbusiness@nku.edu
Financial aid: (859) 572-6364
Tuition: N/A
Room/board/expenses: N/A
Enrollment: N/A

University of Kentucky (Gatton)

145 Gatton College of Business
and Economics
Lexington, KY 40506-0034
http://gatton.uky.edu
Public
Admissions: (859) 257-1306
E-mail: ukmba@uky.edu
Financial aid: (859) 257-1306
Application deadline: 05/12
In-state tuition: full time: $19,977;
part time: $642/credit hour
Out-of-state tuition: full time:
$31,049
Room/board/expenses: $13,000
College-funded aid: Yes
International student aid: Yes
Full-time enrollment: 80
men: 70%; women: 30%;
minorities:5%; international: 10%
Part-time enrollment: 49
men: 65%; women: 35%;
minorities:8%; international: 0%
Acceptance rate (full time): 78%
Average GMAT (full time): 609
Average GMAT (part time): 583
Average GPA (full time): 3.37
**Average age of entrants to full-time
program:** 24
**Average months of prior work
experience (full time):** 14
TOEFL requirement: Yes
Minimum TOEFL score: 550
Most popular departments: finance,
general management, marketing,
operations management, supply
chain management
**Mean starting base salary for 2012
full-time graduates:** $54,811
Employment location for 2012 class:
Intl. 0%; N.E. 0%; M.A. 5%; S.
75%; M.W. 13%; S.W. 3%; W. 5%

University of Louisville

Belknap Campus
Louisville, KY 40292
http://business.louisville.edu/mba
Public
Admissions: (502) 852-7257
E-mail: mba@louisville.edu
Financial aid: (502) 852-5511
Application deadline: 07/01
In-state tuition: total program:
$32,000 (full-time); $32,000
(part-time)
Out-of-state tuition: total program:
$32,000 (full-time)

Room/board/expenses: $13,000
College-funded aid: Yes
International student aid: Yes
**Average student indebtedness at
graduation:** $29,982
Full-time enrollment: 40
men: 70%; women: 30%;
minorities:10%; international: 10%
Part-time enrollment: 111
men: 63%; women: 37%;
minorities:14%; international: 7%
Acceptance rate (full time): 29%
Average GMAT (full time): 556
Average GMAT (part time): 544
Average GPA (full time): 3.42
**Average age of entrants to full-time
program:** 26
**Average months of prior work
experience (full time):** 34
TOEFL requirement: Yes
Minimum TOEFL score: 550
Most popular departments: en-
trepreneurship, finance, health
care administration, leadership,
portfolio management
**Mean starting base salary for 2012
full-time graduates:** $65,955
Employment location for 2012 class:
Intl. 0%; N.E. 0%; M.A. 0%; S.
89%; M.W. 11%; S.W. 0%; W. 0%

Western Kentucky University (Ford)[1]

434 A. Grise Hall
Bowling Green, KY 42101-1056
http://www.wku.edu/gfcb/
Public
Admissions: (270) 745-2446
E-mail: mba@wku.edu
Financial aid: (270) 745-2755
Tuition: N/A
Room/board/expenses: N/A
Enrollment: N/A

LOUISIANA

Louisiana State University– Baton Rouge (Ourso)

3304 Patrick F. Taylor Hall
Baton Rouge, LA 70803
http://mba.lsu.edu
Public
Admissions: (225) 578-8867
E-mail: busmba@lsu.edu
Financial aid: (225) 578-3103
Application deadline: 05/15
In-state tuition: total program:
$26,750 (full-time); $47,650
(part-time)
Out-of-state tuition: total program:
$58,570 (full-time)
Room/board/expenses: $19,500
College-funded aid: Yes
International student aid: Yes
**Average student indebtedness at
graduation:** $8,181
Full-time enrollment: 93
men: 53%; women: 47%;
minorities:4%; international: 23%
Part-time enrollment: 109
men: 70%; women: 30%;
minorities:17%; international: 7%
Acceptance rate (full time): 36%
Average GMAT (full time): 632
Average GMAT (part time): 511
Average GPA (full time): 3.42
**Average age of entrants to full-time
program:** 24
**Average months of prior work
experience (full time):** 25
TOEFL requirement: Yes
Minimum TOEFL score: 550
Most popular departments:
consulting, finance, interna-
tional business, statistics and
operations research, other
**Mean starting base salary for 2012
full-time graduates:** $59,762
Employment location for 2012 class:
Intl. 0%; N.E. 0%; M.A. 5%; S.
70%; M.W. 7%; S.W. 14%; W. 4%

Louisiana State University– Shreveport

1 University Place
Shreveport, LA 71115
http://www.lsus.edu/ba/mba
Public
Admissions: (318) 797-5213
E-mail: bill.bigler@lsus.edu
Financial aid: (318) 797-5363
Application deadline: 06/30
In-state tuition: full time: $231/
credit hour; part time: $231/
credit hour
Out-of-state tuition: full time: $231/
credit hour
Room/board/expenses: N/A
College-funded aid: Yes
International student aid: No
Full-time enrollment: 54
men: 50%; women: 50%;
minorities:7%; international: 19%
Part-time enrollment: 54
men: N/A; women: N/A;
minorities:N/A; international: N/A
Acceptance rate (full time): 95%
**Average age of entrants to full-time
program:** 27
TOEFL requirement: Yes
Minimum TOEFL score: 500

Louisiana Tech University

PO Box 10318
Ruston, LA 71272
http://www.
latech.edu/graduate_school
Public
Admissions: (318) 257-2924
E-mail: gschool@latech.edu
Financial aid: (318) 257-2641
Application deadline: 08/01
In-state tuition: full time: $8,213;
part time: $4,581
Out-of-state tuition: full time:
$14,252
Room/board/expenses: $9,580
College-funded aid: Yes
International student aid: Yes
Full-time enrollment: 49
men: 69%; women: 31%;
minorities:4%; international: 31%
Part-time enrollment: 2
men: 100%; women: 0%;
minorities:0%; international: 0%
Acceptance rate (full time): 72%
Average GMAT (full time): 563
Average GMAT (part time): 550
Average GPA (full time): 3.35
TOEFL requirement: Yes
Minimum TOEFL score: 550

Loyola University New Orleans (Butt)

6363 St. Charles Avenue
Campus Box 15
New Orleans, LA 70118
http://www.business.loyno.edu
Private
Admissions: (504) 864-7953
E-mail: mba@loyno.edu
Financial aid: (504) 865-3231
Application deadline: 06/30
Tuition: full time: N/A; part time:
$958/credit hour
Room/board/expenses: N/A
College-funded aid: Yes
International student aid: Yes
Full-time enrollment: N/A
men: N/A; women: N/A;
minorities:N/A; international: N/A
Part-time enrollment: 67
men: 58%; women: 42%;
minorities:16%; international: 4%
Average GMAT (part time): 560
TOEFL requirement: Yes
Minimum TOEFL score: 580
Most popular departments: en-
trepreneurship, finance, leader-
ship, statistics and operations
research, other

McNeese State University

PO Box 91660
Lake Charles, LA 70609
http://www.
mcneese.edu/colleges/bus
Public
Admissions: (337) 475-5576
E-mail: mba@mcneese.edu
Financial aid: (337) 475-5065
Application deadline: 01/07
In-state tuition: full time: $5,464;
part time: $4,202
Out-of-state tuition: full time:
$15,546
Room/board/expenses: $11,418
College-funded aid: Yes
International student aid: No
Full-time enrollment: 62
men: 52%; women: 48%;
minorities:68%; international:
63%
Part-time enrollment: 34
men: 44%; women: 56%;
minorities:21%; international: 3%
Acceptance rate (full time): 88%
Average GMAT (full time): 482
Average GMAT (part time): 473
Average GPA (full time): 3.23
**Average age of entrants to full-time
program:** 25
TOEFL requirement: Yes
Minimum TOEFL score: 550

Nicholls State University

PO Box 2015
Thibodaux, LA 70310
http://www.nicholls.edu/business/
Public
Admissions: (985) 448-4507
E-mail: becky.leblanc-durocher@
nicholls.edu
Financial aid: (985) 448-4048
Application deadline: rolling
In-state tuition: full time: $6,348;
part time: $3,474
Out-of-state tuition: full time:
$15,196
Room/board/expenses: N/A
College-funded aid: Yes
International student aid: Yes
Full-time enrollment: 44
men: 59%; women: 41%;
minorities:N/A; international: N/A
Part-time enrollment: 48
men: 52%; women: 48%;
minorities:N/A; international: N/A
Acceptance rate (full time): 100%
Average GMAT (full time): 491
Average GPA (full time): 3.21
TOEFL requirement: Yes
Minimum TOEFL score: 550

Southeastern Louisiana University

SLU 10735
Hammond, LA 70402
http://www.selu.edu/
acad_research/programs/
grad_bus
Public
Admissions: (985) 549-5637
E-mail: admissions@selu.edu
Financial aid: (985) 549-2244
Application deadline: 08/01
In-state tuition: full time: $5,726;
part time: $318/credit hour
Out-of-state tuition: full time:
$16,584
Room/board/expenses: $11,582
College-funded aid: Yes
International student aid: No
**Average student indebtedness at
graduation:** $21,039
Full-time enrollment: 66
men: 41%; women: 59%;
minorities:14%; international: 11%
Part-time enrollment: 13
men: 69%; women: 31%;
minorities:8%; international: 0%
Acceptance rate (full time): 98%

Average GMAT (full time): 502
Average GPA (full time): 3.42
Average age of entrants to full-time program: 23
TOEFL requirement: Yes
Minimum TOEFL score: 500

Southern University and A&M College[1]

PO Box 9723
Baton Rouge, LA 70813
http://www.business.subr.edu
Public
Admissions: (225) 771-5390
E-mail: gradschool@subr.edu
Financial aid: (225) 771-2790
Tuition: N/A
Room/board/expenses: N/A
Enrollment: N/A

Tulane University (Freeman)

7 McAlister Drive
New Orleans, LA 70118-5669
http://freeman.tulane.edu
Private
Admissions: (504) 865-5410
E-mail: freeman.admissions@tulane.edu
Financial aid: (504) 865-5410
Application deadline: 05/06
Tuition: full time: $51,291; part time: $1,544/credit hour
Room/board/expenses: $16,300
College-funded aid: Yes
International student aid: Yes
Full-time enrollment: 169
men: 64%; women: 36%;
minorities:18%; international: 32%
Part-time enrollment: N/A
men: N/A; women: N/A;
minorities:N/A; international: N/A
Acceptance rate (full time): 83%
Average GMAT (full time): 629
Average GPA (full time): 3.24
Average age of entrants to full-time program: 27
Average months of prior work experience (full time): 46
TOEFL requirement: Yes
Minimum TOEFL score: 600
Most popular departments: entrepreneurship, finance, general management, international business, other
Mean starting base salary for 2012 full-time graduates: $75,000
Employment location for 2012 class: Intl. 7%; N.E. 5%; M.A. 5%; S. 64%; M.W. 11%; S.W. 5%; W. 5%

University of Louisiana–Lafayette (Moody)

USL Box 44568
Lafayette, LA 70504-4568
http://gradschool.louisiana.edu/
Public
Admissions: (337) 482-6965
E-mail: gradschool@louisiana.edu
Financial aid: (337) 482-6506
Application deadline: 07/15
In-state tuition: full time: $5,830; part time: $4,154
Out-of-state tuition: full time: $14,800
Room/board/expenses: $6,000
College-funded aid: Yes
International student aid: Yes
Full-time enrollment: N/A
men: N/A; women: N/A;
minorities:N/A; international: N/A
Part-time enrollment: 239
men: 57%; women: 43%;
minorities:18%; international: 6%
Average GMAT (part time): 508
TOEFL requirement: Yes
Minimum TOEFL score: 550

University of Louisiana–Monroe[1]

700 University Avenue
Monroe, LA 71209
http://ele.ulm.edu
Public
Admissions: (318) 342-1100
E-mail: pena@ulm.edu
Financial aid: (318) 342-5320
Tuition: N/A
Room/board/expenses: N/A
Enrollment: N/A

University of New Orleans

2000 Lakeshore Drive
New Orleans, LA 70148
http://grad.uno.edu/
Public
Admissions: (504) 280-6595
E-mail: admissions@uno.edu
Financial aid: (504) 280-6209
Application deadline: 07/01
In-state tuition: total program: $18,560 (full-time); $17,681 (part-time)
Out-of-state tuition: total program: $39,587 (full-time)
Room/board/expenses: N/A
College-funded aid: Yes
International student aid: Yes
Full-time enrollment: 300
men: N/A; women: N/A;
minorities:N/A; international: N/A
Part-time enrollment: N/A
men: N/A; women: N/A;
minorities:N/A; international: N/A
TOEFL requirement: Yes
Minimum TOEFL score: 550

MAINE

University of Maine[1]

Donald P. Corbett Business Building
Orono, ME 04469-5723
http://www.umaine.edu/business
Public
Admissions: (207) 581-1973
E-mail: mba@maine.edu
Financial aid: (207) 581-1324
Tuition: N/A
Room/board/expenses: N/A
Enrollment: N/A

University of Southern Maine[1]

PO Box 9300
Portland, ME 04104
http://www.usm.maine.edu/sb
Public
Admissions: (207) 780-4184
E-mail: mba@usm.maine.edu
Financial aid: (207) 780-5250
Tuition: N/A
Room/board/expenses: N/A
Enrollment: N/A

MARYLAND

Frostburg State University

125 Guild Center
101 Braddock Road
Frostburg, MD 21532-2303
http://www.frostburg.edu/colleges/cob/mba/
Public
Admissions: (301) 687-7053
E-mail: gradservices@frostburg.edu
Financial aid: (301) 687-4301
Application deadline: rolling
In-state tuition: full time: $327/credit hour; part time: $327/credit hour
Out-of-state tuition: full time: $420/credit hour
Room/board/expenses: $3,694

College-funded aid: Yes
International student aid: Yes
Full-time enrollment: 77
men: 64%; women: 36%;
minorities:17%; international: 22%
Part-time enrollment: 236
men: 49%; women: 51%;
minorities:17%; international: 3%
Acceptance rate (full time): 81%
Average GMAT (full time): 493
Average GMAT (part time): 520
Average GPA (full time): 3.46
Average age of entrants to full-time program: 28
TOEFL requirement: Yes
Minimum TOEFL score: 550

Loyola University Maryland (Sellinger)

4501 N. Charles Street
Baltimore, MD 21210-2699
http://www.loyola.edu/sellinger
Private
Admissions: (410) 617-5020
E-mail: graduate@loyola.edu
Financial aid: (410) 617-2576
Application deadline: rolling
Tuition: total program: $62,000 (full-time); part time: $895/credit hour
Room/board/expenses: N/A
College-funded aid: Yes
International student aid: No
Average student indebtedness at graduation: $58,260
Full-time enrollment: 21
men: 38%; women: 62%;
minorities:19%; international: 0%
Part-time enrollment: 472
men: 63%; women: 37%;
minorities:18%; international: 2%
Acceptance rate (full time): 77%
Average GMAT (full time): 549
Average GMAT (part time): 543
Average GPA (full time): 3.28
Average age of entrants to full-time program: 24
Average months of prior work experience (full time): 17
TOEFL requirement: Yes
Minimum TOEFL score: 550
Employment location for 2012 class: Intl. N/A; N.E. N/A; M.A. 100%; S. N/A; M.W. N/A; S.W. N/A; W. N/A

Morgan State University (Graves)

1700 E. Cold Spring Lane
Baltimore, MD 21251
http://web.morgan.edu/graduate
Public
Admissions: (443) 885-3185
Financial aid: (443) 885-3170
Application deadline: 07/01
In-state tuition: full time: $348/credit hour; part time: $348/credit hour
Out-of-state tuition: full time: $678/credit hour
Room/board/expenses: $23,000
College-funded aid: Yes
International student aid: Yes
Full-time enrollment: 28
men: 64%; women: 36%;
minorities:100%; international: 68%
Part-time enrollment: 12
men: 50%; women: 50%;
minorities:100%; international: 0%
Acceptance rate (full time): 74%
Average GMAT (full time): 550
Average GMAT (part time): 530
Average GPA (full time): 3.60
Average age of entrants to full-time program: 27
Average months of prior work experience (full time): 24
TOEFL requirement: Yes
Minimum TOEFL score: 550

Salisbury University (Perdue)

1101 Camden Avenue
Salisbury, MD 21801-6860
http://www.salisbury.edu/Schools/perdue/welcome.html
Public
Admissions: (410) 543-6161
E-mail: admissions@salisbury.edu
Financial aid: (410) 543-6165
Application deadline: N/A
In-state tuition: full time: $324/credit hour; part time: $324/credit hour
Out-of-state tuition: full time: $613/credit hour
Room/board/expenses: N/A
College-funded aid: Yes
International student aid: Yes
Full-time enrollment: 16
men: 56%; women: 44%;
minorities:N/A; international: 6%
Part-time enrollment: 26
men: 65%; women: 35%;
minorities:N/A; international: 0%
Average GMAT (full time): 530
Average GMAT (part time): 530
Average GPA (full time): 3.40
TOEFL requirement: Yes
Minimum TOEFL score: 550

University of Baltimore-Towson University[1]

1420 N. Charles Street
Baltimore, MD 21201
http://mba.ubalt.towson.edu/
Public
Admissions: (410) 837-6565
E-mail: gradadmissions@ubalt.edu
Financial aid: (410) 837-4763
Tuition: N/A
Room/board/expenses: N/A
Enrollment: N/A

University of Maryland– College Park (Smith)

2308 Van Munching Hall
College Park, MD 20742
http://www.rhsmith.umd.edu
Public
Admissions: (301) 405-2559
E-mail: mba_info@rhsmith.umd.edu
Financial aid: (301) 314-8297
Application deadline: 01/15
In-state tuition: full time: $40,158; part time: $1,425/credit hour
Out-of-state tuition: full time: $47,448
Room/board/expenses: N/A
College-funded aid: Yes
International student aid: Yes
Full-time enrollment: 230
men: 70%; women: 30%;
minorities:15%; international: 43%
Part-time enrollment: 819
men: 68%; women: 32%;
minorities:26%; international: 15%
Acceptance rate (full time): 44%
Average GMAT (full time): 656
Average GMAT (part time): 579
Average GPA (full time): 3.30
Average age of entrants to full-time program: 29
Average months of prior work experience (full time): 66
TOEFL requirement: Yes
Minimum TOEFL score: 600
Most popular departments: consulting, entrepreneurship, finance, marketing, supply chain management
Mean starting base salary for 2012 full-time graduates: $92,938
Employment location for 2012 class: Intl. 9%; N.E. 23%; M.A. 54%; S. 4%; M.W. 6%; S.W. 3%; W. 3%

MASSACHUSETTS

Babson College (Olin)

231 Forest Street
Babson Park, MA 02457-0310
http://mba.babson.edu
Private
Admissions: (781) 239-4317
E-mail: mbaadmission@babson.edu
Financial aid: (781) 239-4219
Application deadline: 04/01
Tuition: total program: $91,180 (full-time); part time: $1,440/credit hour
Room/board/expenses: $48,566
College-funded aid: Yes
International student aid: Yes
Average student indebtedness at graduation: $62,888
Full-time enrollment: 408
men: 72%; women: 28%;
minorities:11%; international: 55%
Part-time enrollment: 421
men: 67%; women: 33%;
minorities:13%; international: 9%
Acceptance rate (full time): 73%
Average GMAT (full time): 618
Average GMAT (part time): 569
Average GPA (full time): 3.23
Average age of entrants to full-time program: 28
Average months of prior work experience (full time): 54
TOEFL requirement: Yes
Minimum TOEFL score: N/A
Most popular departments: economics, entrepreneurship, finance, general management, marketing
Mean starting base salary for 2012 full-time graduates: $89,742
Employment location for 2012 class: Intl. 21%; N.E. 66%; M.A. 2%; S. 1%; M.W. 4%; S.W. 3%; W. 4%

Bentley University (McCallum)

175 Forest Street
Waltham, MA 02452-4705
http://graduate.bentley.edu
Private
Admissions: (781) 891-2108
E-mail: bentleygraduateadmissions@bentley.edu
Financial aid: (781) 891-3441
Application deadline: 03/15
Tuition: full time: $34,904; part time: $1,218/credit hour
Room/board/expenses: $17,520
College-funded aid: Yes
International student aid: Yes
Full-time enrollment: 136
men: 65%; women: 35%;
minorities:7%; international: 54%
Part-time enrollment: 327
men: 59%; women: 41%;
minorities:14%; international: 5%
Acceptance rate (full time): 69%
Average GMAT (full time): 596
Average GMAT (part time): 585
Average GPA (full time): 3.27
Average age of entrants to full-time program: 26
Average months of prior work experience (full time): 41
TOEFL requirement: Yes
Minimum TOEFL score: 600
Most popular departments: accounting, finance, general management, marketing, management information systems
Mean starting base salary for 2012 full-time graduates: $75,616
Employment location for 2012 class: Intl. 29%; N.E. 59%; M.A. 0%; S. 0%; M.W. 0%; S.W. 6%; W. 6%

Boston College (Carroll)

140 Commonwealth Avenue
Fulton Hall 320
Chestnut Hill, MA 02467
http://www.bc.edu/mba
Private
Admissions: (617) 552-3920
E-mail: bcmba@bc.edu
Financial aid: (800) 294-0294
Application deadline: 03/15
Tuition: full time: $38,566; part time: $1,372/credit hour
Room/board/expenses: $19,565
College-funded aid: Yes
International student aid: Yes
Average student indebtedness at graduation: $61,400
Full-time enrollment: 195
men: 67%; women: 33%; minorities:10%; international: 33%
Part-time enrollment: 407
men: 63%; women: 37%; minorities:18%; international: 6%
Acceptance rate (full time): 35%
Average GMAT (full time): 666
Average GMAT (part time): 590
Average GPA (full time): 3.41
Average age of entrants to full-time program: 28
Average months of prior work experience (full time): 52
TOEFL requirement: Yes
Minimum TOEFL score: 600
Most popular departments: accounting, consulting, finance, general management, marketing
Mean starting base salary for 2012 full-time graduates: $94,147
Employment location for 2012 class: Intl. 12%; N.E. 71%; M.A. 4%; S. 4%; M.W. 3%; S.W. 0%; W. 6%

Boston University

595 Commonwealth Avenue
Boston, MA 02215-1704
http://management.bu.edu
Private
Admissions: (617) 353-2670
E-mail: mba@bu.edu
Financial aid: (617) 353-2670
Application deadline: N/A
Tuition: full time: $42,934; part time: $1,325/credit hour
Room/board/expenses: $17,954
College-funded aid: Yes
International student aid: Yes
Full-time enrollment: 297
men: 67%; women: 33%; minorities:15%; international: 35%
Part-time enrollment: 707
men: 63%; women: 37%; minorities:15%; international: 7%
Acceptance rate (full time): 33%
Average GMAT (full time): 680
Average GMAT (part time): 606
Average GPA (full time): 3.35
Average age of entrants to full-time program: 28
Average months of prior work experience (full time): 63
TOEFL requirement: Yes
Minimum TOEFL score: 600
Most popular departments: finance, health care administration, marketing, management information systems, non-profit management
Mean starting base salary for 2012 full-time graduates: $93,591
Employment location for 2012 class: Intl. 7%; N.E. 72%; M.A. 3%; S. 4%; M.W. 2%; S.W. 3%; W. 10%

Brandeis University[1]

415 South Street
Waltham, MA 02454-9110
http://www.brandeis.edu/global
Private
Admissions: (781) 736-4829
E-mail: hchase@brandeis.edu
Financial aid: N/A

Tuition: N/A
Room/board/expenses: N/A
Enrollment: N/A

Clark University

950 Main Street
Worcester, MA 01610
http://www.clarku.edu/gsom
Private
Admissions: (508) 793-7406
E-mail: clarkmba@clarku.edu
Financial aid: (508) 793-7406
Application deadline: 06/01
Tuition: full time: $1,250/credit hour; part time: $1,250/credit hour
Room/board/expenses: $13,100
College-funded aid: Yes
International student aid: Yes
Full-time enrollment: 132
men: 52%; women: 48%; minorities:8%; international: 55%
Part-time enrollment: 143
men: 53%; women: 47%; minorities:6%; international: 8%
Acceptance rate (full time): 44%
Average GMAT (full time): 510
Average GMAT (part time): 565
Average GPA (full time): 3.30
Average age of entrants to full-time program: 26
Average months of prior work experience (full time): 45
TOEFL requirement: Yes
Minimum TOEFL score: 577
Most popular departments: finance, general management, international business, marketing, other
Mean starting base salary for 2012 full-time graduates: $49,700
Employment location for 2012 class: Intl. N/A; N.E. 83%; M.A. 9%; S. N/A; M.W. N/A; S.W. N/A; W. 9%

Harvard University

Soldiers Field
Boston, MA 02163
http://www.hbs.edu
Private
Admissions: (617) 495-6128
E-mail: admissions@hbs.edu
Financial aid: (617) 495-6640
Application deadline: N/A
Tuition: full time: $63,288; part time: N/A
Room/board/expenses: $23,912
College-funded aid: Yes
International student aid: Yes
Average student indebtedness at graduation: $70,731
Full-time enrollment: 1,824
men: 60%; women: 40%; minorities:22%; international: 34%
Part-time enrollment: N/A
men: N/A; women: N/A; minorities:N/A; international: N/A
Acceptance rate (full time): 11%
Average GMAT (full time): 724
Average GPA (full time): 3.67
Average age of entrants to full-time program: 26
Average months of prior work experience (full time): 50
TOEFL requirement: Yes
Minimum TOEFL score: N/A
Mean starting base salary for 2012 full-time graduates: $124,085
Employment location for 2012 class: Intl. 20%; N.E. 40%; M.A. 5%; S. 5%; M.W. 6%; S.W. 4%; W. 21%

Massachusetts Institute of Technology (Sloan)

50 Memorial Drive
Cambridge, MA 02142
http://mitsloan.mit.edu/mba
Private
Admissions: (617) 258-5434
E-mail: mbaadmissions@sloan.mit.edu
Financial aid: (617) 253-4971

Application deadline: N/A
Tuition: full time: $58,200; part time: N/A
Room/board/expenses: $30,749
College-funded aid: Yes
International student aid: Yes
Average student indebtedness at graduation: $100,212
Full-time enrollment: 816
men: 65%; women: 35%; minorities:27%; international: 40%
Part-time enrollment: N/A
men: N/A; women: N/A; minorities:N/A; international: N/A
Acceptance rate (full time): 16%
Average GMAT (full time): 710
Average GPA (full time): 3.53
Average age of entrants to full-time program: 28
Average months of prior work experience (full time): 60
TOEFL requirement: No
Minimum TOEFL score: N/A
Most popular departments: entrepreneurship, finance, manufacturing and technology management, operations management, technology
Mean starting base salary for 2012 full-time graduates: $118,406
Employment location for 2012 class: Intl. 16%; N.E. 43%; M.A. 5%; S. 4%; M.W. 5%; S.W. 4%; W. 23%

Northeastern University

360 Huntington Avenue
350 Dodge Hall
Boston, MA 02115
http://www.mba.northeastern.edu
Private
Admissions: (617) 373-5992
E-mail: gradbusiness@neu.edu
Financial aid: (617) 373-5899
Application deadline: 04/15
Tuition: full time: $1,345/credit hour; part time: $1,345/credit hour
Room/board/expenses: $21,700
College-funded aid: Yes
International student aid: Yes
Full-time enrollment: 219
men: 67%; women: 33%; minorities:11%; international: 21%
Part-time enrollment: 400
men: 59%; women: 41%; minorities:17%; international: 2%
Acceptance rate (full time): 28%
Average GMAT (full time): 643
Average GMAT (part time): 562
Average GPA (full time): 3.27
Average age of entrants to full-time program: 26
Average months of prior work experience (full time): 48
TOEFL requirement: Yes
Minimum TOEFL score: 600
Most popular departments: entrepreneurship, finance, international business, marketing, supply chain management
Mean starting base salary for 2012 full-time graduates: $72,191
Employment location for 2012 class: Intl. 7%; N.E. 84%; M.A. 3%; S. 0%; M.W. 0%; S.W. 2%; W. 3%

Simmons College[1]

300 The Fenway
Boston, MA 02115
http://www.simmons.edu/som/
Private
Admissions: (617) 521-2000
E-mail: som@simmons.edu
Financial aid: N/A
Tuition: N/A
Room/board/expenses: N/A
Enrollment: N/A

Suffolk University (Sawyer)

8 Ashburton Place
Boston, MA 02108
http://www.suffolk.edu/business
Private
Admissions: (617) 573-8302
E-mail: grad.admission@suffolk.edu
Financial aid: (617) 573-8470
Application deadline: 06/15
Tuition: full time: $37,570; part time: $1,251/credit hour
Room/board/expenses: $20,400
College-funded aid: Yes
International student aid: Yes
Full-time enrollment: 102
men: 59%; women: 41%; minorities:10%; international: 49%
Part-time enrollment: 286
men: 51%; women: 49%; minorities:12%; international: 1%
Acceptance rate (full time): 44%
Average GMAT (full time): 532
Average GMAT (part time): 486
Average GPA (full time): 3.24
Average age of entrants to full-time program: 28
Average months of prior work experience (full time): 44
TOEFL requirement: Yes
Minimum TOEFL score: 550
Mean starting base salary for 2012 full-time graduates: $73,700
Employment location for 2012 class: Intl. 20%; N.E. 40%; M.A. 20%; S. N/A; M.W. 10%; S.W. 10%; W. N/A

University of Massachusetts–Amherst (Isenberg)

121 Presidents Drive
Amherst, MA 01003
http://www.isenberg.umass.edu/mba
Public
Admissions: (413) 545-5608
E-mail: mba@isenberg.umass.edu
Financial aid: (413) 577-0555
Application deadline: 02/01
In-state tuition: full time: $2,640; part time: $667/credit hour
Out-of-state tuition: full time: $9,937
Room/board/expenses: $16,200
College-funded aid: Yes
International student aid: Yes
Average student indebtedness at graduation: $20,447
Full-time enrollment: 65
men: 57%; women: 43%; minorities:5%; international: 37%
Part-time enrollment: 1,179
men: 72%; women: 28%; minorities:17%; international: 6%
Acceptance rate (full time): 25%
Average GMAT (full time): 655
Average GMAT (part time): 572
Average GPA (full time): 3.40
Average age of entrants to full-time program: 28
Average months of prior work experience (full time): 64
TOEFL requirement: Yes
Minimum TOEFL score: 600
Most popular departments: entrepreneurship, finance, health care administration, marketing, sports business
Mean starting base salary for 2012 full-time graduates: $82,900
Employment location for 2012 class: Intl. 16%; N.E. 68%; M.A. 5%; S. 0%; M.W. 5%; S.W. 0%; W. 5%

University of Massachusetts–Boston

100 Morrissey Boulevard
Boston, MA 02125-3393
http://www.umb.edu/academic/cm
Public
Admissions: (617) 287-7760
E-mail: gradcm@umb.edu
Financial aid: (617) 287-6300
Application deadline: rolling
In-state tuition: full time: $17,814; part time: $563/credit hour
Out-of-state tuition: full time: $30,472
Room/board/expenses: $14,989
College-funded aid: Yes
International student aid: Yes
Full-time enrollment: 256
men: 48%; women: 52%; minorities:N/A; international: N/A
Part-time enrollment: 288
men: 60%; women: 40%; minorities:N/A; international: N/A
Acceptance rate (full time): 42%
Average GMAT (full time): 580
Average GMAT (part time): 580
Average GPA (full time): 3.30
Average age of entrants to full-time program: 27
Average months of prior work experience (full time): 55
TOEFL requirement: Yes
Minimum TOEFL score: 600
Most popular departments: accounting, entrepreneurship, finance, health care administration, management information systems

University of Massachusetts–Dartmouth (Charlton)

285 Old Westport Road
North Dartmouth, MA 02747-2300
http://www.umassd.edu/charlton/
Public
Admissions: (508) 999-8604
E-mail: graduate@umassd.edu
Financial aid: (508) 999-8632
Application deadline: 03/01
In-state tuition: full time: $12,988; part time: $550/credit hour
Out-of-state tuition: full time: $23,028
Room/board/expenses: $13,825
College-funded aid: Yes
International student aid: Yes
Full-time enrollment: 92
men: 54%; women: 46%; minorities:8%; international: 60%
Part-time enrollment: 92
men: 50%; women: 50%; minorities:11%; international: 7%
Acceptance rate (full time): 100%
Average GMAT (full time): 472
Average GMAT (part time): 474
Average GPA (full time): 3.27
Average age of entrants to full-time program: 25
TOEFL requirement: Yes
Minimum TOEFL score: 500

University of Massachusetts–Lowell

1 University Avenue
Lowell, MA 01854
http://www.uml.edu/grad
Public
Admissions: (978) 934-2381
E-mail: graduate_school@uml.edu
Financial aid: (978) 934-4220
Application deadline: rolling
In-state tuition: full time: $1,637; part time: $91/credit hour
Out-of-state tuition: full time: $6,425
Room/board/expenses: $9,550
College-funded aid: Yes
International student aid: Yes

Full-time enrollment: 66
men: 52%; women: 48%;
minorities:21%; international: 41%
Part-time enrollment: 458
men: 69%; women: 31%;
minorities:26%; international: 3%
Acceptance rate (full time): 71%
Average GMAT (full time): 550
Average GMAT (part time): 580
Average GPA (full time): 3.27
Average age of entrants to full-time
program: 26
Average months of prior work
experience (full time): 37
TOEFL requirement: Yes
Minimum TOEFL score: 600
Most popular departments: ac-
counting, entrepreneurship,
finance, general management,
management information systems

Western
New England
University

1215 Wilbraham Road
Springfield, MA 01119-2684
http://www1.wne.edu/business/
Private
Admissions: (800) 325-1122
E-mail: study@wne.edu
Financial aid: (413) 796-2080
Application deadline: rolling
Tuition: total program: $26,460
(full-time); part time: $735/credit
hour
Room/board/expenses: N/A
College-funded aid: Yes
International student aid: Yes
Full-time enrollment: 5
men: N/A; women: N/A;
minorities:N/A; international: N/A
Part-time enrollment: 169
men: 49%; women: 51%;
minorities:10%; international: 2%
Acceptance rate (full time): 60%
Average GMAT (full time): 570
Average GMAT (part time): 518
Average age of entrants to full-time
program: 27
TOEFL requirement: Yes
Minimum TOEFL score: 550
Most popular departments: general
management, sports business

Worcester
Polytechnic Institute

100 Institute Road
Worcester, MA 01609
http://business.wpi.edu
Private
Admissions: (508) 831-4665
E-mail: business@wpi.edu
Financial aid: (508) 831-5469
Application deadline: 07/01
Tuition: full time: $1,239/credit
hour; part time: $1,239/credit hour
Room/board/expenses: $13,500
College-funded aid: Yes
International student aid: Yes
Full-time enrollment: 184
men: 46%; women: 54%;
minorities:5%; international: 84%
Part-time enrollment: 278
men: 78%; women: 22%;
minorities:6%; international: 5%
Acceptance rate (full time): 36%
Average GMAT (full time): 635
Average GMAT (part time): 592
Average GPA (full time): 3.35
Average age of entrants to full-time
program: 23
Average months of prior work
experience (full time): 18
TOEFL requirement: Yes
Minimum TOEFL score: 563
Most popular departments: entre-
preneurship, manufacturing and
technology management, market-
ing, management information
systems, technology

MICHIGAN

Central Michigan
University[1]

252 ABSC - Grawn Hall
Mount Pleasant, MI 48859
http://www.cba.cmich.edu/mba/
Public
Admissions: (989) 774-3150
E-mail: pamela.stambersky@
cmich.edu
Financial aid: (989) 774-3674
Tuition: N/A
Room/board/expenses: N/A
Enrollment: N/A

Eastern Michigan
University

404 Gary M. Owen Building
Ypsilanti, MI 48197
http://www.cob.emich.edu
Public
Admissions: (734) 487-4444
E-mail: cob.graduate@emich.edu
Financial aid: (734) 487-0455
Application deadline: rolling
In-state tuition: full time: $606/
credit hour; part time: $606/
credit hour
Out-of-state tuition: full time:
$1,042/credit hour
Room/board/expenses: $9,000
College-funded aid: Yes
International student aid: Yes
Full-time enrollment: N/A
men: N/A; women: N/A;
minorities:N/A; international: N/A
Part-time enrollment: 206
men: 64%; women: 36%;
minorities:33%; international: 14%
Average GMAT (part time): 508
TOEFL requirement: Yes
Minimum TOEFL score: 550
Most popular departments: general
management, human resources
management, marketing, opera-
tions management, supply chain
management

Grand Valley State
University (Seidman)

401 Fulton Street West
Grand Rapids, MI 49504-6431
http://www.gvsu.edu
Public
Admissions: (616) 331-7400
E-mail: go2gvmba@gvsu.edu
Financial aid: (616) 331-3234
Application deadline: 08/01
In-state tuition: total program:
$34,332 (full-time); part time:
$547/credit hour
Out-of-state tuition: total program:
$42,018 (full-time)
Room/board/expenses: $13,000
College-funded aid: Yes
International student aid: Yes
Full-time enrollment: 16
men: 75%; women: 25%;
minorities:19%; international: 0%
Part-time enrollment: 198
men: 74%; women: 26%;
minorities:7%; international: 4%
Acceptance rate (full time): 87%
Average GMAT (full time): 581
Average GMAT (part time): 571
Average GPA (full time): 3.50
Average age of entrants to full-time
program: 23
Average months of prior work
experience (full time): 12
TOEFL requirement: Yes
Minimum TOEFL score: 550

Michigan State
University (Broad)

Eppley Center
645 N. Shaw Lane, Rm 211
East Lansing, MI 48824-1121
http://www.mba.msu.edu
Public
Admissions: (800) 467-8622
E-mail: mba@msu.edu
Financial aid: (517) 355-7604
Application deadline: rolling
In-state tuition: full time: $26,181;
part time: N/A
Out-of-state tuition: full time:
$41,511
Room/board/expenses: $21,530
College-funded aid: Yes
International student aid: Yes
Average student indebtedness at
graduation: $59,785
Full-time enrollment: 180
men: 81%; women: 19%;
minorities:11%; international: 34%
Part-time enrollment: N/A
men: N/A; women: N/A;
minorities:N/A; international: N/A
Acceptance rate (full time): 41%
Average GMAT (full time): 641
Average GPA (full time): 3.30
Average age of entrants to full-time
program: 28
Average months of prior work
experience (full time): 48
TOEFL requirement: Yes
Minimum TOEFL score: 600
Most popular departments: finance,
human resources management,
leadership, marketing, supply
chain management
Mean starting base salary for 2012
full-time graduates: $86,508
Employment location for 2012 class:
Intl. 6%; N.E. 7%; M.A. 4%; S. 3%;
M.W. 47%; S.W. 11%; W. 21%

Michigan
Technological
University

1400 Townsend Drive
Houghton, MI 49931-1295
http://www.mba.mtu.edu
Public
Admissions: (906) 487-3055
E-mail: mba@mtu.edu
Financial aid: (906) 487-3055
Application deadline: rolling
In-state tuition: full time: $13,630;
part time: $744/credit hour
Out-of-state tuition: full time:
$13,630
Room/board/expenses: $12,863
College-funded aid: Yes
International student aid: Yes
Average student indebtedness at
graduation: $26,077
Full-time enrollment: 35
men: 57%; women: 43%;
minorities:3%; international: 51%
Part-time enrollment: 17
men: 82%; women: 18%;
minorities:12%; international: 6%
Acceptance rate (full time): 35%
Average GMAT (full time): 548
Average GMAT (part time): 560
Average GPA (full time): 3.40
Average age of entrants to full-time
program: 24
Average months of prior work
experience (full time): 15
TOEFL requirement: Yes
Minimum TOEFL score: 590
Most popular departments:
economics, entrepreneurship,
manufacturing and technology
management, technology
Mean starting base salary for 2012
full-time graduates: $78,800
Employment location for 2012 class:
Intl. 0%; N.E. 0%; M.A. 0%; S. 0%;
M.W. 82%; S.W. 18%; W. 0%

Northern Michigan
University

1401 Presque Isle Avenue
Marquette, MI 49855
http://www.
nmu.edu/graduatestudies
Public
Admissions: (906) 277-2300
E-mail: gradapp@nmu.edu
Financial aid: (906) 227-2327
Application deadline: 07/01
In-state tuition: full time: $599/
credit hour; part time: $599/
credit hour
Out-of-state tuition: full time: $599/
credit hour
Room/board/expenses: $8,779
College-funded aid: Yes
International student aid: Yes
Average student indebtedness at
graduation: $8,840
Full-time enrollment: 22
men: 73%; women: 27%;
minorities:0%; international: 0%
Part-time enrollment: 4
men: 25%; women: 75%;
minorities:0%; international: 0%
Acceptance rate (full time): 35%
Average GMAT (full time): 643
Average GPA (full time): 3.45
Average age of entrants to full-time
program: 28
Average months of prior work
experience (full time): 90
TOEFL requirement: Yes
Minimum TOEFL score: 550
Most popular departments: general
management
Mean starting base salary for 2012
full-time graduates: $40,000
Employment location for 2012 class:
Intl. 14%; N.E. 0%; M.A. 0%; S.
0%; M.W. 86%; S.W. 0%; W. 0%

Oakland University

238 Elliott Hall
Rochester, MI 48309-4493
http://www.sba.oakland.edu/grad/
Public
Admissions: (248) 370-3287
E-mail: gbp@lists.oakland.edu
Financial aid: (248) 370-2550
Application deadline: 07/15
In-state tuition: full time: N/A; part
time: $595/credit hour
Out-of-state tuition: full time: N/A
Room/board/expenses: $11,486
College-funded aid: Yes
International student aid: Yes
Full-time enrollment: N/A
men: N/A; women: N/A;
minorities:N/A; international: N/A
Part-time enrollment: 267
men: 72%; women: 28%;
minorities:15%; international: 5%
Average GMAT (part time): 550
TOEFL requirement: Yes
Minimum TOEFL score: 550
Most popular departments: ac-
counting, finance, international
business, marketing, management
information systems

Saginaw Valley
State University

7400 Bay Road
University Center, MI 48710
http://www.svsu.edu/cbm/
Public
Admissions: (989) 964-4064
E-mail: cbmdean@svsu.edu
Financial aid: (989) 964-4103
Application deadline: rolling
In-state tuition: full time: $464/
credit hour; part time: $464/
credit hour
Out-of-state tuition: full time: $885/
credit hour
Room/board/expenses: $10,476
College-funded aid: Yes
International student aid: Yes

Full-time enrollment: 64
men: 63%; women: 38%;
minorities:3%; international: 77%
Part-time enrollment: 69
men: 54%; women: 46%;
minorities:20%; international: 22%
Acceptance rate (full time): 96%
Average age of entrants to full-time
program: 27
TOEFL requirement: Yes
Minimum TOEFL score: 525

University of
Detroit Mercy[1]

4001 W. McNichols Road
Detroit, MI 48221-3038
http://business.udmercy.edu
Private
Admissions: (313) 993-1202
E-mail: naskibom@udmercy.edu
Financial aid: (313) 993-3350
Tuition: N/A
Room/board/expenses: N/A
Enrollment: N/A

University of
Michigan–Ann Arbor
(Ross)

701 Tappan Street
Ann Arbor, MI 48109-1234
http://www.bus.umich.edu
Public
Admissions: (734) 763-5796
E-mail: rossmba@umich.edu
Financial aid: (734) 764-5796
Application deadline: 03/04
In-state tuition: full time: $50,194;
part time: $1,638/credit hour
Out-of-state tuition: full time:
$55,194
Room/board/expenses: $18,714
College-funded aid: Yes
International student aid: Yes
Average student indebtedness at
graduation: $95,720
Full-time enrollment: 992
men: 69%; women: 31%;
minorities:28%; international: 32%
Part-time enrollment: 366
men: 81%; women: 19%;
minorities:18%; international: 19%
Acceptance rate (full time): 41%
Average GMAT (full time): 703
Average GMAT (part time): 648
Average GPA (full time): 3.40
Average age of entrants to full-time
program: 28
Average months of prior work
experience (full time): 64
TOEFL requirement: Yes
Minimum TOEFL score: 600
Mean starting base salary for 2012
full-time graduates: $111,047
Employment location for 2012 class:
Intl. 8%; N.E. 22%; M.A. 4%; S.
3%; M.W. 34%; S.W. 5%; W. 24%

University of
Michigan–Dearborn

19000 Hubbard Drive
Dearborn, MI 48126-2638
http://www.
cob.umd.umich.edu/grad
Public
Admissions: (313) 593-5460
E-mail: gradbusiness@
umd.umich.edu
Financial aid: (313) 593-5300
Application deadline: 08/01
In-state tuition: full time: N/A; part
time: $575/credit hour
Out-of-state tuition: full time: N/A
Room/board/expenses: $12,500
College-funded aid: Yes
International student aid: Yes
Full-time enrollment: N/A
men: N/A; women: N/A;
minorities:N/A; international: N/A
Part-time enrollment: 193
men: 62%; women: 38%;
minorities:20%; international: 2%

Average GMAT (part time): 577
TOEFL requirement: Yes
Minimum TOEFL score: 560
Most popular departments: accounting, finance, general management, management information systems, supply chain management

University of Michigan–Flint
303 E. Kearsley Street
Flint, MI 48502-1950
http://mba.umflint.edu
Public
Admissions: (810) 762-3171
E-mail: graduate@umflint.edu
Financial aid: (810) 762-3444
Application deadline: rolling
In-state tuition: full time: $10,942; part time: $585/credit hour
Out-of-state tuition: full time: $10,942
Room/board/expenses: $7,506
College-funded aid: Yes
International student aid: No
Full-time enrollment: N/A
men: N/A; women: N/A;
minorities:N/A; international: N/A
Part-time enrollment: 183
men: 72%; women: 28%;
minorities:21%; international: 8%
Average GMAT (part time): 539
TOEFL requirement: Yes
Minimum TOEFL score: 560
Most popular departments: accounting, finance, general management, health care administration, international business

Wayne State University
5201 Cass Avenue
Prentis Building
Detroit, MI 48202
http://www.business.wayne.edu
Public
Admissions: (313) 577-4511
E-mail: gradbusiness@wayne.edu
Financial aid: (313) 577-3378
Application deadline: 08/01
In-state tuition: full time: $618/credit hour; part time: $618/credit hour
Out-of-state tuition: full time: $1,262/credit hour
Room/board/expenses: $16,257
College-funded aid: Yes
International student aid: Yes
Full-time enrollment: N/A
men: N/A; women: N/A;
minorities:N/A; international: N/A
Part-time enrollment: 635
men: 59%; women: 41%;
minorities:26%; international: 5%
Average GMAT (part time): 488
TOEFL requirement: Yes
Minimum TOEFL score: 550
Most popular departments: finance, general management, international business, marketing, supply chain management

Western Michigan University (Haworth)
1903 W. Michigan Avenue
Kalamazoo, MI 49008-5480
http://www.wmich.edu/mba
Public
Admissions: (269) 387-5133
E-mail: mba-advising@wmich.edu
Financial aid: (269) 387-6000
Application deadline: 07/15
In-state tuition: full time: N/A; part time: $480/credit hour
Out-of-state tuition: full time: N/A
Room/board/expenses: $13,341
College-funded aid: Yes
International student aid: No

Full-time enrollment: N/A
men: N/A; women: N/A;
minorities:N/A; international: N/A
Part-time enrollment: 381
men: 65%; women: 35%;
minorities:12%; international: 12%
Average GMAT (part time): 526
TOEFL requirement: Yes
Minimum TOEFL score: 550
Most popular departments: finance, general management, international business, marketing, management information systems

MINNESOTA

Minnesota State University–Mankato
120 Morris Hall
Mankato, MN 56001
http://cob.mnsu.edu/mba/
Public
Admissions: (507) 389-2967
E-mail: mba@mnsu.edu
Financial aid: (507) 389-1419
Application deadline: 07/01
In-state tuition: full time: $529/credit hour; part time: $529/credit hour
Out-of-state tuition: full time: $529/credit hour
Room/board/expenses: N/A
College-funded aid: Yes
International student aid: Yes
Full-time enrollment: 119
men: 73%; women: 27%;
minorities:N/A; international: N/A
Part-time enrollment: 119
men: 73%; women: 27%;
minorities:N/A; international: N/A
Acceptance rate (full time): 71%
Average GMAT (full time): 537
Average GPA (full time): 3.26
Average age of entrants to full-time program: 29
Average months of prior work experience (full time): 66
TOEFL requirement: Yes
Minimum TOEFL score: 550
Most popular departments: international business, leadership

St. Cloud State University (Herberger)[1]
720 Fourth Avenue S
St. Cloud, MN 56301-4498
http://www.stcloudstate.edu/mba
Public
Admissions: (320) 308-3212
E-mail: mba@stcloudstate.edu
Financial aid: (320) 308-2047
Tuition: N/A
Room/board/expenses: N/A
Enrollment: N/A

University of Minnesota–Duluth (Labovitz)
1318 Kirby Drive
Duluth, MN 55812-2496
https://lsbe.d.umn.edu/mba/mba.php
Public
Admissions: (218) 726-8839
E-mail: grad@d.umn.edu
Financial aid: (218) 726-8000
Application deadline: rolling
In-state tuition: full time: N/A; part time: $1,120/credit hour
Out-of-state tuition: full time: N/A
Room/board/expenses: $9,500
College-funded aid: Yes
International student aid: No
Full-time enrollment: 77
men: 66%; women: 34%;
minorities:16%; international: 6%
Part-time enrollment: N/A
men: N/A; women: N/A;
minorities:N/A; international: N/A

Average GMAT (part time): 560
TOEFL requirement: Yes
Minimum TOEFL score: 550

University of Minnesota–Twin Cities (Carlson)
321 19th Avenue S, Office 4-300
Minneapolis, MN 55455
http://www.carlsonschool.umn.edu/mba
Public
Admissions: (612) 625-5555
E-mail: mba@umn.edu
Financial aid: (612) 624-1111
Application deadline: 04/01
In-state tuition: full time: $37,264; part time: $1,200/credit hour
Out-of-state tuition: full time: $49,034
Room/board/expenses: $16,500
College-funded aid: Yes
International student aid: Yes
Average student indebtedness at graduation: $61,916
Full-time enrollment: 206
men: 72%; women: 28%;
minorities:11%; international: 26%
Part-time enrollment: 1,342
men: 68%; women: 32%;
minorities:7%; international: 5%
Acceptance rate (full time): 43%
Average GMAT (full time): 692
Average GMAT (part time): 607
Average GPA (full time): 3.40
Average age of entrants to full-time program: 28
Average months of prior work experience (full time): 52
TOEFL requirement: Yes
Minimum TOEFL score: 580
Most popular departments: consulting, finance, general management, marketing, supply chain management
Mean starting base salary for 2012 full-time graduates: $100,843
Employment location for 2012 class: Intl. 0%; N.E. 4%; M.A. 0%; S. 4%; M.W. 86%; S.W. 4%; W. 2%

University of St. Thomas
1000 LaSalle Avenue SCH200
Minneapolis, MN 55403
http://www.stthomas.edu/business
Private
Admissions: (651) 962-8800
E-mail: ustmba@stthomas.edu
Financial aid: (651) 962-6550
Application deadline: 06/15
Tuition: full time: $29,400; part time: $929/credit hour
Room/board/expenses: $15,712
College-funded aid: Yes
International student aid: Yes
Average student indebtedness at graduation: $56,182
Full-time enrollment: 82
men: 60%; women: 40%;
minorities:28%; international: 11%
Part-time enrollment: 841
men: 61%; women: 39%;
minorities:15%; international: 2%
Acceptance rate (full time): 69%
Average GMAT (full time): 555
Average GMAT (part time): 544
Average GPA (full time): 3.20
Average age of entrants to full-time program: 27
Average months of prior work experience (full time): 55
TOEFL requirement: Yes
Minimum TOEFL score: 550
Most popular departments: accounting, entrepreneurship, finance, general management, marketing
Mean starting base salary for 2012 full-time graduates: $64,193

Employment location for 2012 class: Intl. 0%; N.E. 5%; M.A. 0%; S. 0%; M.W. 92%; S.W. 3%; W. 0%

MISSISSIPPI

Jackson State University (Moore)[1]
1400 J.R. Lynch Street
Jackson, MS 39217
http://ccaix.jsums.edu/business
Public
Admissions: (601) 432-6315
E-mail: gadmappl@ccaix.jsums.edu
Financial aid: (601) 979-2227
Tuition: N/A
Room/board/expenses: N/A
Enrollment: N/A

Millsaps College (Else)
1701 N. State Street
Jackson, MS 39210
http://millsaps.edu/esom
Private
Admissions: (601) 974-1253
E-mail: mbamacc@millsaps.edu
Financial aid: (601) 974-1220
Application deadline: rolling
Tuition: full time: $968/credit hour; part time: $968/credit hour
Room/board/expenses: $15,000
College-funded aid: Yes
International student aid: Yes
Full-time enrollment: 32
men: 56%; women: 44%;
minorities:3%; international: 3%
Part-time enrollment: 22
men: 73%; women: 27%;
minorities:5%; international: 0%
Acceptance rate (full time): 94%
Average GMAT (full time): 564
Average GMAT (part time): 550
Average GPA (full time): 3.24
TOEFL requirement: Yes
Minimum TOEFL score: 550

Mississippi State University
PO Box 5288
Mississippi State, MS 39762
http://www.business.msstate.edu/gsb
Public
Admissions: (662) 325-1891
E-mail: gsb@cobilan.msstate.edu
Financial aid: (662) 325-2450
Application deadline: 03/01
In-state tuition: total program: $9,675 (full-time); part time: $348/credit hour
Out-of-state tuition: total program: $24,450 (full-time)
Room/board/expenses: N/A
College-funded aid: Yes
International student aid: Yes
Average student indebtedness at graduation: $11,255
Full-time enrollment: 63
men: 65%; women: 35%;
minorities:10%; international: 11%
Part-time enrollment: 8
men: 50%; women: 50%;
minorities:13%; international: 0%
TOEFL requirement: Yes
Minimum TOEFL score: 575
Most popular departments: accounting, general management, management information systems, tax

University of Mississippi
253 Holman Hall
University, MS 33677
http://www.olemissbusiness.com/mba
Public
Admissions: (662) 915-5483
E-mail: bcooper@bus.olemiss.edu

Financial aid: (800) 891-4596
Application deadline: 07/01
In-state tuition: total program: $12,540 (full-time); part time: $418/credit hour
Out-of-state tuition: total program: $30,780 (full-time)
Room/board/expenses: N/A
College-funded aid: Yes
International student aid: Yes
Average student indebtedness at graduation: $22,885
Full-time enrollment: 65
men: 55%; women: 45%;
minorities:6%; international: 11%
Part-time enrollment: N/A
men: N/A; women: N/A;
minorities:N/A; international: N/A
Acceptance rate (full time): 81%
Average GMAT (full time): 544
Average GPA (full time): 3.34
Average age of entrants to full-time program: 23
TOEFL requirement: Yes
Minimum TOEFL score: 600
Mean starting base salary for 2012 full-time graduates: $47,434
Employment location for 2012 class: Intl. 5%; N.E. 5%; M.A. 0%; S. 68%; M.W. 5%; S.W. 18%; W. 0%

University of Southern Mississippi
118 College Drive, #5096
Hattiesburg, MS 39406-5096
http://www.usm.edu/gulfcoast/college-business/mba-ap
Public
Admissions: (601) 266-5137
E-mail: gc-business@usm.edu
Financial aid: (601) 266-4774
Application deadline: 06/01
In-state tuition: full time: $352/credit hour; part time: $352/credit hour
Out-of-state tuition: full time: $803/credit hour
Room/board/expenses: N/A
College-funded aid: Yes
International student aid: Yes
Full-time enrollment: N/A
men: N/A; women: N/A;
minorities:N/A; international: N/A
Part-time enrollment: 31
men: 45%; women: 55%;
minorities:6%; international: 3%
Average GMAT (part time): 485
TOEFL requirement: Yes
Minimum TOEFL score: 550

MISSOURI

Drury University
900 North Benton Avenue
Springfield, MO 65802

Private
Admissions: N/A
Financial aid: N/A
Application deadline: 12/31
Tuition: full time: $662/credit hour; part time: N/A
Room/board/expenses: N/A
College-funded aid: Yes
International student aid: Yes
Average student indebtedness at graduation: $5,000
Full-time enrollment: 53
men: 26%; women: 74%;
minorities:N/A; international: 15%
Part-time enrollment: N/A
men: N/A; women: N/A;
minorities:N/A; international: N/A
Acceptance rate (full time): 50%
Average GMAT (full time): 530
Average GPA (full time): 3.52
Average age of entrants to full-time program: 26
Average months of prior work experience (full time): 36
TOEFL requirement: Yes
Minimum TOEFL score: 550

Missouri State University

901 S. National Avenue
Glass Hall 400
Springfield, MO 65897
http://www.mba.missouristate.edu
Public
Admissions: (417) 836-5331
E-mail: graduatecollege@missouristate.edu
Financial aid: (417) 836-5262
Application deadline: 07/15
In-state tuition: full time: $274/credit hour; part time: $274/credit hour
Out-of-state tuition: full time: $516/credit hour
Room/board/expenses: $13,540
College-funded aid: Yes
International student aid: Yes
Average student indebtedness at graduation: $39,600
Full-time enrollment: 245
men: 51%; women: 49%;
minorities:4%; international: 54%
Part-time enrollment: 123
men: 56%; women: 44%;
minorities:6%; international: 22%
Acceptance rate (full time): 79%
Average age of entrants to full-time program: 27
TOEFL requirement: Yes
Minimum TOEFL score: 550
Most popular departments: finance, general management, marketing, management information systems, supply chain management

Rockhurst University (Helzberg)

1100 Rockhurst Road
Kansas City, MO 64110
http://www.rockhurst.edu/hsom/
Private
Admissions: (816) 501-4823
E-mail: mba@rockhurst.edu
Financial aid: N/A
Application deadline: rolling
Tuition: full time: N/A; part time: $575/credit hour
Room/board/expenses: $600
College-funded aid: Yes
International student aid: Yes
Full-time enrollment: N/A
men: N/A; women: N/A;
minorities:N/A; international: N/A
Part-time enrollment: 199
men: 68%; women: 32%;
minorities:16%; international: 0%
Average GMAT (part time): 524
TOEFL requirement: Yes
Minimum TOEFL score: 550
Most popular departments: accounting, finance, general management, health care administration, international business

Southeast Missouri State University (Harrison)

1 University Plaza, MS 5890
Cape Girardeau, MO 63701
http://www.semo.edu/mba
Public
Admissions: (573) 651-2590
E-mail: mba@semo.edu
Financial aid: (573) 651-2039
Application deadline: 08/01
In-state tuition: full time: $281/credit hour; part time: $281/credit hour
Out-of-state tuition: full time: $497/credit hour
Room/board/expenses: $8,500
College-funded aid: Yes
International student aid: Yes
Full-time enrollment: N/A
men: N/A; women: N/A;
minorities:N/A; international: N/A

Part-time enrollment: 123
men: 63%; women: 37%;
minorities:9%; international: 23%
Average GMAT (part time): 513
TOEFL requirement: Yes
Minimum TOEFL score: 550
Most popular departments: accounting, entrepreneurship, general management, health care administration, international business

St. Louis University (Cook)

3674 Lindell Boulevard
St. Louis, MO 63108
http://www.slu.edu/gradbiz.xml
Private
Admissions: (314) 977-2125
E-mail: gradbiz@slu.edu
Financial aid: (314) 977-2350
Application deadline: 08/01
Tuition: full time: $52,481; part time: $935/credit hour
Room/board/expenses: $16,188
College-funded aid: Yes
International student aid: Yes
Average student indebtedness at graduation: $55,006
Full-time enrollment: 37
men: 65%; women: 35%;
minorities:14%; international: 11%
Part-time enrollment: 251
men: 66%; women: 34%;
minorities:12%; international: 2%
Acceptance rate (full time): 47%
Average GMAT (full time): 568
Average GMAT (part time): 577
Average GPA (full time): 3.70
Average months of prior work experience (full time): 41
TOEFL requirement: Yes
Minimum TOEFL score: 570
Most popular departments: finance, general management, international business, marketing, supply chain management
Mean starting base salary for 2012 full-time graduates: $54,984
Employment location for 2012 class: Intl. N/A; N.E. N/A; M.A. 5%; S. N/A; M.W. 90%; S.W. N/A; W. 5%

Truman State University

100 E. Normal
Kirksville, MO 63501
http://gradstudies.truman.edu
Public
Admissions: (660) 785-4109
E-mail: gradinfo@truman.edu
Financial aid: (660) 785-4130
Application deadline: rolling
In-state tuition: full time: $327/credit hour; part time: N/A
Out-of-state tuition: full time: $561/credit hour
Room/board/expenses: $7,000
College-funded aid: Yes
International student aid: Yes
Full-time enrollment: 45
men: 44%; women: 56%;
minorities:4%; international: 11%
Part-time enrollment: N/A
men: N/A; women: N/A;
minorities:N/A; international: N/A
Acceptance rate (full time): 90%
Average GMAT (full time): 590
Average GPA (full time): 3.56
Average age of entrants to full-time program: 22
Average months of prior work experience (full time): N/A
TOEFL requirement: Yes
Minimum TOEFL score: 550

University of Central Missouri (Harmon)

Ward Edwards 1600
Warrensburg, MO 64093
http://www.ucmo.edu/mba
Public
Admissions: (660) 543-8617
E-mail: mba@ucmo.edu
Financial aid: (800) 729-2678
Application deadline: rolling
In-state tuition: full time: N/A; part time: N/A
Out-of-state tuition: full time: N/A
Room/board/expenses: N/A
College-funded aid: Yes
International student aid: Yes
Full-time enrollment: 89
men: N/A; women: N/A;
minorities:N/A; international: N/A
Part-time enrollment: N/A
men: N/A; women: N/A;
minorities:N/A; international: N/A
TOEFL requirement: Yes
Minimum TOEFL score: 550

University of Missouri–Kansas City (Bloch)

5100 Rockhill Road
Kansas City, MO 64110
http://www.bsbpa.umkc.edu/
Public
Admissions: (816) 235-1111
E-mail: admit@umkc.edu
Financial aid: (816) 235-1154
Application deadline: rolling
In-state tuition: full time: $332/credit hour; part time: $332/credit hour
Out-of-state tuition: full time: $857/credit hour
Room/board/expenses: $19,068
College-funded aid: Yes
International student aid: Yes
Full-time enrollment: N/A
men: N/A; women: N/A;
minorities:N/A; international: N/A
Part-time enrollment: 278
men: 63%; women: 37%;
minorities:11%; international: 7%
Average GMAT (part time): 560
TOEFL requirement: Yes
Minimum TOEFL score: 550
Most popular departments: entrepreneurship, finance, general management, international business, marketing

University of Missouri–St. Louis

1 University Boulevard
St. Louis, MO 63121
http://mba.umsl.edu
Public
Admissions: (314) 516-5885
E-mail: mba@umsl.edu
Financial aid: (314) 516-5526
Application deadline: 07/01
In-state tuition: full time: N/A; part time: $349/credit hour
Out-of-state tuition: full time: N/A
Room/board/expenses: $11,700
College-funded aid: Yes
International student aid: Yes
Full-time enrollment: N/A
men: N/A; women: N/A;
minorities:N/A; international: N/A
Part-time enrollment: 487
men: 58%; women: 42%;
minorities:13%; international: 13%
Average GMAT (part time): 524
TOEFL requirement: Yes
Minimum TOEFL score: 550

University of Missouri (Trulaske)

213 Cornell Hall
Columbia, MO 65211
http://mba.missouri.edu
Public
Admissions: (573) 882-2750
E-mail: mba@mso.umt.edu
Financial aid: (573) 882-2750
Application deadline: 01/15
In-state tuition: full time: $12,833; part time: $337/credit hour
Out-of-state tuition: full time: $27,737
Room/board/expenses: $9,768
College-funded aid: Yes
International student aid: Yes
Average student indebtedness at graduation: $24,200
Full-time enrollment: 195
men: 67%; women: 33%;
minorities:6%; international: 28%
Part-time enrollment: N/A
men: N/A; women: N/A;
minorities:N/A; international: N/A
Acceptance rate (full time): 43%
Average GMAT (full time): 658
Average GPA (full time): 3.50
Average age of entrants to full-time program: 26
Average months of prior work experience (full time): 31
TOEFL requirement: Yes
Minimum TOEFL score: 550
Most popular departments: entrepreneurship, finance, general management, marketing, portfolio management
Mean starting base salary for 2012 full-time graduates: $59,696
Employment location for 2012 class: Intl. 0%; N.E. 2%; M.A. 0%; S. 5%; M.W. 86%; S.W. 7%; W. 0%

Washington University in St. Louis (Olin)

1 Brookings Drive
Campus Box 1133
St. Louis, MO 63130-4899
http://www.olin.wustl.edu/academicprograms/MBA/Pages/default.aspx
Private
Admissions: (314) 935-7301
E-mail: mba@wustl.edu
Financial aid: (314) 935-7301
Application deadline: 04/01
Tuition: full time: $48,900; part time: $1,400/credit hour
Room/board/expenses: $24,068
College-funded aid: Yes
International student aid: Yes
Average student indebtedness at graduation: $68,732
Full-time enrollment: 279
men: 70%; women: 30%;
minorities:18%; international: 34%
Part-time enrollment: 357
men: 74%; women: 26%;
minorities:23%; international: 6%
Acceptance rate (full time): 34%
Average GMAT (full time): 698
Average GMAT (part time): 587
Average GPA (full time): 3.43
Average age of entrants to full-time program: 28
Average months of prior work experience (full time): 57
TOEFL requirement: No
Minimum TOEFL score: N/A
Most popular departments: consulting, finance, general management, marketing, supply chain management
Mean starting base salary for 2012 full-time graduates: $94,762
Employment location for 2012 class: Intl. 9%; N.E. 8%; M.A. 4%; S. 4%; M.W. 58%; S.W. 5%; W. 10%

University of Montana

32 Campus Drive
Missoula, MT 59812-6808
http://www.mba-macct.umt.edu/
Public
Admissions: (406) 243-2361
E-mail: jliston@mso.umt.edu
Financial aid: (406) 243-5373
Application deadline: N/A
In-state tuition: full time: N/A; part time: N/A
Out-of-state tuition: full time: N/A
Room/board/expenses: N/A
College-funded aid: Yes
International student aid: Yes
Full-time enrollment: 60
men: N/A; women: N/A;
minorities:N/A; international: 8%
Part-time enrollment: 47
men: N/A; women: N/A;
minorities:N/A; international: N/A
Acceptance rate (full time): 89%
Average GMAT (full time): 545
Average GMAT (part time): 559
Average GPA (full time): 3.40
TOEFL requirement: Yes
Minimum TOEFL score: 580
Most popular departments: accounting, entrepreneurship, general management, marketing, management information systems

Creighton University

2500 California Plaza
Omaha, NE 68178-0130
http://business.creighton.edu
Private
Admissions: (402) 280-2841
E-mail: busgradadmit@creighton.edu
Financial aid: (402) 280-2731
Application deadline: 07/01
Tuition: full time: N/A; part time: $730/credit hour
Room/board/expenses: $28,100
College-funded aid: Yes
International student aid: Yes
Full-time enrollment: N/A
men: N/A; women: N/A;
minorities:N/A; international: N/A
Part-time enrollment: 160
men: 66%; women: 34%;
minorities:10%; international: 5%
Average GMAT (part time): 522
TOEFL requirement: Yes
Minimum TOEFL score: 550
Most popular departments: accounting, finance, leadership, management information systems, portfolio management

University of Nebraska–Kearney[1]

905 West 25th Street
Kearney, NE 68849
http://www.unk.edu/acad/bt/index.php?id=107
Public
Admissions: (800) 717-7881
E-mail: unkbt@unk.edu
Financial aid: N/A
Tuition: N/A
Room/board/expenses: N/A
Enrollment: N/A

University of Nebraska–Lincoln

P.O. Box 880405
Lincoln, NE 68588-0405
http://www.mba.unl.edu
Public
Admissions: (402) 472-2338
E-mail: cbagrad@unl.edu
Financial aid: (402) 472-2030
Application deadline: 12/31
In-state tuition: full time: N/A; part time: $353/credit hour
Out-of-state tuition: full time: N/A

Room/board/expenses: $14,000
College-funded aid: Yes
International student aid: Yes
Full-time enrollment: N/A
men: N/A; women: N/A;
minorities:N/A; international: N/A
Part-time enrollment: 77
men: 73%; women: 27%;
minorities:4%; international: 13%
Average GMAT (part time): 610
TOEFL requirement: Yes
Minimum TOEFL score: 550
Most popular departments: finance, human resources management, international business, marketing, other

University of Nebraska–Omaha

6708 Pine St
Omaha, NE 68182-0048
http://cba.unomaha.edu/mba
Public
Admissions: (402) 554-2303
E-mail: mba@unomaha.edu
Financial aid: (402) 554-2327
Application deadline: 07/01
In-state tuition: full time: $255/
credit hour; part time: $245/
credit hour
Out-of-state tuition: full time: $646/
credit hour
Room/board/expenses: $13,026
College-funded aid: Yes
International student aid: Yes
Full-time enrollment: N/A
men: N/A; women: N/A;
minorities:N/A; international: N/A
Part-time enrollment: 258
men: 67%; women: 33%;
minorities:6%; international: 7%
Average GMAT (part time): 564
TOEFL requirement: Yes
Minimum TOEFL score: 550
Most popular departments: e-commerce, health care administration, human resources management, international business, other

NEVADA

University of Nevada–Las Vegas

4505 Maryland Parkway
PO Box 456031
Las Vegas, NV 89154-6031
http://business.unlv.edu
Public
Admissions: (702) 895-3655
E-mail: cobmba@unlv.edu
Financial aid: (702) 895-3682
Application deadline: 06/01
In-state tuition: full time: $364/
credit hour; part time: $364/
credit hour
Out-of-state tuition: full time:
$22,646
Room/board/expenses: $20,000
College-funded aid: Yes
International student aid: Yes
Full-time enrollment: N/A
men: N/A; women: N/A;
minorities:N/A; international: N/A
Part-time enrollment: 186
men: 67%; women: 33%;
minorities:19%; international: 7%
Average GMAT (part time): 600
TOEFL requirement: Yes
Minimum TOEFL score: 550

University of Nevada–Reno[1]

1664 N. Virginia Street
Reno, NV 89557
http://www.coba.unr.edu
Public
Admissions: (775) 784-4912
E-mail: vkrentz@unr.edu
Financial aid: (775) 784-4666
Tuition: N/A
Room/board/expenses: N/A
Enrollment: N/A

NEW HAMPSHIRE

Dartmouth College (Tuck)

100 Tuck Hall
Hanover, NH 03755-9000
http://www.tuck.dartmouth.edu
Private
Admissions: (603) 646-3162
E-mail: tuck.admissions@
dartmouth.edu
Financial aid: (603) 646-0640
Application deadline: 04/02
Tuition: full time: $60,510; part
time: N/A
Room/board/expenses: $12,075
College-funded aid: Yes
International student aid: Yes
Average student indebtedness at
graduation: $94,512
Full-time enrollment: 549
men: 67%; women: 33%;
minorities:17%; international: 33%
Part-time enrollment: N/A
men: N/A; women: N/A;
minorities:N/A; international: N/A
Acceptance rate (full time): 20%
Average GMAT (full time): 717
Average GPA (full time): 3.49
Average age of entrants to full-time
program: 28
Average months of prior work
experience (full time): 63
TOEFL requirement: Yes
Minimum TOEFL score: N/A
Mean starting base salary for 2012
full-time graduates: $115,302
Employment location for 2012 class:
Intl. 15%; N.E. 49%; M.A. 7%; S.
2%; M.W. 11%; S.W. 1%; W. 15%

University of New Hampshire (Paul)

McConnell Hall, 15 College Road
Durham, NH 03824
http://www.mba.unh.edu
Public
Admissions: (603) 862-1367
E-mail: wsbe.grad@unh.edu
Financial aid: (603) 862-3600
Application deadline: 06/01
In-state tuition: total program:
$28,000 (full-time); part time:
$800/credit hour
Out-of-state tuition: total program:
$42,000 (full-time)
Room/board/expenses: $12,010
College-funded aid: Yes
International student aid: Yes
Full-time enrollment: 33
men: 67%; women: 33%;
minorities:42%; international: 33%
Part-time enrollment: 52
men: 54%; women: 46%;
minorities:23%; international: 12%
Acceptance rate (full time): 72%
Average GMAT (full time): 577
Average GMAT (part time): 561
Average GPA (full time): 3.25
TOEFL requirement: Yes
Minimum TOEFL score: 550
Most popular departments: entrepreneurship, finance, general management, other
Employment location for 2012 class:
Intl. N/A; N.E. 94%; M.A. N/A; S.
6%; M.W. N/A; S.W. N/A; W. N/A

NEW JERSEY

Fairleigh Dickinson University (Silberman)[1]

1000 River Road
Teaneck, NJ 07666
http://www.fduinfo.com/depts/
sctab.php
Private
Admissions: (201) 692-2554
E-mail: grad@fdu.edu
Financial aid: (201) 692-2363

Tuition: N/A
Room/board/expenses: N/A
Enrollment: N/A

Monmouth University

400 Cedar Avenue
West Long Branch, NJ 07764-
1898
http://www.monmouth.edu
Private
Admissions: (732) 571-3452
E-mail: gradadm@monmouth.edu
Financial aid: (732) 571-3463
Application deadline: 07/15
Tuition: full time: $922/credit hour;
part time: $922/credit hour
Room/board/expenses: $17,942
College-funded aid: Yes
International student aid: Yes
Average student indebtedness at
graduation: $17,324
Full-time enrollment: 29
men: 48%; women: 52%;
minorities:14%; international: 0%
Part-time enrollment: 203
men: 62%; women: 38%;
minorities:17%; international: 6%
Acceptance rate (full time): 78%
Average GMAT (full time): 503
Average GMAT (part time): 463
Average GPA (full time): 3.49
Average age of entrants to full-time
program: 22
TOEFL requirement: Yes
Minimum TOEFL score: 550
Most popular departments: accounting, finance, general management, health care administration, real estate

Montclair State University

Partridge Hall, 1 Normal Avenue
Montclair, NJ 07043
http://www.montclair.edu/mba
Public
Admissions: (973) 655-5147
E-mail: graduate.school@mont-
clair.edu
Financial aid: (973) 655-4461
Application deadline: rolling
In-state tuition: full time: $640/
credit hour; part time: $640/
credit hour
Out-of-state tuition: full time: $880/
credit hour
Room/board/expenses: N/A
College-funded aid: Yes
International student aid: Yes
Average student indebtedness at
graduation: $38,800
Full-time enrollment: 88
men: 53%; women: 47%;
minorities:32%; international: 24%
Part-time enrollment: 234
men: 62%; women: 38%;
minorities:29%; international: 3%
Average GMAT (full time): 497
Average GMAT (part time): 486
Average GPA (full time): 3.22
Average age of entrants to full-time
program: 27
TOEFL requirement: Yes
Minimum TOEFL score: 380

New Jersey Institute of Technology[1]

University Heights
Newark, NJ 07102
http://management.njit.edu/
Public
Admissions: (973) 596-3300
E-mail: admissions@njit.edu
Financial aid: (973) 596-3479
Tuition: N/A
Room/board/expenses: N/A
Enrollment: N/A

Rider University

2083 Lawrenceville Road
Lawrenceville, NJ 08648-3099
http://www.rider.edu/mba
Private
Admissions: (609) 896-5036
E-mail: gradadm@rider.edu
Financial aid: (609) 896-5360
Application deadline: rolling
Tuition: full time: N/A; part time:
N/A
Room/board/expenses: N/A
College-funded aid: Yes
International student aid: Yes
Full-time enrollment: N/A
men: N/A; women: N/A;
minorities:N/A; international: N/A
Part-time enrollment: 142
men: 58%; women: 42%;
minorities:15%; international: 15%
Average GMAT (part time): 478
TOEFL requirement: Yes
Minimum TOEFL score: 550
Most popular departments: accounting, finance, general management, international business, management information systems, technology

Rowan University (Rohrer)

201 Mullica Hill Road
Glassboro, NJ 08028
http://www.rowan.edu/
graduateschool
Public
Admissions: (856) 256-4050
E-mail: gradoffice@rowan.edu
Financial aid: (856) 256-4250
Application deadline: rolling
In-state tuition: full time: $670/
credit hour; part time: $670/
credit hour
Out-of-state tuition: full time: $670/
credit hour
Room/board/expenses: $13,442
College-funded aid: Yes
International student aid: No
Full-time enrollment: N/A
men: N/A; women: N/A;
minorities:N/A; international: N/A
Part-time enrollment: 173
men: 64%; women: 36%;
minorities:21%; international: 5%
Average GMAT (part time): 532
TOEFL requirement: Yes
Minimum TOEFL score: 550
Most popular departments: accounting, finance, general management, marketing, management information systems

Rutgers, the State University of New Jersey–Camden

227 Penn Street
Camden, NJ 08102
http://camden-sbc.rutgers.edu
Public
Admissions: (856) 225-6104
E-mail: camden@
camuga.rutgers.edu
Financial aid: (856) 225-6039
Application deadline: 01/07
In-state tuition: full time: N/A; part
time: N/A
Out-of-state tuition: full time: N/A
Room/board/expenses: N/A
College-funded aid: Yes
International student aid: Yes
Full-time enrollment: N/A
men: N/A; women: N/A;
minorities:N/A; international: N/A
Part-time enrollment: 225
men: 63%; women: 37%;
minorities:26%; international: 4%
Average GMAT (part time): 520
TOEFL requirement: Yes
Minimum TOEFL score: 550

Rutgers, the State University of New Jersey–New Brunswick and Newark

1 Washington Park
Newark, NJ 07102-3122
http://www.business.rutgers.edu
Public
Admissions: (973) 353-1234
E-mail: admit@
business.rutgers.edu
Financial aid: (973) 353-5151
Application deadline: 05/01
In-state tuition: full time: $27,810;
part time: $951/credit hour
Out-of-state tuition: full time:
$41,347
Room/board/expenses: $28,000
College-funded aid: Yes
International student aid: No
Average student indebtedness at
graduation: $42,500
Full-time enrollment: 244
men: 63%; women: 37%;
minorities:32%; international: 25%
Part-time enrollment: 1,013
men: 66%; women: 34%;
minorities:36%; international: 3%
Acceptance rate (full time): 44%
Average GMAT (full time): 643
Average GMAT (part time): 579
Average GPA (full time): 3.31
Average age of entrants to full-time
program: 28
Average months of prior work
experience (full time): 53
TOEFL requirement: Yes
Minimum TOEFL score: 600
Most popular departments: finance, international business, marketing, supply chain management, other
Mean starting base salary for 2012
full-time graduates: $85,530
Employment location for 2012 class:
Intl. 2%; N.E. 80%; M.A. 7%; S.
4%; M.W. 0%; S.W. 5%; W. 2%

Seton Hall University (Stillman)

400 S. Orange Avenue
South Orange, NJ 07079
http://www.shu.edu/academics/
business/
Private
Admissions: (973) 761-9262
E-mail: mba@shu.edu
Financial aid: (973) 761-9350
Application deadline: 05/31
Tuition: full time: N/A; part time:
$1,111/credit hour
Room/board/expenses: $17,600
College-funded aid: Yes
International student aid: Yes
Full-time enrollment: N/A
men: N/A; women: N/A;
minorities:N/A; international: N/A
Part-time enrollment: 372
men: 65%; women: 35%;
minorities:3%; international: 12%
Average GMAT (part time): 558
TOEFL requirement: Yes
Minimum TOEFL score: 607
Most popular departments: accounting, finance, general management, international business, marketing

William Paterson University (Cotsakos)

1600 Valley Road
Wayne, NJ 07474
http://www.wpunj.edu/cob/
Public
Admissions: (973) 720-2237
E-mail: graduate@wpunj.edu
Financial aid: (973) 720-2928
Application deadline: 08/01
In-state tuition: full time: $500/
credit hour; part time: $500/
credit hour

Out-of-state tuition: full time: $854/ credit hour
Room/board/expenses: $14,266
College-funded aid: Yes
International student aid: Yes
Average student indebtedness at graduation: $20,550
Full-time enrollment: 26
men: 50%; women: 50%; minorities:46%; international: 27%
Part-time enrollment: 74
men: 64%; women: 36%; minorities:39%; international: 4%
Average GMAT (part time): 519
TOEFL requirement: Yes
Minimum TOEFL score: 550

NEW MEXICO

New Mexico State University
P.O. Box 30001, MSC 3GSP
Las Cruces, NM 88003
http://business.nmsu.edu/mba
Public
Admissions: (505) 646-8003
E-mail: mba@nmsu.edu
Financial aid: (505) 646-4105
Application deadline: 07/15
In-state tuition: full time: $11,752; part time: $271/credit hour
Out-of-state tuition: full time: $19,540
Room/board/expenses: $13,064
College-funded aid: Yes
International student aid: Yes
Full-time enrollment: N/A
men: N/A; women: N/A; minorities:N/A; international: N/A
Part-time enrollment: 157
men: 51%; women: 49%; minorities:41%; international: 12%
Average GMAT (part time): 471
TOEFL requirement: Yes
Minimum TOEFL score: 550

University of New Mexico (Anderson)
MSC05 3090
1 University of New Mexico
Albuquerque, NM 87131-0001
http://www.mgt.unm.edu
Public
Admissions: (505) 277-3290
E-mail: mba@mgt.unm.edu
Financial aid: (505) 277-8900
Application deadline: 04/01
In-state tuition: full time: $436/ credit hour; part time: $436/ credit hour
Out-of-state tuition: full time: $1,051/credit hour
Room/board/expenses: $12,725
College-funded aid: Yes
International student aid: Yes
Full-time enrollment: 269
men: 55%; women: 45%; minorities:43%; international: 8%
Part-time enrollment: 210
men: 53%; women: 47%; minorities:48%; international: 3%
Average GMAT (full time): 559
Average GMAT (part time): 545
Average age of entrants to full-time program: 27
TOEFL requirement: Yes
Minimum TOEFL score: 550
Most popular departments: finance, general management, human resources management, public policy, other
Mean starting base salary for 2012 full-time graduates: $53,522
Employment location for 2012 class: Intl. 2%; N.E. 2%; M.A. 0%; S. 0%; M.W. 2%; S.W. 91%; W. 2%

NEW YORK

Adelphi University
1 South Avenue
Garden City, NY 11530
http://www.adelphi.edu
Private
Admissions: (516) 877-3050
E-mail: admissions@adelphi.edu
Financial aid: (516) 877-3080
Application deadline: rolling
Tuition: full time: N/A; part time: $960/credit hour
Room/board/expenses: N/A
College-funded aid: Yes
International student aid: Yes
Full-time enrollment: N/A
men: N/A; women: N/A; minorities:N/A; international: N/A
Part-time enrollment: 438
men: 51%; women: 49%; minorities:16%; international: 53%
Average GMAT (part time): 490
TOEFL requirement: Yes
Minimum TOEFL score: 550

Alfred University
Saxon Drive
Alfred, NY 14802
http://business.alfred.edu/ mba.html
Private
Admissions: (800) 541-9229
E-mail: gradinquiry@alfred.edu
Financial aid: (607) 871-2159
Application deadline: 08/01
Tuition: full time: $37,646; part time: $782/credit hour
Room/board/expenses: $49,144
College-funded aid: Yes
International student aid: Yes
Average student indebtedness at graduation: $22,000
Full-time enrollment: 31
men: 52%; women: 48%; minorities:13%; international: 13%
Part-time enrollment: 21
men: 71%; women: 29%; minorities:5%; international: 0%
Acceptance rate (full time): 93%
Average GMAT (full time): 488
Average GMAT (part time): 455
Average GPA (full time): 3.29
Average age of entrants to full-time program: 23
Average months of prior work experience (full time): 24
TOEFL requirement: Yes
Minimum TOEFL score: 590
Most popular departments: accounting, general management

Binghamton University–SUNY
PO Box 6000
Binghamton, NY 13902-6000
http://www2. binghamton.edu/som/
Public
Admissions: (607) 777-2317
E-mail: somadvis@ binghamton.edu
Financial aid: (607) 777-2470
Application deadline: 03/01
In-state tuition: full time: $12,825; part time: $464/credit hour
Out-of-state tuition: full time: $20,015
Room/board/expenses: $16,500
College-funded aid: Yes
International student aid: Yes
Average student indebtedness at graduation: $23,762
Full-time enrollment: 60
men: 58%; women: 42%; minorities:12%; international: 28%
Part-time enrollment: N/A
men: N/A; women: N/A; minorities:N/A; international: N/A
Acceptance rate (full time): 44%
Average GMAT (full time): 614
Average GPA (full time): 3.48
Average age of entrants to full-time program: 23
Average months of prior work experience (full time): 33
TOEFL requirement: Yes
Minimum TOEFL score: 590
Most popular departments: finance, marketing, management information systems
Mean starting base salary for 2012 full-time graduates: $57,500
Employment location for 2012 class: Intl. 5%; N.E. 70%; M.A. 5%; S. 5%; M.W. 15%; S.W. 0%; W. 0%

Canisius College (Wehle)
2001 Main Street
Buffalo, NY 14208
http://www.canisius.edu/ business/graduate_programs.asp
Private
Admissions: (800) 950-2505
E-mail: gradubus@canisius.edu
Financial aid: (716) 888-2300
Application deadline: rolling
Tuition: total program: $35,800 (full-time); part time: $722/credit hour
Room/board/expenses: $13,220
College-funded aid: Yes
International student aid: Yes
Full-time enrollment: 21
men: 71%; women: 29%; minorities:29%; international: 0%
Part-time enrollment: 290
men: 58%; women: 42%; minorities:11%; international: 4%
Acceptance rate (full time): 61%
Average GMAT (full time): 503
Average GMAT (part time): 507
Average GPA (full time): 3.18
Average age of entrants to full-time program: 25
TOEFL requirement: Yes
Minimum TOEFL score: 550
Most popular departments: accounting, finance, general management, international business, marketing

Clarkson University
Snell Hall 322E, Box 5770
Potsdam, NY 13699-5770
http://www.clarkson.edu/ business/graduate
Private
Admissions: (315) 268-6613
E-mail: busgrad@clarkson.edu
Financial aid: (315) 268-7699
Application deadline: rolling
Tuition: full time: $48,432; part time: $1,259/credit hour
Room/board/expenses: $13,888
College-funded aid: Yes
International student aid: Yes
Average student indebtedness at graduation: $22,791
Full-time enrollment: 86
men: 57%; women: 43%; minorities:5%; international: 55%
Part-time enrollment: 59
men: 69%; women: 31%; minorities:7%; international: 7%
Acceptance rate (full time): 69%
Average GMAT (full time): 538
Average GMAT (part time): 540
Average GPA (full time): 3.34
Average age of entrants to full-time program: 24
Average months of prior work experience (full time): 31
TOEFL requirement: Yes
Minimum TOEFL score: 550
Most popular departments: accounting, entrepreneurship, general management, supply chain management, other
Mean starting base salary for 2012 full-time graduates: $64,594
Employment location for 2012 class: Intl. 3%; N.E. 67%; M.A. 3%; S. 3%; M.W. 13%; S.W. 3%; W. 7%

College at Brockport–SUNY[1]
119 Hartwell Hall
Brockport, NY 14420
http://www.brockport.edu/ bus-econ
Private
Admissions: N/A
Financial aid: N/A
Tuition: N/A
Room/board/expenses: N/A
Enrollment: N/A

Columbia University
3022 Broadway, 216 Uris Hall
New York, NY 10027
http://www.gsb.columbia.edu
Private
Admissions: (212) 854-1961
E-mail: apply@gsb.columbia.edu
Financial aid: (212) 854-4057
Application deadline: 04/09
Tuition: full time: $60,896; part time: N/A
Room/board/expenses: $26,190
College-funded aid: Yes
International student aid: Yes
Full-time enrollment: 1,274
men: 64%; women: 36%; minorities:23%; international: 32%
Part-time enrollment: N/A
men: N/A; women: N/A; minorities:N/A; international: N/A
Acceptance rate (full time): 21%
Average GMAT (full time): 715
Average GPA (full time): 3.50
Average age of entrants to full-time program: 28
Average months of prior work experience (full time): 58
TOEFL requirement: Yes
Minimum TOEFL score: N/A
Most popular departments: consulting, entrepreneurship, finance, general management, marketing
Mean starting base salary for 2012 full-time graduates: $112,728

Cornell University (Johnson)
Sage Hall, Cornell University
Ithaca, NY 14853-6201
http://www.johnson.cornell.edu
Private
Admissions: (607) 255-0600
E-mail: mba@cornell.edu
Financial aid: (607) 255-6116
Application deadline: 03/27
Tuition: full time: $56,811; part time: N/A
Room/board/expenses: $20,460
College-funded aid: Yes
International student aid: Yes
Average student indebtedness at graduation: $95,600
Full-time enrollment: 568
men: 70%; women: 30%; minorities:29%; international: 31%
Part-time enrollment: N/A
men: N/A; women: N/A; minorities:N/A; international: N/A
Acceptance rate (full time): 28%
Average GMAT (full time): 694
Average GPA (full time): 3.29
Average age of entrants to full-time program: 27
Average months of prior work experience (full time): 56
TOEFL requirement: Yes
Minimum TOEFL score: 600
Most popular departments: consulting, finance, international business, marketing, portfolio management
Mean starting base salary for 2012 full-time graduates: $106,064
Employment location for 2012 class: Intl. 14%; N.E. 55%; M.A. 4%; S. 1%; M.W. 6%; S.W. 4%; W. 15%

CUNY Bernard M. Baruch College (Zicklin)
1 Bernard Baruch Way
New York, NY 10010
http://zicklin.baruch.cuny.edu
Public
Admissions: (646) 312-1300
E-mail: zicklingradadmissions@ baruch.cuny.edu
Financial aid: (646) 312-1370
Application deadline: 04/15
In-state tuition: full time: $13,970; part time: $575/credit hour
Out-of-state tuition: full time: $26,100
Room/board/expenses: N/A
College-funded aid: Yes
International student aid: Yes
Average student indebtedness at graduation: $18,827
Full-time enrollment: 121
men: 67%; women: 33%; minorities:23%; international: 33%
Part-time enrollment: 1,198
men: 60%; women: 40%; minorities:37%; international: 2%
Acceptance rate (full time): 37%
Average GMAT (full time): 629
Average GMAT (part time): 578
Average GPA (full time): 3.20
Average age of entrants to full-time program: 29
Average months of prior work experience (full time): 57
TOEFL requirement: Yes
Minimum TOEFL score: 600
Most popular departments: accounting, entrepreneurship, finance, marketing, organizational behavior
Mean starting base salary for 2012 full-time graduates: $77,652
Employment location for 2012 class: Intl. 3%; N.E. 91%; M.A. 0%; S. 3%; M.W. 0%; S.W. 3%; W. 0%

Fordham University
113 W. 60th Street, Room 624
New York, NY 10023
http://www.bnet.fordham.edu
Private
Admissions: (212) 636-6200
E-mail: admissionsgb@ fordham.edu
Financial aid: (212) 636-6700
Application deadline: 06/01
Tuition: full time: $1,199/credit hour; part time: $1,199/credit hour
Room/board/expenses: $25,152
College-funded aid: Yes
International student aid: Yes
Average student indebtedness at graduation: $69,637
Full-time enrollment: 1,103
men: 48%; women: 52%; minorities:18%; international: 50%
Part-time enrollment: 551
men: 53%; women: 47%; minorities:29%; international: 23%
Acceptance rate (full time): 45%
Average GMAT (full time): 648
Average GMAT (part time): 598
Average GPA (full time): 3.38
Average age of entrants to full-time program: 25
Average months of prior work experience (full time): 30
TOEFL requirement: Yes
Minimum TOEFL score: N/A
Most popular departments: accounting, finance, marketing, tax, other
Mean starting base salary for 2012 full-time graduates: $80,589
Employment location for 2012 class: Intl. 5%; N.E. 87%; M.A. 2%; S. 1%; M.W. 1%; S.W. 1%; W. 4%

Hofstra University (Zarb)
300 Weller Hall
Hempstead, NY 11549
http://www.hofstra.edu/graduate
Private
Admissions: (800) 463-7872
E-mail: gradstudent@hofstra.edu
Financial aid: (516) 463-4335
Application deadline: rolling
Tuition: full time: $1,080/credit hour; part time: $1,080/credit hour
Room/board/expenses: $20,435
College-funded aid: Yes
International student aid: Yes
Full-time enrollment: 99
men: 61%; women: 39%; minorities:10%; international: 58%
Part-time enrollment: 946
men: 53%; women: 47%; minorities:13%; international: 50%
Acceptance rate (full time): 43%
Average GMAT (full time): 603
Average GMAT (part time): 582
Average GPA (full time): 3.11
Average age of entrants to full-time program: 25
Average months of prior work experience (full time): 43
TOEFL requirement: Yes
Minimum TOEFL score: 550
Most popular departments: accounting, finance, marketing, statistics and operations research, tax
Mean starting base salary for 2012 full-time graduates: $66,938
Employment location for 2012 class: Intl. 19%; N.E. 76%; M.A. 0%; S. 0%; M.W. 5%; S.W. 0%; W. 0%

Iona College (Hagan)
715 North Avenue
New Rochelle, NY 10801
http://www.iona.edu/hagan
Private
Admissions: (914) 633-2288
E-mail: sfan@iona.edu
Financial aid: (914) 633-2497
Application deadline: 08/15
Tuition: full time: N/A; part time: $912/credit hour
Room/board/expenses: N/A
College-funded aid: Yes
International student aid: Yes
Full-time enrollment: N/A
men: N/A; women: N/A; minorities:N/A; international: N/A
Part-time enrollment: 415
men: 55%; women: 45%; minorities:17%; international: 1%
Average GMAT (part time): 437
TOEFL requirement: Yes
Minimum TOEFL score: 580
Most popular departments: accounting, finance, general management, marketing, management information systems

Ithaca College
953 Danby Road
Ithaca, NY 14850-7000
http://www.ithaca.edu/gps
Private
Admissions: (607) 274-3527
E-mail: gps@ithaca.edu
Financial aid: (607) 274-3131
Application deadline: 03/01
Tuition: full time: $821/credit hour; part time: $821/credit hour
Room/board/expenses: N/A
College-funded aid: Yes
International student aid: Yes
Full-time enrollment: 35
men: 74%; women: 26%; minorities:14%; international: 3%
Part-time enrollment: 9
men: 56%; women: 44%; minorities:N/A; international: N/A
Acceptance rate (full time): 95%
Average GMAT (full time): 508
Average GMAT (part time): 510

Average GPA (full time): 3.37
Average age of entrants to full-time program: 23
TOEFL requirement: Yes
Minimum TOEFL score: 550

Le Moyne College
1419 Salt Springs Road
Syracuse, NY 13214-1301
http://www.lemoyne.edu/mba
Private
Admissions: (315) 445-5444
E-mail: mba@lemoyne.edu
Financial aid: (315) 445-4400
Application deadline: 07/01
Tuition: full time: N/A; part time: $708/credit hour
Room/board/expenses: N/A
College-funded aid: Yes
International student aid: Yes
Average student indebtedness at graduation: $19,287
Full-time enrollment: N/A
men: N/A; women: N/A; minorities:N/A; international: N/A
Part-time enrollment: 133
men: 59%; women: 41%; minorities:5%; international: 1%
Average GMAT (part time): 497
TOEFL requirement: Yes
Minimum TOEFL score: 550

LIU Post
720 Northern Boulevard
Brookville, NY 11548-1300
http://www.liu.edu/postmba
Private
Admissions: (516) 299-2900
E-mail: enroll@cwpost.liu.edu
Financial aid: (516) 299-2338
Application deadline: 08/15
Tuition: full time: $1,068/credit hour; part time: $1,068/credit hour
Room/board/expenses: $17,380
College-funded aid: Yes
International student aid: Yes
Full-time enrollment: 164
men: 56%; women: 44%; minorities:13%; international: 53%
Part-time enrollment: 64
men: 66%; women: 34%; minorities:25%; international: 0%
Acceptance rate (full time): 74%
Average GMAT (full time): 471
Average GMAT (part time): 459
Average GPA (full time): 3.20
Average age of entrants to full-time program: 25
Average months of prior work experience (full time): 35
TOEFL requirement: Yes
Minimum TOEFL score: 563

Marist College
149 Dyson Center
Poughkeepsie, NY 12601
http://www.marist.edu/mba
Private
Admissions: (845) 575-3800
E-mail: graduate@marist.edu
Financial aid: (845) 575-3230
Application deadline: rolling
Tuition: full time: N/A; part time: $720/credit hour
Room/board/expenses: N/A
College-funded aid: Yes
International student aid: No
Full-time enrollment: N/A
men: N/A; women: N/A; minorities:N/A; international: N/A
Part-time enrollment: 166
men: 59%; women: 41%; minorities:16%; international: 1%
Average GMAT (part time): 524
TOEFL requirement: Yes
Minimum TOEFL score: 550
Most popular departments: finance, general management, health care administration, international business, leadership

New York University (Stern)
44 W. Fourth Street
New York, NY 10012-1126
http://www.stern.nyu.edu
Private
Admissions: (212) 998-0600
E-mail: sternmba@stern.nyu.edu
Financial aid: (212) 998-0790
Application deadline: 03/15
Tuition: full time: $55,154; part time: $1,738/credit hour
Room/board/expenses: $35,712
College-funded aid: Yes
International student aid: Yes
Average student indebtedness at graduation: $105,782
Full-time enrollment: 780
men: 65%; women: 35%; minorities:30%; international: 26%
Part-time enrollment: 2,031
men: 67%; women: 33%; minorities:24%; international: 13%
Acceptance rate (full time): 16%
Average GMAT (full time): 720
Average GMAT (part time): 671
Average GPA (full time): 3.51
Average age of entrants to full-time program: 28
Average months of prior work experience (full time): 58
TOEFL requirement: Yes
Minimum TOEFL score: N/A
Most popular departments: accounting, entrepreneurship, finance, general management, marketing
Mean starting base salary for 2012 full-time graduates: $107,875
Employment location for 2012 class: Intl. 11%; N.E. 78%; M.A. 3%; S. 2%; M.W. 1%; S.W. 1%; W. 4%

Niagara University[1]
PO Box 1909
Niagara University, NY 14109
http://www.niagara.edu/mba
Private
Admissions: (716) 286-8051
E-mail: mbadirector@niagara.edu
Financial aid: (716) 286-8686
Tuition: N/A
Room/board/expenses: N/A
Enrollment: N/A

Pace University (Lubin)
1 Pace Plaza
New York, NY 10038
http://www.pace.edu/lubin/
Private
Admissions: (212) 346-1531
E-mail: gradnyc@pace.edu
Financial aid: (914) 773-3751
Application deadline: 08/01
Tuition: full time: $1,035/credit hour; part time: $1,035/credit hour
Room/board/expenses: $20,704
College-funded aid: Yes
International student aid: Yes
Average student indebtedness at graduation: $52,906
Full-time enrollment: 146
men: 49%; women: 51%; minorities:19%; international: 49%
Part-time enrollment: 369
men: 52%; women: 48%; minorities:26%; international: 31%
Acceptance rate (full time): 44%
Average GMAT (full time): 556
Average GMAT (part time): 549
Average GPA (full time): 3.32
Average age of entrants to full-time program: 24
TOEFL requirement: Yes
Minimum TOEFL score: 600
Most popular departments: accounting, finance, general management, human resources management, portfolio management

Mean starting base salary for 2012 full-time graduates: $63,600
Employment location for 2012 class: Intl. 2%; N.E. 98%; M.A. N/A; S. N/A; M.W. N/A; S.W. N/A; W. N/A

Rensselaer Polytechnic Institute (Lally)
110 Eighth Street
Pittsburgh Building 5202
Troy, NY 12180-3590
http://lallyschool.rpi.edu
Private
Admissions: (518) 276-6565
E-mail: lallymba@rpi.edu
Financial aid: (518) 276-6586
Application deadline: 06/15
Tuition: full time: $45,299; part time: $1,805/credit hour
Room/board/expenses: $15,840
College-funded aid: Yes
International student aid: Yes
Full-time enrollment: 78
men: 51%; women: 49%; minorities:6%; international: 69%
Part-time enrollment: 84
men: 71%; women: 29%; minorities:23%; international: 0%
Acceptance rate (full time): 55%
Average GMAT (full time): 652
Average GPA (full time): 3.22
Average age of entrants to full-time program: 25
Average months of prior work experience (full time): 34
TOEFL requirement: Yes
Minimum TOEFL score: 577
Most popular departments: entrepreneurship, finance, management information systems, supply chain management, technology
Mean starting base salary for 2012 full-time graduates: $65,133
Employment location for 2012 class: Intl. 10%; N.E. 60%; M.A. 5%; S. 20%; M.W. 5%; S.W. 0%; W. 0%

Rochester Institute of Technology (Saunders)
105 Lomb Memorial Drive
Rochester, NY 14623-5608
http://www.cob.rit.edu
Private
Admissions: (585) 475-7284
E-mail: gradinfo@rit.edu
Financial aid: (585) 475-2186
Application deadline: 07/26
Tuition: full time: $36,216; part time: $999/credit hour
Room/board/expenses: $14,967
College-funded aid: Yes
International student aid: Yes
Full-time enrollment: 169
men: 66%; women: 34%; minorities:N/A; international: N/A
Part-time enrollment: 88
men: 65%; women: 35%; minorities:N/A; international: N/A
Acceptance rate (full time): 59%
Average GMAT (full time): 579
Average GMAT (part time): 565
Average GPA (full time): 3.30
Average age of entrants to full-time program: 24
Average months of prior work experience (full time): 30
TOEFL requirement: Yes
Minimum TOEFL score: 580
Most popular departments: entrepreneurship, finance, general management, marketing, technology
Mean starting base salary for 2012 full-time graduates: $59,922
Employment location for 2012 class: Intl. 7%; N.E. 83%; M.A. 2%; S. 0%; M.W. 0%; S.W. 0%; W. 7%

Siena College[1]
515 Loudon Road
Loudonville, NY 12211
http://www.siena.edu
Private
Admissions: N/A
Financial aid: N/A
Tuition: N/A
Room/board/expenses: N/A
Enrollment: N/A

St. Bonaventure University
St. Bonaventure, NY 14778
http://www.sbu.edu/business
Private
Admissions: (716) 375-2021
E-mail: gradsch@sbu.edu
Financial aid: (716) 375-2528
Application deadline: 08/15
Tuition: full time: $690/credit hour; part time: $690/credit hour
Room/board/expenses: $12,159
College-funded aid: Yes
International student aid: Yes
Average student indebtedness at graduation: $21,615
Full-time enrollment: 78
men: 68%; women: 32%; minorities:4%; international: 9%
Part-time enrollment: 41
men: 56%; women: 44%; minorities:0%; international: 0%
Average GMAT (full time): 446
Average GMAT (part time): 420
Average GPA (full time): 3.23
TOEFL requirement: Yes
Minimum TOEFL score: 550

St. John Fisher College (Bittner)
3690 East Avenue
Rochester, NY 14618
http://www.sjfc.edu/bittner
Private
Admissions: (585) 385-8161
E-mail: grad@sjfc.edu
Financial aid: (585) 385-8042
Application deadline: rolling
Tuition: full time: $765/credit hour; part time: $765/credit hour
Room/board/expenses: N/A
College-funded aid: Yes
International student aid: Yes
Full-time enrollment: 67
men: 58%; women: 42%; minorities:10%; international: 3%
Part-time enrollment: 95
men: 47%; women: 53%; minorities:11%; international: 0%
Acceptance rate (full time): 82%
Average GMAT (full time): 476
Average GMAT (part time): 443
Average GPA (full time): 3.37
Average age of entrants to full-time program: 23
TOEFL requirement: Yes
Minimum TOEFL score: 575
Most popular departments: accounting, general management, health care administration, international business

St. John's University (Tobin)
8000 Utopia Parkway
Queens, NY 11439
http://www.stjohns.edu/tobin
Private
Admissions: (718) 990-1345
E-mail: tobingradnyc@stjohns.edu
Financial aid: (718) 990-2000
Application deadline: 05/01
Tuition: full time: $1,060/credit hour; part time: $1,060/credit hour
Room/board/expenses: $22,637
College-funded aid: Yes
International student aid: Yes
Average student indebtedness at graduation: $31,932

Full-time enrollment: 517
men: 43%; women: 57%;
minorities:14%; international: 59%
Part-time enrollment: 222
men: 61%; women: 39%;
minorities:34%; international: 19%
Acceptance rate (full time): 83%
Average GMAT (full time): 545
Average GMAT (part time): 526
Average GPA (full time): 3.22
Average age of entrants to full-time program: 24
TOEFL requirement: Yes
Minimum TOEFL score: 600
Most popular departments: accounting, finance, marketing, tax, other
Mean starting base salary for 2012 full-time graduates: $51,922
Employment location for 2012 class: Intl. 3%; N.E. 88%; M.A. 0%; S. 1%; M.W. 3%; S.W. 3%; W. 1%

SUNY Institute of Technology–Utica/Rome

100 Seymour Road
Utica, NY 13502
http://www.sunyit.edu/business/
Public
Admissions: (315) 792-7347
E-mail: gradcenter@sunyit.edu
Financial aid: (315) 792-7210
Application deadline: 08/01
In-state tuition: full time: $12,023; part time: $464/credit hour
Out-of-state tuition: full time: $19,213
Room/board/expenses: $14,200
College-funded aid: Yes
International student aid: Yes
Average student indebtedness at graduation: $18,200
Full-time enrollment: 70
men: 53%; women: 47%;
minorities:20%; international: 1%
Part-time enrollment: 175
men: 55%; women: 45%;
minorities:9%; international: 1%
Acceptance rate (full time): 48%
Average GMAT (full time): 485
Average GMAT (part time): 493
Average GPA (full time): 3.33
Average age of entrants to full-time program: 28
TOEFL requirement: Yes
Minimum TOEFL score: 550

SUNY–Oswego

238 Rich Hall
Oswego, NY 13126
http://www.oswego.edu/academics/colleges_and_departments/business/index.html
Public
Admissions: (315) 312-3152
E-mail: gradoff@oswego.edu
Financial aid: (315) 312-2248
Application deadline: rolling
In-state tuition: full time: $11,130; part time: $464/credit hour
Out-of-state tuition: full time: $18,320
Room/board/expenses: $15,910
College-funded aid: Yes
International student aid: Yes
Average student indebtedness at graduation: $16,993
Full-time enrollment: 54
men: 57%; women: 43%;
minorities:13%; international: 7%
Part-time enrollment: 63
men: 49%; women: 51%;
minorities:16%; international: 0%
Acceptance rate (full time): 95%
Average GMAT (full time): 530
Average GMAT (part time): 541
Average GPA (full time): 3.23
Average age of entrants to full-time program: 25
TOEFL requirement: Yes
Minimum TOEFL score: 560

Most popular departments: accounting, general management, human resources management, marketing, operations management

Syracuse University (Whitman)

721 University Avenue, Suite 315
Syracuse, NY 13244-2450
http://whitman.syr.edu/mba/fulltime
Private
Admissions: (315) 443-4327
E-mail: mbainfo@syr.edu
Financial aid: (315) 443-3727
Application deadline: 04/19
Tuition: full time: $38,864; part time: $1,249/credit hour
Room/board/expenses: $19,230
College-funded aid: Yes
International student aid: Yes
Average student indebtedness at graduation: $36,228
Full-time enrollment: 77
men: 57%; women: 43%;
minorities:12%; international: 56%
Part-time enrollment: N/A
men: N/A; women: N/A;
minorities:N/A; international: N/A
Acceptance rate (full time): 56%
Average GMAT (full time): 627
Average GPA (full time): 3.53
Average age of entrants to full-time program: 25
Average months of prior work experience (full time): 44
TOEFL requirement: Yes
Minimum TOEFL score: 600
Most popular departments: accounting, entrepreneurship, finance, marketing, supply chain management
Mean starting base salary for 2012 full-time graduates: $71,419
Employment location for 2012 class: Intl. 6%; N.E. 69%; M.A. 6%; S. 6%; M.W. 6%; S.W. 0%; W. 6%

Union Graduate College[1]

80 Nott Terrace
Schenectady, NY 12308-3107
http://www.uniongraduatecollege.edu
Private
Admissions: (518) 631-9831
E-mail: sheehanr@uniongraduatecollege.edu
Financial aid: (518) 631-9836
Tuition: N/A
Room/board/expenses: N/A
Enrollment: N/A

University at Albany–SUNY

1400 Washington Avenue
Albany, NY 12222
http://www.albany.edu/business
Public
Admissions: (518) 442-4961
E-mail: busweb@uamail.albany.edu
Financial aid: (518) 442-5757
Application deadline: 03/01
In-state tuition: full time: $464/credit hour; part time: $464/credit hour
Out-of-state tuition: full time: $763/credit hour
Room/board/expenses: N/A
College-funded aid: Yes
International student aid: No
Full-time enrollment: 63
men: 51%; women: 49%;
minorities:N/A; international: 11%
Part-time enrollment: 216
men: 66%; women: 34%;
minorities:N/A; international: 0%
Acceptance rate (full time): 45%
Average GMAT (full time): 559
Average GMAT (part time): 540

Average GPA (full time): 3.46
Average months of prior work experience (full time): 24
TOEFL requirement: Yes
Minimum TOEFL score: 600
Mean starting base salary for 2012 full-time graduates: $57,125
Employment location for 2012 class: Intl. N/A; N.E. 89%; M.A. 7%; S. N/A; M.W. 4%; S.W. N/A; W. N/A

University at Buffalo–SUNY

203 Alfiero Center
Buffalo, NY 14260-4010
http://www.mgt.buffalo.edu
Public
Admissions: (716) 645-3204
E-mail: som-apps@buffalo.edu
Financial aid: (716) 645-2450
Application deadline: 05/30
In-state tuition: full time: $14,130; part time: $725/credit hour
Out-of-state tuition: full time: $21,320
Room/board/expenses: $13,000
College-funded aid: Yes
International student aid: Yes
Full-time enrollment: 173
men: 65%; women: 35%;
minorities:8%; international: 33%
Part-time enrollment: 192
men: 65%; women: 35%;
minorities:7%; international: 5%
Acceptance rate (full time): 47%
Average GMAT (full time): 613
Average GMAT (part time): 551
Average GPA (full time): 3.40
Average age of entrants to full-time program: 24
Average months of prior work experience (full time): 24
TOEFL requirement: Yes
Minimum TOEFL score: 570
Most popular departments: consulting, finance, human resources management, marketing, supply chain management
Mean starting base salary for 2012 full-time graduates: $58,209
Employment location for 2012 class: Intl. 6%; N.E. 75%; M.A. 6%; S. 0%; M.W. 4%; S.W. 4%; W. 6%

University of Rochester (Simon)

Schlegel Hall
Rochester, NY 14627
http://www.simon.rochester.edu
Private
Admissions: (585) 275-3533
E-mail: admissions@simon.rochester.edu
Financial aid: (585) 275-3533
Application deadline: 05/15
Tuition: full time: $49,012; part time: $1,574/credit hour
Room/board/expenses: $16,900
College-funded aid: Yes
International student aid: Yes
Average student indebtedness at graduation: $31,348
Full-time enrollment: 267
men: 72%; women: 28%;
minorities:18%; international: 51%
Part-time enrollment: 229
men: 76%; women: 24%;
minorities:11%; international: 7%
Acceptance rate (full time): 34%
Average GMAT (full time): 680
Average GMAT (part time): 558
Average GPA (full time): 3.45
Average age of entrants to full-time program: 27
Average months of prior work experience (full time): 57
TOEFL requirement: Yes
Minimum TOEFL score: N/A
Most popular departments: accounting, consulting, finance, marketing, other
Mean starting base salary for 2012 full-time graduates: $86,553

Employment location for 2012 class: Intl. 9%; N.E. 60%; M.A. 6%; S. 10%; M.W. 6%; S.W. 2%; W. 9%

SUNY–Geneseo[1]

1 College Circle
Geneseo, NY 14454
http://www.geneseo.edu/business
Public
Admissions: N/A
Financial aid: N/A
Tuition: N/A
Room/board/expenses: N/A
Enrollment: N/A

NORTH CAROLINA

Appalachian State University (Walker)[1]

Box 32037
Boone, NC 28608-2037
http://www.business.appstate.edu/grad/mba.asp
Public
Admissions: (828) 262-2130
E-mail: mba@appstate.edu
Financial aid: (828) 262-2190
Tuition: N/A
Room/board/expenses: N/A
Enrollment: N/A

Duke University (Fuqua)

100 Fuqua Drive Box 90120
Durham, NC 27708-0120
http://www.fuqua.duke.edu
Private
Admissions: (919) 660-7705
E-mail: admissions-info@fuqua.duke.edu
Financial aid: (919) 660-7687
Application deadline: 12/31
Tuition: full time: $54,922; part time: N/A
Room/board/expenses: $20,179
College-funded aid: Yes
International student aid: Yes
Average student indebtedness at graduation: $102,054
Full-time enrollment: 874
men: 65%; women: 35%;
minorities:23%; international: 34%
Part-time enrollment: N/A
men: N/A; women: N/A;
minorities:N/A; international: N/A
Acceptance rate (full time): 27%
Average GMAT (full time): 690
Average GPA (full time): 3.42
Average age of entrants to full-time program: 29
Average months of prior work experience (full time): 65
TOEFL requirement: Yes
Minimum TOEFL score: N/A
Most popular departments: consulting, finance, health care administration, marketing, statistics and operations research
Mean starting base salary for 2012 full-time graduates: $111,812
Employment location for 2012 class: Intl. 16%; N.E. 24%; M.A. 8%; S. 17%; M.W. 13%; S.W. 6%; W. 14%

East Carolina University

3203 Bate Building
Greenville, NC 27858-4353
http://www.business.ecu.edu/grad/
Public
Admissions: (252) 328-6970
E-mail: gradbus@ecu.edu
Financial aid: (252) 328-6610
Application deadline: 06/01
In-state tuition: full time: $440/credit hour; part time: $312/credit hour

Out-of-state tuition: full time: $1,097/credit hour
Room/board/expenses: $8,000
College-funded aid: Yes
International student aid: Yes
Full-time enrollment: 304
men: 59%; women: 41%;
minorities:15%; international: 6%
Part-time enrollment: 612
men: 59%; women: 41%;
minorities:11%; international: 2%
Acceptance rate (full time): 63%
Average GMAT (full time): 550
Average GMAT (part time): 530
Average GPA (full time): 3.20
Average age of entrants to full-time program: 31
TOEFL requirement: Yes
Minimum TOEFL score: 550
Most popular departments: finance, health care administration, management information systems, supply chain management

Elon University (Love)

100 Campus Drive
Elon, NC 27244-2010
http://www.elon.edu/mba
Private
Admissions: (800) 334-8448
E-mail: gradadm@elon.edu
Financial aid: (800) 334-8448
Application deadline: rolling
Tuition: full time: N/A; part time: $767/credit hour
Room/board/expenses: N/A
College-funded aid: No
International student aid: No
Full-time enrollment: N/A
men: N/A; women: N/A;
minorities:N/A; international: N/A
Part-time enrollment: 137
men: 58%; women: 42%;
minorities:26%; international: 14%
Average GMAT (part time): 563
TOEFL requirement: Yes
Minimum TOEFL score: 550
Most popular departments: entrepreneurship, general management, human resources management, leadership, operations management

Fayetteville State University

1200 Murchison Road
Newbold Station
Fayetteville, NC 28301-1033
http://www.uncfsu.edu/sbe/academics/graduate.asp
Private
Admissions: (910) 672-1197
E-mail: mbaprogram@uncfsu.edu
Financial aid: N/A
Application deadline: 04/15
Tuition: full time: N/A; part time: $188/credit hour
Room/board/expenses: N/A
College-funded aid: Yes
International student aid: Yes
Full-time enrollment: N/A
men: N/A; women: N/A;
minorities:N/A; international: N/A
Part-time enrollment: 109
men: 40%; women: 60%;
minorities:66%; international: N/A
Average GMAT (part time): 498
TOEFL requirement: Yes
Minimum TOEFL score: 550
Most popular departments: accounting, finance, general management, health care administration, marketing

Meredith College[1]

3800 Hillsborough St.
Raleigh, NC 27607
http://www.meredith.edu/mba
Private
Admissions: (919) 760-8212
E-mail: mba@meredith.edu
Financial aid: (919) 760-8565

Tuition: N/A
Room/board/expenses: N/A
Enrollment: N/A

North Carolina A&T State University

1601 E. Market Street
Greensboro, NC 27411
http://www.ncat.edu/~business/
Public
Admissions: (336) 334-7920
E-mail: jjtaylor@ncat.edu
Financial aid: (336) 334-7973
Application deadline: 04/01
In-state tuition: full time: $9,648; part time: N/A
Out-of-state tuition: full time: $19,176
Room/board/expenses: $13,317
College-funded aid: Yes
International student aid: Yes
Average student indebtedness at graduation: N/A
Full-time enrollment: 17
men: 41%; women: 59%; minorities:65%; international: 35%
Part-time enrollment: 11
men: 18%; women: 82%; minorities:100%; international: 0%
Acceptance rate (full time): 87%
Average GMAT (full time): 520
Average GPA (full time): 3.31
Average age of entrants to full-time program: 25
Average months of prior work experience (full time): 180
TOEFL requirement: Yes
Minimum TOEFL score: 550
Most popular departments: accounting, human resources management, supply chain management
Employment location for 2012 class: Intl. N/A; N.E. N/A; M.A. N/A; S. 100%; M.W. N/A; S.W. N/A; W. N/A

North Carolina Central University[1]

1801 Fayetteville Street
Durham, NC 27707
http://www.nccu.edu/academics/business/index.cfm
Public
Admissions: (919) 530-6405
E-mail: mba@nccu.edu
Financial aid: N/A
Tuition: N/A
Room/board/expenses: N/A
Enrollment: N/A

North Carolina State University (Jenkins)

2130 Nelson Hall
Campus Box 8114
Raleigh, NC 27695-8114
http://www.mba.ncsu.edu
Public
Admissions: (919) 515-5584
E-mail: mba@ncsu.edu
Financial aid: (919) 515-2421
Application deadline: rolling
In-state tuition: total program: $37,317 (full-time); $42,993 (part-time)
Out-of-state tuition: total program: $62,383 (full-time)
Room/board/expenses: $15,000
College-funded aid: Yes
International student aid: Yes
Average student indebtedness at graduation: $36,448
Full-time enrollment: 92
men: 68%; women: 32%; minorities:8%; international: 16%
Part-time enrollment: 254
men: 74%; women: 26%; minorities:17%; international: 14%
Acceptance rate (full time): 52%
Average GMAT (full time): 600
Average GMAT (part time): 577
Average GPA (full time): 3.30
Average age of entrants to full-time program: 27
Average months of prior work experience (full time): 53
TOEFL requirement: Yes
Minimum TOEFL score: 600
Most popular departments: entrepreneurship, finance, marketing, supply chain management, technology
Mean starting base salary for 2012 full-time graduates: $70,474
Employment location for 2012 class: Intl. 3%; N.E. 0%; M.A. 3%; S. 82%; M.W. 6%; S.W. 3%; W. 3%

Queens University of Charlotte (McColl)

1900 Selwyn Avenue
Charlotte, NC 28274
http://mccoll.queens.edu/
Private
Admissions: (704) 337-2352
E-mail: MBA@Queens.edu
Financial aid: (704) 337-2225
Application deadline: 08/15
Tuition: full time: N/A; part time: $925/credit hour
Room/board/expenses: N/A
College-funded aid: Yes
International student aid: Yes
Full-time enrollment: N/A
men: N/A; women: N/A; minorities:N/A; international: N/A
Part-time enrollment: 131
men: 62%; women: 38%; minorities:18%; international: 10%
Average GMAT (part time): 511
TOEFL requirement: Yes
Minimum TOEFL score: 550
Most popular departments: entrepreneurship, finance, general management, international business, marketing

University of North Carolina–Chapel Hill (Kenan-Flagler)

CB 3490, McColl Building
Chapel Hill, NC 27599-3490
http://www.kenan-flagler.unc.edu
Public
Admissions: (919) 962-3236
E-mail: mba_info@unc.edu
Financial aid: (919) 962-9096
Application deadline: 03/15
In-state tuition: full time: $30,793; part time: N/A
Out-of-state tuition: full time: $52,074
Room/board/expenses: $24,338
College-funded aid: Yes
International student aid: Yes
Average student indebtedness at graduation: $82,784
Full-time enrollment: 580
men: 73%; women: 27%; minorities:14%; international: 33%
Part-time enrollment: N/A
men: N/A; women: N/A; minorities:N/A; international: N/A
Acceptance rate (full time): 43%
Average GMAT (full time): 692
Average GPA (full time): 3.34
Average age of entrants to full-time program: 28
Average months of prior work experience (full time): 66
TOEFL requirement: Yes
Minimum TOEFL score: 600
Most popular departments: consulting, finance, general management, marketing, real estate
Mean starting base salary for 2012 full-time graduates: $102,170
Employment location for 2012 class: Intl. 6%; N.E. 27%; M.A. 10%; S. 37%; M.W. 8%; S.W. 4%; W. 8%

University of North Carolina–Charlotte (Belk)

9201 University City Boulevard
Charlotte, NC 28223
http://www.mba.uncc.edu
Public
Admissions: (704) 687-7566
E-mail: mba@uncc.edu
Financial aid: (704) 687-2461
Application deadline: rolling
In-state tuition: full time: $11,394; part time: $8,144
Out-of-state tuition: full time: $23,636
Room/board/expenses: N/A
College-funded aid: Yes
International student aid: Yes
Full-time enrollment: N/A
men: N/A; women: N/A; minorities:N/A; international: N/A
Part-time enrollment: 305
men: 64%; women: 36%; minorities:21%; international: 14%
Average GMAT (part time): 585
TOEFL requirement: Yes
Minimum TOEFL score: 557
Most popular departments: finance, general management, international business, marketing, real estate

University of North Carolina–Greensboro (Bryan)

PO Box 26170
Greensboro, NC 27402-6170
http://bryanmba.uncg.edu
Public
Admissions: (336) 334-5390
E-mail: bryanmba@uncg.edu
Financial aid: (336) 334-5702
Application deadline: 07/01
In-state tuition: full time: $8,206; part time: $706/credit hour
Out-of-state tuition: full time: $21,655
Room/board/expenses: $8,982
College-funded aid: Yes
International student aid: Yes
Full-time enrollment: 65
men: 57%; women: 43%; minorities:34%; international: 22%
Part-time enrollment: 108
men: 74%; women: 26%; minorities:19%; international: 2%
Acceptance rate (full time): 73%
Average GMAT (full time): 565
Average GMAT (part time): 548
Average GPA (full time): 3.37
Average age of entrants to full-time program: 25
Average months of prior work experience (full time): 18
TOEFL requirement: Yes
Minimum TOEFL score: 550
Most popular departments: finance, general management, marketing, management information systems, supply chain management
Mean starting base salary for 2012 full-time graduates: $52,000
Employment location for 2012 class: Intl. 13%; N.E. 6%; M.A. N/A; S. 63%; M.W. 13%; S.W. N/A; W. 6%

University of North Carolina–Wilmington (Cameron)

601 S. College Road
Wilmington, NC 28403-5680
http://www.csb.uncw.edu/gradprograms
Public
Admissions: (910) 962-3903
E-mail: barnhillk@uncw.edu
Financial aid: (910) 962-3177
Application deadline: 04/01
In-state tuition: full time: $20,673; part time: $6,408
Out-of-state tuition: full time: $20,673
Room/board/expenses: N/A
College-funded aid: Yes
International student aid: Yes
Average student indebtedness at graduation: $44,219
Full-time enrollment: 53
men: 68%; women: 32%; minorities:8%; international: 23%
Part-time enrollment: 38
men: 61%; women: 39%; minorities:13%; international: 3%
Acceptance rate (full time): 73%
Average GMAT (full time): 558
Average GMAT (part time): 534
Average GPA (full time): 3.24
Average age of entrants to full-time program: 25
Average months of prior work experience (full time): 20
TOEFL requirement: Yes
Minimum TOEFL score: 550
Most popular departments: consulting, finance, general management, marketing, supply chain management

Wake Forest University (Babcock)

PO Box 7659
Winston-Salem, NC 27109-7659
http://www.business.wfu.edu
Private
Admissions: (336) 758-5422
E-mail: busadmissions@wfu.edu
Financial aid: (336) 758-4424
Application deadline: rolling
Tuition: full time: $41,132; part time: $35,594
Room/board/expenses: $19,500
College-funded aid: Yes
International student aid: Yes
Full-time enrollment: 123
men: 71%; women: 29%; minorities:15%; international: 22%
Part-time enrollment: 250
men: 72%; women: 28%; minorities:20%; international: 6%
Acceptance rate (full time): 54%
Average GMAT (full time): 648
Average GMAT (part time): 582
Average GPA (full time): 3.25
Average age of entrants to full-time program: 27
Average months of prior work experience (full time): 52
TOEFL requirement: Yes
Minimum TOEFL score: 600
Most popular departments: consulting, finance, marketing, operations management, other
Mean starting base salary for 2012 full-time graduates: $88,693
Employment location for 2012 class: Intl. 0%; N.E. 16%; M.A. 11%; S. 50%; M.W. 7%; S.W. 7%; W. 9%

Western Carolina University

Forsyth Building
Cullowhee, NC 28723
http://www.wcu.edu/43.asp
Public
Admissions: (828) 227-3174
E-mail: gradsch@email.wcu.edu
Financial aid: (828) 227-7290
Application deadline: rolling
In-state tuition: full time: $6,322; part time: N/A
Out-of-state tuition: full time: $15,907
Room/board/expenses: $10,420
College-funded aid: Yes
International student aid: No
Full-time enrollment: 46
men: 54%; women: 46%; minorities:9%; international: 9%
Part-time enrollment: 179
men: 61%; women: 39%; minorities:17%; international: 2%
Average GMAT (full time): 532
Average GMAT (part time): 504
Average GPA (full time): 3.26
Average age of entrants to full-time program: 27
TOEFL requirement: Yes
Minimum TOEFL score: 550

Winston-Salem State University

RJR Center Suite 109
Winston-Salem, NC 27110
http://www.wssu.edu/mba
Public
Admissions: (336) 750-3045
E-mail: graduate@wssu.edu
Financial aid: (336) 750-3280
Application deadline: 06/15
In-state tuition: full time: N/A; total program: $10,340 (part-time)
Out-of-state tuition: full time: N/A
Room/board/expenses: N/A
College-funded aid: Yes
International student aid: No
Full-time enrollment: N/A
men: N/A; women: N/A; minorities:N/A; international: N/A
Part-time enrollment: 69
men: 52%; women: 48%; minorities:78%; international: 12%
Average GMAT (part time): 435
TOEFL requirement: Yes
Minimum TOEFL score: 550

NORTH DAKOTA

North Dakota State University

NDSU Department 2400
PO Box 6050
Fargo, ND 58108-6050
http://www.ndsu.nodak.edu/cba/mba
Public
Admissions: (701) 231-7681
E-mail: Melissa.J.Erickson@ndsu.edu
Financial aid: (800) 726-3188
Application deadline: rolling
In-state tuition: full time: N/A; part time: N/A
Out-of-state tuition: full time: N/A
Room/board/expenses: N/A
College-funded aid: Yes
International student aid: Yes
Full-time enrollment: 20
men: 65%; women: 35%; minorities:5%; international: 45%
Part-time enrollment: 60
men: 73%; women: 27%; minorities:13%; international: 8%
TOEFL requirement: Yes
Minimum TOEFL score: 550

University of North Dakota

293 Centennial Drive Stop 8098
Grand Forks, ND 58202-8098
http://business.und.edu/academics/academic-programs/graduate-programs.cfm
Public
Admissions: (701) 777-2784
E-mail: questions@gradschool.und.edu
Financial aid: (701) 777-3121
Application deadline: 03/15
In-state tuition: full time: $266/credit hour; part time: $266/credit hour
Out-of-state tuition: full time: $710/credit hour
Room/board/expenses: N/A
College-funded aid: Yes
International student aid: Yes
Full-time enrollment: 38
men: 66%; women: 34%; minorities:11%; international: 21%
Part-time enrollment: 77
men: 65%; women: 35%; minorities:9%; international: 5%
TOEFL requirement: Yes
Minimum TOEFL score: 550

More at www.usnews.com/grad

OHIO

Bowling Green State University

371 Business Administration Building
Bowling Green, OH 43403-0001
http://www.bgsumba.com
Public
Admissions: (800) 247-8622
E-mail: mba-info@bgsu.edu
Financial aid: (419) 372-2651
Application deadline: 03/15
In-state tuition: total program: $17,448 (full-time); part time: $652/credit hour
Out-of-state tuition: total program: $28,410 (full-time)
Room/board/expenses: N/A
College-funded aid: Yes
International student aid: Yes
Full-time enrollment: 34
men: 68%; women: 32%; minorities:6%; international: 32%
Part-time enrollment: 45
men: 58%; women: 42%; minorities:2%; international: 0%
Acceptance rate (full time): 40%
Average GMAT (full time): 563
Average GMAT (part time): 538
Average GPA (full time): 3.34
Average age of entrants to full-time program: 26
Average months of prior work experience (full time): 32
TOEFL requirement: Yes
Minimum TOEFL score: 550
Most popular departments: accounting, finance

Case Western Reserve University (Weatherhead)

Peter B. Lewis Building
10900 Euclid Avenue
Cleveland, OH 44106-7235
http://www.weatherhead.case.edu
Private
Admissions: (216) 368-6702
E-mail: wsomadmission@case.edu
Financial aid: (216) 368-8907
Application deadline: 03/15
Tuition: full time: $45,640; part time: $1,833/credit hour
Room/board/expenses: $13,000
College-funded aid: Yes
International student aid: Yes
Average student indebtedness at graduation: $64,066
Full-time enrollment: 122
men: 68%; women: 32%; minorities:10%; international: 48%
Part-time enrollment: 167
men: 66%; women: 34%; minorities:8%; international: 7%
Acceptance rate (full time): 24%
Average GMAT (full time): 631
Average GMAT (part time): 585
Average GPA (full time): 3.30
Average age of entrants to full-time program: 27
Average months of prior work experience (full time): 52
TOEFL requirement: Yes
Minimum TOEFL score: 600
Most popular departments: accounting, finance, leadership, organizational behavior, supply chain management
Mean starting base salary for 2012 full-time graduates: $80,762
Employment location for 2012 class: Intl. 12%; N.E. 9%; M.A. 3%; S. 0%; M.W. 74%; S.W. 0%; W. 3%

Cleveland State University (Ahuja)

1860 E. 18th Street, BU420
Cleveland, OH 44115
http://www.csuohio.edu/business/mba
Public
Admissions: (216) 687-5599
E-mail: cbacsu@csuohio.edu
Financial aid: (216) 687-3764
Application deadline: 07/01
In-state tuition: full time: $14,222; part time: $547/credit hour
Out-of-state tuition: full time: $26,565
Room/board/expenses: $13,748
College-funded aid: Yes
International student aid: Yes
Average student indebtedness at graduation: $26,397
Full-time enrollment: 229
men: 52%; women: 48%; minorities:17%; international: 20%
Part-time enrollment: 474
men: 60%; women: 40%; minorities:17%; international: 8%
Acceptance rate (full time): 62%
Average GMAT (full time): 500
Average GMAT (part time): 515
Average GPA (full time): 3.15
Average age of entrants to full-time program: 27
Average months of prior work experience (full time): 36
TOEFL requirement: Yes
Minimum TOEFL score: 525
Most popular departments: finance, general management, international business, marketing, supply chain management
Mean starting base salary for 2012 full-time graduates: $50,000
Employment location for 2012 class: Intl. N/A; N.E. N/A; M.A. N/A; S. N/A; M.W. 100%; S.W. N/A; W. N/A

John Carroll University (Boler)

1 John Carroll Boulevard
University Heights, OH 44118
http://www.jcu.edu/mba
Private
Admissions: (216) 397-1970
E-mail: gradbusiness@jcu.edu
Financial aid: (216) 397-4248
Application deadline: 07/15
Tuition: full time: N/A; part time: $855/credit hour
Room/board/expenses: N/A
College-funded aid: Yes
International student aid: Yes
Full-time enrollment: N/A
men: N/A; women: N/A; minorities:N/A; international: N/A
Part-time enrollment: 116
men: 68%; women: 32%; minorities:9%; international: 5%
Average GMAT (part time): 539
TOEFL requirement: Yes
Minimum TOEFL score: 550
Most popular departments: accounting, finance, human resources management, international business, marketing

Kent State University

PO Box 5190
Kent, OH 44242-0001
http://www.kent.edu/business/grad
Public
Admissions: (330) 672-2282
E-mail: gradbus@kent.edu
Financial aid: (330) 672-2972
Application deadline: 04/01
In-state tuition: full time: $11,490; part time: $468/credit hour
Out-of-state tuition: full time: $19,006
Room/board/expenses: $10,500
College-funded aid: Yes
International student aid: Yes
Full-time enrollment: 51
men: 59%; women: 41%; minorities:2%; international: 35%
Part-time enrollment: 90
men: 54%; women: 46%; minorities:4%; international: 0%
Acceptance rate (full time): 43%
Average GMAT (full time): 569
Average GMAT (part time): 555
Average GPA (full time): 3.27
Average age of entrants to full-time program: 25
Average months of prior work experience (full time): 21
TOEFL requirement: Yes
Minimum TOEFL score: 550
Most popular departments: accounting, finance, human resources management, international business, marketing
Mean starting base salary for 2012 full-time graduates: $51,111

Miami University (Farmer)

800 E. High Street
Oxford, OH 45056
http://mba.muohio.edu
Public
Admissions: (513) 895-8876
E-mail: miamimba@muohio.edu
Financial aid: (513) 529-8710
Application deadline: rolling
In-state tuition: full time: N/A; total program: $28,800 (part-time)
Out-of-state tuition: full time: N/A
Room/board/expenses: N/A
College-funded aid: No
International student aid: No
Full-time enrollment: N/A
men: N/A; women: N/A; minorities:N/A; international: N/A
Part-time enrollment: 68
men: 69%; women: 31%; minorities:6%; international: 1%
Average GMAT (part time): 567
TOEFL requirement: Yes
Minimum TOEFL score: 550
Most popular departments: finance, general management, marketing

Ohio State University (Fisher)

100 Gerlach Hall, 2108 Neil Avenue
Columbus, OH 43210-1144
http://fishermba.osu.edu
Public
Admissions: (614) 292-8511
E-mail: mba@fisher.osu.edu
Financial aid: (614) 292-8511
Application deadline: 04/15
In-state tuition: full time: $28,355; part time: $1,399/credit hour
Out-of-state tuition: full time: $45,667
Room/board/expenses: $19,386
College-funded aid: Yes
International student aid: Yes
Average student indebtedness at graduation: $40,009
Full-time enrollment: 229
men: 72%; women: 28%; minorities:14%; international: 33%
Part-time enrollment: 318
men: 73%; women: 27%; minorities:19%; international: 20%
Acceptance rate (full time): 32%
Average GMAT (full time): 668
Average GMAT (part time): 621
Average GPA (full time): 3.38
Average age of entrants to full-time program: 28
Average months of prior work experience (full time): 65
TOEFL requirement: Yes
Minimum TOEFL score: 600
Most popular departments: consulting, finance, marketing, operations management, supply chain management
Mean starting base salary for 2012 full-time graduates: $91,312
Employment location for 2012 class: Intl. 4%; N.E. 10%; M.A. 3%; S. 2%; M.W. 72%; S.W. 3%; W. 6%

Ohio University

514 Copeland Hall
Athens, OH 45701
http://www.cob.ohiou.edu
Public
Admissions: (740) 593-2053
E-mail: rossj@ohio.edu
Financial aid: (740) 593-4141
Application deadline: rolling
In-state tuition: full time: N/A; part time: N/A
Out-of-state tuition: full time: N/A
Room/board/expenses: N/A
College-funded aid: Yes
International student aid: Yes
Full-time enrollment: N/A
men: N/A; women: N/A; minorities:N/A; international: N/A
Part-time enrollment: 133
men: 64%; women: 36%; minorities:14%; international: 0%
TOEFL requirement: Yes
Minimum TOEFL score: 600
Most popular departments: finance, general management, health care administration

University of Akron

CBA 412
Akron, OH 44325-4805
http://mba.uakron.edu
Public
Admissions: (330) 972-7043
E-mail: gradcba@uakron.edu
Financial aid: (330) 972-7032
Application deadline: 07/15
In-state tuition: full time: N/A; part time: $443/credit hour
Out-of-state tuition: full time: N/A
Room/board/expenses: $12,600
College-funded aid: Yes
International student aid: Yes
Full-time enrollment: N/A
men: N/A; women: N/A; minorities:N/A; international: N/A
Part-time enrollment: 290
men: 67%; women: 33%; minorities:9%; international: 19%
Average GMAT (part time): 582
TOEFL requirement: Yes
Minimum TOEFL score: 550

University of Cincinnati

606 Lindner Hall
Cincinnati, OH 45221-0020
http://www.business.uc.edu/mba
Public
Admissions: (513) 556-7024
E-mail: graduate@uc.edu
Financial aid: (513) 556-6982
Application deadline: 07/15
In-state tuition: total program: $30,819 (full-time); part time: $873/credit hour
Out-of-state tuition: total program: $37,935 (full-time)
Room/board/expenses: $25,000
College-funded aid: Yes
International student aid: Yes
Average student indebtedness at graduation: $24,766
Full-time enrollment: 109
men: 68%; women: 32%; minorities:14%; international: 27%
Part-time enrollment: 152
men: 65%; women: 35%; minorities:15%; international: 18%
Acceptance rate (full time): 92%
Average GMAT (full time): 565
Average GMAT (part time): 522
Average GPA (full time): 3.42
Average age of entrants to full-time program: 26
Average months of prior work experience (full time): 48
TOEFL requirement: Yes
Minimum TOEFL score: 600
Most popular departments: finance, general management, international business, marketing, real estate
Mean starting base salary for 2012 full-time graduates: $56,791
Employment location for 2012 class: Intl. 3%; N.E. 3%; M.A. 3%; S. 11%; M.W. 74%; S.W. 0%; W. 6%

University of Dayton

300 College Park Avenue
Dayton, OH 45469-2234
http://business.udayton.edu/mba
Private
Admissions: (937) 229-3733
E-mail: mba@udayton.edu
Financial aid: (937) 229-4311
Application deadline: rolling
Tuition: full time: $858/credit hour; part time: $858/credit hour
Room/board/expenses: N/A
College-funded aid: Yes
International student aid: Yes
Full-time enrollment: 118
men: 56%; women: 44%; minorities:8%; international: 79%
Part-time enrollment: 176
men: 56%; women: 44%; minorities:8%; international: 4%
Acceptance rate (full time): 79%
Average GMAT (full time): 560
Average GMAT (part time): 560
Average GPA (full time): 3.25
Average age of entrants to full-time program: 23
Average months of prior work experience (full time): 6
TOEFL requirement: Yes
Minimum TOEFL score: 550

University of Toledo

Stranahan Hall North, Room 3130
Toledo, OH 43606-3390
http://utoledo.edu/business/gradprograms/
Public
Admissions: (419) 530-2087
E-mail: robert.detwiler@utoledo.edu
Financial aid: (419) 530-5800
Application deadline: rolling
In-state tuition: full time: $504/credit hour; part time: $504/credit hour
Out-of-state tuition: full time: $916/credit hour
Room/board/expenses: $9,500
College-funded aid: Yes
International student aid: Yes
Average student indebtedness at graduation: $15,000
Full-time enrollment: 345
men: 54%; women: 46%; minorities:N/A; international: N/A
Part-time enrollment: 160
men: 50%; women: 50%; minorities:N/A; international: N/A
Acceptance rate (full time): 84%
Average GMAT (full time): 450
Average GPA (full time): 3.15
Average age of entrants to full-time program: 26
Average months of prior work experience (full time): 36
TOEFL requirement: Yes
Minimum TOEFL score: 550
Most popular departments: finance, general management, human resources management, leadership, marketing

Wright State University (Soin)

3640 Colonel Glenn Highway
Dayton, OH 45435-0001
http://www.wright.edu/business
Public
Admissions: (937) 775-2437
E-mail: mba@wright.edu
Financial aid: (937) 775-5721
Application deadline: 08/01

In-state tuition: full time: $556/credit hour; part time: $564/credit hour
Out-of-state tuition: full time: $942/credit hour
Room/board/expenses: $12,200
College-funded aid: Yes
International student aid: Yes
Average student indebtedness at graduation: $44,886
Full-time enrollment: 103
men: 59%; women: 41%; minorities:11%; international: 22%
Part-time enrollment: 346
men: 58%; women: 42%; minorities:10%; international: 10%
Acceptance rate (full time): 62%
Average GMAT (full time): 470
Average GMAT (part time): 482
Average GPA (full time): 3.26
Average age of entrants to full-time program: 28
Average months of prior work experience (full time): 30
TOEFL requirement: Yes
Minimum TOEFL score: 550
Most popular departments: finance, general management, international business, marketing, other
Mean starting base salary for 2012 full-time graduates: $54,000
Employment location for 2012 class: Intl. N/A; N.E. N/A; M.A. 8%; S. N/A; M.W. 92%; S.W. N/A; W. N/A

Xavier University (Williams)

3800 Victory Parkway
Cincinnati, OH 45207-3221
http://www.xavier.edu/MBA
Private
Admissions: (513) 745-3525
E-mail: xumba@xu.edu
Financial aid: (513) 745-3142
Application deadline: 08/01
Tuition: full time: $740/credit hour; part time: $740/credit hour
Room/board/expenses: $2,500
College-funded aid: Yes
International student aid: Yes
Full-time enrollment: N/A
men: N/A; women: N/A; minorities:N/A; international: N/A
Part-time enrollment: 748
men: 64%; women: 36%; minorities:14%; international: 7%
Average GMAT (part time): 538
TOEFL requirement: Yes
Minimum TOEFL score: 550
Most popular departments: finance, general management, international business, marketing, other

Youngstown State University (Williamson)[1]

1 University Plaza
Youngstown, OH 44555
http://www.wcba.ysu.edu
Public
Admissions: (330) 941-3091
E-mail: graduateschool@cc.ysu.edu
Financial aid: (330) 941-3505
Tuition: N/A
Room/board/expenses: N/A
Enrollment: N/A

OKLAHOMA

Oklahoma State University (Spears)

102 Gundersen
Stillwater, OK 74078-4022
http://spears.okstate.edu/
Public
Admissions: (405) 744-2951
E-mail: spearsmasters@okstate.edu
Financial aid: (405) 744-6604

Application deadline: 07/01
In-state tuition: full time: $178/credit hour; part time: $178/credit hour
Out-of-state tuition: full time: $709/credit hour
Room/board/expenses: $13,910
College-funded aid: Yes
International student aid: No
Full-time enrollment: 76
men: 66%; women: 34%; minorities:16%; international: 36%
Part-time enrollment: 144
men: 63%; women: 38%; minorities:21%; international: 9%
Acceptance rate (full time): 74%
Average GMAT (full time): 562
Average GMAT (part time): 544
Average GPA (full time): 3.38
Average age of entrants to full-time program: 24
Average months of prior work experience (full time): 25
TOEFL requirement: Yes
Minimum TOEFL score: 575
Mean starting base salary for 2012 full-time graduates: $54,206
Employment location for 2012 class: Intl. 6%; N.E. 6%; M.A. 6%; S. 6%; M.W. 6%; S.W. 76%; W. 0%

Southeastern Oklahoma State University

1405 N. Fourth Avenue, PMB 4205
Durant, OK 74701-0609
http://www.se.edu/bus/
Public
Admissions: N/A
E-mail: kluke@se.edu
Financial aid: (580) 745-2186
Application deadline: N/A
In-state tuition: full time: $187/credit hour; part time: $187/credit hour
Out-of-state tuition: full time: $492/credit hour
Room/board/expenses: $2,985
College-funded aid: Yes
International student aid: No
Full-time enrollment: 49
men: 53%; women: 47%; minorities:24%; international: 22%
Part-time enrollment: N/A
men: N/A; women: N/A; minorities:N/A; international: N/A
Average age of entrants to full-time program: 29
TOEFL requirement: Yes
Minimum TOEFL score: 550

University of Oklahoma (Price)

Price Hall
1003 Asp Avenue, Suite 1040
Norman, OK 73019-4302
http://price.ou.edu/mba
Public
Admissions: (405) 325-4107
E-mail: gamundson@ou.edu
Financial aid: (405) 325-4521
Application deadline: 06/01
In-state tuition: full time: $175/credit hour; part time: $175/credit hour
Out-of-state tuition: full time: $652/credit hour
Room/board/expenses: $13,420
College-funded aid: Yes
International student aid: Yes
Full-time enrollment: 107
men: 73%; women: 27%; minorities:16%; international: 18%
Part-time enrollment: 160
men: 74%; women: 26%; minorities:18%; international: 3%
Acceptance rate (full time): 73%
Average GMAT (full time): 616
Average GMAT (part time): 587
Average GPA (full time): 3.49
Average age of entrants to full-time program: 25

Average months of prior work experience (full time): 21
TOEFL requirement: Yes
Minimum TOEFL score: 600
Most popular departments: entrepreneurship, finance, management information systems, other
Mean starting base salary for 2012 full-time graduates: $67,758
Employment location for 2012 class: Intl. 3%; N.E. 3%; M.A. 3%; S. 0%; M.W. 3%; S.W. 86%; W. 3%

University of Tulsa (Collins)

800 S. Tucker Drive
Tulsa, OK 74104-9700
http://www.utulsa.edu/graduate/business
Private
Admissions: (918) 631-2242
E-mail: graduate-business@utulsa.edu
Financial aid: (918) 631-2526
Application deadline: 07/01
Tuition: full time: $1,035/credit hour; part time: $1,035/credit hour
Room/board/expenses: $13,034
College-funded aid: Yes
International student aid: Yes
Average student indebtedness at graduation: $24,921
Full-time enrollment: 56
men: 52%; women: 48%; minorities:9%; international: 30%
Part-time enrollment: 34
men: 76%; women: 24%; minorities:6%; international: 3%
Acceptance rate (full time): 95%
Average GMAT (full time): 579
Average GMAT (part time): 598
Average GPA (full time): 3.42
Average age of entrants to full-time program: 24
TOEFL requirement: Yes
Minimum TOEFL score: 575
Mean starting base salary for 2012 full-time graduates: $58,202
Employment location for 2012 class: Intl. 0%; N.E. 0%; M.A. 5%; S. 5%; M.W. 5%; S.W. 85%; W. 0%

OREGON

Oregon State University

Bexell Hall 200
Corvallis, OR 97331
http://business.oregonstate.edu/mba/
Public
Admissions: (541) 737-5510
E-mail: osumba@bus.oregonstate.edu
Financial aid: (541) 737-2241
Application deadline: 08/30
In-state tuition: total program: $20,106 (full-time); part time: N/A
Out-of-state tuition: total program: $30,852 (full-time)
Room/board/expenses: $12,300
College-funded aid: Yes
International student aid: Yes
Full-time enrollment: 148
men: 53%; women: 47%; minorities:9%; international: 51%
Part-time enrollment: N/A
men: N/A; women: N/A; minorities:N/A; international: N/A
Acceptance rate (full time): 40%
Average GMAT (full time): 560
Average GPA (full time): 3.25
Average age of entrants to full-time program: 29
Average months of prior work experience (full time): 84
TOEFL requirement: Yes
Minimum TOEFL score: 575
Mean starting base salary for 2012 full-time graduates: $55,897

Employment location for 2012 class: Intl. 12%; N.E. 0%; M.A. 0%; S. 0%; M.W. 0%; S.W. 0%; W. 88%

Portland State University

PO Box 751
Portland, OR 97207-0751
http://www.mba.pdx.edu
Public
Admissions: (503) 725-3714
E-mail: gradinfo@sba.pdx.edu
Financial aid: (503) 725-5442
Application deadline: 05/01
In-state tuition: full time: $572/credit hour; part time: $572/credit hour
Out-of-state tuition: full time: $685/credit hour
Room/board/expenses: $20,000
College-funded aid: Yes
International student aid: Yes
Full-time enrollment: 81
men: 53%; women: 47%; minorities:9%; international: 33%
Part-time enrollment: 116
men: 68%; women: 32%; minorities:9%; international: 9%
Acceptance rate (full time): 46%
Average GMAT (full time): 613
Average GMAT (part time): 627
Average GPA (full time): 3.31
Average age of entrants to full-time program: 30
Average months of prior work experience (full time): 55
TOEFL requirement: Yes
Minimum TOEFL score: 550
Most popular departments: entrepreneurship, finance, international business, marketing, supply chain management
Mean starting base salary for 2012 full-time graduates: $66,409
Employment location for 2012 class: Intl. 25%; N.E. 0%; M.A. 8%; S. 4%; M.W. 0%; S.W. 0%; W. 63%

University of Oregon (Lundquist)

1208 University of Oregon
Eugene, OR 97403-1208
http://oregonmba.com
Public
Admissions: (541) 346-3306
E-mail: info@oregonmba.com
Financial aid: (541) 346-3221
Application deadline: 04/15
In-state tuition: full time: $22,188; part time: N/A
Out-of-state tuition: full time: $30,216
Room/board/expenses: $14,500
College-funded aid: Yes
International student aid: Yes
Average student indebtedness at graduation: $16,950
Full-time enrollment: 82
men: 65%; women: 35%; minorities:16%; international: 15%
Part-time enrollment: N/A
men: N/A; women: N/A; minorities:N/A; international: N/A
Acceptance rate (full time): 43%
Average GMAT (full time): 628
Average GPA (full time): 3.37
Average age of entrants to full-time program: 27
Average months of prior work experience (full time): 47
TOEFL requirement: Yes
Minimum TOEFL score: 600
Mean starting base salary for 2012 full-time graduates: $61,140
Employment location for 2012 class: Intl. 11%; N.E. 11%; M.A. 8%; S. N/A; M.W. 3%; S.W. 14%; W. 53%

University of Portland (Pamplin)

5000 N. Willamette Boulevard
Portland, OR 97203-5798
http://business.up.edu
Private
Admissions: (503) 943-7225
E-mail: mba-up@up.edu
Financial aid: (503) 943-7311
Application deadline: 07/15
Tuition: full time: $1,030/credit hour; part time: $1,030/credit hour
Room/board/expenses: $13,000
College-funded aid: Yes
International student aid: Yes
Average student indebtedness at graduation: $33,755
Full-time enrollment: 50
men: 70%; women: 30%; minorities:12%; international: 38%
Part-time enrollment: 78
men: 58%; women: 42%; minorities:8%; international: 4%
Acceptance rate (full time): 45%
Average GMAT (full time): 551
Average GMAT (part time): 551
Average GPA (full time): 3.58
Average age of entrants to full-time program: 32
Average months of prior work experience (full time): 108
TOEFL requirement: Yes
Minimum TOEFL score: 570
Most popular departments: entrepreneurship, finance, health care administration, marketing, operations management

Willamette University (Atkinson)

900 State Street
Salem, OR 97301-3922
http://www.willamette.edu/mba
Private
Admissions: (503) 370-6167
E-mail: mba-admission@willamette.edu
Financial aid: (503) 370-6273
Application deadline: 05/01
Tuition: full time: $33,206; total program: $57,774 (part-time)
Room/board/expenses: $13,000
College-funded aid: Yes
International student aid: Yes
Average student indebtedness at graduation: $63,678
Full-time enrollment: 215
men: 62%; women: 38%; minorities:15%; international: 34%
Part-time enrollment: 105
men: 59%; women: 41%; minorities:15%; international: 0%
Acceptance rate (full time): 80%
Average GMAT (full time): 592
Average GMAT (part time): 512
Average GPA (full time): 3.24
Average age of entrants to full-time program: 25
Average months of prior work experience (full time): 18
TOEFL requirement: Yes
Minimum TOEFL score: 570
Most popular departments: accounting, entrepreneurship, finance, marketing, operations management
Mean starting base salary for 2012 full-time graduates: $56,127
Employment location for 2012 class: Intl. 15%; N.E. 2%; M.A. 2%; S. 4%; M.W. 2%; S.W. 4%; W. 71%

PENNSYLVANIA

Bloomsburg University of Pennsylvania

Sutliff Hall, Room 212
400 Second Street
Bloomsburg, PA 17815-1301
http://cob.bloomu.edu/
Public
Admissions: N/A
Financial aid: N/A
Application deadline: rolling
In-state tuition: full time: N/A; part time: N/A
Out-of-state tuition: full time: N/A
Room/board/expenses: N/A
College-funded aid: Yes
International student aid: Yes
Full-time enrollment: N/A
men: N/A; women: N/A;
minorities:N/A; international: N/A
Part-time enrollment: 60
men: 82%; women: 18%;
minorities:5%; international: 7%
Average GMAT (part time): 490
TOEFL requirement: Yes
Minimum TOEFL score: 550

Carnegie Mellon University (Tepper)

5000 Forbes Avenue
Pittsburgh, PA 15213
http://www.tepper.cmu.edu
Private
Admissions: (412) 268-2272
E-mail: mba-admissions@
andrew.cmu.edu
Financial aid: (412) 268-7581
Application deadline: 04/21
Tuition: full time: $55,800; part time: $1,815/credit hour
Room/board/expenses: $23,166
College-funded aid: Yes
International student aid: Yes
Average student indebtedness at graduation: $88,156
Full-time enrollment: 418
men: 72%; women: 28%;
minorities:22%; international: 33%
Part-time enrollment: 172
men: 84%; women: 16%;
minorities:4%; international: 13%
Acceptance rate (full time): 27%
Average GMAT (full time): 693
Average GMAT (part time): 646
Average GPA (full time): 3.26
Average age of entrants to full-time program: 29
Average months of prior work experience (full time): 52
TOEFL requirement: Yes
Minimum TOEFL score: 600
Most popular departments: entrepreneurship, finance, marketing, operations management, other
Mean starting base salary for 2012 full-time graduates: $107,700
Employment location for 2012 class: Intl. 5%; N.E. 29%; M.A. 22%; S. 4%; M.W. 14%; S.W. 4%; W. 21%

Clarion University of Pennsylvania[1]

Still Hall
Clarion, PA 16214
http://www.clarion.edu/mba
Public
Admissions: (814) 393-2605
E-mail: mba@clarion.edu
Financial aid: (814) 393-2315
Tuition: N/A
Room/board/expenses: N/A
Enrollment: N/A

Drexel University (LeBow)[1]

3141 Chestnut Street
Philadelphia, PA 19104
http://www.lebow.drexel.edu/
Private
Admissions: (215) 895-0562
E-mail: mba@drexel.edu
Financial aid: (215) 895-6395
Tuition: N/A
Room/board/expenses: N/A
Enrollment: N/A

Duquesne University (Donahue)

704 Rockwell Hall
Pittsburgh, PA 15282
http://www.
duq.edu/business/grad
Private
Admissions: (412) 396-6276
E-mail: grad-bus@duq.edu
Financial aid: (412) 396-6607
Application deadline: 01/02
Tuition: total program: $46,971 (full-time); part time: $725/credit hour
Room/board/expenses: $20,000
College-funded aid: Yes
International student aid: Yes
Full-time enrollment: 22
men: 64%; women: 36%;
minorities:14%; international: 0%
Part-time enrollment: 213
men: 64%; women: 36%;
minorities:5%; international: 11%
TOEFL requirement: Yes
Minimum TOEFL score: 577
Most popular departments: finance, general management, marketing, supply chain management

Indiana University of Pennsylvania (Eberly)

664 Pratt Drive, Room 402
Indiana, PA 15705
http://www.eberly.iup.edu/mba
Public
Admissions: (724) 357-2522
E-mail: iup-mba@iup.edu
Financial aid: (724) 357-2218
Application deadline: rolling
In-state tuition: full time: $10,368; part time: $452/credit hour
Out-of-state tuition: full time: $14,436
Room/board/expenses: $14,409
College-funded aid: Yes
International student aid: Yes
Full-time enrollment: 147
men: 62%; women: 38%;
minorities:2%; international: 82%
Part-time enrollment: 13
men: 46%; women: 54%;
minorities:0%; international: 8%
Acceptance rate (full time): 47%
Average GMAT (full time): 502
Average GMAT (part time): 480
Average age of entrants to full-time program: 23
TOEFL requirement: Yes
Minimum TOEFL score: 540

King's College (McGowan)[1]

133 N. River Street
Wilkes-Barre, PA 18711
http://www.kings.edu/academics/
mcgowan.htm
Private
Admissions: (570) 208-5991
E-mail: elizabethlott@kings.edu
Financial aid: N/A
Tuition: N/A
Room/board/expenses: N/A
Enrollment: N/A

La Salle University

1900 W. Olney Avenue
Philadelphia, PA 19141
http://www.lasalle.edu/mba
Private
Admissions: (215) 951-1057
E-mail: mba@lasalle.edu
Financial aid: (215) 951-1070
Application deadline: rolling
Tuition: full time: $20,350; part time: $840/credit hour
Room/board/expenses: N/A
College-funded aid: Yes
International student aid: Yes
Average student indebtedness at graduation: $40,778
Full-time enrollment: 77
men: 58%; women: 42%;
minorities:18%; international: 38%
Part-time enrollment: 443
men: 51%; women: 49%;
minorities:15%; international: 0%
Acceptance rate (full time): 86%
Average GMAT (full time): 421
Average GMAT (part time): 454
Average GPA (full time): 3.18
Average age of entrants to full-time program: 25
TOEFL requirement: Yes
Minimum TOEFL score: 573
Most popular departments: accounting, finance, general management, international business, marketing

Lehigh University

621 Taylor Street
Bethlehem, PA 18015
http://www.lehigh.edu/mba
Private
Admissions: (610) 758-5280
E-mail: mba.admissions@
lehigh.edu
Financial aid: (610) 758-4450
Application deadline: 07/15
Tuition: full time: $950/credit hour; part time: $950/credit hour
Room/board/expenses: $17,000
College-funded aid: Yes
International student aid: Yes
Average student indebtedness at graduation: $22,240
Full-time enrollment: 25
men: 72%; women: 28%;
minorities:4%; international: 52%
Part-time enrollment: 219
men: 69%; women: 31%;
minorities:16%; international: 8%
Acceptance rate (full time): 46%
Average GMAT (full time): 608
Average GMAT (part time): 620
Average GPA (full time): 3.29
Average age of entrants to full-time program: 26
Average months of prior work experience (full time): 42
TOEFL requirement: Yes
Minimum TOEFL score: 600
Most popular departments: entrepreneurship, finance, marketing, supply chain management, other
Employment location for 2012 class: Intl. 13%; N.E. 13%; M.A. 75%; S. N/A; M.W. N/A; S.W. N/A; W. N/A

Pennsylvania State University–Erie, The Behrend College (Black)

5101 Jordan Road
Erie, PA 16563
http://www.
pennstatebehrend.psu.edu
Public
Admissions: (814) 898-7255
E-mail:
behrend.admissions@psu.edu
Financial aid: (814) 898-6162
Application deadline: 06/25
In-state tuition: full time: $773/credit hour; part time: $773/credit hour

Out-of-state tuition: full time: $1,198/credit hour
Room/board/expenses: $13,010
College-funded aid: Yes
International student aid: Yes
Average student indebtedness at graduation: $24,616
Full-time enrollment: 25
men: 76%; women: 24%;
minorities:8%; international: 4%
Part-time enrollment: 63
men: 81%; women: 19%;
minorities:14%; international: 6%
Acceptance rate (full time): 95%
Average GMAT (full time): 531
Average GMAT (part time): 585
Average GPA (full time): 3.36
Average age of entrants to full-time program: 24
TOEFL requirement: Yes
Minimum TOEFL score: 550
Most popular departments: other

Pennsylvania State University–Great Valley[1]

30 E. Swedesford Road
Malvern, PA 19355
http://www.sgps.psu.edu
Public
Admissions: (610) 648-3242
E-mail: gvadmiss@psu.edu
Financial aid: (610) 648-3311
Tuition: N/A
Room/board/expenses: N/A
Enrollment: N/A

Pennsylvania State University–Harrisburg

777 W. Harrisburg Pike
Middletown, PA 17057-4898
http://php.scripts.psu.edu/dept/lit/
cl/sba/Graduate.php
Public
Admissions: (717) 948-6250
E-mail: mbahbg@psu.edu
Financial aid: (717) 948-6307
Application deadline: rolling
In-state tuition: full time: N/A; part time: $773/credit hour
Out-of-state tuition: full time: N/A
Room/board/expenses: N/A
College-funded aid: Yes
International student aid: Yes
Full-time enrollment: N/A
men: N/A; women: N/A;
minorities:N/A; international: N/A
Part-time enrollment: 187
men: 70%; women: 30%;
minorities:8%; international: 4%
Average GMAT (part time): 575
TOEFL requirement: Yes
Minimum TOEFL score: 550
Most popular departments: accounting, finance, general management, human resources management, supply chain management

Pennsylvania State University– University Park (Smeal)

220 Business Building
University Park, PA 16802-3000
http://www.smeal.psu.edu/mba
Public
Admissions: (814) 863-0474
E-mail: smealmba@psu.edu
Financial aid: (814) 865-6301
Application deadline: 04/11
In-state tuition: full time: $22,758; part time: N/A
Out-of-state tuition: full time: $35,968
Room/board/expenses: $19,900
College-funded aid: Yes
International student aid: Yes
Average student indebtedness at graduation: $51,333

Full-time enrollment: 159
men: 72%; women: 28%;
minorities:16%; international: 37%
Part-time enrollment: N/A
men: N/A; women: N/A;
minorities:N/A; international: N/A
Acceptance rate (full time): 29%
Average GMAT (full time): 643
Average GPA (full time): 3.23
Average age of entrants to full-time program: 28
Average months of prior work experience (full time): 54
TOEFL requirement: Yes
Minimum TOEFL score: 600
Most popular departments: entrepreneurship, finance, leadership, marketing, supply chain management
Mean starting base salary for 2012 full-time graduates: $84,345
Employment location for 2012 class: Intl. 6%; N.E. 14%; M.A. 30%; S. 6%; M.W. 15%; S.W. 20%; W. 9%

Robert Morris University

6001 University Boulevard
Moon Township, PA 15108-1189
http://mba.rmu.edu/
Private
Admissions: (800) 762-0097
E-mail: enrollmentoffice@rmu.edu
Financial aid: N/A
Application deadline: rolling
Tuition: full time: N/A; part time: $810/credit hour
Room/board/expenses: N/A
College-funded aid: Yes
International student aid: Yes
Full-time enrollment: N/A
men: N/A; women: N/A;
minorities:N/A; international: N/A
Part-time enrollment: 173
men: 62%; women: 38%;
minorities:2%; international: 3%
Average age of entrants to full-time program: N/A
TOEFL requirement: Yes
Minimum TOEFL score: 500
Most popular departments: general management, human resources management

Shippensburg University of Pennsylvania (Grove)

1871 Old Main Drive
Shippensburg, PA 17257
http://www.ship.edu/mba
Public
Admissions: (717) 477-1231
E-mail: admiss@ship.edu
Financial aid: (717) 477-1131
Application deadline: rolling
In-state tuition: full time: $429/credit hour; part time: $429/credit hour
Out-of-state tuition: full time: $624/credit hour
Room/board/expenses: N/A
College-funded aid: Yes
International student aid: Yes
Full-time enrollment: 20
men: 85%; women: 15%;
minorities:5%; international: 30%
Part-time enrollment: 68
men: 60%; women: 40%;
minorities:7%; international: 6%
Acceptance rate (full time): 76%
Average GMAT (full time): 513
Average GMAT (part time): 523
Average GPA (full time): 3.18
TOEFL requirement: Yes
Minimum TOEFL score: 500

St. Joseph's University (Haub)
5600 City Avenue
Philadelphia, PA 19131
http://www.sju.edu/mba
Private
Admissions: (610) 660-1690
E-mail: sjumba@sju.edu
Financial aid: (610) 660-1555
Application deadline: 07/15
Tuition: full time: $892/credit hour; part time: $892/credit hour
Room/board/expenses: N/A
College-funded aid: Yes
International student aid: Yes
Full-time enrollment: N/A
men: N/A; women: N/A; minorities:N/A; international: N/A
Part-time enrollment: 1,261
men: 55%; women: 45%; minorities:32%; international: 20%
Average GMAT (part time): 546
TOEFL requirement: Yes
Minimum TOEFL score: 550
Most popular departments: finance, general management, human resources management, marketing, management information systems

Temple University (Fox)
Alter Hall
1801 Liacouras Walk, Suite A701
Philadelphia, PA 19122-6083
http://sbm.temple.edu/
Public
Admissions: (215) 204-7678
E-mail: foxinfo@temple.edu
Financial aid: (215) 204-7678
Application deadline: 12/10
In-state tuition: full time: $26,102; part time: $931/credit hour
Out-of-state tuition: full time: $36,821
Room/board/expenses: $16,379
College-funded aid: Yes
International student aid: Yes
Average student indebtedness at graduation: $26,040
Full-time enrollment: 90
men: 69%; women: 31%; minorities:14%; international: 18%
Part-time enrollment: 364
men: 61%; women: 39%; minorities:12%; international: 18%
Acceptance rate (full time): 34%
Average GMAT (full time): 643
Average GMAT (part time): 596
Average GPA (full time): 3.42
Average age of entrants to full-time program: 27
Average months of prior work experience (full time): 42
TOEFL requirement: Yes
Minimum TOEFL score: 600
Most popular departments: finance, general management, health care administration, international business, marketing
Mean starting base salary for 2012 full-time graduates: $79,078
Employment location for 2012 class: Intl. N/A; N.E. 35%; M.A. 62%; S. 3%; M.W. N/A; S.W. N/A; W. N/A

University of Pennsylvania (Wharton)
420 Jon M. Huntsman Hall
3730 Walnut Street
Philadelphia, PA 19104
http://www.wharton.upenn.edu/mba/admissions
Private
Admissions: (215) 898-6183
E-mail: http://engage.wharton.upenn.edu/MBA/forums/
Financial aid: (215) 898-6183
Application deadline: 03/05
Tuition: full time: $62,034; part time: N/A
Room/board/expenses: $30,966
College-funded aid: Yes
International student aid: Yes
Full-time enrollment: 1,685
men: 57%; women: 43%; minorities:N/A; international: 38%
Part-time enrollment: N/A
men: N/A; women: N/A; minorities:N/A; international: N/A
Acceptance rate (full time): 20%
Average GMAT (full time): 718
Average GPA (full time): 3.60
Average age of entrants to full-time program: 28
Average months of prior work experience (full time): 56
TOEFL requirement: Yes
Minimum TOEFL score: N/A
Most popular departments: entrepreneurship, finance, general management, health care administration, other
Mean starting base salary for 2012 full-time graduates: $120,605
Employment location for 2012 class: Intl. 22%; N.E. 42%; M.A. 8%; S. 4%; M.W. 5%; S.W. 3%; W. 16%

University of Pittsburgh (Katz)
372 Mervis Hall
Pittsburgh, PA 15260
http://www.business.pitt.edu/katz
Public
Admissions: (412) 648-1700
E-mail: mba@katz.pitt.edu
Financial aid: (412) 648-1700
Application deadline: 04/08
In-state tuition: total program: $49,520 (full-time); part time: $1,107/credit hour
Out-of-state tuition: total program: $63,196 (full-time)
Room/board/expenses: $34,368
College-funded aid: Yes
International student aid: Yes
Full-time enrollment: 171
men: 70%; women: 30%; minorities:14%; international: 37%
Part-time enrollment: 571
men: 65%; women: 35%; minorities:5%; international: 3%
Acceptance rate (full time): 35%
Average GMAT (full time): 608
Average GMAT (part time): 539
Average GPA (full time): 3.24
Average age of entrants to full-time program: 26
Average months of prior work experience (full time): 34
TOEFL requirement: Yes
Minimum TOEFL score: 600
Most popular departments: finance, marketing, management information systems, operations management, supply chain management
Mean starting base salary for 2012 full-time graduates: $76,136
Employment location for 2012 class: Intl. 13%; N.E. 11%; M.A. 49%; S. 3%; M.W. 11%; S.W. 10%; W. 3%

University of Scranton
800 Linden Street
Scranton, PA 18510-4632
http://www.scranton.edu
Private
Admissions: (570) 941-7540
E-mail: robackj2@scranton.edu
Financial aid: (570) 941-7700
Application deadline: 08/01
Tuition: full time: $887/credit hour; part time: $887/credit hour
Room/board/expenses: $9,240
College-funded aid: Yes
International student aid: Yes
Average student indebtedness at graduation: $18,303
Full-time enrollment: 506
men: 72%; women: 28%; minorities:16%; international: 10%
Part-time enrollment: 155
men: 72%; women: 28%; minorities:9%; international: 0%
Acceptance rate (full time): 82%
Average GMAT (full time): 500
Average GMAT (part time): 500
Average GPA (full time): 3.15
Average age of entrants to full-time program: 34
Average months of prior work experience (full time): 112
TOEFL requirement: Yes
Minimum TOEFL score: 500
Most popular departments: accounting, general management, health care administration, operations management, other
Mean starting base salary for 2012 full-time graduates: $75,983
Employment location for 2012 class: Intl. 0%; N.E. 25%; M.A. 51%; S. 9%; M.W. 7%; S.W. 2%; W. 6%

Villanova University
Bartley Hall
800 Lancaster Avenue
Villanova, PA 19085
http://mba.villanova.edu
Private
Admissions: (610) 519-4336
E-mail: meredith.lockyer@villanova.edu
Financial aid: (610) 519-4010
Application deadline: 06/30
Tuition: full time: N/A; part time: $975/credit hour
Room/board/expenses: $46,920
College-funded aid: Yes
International student aid: Yes
Full-time enrollment: N/A
men: N/A; women: N/A; minorities:N/A; international: N/A
Part-time enrollment: 134
men: 66%; women: 34%; minorities:14%; international: 3%
Average GMAT (part time): 623
TOEFL requirement: Yes
Minimum TOEFL score: 550
Most popular departments: finance, general management, international business, marketing, management information systems

West Chester University of Pennsylvania
1160 McDermott Drive
West Chester, PA 19383
http://www.wcumba.org/
Public
Admissions: (610) 436-2943
E-mail: gradstudy@wcupa.edu
Financial aid: (610) 436-2627
Application deadline: rolling
In-state tuition: full time: $429/credit hour; part time: $429/credit hour
Out-of-state tuition: full time: $644/credit hour
Room/board/expenses: N/A
College-funded aid: Yes
International student aid: Yes
Full-time enrollment: 7
men: 71%; women: 29%; minorities:29%; international: 29%
Part-time enrollment: 79
men: 71%; women: 29%; minorities:19%; international: 1%
Average GMAT (part time): 530
Average age of entrants to full-time program: N/A
TOEFL requirement: Yes
Minimum TOEFL score: 550

Widener University
1 University Place
Chester, PA 19013
http://www.widener.edu/sba
Private
Admissions: (610) 499-4305
E-mail: sbagradv@mail.widener.edu
Financial aid: (610) 499-4174
Application deadline: rolling
Tuition: full time: $874/credit hour; part time: $874/credit hour
Room/board/expenses: $1,000
College-funded aid: Yes
International student aid: Yes
Full-time enrollment: 35
men: N/A; women: N/A; minorities:N/A; international: N/A
Part-time enrollment: 107
men: N/A; women: N/A; minorities:N/A; international: N/A
TOEFL requirement: Yes
Minimum TOEFL score: 587

RHODE ISLAND

Bryant University
1150 Douglas Pike
Smithfield, RI 02917
http://www.bryant.edu/
Private
Admissions: (401) 232-6230
E-mail: gradprog@bryant.edu
Financial aid: (401) 232-6020
Application deadline: rolling
Tuition: full time: $1,065/credit hour; part time: $1,029/credit hour
Room/board/expenses: $14,900
College-funded aid: Yes
International student aid: Yes
Average student indebtedness at graduation: $31,238
Full-time enrollment: 47
men: 62%; women: 38%; minorities:4%; international: 9%
Part-time enrollment: 29
men: 59%; women: 41%; minorities:7%; international: 3%
Acceptance rate (full time): 97%
Average GMAT (full time): 480
Average GMAT (part time): 522
Average GPA (full time): 3.21
Average age of entrants to full-time program: 23
Average months of prior work experience (full time): 9
TOEFL requirement: Yes
Minimum TOEFL score: 580
Most popular departments: finance, general management, international business, supply chain management

University of Rhode Island[1]
7 Lippitt Road
Kingston, RI 02881
http://www.cba.uri.edu/mba
Public
Admissions: (401) 874-5000
E-mail: hadz@uri.edu
Financial aid: (401) 874-9500
Tuition: N/A
Room/board/expenses: N/A
Enrollment: N/A

Providence College[1]
1 Cunningham Square
Providence, RI 02918
http://www.providence.edu/business/mba
Private
Admissions: N/A
Financial aid: N/A
Tuition: N/A
Room/board/expenses: N/A
Enrollment: N/A

SOUTH CAROLINA

The Citadel
171 Moultrie Street
Charleston, SC 29409
http://www.citadel.edu/csba/
Public
Admissions: (843) 953-5089
E-mail: cgc@citadel.edu
Financial aid: (843) 953-5187
Application deadline: 07/15
In-state tuition: full time: $510/credit hour; part time: $510/credit hour
Out-of-state tuition: full time: $840/credit hour
Room/board/expenses: $15,000
College-funded aid: Yes
International student aid: Yes
Average student indebtedness at graduation: $39,958
Full-time enrollment: 25
men: 76%; women: 24%; minorities:32%; international: 12%
Part-time enrollment: 233
men: 62%; women: 38%; minorities:9%; international: 1%
Acceptance rate (full time): 100%
Average GMAT (full time): 461
Average GMAT (part time): 498
Average GPA (full time): 3.26
Average age of entrants to full-time program: 24
Average months of prior work experience (full time): N/A
TOEFL requirement: Yes
Minimum TOEFL score: 550

Clemson University
55 East Camperdown Way
Greenville, SC 29601
http://www.clemson.edu/cbbs/departments/mba
Public
Admissions: (864) 656-8173
E-mail: mba@clemson.edu
Financial aid: (864) 656-2280
Application deadline: 06/01
In-state tuition: full time: $9,744; part time: $604/credit hour
Out-of-state tuition: full time: $19,426
Room/board/expenses: $13,152
College-funded aid: Yes
International student aid: Yes
Full-time enrollment: 87
men: 60%; women: 40%; minorities:21%; international: 17%
Part-time enrollment: 214
men: 63%; women: 37%; minorities:10%; international: 2%
Acceptance rate (full time): 67%
Average GMAT (full time): 559
Average GMAT (part time): 578
Average GPA (full time): 3.29
Average age of entrants to full-time program: 27
Average months of prior work experience (full time): 55
TOEFL requirement: Yes
Minimum TOEFL score: 580
Most popular departments: entrepreneurship, marketing, management information systems, supply chain management, other
Mean starting base salary for 2012 full-time graduates: $53,370
Employment location for 2012 class: Intl. N/A; N.E. N/A; M.A. N/A; S. 89%; M.W. N/A; S.W. 11%; W. N/A

Coastal Carolina University
PO Box 261954
Conway, SC 29528-6054
http://www.coastal.edu/admissions
Public
Admissions: (843) 349-2026
E-mail: admissions@coastal.edu
Financial aid: (843) 349-2313
Application deadline: rolling

More at www.usnews.com/grad

In-state tuition: full time: $13,280; part time: $550/credit hour
Out-of-state tuition: full time: $20,240
Room/board/expenses: $4,747
College-funded aid: Yes
International student aid: Yes
Average student indebtedness at graduation: $20,925
Full-time enrollment: 51
men: 67%; women: 33%; minorities:6%; international: 8%
Part-time enrollment: 42
men: 33%; women: 67%; minorities:7%; international: 7%
Acceptance rate (full time): 91%
Average GMAT (full time): 528
Average GMAT (part time): 484
Average GPA (full time): 3.35
Average age of entrants to full-time program: 24
TOEFL requirement: Yes
Minimum TOEFL score: 575

College of Charleston[1]
Randolph Hall 310
Charleston, SC 29424
http://www.sb.cofc.edu/graduate/accountancy/
Public
Admissions: (843) 953-5614
E-mail: gradsch@cofc.edu
Financial aid: (843) 953-5540
Tuition: N/A
Room/board/expenses: N/A
Enrollment: N/A

Francis Marion University
Box 100547
Florence, SC 29501
http://www.fmarion.edu/academics/mba
Public
Admissions: (843) 661-1419
E-mail: bkyer@fmarion.edu
Financial aid: (843) 661-1190
Application deadline: rolling
In-state tuition: full time: N/A; part time: N/A
Out-of-state tuition: full time: N/A
Room/board/expenses: N/A
College-funded aid: Yes
International student aid: Yes
Full-time enrollment: N/A
men: N/A; women: N/A; minorities:N/A; international: N/A
Part-time enrollment: 30
men: 50%; women: 50%; minorities:N/A; international: N/A
TOEFL requirement: Yes
Minimum TOEFL score: 550

South Carolina State University[1]
300 College Street NE
Orangeburg, SC 29117
http://belcher.scsu.edu
Public
Admissions: (803) 536-8558
E-mail: admissions@scsu.edu
Financial aid: (803) 536-7067
Tuition: N/A
Room/board/expenses: N/A
Enrollment: N/A

University of South Carolina (Moore)
1705 College Street
Columbia, SC 29208
http://moore.sc.edu/
Public
Admissions: (803) 777-4346
E-mail: gradinfo@moore.sc.edu
Financial aid: (803) 777-8134
Application deadline: rolling
In-state tuition: total program: $42,296 (full-time); part time: $622/credit hour

Out-of-state tuition: total program: $70,176 (full-time)
Room/board/expenses: $20,378
College-funded aid: Yes
International student aid: Yes
Average student indebtedness at graduation: $47,769
Full-time enrollment: 180
men: 71%; women: 29%; minorities:32%; international: 20%
Part-time enrollment: 416
men: 71%; women: 29%; minorities:17%; international: 4%
Acceptance rate (full time): 70%
Average GMAT (full time): 624
Average GMAT (part time): 599
Average GPA (full time): 3.28
Average age of entrants to full-time program: 28
Average months of prior work experience (full time): 44
TOEFL requirement: Yes
Minimum TOEFL score: 600
Most popular departments: accounting, entrepreneurship, finance, general management, supply chain management
Mean starting base salary for 2012 full-time graduates: $75,521
Employment location for 2012 class: Intl. N/A; N.E. 4%; M.A. 14%; S. 49%; M.W. 8%; S.W. 12%; W. 12%

Winthrop University[1]
Thurmond Building
Rock Hill, SC 29733
http://www.winthrop.edu/cba
Public
Admissions: (803) 323-2409
E-mail: hagerp@winthrop.edu
Financial aid: (803) 323-2189
Tuition: N/A
Room/board/expenses: N/A
Enrollment: N/A

University of South Dakota
414 E. Clark Street
Vermillion, SD 57069
http://www.usd.edu/mba
Public
Admissions: (605) 677-5232
E-mail: mba@usd.edu
Financial aid: (605) 677-5446
Application deadline: 06/01
In-state tuition: full time: $197/credit hour; part time: $383/credit hour
Out-of-state tuition: full time: $417/credit hour
Room/board/expenses: N/A
College-funded aid: Yes
International student aid: Yes
Average student indebtedness at graduation: $28,500
Full-time enrollment: 49
men: 63%; women: 37%; minorities:0%; international: 6%
Part-time enrollment: 220
men: 62%; women: 38%; minorities:3%; international: 4%
Acceptance rate (full time): 75%
Average GMAT (full time): 518
Average GMAT (part time): 556
Average GPA (full time): 3.34
Average age of entrants to full-time program: 24
Average months of prior work experience (full time): 24
TOEFL requirement: Yes
Minimum TOEFL score: 550
Most popular departments: accounting, general management, health care administration

TENNESSEE

Belmont University (Massey)
1900 Belmont Boulevard
Nashville, TN 37212
http://www.belmont.edu/business/graduatebusiness
Private
Admissions: (615) 460-6480
E-mail: masseyadmissions@belmont.edu
Financial aid: (615) 460-6403
Application deadline: 07/01
Tuition: total program: $46,050 (full-time); $46,050 (part-time)
Room/board/expenses: N/A
College-funded aid: Yes
International student aid: Yes
Average student indebtedness at graduation: $25,500
Full-time enrollment: 25
men: 76%; women: 24%; minorities:4%; international: 8%
Part-time enrollment: 115
men: 57%; women: 43%; minorities:11%; international: 2%
Acceptance rate (full time): 94%
Average GMAT (full time): 548
Average GMAT (part time): 523
Average GPA (full time): 3.27
Average age of entrants to full-time program: 23
Average months of prior work experience (full time): N/A
TOEFL requirement: Yes
Minimum TOEFL score: 550
Most popular departments: entrepreneurship, finance, general management, health care administration, marketing
Mean starting base salary for 2012 full-time graduates: $41,400
Employment location for 2012 class: Intl. 0%; N.E. 0%; M.A. 17%; S. 78%; M.W. 0%; S.W. 0%; W. 6%

East Tennessee State University
PO Box 70699
Johnson City, TN 37614
http://www.etsu.edu/cbat
Public
Admissions: (423) 439-5314
E-mail: business@etsu.edu
Financial aid: (423) 439-4300
Application deadline: 12/31
In-state tuition: full time: $442/credit hour; part time: $442/credit hour
Out-of-state tuition: full time: $1,114/credit hour
Room/board/expenses: $6,500
College-funded aid: Yes
International student aid: Yes
Average student indebtedness at graduation: $10,000
Full-time enrollment: 89
men: 55%; women: 45%; minorities:7%; international: 3%
Part-time enrollment: 18
men: 56%; women: 44%; minorities:0%; international: 0%
Acceptance rate (full time): 52%
Average GMAT (full time): 535
Average GMAT (part time): 535
Average GPA (full time): 3.10
Average age of entrants to full-time program: 28
Average months of prior work experience (full time): 48
TOEFL requirement: Yes
Minimum TOEFL score: 550
Most popular departments: entrepreneurship, general management, health care administration

Middle Tennessee State University
PO Box 290
Murfreesboro, TN 37132
http://www.mtsu.edu
Public
Admissions: (615) 898-2964
E-mail: troy.festervand@mtsu.edu
Financial aid: (615) 898-2422
Application deadline: rolling
In-state tuition: full time: $378/credit hour; part time: N/A
Out-of-state tuition: full time: $1,047/credit hour
Room/board/expenses: $5,500
College-funded aid: Yes
International student aid: Yes
Full-time enrollment: 136
men: N/A; women: N/A; minorities:N/A; international: N/A
Part-time enrollment: 195
men: N/A; women: N/A; minorities:N/A; international: N/A
TOEFL requirement: Yes
Minimum TOEFL score: 525

Tennessee State University[1]
330 N. 10th Avenue
Nashville, TN 37203
http://www.cob.tnstate.edu/grad/gprograms.htm
Public
Admissions: (615) 963-7170
E-mail: rrussell3@tnstate.edu
Financial aid: (615) 963-7544
Tuition: N/A
Room/board/expenses: N/A
Enrollment: N/A

Tennessee Technological University
Box 5023
Cookeville, TN 38505
http://www.tntech.edu/mba
Public
Admissions: (931) 372-3600
E-mail: mbastudies@tntech.edu
Financial aid: (931) 372-3073
Application deadline: 08/01
In-state tuition: full time: $441/credit hour; part time: $441/credit hour
Out-of-state tuition: full time: $1,089/credit hour
Room/board/expenses: $12,000
College-funded aid: Yes
International student aid: Yes
Average student indebtedness at graduation: $12,000
Full-time enrollment: 52
men: 63%; women: 37%; minorities:N/A; international: 8%
Part-time enrollment: 131
men: 61%; women: 39%; minorities:N/A; international: 2%
Acceptance rate (full time): 62%
Average GMAT (full time): 550
Average GMAT (part time): 532
Average GPA (full time): 3.39
Average age of entrants to full-time program: 24
TOEFL requirement: Yes
Minimum TOEFL score: 550
Most popular departments: accounting, finance, general management, human resources management, international business

University of Memphis (Fogelman)
3675 Central Avenue
Memphis, TN 38152
http://fcbe.memphis.edu/
Public
Admissions: (901) 678-3721
E-mail: krishnan@memphis.edu
Financial aid: (901) 678-4825

Application deadline: 08/01
In-state tuition: full time: $510/credit hour; part time: $510/credit hour
Out-of-state tuition: full time: $1,131/credit hour
Room/board/expenses: N/A
College-funded aid: Yes
International student aid: Yes
Average student indebtedness at graduation: $30,445
Full-time enrollment: 49
men: 59%; women: 41%; minorities:22%; international: 29%
Part-time enrollment: 257
men: 69%; women: 31%; minorities:27%; international: 7%
Acceptance rate (full time): 11%
Average GMAT (full time): 603
Average GMAT (part time): 569
Average GPA (full time): 3.16
Average months of prior work experience (full time): 29
TOEFL requirement: Yes
Minimum TOEFL score: 550
Most popular departments: accounting, finance, marketing, management information systems, other
Mean starting base salary for 2012 full-time graduates: $81,833
Employment location for 2012 class: Intl. 11%; N.E. N/A; M.A. N/A; S. 89%; M.W. N/A; S.W. N/A; W. N/A

University of Tennessee–Chattanooga
615 McCallie Avenue
Chattanooga, TN 37403
http://www.utc.edu/Academic/Business/
Public
Admissions: (423) 425-4210
E-mail: Michael-Owens@utc.edu
Financial aid: (423) 425-4677
Application deadline: 07/01
In-state tuition: full time: N/A; part time: $1,143/credit hour
Out-of-state tuition: full time: N/A
Room/board/expenses: N/A
College-funded aid: Yes
International student aid: No
Full-time enrollment: N/A
men: N/A; women: N/A; minorities:N/A; international: N/A
Part-time enrollment: 280
men: 59%; women: 41%; minorities:N/A; international: 3%
Average GMAT (part time): 492
TOEFL requirement: Yes
Minimum TOEFL score: 550
Most popular departments: entrepreneurship, finance, human resources management, leadership, marketing

University of Tennessee–Knoxville
504 Haslam Business Building
Knoxville, TN 37996-0552
http://mba.utk.edu
Public
Admissions: (865) 974-5033
E-mail: mba@utk.edu
Financial aid: (865) 974-3131
Application deadline: 02/01
In-state tuition: total program: $35,539 (full-time); part time: N/A
Out-of-state tuition: total program: $66,355 (full-time)
Room/board/expenses: $16,000
College-funded aid: Yes
International student aid: Yes
Average student indebtedness at graduation: $37,145
Full-time enrollment: 149
men: 72%; women: 28%; minorities:17%; international: 8%
Part-time enrollment: N/A
men: N/A; women: N/A; minorities:N/A; international: N/A
Acceptance rate (full time): 70%

Average GMAT (full time): 608
Average GPA (full time): 3.40
Average age of entrants to full-time program: 26
Average months of prior work experience (full time): 36
TOEFL requirement: Yes
Minimum TOEFL score: 600
Most popular departments: entrepreneurship, finance, marketing, supply chain management, other
Mean starting base salary for 2012 full-time graduates: $76,910
Employment location for 2012 class: Intl. 2%; N.E. 3%; M.A. N/A; S. 69%; M.W. 13%; S.W. 10%; W. 3%

University of Tennessee–Martin

103 Business Administration Building
Martin, TN 38238
http://www.utm.edu/departments/cbga/mba
Public
Admissions: (731) 881-7012
E-mail: larant@utm.edu
Financial aid: (731) 881-7040
Application deadline: 08/01
In-state tuition: full time: $457/credit hour; part time: $457/credit hour
Out-of-state tuition: full time: $1,188/credit hour
Room/board/expenses: N/A
College-funded aid: Yes
International student aid: Yes
Full-time enrollment: 19
men: 68%; women: 32%; minorities:5%; international: 21%
Part-time enrollment: 53
men: 53%; women: 47%; minorities:9%; international: 11%
Acceptance rate (full time): 80%
Average GMAT (full time): 510
Average GMAT (part time): 500
Average GPA (full time): 3.48
Average age of entrants to full-time program: 24
Average months of prior work experience (full time): 18
TOEFL requirement: Yes
Minimum TOEFL score: 525

Vanderbilt University (Owen)

401 21st Avenue S
Nashville, TN 37203
http://www.owen.vanderbilt.edu
Private
Admissions: (615) 322-6469
E-mail: admissions@owen.vanderbilt.edu
Financial aid: (615) 322-3591
Application deadline: 03/05
Tuition: full time: $45,000; part time: N/A
Room/board/expenses: $23,746
College-funded aid: Yes
International student aid: Yes
Average student indebtedness at graduation: $84,342
Full-time enrollment: 336
men: 64%; women: 36%; minorities:11%; international: 22%
Part-time enrollment: N/A
men: N/A; women: N/A; minorities:N/A; international: N/A
Acceptance rate (full time): 37%
Average GMAT (full time): 682
Average GPA (full time): 3.37
Average age of entrants to full-time program: 28
Average months of prior work experience (full time): 54
TOEFL requirement: Yes
Minimum TOEFL score: N/A
Most popular departments: consulting, finance, general management, health care administration, marketing
Mean starting base salary for 2012 full-time graduates: $95,134

Employment location for 2012 class: Intl. 3%; N.E. 12%; M.A. 7%; S. 38%; M.W. 9%; S.W. 9%; W. 21%

TEXAS

Abilene Christian University[1]

ACU Box 29300
Abilene, TX 79699-9300
http://www.acu.edu/academics/coba/index.html
Private
Admissions: (325) 674-2245
E-mail: coba@acu.edu
Financial aid: N/A
Tuition: N/A
Room/board/expenses: N/A
Enrollment: N/A

Baylor University (Hankamer)

1 Bear Place #98013
Waco, TX 76798-8013
http://www.baylor.edu/mba
Private
Admissions: (254) 710-3718
E-mail: mba_info@baylor.edu
Financial aid: (254) 710-2611
Application deadline: 06/15
Tuition: full time: $34,116; part time: N/A
Room/board/expenses: $13,500
College-funded aid: Yes
International student aid: Yes
Average student indebtedness at graduation: $20,000
Full-time enrollment: 100
men: 70%; women: 30%; minorities:24%; international: 11%
Part-time enrollment: N/A
men: N/A; women: N/A; minorities:N/A; international: N/A
Acceptance rate (full time): 39%
Average GMAT (full time): 628
Average GPA (full time): 3.31
Average age of entrants to full-time program: 26
Average months of prior work experience (full time): 26
TOEFL requirement: Yes
Minimum TOEFL score: 600
Mean starting base salary for 2012 full-time graduates: $66,426
Employment location for 2012 class: Intl. 3%; N.E. 0%; M.A. 3%; S. 7%; M.W. 3%; S.W. 79%; W. 3%

Lamar University

4400 Martin Luther King Parkway
Beaumont, TX 77710
http://mba.lamar.edu
Public
Admissions: (409) 880-8888
E-mail: gradmissions@lamar.edu
Financial aid: (409) 880-8450
Application deadline: 07/25
In-state tuition: full time: $10,722; part time: $7,325
Out-of-state tuition: full time: $21,669
Room/board/expenses: $11,721
College-funded aid: Yes
International student aid: Yes
Full-time enrollment: 117
men: 66%; women: 34%; minorities:N/A; international: 24%
Part-time enrollment: N/A
men: N/A; women: N/A; minorities:N/A; international: N/A
Average GMAT (full time): 507
Average GPA (full time): 3.06
Average age of entrants to full-time program: 28
TOEFL requirement: Yes
Minimum TOEFL score: 550
Most popular departments: accounting, finance, leadership, marketing, management information systems

Midwestern State University[1]

3410 Taft Boulevard
Wichita Falls, TX 76308
http://business.mwsu.edu
Private
Admissions: N/A
Financial aid: N/A
Tuition: N/A
Room/board/expenses: N/A
Enrollment: N/A

Prairie View A&M University

PO Box 519; MS 2300
Prairie View, TX 77446
http://www.pvamu.edu/pages/129.asp
Public
Admissions: (936) 261-9200
Financial aid: N/A
Application deadline: 07/01
In-state tuition: full time: $230/credit hour; part time: $230/credit hour
Out-of-state tuition: full time: $583/credit hour
Room/board/expenses: N/A
College-funded aid: Yes
International student aid: Yes
Full-time enrollment: 44
men: 41%; women: 59%; minorities:66%; international: 18%
Part-time enrollment: 150
men: 42%; women: 58%; minorities:93%; international: 2%
Acceptance rate (full time): 97%
Average GPA (full time): 3.66
Average age of entrants to full-time program: 27
TOEFL requirement: Yes
Minimum TOEFL score: 500

Rice University (Jones)

PO Box 2932
Houston, TX 77252-2932
http://business.rice.edu
Private
Admissions: (713) 348-4918
E-mail: ricemba@rice.edu
Financial aid: (713) 348-4958
Application deadline: 04/07
Tuition: full time: $48,903; total program: $94,000 (part-time)
Room/board/expenses: $28,731
College-funded aid: Yes
International student aid: Yes
Average student indebtedness at graduation: $55,291
Full-time enrollment: 231
men: 72%; women: 28%; minorities:24%; international: 25%
Part-time enrollment: 311
men: 73%; women: 27%; minorities:28%; international: 14%
Acceptance rate (full time): 27%
Average GMAT (full time): 673
Average GMAT (part time): 615
Average GPA (full time): 3.40
Average age of entrants to full-time program: 28
Average months of prior work experience (full time): 57
TOEFL requirement: Yes
Minimum TOEFL score: 600
Most popular departments: accounting, consulting, entrepreneurship, finance, other
Mean starting base salary for 2012 full-time graduates: $99,506
Employment location for 2012 class: Intl. 2%; N.E. 0%; M.A. 1%; S. 2%; M.W. 1%; S.W. 89%; W. 4%

Sam Houston State University

PO Box 2056
Huntsville, TX 77341
http://coba.shsu.edu/
Public
Admissions: (936) 294-1246
E-mail: busgrad@shsu.edu
Financial aid: (936) 294-1724
Application deadline: 08/01
In-state tuition: full time: $237/credit hour; part time: $237/credit hour
Out-of-state tuition: full time: $588/credit hour
Room/board/expenses: $11,062
College-funded aid: Yes
International student aid: Yes
Full-time enrollment: 71
men: 51%; women: 49%; minorities:23%; international: 15%
Part-time enrollment: 251
men: 53%; women: 47%; minorities:27%; international: 3%
Acceptance rate (full time): 81%
Average GMAT (full time): 495
Average GPA (full time): 3.14
Average age of entrants to full-time program: 30
TOEFL requirement: Yes
Minimum TOEFL score: 550

Southern Methodist University (Cox)

PO Box 750333
Dallas, TX 75275-0333
http://www.coxmba.com
Private
Admissions: (214) 768-1214
E-mail: mbainfo@cox.smu.edu
Financial aid: (214) 768-2371
Application deadline: 05/01
Tuition: full time: $46,708; part time: $44,040
Room/board/expenses: $16,400
College-funded aid: Yes
International student aid: Yes
Full-time enrollment: 216
men: 76%; women: 24%; minorities:17%; international: 19%
Part-time enrollment: 344
men: 76%; women: 24%; minorities:23%; international: 5%
Acceptance rate (full time): 49%
Average GMAT (full time): 639
Average GMAT (part time): 591
Average GPA (full time): 3.40
Average age of entrants to full-time program: 27
Average months of prior work experience (full time): 63
TOEFL requirement: Yes
Minimum TOEFL score: 600
Most popular departments: entrepreneurship, finance, general management, marketing, real estate
Mean starting base salary for 2012 full-time graduates: $87,694
Employment location for 2012 class: Intl. 1%; N.E. 5%; M.A. 1%; S. 1%; M.W. 4%; S.W. 82%; W. 5%

Stephen F. Austin State University[1]

PO Box 13004, SFA Station
Nacogdoches, TX 75962-3004
http://www.cob.sfasu.edu
Public
Admissions: (936) 468-2807
E-mail: gschool@titan.sfasu.edu
Financial aid: (936) 468-2768
Tuition: N/A
Room/board/expenses: N/A
Enrollment: N/A

St. Mary's University (Greehey)

1 Camino Santa Maria
San Antonio, TX 78228-8607
http://www.stmarytx.edu/mba
Private
Admissions: (210) 436-3708
E-mail: ebroughton@stmarytx.edu
Financial aid: (210) 436-3141
Application deadline: 08/01
Tuition: full time: $740/credit hour; part time: $740/credit hour
Room/board/expenses: $27,000
College-funded aid: Yes
International student aid: Yes
Full-time enrollment: 28
men: 64%; women: 36%; minorities:39%; international: 25%
Part-time enrollment: 2
men: 50%; women: 50%; minorities:50%; international: 0%
Acceptance rate (full time): 72%
Average GMAT (full time): 550
Average GMAT (part time): 582
Average GPA (full time): 3.18
Average age of entrants to full-time program: 28
Average months of prior work experience (full time): 27
TOEFL requirement: Yes
Minimum TOEFL score: 570
Most popular departments: accounting, general management, other

Texas A&M International University

5201 University Boulevard
Western Hemispheric Trade Center, Suite 203
Laredo, TX 78041-1900
http://www.tamiu.edu
Public
Admissions: (956) 326-2200
E-mail: adms@tamiu.edu
Financial aid: (956) 326-2225
Application deadline: 04/30
In-state tuition: full time: $77/credit hour; part time: $72/credit hour
Out-of-state tuition: full time: $422/credit hour
Room/board/expenses: $12,102
College-funded aid: Yes
International student aid: Yes
Full-time enrollment: 40
men: 75%; women: 25%; minorities:45%; international: 53%
Part-time enrollment: 158
men: 59%; women: 41%; minorities:63%; international: 35%
Acceptance rate (full time): 97%
Average GMAT (full time): 435
Average GPA (full time): 3.32
Average age of entrants to full-time program: 26
Average months of prior work experience (full time): 58
TOEFL requirement: Yes
Minimum TOEFL score: 550
Most popular departments: accounting, finance, general management, international business, management information systems

Texas A&M University–College Station (Mays)

4117 TAMU, 390 Wehner Building
College Station, TX 77843-4117
http://ftmba.tamu.edu
Public
Admissions: (979) 845-4714
E-mail: ftmba@tamu.edu
Financial aid: (979) 845-3236
Application deadline: 04/15
In-state tuition: full time: $22,213; part time: $93,557

Out-of-state tuition: full time: $34,849
Room/board/expenses: $14,776
College-funded aid: Yes
International student aid: Yes
Average student indebtedness at graduation: $32,278
Full-time enrollment: 132
men: 77%; women: 23%; minorities:20%; international: 31%
Part-time enrollment: 36
men: 81%; women: 19%; minorities:25%; international: 3%
Acceptance rate (full time): 25%
Average GMAT (full time): 649
Average GMAT (part time): 611
Average GPA (full time): 3.40
Average age of entrants to full-time program: 28
Average months of prior work experience (full time): 58
TOEFL requirement: Yes
Minimum TOEFL score: 600
Most popular departments: finance, general management, leadership, marketing, supply chain management
Mean starting base salary for 2012 full-time graduates: $93,511
Employment location for 2012 class: Intl. 2%; N.E. 2%; M.A. 0%; S. 9%; M.W. 4%; S.W. 74%; W. 9%

Texas A&M University–Commerce

PO Box 3011
Commerce, TX 75429-3011
http://www.tamu-commerce.edu/graduateprograms
Public
Admissions: (903) 886-5163
E-mail: graduate_school@tamu-commerce.edu
Financial aid: (903) 886-5096
Application deadline: 08/18
In-state tuition: full time: $402/credit hour; part time: $402/credit hour
Out-of-state tuition: full time: $753/credit hour
Room/board/expenses: N/A
College-funded aid: Yes
International student aid: Yes
Full-time enrollment: 343
men: 67%; women: 33%; minorities:51%; international: 10%
Part-time enrollment: 1,001
men: 54%; women: 46%; minorities:30%; international: 23%
TOEFL requirement: Yes
Minimum TOEFL score: 550

Texas A&M University–Corpus Christi

6300 Ocean Drive
Corpus Christi, TX 78412-5807
http://www.cob.tamucc.edu/prstudents/graduate.html
Public
Admissions: (361) 825-2177
E-mail: maria.martinez@tamucc.edu
Financial aid: (361) 825-2338
Application deadline: 07/15
In-state tuition: full time: $196/credit hour; part time: $196/credit hour
Out-of-state tuition: full time: $547/credit hour
Room/board/expenses: N/A
College-funded aid: Yes
International student aid: Yes
Full-time enrollment: N/A
men: N/A; women: N/A; minorities:N/A; international: N/A
Part-time enrollment: 163
men: 55%; women: 45%; minorities:25%; international: 36%

Average GMAT (part time): 484
TOEFL requirement: Yes
Minimum TOEFL score: 550
Most popular departments: finance, health care administration, international business

Texas Christian University (Neeley)

PO Box 298540
Fort Worth, TX 76129
http://www.mba.tcu.edu
Private
Admissions: (817) 257-7531
E-mail: mbainfo@tcu.edu
Financial aid: (817) 257-7531
Application deadline: 04/15
Tuition: full time: $41,800; part time: $27,400
Room/board/expenses: $13,000
College-funded aid: Yes
International student aid: Yes
Average student indebtedness at graduation: $32,107
Full-time enrollment: 82
men: 68%; women: 32%; minorities:15%; international: 33%
Part-time enrollment: 127
men: 72%; women: 28%; minorities:13%; international: 1%
Acceptance rate (full time): 56%
Average GMAT (full time): 641
Average GMAT (part time): 579
Average GPA (full time): 3.18
Average age of entrants to full-time program: 27
Average months of prior work experience (full time): 51
TOEFL requirement: Yes
Minimum TOEFL score: 600
Most popular departments: consulting, finance, marketing, portfolio management, supply chain management
Mean starting base salary for 2012 full-time graduates: $81,331
Employment location for 2012 class: Intl. 3%; N.E. 0%; M.A. 0%; S. 5%; M.W. 3%; S.W. 87%; W. 3%

Texas Southern University (Jones)

3100 Cleburne Avenue
Houston, TX 77004
http://www.tsu.edu/academics/colleges_schools/Jesse_H_Jones_School_of_Business/
Public
Admissions: (713) 313-7590
E-mail: richardson_bj@tsu.edu
Financial aid: (713) 313-7480
Application deadline: rolling
In-state tuition: full time: N/A; part time: N/A
Out-of-state tuition: full time: N/A
Room/board/expenses: N/A
College-funded aid: Yes
International student aid: Yes
Full-time enrollment: 179
men: 51%; women: 49%; minorities:91%; international: 6%
Part-time enrollment: N/A
men: N/A; women: N/A; minorities:N/A; international: N/A
Acceptance rate (full time): 44%
Average GMAT (full time): 375
Average GPA (full time): 3.04
Average age of entrants to full-time program: 26
Average months of prior work experience (full time): 12
TOEFL requirement: Yes
Minimum TOEFL score: 550

Texas State University–San Marcos (McCoy)

601 University Drive
San Marcos, TX 78666-4616
http://www.txstate.edu
Public
Admissions: (512) 245-3591
E-mail: nw04@txstate.edu
Financial aid: (512) 245-2315
Application deadline: 06/01
In-state tuition: full time: N/A; total program: $15,540 (part-time)
Out-of-state tuition: full time: N/A
Room/board/expenses: N/A
College-funded aid: Yes
International student aid: Yes
Full-time enrollment: N/A
men: N/A; women: N/A; minorities:N/A; international: N/A
Part-time enrollment: 334
men: 60%; women: 40%; minorities:28%; international: 5%
Average GMAT (part time): 523
TOEFL requirement: Yes
Minimum TOEFL score: 550
Most popular departments: general management, health care administration, human resources management, international business, manufacturing and technology management

Texas Tech University (Rawls)

PO Box 42101
Lubbock, TX 79409-2101
http://mba.ba.ttu.edu/MBAhome.asp
Public
Admissions: (806) 742-2787
E-mail: graduate.admissions@ttu.edu
Financial aid: (806) 742-0454
Application deadline: rolling
In-state tuition: full time: $252/credit hour; part time: $252/credit hour
Out-of-state tuition: full time: $252/credit hour
Room/board/expenses: $14,200
College-funded aid: Yes
International student aid: Yes
Average student indebtedness at graduation: $12,365
Full-time enrollment: 37
men: 65%; women: 35%; minorities:41%; international: 14%
Part-time enrollment: 460
men: 70%; women: 30%; minorities:28%; international: 5%
Acceptance rate (full time): 58%
Average GMAT (full time): 613
Average GMAT (part time): 530
Average GPA (full time): 3.56
Average age of entrants to full-time program: 25
Average months of prior work experience (full time): 39
TOEFL requirement: Yes
Minimum TOEFL score: 550
Mean starting base salary for 2012 full-time graduates: $52,127
Employment location for 2012 class: Intl. 0%; N.E. 16%; M.A. 4%; S. 4%; M.W. 4%; S.W. 68%; W. 4%

University of Houston (Bauer)

334 Melcher Hall, Suite 330
Houston, TX 77204-6021
http://www.bauer.uh.edu/graduate
Public
Admissions: (713) 743-4638
E-mail: houstonmba@uh.edu
Financial aid: (713) 743-5158
Application deadline: 06/01
In-state tuition: full time: $21,134; part time: $17,258
Out-of-state tuition: full time: $29,558

Room/board/expenses: $14,682
College-funded aid: Yes
International student aid: Yes
Average student indebtedness at graduation: $36,666
Full-time enrollment: 161
men: 60%; women: 40%; minorities:29%; international: 30%
Part-time enrollment: 615
men: 71%; women: 29%; minorities:34%; international: 16%
Acceptance rate (full time): 57%
Average GMAT (full time): 596
Average GMAT (part time): 588
Average GPA (full time): 3.27
Average age of entrants to full-time program: 28
Average months of prior work experience (full time): 53
TOEFL requirement: Yes
Minimum TOEFL score: 603
Mean starting base salary for 2012 full-time graduates: $67,034
Employment location for 2012 class: Intl. 3%; N.E. 0%; M.A. 0%; S. 0%; M.W. 0%; S.W. 94%; W. 3%

University of Houston–Clear Lake

2700 Bay Area Boulevard, Box 71
Houston, TX 77058
http://www.uhcl.edu/admissions
Public
Admissions: (281) 283-2500
E-mail: admissions@uhcl.edu
Financial aid: (281) 283-2480
Application deadline: 08/01
In-state tuition: full time: N/A; part time: $350/credit hour
Out-of-state tuition: full time: N/A
Room/board/expenses: $15,782
College-funded aid: Yes
International student aid: Yes
Full-time enrollment: N/A
men: N/A; women: N/A; minorities:N/A; international: N/A
Part-time enrollment: 404
men: 53%; women: 47%; minorities:34%; international: 16%
Average GMAT (part time): 503
TOEFL requirement: Yes
Minimum TOEFL score: 550
Most popular departments: finance, human resources management, international business, manufacturing and technology management, other

University of Houston–Downtown

One Main St.
Houston, TX 77002
http://uhd.edu/admissions/graduate.htm
Public
Admissions: (713) 221-8093
E-mail: gradadmissions@uhd.edu
Financial aid: (713) 221-8041
Application deadline: 07/28
In-state tuition: full time: $6,762; part time: $358/credit hour
Out-of-state tuition: full time: $11,818
Room/board/expenses: $17,998
College-funded aid: Yes
International student aid: Yes
Full-time enrollment: N/A
men: N/A; women: N/A; minorities:N/A; international: N/A
Part-time enrollment: 49
men: 67%; women: 33%; minorities:65%; international: 2%
Average GMAT (part time): 458
TOEFL requirement: Yes
Minimum TOEFL score: 550

University of Houston–Victoria

University West Room 214
3007 N. Ben Wilson
Victoria, TX 77901
http://www.uhv.edu/bus/default.asp
Public
Admissions: (361) 570-4110
E-mail: admissions@uhv.edu
Financial aid: (361) 570-4131
Application deadline: rolling
In-state tuition: full time: $244/credit hour; part time: $244/credit hour
Out-of-state tuition: full time: $595/credit hour
Room/board/expenses: $23,000
College-funded aid: Yes
International student aid: Yes
Full-time enrollment: 340
men: 51%; women: 49%; minorities:80%; international: 18%
Part-time enrollment: 1,001
men: 52%; women: 48%; minorities:70%; international: 15%
Acceptance rate (full time): 80%
Average GMAT (full time): 414
Average GMAT (part time): 409
Average age of entrants to full-time program: 30
TOEFL requirement: Yes
Minimum TOEFL score: 550
Most popular departments: accounting, finance, general management, international business, marketing

University of North Texas

1155 Union Circle #311160
Denton, TX 76203-5017
http://www.cob.unt.edu
Public
Admissions: (940) 369-8977
E-mail: mbacob@unt.edu
Financial aid: (940) 565-2302
Application deadline: 06/15
In-state tuition: full time: $291/credit hour; part time: $291/credit hour
Out-of-state tuition: full time: $642/credit hour
Room/board/expenses: $11,166
College-funded aid: Yes
International student aid: Yes
Full-time enrollment: N/A
men: N/A; women: N/A; minorities:N/A; international: N/A
Part-time enrollment: 633
men: 53%; women: 47%; minorities:27%; international: 17%
Average GMAT (part time): 526
TOEFL requirement: Yes
Minimum TOEFL score: 550
Most popular departments: accounting, finance, general management, marketing, other

University of St. Thomas–Houston

3800 Montrose Blvd.
Houston, TX 77006
http://www.stthom.edu/bschool
Private
Admissions: (713) 525-2100
E-mail: cameron@stthom.edu
Financial aid: (713) 525-2170
Application deadline: 07/15
Tuition: full time: $990/credit hour; part time: $990/credit hour
Room/board/expenses: $14,254
College-funded aid: Yes
International student aid: Yes
Full-time enrollment: 364
men: 51%; women: 49%; minorities:32%; international: 43%
Part-time enrollment: N/A
men: N/A; women: N/A; minorities:N/A; international: N/A
Acceptance rate (full time): 100%
Average GMAT (full time): 436

Average GPA (full time): 3.00
Average age of entrants to full-time program: 29
TOEFL requirement: Yes
Minimum TOEFL score: 550
Most popular departments: accounting, finance, general management, international business, marketing

University of Texas–Arlington

UTA Box 19377
Arlington, TX 76019-0376
http://wweb.uta.edu/business/gradbiz
Public
Admissions: (817) 272-3649
E-mail: admit@uta.edu
Financial aid: (817) 272-3561
Application deadline: 06/15
In-state tuition: full time: $8,918; part time: $6,112
Out-of-state tuition: full time: $15,236
Room/board/expenses: $13,106
College-funded aid: Yes
International student aid: Yes
Full-time enrollment: 514
men: 60%; women: 40%; minorities:26%; international: 35%
Part-time enrollment: 483
men: 59%; women: 41%; minorities:31%; international: 33%
Acceptance rate (full time): 79%
Average GMAT (full time): 521
Average GMAT (part time): 508
Average age of entrants to full-time program: 29
TOEFL requirement: Yes
Minimum TOEFL score: 550
Most popular departments: accounting, finance, general management, human resources management, international business

University of Texas–Austin (McCombs)

MBA Program
2100 Speedway, Stop B6004
Austin, TX 78712-1750
http://www.mccombs.utexas.edu/mba/full-time
Public
Admissions: (512) 471-7698
E-mail: TexasMBA@mccombs.utexas.edu
Financial aid: (512) 471-7605
Application deadline: 03/24
In-state tuition: full time: $33,926; total program: $93,100 (part-time)
Out-of-state tuition: full time: $48,832
Room/board/expenses: $18,004
College-funded aid: Yes
International student aid: Yes
Average student indebtedness at graduation: $80,589
Full-time enrollment: 504
men: 71%; women: 29%; minorities:20%; international: 21%
Part-time enrollment: 199
men: 80%; women: 20%; minorities:24%; international: 13%
Acceptance rate (full time): 29%
Average GMAT (full time): 692
Average GMAT (part time): 643
Average GPA (full time): 3.40
Average age of entrants to full-time program: 28
Average months of prior work experience (full time): 61
TOEFL requirement: Yes
Minimum TOEFL score: 620
Most popular departments: consulting, entrepreneurship, finance, general management, marketing
Mean starting base salary for 2012 full-time graduates: $105,112
Employment location for 2012 class: Intl. 3%; N.E. 8%; M.A. 1%; S. 5%; M.W. 7%; S.W. 60%; W. 15%

University of Texas–Dallas

800 W. Campbell Road
Richardson, TX 75080-3021
http://www.som.utdallas.edu/
Public
Admissions: (972) 883-6191
E-mail: mba@utdallas.edu
Financial aid: (972) 883-2941
Application deadline: 07/01
In-state tuition: full time: $14,258; part time: $12,714
Out-of-state tuition: full time: $28,118
Room/board/expenses: $15,000
College-funded aid: Yes
International student aid: Yes
Average student indebtedness at graduation: $15,500
Full-time enrollment: 112
men: 64%; women: 36%; minorities:13%; international: 43%
Part-time enrollment: 681
men: 60%; women: 40%; minorities:28%; international: 28%
Acceptance rate (full time): 26%
Average GMAT (full time): 669
Average GMAT (part time): 654
Average GPA (full time): 3.50
Average age of entrants to full-time program: 27
Average months of prior work experience (full time): 48
TOEFL requirement: Yes
Minimum TOEFL score: 550
Most popular departments: accounting, finance, marketing, management information systems, supply chain management
Mean starting base salary for 2012 full-time graduates: $78,107
Employment location for 2012 class: Intl. 0%; N.E. 6%; M.A. 6%; S. 6%; M.W. 3%; S.W. 74%; W. 6%

University of Texas–El Paso

500 W. University Avenue
El Paso, TX 79968
http://mba.utep.edu
Public
Admissions: (915) 747-7726
E-mail: mba@utep.edu
Financial aid: (915) 747-5204
Application deadline: 06/15
In-state tuition: full time: $248/credit hour; part time: N/A
Out-of-state tuition: full time: $599/credit hour
Room/board/expenses: N/A
College-funded aid: Yes
International student aid: Yes
Average student indebtedness at graduation: $24,448
Full-time enrollment: 199
men: 58%; women: 42%; minorities:69%; international: 20%
Part-time enrollment: 46
men: 48%; women: 52%; minorities:50%; international: 39%
Acceptance rate (full time): 56%
Average GMAT (full time): 479
Average GPA (full time): 3.17
Average age of entrants to full-time program: 29
Average months of prior work experience (full time): 89
TOEFL requirement: Yes
Minimum TOEFL score: 600
Most popular departments: finance, general management, international business, management information systems, supply chain management
Mean starting base salary for 2012 full-time graduates: $66,836
Employment location for 2012 class: Intl. 20%; N.E. 7%; M.A. 7%; S. N/A; M.W. N/A; S.W. 60%; W. 7%

University of Texas of the Permian Basin[1]

4901 E. University
Odessa, TX 79762
http://ss.utpb.edu/admissions
Private
Admissions: (432) 552-2608
E-mail: admissions@utpb.edu
Financial aid: (432) 552-2620
Tuition: N/A
Room/board/expenses: N/A
Enrollment: N/A

University of Texas–Pan American[1]

1201 W. University Drive
Edinburg, TX 78539
http://www.coba.panam.edu/mba
Public
Admissions: (956) 381-3313
E-mail: mbaprog@panam.edu
Financial aid: (956) 381-5372
Tuition: N/A
Room/board/expenses: N/A
Enrollment: N/A

University of Texas–San Antonio

1 UTSA Circle
San Antonio, TX 78249
http://www.graduateschool.utsa.edu
Public
Admissions: (210) 458-4331
E-mail: graduatestudies@utsa.edu
Financial aid: (210) 458-8000
Application deadline: 07/01
In-state tuition: full time: $322/credit hour; part time: $322/credit hour
Out-of-state tuition: full time: $1,024/credit hour
Room/board/expenses: N/A
College-funded aid: Yes
International student aid: Yes
Full-time enrollment: 12
men: 58%; women: 42%; minorities:25%; international: 33%
Part-time enrollment: 244
men: 73%; women: 27%; minorities:30%; international: 5%
Acceptance rate (full time): 84%
Average GMAT (full time): 544
Average GMAT (part time): 585
Average GPA (full time): 3.25
Average age of entrants to full-time program: 24
Average months of prior work experience (full time): 15
TOEFL requirement: Yes
Minimum TOEFL score: 550
Most popular departments: finance, health care administration, international business, marketing, other
Mean starting base salary for 2012 full-time graduates: $62,500
Employment location for 2012 class: Intl. 20%; N.E. 0%; M.A. 0%; S. 0%; M.W. 0%; S.W. 60%; W. 20%

University of Texas–Tyler[1]

3900 University Boulevard
Tyler, TX 75799
http://www.uttyler.edu/cbt/index.html
Public
Admissions: (903) 566-7202
E-mail: arusso@uttyler.edu
Financial aid: (903) 566-7221
Tuition: N/A
Room/board/expenses: N/A
Enrollment: N/A

University of Texas–Brownsville

80 Fort Brown
Brownsville, TX 78520
http://utb.edu/vpaa/cob/Pages/default.aspx
Public
Admissions: N/A
Financial aid: N/A
Application deadline: 07/01
In-state tuition: full time: N/A; part time: N/A
Out-of-state tuition: full time: N/A
Room/board/expenses: N/A
Full-time enrollment: 158
men: 54%; women: 46%; minorities:80%; international: 1%
Part-time enrollment: N/A
men: N/A; women: N/A; minorities:N/A; international: N/A
Acceptance rate (full time): 100%
Average GMAT (full time): 440
Average GPA (full time): 3.10
Average age of entrants to full-time program: 29
TOEFL requirement: Yes
Minimum TOEFL score: 550

West Texas A&M University

WTAMU Box 60768
Canyon, TX 79016
http://www.wtamu.edu/academics/college-business.aspx
Public
Admissions: N/A
Financial aid: N/A
Application deadline: 06/01
In-state tuition: total program: $15,500 (full-time); $17,000 (part-time)
Out-of-state tuition: total program: $17,500 (full-time)
Room/board/expenses: $15,000
College-funded aid: Yes
International student aid: Yes
Average student indebtedness at graduation: $20,000
Full-time enrollment: 90
men: 56%; women: 44%; minorities:28%; international: 31%
Part-time enrollment: 110
men: 68%; women: 32%; minorities:41%; international: 2%
Acceptance rate (full time): 73%
Average GMAT (full time): 540
Average GMAT (part time): 520
Average GPA (full time): 3.48
Average age of entrants to full-time program: 25
Average months of prior work experience (full time): 12
TOEFL requirement: Yes
Minimum TOEFL score: 525
Most popular departments: accounting, finance, health care administration, management information systems, organizational behavior
Mean starting base salary for 2012 full-time graduates: $63,000
Employment location for 2012 class: Intl. 16%; N.E. 6%; M.A. 0%; S. 0%; M.W. 10%; S.W. 61%; W. 6%

UTAH

Brigham Young University (Marriott)

W-437 TNRB
Provo, UT 84602
http://mba.byu.edu
Private
Admissions: (801) 422-3500
E-mail: mba@byu.edu
Financial aid: (801) 422-3509
Application deadline: 05/01
Tuition: full time: $10,950; part time: N/A
Room/board/expenses: $13,136
College-funded aid: Yes
International student aid: Yes
Average student indebtedness at graduation: $27,425
Full-time enrollment: 325
men: 85%; women: 15%; minorities:8%; international: 14%
Part-time enrollment: N/A
men: N/A; women: N/A; minorities:N/A; international: N/A
Acceptance rate (full time): 54%
Average GMAT (full time): 672
Average GPA (full time): 3.50
Average age of entrants to full-time program: 29
Average months of prior work experience (full time): 50
TOEFL requirement: Yes
Minimum TOEFL score: 590
Most popular departments: finance, human resources management, marketing, organizational behavior, supply chain management
Mean starting base salary for 2012 full-time graduates: $95,721
Employment location for 2012 class: Intl. 4%; N.E. 10%; M.A. 2%; S. 7%; M.W. 16%; S.W. 13%; W. 48%

Southern Utah University

351 W. University Boulevard
Cedar City, UT 84720
http://www.suu.edu/business
Public
Admissions: (435) 586-5462
Financial aid: N/A
Application deadline: 03/01
In-state tuition: total program: $10,356 (full-time); part time: $652/credit hour
Out-of-state tuition: total program: $29,805 (full-time)
Room/board/expenses: $8,900
College-funded aid: Yes
International student aid: No
Average student indebtedness at graduation: $18,860
Full-time enrollment: 33
men: 73%; women: 27%; minorities:6%; international: 30%
Part-time enrollment: 13
men: 85%; women: 15%; minorities:0%; international: 0%
Acceptance rate (full time): 90%
Average GMAT (full time): 517
Average GPA (full time): 3.49
Average age of entrants to full-time program: 26
TOEFL requirement: Yes
Minimum TOEFL score: 525

University of Utah (Eccles)

1655 E. Campus Center Drive
Room 1113
Salt Lake City, UT 84112-9301
http://www.business.utah.edu
Public
Admissions: (801) 581-7785
E-mail: mastersinfo@business.utah.edu
Financial aid: (801) 581-7785
Application deadline: 12/01
In-state tuition: total program: $45,000 (full-time); $48,000 (part-time)
Out-of-state tuition: total program: $78,000 (full-time)
Room/board/expenses: $17,864
College-funded aid: Yes
International student aid: Yes
Average student indebtedness at graduation: $27,500
Full-time enrollment: 139
men: 81%; women: 19%; minorities:4%; international: 4%
Part-time enrollment: 330
men: 85%; women: 15%; minorities:8%; international: 3%
Acceptance rate (full time): 54%
Average GMAT (full time): 615
Average GMAT (part time): 570
Average GPA (full time): 3.43
Average age of entrants to full-time program: 29

More at www.usnews.com/grad

Average months of prior work experience (full time): 47
TOEFL requirement: Yes
Minimum TOEFL score: 600
Most popular departments: accounting, entrepreneurship, finance, leadership, marketing
Mean starting base salary for 2012 full-time graduates: $69,362
Employment location for 2012 class: Intl. 4%; N.E. 4%; M.A. 2%; S. 0%; M.W. 10%; S.W. 2%; W. 78%

Utah State University (Huntsman)

3500 Old Main Hill
Logan, UT 84322-3500
http://www.huntsman.usu.edu/mba/
Public
Admissions: (435) 797-2360
E-mail: katherine.mcconkie@usu.edu
Financial aid: (435) 797-0173
Application deadline: 07/01
In-state tuition: total program: $24,682 (full-time); $23,600 (part-time)
Out-of-state tuition: total program: $40,051 (full-time)
Room/board/expenses: $15,000
College-funded aid: Yes
International student aid: Yes
Average student indebtedness at graduation: $27,000
Full-time enrollment: 68
men: 74%; women: 26%;
minorities:3%; international: 26%
Part-time enrollment: 73
men: 85%; women: 15%;
minorities:4%; international: 3%
Acceptance rate (full time): 66%
Average GMAT (full time): 564
Average GMAT (part time): 525
Average GPA (full time): 3.51
Average age of entrants to full-time program: 27
Average months of prior work experience (full time): 55
TOEFL requirement: Yes
Minimum TOEFL score: 550
Mean starting base salary for 2012 full-time graduates: $50,444
Employment location for 2012 class: Intl. N/A; N.E. N/A; M.A. N/A; S. N/A; M.W. N/A; S.W. 14%; W. 86%

Utah Valley University

800 W. University Parkway
Orem, UT 84058
http://www.uvu.edu/woodbury
Public
Admissions: (801) 863-8367
Financial aid: N/A
Application deadline: 04/01
In-state tuition: full time: N/A; part time: $404/credit hour
Out-of-state tuition: full time: N/A
Room/board/expenses: $16,052
College-funded aid: No
International student aid: No
Full-time enrollment: 43
men: 88%; women: 12%;
minorities:2%; international: 0%
Part-time enrollment: N/A
men: N/A; women: N/A;
minorities:N/A; international: N/A
Average GMAT (part time): 556
TOEFL requirement: Yes
Minimum TOEFL score: N/A
Most popular departments: accounting, general management

Weber State University (Goddard)

2750 N. University Park Boulevard—MC102
Layton, UT 84041-9099
http://weber.edu/mba
Public
Admissions: (801) 395-3528
E-mail: mba@weber.edu
Financial aid: (801) 626-7569
Application deadline: 05/03
In-state tuition: full time: N/A; part time: $583/credit hour
Out-of-state tuition: full time: N/A
Room/board/expenses: $13,000
College-funded aid: Yes
International student aid: Yes
Full-time enrollment: N/A
men: N/A; women: N/A;
minorities:N/A; international: N/A
Part-time enrollment: 203
men: 81%; women: 19%;
minorities:N/A; international: 1%
Average GMAT (part time): 558
TOEFL requirement: Yes
Minimum TOEFL score: 550
Most popular departments: accounting, health care administration, management information systems, other

VERMONT

University of Vermont[1]

55 Colchester Avenue
Burlington, VT 05405
http://www.bsad.uvm.edu/mba
Public
Admissions: (802) 656-0513
E-mail: studentservices@bsad.uvm.edu
Financial aid: (802) 656-1340
Tuition: N/A
Room/board/expenses: N/A
Enrollment: N/A

VIRGINIA

College of William and Mary (Mason)

PO Box 8795
Williamsburg, VA 23187-8795
http://mason.wm.edu
Public
Admissions: (757) 221-2900
E-mail: admissions@mason.wm.edu
Financial aid: (757) 221-2900
Application deadline: N/A
In-state tuition: full time: $29,350; part time: $700/credit hour
Out-of-state tuition: full time: $39,750
Room/board/expenses: $16,300
College-funded aid: Yes
International student aid: Yes
Average student indebtedness at graduation: $53,674
Full-time enrollment: 206
men: 66%; women: 34%;
minorities:23%; international: 37%
Part-time enrollment: 180
men: 69%; women: 31%;
minorities:15%; international: 4%
Acceptance rate (full time): 58%
Average GMAT (full time): 610
Average GMAT (part time): 593
Average GPA (full time): 3.30
Average age of entrants to full-time program: 27
Average months of prior work experience (full time): 46
TOEFL requirement: Yes
Minimum TOEFL score: 600
Most popular departments: entrepreneurship, finance, marketing, real estate, supply chain management
Mean starting base salary for 2012 full-time graduates: $75,674

Employment location for 2012 class: Intl. 2%; N.E. 15%; M.A. 63%; S. 7%; M.W. 2%; S.W. 6%; W. 6%

George Mason University

4400 University Drive
Fairfax, VA 22030
http://www.som.gmu.edu
Public
Admissions: (703) 993-2136
E-mail: somgrad@gmu.edu
Financial aid: (703) 993-2353
Application deadline: rolling
In-state tuition: full time: $830/credit hour; part time: $830/credit hour
Out-of-state tuition: full time: $1,486/credit hour
Room/board/expenses: $23,344
College-funded aid: Yes
International student aid: Yes
Full-time enrollment: 82
men: 62%; women: 38%;
minorities:21%; international: 33%
Part-time enrollment: 310
men: 69%; women: 31%;
minorities:21%; international: 3%
Acceptance rate (full time): 55%
Average GMAT (full time): 571
Average GMAT (part time): 550
Average GPA (full time): 3.11
Average age of entrants to full-time program: 27
Average months of prior work experience (full time): 48
TOEFL requirement: Yes
Minimum TOEFL score: 570
Most popular departments: accounting, finance, management information systems, real estate, other
Mean starting base salary for 2012 full-time graduates: $70,417
Employment location for 2012 class: Intl. N/A; N.E. N/A; M.A. 100%; S. N/A; M.W. N/A; S.W. N/A; W. N/A

James Madison University[1]

Showker Hall
Harrisonburg, VA 22807
http://www.jmu.edu/cob/mba
Public
Admissions: (540) 568-3236
E-mail: busingme@jmu.edu
Financial aid: (540) 568-3139
Tuition: N/A
Room/board/expenses: N/A
Enrollment: N/A

Longwood University[1]

201 High Street
Farmville, VA 23909
http://www.longwood.edu/business/
Public
Admissions: (877) 267-7883
E-mail: graduate@longwood.edu
Financial aid: N/A
Tuition: N/A
Room/board/expenses: N/A
Enrollment: N/A

Old Dominion University

1026 Constant Hall
Norfolk, VA 23529
http://bpa.odu.edu/mba
Public
Admissions: (757) 683-3585
E-mail: mbainfo@odu.edu
Financial aid: (757) 683-3683
Application deadline: 06/01
In-state tuition: full time: $393/credit hour; part time: $393/credit hour
Out-of-state tuition: full time: $997/credit hour
Room/board/expenses: $15,000

College-funded aid: Yes
International student aid: Yes
Average student indebtedness at graduation: $38,177
Full-time enrollment: N/A
men: N/A; women: N/A;
minorities:N/A; international: N/A
Part-time enrollment: 219
men: 57%; women: 43%;
minorities:28%; international: 8%
Average GMAT (part time): 547
TOEFL requirement: Yes
Minimum TOEFL score: 550
Most popular departments: accounting, health care administration, international business, public administration

Radford University

PO Box 6956
Radford, VA 24142
http://www.radford.edu
Public
Admissions: (540) 831-6296
E-mail: gradcoll@radford.edu
Financial aid: (540) 831-5408
Application deadline: rolling
In-state tuition: full time: $270/credit hour; part time: $270/credit hour
Out-of-state tuition: full time: $627/credit hour
Room/board/expenses: $18,290
College-funded aid: Yes
International student aid: Yes
Full-time enrollment: 37
men: 68%; women: 32%;
minorities:30%; international: 22%
Part-time enrollment: 47
men: 64%; women: 36%;
minorities:11%; international: 4%
Acceptance rate (full time): 79%
Average GMAT (full time): 488
Average GMAT (part time): 510
Average GPA (full time): 3.21
Average age of entrants to full-time program: 23
Average months of prior work experience (full time): 26
TOEFL requirement: Yes
Minimum TOEFL score: 550
Most popular departments: general management

Shenandoah University (Byrd)

Halpin Harrison, Room 103
Winchester, VA 22601
http://www.su.edu/
Private
Admissions: (540) 665-4581
E-mail: admit@su.edu
Financial aid: (540) 665-4538
Application deadline: rolling
Tuition: full time: $11,052; part time: $614/credit hour
Room/board/expenses: $13,820
College-funded aid: Yes
International student aid: Yes
Average student indebtedness at graduation: $4,908
Full-time enrollment: 58
men: 59%; women: 41%;
minorities:28%; international: 28%
Part-time enrollment: 52
men: 56%; women: 44%;
minorities:17%; international: 6%
Acceptance rate (full time): 53%
Average GPA (full time): 3.70
Average age of entrants to full-time program: 25
TOEFL requirement: Yes
Minimum TOEFL score: 527
Most popular departments: general management

University of Richmond (Robins)

1 Gateway Road
Richmond, VA 23173
http://robins.richmond.edu/mba/
Private
Admissions: (804) 289-8553
E-mail: mba@richmond.edu
Financial aid: (804) 289-8438
Application deadline: 05/12
Tuition: full time: $37,350; part time: $1,230/credit hour
Room/board/expenses: $5,230
College-funded aid: Yes
International student aid: Yes
Full-time enrollment: N/A
men: N/A; women: N/A;
minorities:N/A; international: N/A
Part-time enrollment: 113
men: 73%; women: 27%;
minorities:9%; international: 1%
Average GMAT (part time): 604
TOEFL requirement: Yes
Minimum TOEFL score: 600

University of Virginia (Darden)

PO Box 6550
Charlottesville, VA 22906-6550
http://www.darden.virginia.edu
Public
Admissions: (434) 924-7281
E-mail: darden@virginia.edu
Financial aid: (434) 924-7739
Application deadline: N/A
In-state tuition: full time: $49,582; part time: N/A
Out-of-state tuition: full time: $53,900
Room/board/expenses: $22,607
College-funded aid: Yes
International student aid: Yes
Average student indebtedness at graduation: $105,490
Full-time enrollment: 637
men: 68%; women: 32%;
minorities:20%; international: 26%
Part-time enrollment: N/A
men: N/A; women: N/A;
minorities:N/A; international: N/A
Acceptance rate (full time): 27%
Average GMAT (full time): 703
Average GPA (full time): 3.45
Average age of entrants to full-time program: 27
Average months of prior work experience (full time): 55
TOEFL requirement: No
Minimum TOEFL score: N/A
Mean starting base salary for 2012 full-time graduates: $109,335
Employment location for 2012 class: Intl. 11%; N.E. 30%; M.A. 20%; S. 11%; M.W. 9%; S.W. 8%; W. 11%

Virginia Commonwealth University

301 W. Main Street
Richmond, VA 23284-4000
http://www.business.vcu.edu/graduate
Public
Admissions: (804) 828-4622
E-mail: gsib@vcu.edu
Financial aid: (804) 828-6669
Application deadline: 07/01
In-state tuition: full time: $11,912; part time: $529/credit hour
Out-of-state tuition: full time: $21,976
Room/board/expenses: $18,500
College-funded aid: Yes
International student aid: Yes
Full-time enrollment: N/A
men: N/A; women: N/A;
minorities:N/A; international: N/A
Part-time enrollment: 180
men: 68%; women: 32%;
minorities:14%; international: 13%
Average GMAT (part time): 528

TOEFL requirement: Yes
Minimum TOEFL score: 600
Most popular departments: finance, human resources management, international business, real estate, statistics and operations research

Virginia Tech (Pamplin)

1044 Pamplin Hall (0209)
Blacksburg, VA 24061
http://www.mba.vt.edu
Public
Admissions: (540) 231-6152
E-mail: mba_info@vt.edu
Financial aid: (540) 231-5179
Application deadline: 06/01
In-state tuition: full time: $16,917; part time: $657/credit hour
Out-of-state tuition: full time: $27,166
Room/board/expenses: $17,160
College-funded aid: Yes
International student aid: Yes
Average student indebtedness at graduation: $34,375
Full-time enrollment: 80
men: 68%; women: 33%;
minorities:6%; international: 50%
Part-time enrollment: 150
men: 63%; women: 37%;
minorities:25%; international: 9%
Acceptance rate (full time): 52%
Average GMAT (full time): 627
Average GMAT (part time): 609
Average GPA (full time): 3.46
Average age of entrants to full-time program: 26
Average months of prior work experience (full time): 24
TOEFL requirement: Yes
Minimum TOEFL score: 550
Most popular departments: finance, marketing, management information systems
Mean starting base salary for 2012 full-time graduates: $67,392
Employment location for 2012 class: Intl. 8%; N.E. 4%; M.A. 64%; S. 12%; M.W. 4%; S.W. 4%; W. 4%

WASHINGTON

Eastern Washington University

668 N. Riverpoint Boulevard, Suite A
Spokane, WA 99202-1677
http://www.ewu.edu/mba
Public
Admissions: (509) 828-1248
E-mail: mbaprogram@ewu.edu
Financial aid: (509) 359-2314
Application deadline: rolling
In-state tuition: total program: $22,500 (full-time); part time: $450/credit hour
Out-of-state tuition: total program: $22,500 (full-time)
Room/board/expenses: $18,000
College-funded aid: Yes
International student aid: Yes
Full-time enrollment: N/A
men: N/A; women: N/A;
minorities:N/A; international: N/A
Part-time enrollment: 80
men: 69%; women: 31%;
minorities:10%; international: 26%
Average GMAT (part time): 505
TOEFL requirement: Yes
Minimum TOEFL score: 580
Most popular departments: economics, finance, health care administration, marketing, public administration

Gonzaga University

502 E. Boone Avenue
Spokane, WA 99258-0009
http://www.gonzaga.edu/mba
Private
Admissions: (509) 313-4622
E-mail: chatman@gonzaga.edu
Financial aid: (509) 313-6581
Application deadline: 08/01
Tuition: full time: $840/credit hour; part time: $840/credit hour
Room/board/expenses: $12,500
College-funded aid: Yes
International student aid: Yes
Average student indebtedness at graduation: $32,000
Full-time enrollment: N/A
men: N/A; women: N/A;
minorities:N/A; international: N/A
Part-time enrollment: 276
men: 60%; women: 40%;
minorities:11%; international: 8%
Average GMAT (part time): 569
TOEFL requirement: Yes
Minimum TOEFL score: 570
Most popular departments: accounting, entrepreneurship, finance, general management, health care administration

Pacific Lutheran University

Morken Center for Learning and Technology, Room 176
Tacoma, WA 98447
http://www.plu.edu/mba/home.php
Private
Admissions: (253) 535-7330
E-mail: plumba@plu.edu
Financial aid: (253) 535-7134
Application deadline: rolling
Tuition: full time: N/A; total program: $48,645 (part-time)
Room/board/expenses: $5,200
College-funded aid: Yes
International student aid: Yes
Full-time enrollment: N/A
men: N/A; women: N/A;
minorities:N/A; international: N/A
Part-time enrollment: 63
men: 56%; women: 44%;
minorities:21%; international: 8%
Average GMAT (part time): 556
TOEFL requirement: Yes
Minimum TOEFL score: 570
Most popular departments: entrepreneurship, general management, health care administration, technology

Seattle Pacific University

3307 Third Avenue W, Suite 201
Seattle, WA 98119-1950
http://www.spu.edu/sbe
Private
Admissions: (206) 281-2753
E-mail: lpeterso@spu.edu
Financial aid: (206) 281-2469
Application deadline: 08/01
Tuition: full time: N/A; part time: N/A
Room/board/expenses: N/A
College-funded aid: No
International student aid: No
Full-time enrollment: 8
men: 13%; women: 88%;
minorities:25%; international: N/A
Part-time enrollment: 125
men: 62%; women: 38%;
minorities:27%; international: 13%
TOEFL requirement: Yes
Minimum TOEFL score: 577

Seattle University (Albers)

901 12th Avenue, PO Box 222000
Seattle, WA 98122-1090
http://www.seattleu.edu/albers/gradoverview/
Private
Admissions: (206) 296-5708
E-mail: millardj@seattleu.edu
Financial aid: (206) 296-5845
Application deadline: 08/20
Tuition: full time: N/A; part time: $778/credit hour
Room/board/expenses: $16,512
College-funded aid: Yes
International student aid: Yes
Average student indebtedness at graduation: $21,552
Full-time enrollment: N/A
men: N/A; women: N/A;
minorities:N/A; international: N/A
Part-time enrollment: 584
men: 62%; women: 38%;
minorities:25%; international: 14%
Average GMAT (part time): 585
TOEFL requirement: Yes
Minimum TOEFL score: 580
Most popular departments: accounting, entrepreneurship, finance, international business, leadership

University of Washington–Bothell

18115 Campus Way NW
Box 358533
Bothell, WA 98011
http://www.uwb.edu/mba/mbaadmissions
Public
Admissions: (425) 352-5394
E-mail: vtolbert@uwb.edu
Financial aid: N/A
Application deadline: 04/26
In-state tuition: full time: N/A; part time: $22,215
Out-of-state tuition: full time: N/A
Room/board/expenses: N/A
College-funded aid: Yes
Full-time enrollment: N/A
men: N/A; women: N/A;
minorities:N/A; international: N/A
Part-time enrollment: 122
men: 57%; women: 43%;
minorities:20%; international: 8%
Average GMAT (part time): 548
TOEFL requirement: Yes
Minimum TOEFL score: 580
Most popular departments: entrepreneurship, leadership, marketing, supply chain management, technology

University of Washington (Foster)

PO Box 353200
Seattle, WA 98195-3200
http://foster.washington.edu/mba/
Public
Admissions: (206) 543-4661
E-mail: mba@uw.edu
Financial aid: (206) 543-4661
Application deadline: 03/15
In-state tuition: full time: $27,621; part time: $21,126
Out-of-state tuition: full time: $40,170
Room/board/expenses: $22,341
College-funded aid: Yes
International student aid: Yes
Average student indebtedness at graduation: $40,015
Full-time enrollment: 230
men: 58%; women: 42%;
minorities:23%; international: 24%
Part-time enrollment: 305
men: 77%; women: 23%;
minorities:37%; international: 14%
Acceptance rate (full time): 43%
Average GMAT (full time): 670

Average GMAT (part time): 638
Average GPA (full time): 3.37
Average age of entrants to full-time program: 29
Average months of prior work experience (full time): 74
TOEFL requirement: Yes
Minimum TOEFL score: 600
Most popular departments: entrepreneurship, finance, general management, international business, marketing
Mean starting base salary for 2012 full-time graduates: $96,814
Employment location for 2012 class: Intl. 1%; N.E. 4%; M.A. N/A; S. N/A; M.W. N/A; S.W. N/A; W. 95%

University of Washington–Tacoma

1900 Commerce Street
Box 358420
Tacoma, WA 98402
http://www.tacoma.uw.edu/milgard-school-business
Public
Admissions: N/A
Financial aid: N/A
Application deadline: 07/01
In-state tuition: full time: N/A; part time: $26,092
Out-of-state tuition: full time: N/A
Room/board/expenses: N/A
College-funded aid: Yes
International student aid: Yes
Full-time enrollment: N/A
men: N/A; women: N/A;
minorities:N/A; international: N/A
Part-time enrollment: 59
men: 61%; women: 39%;
minorities:20%; international: 0%
Average GMAT (part time): 502
Minimum TOEFL score: N/A

Washington State University

PO Box 644744
Pullman, WA 99164-4744
http://www.business.wsu.edu/graduate
Public
Admissions: (509) 335-7617
E-mail: mba@wsu.edu
Financial aid: (509) 335-9711
Application deadline: 05/03
In-state tuition: full time: N/A; part time: $587/credit hour
Out-of-state tuition: full time: N/A
Room/board/expenses: $15,536
College-funded aid: Yes
International student aid: Yes
Full-time enrollment: N/A
men: N/A; women: N/A;
minorities:N/A; international: N/A
Part-time enrollment: 73
men: 59%; women: 41%;
minorities:19%; international: 3%
TOEFL requirement: Yes
Minimum TOEFL score: 580

Western Washington University[1]

516 High Street, MS 9072
Bellingham, WA 98225-9072
http://www.cbe.wwu.edu/mba/
Public
Admissions: (360) 650-3898
E-mail: mba@wwu.edu
Financial aid: (360) 650-3470
Tuition: N/A
Room/board/expenses: N/A
Enrollment: N/A

WEST VIRGINIA

Marshall University (Lewis)

1 John Marshall Drive
Huntington, WV 25755-2020
http://www.marshall.edu/lcob/
Public
Admissions: (800) 642-9842
E-mail: johnson73@marshall.edu
Financial aid: (800) 438-5390
Application deadline: 08/01
In-state tuition: full time: $7,588; part time: $374/credit hour
Out-of-state tuition: full time: $17,090
Room/board/expenses: N/A
College-funded aid: Yes
International student aid: Yes
Full-time enrollment: 45
men: 71%; women: 29%;
minorities:7%; international: 27%
Part-time enrollment: 52
men: 60%; women: 40%;
minorities:10%; international: 4%
Average GMAT (part time): 530
TOEFL requirement: Yes
Minimum TOEFL score: 550

West Virginia University

PO Box 6027
Morgantown, WV 26506
http://www.be.wvu.edu
Public
Admissions: (304) 293-7937
E-mail: mba@wvu.edu
Financial aid: (304) 293-5242
Application deadline: 03/01
In-state tuition: total program: $21,720 (full-time); part time: N/A
Out-of-state tuition: total program: $54,100 (full-time)
Room/board/expenses: $15,750
College-funded aid: Yes
International student aid: Yes
Full-time enrollment: 34
men: 65%; women: 35%;
minorities:6%; international: 41%
Part-time enrollment: N/A
men: N/A; women: N/A;
minorities:N/A; international: N/A
Acceptance rate (full time): 43%
Average GMAT (full time): 617
Average GPA (full time): 3.41
Average age of entrants to full-time program: 25
Average months of prior work experience (full time): 20
TOEFL requirement: Yes
Minimum TOEFL score: 580
Mean starting base salary for 2012 full-time graduates: $56,340
Employment location for 2012 class: Intl. 0%; N.E. 0%; M.A. 81%; S. 10%; M.W. 10%; S.W. 0%; W. 0%

WISCONSIN

Marquette University

PO Box 1881
Milwaukee, WI 53201-1881
http://www.marquette.edu/gsm
Private
Admissions: (414) 288-7145
E-mail: mba@Marquette.edu
Financial aid: (414) 288-7137
Application deadline: rolling
Tuition: full time: $985/credit hour; part time: $985/credit hour
Room/board/expenses: $16,206
College-funded aid: Yes
International student aid: Yes
Full-time enrollment: N/A
men: N/A; women: N/A;
minorities:N/A; international: N/A
Part-time enrollment: 346
men: 75%; women: 25%;
minorities:8%; international: 5%
Average GMAT (part time): 577
TOEFL requirement: Yes
Minimum TOEFL score: 550

Most popular departments: finance, human resources management, international business, marketing, management information systems

University of Wisconsin–Eau Claire

Schneider Hall 215
Eau Claire, WI 54702-4004
http://www.uwec.edu/COB/
graduate/index.htm
Public
Admissions: (715) 836-5415
E-mail: uwecmba@uwec.edu
Financial aid: (715) 836-3373
Application deadline: 07/01
In-state tuition: full time: $521/
credit hour; part time: $521/
credit hour
Out-of-state tuition: full time:
$1,030/credit hour
Room/board/expenses: $9,750
College-funded aid: Yes
International student aid: Yes
Full-time enrollment: 7
men: 71%; women: 29%;
minorities:0%; international: 57%
Part-time enrollment: 256
men: 58%; women: 42%;
minorities:11%; international: 0%
Acceptance rate (full time): 75%
Average GMAT (part time): 540
Average age of entrants to full-time program: 25
TOEFL requirement: Yes
Minimum TOEFL score: 550
Most popular departments:
accounting, finance, general
management, health care
administration, marketing

University of Wisconsin–La Crosse

1725 State Street
La Crosse, WI 54601
http://www.uwlax.edu
Public
Admissions: (608) 785-8939
E-mail: admissions@uwlax.edu
Financial aid: (608) 785-8604
Application deadline: 06/15
In-state tuition: full time: N/A; part
time: $506/credit hour
Out-of-state tuition: full time: N/A
Room/board/expenses: N/A
College-funded aid: Yes
International student aid: Yes
Full-time enrollment: 46
men: 57%; women: 43%;
minorities:N/A; international: 50%

Part-time enrollment: N/A
men: N/A; women: N/A;
minorities:N/A; international: N/A
Acceptance rate (full time): 80%
Average age of entrants to full-time program: 25
Average months of prior work experience (full time): 34
TOEFL requirement: Yes
Minimum TOEFL score: 550

University of Wisconsin–Madison

2450 Grainger Hall
975 University Avenue
Madison, WI 53706-1323
http://www.bus.wisc.edu/mba
Public
Admissions: (608) 262-4000
E-mail: mba@bus.wisc.edu
Financial aid: (608) 262-4000
Application deadline: 04/25
In-state tuition: full time: $15,295;
part time: $21,911
Out-of-state tuition: full time:
$27,789
Room/board/expenses: $15,780
College-funded aid: Yes
International student aid: Yes
Average student indebtedness at graduation: $29,976
Full-time enrollment: 203
men: 72%; women: 28%;
minorities:16%; international: 18%
Part-time enrollment: 149
men: 70%; women: 30%;
minorities:13%; international: 4%
Acceptance rate (full time): 24%
Average GMAT (full time): 675
Average GMAT (part time): 593
Average GPA (full time): 3.32
Average age of entrants to full-time program: 25
Average months of prior work experience (full time): 62
TOEFL requirement: Yes
Minimum TOEFL score: 600
Most popular departments: finance,
marketing, operations management, portfolio management,
real estate
Mean starting base salary for 2012 full-time graduates: $91,625
Employment location for 2012 class:
Intl. 2%; N.E. 11%; M.A. 1%; S. 4%;
M.W. 60%; S.W. 3%; W. 18%

University of Wisconsin–Milwaukee (Lubar)

PO Box 742
Milwaukee, WI 53201-9863
http://www4.uwm.edu/business/
Public
Admissions: (414) 229-5403
E-mail: mba-ms@uwm.edu
Financial aid: (414) 229-4541
Application deadline: 08/01
In-state tuition: full time: N/A; part
time: $12,886
Out-of-state tuition: full time: N/A
Room/board/expenses: $13,000
College-funded aid: Yes
International student aid: Yes
Full-time enrollment: N/A
men: N/A; women: N/A;
minorities:N/A; international: N/A
Part-time enrollment: 464
men: 61%; women: 39%;
minorities:12%; international: 11%
Average GMAT (part time): 560
TOEFL requirement: Yes
Minimum TOEFL score: 550

University of Wisconsin–Oshkosh

800 Algoma Boulevard
Oshkosh, WI 54901
http://www.uwosh.edu/coba/
Public
Admissions: (800) 633-1430
E-mail: mba@uwosh.edu
Financial aid: (920) 424-3377
Application deadline: rolling
In-state tuition: full time: N/A; total
program: $24,500 (part-time)
Out-of-state tuition: full time: N/A
Room/board/expenses: N/A
College-funded aid: Yes
International student aid: Yes
Full-time enrollment: N/A
men: N/A; women: N/A;
minorities:N/A; international: N/A
Part-time enrollment: 433
men: 58%; women: 42%;
minorities:7%; international: 2%
Average GMAT (part time): 583
TOEFL requirement: Yes
Minimum TOEFL score: 550
Most popular departments:
finance, health care administration, human resources management, international business,
marketing

University of Wisconsin–Parkside

PO Box 2000
Kenosha, WI 53141-2000
http://www.uwp.edu/
departments/business
Public
Admissions: (262) 595-2280
E-mail: mba@uwp.edu
Financial aid: (262) 595-2574
Application deadline: 08/01
In-state tuition: full time: $482/
credit hour; part time: $482/
credit hour
Out-of-state tuition: full time: $990/
credit hour
Room/board/expenses: $9,000
College-funded aid: Yes
International student aid: Yes
Full-time enrollment: 33
men: 42%; women: 58%;
minorities:6%; international: 48%
Part-time enrollment: 76
men: 59%; women: 41%;
minorities:13%; international: 0%
Acceptance rate (full time): 92%
Average GMAT (full time): 479
Average GMAT (part time): 413
Average GPA (full time): 3.29
Average age of entrants to full-time program: 26
Average months of prior work experience (full time): 48
TOEFL requirement: Yes
Minimum TOEFL score: 550

University of Wisconsin–River Falls

410 S. Third Street
River Falls, WI 54022-5001
http://www.uwrf.edu/mba
Public
Admissions: (715) 425-3335
E-mail: mmcbe@uwrf.edu
Financial aid: (715) 425-3141
Application deadline: 06/15
In-state tuition: full time: N/A; part
time: $665/credit hour
Out-of-state tuition: full time: N/A
Room/board/expenses: N/A
College-funded aid: Yes
International student aid: Yes
Full-time enrollment: N/A
men: N/A; women: N/A;
minorities:N/A; international: N/A
Part-time enrollment: 112
men: 57%; women: 43%;
minorities:3%; international: 4%
Average GMAT (part time): 484
TOEFL requirement: Yes
Minimum TOEFL score: 550

University of Wisconsin–Whitewater

800 W. Main Street
Whitewater, WI 53190
http://www.uww.edu/
Public
Admissions: (262) 472-1945
E-mail: chenowej@uww.edu
Financial aid: (262) 472-1130
Application deadline: rolling
In-state tuition: full time: N/A; part
time: N/A
Out-of-state tuition: full time: N/A
Room/board/expenses: N/A
College-funded aid: Yes
International student aid: Yes
Full-time enrollment: 285
men: N/A; women: N/A;
minorities:N/A; international: N/A
Part-time enrollment: 390
men: N/A; women: N/A;
minorities:N/A; international: N/A
TOEFL requirement: Yes
Minimum TOEFL score: 550
Most popular departments:
finance, general management,
marketing, management information systems, supply chain
management

WYOMING

University of Wyoming[1]

PO Box 3275
Laramie, WY 82071-3275
http://business.uwyo.edu/
MBA_index.html
Public
Admissions: (307) 766-2449
E-mail: mba@uwyo.edu
Financial aid: (307) 766-3886
Tuition: N/A
Room/board/expenses: N/A
Enrollment: N/A

EDUCATION

Here you'll find information on 278 schools nationwide that offer doctoral programs in education. Two hundred thirty-nine responded to the *U.S. News* survey, which was conducted in the fall of 2012 and early 2013. They provided information on matters of interest to applicants such as entrance requirements, enrollment, costs, location, and specialties. Schools that did not respond to the survey have abbreviated entries.

KEY TO THE TERMINOLOGY

1. A school whose name has been footnoted with the numeral 1 did not return the *U.S. News* statistical survey; limited data appear in its entry.

N/A. Not available from the school or not applicable.

Admissions. The admissions office phone number.

E-mail. The address of the admissions office. If instead of an E-mail address a website is listed, the website will automatically present an E-mail screen programmed to reach the admissions office.

Financial aid. The financial aid office phone number.

Application deadline. For fall 2014 enrollment. "Rolling" means there is no deadline; the school acts on applications as they are received. "Varies" means deadlines vary according to department or whether applicants are U.S. citizens or foreign nationals.

Tuition. For the 2012-13 academic year. Includes fees.

Credit hour. The cost per credit hour for the 2012-13 academic year.

Room/board/expenses. For the 2012-13 academic year.

Enrollment. Full-time and part-time graduate-level enrollment at the education school for fall 2012.

Minorities. Full-time and part-time graduate-level minority enrollment percentage for fall 2012. It is the share of students who are black or African-American, Asian, American Indian or Alaskan Native, Native Hawaiian or other Pacific Islander, Hispanic/Latino, or two or more races. The minority percentage was reported by each school.

Acceptance rate. Percentage of applicants who were accepted among those who applied for fall 2012 for both master's and doctoral programs.

Entrance test required. GRE means that scores on the Graduate Record Examination are required by some or all departments. GRE scores displayed are for both the master's and Ph.D. students and are only for those GRE exams taken by the fall 2012 entering students during or after August 2011 using the new GRE 130-170 score scale. MAT means that the Miller Analogies Test is required by some or all departments. GRE or MAT means that some or all departments require either the GRE or MAT.

Average GRE scores. Average verbal and quantitative scores for students who entered in fall 2012. Averages are based on the number of students who provided the school with scores. That number may be less than the total number of students who entered in fall 2012. (The GRE scores published in the ranking table refer to the scores of a school's entering doctoral students and may not be the same as the average GRE scores for the overall entering class printed in the directory.)

Total research assistantships. For the 2012-13 academic year.

Students reporting specialty. The percentage of graduate students, both full and part time, reporting a program specialization in fall 2012. If a school's figure is less than 50 percent, then its directory entry does not include this information or an enumeration of student specialties.

Student specialties. Proportion of students in the specialty-reporting population (not necessarily the entire student body) who are enrolled in a particular specialty. Numbers may not add up to 100 percent because of rounding or students enrolled in multiple specialties. The largest specialty areas in graduate education are listed.

ALABAMA

Alabama A&M University[1]
PO Box 1357
Normal, AL 35762
http://www.aamu.edu/
Public
Admissions: N/A
Financial aid: N/A
Tuition: N/A
Room/board expenses: N/A
Enrollment: N/A

Alabama State University
915 S. Jackson Street
Montgomery, AL 36101
http://www.alasu.edu/Education/
Public
Admissions: (334) 229-4275
Financial aid: (334) 229-4324
Application deadline: rolling
In-state tuition: full time: $312/credit hour; part time: $312/credit hour
Out-of-state tuition: full time: $624/credit hour
Room/board/expenses: $7,746
Full-time enrollment: 112
doctoral students: 23%; master's students: 71%; education specialists: 6%; men: 28%; women: 72%; minorities: 93%; international: N/A
Part-time enrollment: 341
doctoral students: 14%; master's students: 67%; education specialists: 19%; men: 25%; women: 75%; minorities: 94%; international: N/A
Acceptance rate (master's): 51%
Acceptance rate (doctoral): 28%
Entrance test required: GRE
Avg. GRE (of all entering students with scores): quantitative: 139; verbal: 141
Research assistantships: 2
Students reporting specialty: 100%
Students specializing in: admin.: 17%; counseling: 22%; curriculum/instr.: 7%; educational tech.: 2%; elementary: 17%; secondary: 18%; special: 5%; instructional media design: 3%; other: 10%

Auburn University
3084 Haley Center
Auburn, AL 36849-5218
http://www.auburn.edu/
Public
Admissions: (334) 844-4700
E-mail: gradadm@auburn.edu
Financial aid: (334) 844-4367
Application deadline: 11/25
In-state tuition: full time: $9,440; part time: $437/credit hour
Out-of-state tuition: full time: $25,172
Room/board/expenses: $17,102
Full-time enrollment: 355
doctoral students: 34%; master's students: 65%; education specialists: 1%; men: 31%; women: 69%; minorities: 21%; international: 4%
Part-time enrollment: 506
doctoral students: 53%; master's students: 36%; education specialists: 11%; men: 36%; women: 64%; minorities: 27%; international: 2%
Acceptance rate (master's): 66%
Acceptance rate (doctoral): 27%

Entrance test required: GRE
Avg. GRE (of all entering students with scores): quantitative: 145; verbal: 148
Research assistantships: 53
Students reporting specialty: 100%
Students specializing in: admin.: 11%; counseling: 9%; educational psych: 7%; elementary: 6%; higher education admin.: 12%; secondary: 15%; special: 13%; technical (vocational): 5%; instructional media design: 1%; other: 21%

Samford University (Beeson)
800 Lakeshore Drive
Birmingham, AL 35229
http://education.samford.edu
Private
Admissions: (205) 726-2019
E-mail: jmpersal@samford.edu
Financial aid: (205) 726-2905
Application deadline: 07/28
Tuition: full time: $688/credit hour; part time: $688/credit hour
Room/board/expenses: N/A
Full-time enrollment: 48
doctoral students: 4%; master's students: 96%; education specialists: 0%; men: 33%; women: 67%; minorities: 8%; international: 2%
Part-time enrollment: 188
doctoral students: 42%; master's students: 48%; education specialists: 10%; men: 28%; women: 72%; minorities: 14%; international: 3%
Acceptance rate (master's): N/A
Acceptance rate (doctoral): 83%
Entrance test required: GRE
Avg. GRE (of all entering students with scores): quantitative: 150; verbal: 152
Research assistantships: 0
Students reporting specialty: 100%
Students specializing in: admin.: 66%; elementary: 1%; secondary: 21%; special: 4%; other: 8%

University of Alabama
Box 870231
Tuscaloosa, AL 35487-0231
http://graduate.ua.edu
Public
Admissions: (205) 348-5921
E-mail: usgradapply@aalan.ua.edu
Financial aid: (205) 348-6756
Application deadline: 07/01
In-state tuition: full time: $9,200; part time: N/A
Out-of-state tuition: full time: $22,950
Room/board/expenses: $12,758
Full-time enrollment: 391
doctoral students: 53%; master's students: 41%; education specialists: 6%; men: 32%; women: 68%; minorities: 21%; international: 6%
Part-time enrollment: 633
doctoral students: 56%; master's students: 33%; education specialists: 10%; men: 25%; women: 75%; minorities: 20%; international: 2%
Acceptance rate (master's): 53%
Acceptance rate (doctoral): 54%
Entrance test required: GRE
Avg. GRE (of all entering students with scores): quantitative: 150; verbal: 151
Research assistantships: 54

More at www.usnews.com/grad

Students reporting specialty: 100%
Students specializing in: admin.: 31%; counseling: 3%; evaluation/research/statistics: 1%; educational psych: 9%; elementary: 6%; higher education admin.: 14%; secondary: 15%; special: 7%; other: 17%

University of Alabama–Birmingham

1530 Third Avenue S, EB 217
Birmingham, AL 35294-1250
http://www.uab.edu/graduate
Public
Admissions: (205) 934-8227
E-mail: gradschool@uab.edu
Financial aid: (205) 934-8223
Application deadline: rolling
In-state tuition: full time: $6,420; part time: N/A
Out-of-state tuition: full time: $14,574
Room/board/expenses: $13,144
Full-time enrollment: 259
doctoral students: 5%; master's students: 94%; education specialists: 1%; men: 21%; women: 79%; minorities: 19%; international: 2%
Part-time enrollment: 481
doctoral students: 15%; master's students: 67%; education specialists: 18%; men: 24%; women: 76%; minorities: 31%; international: 0%
Acceptance rate (master's): 95%
Acceptance rate (doctoral): 93%
Entrance test required: GRE
Avg. GRE (of all entering students with scores): quantitative: 146; verbal: 148
Research assistantships: 0
Students reporting specialty: 100%
Students specializing in: admin.: 16%; counseling: 12%; elementary: 12%; secondary: 13%; special: 11%; other: 36%

University of South Alabama

UCOM 3600
Mobile, AL 36688
http://www.southalabama.edu/
Public
Admissions: (251) 460-6141
E-mail: admiss@usouthal.edu
Financial aid: (251) 460-6231
Application deadline: rolling
In-state tuition: full time: $358/credit hour; part time: $358/credit hour
Out-of-state tuition: full time: $716/credit hour
Room/board/expenses: N/A
Full-time enrollment: 246
doctoral students: 4%; master's students: 91%; education specialists: 5%; men: 22%; women: 78%; minorities: 18%; international: 3%
Part-time enrollment: 163
doctoral students: 13%; master's students: 79%; education specialists: 8%; men: 23%; women: 77%; minorities: 16%; international: 1%
Acceptance rate (master's): 85%
Acceptance rate (doctoral): 50%
Entrance test required: GRE
Avg. GRE (of all entering students with scores): quantitative: 144; verbal: 149
Research assistantships: 3
Students reporting specialty: 100%
Students specializing in: admin.: 11%; counseling: 8%; elementary: 13%; secondary: 17%; special: 2%; other: 49%

ARIZONA

Arizona State University

PO Box 37100, MC 1252
Phoenix, AZ 85069-7100
http://www.asu.edu/graduate
Public
Admissions: (480) 965-6113
E-mail: asugrad@asu.edu
Financial aid: (480) 965-3521
Application deadline: rolling
In-state tuition: full time: $10,518; part time: $714/credit hour
Out-of-state tuition: full time: $25,066
Room/board/expenses: $18,306
Full-time enrollment: 903
doctoral students: 16%; master's students: 84%; education specialists: N/A; men: 29%; women: 71%; minorities: 28%; international: 4%
Part-time enrollment: 1,463
doctoral students: 15%; master's students: 85%; education specialists: N/A; men: 21%; women: 79%; minorities: 25%; international: 2%
Acceptance rate (master's): 88%
Acceptance rate (doctoral): 29%
Entrance test required: GRE
Avg. GRE (of all entering students with scores): quantitative: 148; verbal: 154
Research assistantships: 54
Students reporting specialty: 100%
Students specializing in: admin.: 18%; curriculum/instr.: 38%; social/philosophical foundations: 0%; policy: 2%; educational psych: 7%; elementary: 7%; higher education admin.: 4%; secondary: 10%; special: 8%; instructional media design: 3%; other: 6%

Northern Arizona University

PO Box 5774
Flagstaff, AZ 86011-5774
http://nau.edu/GradCol/Welcome/
Public
Admissions: (928) 523-4348
E-mail: Graduate@nau.edu
Financial aid: (928) 523-4951
Application deadline: rolling
In-state tuition: full time: $9,132; part time: $373/credit hour
Out-of-state tuition: full time: $20,226
Room/board/expenses: $14,316
Full-time enrollment: 838
doctoral students: 8%; master's students: 91%; education specialists: 1%; men: 26%; women: 74%; minorities: 30%; international: 3%
Part-time enrollment: 1,285
doctoral students: 10%; master's students: 90%; education specialists: N/A; men: 25%; women: 75%; minorities: 31%; international: 1%
Acceptance rate (master's): 87%
Acceptance rate (doctoral): 70%
Entrance test required: GRE
Avg. GRE (of all entering students with scores): quantitative: 146; verbal: 153
Research assistantships: 3
Students reporting specialty: 100%
Students specializing in: admin.: 37%; counseling: 20%; curriculum/instr.: 2%; educational tech.: 4%; educational psych: 2%; elementary: 11%; secondary: 2%; special: 5%; technical (vocational): 0%; other: 19%

University of Arizona

Box 210069
1430 E. Second Street
Tucson, AZ 85721-0069
http://coe.arizona.edu/
Public
Admissions: (520) 626-8851
E-mail: tembry@grad.arizona.edu
Financial aid: (520) 621-5200
Application deadline: 12/01
In-state tuition: full time: $12,072; part time: $729/credit hour
Out-of-state tuition: full time: $27,483
Room/board/expenses: $12,214
Full-time enrollment: 460
doctoral students: 47%; master's students: 50%; education specialists: 3%; men: 29%; women: 71%; minorities: 43%; international: 8%
Part-time enrollment: 251
doctoral students: 41%; master's students: 56%; education specialists: 2%; men: 27%; women: 73%; minorities: 37%; international: 1%
Acceptance rate (master's): 76%
Acceptance rate (doctoral): 66%
Entrance test required: GRE
Avg. GRE (of all entering students with scores): quantitative: 146; verbal: 150
Research assistantships: 30
Students reporting specialty: 100%
Students specializing in: admin.: 11%; counseling: 14%; curriculum/instr.: 23%; social/philosophical foundations: 14%; policy: 1%; educational psych: 7%; higher education admin.: 13%; junior high: 1%; secondary: 10%; special: 13%; instructional media design: 0%; other: 7%

ARKANSAS

University of Arkansas–Fayetteville

324 Graduate Education Building
Fayetteville, AR 72701
http://coehp.uark.edu
Public
Admissions: (479) 575-6247
E-mail: gradinfo@uark.edu
Financial aid: (479) 575-3276
Application deadline: rolling
In-state tuition: full time: $349/credit hour; part time: $349/credit hour
Out-of-state tuition: full time: $827/credit hour
Room/board/expenses: $13,918
Full-time enrollment: 448
doctoral students: 17%; master's students: 83%; education specialists: 0%; men: 23%; women: 77%; minorities: 16%; international: 6%
Part-time enrollment: 621
doctoral students: 36%; master's students: 61%; education specialists: 3%; men: 35%; women: 65%; minorities: 20%; international: 3%
Acceptance rate (master's): 95%
Acceptance rate (doctoral): 62%
Entrance test required: GRE
Avg. GRE (of all entering students with scores): quantitative: 148; verbal: 153
Research assistantships: 39
Students reporting specialty: 68%
Students specializing in: admin.: 9%; counseling: 18%; curriculum/instr.: 9%; evaluation/research/statistics: 2%; policy: 2%; educational tech.: 6%; elementary: 8%; higher education admin.: 6%; secondary: 11%; special: 6%; other: 42%

University of Arkansas–Little Rock[1]

2801 S. University Avenue
Little Rock, AR 72204
http://www.ualr.edu/%7Egraddept/gsprodegs.html
Public
Admissions: (501) 569-3127
E-mail: gradinfo@ualr.edu
Financial aid: (501) 569-3450
Tuition: N/A
Room/board expenses: N/A
Enrollment: N/A

University of Central Arkansas[1]

201 Donaghey Avenue
Conway, AR 72035
http://www.uca.edu/index.php
Public
Admissions: (501) 450-3124
E-mail: bherring@uca.edu
Financial aid: (501) 450-3140
Tuition: N/A
Room/board expenses: N/A
Enrollment: N/A

CALIFORNIA

Alliant International University

1 Beach Street
San Francisco, CA 94133-1221
http://www.alliant.edu/
Private
Admissions: (866) 825-5426
E-mail: admissions@alliant.edu
Financial aid: (858) 635-4559
Application deadline: rolling
Tuition: full time: $580/credit hour; part time: $580/credit hour
Room/board/expenses: $24,146
Full-time enrollment: 124
doctoral students: 27%; master's students: 73%; education specialists: N/A; men: 24%; women: 76%; minorities: 31%; international: 16%
Part-time enrollment: 181
doctoral students: 54%; master's students: 46%; education specialists: N/A; men: 26%; women: 74%; minorities: 42%; international: 8%
Acceptance rate (master's): N/A
Acceptance rate (doctoral): 79%
Entrance test required: N/A
Avg. GRE (of all entering students with scores): quantitative: N/A; verbal: N/A
Research assistantships: 1
Students reporting specialty: 100%
Students specializing in: admin.: 13%; educational psych: 15%; elementary: 1%; higher education admin.: 2%; special: 19%; other: 50%

California Polytechnic State University–San Luis Obispo

1 Grand Avenue
San Luis Obispo, CA 93407
http://www.calpoly.edu
Public
Admissions: (805) 756-2311
E-mail: admissions@calpoly.edu
Financial aid: (805) 756-2927
Application deadline: 11/30
In-state tuition: full time: $8,523; part time: $6,225
Out-of-state tuition: full time: $19,683
Room/board/expenses: $15,839
Full-time enrollment: 80
doctoral students: N/A; master's students: 100%; education

specialists: N/A; men: 15%; women: 85%; minorities: 34%; international: N/A
Part-time enrollment: 2
doctoral students: N/A; master's students: 100%; education specialists: N/A; men: 50%; women: 50%; minorities: N/A; international: N/A
Acceptance rate (master's): 69%
Acceptance rate (doctoral): N/A
Entrance test required: N/A
Avg. GRE (of all entering students with scores): quantitative: N/A; verbal: N/A
Students reporting specialty: 0%
Students specializing in: N/A

California State University–Fullerton[1]

800 N. State College Boulevard
Fullerton, CA 92831-3599
http://ed.fullerton.edu/
Public
Admissions: (657) 278-3352
E-mail: coeadmissions@fullerton.edu
Financial aid: (657) 278-3125
Tuition: N/A
Room/board expenses: N/A
Enrollment: N/A

California State University–Long Beach

1250 Bellflower Boulevard
Long Beach, CA 90840
http://www.ced.csulb.edu
Public
Admissions: (562) 985-4547
E-mail: nmcgloth@csulb.edu
Financial aid: (562) 985-8403
Application deadline: rolling
In-state tuition: full time: $7,506; part time: $4,674
Out-of-state tuition: full time: $16,434
Room/board/expenses: N/A
Full-time enrollment: 239
doctoral students: 0%; master's students: 99%; education specialists: 1%; men: 24%; women: 76%; minorities: 70%; international: 4%
Part-time enrollment: 458
doctoral students: 17%; master's students: 74%; education specialists: 8%; men: 24%; women: 76%; minorities: 62%; international: 2%
Acceptance rate (master's): 37%
Acceptance rate (doctoral): 50%
Entrance test required: GRE
Avg. GRE (of all entering students with scores): quantitative: N/A; verbal: N/A
Research assistantships: 0
Students reporting specialty: 100%
Students specializing in: admin.: 19%; counseling: 8%; curriculum/instr.: 3%; social/philosophical foundations: 3%; educational psych: 3%; elementary: 9%; secondary: 36%; special: 2%; instructional media design: 3%; other: 14%

California State University–Los Angeles[1]

5151 State University Drive
Los Angeles, CA 90032
http://www.calstatela.edu/academic/ccoe/
Public
Admissions: (323) 343-3940
Financial aid: (323) 343-3245
Tuition: N/A
Room/board expenses: N/A
Enrollment: N/A

Chapman University

1 University Drive
Orange, CA 92866
http://www.chapman.edu/ces
Private
Admissions: (888) 282-7759
E-mail: admit@chapman.edu
Financial aid: (714) 997-6741
Application deadline: rolling
Tuition: full time: $849/credit hour; part time: $849/credit hour
Room/board/expenses: N/A
Full-time enrollment: 217
doctoral students: 5%; master's students: 73%; education specialists: 23%; men: 21%; women: 79%; minorities: 42%; international: N/A
Part-time enrollment: 150
doctoral students: 43%; master's students: 53%; education specialists: 5%; men: 19%; women: 81%; minorities: 37%; international: 1%
Acceptance rate (master's): 32%
Acceptance rate (doctoral): 51%
Entrance test required: GRE
Avg. GRE (of all entering students with scores): quantitative: 146; verbal: 151
Research assistantships: 25
Students reporting specialty: 100%
Students specializing in: admin.: 0%; counseling: 7%; curriculum/instr.: 8%; social/philosophical foundations: 2%; educational psych: 17%; elementary: 13%; secondary: 13%; special: 21%; other: 21%

Claremont Graduate University

150 E. 10th Street
Claremont, CA 91711
http://www.cgu.edu/pages/267.asp
Private
Admissions: (909) 621-8263
E-mail: admiss@cgu.edu
Financial aid: (909) 621-8337
Application deadline: rolling
Tuition: full time: $38,140; part time: $1,636/credit hour
Room/board/expenses: $14,950
Full-time enrollment: 116
doctoral students: 70%; master's students: 30%; education specialists: N/A; men: 23%; women: 77%; minorities: 58%; international: 5%
Part-time enrollment: 313
doctoral students: 77%; master's students: 23%; education specialists: N/A; men: 29%; women: 71%; minorities: 52%; international: 4%
Acceptance rate (master's): 84%
Acceptance rate (doctoral): 65%
Entrance test required: GRE
Avg. GRE (of all entering students with scores): quantitative: 147; verbal: 152
Research assistantships: 19
Students reporting specialty: 100%
Students specializing in: admin.: 13%; curriculum/instr.: 8%; evaluation/research/statistics: 0%; policy: 3%; educational psych: 1%; elementary: 7%; higher education admin.: 11%; secondary: 10%; special: 10%; other: 36%

Fielding Graduate University

20 De La Vina St.
Santa Barbara, CA 93105
http://www.fielding.edu/programs/elc/default.aspx
Private
Admissions: (800) 340-1099
E-mail: admission@fielding.edu
Financial aid: (805) 898-4009

Application deadline: 08/01
Tuition: full time: $21,945; part time: $21,945
Room/board/expenses: $24,800
Full-time enrollment: 164
doctoral students: 100%; master's students: 0%; education specialists: N/A; men: 32%; women: 68%; minorities: 48%; international: N/A
Part-time enrollment: 14
doctoral students: 100%; master's students: 0%; education specialists: N/A; men: 29%; women: 71%; minorities: 57%; international: N/A
Acceptance rate (master's): N/A
Acceptance rate (doctoral): 86%
Entrance test required: N/A
Avg. GRE (of all entering students with scores): quantitative: N/A; verbal: N/A
Research assistantships: 0
Students reporting specialty: 100%
Students specializing in: admin.: 100%

Loyola Marymount University

1 LMU Drive
Los Angeles, CA 90045
http://soe.lmu.edu
Private
Admissions: (310) 338-7845
E-mail: soeinfo@lmu.edu
Financial aid: (310) 338-2753
Application deadline: 06/15
Tuition: full time: $1,009/credit hour; part time: $1,009/credit hour
Room/board/expenses: $19,379
Full-time enrollment: 983
doctoral students: 7%; master's students: 88%; education specialists: 5%; men: 23%; women: 77%; minorities: 55%; international: 3%
Part-time enrollment: 189
doctoral students: 0%; master's students: 100%; education specialists: 0%; men: 25%; women: 75%; minorities: 58%; international: 1%
Acceptance rate (master's): 25%
Acceptance rate (doctoral): 40%
Entrance test required: GRE
Avg. GRE (of all entering students with scores): quantitative: 152; verbal: 152
Research assistantships: 27
Students reporting specialty: 100%
Students specializing in: admin.: 11%; counseling: 14%; educational psych: 3%; elementary: 23%; secondary: 25%; special: 9%; other: 18%

Mills College

5000 MacArthur Boulevard
Oakland, CA 94613
http://www.mills.edu/
Private
Admissions: (510) 430-3309
E-mail: grad-studies@mills.edu
Financial aid: (510) 430-2000
Application deadline: 12/31
Tuition: full time: $29,930; part time: $7,214/credit hour
Room/board/expenses: N/A
Full-time enrollment: 164
doctoral students: 13%; master's students: 87%; education specialists: N/A; men: 10%; women: 90%; minorities: 8%; international: 1%
Part-time enrollment: 56
doctoral students: 46%; master's students: 54%; education specialists: N/A; men: 9%; women: 91%; minorities: 63%; international: N/A
Acceptance rate (master's): 55%
Acceptance rate (doctoral): 73%
Entrance test required: N/A

Avg. GRE (of all entering students with scores): quantitative: N/A; verbal: N/A
Research assistantships: 39
Students reporting specialty: 0%
Students specializing in: N/A

Pepperdine University[1]

6100 Center Drive, Fifth Floor
Los Angeles, CA 90045-4301
http://gsep.pepperdine.edu/
Private
Admissions: (310) 568-5744
E-mail: gsepdad@pepperdine.edu
Financial aid: (310) 568-5735
Tuition: N/A
Room/board expenses: N/A
Enrollment: N/A

San Diego State University

5500 Campanile Drive
San Diego, CA 92182
http://edweb.sdsu.edu/
Public
Admissions: (619) 594-6336
E-mail: barata@mail.sdsu.edu
Financial aid: (619) 594-6323
Application deadline: N/A
In-state tuition: full time: $7,844; part time: $5,012
Out-of-state tuition: full time: $372/credit hour
Room/board/expenses: $16,714
Full-time enrollment: 351
doctoral students: 10%; master's students: 79%; education specialists: 11%; men: 27%; women: 73%; minorities: 58%; international: 6%
Part-time enrollment: 286
doctoral students: 21%; master's students: 78%; education specialists: 0%; men: 24%; women: 76%; minorities: 45%; international: 5%
Acceptance rate (master's): 48%
Acceptance rate (doctoral): 50%
Entrance test required: GRE
Avg. GRE (of all entering students with scores): quantitative: 145; verbal: 149
Research assistantships: 22
Students reporting specialty: 53%
Students specializing in: admin.: 26%; counseling: 28%; curriculum/instr.: 13%; policy: 1%; educational tech.: 8%; special: 13%; technical (vocational): 0%; other: 12%

San Francisco State University[1]

1600 Holloway Avenue
San Francisco, CA 94132
http://www.sfsu.edu/~gradstdy
Public
Admissions: (415) 338-2234
E-mail: gradstdy@sfsu.edu
Financial aid: (415) 338-7000
Tuition: N/A
Room/board expenses: N/A
Enrollment: N/A

Stanford University

485 Lasuen Mall
Stanford, CA 94305-3096
http://ed.stanford.edu
Private
Admissions: (650) 723-4794
E-mail: info@suse.stanford.edu
Financial aid: (650) 723-4794
Application deadline: 12/04
Tuition: full time: $41,787; part time: N/A
Room/board/expenses: $21,945
Full-time enrollment: 380
doctoral students: 49%; master's students: 51%; education

specialists: N/A; men: 35%; women: 65%; minorities: 37%; international: 13%
Part-time enrollment: N/A
doctoral students: N/A; master's students: N/A; education specialists: N/A; men: N/A; women: N/A; minorities: N/A; international: N/A
Acceptance rate (master's): 33%
Acceptance rate (doctoral): 6%
Entrance test required: GRE
Avg. GRE (of all entering students with scores): quantitative: 157; verbal: 160
Research assistantships: 446
Students reporting specialty: 78%
Students specializing in: admin.: 26%; curriculum/instr.: 47%; evaluation/research/statistics: 12%; social/philosophical foundations: 54%; policy: 25%; educational tech.: 16%; educational psych: 14%; elementary: 12%; higher education admin.: 5%; junior high: 37%; secondary: 37%; special: 28%; technical (vocational): 28%; instructional media design: 16%

University of California–Berkeley

1600 Tolman Hall, MC #1670
Berkeley, CA 94720-1670
http://gse.berkeley.edu
Public
Admissions: (510) 642-0841
E-mail: gse_info@berkeley.edu
Financial aid: (510) 643-1720
Application deadline: 12/04
In-state tuition: full time: $15,180; part time: N/A
Out-of-state tuition: full time: $30,282
Room/board/expenses: $21,574
Full-time enrollment: 344
doctoral students: 70%; master's students: 30%; education specialists: N/A; men: 31%; women: 69%; minorities: 44%; international: 9%
Part-time enrollment: N/A
doctoral students: N/A; master's students: N/A; education specialists: N/A; men: N/A; women: N/A; minorities: N/A; international: N/A
Acceptance rate (master's): 30%
Acceptance rate (doctoral): 17%
Entrance test required: GRE
Avg. GRE (of all entering students with scores): quantitative: 152; verbal: 159
Research assistantships: 107
Students reporting specialty: 100%
Students specializing in: admin.: 17%; evaluation/research/statistics: 7%; social/philosophical foundations: 9%; policy: 11%; educational psych: 15%; elementary: 5%; secondary: 12%; special: 3%; other: 21%

University of California–Davis

School of Education
1 Shields Avenue
Davis, CA 95616
http://education.ucdavis.edu
Public
Admissions: (530) 752-5887
E-mail: eduadvising@ucdavis.edu
Financial aid: (530) 752-2396
Application deadline: rolling
In-state tuition: full time: $30,774; part time: $25,164
Out-of-state tuition: full time: $45,876
Room/board/expenses: $17,177
Full-time enrollment: 146
doctoral students: 92%; master's students: 8%; education

specialists: N/A; men: 30%; women: 70%; minorities: 42%; international: 2%
Part-time enrollment: 132
doctoral students: 13%; master's students: 87%; education specialists: N/A; men: 24%; women: 76%; minorities: 34%; international: N/A
Acceptance rate (master's): 50%
Acceptance rate (doctoral): 34%
Entrance test required: GRE
Avg. GRE (of all entering students with scores): quantitative: 149; verbal: 154
Research assistantships: 86
Students reporting specialty: 0%
Students specializing in: N/A

University of California–Irvine

3200 Education
Irvine, CA 92697-5500
http://www.gse.uci.edu/
Public
Admissions: (949) 824-7465
E-mail: judi.conroy@uci.edu
Financial aid: (949) 824-5337
Application deadline: rolling
In-state tuition: full time: $15,230; part time: $9,620
Out-of-state tuition: full time: $30,332
Room/board/expenses: $17,709
Full-time enrollment: 131
doctoral students: 56%; master's students: 44%; education specialists: N/A; men: 27%; women: 73%; minorities: 44%; international: 6%
Part-time enrollment: 5
doctoral students: 20%; master's students: 80%; education specialists: N/A; men: 80%; women: 20%; minorities: 60%; international: N/A
Acceptance rate (master's): 90%
Acceptance rate (doctoral): 13%
Entrance test required: GRE
Avg. GRE (of all entering students with scores): quantitative: 152; verbal: 153
Research assistantships: 36
Students reporting specialty: 100%
Students specializing in: admin.: 3%; other: 97%

University of California–Los Angeles

1009 Moore Hall, MB 951521
Los Angeles, CA 90095-1521
http://www.gseis.ucla.edu
Public
Admissions: (310) 825-8326
E-mail: info@gseis.ucla.edu
Financial aid: (310) 206-0400
Application deadline: 12/02
In-state tuition: full time: $14,809; part time: N/A
Out-of-state tuition: full time: $18,691
Room/board/expenses: $20,424
Full-time enrollment: 795
doctoral students: 53%; master's students: 47%; education specialists: N/A; men: 31%; women: 69%; minorities: 60%; international: 4%
Part-time enrollment: N/A
doctoral students: N/A; master's students: N/A; education specialists: N/A; men: N/A; women: N/A; minorities: N/A; international: N/A
Acceptance rate (master's): 62%
Acceptance rate (doctoral): 29%
Entrance test required: GRE
Avg. GRE (of all entering students with scores): quantitative: 152; verbal: 154
Research assistantships: 130
Students reporting specialty: 99%

Students specializing in: admin.: 14%; counseling: 2%; curriculum/instr.: 3%; evaluation/research/statistics: 5%; social/philosophical foundations: 11%; policy: 15%; educational tech.: 1%; educational psych: 7%; elementary: 12%; higher education admin.: 14%; secondary: 23%; special: 3%; instructional media design: 1%

University of California–Riverside

1207 Sproul Hall
Riverside, CA 92521
http://www.education.ucr.edu
Public
Admissions: (951) 827-6362
E-mail: edgrad@ucr.edu
Financial aid: (951) 827-6362
Application deadline: N/A
In-state tuition: full time: $14,647; part time: N/A
Out-of-state tuition: full time: $29,749
Room/board/expenses: $18,000
Full-time enrollment: 168
doctoral students: 57%; master's students: 43%; education specialists: N/A; men: 32%; women: 68%; minorities: 45%; international: 5%
Part-time enrollment: N/A
doctoral students: N/A; master's students: N/A; education specialists: N/A; men: N/A; women: N/A; minorities: N/A; international: N/A
Acceptance rate (master's): 57%
Acceptance rate (doctoral): 43%
Entrance test required: GRE
Avg. GRE (of all entering students with scores): quantitative: 152; verbal: 152
Research assistantships: 24
Students reporting specialty: 100%
Students specializing in: admin.: 3%; counseling: 12%; curriculum/instr.: 11%; educational psych: 10%; elementary: 11%; higher education admin.: 16%; secondary: 25%; special: 13%

University of California–Santa Barbara (Gevirtz)

Phelps Hall 1190
Santa Barbara, CA 93106-9490
http://www.education.ucsb.edu
Public
Admissions: (805) 893-2137
E-mail: sao@education.ucsb.edu
Financial aid: (805) 893-2432
Application deadline: N/A
In-state tuition: full time: $15,497; part time: N/A
Out-of-state tuition: full time: $30,599
Room/board/expenses: $20,726
Full-time enrollment: 344
doctoral students: 70%; master's students: 27%; education specialists: 3%; men: 22%; women: 78%; minorities: 37%; international: 8%
Part-time enrollment: N/A
doctoral students: N/A; master's students: N/A; education specialists: N/A; men: N/A; women: N/A; minorities: N/A; international: N/A
Acceptance rate (master's): 57%
Acceptance rate (doctoral): 15%
Entrance test required: GRE
Avg. GRE (of all entering students with scores): quantitative: 149; verbal: 153
Research assistantships: 108
Students reporting specialty: 100%
Students specializing in: admin.: 3%; counseling: 15%; curriculum/instr.: 16%; evaluation/research/statistics: 3%; social/philosophical foundations: 14%; policy: 9%; elementary: 9%; secondary: 8%; special: 11%; other: 13%

University of California–Santa Cruz

1156 High Street
Santa Cruz, CA 95064
http://www.graddiv.ucsc.edu/
Public
Admissions: (831) 459-5905
E-mail: gradadm@ucsc.edu
Financial aid: (831) 459-2963
Application deadline: N/A
In-state tuition: full time: $16,257; part time: $10,161
Out-of-state tuition: full time: $19,167
Room/board/expenses: $22,140
Full-time enrollment: 90
doctoral students: 32%; master's students: 68%; education specialists: N/A; men: 29%; women: 71%; minorities: 43%; international: N/A
Part-time enrollment: 3
doctoral students: 100%; master's students: 0%; education specialists: N/A; men: N/A; women: 100%; minorities: N/A; international: N/A
Acceptance rate (master's): 80%
Acceptance rate (doctoral): 39%
Entrance test required: GRE
Avg. GRE (of all entering students with scores): quantitative: 148; verbal: 158
Research assistantships: 11
Students reporting specialty: 84%
Students specializing in: social/philosophical foundations: 18%; elementary: 33%; higher education admin.: 4%; secondary: 45%

University of La Verne

1950 Third Street
La Verne, CA 91750
http://www.laverne.edu/academics/education/
Private
Admissions: (909) 593-3511
E-mail: gradadm@ulv.edu
Financial aid: (909) 593-3511
Application deadline: rolling
Tuition: full time: $615/credit hour; part time: $615/credit hour
Room/board/expenses: N/A
Full-time enrollment: 459
doctoral students: 27%; master's students: 57%; education specialists: 15%; men: 21%; women: 79%; minorities: 53%; international: N/A
Part-time enrollment: 454
doctoral students: 2%; master's students: 82%; education specialists: 17%; men: 15%; women: 85%; minorities: 57%; international: N/A
Acceptance rate (master's): 50%
Acceptance rate (doctoral): 61%
Entrance test required: N/A
Avg. GRE (of all entering students with scores): quantitative: N/A; verbal: N/A
Research assistantships: 0
Students reporting specialty: 100%
Students specializing in: admin.: 5%; counseling: 22%; educational tech.: 0%; educational psych: 4%; elementary: 16%; higher education admin.: 10%; secondary: 13%; special: 11%; other: 20%

University of San Diego

5998 Alcala Park
San Diego, CA 92110-2492
http://www.sandiego.edu/soles/
Private
Admissions: (619) 260-4506
E-mail: grads@sandiego.edu
Financial aid: (619) 260-4514
Application deadline: 03/01
Tuition: full time: $1,280/credit hour; part time: $1,280/credit hour
Room/board/expenses: $16,743
Full-time enrollment: 310
doctoral students: 15%; master's students: 85%; education specialists: N/A; men: 19%; women: 81%; minorities: 32%; international: 8%
Part-time enrollment: 206
doctoral students: 20%; master's students: 80%; education specialists: N/A; men: 26%; women: 74%; minorities: 34%; international: 2%
Acceptance rate (master's): 58%
Acceptance rate (doctoral): 46%
Entrance test required: GRE
Avg. GRE (of all entering students with scores): quantitative: 149; verbal: 154
Research assistantships: 15
Students reporting specialty: 100%
Students specializing in: admin.: 38%; counseling: 17%; curriculum/instr.: 16%; elementary: 13%; higher education admin.: 5%; secondary: 1%; special: 5%; other: 19%

University of San Francisco

2130 Fulton Street
San Francisco, CA 94117-1080
http://www.usfca.edu
Private
Admissions: (415) 422-6563
E-mail: graduate@usfca.edu
Financial aid: (415) 422-6303
Application deadline: N/A
Tuition: full time: $1,035/credit hour; part time: $1,035/credit hour
Room/board/expenses: $19,440
Full-time enrollment: 764
doctoral students: 14%; master's students: 86%; education specialists: N/A; men: 21%; women: 79%; minorities: 38%; international: 5%
Part-time enrollment: 195
doctoral students: 48%; master's students: 52%; education specialists: N/A; men: 30%; women: 70%; minorities: 41%; international: 6%
Acceptance rate (master's): 60%
Acceptance rate (doctoral): 65%
Entrance test required: GRE
Avg. GRE (of all entering students with scores): quantitative: N/A; verbal: N/A
Research assistantships: 19
Students reporting specialty: 100%
Students specializing in: admin.: 3%; counseling: 6%; curriculum/instr.: 6%; educational psych: 23%; elementary: 15%; higher education admin.: 13%; secondary: 6%; special: 3%; instructional media design: 2%; other: 24%

University of Southern California (Rossier)

3470 Trousdale Parkway
Waite Phillips Hall
Los Angeles, CA 90089-0031
http://rossier.usc.edu
Private
Admissions: (213) 740-0224
E-mail: soeinfo@usc.edu
Financial aid: (213) 740-1111
Application deadline: rolling
Tuition: full time: $1,473/credit hour; part time: $1,473/credit hour
Room/board/expenses: $21,547
Full-time enrollment: 798
doctoral students: 4%; master's students: 96%; education specialists: N/A; men: 23%; women: 77%; minorities: 46%; international: 7%
Part-time enrollment: 1,195
doctoral students: 53%; master's students: 47%; education specialists: N/A; men: 33%; women: 67%; minorities: 49%; international: 3%
Acceptance rate (master's): 68%
Acceptance rate (doctoral): 16%
Entrance test required: GRE
Avg. GRE (of all entering students with scores): quantitative: 151; verbal: 153
Research assistantships: 46
Students reporting specialty: 100%
Students specializing in: admin.: 31%; counseling: 3%; curriculum/instr.: 1%; policy: 3%; elementary: 13%; higher education admin.: 5%; secondary: 28%; other: 17%

University of the Pacific

3601 Pacific Avenue
Stockton, CA 95211
http://www.pacific.edu
Private
Admissions: (209) 946-2683
E-mail: gradschool@pacific.edu
Financial aid: (209) 946-2421
Application deadline: rolling
Tuition: full time: $1,303/credit hour; part time: $1,303/credit hour
Room/board/expenses: $13,703
Full-time enrollment: 147
doctoral students: 15%; master's students: 84%; education specialists: 1%; men: 24%; women: 76%; minorities: 31%; international: 22%
Part-time enrollment: 250
doctoral students: 32%; master's students: 66%; education specialists: 2%; men: 27%; women: 73%; minorities: 48%; international: 0%
Acceptance rate (master's): 79%
Acceptance rate (doctoral): 79%
Entrance test required: GRE
Avg. GRE (of all entering students with scores): quantitative: N/A; verbal: N/A
Students reporting specialty: 100%
Students specializing in: admin.: 28%; curriculum/instr.: 56%; educational psych: 5%; elementary: 0%; special: 7%; other: 3%

COLORADO

Colorado State University

Room 209 Education Building
Fort Collins, CO 80523-2015
http://www.colostate.edu/
Public
Admissions: (970) 491-6909
E-mail: gschool@grad.colostate.edu
Financial aid: (970) 491-6321
Application deadline: rolling
In-state tuition: full time: $9,986; part time: N/A
Out-of-state tuition: full time: $22,165
Room/board/expenses: N/A
Full-time enrollment: 111
doctoral students: 25%; master's students: 75%; education specialists: N/A; men: N/A; women: N/A; minorities: N/A; international: N/A
Part-time enrollment: 489
doctoral students: 51%; master's students: 49%; education specialists: N/A; men: N/A; women: N/A; minorities: N/A; international: N/A
Acceptance rate (master's): 31%
Acceptance rate (doctoral): 7%
Entrance test required: GRE
Avg. GRE (of all entering students with scores): quantitative: N/A; verbal: N/A
Research assistantships: 3
Students reporting specialty: 100%
Students specializing in: admin.: 5%; counseling: 7%; curriculum/instr.: 9%; evaluation/research/statistics: 2%; higher education admin.: 29%; secondary: 3%; other: 46%

University of Colorado–Boulder

Campus Box 249
Boulder, CO 80309-0249
http://www.colorado.edu/education
Public
Admissions: (303) 492-6555
E-mail: edadvise@colorado.edu
Financial aid: (303) 492-5091
Application deadline: 01/01
In-state tuition: full time: $11,172; part time: $541/credit hour
Out-of-state tuition: full time: $27,642
Room/board/expenses: $18,372
Full-time enrollment: 170
doctoral students: 46%; master's students: 54%; education specialists: N/A; men: 35%; women: 65%; minorities: 28%; international: 1%
Part-time enrollment: 184
doctoral students: 8%; master's students: 92%; education specialists: N/A; men: 11%; women: 89%; minorities: 29%; international: 2%
Acceptance rate (master's): 82%
Acceptance rate (doctoral): 16%
Entrance test required: GRE
Avg. GRE (of all entering students with scores): quantitative: 151; verbal: 159
Research assistantships: 236
Students reporting specialty: 100%
Students specializing in: curriculum/instr.: 23%; evaluation/research/statistics: 2%; social/philosophical foundations: 13%; educational psych: 3%; secondary: 8%; special: 6%; other: 45%

University of Colorado–Denver

PO Box 173364, Campus Box 106
Denver, CO 80217-3364
http://www.ucdenver.edu/education
Public
Admissions: (303) 315-6300
E-mail: education@ucdenver.edu
Financial aid: (303) 556-2886
Application deadline: rolling
In-state tuition: full time: $349/credit hour; part time: $349/credit hour
Out-of-state tuition: full time: $1,160/credit hour
Room/board/expenses: $14,707
Full-time enrollment: 870
doctoral students: 4%; master's students: 86%; education specialists: 9%; men: 16%; women: 84%; minorities: 12%; international: 3%
Part-time enrollment: 444
doctoral students: 3%; master's students: 94%; education

specialists: 3%; men: 20%; women: 80%; minorities: 12%; international: 0%
Acceptance rate (master's): 71%
Acceptance rate (doctoral): 56%
Entrance test required: GRE
Avg. GRE (of all entering students with scores): quantitative: N/A; verbal: N/A
Research assistantships: 24
Students reporting specialty: 100%
Students specializing in: admin.: 10%; counseling: 7%; curriculum/instr.: 11%; evaluation/research/statistics: 1%; policy: 1%; educational tech.: 7%; educational psych: 11%; elementary: 24%; secondary: 16%; special: 12%; instructional media design: 2%; other: 28%

University of Denver (Morgridge)
Graduate Office, A. Hyde Building
Denver, CO 80208
http://www.du.edu/education/
Private
Admissions: (303) 871-2509
E-mail: edinfo@du.edu
Financial aid: (303) 871-2509
Application deadline: rolling
Tuition: full time: $38,478; part time: $1,062/credit hour
Room/board/expenses: N/A
Full-time enrollment: 374
doctoral students: 23%; master's students: 64%; education specialists: 13%; men: 21%; women: 79%; minorities: 18%; international: 3%
Part-time enrollment: 362
doctoral students: 40%; master's students: 60%; education specialists: 0%; men: 25%; women: 75%; minorities: 22%; international: 2%
Acceptance rate (master's): 74%
Acceptance rate (doctoral): 41%
Entrance test required: GRE
Avg. GRE (of all entering students with scores): quantitative: 149; verbal: 154
Students reporting specialty: 0%
Students specializing in: N/A

University of Northern Colorado
McKee 125
Greeley, CO 80639
http://www.unco.edu/grad/index.html
Public
Admissions: (970) 351-2831
E-mail: gradsch@unco.edu
Financial aid: (970) 351-2502
Application deadline: rolling
In-state tuition: full time: $8,806; part time: $426/credit hour
Out-of-state tuition: full time: $18,742
Room/board/expenses: $14,990
Full-time enrollment: 446
doctoral students: 35%; master's students: 59%; education specialists: 6%; men: 26%; women: 74%; minorities: 19%; international: 10%
Part-time enrollment: 655
doctoral students: 25%; master's students: 64%; education specialists: 11%; men: 21%; women: 79%; minorities: 15%; international: 3%
Acceptance rate (master's): 87%
Acceptance rate (doctoral): 50%
Entrance test required: GRE
Avg. GRE (of all entering students with scores): quantitative: N/A; verbal: N/A
Students reporting specialty: 62%
Students specializing in: admin.: 25%; counseling: 7%; evaluation/research/statistics: 2%; educational psych: 20%; elementary: 3%; special: 40%; other: 4%

CONNECTICUT

Central Connecticut State University
1615 Stanley Street
New Britain, CT 06050
http://www.ccsu.edu/page.cfm?p=532
Public
Admissions: (860) 832-2350
E-mail: graduateadmissions@mail.ccsu.edu
Financial aid: (860) 832-2200
Application deadline: 06/01
In-state tuition: full time: $9,307; part time: $498/credit hour
Out-of-state tuition: full time: $18,839
Room/board/expenses: $13,052
Full-time enrollment: 217
doctoral students: 0%; master's students: 100%; education specialists: N/A; men: 22%; women: 78%; minorities: 24%; international: 3%
Part-time enrollment: 610
doctoral students: 7%; master's students: 93%; education specialists: N/A; men: 26%; women: 74%; minorities: 16%; international: 0%
Acceptance rate (master's): 58%
Acceptance rate (doctoral): N/A
Entrance test required: GRE
Avg. GRE (of all entering students with scores): quantitative: N/A; verbal: N/A
Students reporting specialty: 100%
Students specializing in: admin.: 10%; counseling: 19%; social/philosophical foundations: 1%; elementary: 2%; secondary: 15%; special: 17%; instructional media design: 3%; other: 32%

Southern Connecticut State University
501 Crescent Street
New Haven, CT 06515
http://www.southernct.edu/
Public
Admissions: (203) 392-5240
E-mail: GradInfo@southernCT.edu
Financial aid: (203) 392-5222
Application deadline: rolling
In-state tuition: full time: $9,477; part time: $539/credit hour
Out-of-state tuition: full time: $19,009
Room/board/expenses: $13,821
Full-time enrollment: 327
doctoral students: 3%; master's students: 85%; education specialists: 13%; men: 17%; women: 83%; minorities: 9%; international: N/A
Part-time enrollment: 757
doctoral students: 6%; master's students: 61%; education specialists: 33%; men: 20%; women: 80%; minorities: 11%; international: 0%
Acceptance rate (master's): 21%
Acceptance rate (doctoral): 29%
Entrance test required: GRE
Avg. GRE (of all entering students with scores): quantitative: N/A; verbal: N/A
Research assistantships: 12
Students reporting specialty: 0%
Students specializing in: N/A

University of Bridgeport
126 Park Avenue
Bridgeport, CT 06604
http://www.bridgeport.edu/
Private
Admissions: (203) 576-4552
E-mail: admit@bridgeport.edu
Financial aid: (203) 576-4568
Application deadline: rolling
Tuition: full time: $620/credit hour; part time: $620/credit hour
Room/board/expenses: $15,150
Full-time enrollment: 240
doctoral students: 7%; master's students: 83%; education specialists: 10%; men: 24%; women: 76%; minorities: 23%; international: 8%
Part-time enrollment: 368
doctoral students: 4%; master's students: 67%; education specialists: 29%; men: 32%; women: 68%; minorities: 27%; international: 2%
Acceptance rate (master's): 57%
Acceptance rate (doctoral): 47%
Entrance test required: N/A
Avg. GRE (of all entering students with scores): quantitative: N/A; verbal: N/A
Students reporting specialty: 100%
Students specializing in: admin.: 22%; counseling: 19%; educational tech.: 1%; elementary: 35%; junior high: 2%; secondary: 15%; other: 6%

University of Connecticut (Neag)
249 Glenbrook Road
Storrs, CT 06269-2064
http://www.grad.uconn.edu
Public
Admissions: (860) 486-3617
E-mail: gradschool@uconn.edu
Financial aid: (860) 486-2819
Application deadline: rolling
In-state tuition: full time: $12,786; part time: $599/credit hour
Out-of-state tuition: full time: $29,994
Room/board/expenses: $18,170
Full-time enrollment: 503
doctoral students: 35%; master's students: 65%; education specialists: N/A; men: 33%; women: 67%; minorities: 12%; international: 5%
Part-time enrollment: 185
doctoral students: 43%; master's students: 57%; education specialists: N/A; men: 26%; women: 74%; minorities: 15%; international: 4%
Acceptance rate (master's): 38%
Acceptance rate (doctoral): 39%
Entrance test required: GRE
Avg. GRE (of all entering students with scores): quantitative: 153; verbal: 156
Research assistantships: 66
Students reporting specialty: 99%
Students specializing in: admin.: 9%; counseling: 7%; curriculum/instr.: 8%; evaluation/research/statistics: 2%; policy: 0%; educational psych: 22%; elementary: 6%; higher education admin.: 5%; secondary: 15%; special: 1%; instructional media design: 1%; other: 23%

University of Hartford
200 Bloomfield Avenue
West Hartford, CT 06117
http://www.hartford.edu/enhp
Private
Admissions: (860) 768-4371
E-mail: gradstudy@hartford.edu
Financial aid: (860) 768-4296
Application deadline: rolling
Tuition: full time: $11,477; part time: $521/credit hour
Room/board/expenses: N/A
Full-time enrollment: 95
doctoral students: 46%; master's students: 54%; education specialists: N/A; men: 21%; women: 79%; minorities: 15%; international: 2%
Part-time enrollment: 105
doctoral students: 25%; master's students: 75%; education specialists: N/A; men: 18%; women: 82%; minorities: 18%; international: 1%
Acceptance rate (master's): 60%
Acceptance rate (doctoral): 55%
Entrance test required: GRE
Avg. GRE (of all entering students with scores): quantitative: 144; verbal: 150
Research assistantships: 10
Students reporting specialty: 100%
Students specializing in: counseling: 16%; educational tech.: 6%; elementary: 15%; higher education admin.: 35%; other: 29%

Western Connecticut State University[1]
181 White Street
Danbury, CT 06810
http://www.wcsu.edu
Public
Admissions: (203) 837-9000
Financial aid: (203) 837-8528
Tuition: N/A
Room/board expenses: N/A
Enrollment: N/A

DELAWARE

University of Delaware
113 Willard Hall Education Building
Newark, DE 19716
http://www.udel.edu/education/
Public
Admissions: (302) 831-2129
E-mail: marym@udel.edu
Financial aid: (302) 831-2129
Application deadline: N/A
In-state tuition: full time: $27,982; part time: $1,513/credit hour
Out-of-state tuition: full time: $27,982
Room/board/expenses: $14,439
Full-time enrollment: 130
doctoral students: 53%; master's students: 41%; education specialists: 6%; men: 18%; women: 82%; minorities: 16%; international: 22%
Part-time enrollment: 233
doctoral students: 60%; master's students: 37%; education specialists: 3%; men: 38%; women: 62%; minorities: 16%; international: 0%
Acceptance rate (master's): 67%
Acceptance rate (doctoral): 42%
Entrance test required: GRE
Avg. GRE (of all entering students with scores): quantitative: 153; verbal: 155
Research assistantships: 19
Students reporting specialty: 0%
Students specializing in: N/A

Wilmington University[1]
320 DuPont Highway
Wilmington, DE 19720
http://www.wilmu.edu
Private
Admissions: (302) 295-1184
E-mail: gradadmissions@wilmu.edu
Financial aid: (302) 328-9437
Tuition: N/A
Room/board expenses: N/A
Enrollment: N/A

DISTRICT OF COLUMBIA

American University
4400 Massachusetts Avenue NW
Washington, DC 20016-8030
http://www.american.edu/education
Private
Admissions: (202) 885-3621
E-mail: casgrad@american.edu
Financial aid: (202) 885-6100
Application deadline: 02/01
Tuition: full time: $25,612; part time: $1,399/credit hour
Room/board/expenses: $18,892
Full-time enrollment: 51
doctoral students: N/A; master's students: 100%; education specialists: N/A; men: 16%; women: 84%; minorities: 14%; international: 6%
Part-time enrollment: 131
doctoral students: N/A; master's students: 100%; education specialists: N/A; men: 25%; women: 75%; minorities: 31%; international: N/A
Acceptance rate (master's): 78%
Acceptance rate (doctoral): N/A
Entrance test required: GRE
Avg. GRE (of all entering students with scores): quantitative: 149; verbal: 154
Students reporting specialty: 100%
Students specializing in: admin.: 0%; curriculum/instr.: 10%; policy: 16%; elementary: 14%; secondary: 21%; special: 16%; other: 27%

Catholic University of America
Cardinal Station
Washington, DC 20064
http://admissions.cua.edu/graduate/
Private
Admissions: (800) 673-2772
E-mail: cua-admissions@cua.edu
Financial aid: (202) 319-5307
Application deadline: rolling
Tuition: full time: $36,720; part time: $1,420/credit hour
Room/board/expenses: $20,210
Full-time enrollment: 2
doctoral students: N/A; master's students: 100%; education specialists: N/A; men: 50%; women: 50%; minorities: N/A; international: N/A
Part-time enrollment: 43
doctoral students: 42%; master's students: 40%; education specialists: 19%; men: 19%; women: 81%; minorities: 26%; international: 2%
Acceptance rate (master's): 55%
Acceptance rate (doctoral): 88%
Entrance test required: GRE
Avg. GRE (of all entering students with scores): quantitative: N/A; verbal: N/A
Research assistantships: 2
Students reporting specialty: 78%
Students specializing in: admin.: 31%; educational psych: 19%; secondary: 6%; special: 22%; other: 36%

Gallaudet University
800 Florida Avenue NE
Washington, DC 20002-3695
http://gradschool.gallaudet.edu
Private
Admissions: (202) 651-5717
E-mail: graduate.school@gallaudet.edu
Financial aid: (202) 651-5290
Application deadline: rolling
Tuition: full time: $14,056; part time: $760/credit hour
Room/board/expenses: $17,332

Full-time enrollment: 85
doctoral students: 8%; master's
students: 79%; education
specialists: 13%; men: 18%;
women: 82%; minorities: 25%;
international: 7%
Part-time enrollment: 32
doctoral students: 53%; master's
students: 34%; education
specialists: 13%; men: 16%;
women: 84%; minorities: 34%;
international: 16%
Acceptance rate (master's): 58%
Acceptance rate (doctoral): 44%
Entrance test required: GRE
Avg. GRE (of all entering students
with scores): quantitative: N/A;
verbal: N/A
Research assistantships: 3
Students reporting specialty: 100%
Students specializing in:
counseling: 15%; special: 51%;
other: 33%

George Washington
University
2134 G Street NW
Washington, DC 20052
http://gsehd.gwu.edu
Private
Admissions: (202) 994-9283
E-mail: gsehdadm@gwu.edu
Financial aid: (202) 994-6822
Application deadline: rolling
Tuition: full time: $1,310/credit
hour; part time: $1,310/credit hour
Room/board expenses: $23,075
Full-time enrollment: 454
doctoral students: 26%; master's
students: 72%; education
specialists: 1%; men: 20%;
women: 80%; minorities: 27%;
international: 11%
Part-time enrollment: 960
doctoral students: 50%; master's
students: 44%; education
specialists: 7%; men: 28%;
women: 72%; minorities: 33%;
international: 3%
Acceptance rate (master's): 70%
Acceptance rate (doctoral): 49%
Entrance test required: GRE
Avg. GRE (of all entering students
with scores): quantitative: 150;
verbal: 154
Research assistantships: 26
Students reporting specialty: 96%
Students specializing in: admin.:
22%; counseling: 29%; curricu-
lum/instr.: 4%; educational tech.:
3%; elementary: 2%; higher education admin.: 10%; secondary:
3%; special: 17%; instructional
media design: 2%; other: 8%

Howard University
2441 Fourth Street NW
Washington, DC 20059
http://www.
howard.edu/schooleducation
Private
Admissions: (202) 806-7340
E-mail: hugsadmission@
howard.edu
Financial aid: (202) 806-2820
Application deadline: rolling
Tuition: full time: $30,323; part
time: $1,615/credit hour
Room/board expenses: $24,373
Full-time enrollment: 167
doctoral students: 51%; master's
students: 49%; education
specialists: N/A; men: 19%;
women: 81%; minorities: 81%;
international: 14%
Part-time enrollment: 121
doctoral students: 54%; master's
students: 46%; education
specialists: N/A; men: 40%;
women: 60%; minorities: 88%;
international: 9%
Acceptance rate (master's): 75%
Acceptance rate (doctoral): 62%
Entrance test required: GRE

Avg. GRE (of all entering students
with scores): quantitative: N/A;
verbal: N/A
Research assistantships: 17
Students reporting specialty: 100%
Students specializing in: admin.:
31%; counseling: 40%; educational psych: 8%; elementary:
9%; secondary: 7%; special: 3%;
other: 2%

FLORIDA

Barry University
(Dominican)[1]
11300 N.E. Second Avenue
Miami Shores, FL 33161-6695
http://www.barry.edu/ed/
Private
Admissions: (305) 899-3100
E-mail:
admissions@mail.barry.edu
Financial aid: (305) 899-3673
Tuition: N/A
Room/board expenses: N/A
Enrollment: N/A

Florida A&M
University
Gore Education Center
Tallahassee, FL 32307
http://www.famu.edu/education/
Public
Admissions: (850) 599-3315
E-mail: adm@famu.edu
Financial aid: (850) 599-3730
Application deadline: 04/01
In-state tuition: full time: $334/
credit hour; part time: $334/
credit hour
Out-of-state tuition: full time: $951/
credit hour
Room/board expenses: $14,564
Full-time enrollment: 47
doctoral students: 30%; master's
students: 66%; education
specialists: 4%; men: 34%;
women: 66%; minorities: 100%;
international: N/A
Part-time enrollment: 64
doctoral students: 44%; master's
students: 55%; education
specialists: 2%; men: 25%;
women: 75%; minorities: 95%;
international: N/A
Acceptance rate (master's): 55%
Acceptance rate (doctoral): 57%
Entrance test required: GRE
Avg. GRE (of all entering students
with scores): quantitative: N/A;
verbal: N/A
Research assistantships: 0
Students reporting specialty: 100%
Students specializing in:
secondary: 9%; other: 91%

Florida Atlantic
University
777 Glades Road, PO Box 3091
Boca Raton, FL 33431-0991
http://www.
coe.fau.edu/menu.htm
Public
Admissions: (561) 297-3624
E-mail: gradadm@fau.edu
Financial aid: (561) 297-3131
Application deadline: N/A
In-state tuition: full time: $369/
credit hour; part time: $369/
credit hour
Out-of-state tuition: full time:
$1,024/credit hour
Room/board expenses: $16,506
Full-time enrollment: 363
doctoral students: 12%; master's
students: 81%; education
specialists: 7%; men: 23%;
women: 77%; minorities: 32%;
international: 3%

Part-time enrollment: 602
doctoral students: 32%; master's
students: 62%; education
specialists: 6%; men: 24%;
women: 76%; minorities: 29%;
international: 1%
Acceptance rate (master's): 36%
Acceptance rate (doctoral): 29%
Entrance test required: GRE
Avg. GRE (of all entering students
with scores): quantitative: N/A;
verbal: N/A
Research assistantships: 50
Students reporting specialty: 100%
Students specializing in: admin.:
36%; counseling: 15%; curriculum/
instr.: 17%; social/philosophical
foundations: 3%; elementary: 4%;
special: 4%; other: 20%

Florida Institute
of Technology
150 W. University Boulevard
Melbourne, FL 32901
http://www.fit.edu
Private
Admissions: (800) 944-4348
E-mail: grad-admissions@fit.edu
Financial aid: (321) 674-8070
Application deadline: rolling
Tuition: full time: $1,123/credit
hour; part time: $1,123/credit hour
Room/board expenses: $16,470
Full-time enrollment: 40
doctoral students: 23%; master's
students: 78%; education
specialists: N/A; men: 33%;
women: 68%; minorities: 13%;
international: 53%
Part-time enrollment: 25
doctoral students: 60%; master's
students: 40%; education
specialists: N/A; men: 52%;
women: 48%; minorities: 24%;
international: 12%
Acceptance rate (master's): 63%
Acceptance rate (doctoral): 52%
Entrance test required: N/A
Avg. GRE (of all entering students
with scores): quantitative: N/A;
verbal: N/A
Research assistantships: 0
Students reporting specialty: 100%
Students specializing in: admin.:
61%; counseling: 26%; educational psych: 3%; secondary: 1%;
other: 9%

Florida International
University
11200 S.W. Eighth Street
Miami, FL 33199
http://education.fiu.edu
Public
Admissions: (305) 348-7442
E-mail: gradadm@fiu.edu
Financial aid: (305) 348-7272
Application deadline: 06/01
In-state tuition: full time: $422/
credit hour; part time: $422/
credit hour
Out-of-state tuition: full time: $926/
credit hour
Room/board expenses: $18,426
Full-time enrollment: 404
doctoral students: 24%; master's
students: 73%; education
specialists: 3%; men: 26%;
women: 74%; minorities: 76%;
international: 8%
Part-time enrollment: 595
doctoral students: 12%; master's
students: 79%; education
specialists: 9%; men: 21%;
women: 79%; minorities: 80%;
international: 1%
Acceptance rate (master's): 75%
Acceptance rate (doctoral): 58%
Entrance test required: GRE
Avg. GRE (of all entering students
with scores): quantitative: 147;
verbal: 151
Research assistantships: 10
Students reporting specialty: 100%

Students specializing in: admin.:
1%; counseling: 2%; curriculum/
instr.: 20%; higher education
admin.: 15%; special: 5%; other:
56%

Florida State
University
Suite 1100 Stone Building
1114 W. Call Street
Tallahassee, FL 32306-4450
http://www.coe.fsu.edu
Public
Admissions: (850) 644-6200
E-mail:
admissions@admin.fsu.edu
Financial aid: (850) 644-0539
Application deadline: rolling
In-state tuition: full time: $404/
credit hour; part time: $404/
credit hour
Out-of-state tuition: full time:
$1,035/credit hour
Room/board/expenses: $14,712
Full-time enrollment: 664
doctoral students: 34%; master's
students: 57%; education
specialists: 9%; men: 35%;
women: 65%; minorities: 43%;
international: 26%
Part-time enrollment: 405
doctoral students: 34%; master's
students: 58%; education
specialists: 9%; men: 35%;
women: 65%; minorities: 30%;
international: 4%
Acceptance rate (master's): 59%
Acceptance rate (doctoral): 36%
Entrance test required: GRE
Avg. GRE (of all entering students
with scores): quantitative: N/A;
verbal: N/A
Research assistantships: 126
Students reporting specialty: 100%
Students specializing in: admin.:
12%; counseling: 11%; evaluation/
research/statistics: 3%; social/
philosophical foundations: 4%;
educational psych: 7%; elementary: 3%; higher education admin.:
10%; special: 9%; instructional
media design: 12%; other: 29%

Lynn University
3601 North Military Trail
Boca Raton, FL 33431
http://www.lynn.edu
Private
Admissions: (561) 237-7900
E-mail: admission@lynn.edu
Financial aid: (561) 237-7816
Application deadline: rolling
Tuition: full time: $640/credit hour;
part time: $640/credit hour
Room/board/expenses: $16,135
Full-time enrollment: 18
doctoral students: N/A; master's
students: 100%; education
specialists: N/A; men: 33%;
women: 67%; minorities: 11%;
international: 11%
Part-time enrollment: 45
doctoral students: 64%; master's
students: 36%; education
specialists: N/A; men: 29%;
women: 71%; minorities: 13%;
international: 11%
Acceptance rate (master's): 100%
Acceptance rate (doctoral): 94%
Entrance test required: N/A
Avg. GRE (of all entering students
with scores): quantitative: N/A;
verbal: N/A
Research assistantships: 1
Students reporting specialty: 100%
Students specializing in: admin.:
79%; special: 21%

Nova Southeastern
University (Fischler)
3301 College Avenue
Fort Lauderdale, FL 33314
http://www.schoolofed.nova.edu
Private
Admissions: (954) 262-8500
Financial aid: (954) 262-3380
Application deadline: rolling
Tuition: full time: $730/credit hour;
part time: $730/credit hour
Room/board expenses: $23,401
Full-time enrollment: N/A
doctoral students: N/A; master's
students: N/A; education
specialists: N/A; men: N/A;
women: N/A; minorities: N/A;
international: N/A
Part-time enrollment: N/A
doctoral students: N/A; master's
students: N/A; education
specialists: N/A; men: N/A;
women: N/A; minorities: N/A;
international: N/A
Acceptance rate (master's): N/A
Acceptance rate (doctoral): N/A
Entrance test required: GRE
Avg. GRE (of all entering students
with scores): quantitative: N/A;
verbal: N/A
Research assistantships: 0
Students reporting specialty: N/A
Students specializing in: N/A

University of
Central Florida
4000 Central Florida Boulevard
Orlando, FL 32816-1250
http://www.graduate.ucf.edu
Public
Admissions: (407) 823-0549
E-mail: graduate@mail.ucf.edu
Financial aid: (407) 823-2827
Application deadline: 07/15
In-state tuition: full time: $357/
credit hour; part time: $357/
credit hour
Out-of-state tuition: full time:
$1,182/credit hour
Room/board/expenses: $14,522
Full-time enrollment: 717
doctoral students: 27%; master's
students: 66%; education
specialists: 6%; men: 24%;
women: 76%; minorities: 26%;
international: 4%
Part-time enrollment: 1,005
doctoral students: 14%; master's
students: 85%; education
specialists: 1%; men: 25%;
women: 75%; minorities: 24%;
international: N/A
Acceptance rate (master's): 60%
Acceptance rate (doctoral): 48%
Entrance test required: GRE
Avg. GRE (of all entering students
with scores): quantitative: N/A;
verbal: N/A
Research assistantships: 16
Students reporting specialty: 100%
Students specializing in: admin.:
16%; counseling: 3%; curriculum/
instr.: 5%; educational tech.: 2%;
educational psych: 2%; elementary: 5%; higher education admin.:
5%; junior high: 2%; secondary:
8%; special: 8%; technical (vocational): 3%; instructional media
design: 6%; other: 34%

University of Florida
140 Norman Hall, PO Box 117040
Gainesville, FL 32611-7040
http://education.ufl.edu/
Public
Admissions: (352) 273-4116
E-mail: tla@coe.ufl.edu
Financial aid: (352) 392-1275
Application deadline: rolling
In-state tuition: full time: $449/
credit hour; part time: $449/
credit hour

Out-of-state tuition: full time: $1,249/credit hour
Room/board/expenses: $15,690
Full-time enrollment: 902
doctoral students: 44%; master's students: 41%; education specialists: 15%; men: 19%; women: 81%; minorities: 22%; international: 7%
Part-time enrollment: 333
doctoral students: 28%; master's students: 56%; education specialists: 16%; men: 17%; women: 83%; minorities: 30%; international: 3%
Acceptance rate (master's): 61%
Acceptance rate (doctoral): 41%
Entrance test required: GRE
Avg. GRE (of all entering students with scores): quantitative: 148; verbal: 154
Research assistantships: 48
Students reporting specialty: 100%
Students specializing in: admin.: 9%; counseling: 6%; curriculum/instr.: 37%; evaluation/research/statistics: 1%; educational psych: 0%; elementary: 9%; higher education admin.: 6%; special: 9%; other: 22%

University of Miami
PO Box 248212
Coral Gables, FL 33124
http://www.education.miami.edu
Private
Admissions: (305) 284-2167
E-mail: soegradadmissions@miami.edu
Financial aid: (305) 284-5212
Application deadline: rolling
Tuition: full time: $1,660/credit hour; part time: $1,660/credit hour
Room/board/expenses: $18,020
Full-time enrollment: 215
doctoral students: 47%; master's students: 53%; education specialists: 0%; men: 36%; women: 64%; minorities: 40%; international: 11%
Part-time enrollment: 93
doctoral students: 4%; master's students: 96%; education specialists: 0%; men: 22%; women: 78%; minorities: 51%; international: 4%
Acceptance rate (master's): 58%
Acceptance rate (doctoral): 16%
Entrance test required: GRE
Avg. GRE (of all entering students with scores): quantitative: 150; verbal: 153
Research assistantships: 39
Students reporting specialty: 100%
Students specializing in: admin.: 6%; evaluation/research/statistics: 3%; higher education admin.: 17%; special: 3%; other: 71%

University of North Florida
1 UNF Drive
Jacksonville, FL 32224-2676
http://www.unf.edu/graduatestudies
Public
Admissions: (904) 620-1360
E-mail: graduatestudies@unf.edu
Financial aid: (904) 620-5555
Application deadline: rolling
In-state tuition: full time: $483/credit hour; part time: $483/credit hour
Out-of-state tuition: full time: $1,041/credit hour
Room/board/expenses: $13,881
Full-time enrollment: 94
doctoral students: 5%; master's students: 95%; education specialists: N/A; men: 13%; women: 87%; minorities: 22%; international: 11%

Part-time enrollment: 325
doctoral students: 31%; master's students: 69%; education specialists: N/A; men: 24%; women: 76%; minorities: 27%; international: 1%
Acceptance rate (master's): 61%
Acceptance rate (doctoral): 27%
Entrance test required: GRE
Avg. GRE (of all entering students with scores): quantitative: 146; verbal: 150
Research assistantships: 10
Students reporting specialty: 100%
Students specializing in: admin.: 45%; counseling: 8%; elementary: 10%; secondary: 1%; special: 21%; other: 14%

University of South Florida
4202 E. Fowler Avenue, EDU 162
Tampa, FL 33620
http://www.grad.usf.edu
Public
Admissions: (813) 974-8800
E-mail: admissions@grad.usf.edu
Financial aid: (813) 974-4700
Application deadline: rolling
In-state tuition: full time: $431/credit hour; part time: $431/credit hour
Out-of-state tuition: full time: $855/credit hour
Room/board/expenses: $15,500
Full-time enrollment: 606
doctoral students: 37%; master's students: 62%; education specialists: 1%; men: 28%; women: 72%; minorities: 29%; international: 10%
Part-time enrollment: 884
doctoral students: 34%; master's students: 64%; education specialists: 2%; men: 30%; women: 70%; minorities: 26%; international: 1%
Acceptance rate (master's): 46%
Acceptance rate (doctoral): 32%
Entrance test required: GRE
Avg. GRE (of all entering students with scores): quantitative: 150; verbal: 155
Research assistantships: 34
Students reporting specialty: 100%
Students specializing in: admin.: 7%; counseling: 3%; curriculum/instr.: 1%; evaluation/research/statistics: 3%; educational tech.: 8%; educational psych: 3%; elementary: 6%; higher education admin.: 4%; junior high: 1%; secondary: 15%; special: 7%; technical (vocational): 4%; other: 37%

University of West Florida
11000 University Parkway
Pensacola, FL 32514-5750
http://uwf.edu
Public
Admissions: (850) 474-2230
E-mail: admissions@uwf.edu
Financial aid: (850) 474-2400
Application deadline: rolling
In-state tuition: full time: $353/credit hour; part time: $353/credit hour
Out-of-state tuition: full time: $1,013/credit hour
Room/board/expenses: $13,718
Full-time enrollment: 145
doctoral students: 12%; master's students: 86%; education specialists: 2%; men: 25%; women: 75%; minorities: 21%; international: 3%
Part-time enrollment: 516
doctoral students: 33%; master's students: 60%; education

specialists: 7%; men: 27%; women: 73%; minorities: 20%; international: N/A
Acceptance rate (master's): 99%
Acceptance rate (doctoral): 88%
Entrance test required: GRE
Avg. GRE (of all entering students with scores): quantitative: N/A; verbal: N/A
Research assistantships: 7
Students reporting specialty: 100%
Students specializing in: admin.: 31%; counseling: 4%; curriculum/instr.: 33%; special: 27%; instructional media design: 3%; other: 1%

GEORGIA

Clark Atlanta University
223 James P. Brawley Drive SW
Atlanta, GA 30314
http://www.cau.edu/
Private
Admissions: (404) 880-6605
E-mail: cauadmissions@cau.edu
Financial aid: (404) 880-8992
Application deadline: rolling
Tuition: full time: $792/credit hour; part time: $792/credit hour
Room/board/expenses: $16,402
Full-time enrollment: 55
doctoral students: 44%; master's students: 56%; education specialists: 0%; men: 18%; women: 82%; minorities: 93%; international: 2%
Part-time enrollment: 62
doctoral students: 53%; master's students: 44%; education specialists: 3%; men: 39%; women: 61%; minorities: 98%; international: N/A
Acceptance rate (master's): 100%
Acceptance rate (doctoral): 92%
Entrance test required: GRE
Avg. GRE (of all entering students with scores): quantitative: N/A; verbal: N/A
Research assistantships: 0
Students reporting specialty: 100%
Students specializing in: admin.: 62%; counseling: 29%; curriculum/instr.: 3%; junior high: 3%; secondary: 3%; other: 1%

Columbus State University
4225 University Ave.
Columbus, GA 31907
http://www.columbusstate.edu
Public
Admissions: (706) 507-8800
Financial aid: (706) 507-8800
Application deadline: 06/30
In-state tuition: full time: $185/credit hour; part time: $185/credit hour
Out-of-state tuition: full time: $740/credit hour
Room/board/expenses: N/A
Full-time enrollment: 197
doctoral students: 2%; master's students: 70%; education specialists: 28%; men: 22%; women: 78%; minorities: 31%; international: 1%
Part-time enrollment: 355
doctoral students: 10%; master's students: 66%; education specialists: 24%; men: 21%; women: 79%; minorities: 35%; international: 1%
Acceptance rate (master's): 60%
Acceptance rate (doctoral): 29%
Entrance test required: GRE
Avg. GRE (of all entering students with scores): quantitative: N/A; verbal: N/A
Students reporting specialty: 89%

Students specializing in: admin.: 18%; counseling: 10%; curriculum/instr.: 13%; elementary: 13%; junior high: 8%; secondary: 23%; special: 13%; instructional media design: 2%

Georgia State University
PO Box 3980
Atlanta, GA 30302-3980
http://education.gsu.edu/coe/
Public
Admissions: (404) 413-8000
E-mail: educadmissions@gsu.edu
Financial aid: (404) 413-2400
Application deadline: N/A
In-state tuition: full time: $8,176; part time: $336/credit hour
Out-of-state tuition: full time: $23,728
Room/board/expenses: $14,357
Full-time enrollment: 841
doctoral students: 21%; master's students: 77%; education specialists: 1%; men: 24%; women: 76%; minorities: 23%; international: 3%
Part-time enrollment: 606
doctoral students: 32%; master's students: 58%; education specialists: 9%; men: 23%; women: 77%; minorities: 29%; international: 0%
Acceptance rate (master's): 61%
Acceptance rate (doctoral): 39%
Entrance test required: GRE
Avg. GRE (of all entering students with scores): quantitative: 147; verbal: 151
Research assistantships: 345
Students reporting specialty: 98%
Students specializing in: admin.: 5%; counseling: 13%; curriculum/instr.: 9%; evaluation/research/statistics: 1%; social/philosophical foundations: 0%; policy: 5%; educational tech.: 4%; educational psych: 3%; elementary: 10%; junior high: 3%; secondary: 13%; special: 17%; instructional media design: 0%; other: 18%

University of Georgia
G-3 Aderhold Hall
Athens, GA 30602-7101
http://www.coe.uga.edu/
Public
Admissions: (706) 542-1739
E-mail: gradadm@uga.edu
Financial aid: (706) 542-6147
Application deadline: rolling
In-state tuition: full time: $9,596; part time: $309/credit hour
Out-of-state tuition: full time: $24,596
Room/board/expenses: $12,070
Full-time enrollment: 952
doctoral students: 47%; master's students: 52%; education specialists: 2%; men: 31%; women: 69%; minorities: 23%; international: 18%
Part-time enrollment: 854
doctoral students: 53%; master's students: 34%; education specialists: 12%; men: 30%; women: 70%; minorities: 27%; international: 2%
Acceptance rate (master's): 40%
Acceptance rate (doctoral): 34%
Entrance test required: GRE
Avg. GRE (of all entering students with scores): quantitative: 149; verbal: 153
Research assistantships: 163
Students reporting specialty: 100%
Students specializing in: admin.: 4%; counseling: 16%; evaluation/research/statistics: 1%; social/philosophical foundations: 1%; policy: 2%; educational tech.: 3%; educational psych: 5%; elementary: 7%; higher education admin.: 9%; junior high: 2%; secondary: 27%; special: 4%; technical (vocational): 4%; instructional media design: 2%; other: 20%

University of West Georgia
1601 Maple Street
Carrollton, GA 30118
http://www.westga.edu/coegrad/
Public
Admissions: (678) 839-5430
E-mail: coegrads@westga.edu
Financial aid: (678) 839-6421
Application deadline: rolling
In-state tuition: full time: $6,324; part time: $187/credit hour
Out-of-state tuition: full time: $19,738
Room/board/expenses: $8,482
Full-time enrollment: 320
doctoral students: 0%; master's students: 76%; education specialists: 24%; men: 19%; women: 81%; minorities: 37%; international: 1%
Part-time enrollment: 722
doctoral students: 14%; master's students: 44%; education specialists: 42%; men: 20%; women: 80%; minorities: 34%; international: 0%
Acceptance rate (master's): 46%
Acceptance rate (doctoral): 50%
Entrance test required: GRE
Avg. GRE (of all entering students with scores): quantitative: N/A; verbal: N/A
Students reporting specialty: 100%
Students specializing in: admin.: 6%; counseling: 17%; elementary: 7%; junior high: 1%; secondary: 2%; special: 14%; instructional media design: 24%; other: 30%

HAWAII

University of Hawaii–Manoa
1776 University Avenue
Everly Hall 128
Honolulu, HI 96822
http://manoa.hawaii.edu/graduate/
Public
Admissions: (808) 956-8544
E-mail: gradadm@hawaii.edu
Financial aid: (808) 956-7251
Application deadline: 02/01
In-state tuition: full time: $12,332; part time: $483/credit hour
Out-of-state tuition: full time: $28,892
Room/board/expenses: $15,625
Full-time enrollment: 282
doctoral students: 18%; master's students: 82%; education specialists: N/A; men: 30%; women: 70%; minorities: 72%; international: 12%
Part-time enrollment: 567
doctoral students: 39%; master's students: 61%; education specialists: N/A; men: 32%; women: 68%; minorities: 75%; international: 4%
Acceptance rate (master's): 56%
Acceptance rate (doctoral): 44%
Entrance test required: GRE
Avg. GRE (of all entering students with scores): quantitative: 149; verbal: 152
Research assistantships: 73
Students reporting specialty: 100%
Students specializing in: admin.: 10%; counseling: 1%; curriculum/instr.: 23%; social/philosophical foundations: 5%; policy: 1%; educational tech.: 12%; educational psych: 6%; elementary: 4%; secondary: 10%; special: 17%; other: 12%

IDAHO

Boise State University

1910 University Drive
Boise, ID 83725-1700
http://www.boisestate.edu/
gradcoll/3admis.html
Public
Admissions: (208) 426-1337
E-mail: gradcoll@boisestate.edu
Financial aid: (208) 426-1664
Application deadline: N/A
In-state tuition: full time: $6,972;
part time: $312/credit hour
Out-of-state tuition: full time:
$18,411
Room/board/expenses: $12,808
Full-time enrollment: 108
doctoral students: 18%; master's
students: 82%; education
specialists: N/A; men: 23%;
women: 77%; minorities: 12%;
international: 5%
Part-time enrollment: 603
doctoral students: 8%; master's
students: 92%; education
specialists: 8%; men: 38%;
women: 62%; minorities: 7%;
international: 3%
Acceptance rate (master's): 93%
Acceptance rate (doctoral): 95%
Entrance test required: GRE
Avg. GRE (of all entering students
with scores): quantitative: 151;
verbal: 156
Research assistantships: 10
Students reporting specialty: 29%
Students specializing in: N/A

Idaho State University[1]

921 S. Eighth Avenue
Pocatello, ID 83209-8059
http://www.isu.edu/departments/
graduate
Public
Admissions: (208) 282-2150
E-mail: graddean@isu.edu
Financial aid: (208) 282-2756
Tuition: N/A
Room/board expenses: N/A
Enrollment: N/A

University of Idaho

PO Box 443080
Moscow, ID 83844-3080
http://www.uidaho.edu/ed
Public
Admissions: (208) 885-4001
E-mail: gadms@uidaho.edu
Financial aid: (208) 885-6312
Application deadline: 02/01
In-state tuition: full time: $7,162;
part time: $359/credit hour
Out-of-state tuition: full time:
$19,950
Room/board/expenses: $16,228
Full-time enrollment: 121
doctoral students: 29%; master's
students: 62%; education
specialists: 9%; men: 43%;
women: 57%; minorities: 10%;
international: 10%
Part-time enrollment: 356
doctoral students: 31%; master's
students: 53%; education
specialists: 15%; men: 38%;
women: 62%; minorities: 6%;
international: 0%
Acceptance rate (master's): 47%
Acceptance rate (doctoral): 40%
Entrance test required: GRE
Avg. GRE (of all entering students
with scores): quantitative: N/A;
verbal: N/A
Students reporting specialty: 100%
Students specializing in: admin.:
25%; counseling: 1%; curriculum/
instr.: 9%; special: 3%; technical
(vocational): 2%; other: 59%

ILLINOIS

Aurora University[1]

347 S. Gladstone Avenue
Aurora, IL 60506-4892
http://www.aurora.edu
Private
Admissions: (630) 844-5533
E-mail: admission@aurora.edu
Financial aid: (630) 844-5448
Tuition: N/A
Room/board expenses: N/A
Enrollment: N/A

Concordia University[1]

7400 Augusta Street
River Forest, IL 60305-1499
http://www.cuchicago.edu/
academics/college_of_education/
index.asp
Private
Admissions: (708) 209-4093
E-mail:
grad.admission@cuchicago.edu
Financial aid: (708) 209-3347
Tuition: N/A
Room/board expenses: N/A
Enrollment: N/A

DePaul University

1 E. Jackson Boulevard
Chicago, IL 60604-2287
http://education.depaul.edu
Private
Admissions: (773) 325-4405
E-mail: edgradadmissions@
depaul.edu
Financial aid: N/A
Application deadline: rolling
Tuition: full time: $580/credit hour;
part time: $580/credit hour
Room/board/expenses: $9,662
Full-time enrollment: 753
doctoral students: 3%; master's
students: 97%; education
specialists: N/A; men: 22%;
women: 78%; minorities: 25%;
international: 2%
Part-time enrollment: 366
doctoral students: 17%; master's
students: 83%; education
specialists: N/A; men: 24%;
women: 76%; minorities: 36%;
international: 1%
Acceptance rate (master's): 64%
Acceptance rate (doctoral): 50%
Entrance test required: GRE
Avg. GRE (of all entering students
with scores): quantitative: N/A;
verbal: N/A
Research assistantships: 10
Students reporting specialty: 100%
Students specializing in: admin.:
15%; counseling: 21%; curriculum/
instr.: 7%; social/philosophical
foundations: 2%; elementary:
13%; junior high: 0%; secondary:
21%; special: 11%; other: 10%

Illinois State University

Campus Box 5300
Normal, IL 61790-5300
http://www.illinoisstate.edu
Public
Admissions: (309) 438-2181
E-mail:
admissions@illinoisstate.edu
Financial aid: (309) 438-2231
Application deadline: rolling
In-state tuition: full time: $308/
credit hour; part time: $308/
credit hour
Out-of-state tuition: full time: $639/
credit hour
Room/board/expenses: $13,658
Full-time enrollment: 205
doctoral students: 29%; master's
students: 65%; education
specialists: 6%; men: 20%;
women: 80%; minorities: 16%;
international: 5%

Part-time enrollment: 500
doctoral students: 36%; master's
students: 59%; education
specialists: 5%; men: 23%;
women: 77%; minorities: 11%;
international: 0%
Acceptance rate (master's): 29%
Acceptance rate (doctoral): 63%
Entrance test required: GRE
Avg. GRE (of all entering students
with scores): quantitative: 149;
verbal: 150
Research assistantships: 41
Students reporting specialty: 100%
Students specializing in: admin.:
20%; counseling: 6%; curriculum/
instr.: 17%; special: 15%; other:
41%

Loyola University Chicago

820 N. Michigan Avenue
Chicago, IL 60611
http://www.luc.edu/education/
Private
Admissions: (312) 915-6722
E-mail: schleduc@luc.edu
Financial aid: (773) 508-7704
Application deadline: N/A
Tuition: full time: $905/credit hour;
part time: $905/credit hour
Room/board/expenses: $24,441
Full-time enrollment: 423
doctoral students: 40%; master's
students: 48%; education
specialists: 12%; men: 26%;
women: 74%; minorities: 30%;
international: 3%
Part-time enrollment: 228
doctoral students: 26%; master's
students: 74%; education
specialists: 0%; men: 25%;
women: 75%; minorities: 25%;
international: 0%
Acceptance rate (master's): 72%
Acceptance rate (doctoral): 27%
Entrance test required: GRE
Avg. GRE (of all entering students
with scores): quantitative: 147;
verbal: 151
Research assistantships: 70
Students reporting specialty: 99%
Students specializing in: admin.:
13%; counseling: 13%; curriculum/
instr.: 12%; evaluation/research/
statistics: 3%; social/philosophi-
cal foundations: 7%; policy: 3%;
educational tech.: 1%; educational psych.: 4%; elementary:
5%; higher education admin.:
20%; secondary: 4%; special: 2%;
other: 14%

National-Louis University[1]

122 S. Michigan Avenue
Chicago, IL 60603
http://www.nl.edu/academics/
nce/index.cfm
Private
Admissions: (888) 658-8632
E-mail: nluinfo@nl.edu
Financial aid: (888) 658-8632
Tuition: N/A
Room/board expenses: N/A
Enrollment: N/A

Northern Illinois University[1]

321 Graham Hall
DeKalb, IL 60115
http://www.niu.edu
Public
Admissions: (815) 753-8301
E-mail: gradsch@niu.edu
Financial aid: (815) 753-1300
Tuition: N/A
Room/board expenses: N/A
Enrollment: N/A

Northwestern University

2120 Campus Drive
Evanston, IL 60208
http://www.
sesp.northwestern.edu
Private
Admissions: (847) 467-2789
E-mail: sesp@northwestern.edu
Financial aid: (847) 467-2789
Application deadline: rolling
Tuition: full time: $43,779; part
time: $4,821/credit hour
Room/board/expenses: N/A
Full-time enrollment: 160
doctoral students: 41%; master's
students: 59%; education
specialists: N/A; men: 25%;
women: 75%; minorities: 20%;
international: 9%
Part-time enrollment: 138
doctoral students: 0%; master's
students: 100%; education
specialists: N/A; men: 23%;
women: 77%; minorities: 15%;
international: 3%
Acceptance rate (master's): 56%
Acceptance rate (doctoral): 9%
Entrance test required: GRE
Avg. GRE (of all entering students
with scores): quantitative: 155;
verbal: 160
Research assistantships: 25
Students reporting specialty: 99%
Students specializing in: elementary: 21%; higher education admin.:
16%; secondary: 18%; other: 45%

Roosevelt University

430 S. Michigan Avenue
Chicago, IL 60605
http://www.roosevelt.edu
Private
Admissions: (877) 277-5978
E-mail: applyRU@roosevelt.edu
Financial aid: (866) 421-0935
Application deadline: rolling
Tuition: full time: $16,475; part
time: $795/credit hour
Room/board/expenses: $17,908
Full-time enrollment: 138
doctoral students: 12%; master's
students: 88%; education
specialists: N/A; men: 23%;
women: 77%; minorities: 48%;
international: 1%
Part-time enrollment: 333
doctoral students: 12%; master's
students: 88%; education
specialists: N/A; men: 19%;
women: 81%; minorities: 32%;
international: 0%
Acceptance rate (master's): 55%
Acceptance rate (doctoral): 0%
Entrance test required: GRE
Avg. GRE (of all entering students
with scores): quantitative: N/A;
verbal: N/A
Research assistantships: 8
Students reporting specialty: 77%
Students specializing in: admin.:
32%; counseling: 11%; elementary: 16%; secondary: 18%; special:
11%; other: 17%

Southern Illinois University–Carbondale

Wham Building 115
Carbondale, IL 62901-4624
http://web.coehs.siu.edu/Public/
Public
Admissions: (618) 536-7791
E-mail: gradsch@siu.edu
Financial aid: (618) 453-4334
Application deadline: rolling
In-state tuition: full time: $750/
credit hour; part time: $750/
credit hour
Out-of-state tuition: full time:
$1,876/credit hour

Room/board/expenses: $15,939
Full-time enrollment: 539
doctoral students: 22%; master's
students: 78%; education
specialists: N/A; men: 36%;
women: 64%; minorities: 21%;
international: 23%
Part-time enrollment: 390
doctoral students: 36%; master's
students: 64%; education
specialists: N/A; men: 31%;
women: 69%; minorities: 18%;
international: 6%
Acceptance rate (master's): 58%
Acceptance rate (doctoral): 61%
Entrance test required: GRE
Avg. GRE (of all entering students
with scores): quantitative: 145;
verbal: 147
Research assistantships: 159
Students reporting specialty: 98%
Students specializing in: admin.:
10%; educational tech.: 0%; educational psych: 9%; higher education admin.: 5%; secondary: 60%;
special: 2%; other: 15%

University of Illinois–Chicago

1040 W. Harrison Street
Chicago, IL 60607-7133
http://www.education.uic.edu
Public
Admissions: (312) 996-4532
E-mail: jeisen@uic.edu
Financial aid: (312) 996-3126
Application deadline: rolling
In-state tuition: full time: $13,772;
part time: $10,144
Out-of-state tuition: full time:
$25,770
Room/board/expenses: $17,075
Full-time enrollment: 135
doctoral students: 45%; master's
students: 55%; education
specialists: N/A; men: 30%;
women: 70%; minorities: 46%;
international: 6%
Part-time enrollment: 540
doctoral students: 48%; master's
students: 52%; education
specialists: N/A; men: 27%;
women: 73%; minorities: 37%;
international: 1%
Acceptance rate (master's): 88%
Acceptance rate (doctoral): 56%
Entrance test required: GRE
Avg. GRE (of all entering students
with scores): quantitative: 151;
verbal: 155
Research assistantships: 93
Students reporting specialty: 100%
Students specializing in: admin.:
15%; curriculum/instr.: 11%;
evaluation/research/statistics:
7%; social/philosophical foundations: 4%; policy: 3%; educational
psych: 4%; elementary: 8%;
secondary: 4%; special: 14%;
other: 24%

University of Illinois–Urbana-Champaign

1310 S. Sixth Street
Champaign, IL 61820
http://www.education.illinois.edu
Public
Admissions: (217) 333-2800
E-mail:
saao@education.illinois.edu
Financial aid: (217) 333-2800
Application deadline: N/A
In-state tuition: full time: $14,938;
part time: $11,128
Out-of-state tuition: full time:
$28,204
Room/board/expenses: $16,926
Full-time enrollment: 329
doctoral students: 68%; master's
students: 32%; education
specialists: N/A; men: 29%;
women: 71%; minorities: 41%;
international: 19%

Part-time enrollment: 600
doctoral students: 39%; master's students: 61%; education specialists: N/A; men: 30%; women: 70%; minorities: 27%; international: 10%
Acceptance rate (master's): 76%
Acceptance rate (doctoral): 38%
Entrance test required: GRE
Avg. GRE (of all entering students with scores): quantitative: N/A; verbal: N/A
Research assistantships: 154
Students reporting specialty: 100%
Students specializing in: admin.: 16%; counseling: 3%; curriculum/instr.: 18%; evaluation/research/statistics: 3%; social/philosophical foundations: 26%; policy: 12%; educational tech.: 6%; educational psych: 10%; elementary: 3%; higher education admin.: 8%; junior high: 6%; secondary: 4%; special: 8%; technical (vocational): 0%; other: 14%

INDIANA

Ball State University

2000 W. University Avenue
Muncie, IN 47306
http://www.bsu.edu/gradschool/
Public
Admissions: (765) 285-1297
E-mail: gradschool@bsu.edu
Financial aid: (765) 285-5600
Application deadline: rolling
In-state tuition: full time: $354/credit hour; part time: $354/credit hour
Out-of-state tuition: full time: $990/credit hour
Room/board/expenses: $12,097
Full-time enrollment: 454
doctoral students: 17%; master's students: 79%; education specialists: 3%; men: 26%; women: 74%; minorities: 11%; international: 5%
Part-time enrollment: 1,729
doctoral students: 9%; master's students: 89%; education specialists: 2%; men: 23%; women: 77%; minorities: 9%; international: 2%
Acceptance rate (master's): 50%
Acceptance rate (doctoral): 24%
Entrance test required: GRE
Avg. GRE (of all entering students with scores): quantitative: 147; verbal: 158
Research assistantships: 0
Students reporting specialty: 75%
Students specializing in: admin.: 18%; counseling: 2%; curriculum/instr.: 4%; educational psych: 3%; elementary: 21%; secondary: 2%; special: 9%; technical (vocational): 2%; other: 39%

Indiana State University

401 N. Seventh Street
Terre Haute, IN 47809
http://www.coe.indstate.edu/
Public
Admissions: (800) 444-4723
E-mail: grdstudy@indstate.edu
Financial aid: (800) 841-4744
Application deadline: rolling
In-state tuition: full time: $366/credit hour; part time: $366/credit hour
Out-of-state tuition: full time: $719/credit hour
Room/board/expenses: $11,964
Full-time enrollment: 262
doctoral students: 44%; master's students: 52%; education specialists: 5%; men: 28%; women: 72%; minorities: 12%; international: 15%
Part-time enrollment: 303
doctoral students: 55%; master's

students: 32%; education specialists: 13%; men: 38%; women: 62%; minorities: 11%; international: 6%
Acceptance rate (master's): 40%
Acceptance rate (doctoral): 62%
Entrance test required: GRE
Avg. GRE (of all entering students with scores): quantitative: N/A; verbal: N/A
Research assistantships: 3
Students reporting specialty: 100%
Students specializing in: admin.: 34%; counseling: 20%; curriculum/instr.: 17%; educational tech.: 3%; elementary: 2%; higher education admin.: 2%; special: 9%; instructional media design: 3%; other: 13%

Indiana University–Bloomington

201 N. Rose Avenue
Bloomington, IN 47405-1006
http://education.indiana.edu/
Public
Admissions: (812) 856-8504
E-mail: educate@indiana.edu
Financial aid: (812) 855-3278
Application deadline: 12/01
In-state tuition: full time: $397/credit hour; part time: $397/credit hour
Out-of-state tuition: full time: $1,155/credit hour
Room/board/expenses: $22,142
Full-time enrollment: 454
doctoral students: 51%; master's students: 47%; education specialists: 2%; men: 28%; women: 72%; minorities: 15%; international: 26%
Part-time enrollment: 412
doctoral students: 59%; master's students: 36%; education specialists: 5%; men: 35%; women: 65%; minorities: 17%; international: 18%
Acceptance rate (master's): 38%
Acceptance rate (doctoral): 32%
Entrance test required: GRE
Avg. GRE (of all entering students with scores): quantitative: 152; verbal: 155
Research assistantships: 117
Students reporting specialty: 100%
Students specializing in: admin.: 5%; counseling: 14%; curriculum/instr.: 28%; evaluation/research/statistics: 5%; social/philosophical foundations: 6%; policy: 6%; educational psych: 5%; elementary: 5%; higher education admin.: 13%; secondary: 3%; special: 3%; instructional media design: 14%; other: 1%

Purdue University–West Lafayette

100 N. University Street
West Lafayette, IN 47907-2098
http://www.education.purdue.edu/
Public
Admissions: (765) 494-2345
E-mail: education-gradoffice@purdue.edu
Financial aid: (765) 494-5050
Application deadline: rolling
In-state tuition: full time: $9,900; part time: $348/credit hour
Out-of-state tuition: full time: $28,702
Room/board/expenses: $13,308
Full-time enrollment: 190
doctoral students: 67%; master's students: 33%; education specialists: 0%; men: 25%; women: 75%; minorities: 16%; international: 30%
Part-time enrollment: 287
doctoral students: 34%; master's students: 66%; education

specialists: 0%; men: 37%; women: 63%; minorities: 16%; international: 6%
Acceptance rate (master's): 75%
Acceptance rate (doctoral): 42%
Entrance test required: GRE
Avg. GRE (of all entering students with scores): quantitative: 151; verbal: 153
Research assistantships: 30
Students reporting specialty: 100%
Students specializing in: admin.: 10%; counseling: 9%; curriculum/instr.: 27%; social/philosophical foundations: 1%; educational tech.: 35%; educational psych: 7%; elementary: 1%; higher education admin.: 1%; special: 6%; technical (vocational): 3%

IOWA

Drake University

3206 University Avenue
Des Moines, IA 50311-4505
http://www.drake.edu/soe/
Private
Admissions: (515) 271-2552
E-mail: soegradadmission@drake.edu
Financial aid: (515) 271-2905
Application deadline: rolling
Tuition: full time: $450/credit hour; part time: $450/credit hour
Room/board/expenses: $9,580
Full-time enrollment: 90
doctoral students: 0%; master's students: 100%; education specialists: 0%; men: 22%; women: 78%; minorities: 4%; international: 1%
Part-time enrollment: 402
doctoral students: 12%; master's students: 79%; education specialists: 9%; men: 27%; women: 73%; minorities: 4%; international: 1%
Acceptance rate (master's): 87%
Acceptance rate (doctoral): 57%
Entrance test required: GRE
Avg. GRE (of all entering students with scores): quantitative: 150; verbal: 152
Research assistantships: 2
Students reporting specialty: 98%
Students specializing in: admin.: 18%; counseling: 23%; curriculum/instr.: 9%; elementary: 5%; secondary: 11%; special: 2%; other: 31%

Iowa State University

E262 Lagomarcino Hall
Ames, IA 50011
http://www.grad-college.iastate.edu/
Public
Admissions: (515) 294-5836
E-mail: admissions@iastate.edu
Financial aid: (515) 294-2223
Application deadline: rolling
In-state tuition: full time: $8,756; part time: $431/credit hour
Out-of-state tuition: full time: $20,696
Room/board/expenses: $12,192
Full-time enrollment: 137
doctoral students: 54%; master's students: 46%; education specialists: N/A; men: 33%; women: 67%; minorities: 27%; international: 13%
Part-time enrollment: 468
doctoral students: 36%; master's students: 64%; education specialists: N/A; men: 40%; women: 60%; minorities: 9%; international: 3%
Acceptance rate (master's): 76%
Acceptance rate (doctoral): 85%
Entrance test required: GRE
Avg. GRE (of all entering students with scores): quantitative: 152; verbal: 154

Research assistantships: 51
Students reporting specialty: 99%
Students specializing in: admin.: 22%; curriculum/instr.: 9%; evaluation/research/statistics: 0%; social/philosophical foundations: 1%; educational tech.: 11%; higher education admin.: 42%; junior high: 3%; secondary: 3%; special: 2%; other: 8%

University of Iowa

Lindquist Center
Iowa City, IA 52242
http://www.education.uiowa.edu
Public
Admissions: (319) 335-5359
E-mail: edu-educationservices@uiowa.edu
Financial aid: (319) 335-1450
Application deadline: rolling
In-state tuition: full time: $10,963; part time: $521/credit hour
Out-of-state tuition: full time: $27,215
Room/board/expenses: $17,957
Full-time enrollment: 520
doctoral students: 57%; master's students: 43%; education specialists: 1%; men: 33%; women: 67%; minorities: 13%; international: 17%
Part-time enrollment: 149
doctoral students: 71%; master's students: 26%; education specialists: 3%; men: 34%; women: 66%; minorities: 13%; international: 16%
Acceptance rate (master's): 62%
Acceptance rate (doctoral): 49%
Entrance test required: GRE
Avg. GRE (of all entering students with scores): quantitative: 150; verbal: 155
Research assistantships: 174
Students reporting specialty: 100%
Students specializing in: admin.: 11%; counseling: 9%; curriculum/instr.: 1%; evaluation/research/statistics: 9%; social/philosophical foundations: 4%; policy: 0%; educational psych: 4%; elementary: 1%; higher education admin.: 11%; secondary: 24%; special: 6%; other: 22%

University of Northern Iowa

205 Schindler Center
Cedar Falls, IA 50614-0610
http://www.uni.edu/coe
Public
Admissions: (319) 273-2623
E-mail: registrar@uni.edu
Financial aid: (800) 772-2736
Application deadline: rolling
In-state tuition: full time: $8,743; part time: $431/credit hour
Out-of-state tuition: full time: $18,013
Room/board/expenses: $11,783
Full-time enrollment: 154
doctoral students: 15%; master's students: 81%; education specialists: 5%; men: 35%; women: 65%; minorities: 11%; international: 19%
Part-time enrollment: 322
doctoral students: 23%; master's students: 74%; education specialists: 3%; men: 29%; women: 71%; minorities: 8%; international: 2%
Acceptance rate (master's): 59%
Acceptance rate (doctoral): 58%
Entrance test required: GRE
Avg. GRE (of all entering students with scores): quantitative: 149; verbal: 151
Research assistantships: 12
Students reporting specialty: 100%
Students specializing in: admin.: 24%; counseling: 7%; curriculum/instr.: 4%; social/philosophical

foundations: 7%; educational psych: 2%; elementary: 2%; special: 7%; instructional media design: 7%; other: 40%

KANSAS

Kansas State University

18 Bluemont Hall
Manhattan, KS 66506
http://www.ksu.edu/
Public
Admissions: (785) 532-5595
E-mail: coegrads@ksu.edu
Financial aid: (785) 532-6420
Application deadline: rolling
In-state tuition: full time: $327/credit hour; part time: $327/credit hour
Out-of-state tuition: full time: $738/credit hour
Room/board/expenses: $12,350
Full-time enrollment: 173
doctoral students: 26%; master's students: 74%; education specialists: N/A; men: 31%; women: 69%; minorities: 40%; international: 7%
Part-time enrollment: 618
doctoral students: 27%; master's students: 73%; education specialists: N/A; men: 33%; women: 67%; minorities: 12%; international: 1%
Acceptance rate (master's): 86%
Acceptance rate (doctoral): 73%
Entrance test required: GRE
Avg. GRE (of all entering students with scores): quantitative: 147; verbal: 153
Research assistantships: 9
Students reporting specialty: 82%
Students specializing in: admin.: 12%; counseling: 49%; curriculum/instr.: 19%; special: 3%; other: 16%

University of Kansas

217 Joseph R. Pearson Hall
Lawrence, KS 66045
http://www.soe.ku.edu
Public
Admissions: (785) 864-4510
E-mail: jlicht@ku.edu
Financial aid: (785) 864-4700
Application deadline: N/A
In-state tuition: full time: $330/credit hour; part time: $330/credit hour
Out-of-state tuition: full time: $772/credit hour
Room/board/expenses: N/A
Full-time enrollment: 605
doctoral students: 48%; master's students: 50%; education specialists: 2%; men: 34%; women: 66%; minorities: 13%; international: 18%
Part-time enrollment: 357
doctoral students: 25%; master's students: 75%; education specialists: 0%; men: 23%; women: 77%; minorities: 11%; international: 4%
Acceptance rate (master's): 74%
Acceptance rate (doctoral): 68%
Entrance test required: GRE
Avg. GRE (of all entering students with scores): quantitative: 150; verbal: 152
Research assistantships: 57
Students reporting specialty: 100%
Students specializing in: admin.: 7%; counseling: 7%; curriculum/instr.: 19%; evaluation/research/statistics: 5%; social/philosophical foundations: 2%; policy: 2%; educational tech.: 3%; educational psych: 3%; elementary: 5%; higher education admin.: 11%; junior high: 2%; secondary: 6%; special: 21%; other: 8%

Wichita State University[1]
1845 N. Fairmount
Wichita, KS 67260-0131
http://www.wichita.edu/my/visitors/
Public
Admissions: N/A
Financial aid: N/A
Tuition: N/A
Room/board expenses: N/A
Enrollment: N/A

KENTUCKY

Spalding University[1]
851 S. Fourth Street
Louisville, KY 40203
http://spalding.edu/content.aspx?id=2134&cid=420
Private
Admissions: (502) 585-7111
E-mail: admissions@spalding.edu
Financial aid: (502) 585-9911
Tuition: N/A
Room/board expenses: N/A
Enrollment: N/A

University of Kentucky
103 Dickey Hall
Lexington, KY 40506-0033
http://www.gradschool.uky.edu/
Public
Admissions: (859) 257-4905
E-mail: Brian.Jackson@uky.edu
Financial aid: (859) 257-3172
Application deadline: rolling
In-state tuition: full time: $10,458; part time: $552/credit hour
Out-of-state tuition: full time: $21,546
Room/board/expenses: $15,700
Full-time enrollment: 549
doctoral students: 42%; master's students: 54%; education specialists: 4%; men: 34%; women: 66%; minorities: 19%; international: 4%
Part-time enrollment: 248
doctoral students: 49%; master's students: 46%; education specialists: 5%; men: 35%; women: 65%; minorities: 14%; international: N/A
Acceptance rate (master's): 49%
Acceptance rate (doctoral): 37%
Entrance test required: GRE
Avg. GRE (of all entering students with scores): quantitative: 149; verbal: 152
Research assistantships: 91
Students reporting specialty: 100%
Students specializing in: admin.: 14%; curriculum/instr.: 1%; evaluation/research/statistics: 18%; social/philosophical foundations: 1%; educational psych: 3%; elementary: 0%; higher education admin.: 3%; junior high: 0%; secondary: 7%; special: 5%; instructional media design: 2%; other: 45%

University of Louisville
Cardinal Boulevard and First Street
Louisville, KY 40292
http://www.louisville.edu/education
Public
Admissions: (502) 852-3101
E-mail: gradadm@louisville.edu
Financial aid: (502) 852-5511
Application deadline: rolling
In-state tuition: full time: $10,274; part time: $571/credit hour
Out-of-state tuition: full time: $21,378
Room/board/expenses: $12,710
Full-time enrollment: 476
doctoral students: 21%; master's students: 79%; education specialists: 0%; men: 33%; women: 67%; minorities: 19%; international: 4%
Part-time enrollment: 538
doctoral students: 16%; master's students: 78%; education specialists: 6%; men: 27%; women: 73%; minorities: 12%; international: 0%
Acceptance rate (master's): 62%
Acceptance rate (doctoral): 22%
Entrance test required: GRE
Avg. GRE (of all entering students with scores): quantitative: 142; verbal: 150
Research assistantships: 43
Students reporting specialty: 100%
Students specializing in: admin.: 9%; counseling: 22%; curriculum/instr.: 4%; elementary: 5%; higher education admin.: 5%; special: 8%; other: 47%

Western Kentucky University
1906 College Heights Boulevard
Bowling Green, KY 42101
http://www.wku.edu/cebs
Public
Admissions: (270) 745-2446
E-mail: graduate.studies@wku.edu
Financial aid: (270) 745-2755
Application deadline: rolling
In-state tuition: full time: $467/credit hour; part time: $467/credit hour
Out-of-state tuition: full time: $583/credit hour
Room/board/expenses: $10,100
Full-time enrollment: 190
doctoral students: 2%; master's students: 94%; education specialists: 5%; men: 12%; women: 88%; minorities: 5%; international: 2%
Part-time enrollment: 694
doctoral students: 5%; master's students: 93%; education specialists: 2%; men: 16%; women: 84%; minorities: 10%; international: 0%
Acceptance rate (master's): 37%
Acceptance rate (doctoral): 100%
Entrance test required: GRE
Avg. GRE (of all entering students with scores): quantitative: 147; verbal: 152
Research assistantships: 52
Students reporting specialty: 100%
Students specializing in: admin.: 7%; elementary: 13%; junior high: 2%; secondary: 5%; special: 16%; other: 57%

LOUISIANA

Grambling State University
GSU Box 4305
Grambling, LA 71245
http://www.gram.edu/
Public
Admissions: (318) 274-2457
E-mail: gsugrad@gram.edu
Financial aid: (318) 274-6190
Application deadline: 07/01
In-state tuition: full time: $218/credit hour; part time: $218/credit hour
Out-of-state tuition: full time: $683/credit hour
Room/board/expenses: $16,707
Full-time enrollment: 124
doctoral students: 12%; master's students: 88%; education specialists: N/A; men: 52%; women: 48%; minorities: 86%; international: 11%
Part-time enrollment: 139
doctoral students: 47%; master's students: 53%; education specialists: N/A; men: 25%; women: 75%; minorities: 76%; international: 3%
Acceptance rate (master's): 84%
Acceptance rate (doctoral): 72%
Entrance test required: GRE
Avg. GRE (of all entering students with scores): quantitative: N/A; verbal: N/A
Students reporting specialty: 100%
Students specializing in: admin.: 6%; curriculum/instr.: 7%; elementary: 2%; secondary: 1%; special: 1%; other: 84%

Louisiana State University–Baton Rouge
221 Peabody Hall
Baton Rouge, LA 70803
http://www.lsu.edu/coe
Public
Admissions: (225) 578-1641
E-mail: graddeanoffice@lsu.edu
Financial aid: (225) 578-3103
Application deadline: rolling
In-state tuition: full time: $7,560; part time: $4,402
Out-of-state tuition: full time: $22,948
Room/board/expenses: $13,898
Full-time enrollment: 315
doctoral students: 26%; master's students: 74%; education specialists: 0%; men: 19%; women: 81%; minorities: 23%; international: 2%
Part-time enrollment: 192
doctoral students: 52%; master's students: 39%; education specialists: 9%; men: 20%; women: 80%; minorities: 21%; international: 1%
Acceptance rate (master's): 74%
Acceptance rate (doctoral): 55%
Entrance test required: GRE
Avg. GRE (of all entering students with scores): quantitative: 149; verbal: 153
Research assistantships: 65
Students reporting specialty: 100%
Students specializing in: admin.: 5%; counseling: 6%; curriculum/instr.: 21%; evaluation/research/statistics: 1%; educational tech.: 3%; educational psych: 4%; elementary: 8%; higher education admin.: 15%; secondary: 9%; special: 4%; other: 24%

Louisiana Tech University
PO Box 3163
Ruston, LA 71272-0001
http://www.latech.edu/education/
Public
Admissions: (318) 257-2924
E-mail: gschool@latech.edu
Financial aid: (318) 257-2641
Application deadline: 08/01
In-state tuition: full time: $7,442; part time: $6,126
Out-of-state tuition: full time: $13,734
Room/board/expenses: $12,380
Full-time enrollment: 452
doctoral students: 12%; master's students: 88%; education specialists: N/A; men: 27%; women: 73%; minorities: 23%; international: 1%
Part-time enrollment: 1,079
doctoral students: 5%; master's students: 95%; education specialists: N/A; men: 23%; women: 77%; minorities: 24%; international: 1%
Acceptance rate (master's): 62%
Acceptance rate (doctoral): 38%
Entrance test required: GRE
Avg. GRE (of all entering students with scores): quantitative: 148; verbal: 152
Research assistantships: 23
Students reporting specialty: 30%
Students specializing in: N/A

University of Louisiana–Monroe
Strauss Hall
Monroe, LA 71209-0001
http://www.ulm.edu
Public
Admissions: (318) 342-5252
E-mail: admissions@ulm.edu
Financial aid: (318) 342-5320
Application deadline: rolling
In-state tuition: full time: $5,442; part time: $200/credit hour
Out-of-state tuition: full time: $18,250
Room/board/expenses: $12,018
Full-time enrollment: 93
doctoral students: 10%; master's students: 90%; education specialists: N/A; men: 27%; women: 73%; minorities: 23%; international: 20%
Part-time enrollment: 202
doctoral students: 17%; master's students: 83%; education specialists: N/A; men: 26%; women: 74%; minorities: 22%; international: 0%
Acceptance rate (master's): 96%
Acceptance rate (doctoral): 75%
Entrance test required: GRE
Avg. GRE (of all entering students with scores): quantitative: 143; verbal: 147
Research assistantships: 49
Students reporting specialty: 0%
Students specializing in: N/A

University of New Orleans[1]
2000 Lakeshore Drive
New Orleans, LA 70148
http://coehd.uno.edu/
Public
Admissions: (504) 280-6595
E-mail: admissions@uno.edu
Financial aid: (504) 280-6603
Tuition: N/A
Room/board expenses: N/A
Enrollment: N/A

MAINE

University of Maine
Shibles Hall
Orono, ME 04469-5766
http://www.umaine.edu/edhd/
Public
Admissions: (207) 581-3219
E-mail: graduate@maine.edu
Financial aid: (207) 581-1324
Application deadline: rolling
In-state tuition: full time: $418/credit hour; part time: $418/credit hour
Out-of-state tuition: full time: $1,259/credit hour
Room/board/expenses: $15,560
Full-time enrollment: 192
doctoral students: 14%; master's students: 81%; education specialists: 6%; men: 23%; women: 77%; minorities: 6%; international: 3%
Part-time enrollment: 266
doctoral students: 18%; master's students: 62%; education specialists: 20%; men: 27%; women: 73%; minorities: 3%; international: 2%
Acceptance rate (master's): 69%
Acceptance rate (doctoral): 63%
Entrance test required: GRE
Avg. GRE (of all entering students with scores): quantitative: N/A; verbal: N/A
Research assistantships: 1
Students reporting specialty: 100%
Students specializing in: admin.: 19%; counseling: 16%; curriculum/instr.: 7%; educational tech.: 6%; elementary: 0%; higher education admin.: 5%; secondary: 5%; special: 15%; other: 28%

MARYLAND

Johns Hopkins University
2800 N. Charles Street
Baltimore, MD 21218
http://education.jhu.edu/admission/
Private
Admissions: (877) 548-7631
E-mail: soe.admissions@jhu.edu
Financial aid: (410) 516-9808
Application deadline: 04/01
Tuition: full time: $1,000/credit hour; part time: $635/credit hour
Room/board/expenses: N/A
Full-time enrollment: 285
doctoral students: 4%; master's students: 96%; education specialists: N/A; men: 35%; women: 65%; minorities: 40%; international: 4%
Part-time enrollment: 843
doctoral students: 4%; master's students: 96%; education specialists: N/A; men: 21%; women: 79%; minorities: 29%; international: 3%
Acceptance rate (master's): 55%
Acceptance rate (doctoral): 24%
Entrance test required: GRE
Avg. GRE (of all entering students with scores): quantitative: N/A; verbal: N/A
Research assistantships: 2
Students reporting specialty: 100%
Students specializing in: admin.: 14%; counseling: 9%; curriculum/instr.: 11%; educational tech.: 9%; elementary: 3%; secondary: 5%; special: 12%; other: 45%

Morgan State University[1]
1700 E. Cold Spring Lane
Baltimore, MD 21251
http://www.morgan.edu/academics/Grad-Studies/default.asp
Public
Admissions: (443) 885-3185
E-mail: pshicks@moac.morgan.edu
Financial aid: (443) 885-3185
Tuition: N/A
Room/board expenses: N/A
Enrollment: N/A

Towson University
8000 York Road
Towson, MD 21252
http://www.grad.towson.edu
Public
Admissions: (410) 704-2501
E-mail: grads@towson.edu
Financial aid: (410) 704-4236
Application deadline: rolling
In-state tuition: full time: $351/credit hour; part time: $351/credit hour
Out-of-state tuition: full time: $737/credit hour
Room/board/expenses: $14,838
Full-time enrollment: 358
doctoral students: 18%; master's students: 70%; education specialists: 12%; men: 16%; women: 84%; minorities: 27%; international: 4%
Part-time enrollment: 1,339
doctoral students: 1%; master's students: 92%; education specialists: 7%; men: 15%; women: 85%; minorities: 20%; international: 1%

Acceptance rate (master's): 48%
Acceptance rate (doctoral): 36%
Entrance test required: GRE
Avg. GRE (of all entering students with scores): quantitative: N/A; verbal: N/A
Research assistantships: 3
Students reporting specialty: 95%
Students specializing in: admin.: 12%; educational tech.: 2%; educational psych.: 2%; elementary: 2%; secondary: 3%; special: 10%; instructional media design: 7%; other: 62%

University of Maryland–College Park

3119 Benjamin Building
College Park, MD 20742-1121
http://www.education.umd.edu/graduateprograms/index.html
Public
Admissions: (301) 405-2337
E-mail: mjm@umd.edu
Financial aid: (301) 314-9000
Application deadline: rolling
In-state tuition: full time: $551/credit hour; part time: $551/credit hour
Out-of-state tuition: full time: $1,188/credit hour
Room/board/expenses: $14,185
Full-time enrollment: 584
doctoral students: 64%; master's students: 36%; education specialists: 0%; men: 23%; women: 77%; minorities: 30%; international: 14%
Part-time enrollment: 367
doctoral students: 22%; master's students: 78%; education specialists: 0%; men: 25%; women: 75%; minorities: 31%; international: 5%
Acceptance rate (master's): 55%
Acceptance rate (doctoral): 23%
Entrance test required: GRE
Avg. GRE (of all entering students with scores): quantitative: 153; verbal: 157
Research assistantships: 80
Students reporting specialty: 99%
Students specializing in: admin.: 7%; counseling: 12%; evaluation/research/statistics: 6%; social/philosophical foundations: 2%; policy: 8%; educational psych: 8%; elementary: 5%; higher education admin.: 4%; junior high: 3%; secondary: 36%; special: 11%

University of Maryland–Eastern Shore[1]

1 Backbone Road
Princess Anne, MD 21853
http://www.umes.edu/education/Default.aspx?id=17432
Public
Admissions: (410) 651-6507
E-mail: jmkeanedawes@umes.edu
Financial aid: (410) 651-6174
Tuition: N/A
Room/board expenses: N/A
Enrollment: N/A

MASSACHUSETTS

American International College

1000 State Street
Springfield, MA 01109
http://www.aic.edu
Private
Admissions: (413) 205-3530
E-mail: diane.mendez@aic.edu
Financial aid: (413) 205-3280
Application deadline: rolling

Tuition: full time: $419/credit hour; part time: $419/credit hour
Room/board/expenses: $12,660
Full-time enrollment: 1,219
doctoral students: 4%; master's students: 96%; education specialists: N/A; men: 23%; women: 77%; minorities: 7%; international: 0%
Part-time enrollment: 95
doctoral students: 6%; master's students: 94%; education specialists: N/A; men: 25%; women: 75%; minorities: 8%; international: N/A
Acceptance rate (master's): 74%
Acceptance rate (doctoral): 76%
Entrance test required: N/A
Avg. GRE (of all entering students with scores): quantitative: N/A; verbal: N/A
Research assistantships: 0
Students reporting specialty: 100%
Students specializing in: admin.: 25%; counseling: 4%; curriculum/instr.: 1%; elementary: 22%; junior high: 5%; secondary: 25%; other: 9%

Boston College (Lynch)

Campion Hall
Chestnut Hill, MA 02467-3813
http://www.bc.edu/education
Private
Admissions: (617) 552-4214
E-mail: gsoe@bc.edu
Financial aid: (617) 552-3300
Application deadline: N/A
Tuition: full time: $1,166/credit hour; part time: $1,166/credit hour
Room/board/expenses: $21,652
Full-time enrollment: 635
doctoral students: 28%; master's students: 72%; education specialists: 0%; men: 21%; women: 79%; minorities: 22%; international: 13%
Part-time enrollment: 226
doctoral students: 18%; master's students: 81%; education specialists: 1%; men: 28%; women: 72%; minorities: 16%; international: 4%
Acceptance rate (master's): 64%
Acceptance rate (doctoral): 6%
Entrance test required: GRE
Avg. GRE (of all entering students with scores): quantitative: 151; verbal: 155
Research assistantships: 448
Students reporting specialty: 100%
Students specializing in: admin.: 7%; counseling: 26%; curriculum/instr.: 17%; evaluation/research/statistics: 6%; educational psych: 6%; elementary: 4%; higher education admin.: 13%; secondary: 10%; special: 7%; other: 3%

Boston University

2 Silber Way
Boston, MA 02215
http://www.bu.edu/sed
Private
Admissions: (617) 353-4237
E-mail: sedgrad@bu.edu
Financial aid: (617) 353-4238
Application deadline: 01/15
Tuition: full time: $42,838; part time: $663/credit hour
Room/board/expenses: $20,624
Full-time enrollment: 254
doctoral students: 27%; master's students: 73%; education specialists: 0%; men: 25%; women: 75%; minorities: 15%; international: 29%
Part-time enrollment: 322
doctoral students: 30%; master's students: 65%; education specialists: 5%; men: 25%; women: 75%; minorities: 28%; international: 2%

Acceptance rate (master's): 61%
Acceptance rate (doctoral): 37%
Entrance test required: GRE
Avg. GRE (of all entering students with scores): quantitative: 152; verbal: 154
Research assistantships: 10
Students reporting specialty: 76%
Students specializing in: admin.: 2%; counseling: 2%; curriculum/instr.: 29%; policy: 15%; elementary: 2%; higher education admin.: 9%; secondary: 22%; special: 9%; instructional media design: 3%; other: 7%

Harvard University

Appian Way
Cambridge, MA 02138
http://www.gse.harvard.edu
Private
Admissions: (617) 495-3414
E-mail: gseadmissions@harvard.edu
Financial aid: (617) 495-3416
Application deadline: 12/02
Tuition: full time: $41,578; part time: $22,338
Room/board/expenses: $21,194
Full-time enrollment: 870
doctoral students: 28%; master's students: 72%; education specialists: N/A; men: 25%; women: 75%; minorities: 29%; international: 15%
Part-time enrollment: 75
doctoral students: 9%; master's students: 91%; education specialists: N/A; men: 19%; women: 81%; minorities: 20%; international: N/A
Acceptance rate (master's): 50%
Acceptance rate (doctoral): 6%
Entrance test required: GRE
Avg. GRE (of all entering students with scores): quantitative: 154; verbal: 159
Research assistantships: 145
Students reporting specialty: 100%
Students specializing in: admin.: 21%; counseling: 6%; curriculum/instr.: 5%; evaluation/research/statistics: 2%; policy: 21%; educational tech.: 5%; higher education admin.: 8%; secondary: 5%; other: 41%

Lesley University[1]

29 Everett Street
Cambridge, MA 02138-2790
http://www.lesley.edu/soe.html
Private
Admissions: (617) 349-8544
E-mail: learn@lesley.edu
Financial aid: (800) 999-1959
Tuition: N/A
Room/board expenses: N/A
Enrollment: N/A

Tufts University[1]

Paige Hall, 12 Upper Campus Road
Medford, MA 02155
http://ase.tufts.edu/GradStudy/programs.htm
Private
Admissions: (617) 627-3395
Financial aid: (617) 627-2000
Tuition: N/A
Room/board expenses: N/A
Enrollment: N/A

University of Massachusetts–Amherst

Furcolo Hall
813 N. Pleasant Street
Amherst, MA 01003-9308
http://www.umass.edu/education
Public
Admissions: (413) 545-0722
E-mail: gradadm@grad.umass.edu

Financial aid: (413) 545-0801
Application deadline: 01/15
In-state tuition: full time: $12,978; part time: $110/credit hour
Out-of-state tuition: full time: $20,275
Room/board/expenses: $12,800
Full-time enrollment: 391
doctoral students: 34%; master's students: 66%; education specialists: N/A; men: 29%; women: 71%; minorities: 16%; international: 22%
Part-time enrollment: 316
doctoral students: 58%; master's students: 42%; education specialists: N/A; men: 30%; women: 70%; minorities: 19%; international: 7%
Acceptance rate (master's): 58%
Acceptance rate (doctoral): 45%
Entrance test required: GRE
Avg. GRE (of all entering students with scores): quantitative: 151; verbal: 152
Research assistantships: 156
Students reporting specialty: 96%
Students specializing in: admin.: 5%; counseling: 3%; curriculum/instr.: 28%; evaluation/research/statistics: 3%; social/philosophical foundations: 7%; policy: 18%; educational tech.: 4%; educational psych: 4%; elementary: 7%; higher education admin.: 12%; junior high: 2%; secondary: 13%; special: 7%; other: 13%

University of Massachusetts–Lowell[1]

510 O'Leary Library
61 Wilder Street
Lowell, MA 01854
http://www.uml.edu/gse/
Public
Admissions: (978) 934-4601
E-mail: admissions@uml.edu
Financial aid: (978) 934-4220
Tuition: N/A
Room/board expenses: N/A
Enrollment: N/A

MICHIGAN

Andrews University

Berrien Springs, MI 49104-0103
http://www.andrews.edu/
Private
Admissions: (800) 253-2874
E-mail: enroll@andrews.edu
Financial aid: (269) 471-3334
Application deadline: rolling
Tuition: full time: $1,079/credit hour; part time: $1,079/credit hour
Room/board/expenses: $13,500
Full-time enrollment: 187
doctoral students: 71%; master's students: 24%; education specialists: 5%; men: 39%; women: 61%; minorities: 48%; international: 26%
Part-time enrollment: 89
doctoral students: 54%; master's students: 37%; education specialists: 9%; men: 37%; women: 63%; minorities: 51%; international: 24%
Acceptance rate (master's): 95%
Acceptance rate (doctoral): 75%
Entrance test required: GRE
Avg. GRE (of all entering students with scores): quantitative: 152; verbal: 154
Students reporting specialty: 0%
Students specializing in: N/A

Eastern Michigan University

310 Porter Building
Ypsilanti, MI 48197
http://www.emich.edu/coe/
Public
Admissions: (734) 487-3400
E-mail: graduate.admissions@emich.edu
Financial aid: (734) 487-0455
Application deadline: rolling
In-state tuition: full time: $449/credit hour; part time: $449/credit hour
Out-of-state tuition: full time: $885/credit hour
Room/board/expenses: $13,066
Full-time enrollment: 212
doctoral students: 3%; master's students: 95%; education specialists: 2%; men: 20%; women: 80%; minorities: 12%; international: 4%
Part-time enrollment: 965
doctoral students: 14%; master's students: 79%; education specialists: 7%; men: 23%; women: 77%; minorities: 18%; international: 2%
Acceptance rate (master's): 47%
Acceptance rate (doctoral): 31%
Entrance test required: GRE
Avg. GRE (of all entering students with scores): quantitative: 146; verbal: 150
Research assistantships: 5
Students reporting specialty: 100%
Students specializing in: admin.: 27%; counseling: 7%; curriculum/instr.: 0%; evaluation/research/statistics: 0%; social/philosophical foundations: 1%; elementary: 4%; higher education admin.: 7%; junior high: 0%; secondary: 7%; special: 21%; instructional media design: 4%; other: 22%

Michigan State University

620 Farm Lane, Rm 501
East Lansing, MI 48824-1034
http://www.educ.msu.edu
Public
Admissions: (517) 355-8332
E-mail: admis@msu.edu
Financial aid: (517) 353-5940
Application deadline: N/A
In-state tuition: full time: $630/credit hour; part time: $630/credit hour
Out-of-state tuition: full time: $1,206/credit hour
Room/board/expenses: $12,632
Full-time enrollment: 991
doctoral students: 54%; master's students: 45%; education specialists: 1%; men: 35%; women: 65%; minorities: 16%; international: 19%
Part-time enrollment: 426
doctoral students: 18%; master's students: 81%; education specialists: 1%; men: 25%; women: 75%; minorities: 8%; international: 3%
Acceptance rate (master's): 41%
Acceptance rate (doctoral): 37%
Entrance test required: GRE
Avg. GRE (of all entering students with scores): quantitative: 151; verbal: 157
Research assistantships: 213
Students reporting specialty: 69%
Students specializing in: admin.: 7%; counseling: 7%; curriculum/instr.: 32%; evaluation/research/statistics: 3%; social/philosophical foundations: 2%; policy: 3%; educational tech.: 10%; educational psych: 2%; elementary: 4%; higher education admin.: 14%; secondary: 2%; special: 6%; other: 9%

Oakland University
415 Pawley Hall
Rochester, MI 48309-4494
http://www.oakland.edu/grad
Public
Admissions: (248) 370-3167
E-mail: gradmail@oakland.edu
Financial aid: (248) 370-2550
Application deadline: rolling
In-state tuition: full time: $14,286; part time: $595/credit hour
Out-of-state tuition: full time: $24,648
Room/board/expenses: $11,432
Full-time enrollment: 414
doctoral students: 8%; master's students: 91%; education specialists: 0%; men: 15%; women: 85%; minorities: 14%; international: 1%
Part-time enrollment: 878
doctoral students: 13%; master's students: 73%; education specialists: 14%; men: 22%; women: 78%; minorities: 14%; international: 0%
Acceptance rate (master's): 57%
Acceptance rate (doctoral): 31%
Entrance test required: N/A
Avg. GRE (of all entering students with scores): quantitative: N/A; verbal: N/A
Students reporting specialty: 97%
Students specializing in: admin.: 16%; counseling: 22%; curriculum/instr.: 3%; elementary: 9%; higher education admin.: 1%; secondary: 6%; special: 10%; other: 33%

University of Michigan–Ann Arbor
610 E. University Street
Ann Arbor, MI 48109-1259
http://www.soe.umich.edu/
Public
Admissions: (734) 764-7563
E-mail: ed.grad.admit@umich.edu
Financial aid: (734) 764-7563
Application deadline: N/A
In-state tuition: full time: $19,810; part time: $1,095/credit hour
Out-of-state tuition: full time: $39,860
Room/board/expenses: $18,086
Full-time enrollment: 446
doctoral students: 54%; master's students: 46%; education specialists: N/A; men: 28%; women: 72%; minorities: 28%; international: 11%
Part-time enrollment: 23
doctoral students: 4%; master's students: 96%; education specialists: N/A; men: 35%; women: 65%; minorities: 13%; international: N/A
Acceptance rate (master's): 69%
Acceptance rate (doctoral): 21%
Entrance test required: GRE
Avg. GRE (of all entering students with scores): quantitative: 153; verbal: 157
Research assistantships: 160
Students reporting specialty: 100%
Students specializing in: admin.: 3%; curriculum/instr.: 21%; evaluation/research/statistics: 1%; social/philosophical foundations: 3%; policy: 7%; educational tech.: 3%; educational psych: 8%; elementary: 6%; higher education admin.: 29%; secondary: 10%; special: 0%; other: 8%

Wayne State University
5425 Gullen Mall
Detroit, MI 48202-3489
http://www.coe.wayne.edu/
Public
Admissions: (313) 577-1605
E-mail: gradadmissions@wayne.edu
Financial aid: (313) 577-3378
Application deadline: rolling
In-state tuition: full time: $533/credit hour; part time: $533/credit hour
Out-of-state tuition: full time: $1,177/credit hour
Room/board/expenses: $16,257
Full-time enrollment: 595
doctoral students: 25%; master's students: 71%; education specialists: 4%; men: 27%; women: 73%; minorities: 28%; international: 7%
Part-time enrollment: 981
doctoral students: 11%; master's students: 74%; education specialists: 15%; men: 24%; women: 76%; minorities: 44%; international: 1%
Acceptance rate (master's): 44%
Acceptance rate (doctoral): 11%
Entrance test required: GRE
Avg. GRE (of all entering students with scores): quantitative: 146; verbal: 149
Research assistantships: 12
Students reporting specialty: 100%
Students specializing in: admin.: 11%; counseling: 12%; curriculum/instr.: 5%; evaluation/research/statistics: 3%; policy: 1%; educational tech.: 0%; educational psych: 8%; elementary: 6%; secondary: 10%; special: 11%; technical (vocational): 1%; instructional media design: 8%; other: 26%

Western Michigan University
1903 W. Michigan Avenue
Kalamazoo, MI 49008-5229
http://www.wmich.edu/education/
Public
Admissions: (269) 387-2000
E-mail: ask-wmu@wmich.edu
Financial aid: (269) 387-6000
Application deadline: rolling
In-state tuition: full time: $480/credit hour; part time: $480/credit hour
Out-of-state tuition: full time: $1,016/credit hour
Room/board/expenses: $13,341
Full-time enrollment: 748
doctoral students: 12%; master's students: 88%; education specialists: 0%; men: 29%; women: 71%; minorities: 19%; international: 10%
Part-time enrollment: 874
doctoral students: 22%; master's students: 78%; education specialists: 1%; men: 31%; women: 69%; minorities: 19%; international: 2%
Acceptance rate (master's): 68%
Acceptance rate (doctoral): 30%
Entrance test required: GRE
Avg. GRE (of all entering students with scores): quantitative: N/A; verbal: N/A
Research assistantships: 58
Students reporting specialty: 100%
Students specializing in: admin.: 18%; counseling: 14%; evaluation/research/statistics: 4%; social/philosophical foundations: 1%; elementary: 0%; higher education admin.: 4%; junior high: 0%; special: 6%; technical (vocational): 3%; instructional media design: 5%; other: 46%

MINNESOTA

Bethel University
3900 Bethel Drive
St. Paul, MN 55112-6999
http://gs.bethel.edu
Private
Admissions: (651) 635-8000
E-mail: gs@bethel.edu
Financial aid: (651) 638-6241
Application deadline: rolling
Tuition: full time: $490/credit hour; part time: $490/credit hour
Room/board/expenses: N/A
Full-time enrollment: 200
doctoral students: 36%; master's students: 65%; education specialists: N/A; men: 35%; women: 65%; minorities: 13%; international: 1%
Part-time enrollment: 169
doctoral students: 25%; master's students: 75%; education specialists: N/A; men: 34%; women: 66%; minorities: 7%; international: 1%
Acceptance rate (master's): 73%
Acceptance rate (doctoral): 86%
Entrance test required: N/A
Avg. GRE (of all entering students with scores): quantitative: N/A; verbal: N/A
Research assistantships: 0
Students reporting specialty: 100%
Students specializing in: admin.: 37%; special: 32%; other: 31%

Hamline University
1536 Hewitt Avenue
St. Paul, MN 55104-1284
http://www.hamline.edu
Private
Admissions: (651) 523-2900
E-mail: gradprog@hamline.edu
Financial aid: (651) 523-3000
Application deadline: rolling
Tuition: full time: $484/credit hour; part time: $484/credit hour
Room/board/expenses: $7,900
Full-time enrollment: 95
doctoral students: 2%; master's students: 98%; education specialists: N/A; men: 33%; women: 67%; minorities: 4%; international: 1%
Part-time enrollment: 808
doctoral students: 5%; master's students: 95%; education specialists: N/A; men: 27%; women: 73%; minorities: 8%; international: 1%
Acceptance rate (master's): 86%
Acceptance rate (doctoral): 100%
Entrance test required: N/A
Avg. GRE (of all entering students with scores): quantitative: N/A; verbal: N/A
Students reporting specialty: 100%
Students specializing in: N/A

University of Minnesota–Twin Cities
104 Burton Hall
178 Pillsbury Drive SE
Minneapolis, MN 55455
http://www.cehd.umn.edu
Public
Admissions: (612) 625-3339
E-mail: cehdinfo@umn.edu
Financial aid: (612) 624-1111
Application deadline: rolling
In-state tuition: full time: $15,520; part time: $1,214/credit hour
Out-of-state tuition: full time: $23,270
Room/board/expenses: $13,188
Full-time enrollment: 938
doctoral students: 55%; master's students: 45%; education specialists: 0%; men: 33%; women: 67%; minorities: 14%; international: 16%
Part-time enrollment: 580
doctoral students: 63%; master's students: 36%; education specialists: 1%; men: 35%; women: 65%; minorities: 14%; international: 7%
Acceptance rate (master's): 59%
Acceptance rate (doctoral): 41%
Entrance test required: GRE
Avg. GRE (of all entering students with scores): quantitative: N/A; verbal: N/A
Research assistantships: 233
Students reporting specialty: 100%
Students specializing in: admin.: 4%; counseling: 6%; curriculum/instr.: 11%; evaluation/research/statistics: 2%; social/philosophical foundations: 5%; educational tech.: 3%; educational psych: 6%; elementary: 6%; higher education admin.: 9%; secondary: 13%; special: 7%; instructional media design: 0%; other: 28%

University of St. Thomas
1000 LaSalle Avenue
Minneapolis, MN 55403
http://www.stthomas.edu/education
Private
Admissions: (651) 962-4550
E-mail: education@stthomas.edu
Financial aid: (651) 962-6550
Application deadline: rolling
Tuition: full time: $730/credit hour; part time: $730/credit hour
Room/board/expenses: $1,200
Full-time enrollment: 385
doctoral students: 11%; master's students: 84%; education specialists: 6%; men: 31%; women: 69%; minorities: 11%; international: 8%
Part-time enrollment: 428
doctoral students: 31%; master's students: 60%; education specialists: 9%; men: 31%; women: 69%; minorities: 15%; international: 1%
Acceptance rate (master's): 96%
Acceptance rate (doctoral): 83%
Entrance test required: N/A
Avg. GRE (of all entering students with scores): quantitative: N/A; verbal: N/A
Research assistantships: 3
Students reporting specialty: 98%
Students specializing in: admin.: 34%; curriculum/instr.: 4%; elementary: 14%; higher education admin.: 6%; junior high: 0%; secondary: 7%; special: 35%

MISSISSIPPI

Delta State University
1003 W. Sunflower Road
Cleveland, MS 38733
http://www.deltastate.edu/pages/251.asp
Public
Admissions: (662) 846-4875
E-mail: grad-info@deltastate.edu
Financial aid: (662) 846-4670
Application deadline: rolling
In-state tuition: full time: $5,724; part time: $318/credit hour
Out-of-state tuition: full time: $14,820
Room/board/expenses: $12,025
Full-time enrollment: 107
doctoral students: 3%; master's students: 84%; education specialists: 13%; men: 39%; women: 61%; minorities: 55%; international: 2%
Part-time enrollment: 427
doctoral students: 14%; master's students: 55%; education specialists: 31%; men: 18%; women: 82%; minorities: 51%; international: 1%
Acceptance rate (master's): 97%
Acceptance rate (doctoral): 79%
Entrance test required: GRE
Avg. GRE (of all entering students with scores): quantitative: N/A; verbal: N/A
Research assistantships: 0
Students reporting specialty: 100%
Students specializing in: admin.: 19%; counseling: 13%; elementary: 30%; secondary: 3%; special: 11%; other: 24%

Mississippi State University
PO Box 9710
Mississippi State, MS 39762
http://www.educ.msstate.edu/
Public
Admissions: (662) 325-2224
E-mail: grad@grad.msstate.edu
Financial aid: (662) 325-2450
Application deadline: N/A
In-state tuition: full time: $6,264; part time: $348/credit hour
Out-of-state tuition: full time: $9,564
Room/board/expenses: $17,158
Full-time enrollment: 376
doctoral students: 21%; master's students: 70%; education specialists: 9%; men: 35%; women: 65%; minorities: 29%; international: 3%
Part-time enrollment: 432
doctoral students: 57%; master's students: 36%; education specialists: 7%; men: 22%; women: 78%; minorities: 46%; international: 0%
Acceptance rate (master's): 35%
Acceptance rate (doctoral): 23%
Entrance test required: GRE
Avg. GRE (of all entering students with scores): quantitative: N/A; verbal: N/A
Research assistantships: 19
Students reporting specialty: 100%
Students specializing in: admin.: 26%; counseling: 21%; curriculum/instr.: 5%; educational psych: 6%; elementary: 2%; junior high: 1%; secondary: 12%; special: 2%; technical (vocational): 1%; other: 25%

University of Mississippi
222 Guyton Hall
University, MS 38677
http://education.olemiss.edu
Public
Admissions: (662) 915-7226
E-mail: admissions@olemiss.edu
Financial aid: (662) 915-5788
Application deadline: 03/01
In-state tuition: full time: $349/credit hour; part time: $349/credit hour
Out-of-state tuition: full time: $903/credit hour
Room/board/expenses: $18,798
Full-time enrollment: 260
doctoral students: 18%; master's students: 76%; education specialists: 6%; men: 23%; women: 77%; minorities: 31%; international: 2%
Part-time enrollment: 363
doctoral students: 19%; master's students: 66%; education specialists: 15%; men: 26%; women: 74%; minorities: 31%; international: 0%
Acceptance rate (master's): 41%
Acceptance rate (doctoral): 39%
Entrance test required: GRE
Avg. GRE (of all entering students with scores): quantitative: 141; verbal: 149
Research assistantships: 13
Students reporting specialty: 100%
Students specializing in: admin.: 26%; counseling: 19%; curriculum/instr.: 41%; higher education admin.: 13%

University of Southern Mississippi
118 College Drive, Box 5023
Hattiesburg, MS 39406
http://www.usm.edu
Public
Admissions: (601) 266-4369
Financial aid: (601) 266-4774

Application deadline: 05/01
In-state tuition: full time: $6,618; part time: $325/credit hour
Out-of-state tuition: full time: $14,730
Room/board/expenses: $11,348
Full-time enrollment: 277
doctoral students: 42%; master's students: 56%; education specialists: 2%; men: 23%; women: 77%; minorities: 21%; international: 4%
Part-time enrollment: 572
doctoral students: 53%; master's students: 44%; education specialists: 3%; men: 26%; women: 74%; minorities: 28%; international: 1%
Acceptance rate (master's): N/A
Acceptance rate (doctoral): N/A
Entrance test required: GRE
Avg. GRE (of all entering students with scores): quantitative: N/A; verbal: N/A
Students reporting specialty: 38%
Students specializing in: N/A

MISSOURI

St. Louis University
3500 Lindell Boulevard
St. Louis, MO 63103-3412
http://www.slu.edu/x7039.xml
Private
Admissions: (314) 977-3297
E-mail: swatekp@slu.edu
Financial aid: (314) 977-2350
Application deadline: rolling
Tuition: full time: $990/credit hour; part time: $990/credit hour
Room/board/expenses: $16,188
Full-time enrollment: 135
doctoral students: 81%; master's students: 19%; education specialists: 1%; men: 36%; women: 64%; minorities: 17%; international: 9%
Part-time enrollment: 308
doctoral students: 83%; master's students: 17%; education specialists: 0%; men: 36%; women: 64%; minorities: 19%; international: 3%
Acceptance rate (master's): 64%
Acceptance rate (doctoral): 78%
Entrance test required: GRE
Avg. GRE (of all entering students with scores): quantitative: N/A; verbal: N/A
Research assistantships: 16
Students reporting specialty: 42%
Students specializing in: N/A

University of Central Missouri
Lovinger 2190
Warrensburg, MO 64093
http://www.ucmo.edu/graduate
Public
Admissions: (660) 543-4621
E-mail: Gradinfo@ucmo.edu
Financial aid: (660) 543-4040
Application deadline: rolling
In-state tuition: full time: $272/credit hour; part time: $272/credit hour
Out-of-state tuition: full time: $543/credit hour
Room/board/expenses: $8,100
Full-time enrollment: 122
doctoral students: 1%; master's students: 97%; education specialists: 2%; men: 25%; women: 75%; minorities: 8%; international: N/A
Part-time enrollment: 666
doctoral students: 2%; master's students: 78%; education specialists: 20%; men: 21%; women: 79%; minorities: 6%; international: N/A
Acceptance rate (master's): 70%
Acceptance rate (doctoral): 100%
Entrance test required: GRE
Avg. GRE (of all entering students with scores): quantitative: N/A; verbal: N/A
Research assistantships: 1
Students reporting specialty: 100%
Students specializing in: admin.: 19%; counseling: 3%; curriculum/instr.: 27%; educational tech.: 0%; elementary: 4%; higher education admin.: 7%; secondary: 1%; special: 2%; instructional media design: 11%; other: 26%

University of Missouri
118 Hill Hall
Columbia, MO 65211
http://education.missouri.edu/
Public
Admissions: (573) 882-7832
E-mail: chvalkb@missouri.edu
Financial aid: (573) 882-7506
Application deadline: rolling
In-state tuition: full time: $337/credit hour; part time: $337/credit hour
Out-of-state tuition: full time: $869/credit hour
Room/board/expenses: $16,812
Full-time enrollment: 676
doctoral students: 50%; master's students: 47%; education specialists: 3%; men: 30%; women: 70%; minorities: 11%; international: 13%
Part-time enrollment: 822
doctoral students: 21%; master's students: 66%; education specialists: 13%; men: 29%; women: 71%; minorities: 8%; international: 4%
Acceptance rate (master's): 49%
Acceptance rate (doctoral): 16%
Entrance test required: GRE
Avg. GRE (of all entering students with scores): quantitative: 147; verbal: 155
Research assistantships: 124
Students reporting specialty: 100%
Students specializing in: admin.: 25%; counseling: 17%; curriculum/instr.: 51%; special: 5%; technical (vocational): 1%; other: 0%

University of Missouri–Kansas City
5100 Rockhill Road
Kansas City, MO 64110-2499
http://www.umkc.edu/
Public
Admissions: (816) 235-1111
E-mail: admit@umkc.edu
Financial aid: (816) 235-1154
Application deadline: rolling
In-state tuition: full time: $332/credit hour; part time: $332/credit hour
Out-of-state tuition: full time: $857/credit hour
Room/board/expenses: $19,068
Full-time enrollment: 226
doctoral students: 13%; master's students: 85%; education specialists: 2%; men: 31%; women: 69%; minorities: 20%; international: 4%
Part-time enrollment: 357
doctoral students: 17%; master's students: 68%; education specialists: 15%; men: 27%; women: 73%; minorities: 24%; international: 1%
Acceptance rate (master's): 70%
Acceptance rate (doctoral): 21%
Entrance test required: GRE
Avg. GRE (of all entering students with scores): quantitative: 146; verbal: 151
Research assistantships: 14
Students reporting specialty: 100%
Students specializing in: admin.: 17%; counseling: 20%; curriculum/instr.: 24%; educational psych: 0%; special: 5%; other: 35%

University of Missouri–St. Louis
1 University Boulevard
St. Louis, MO 63121
http://coe.umsl.edu
Public
Admissions: (314) 516-5458
E-mail: gradadm@umsl.edu
Financial aid: (314) 516-5508
Application deadline: rolling
In-state tuition: full time: $349/credit hour; part time: $349/credit hour
Out-of-state tuition: full time: $900/credit hour
Room/board/expenses: $16,711
Full-time enrollment: 189
doctoral students: 8%; master's students: 79%; education specialists: 13%; men: 19%; women: 81%; minorities: 21%; international: 9%
Part-time enrollment: 1,173
doctoral students: 19%; master's students: 78%; education specialists: 3%; men: 25%; women: 75%; minorities: 27%; international: 1%
Acceptance rate (master's): 86%
Acceptance rate (doctoral): 49%
Entrance test required: GRE
Avg. GRE (of all entering students with scores): quantitative: 150; verbal: 151
Research assistantships: 23
Students reporting specialty: 100%
Students specializing in: admin.: 14%; counseling: 13%; evaluation/research/statistics: 0%; elementary: 17%; secondary: 26%; special: 7%; other: 24%

Washington University in St. Louis
1 Brookings Drive, Box 1183
St. Louis, MO 63130-4899
http://education.wustl.edu
Private
Admissions: (314) 935-6791
E-mail: nkolk@artsci.wustl.edu
Financial aid: (314) 935-6880
Application deadline: N/A
Tuition: full time: $43,280; part time: $1,771/credit hour
Room/board/expenses: N/A
Full-time enrollment: 20
doctoral students: 40%; master's students: 60%; education specialists: N/A; men: 25%; women: 75%; minorities: 15%; international: N/A
Part-time enrollment: 1
doctoral students: 100%; master's students: 0%; education specialists: N/A; men: N/A; women: 100%; minorities: N/A; international: N/A
Acceptance rate (master's): 58%
Acceptance rate (doctoral): 15%
Entrance test required: GRE
Avg. GRE (of all entering students with scores): quantitative: 152; verbal: 159
Research assistantships: 0
Students reporting specialty: 100%
Students specializing in: policy: 41%; elementary: 23%; secondary: 36%

MONTANA

Montana State University[1]
215 Reid Hall
Bozeman, MT 59717
http://www.montana.edu/wwweduc/
Public
Admissions: (406) 994-4145
E-mail: gradstudy@montana.edu
Financial aid: (406) 994-2845
Tuition: N/A
Room/board expenses: N/A
Enrollment: N/A

University of Montana
PJWEC Room 321
Missoula, MT 59812
http://www.coehs.umt.edu
Public
Admissions: (406) 243-2572
E-mail: grad.school@umontana.edu
Financial aid: (406) 243-5373
Application deadline: rolling
In-state tuition: full time: $6,788; part time: N/A
Out-of-state tuition: full time: $23,455
Room/board/expenses: $14,290
Full-time enrollment: 169
doctoral students: 9%; master's students: 90%; education specialists: 1%; men: 27%; women: 73%; minorities: 6%; international: 3%
Part-time enrollment: 166
doctoral students: 45%; master's students: 54%; education specialists: 1%; men: 33%; women: 67%; minorities: 12%; international: 1%
Acceptance rate (master's): 31%
Acceptance rate (doctoral): 97%
Entrance test required: GRE
Avg. GRE (of all entering students with scores): quantitative: N/A; verbal: N/A
Research assistantships: 0
Students reporting specialty: 100%
Students specializing in: admin.: 31%; counseling: 12%; curriculum/instr.: 42%; other: 15%

NEBRASKA

University of Nebraska–Lincoln
233 Mabel Lee Hall
Lincoln, NE 68588-0234
http://cehs.unl.edu
Public
Admissions: (402) 472-2878
E-mail: graduate@unl.edu
Financial aid: (402) 472-2030
Application deadline: rolling
In-state tuition: full time: $285/credit hour; part time: $285/credit hour
Out-of-state tuition: full time: $769/credit hour
Room/board/expenses: $10,249
Full-time enrollment: 423
doctoral students: 42%; master's students: 57%; education specialists: 1%; men: 22%; women: 78%; minorities: 18%; international: 5%
Part-time enrollment: 548
doctoral students: 54%; master's students: 41%; education specialists: 4%; men: 35%; women: 65%; minorities: 12%; international: 1%
Acceptance rate (master's): 55%
Acceptance rate (doctoral): 43%
Entrance test required: GRE
Avg. GRE (of all entering students with scores): quantitative: N/A; verbal: N/A
Research assistantships: 41
Students reporting specialty: 100%
Students specializing in: admin.: 12%; counseling: 9%; curriculum/instr.: 12%; evaluation/research/statistics: 3%; educational psych: 6%; elementary: 9%; higher education admin.: 17%; secondary: 8%; special: 7%; instructional media design: 2%; other: 14%

University of Nebraska–Omaha
6001 Dodge Street
Omaha, NE 68182
http://www.unomaha.edu
Public
Admissions: (402) 554-2936
E-mail: graduate@unomaha.edu
Financial aid: (402) 554-3408
Application deadline: rolling
In-state tuition: full time: $245/credit hour; part time: $245/credit hour
Out-of-state tuition: full time: $646/credit hour
Room/board/expenses: $13,026
Full-time enrollment: 65
doctoral students: 6%; master's students: 75%; education specialists: 18%; men: 14%; women: 86%; minorities: 8%; international: 5%
Part-time enrollment: 421
doctoral students: 12%; master's students: 86%; education specialists: 2%; men: 20%; women: 80%; minorities: 5%; international: N/A
Acceptance rate (master's): 39%
Acceptance rate (doctoral): 63%
Entrance test required: GRE
Avg. GRE (of all entering students with scores): quantitative: 144; verbal: 149
Research assistantships: 10
Students reporting specialty: 100%
Students specializing in: admin.: 24%; counseling: 30%; elementary: 23%; secondary: 21%; special: 2%; instructional media design: 0%

NEVADA

University of Nevada–Las Vegas
4505 Maryland Parkway
Box 453001
Las Vegas, NV 89154-3001
http://graduatecollege.unlv.edu/admissions/
Public
Admissions: (702) 895-3320
E-mail: GradAdmissions@unlv.edu
Financial aid: (702) 895-3424
Application deadline: rolling
In-state tuition: full time: $5,500; part time: $264/credit hour
Out-of-state tuition: full time: $19,410
Room/board/expenses: $14,998
Full-time enrollment: 358
doctoral students: 10%; master's students: 87%; education specialists: 3%; men: 28%; women: 72%; minorities: 34%; international: 2%
Part-time enrollment: 557
doctoral students: 33%; master's students: 64%; education specialists: 3%; men: 26%; women: 74%; minorities: 30%; international: 2%
Acceptance rate (master's): 80%
Acceptance rate (doctoral): 69%
Entrance test required: GRE
Avg. GRE (of all entering students with scores): quantitative: 147; verbal: 150
Research assistantships: 21
Students reporting specialty: 0%
Students specializing in: N/A

University of Nevada–Reno
MS278
Reno, NV 89557-0278
http://www.unr.edu/grad
Public
Admissions: (775) 784-6869
E-mail: gradadmissions@unr.edu
Financial aid: (775) 784-4666

Application deadline: rolling
In-state tuition: full time: $240/credit hour; part time: $240/credit hour
Out-of-state tuition: full time: $14,313
Room/board/expenses: $19,303
Full-time enrollment: 277
doctoral students: 13%; master's students: 87%; education specialists: 0%; men: 30%; women: 70%; minorities: 14%; international: 2%
Part-time enrollment: 447
doctoral students: 24%; master's students: 75%; education specialists: 0%; men: 21%; women: 79%; minorities: 9%; international: 1%
Acceptance rate (master's): 85%
Acceptance rate (doctoral): 83%
Entrance test required: GRE
Avg. GRE (of all entering students with scores): quantitative: 151; verbal: 155
Research assistantships: 14
Students reporting specialty: 100%
Students specializing in: admin.: 5%; counseling: 16%; curriculum/instr.: 2%; educational tech.: 2%; educational psych: 2%; elementary: 8%; higher education admin.: 12%; secondary: 12%; special: 9%; other: 32%

NEW HAMPSHIRE

University of New Hampshire

Morrill Hall
Durham, NH 03824-3595
http://www.unh.edu/education/
Public
Admissions: (603) 862-2381
Financial aid: (603) 862-3600
Application deadline: rolling
In-state tuition: full time: $15,199; part time: $750/credit hour
Out-of-state tuition: full time: $27,639
Room/board/expenses: $21,300
Full-time enrollment: 144
doctoral students: 26%; master's students: 73%; education specialists: 1%; men: 23%; women: 77%; minorities: 4%; international: 3%
Part-time enrollment: 199
doctoral students: 7%; master's students: 77%; education specialists: 16%; men: 26%; women: 74%; minorities: 4%; international: N/A
Acceptance rate (master's): 76%
Acceptance rate (doctoral): 47%
Entrance test required: GRE
Avg. GRE (of all entering students with scores): quantitative: N/A; verbal: N/A
Research assistantships: 11
Students reporting specialty: 100%
Students specializing in: admin.: 9%; counseling: 11%; evaluation/research/statistics: 14%; elementary: 19%; secondary: 31%; special: 5%; other: 12%

NEW JERSEY

Montclair State University

1 Normal Avenue
Upper Montclair, NJ 07043
http://cehs.montclair.edu/
Public
Admissions: (973) 655-5147
E-mail: Graduate.School@montclair.edu
Financial aid: (973) 655-4461
Application deadline: rolling
In-state tuition: full time: $532/credit hour; part time: $532/credit hour
Out-of-state tuition: full time: $821/credit hour
Room/board/expenses: $15,421
Full-time enrollment: 485
doctoral students: 4%; master's students: 96%; education specialists: N/A; men: 29%; women: 71%; minorities: 29%; international: 2%
Part-time enrollment: 1,033
doctoral students: 6%; master's students: 94%; education specialists: N/A; men: 20%; women: 80%; minorities: 24%; international: 0%
Acceptance rate (master's): 57%
Acceptance rate (doctoral): 33%
Entrance test required: GRE
Avg. GRE (of all entering students with scores): quantitative: 146; verbal: 149
Research assistantships: 76
Students reporting specialty: 100%
Students specializing in: admin.: 9%; counseling: 20%; educational psych: 0%; special: 11%; other: 60%

Rowan University

201 Mullica Hill Road
Glassboro, NJ 08028
http://www.rowan.edu/
Public
Admissions: (856) 256-4050
E-mail: gradoffice@rowan.edu
Financial aid: (856) 256-4250
Application deadline: rolling
In-state tuition: full time: $630/credit hour; part time: $630/credit hour
Out-of-state tuition: full time: $630/credit hour
Room/board/expenses: N/A
Full-time enrollment: 179
doctoral students: 16%; master's students: 73%; education specialists: 11%; men: 25%; women: 75%; minorities: 26%; international: 1%
Part-time enrollment: 580
doctoral students: 28%; master's students: 68%; education specialists: 4%; men: 27%; women: 73%; minorities: 21%; international: 0%
Acceptance rate (master's): 96%
Acceptance rate (doctoral): 81%
Entrance test required: GRE
Avg. GRE (of all entering students with scores): quantitative: N/A; verbal: N/A
Research assistantships: 15
Students reporting specialty: 61%
Students specializing in: admin.: 74%; counseling: 16%; special: 10%

Rutgers, the State University of New Jersey–New Brunswick

10 Seminary Place
New Brunswick, NJ 08901-1183
http://www.gse.rutgers.edu
Public
Admissions: (732) 932-7711
E-mail: gradadm@rci.rutgers.edu
Financial aid: (732) 932-7057
Application deadline: 02/01
In-state tuition: full time: $16,635; part time: $626/credit hour
Out-of-state tuition: full time: $26,211
Room/board/expenses: $16,340
Full-time enrollment: 392
doctoral students: 14%; master's students: 86%; education specialists: N/A; men: 26%; women: 74%; minorities: 24%; international: 7%
Part-time enrollment: 421
doctoral students: 55%; master's students: 45%; education specialists: N/A; men: 29%; women: 71%; minorities: 21%; international: 2%
Acceptance rate (master's): 58%
Acceptance rate (doctoral): 47%
Entrance test required: GRE
Avg. GRE (of all entering students with scores): quantitative: 148; verbal: 151
Research assistantships: 5
Students reporting specialty: 100%
Students specializing in: admin.: 13%; counseling: 4%; evaluation/research/statistics: 2%; social/philosophical foundations: 4%; policy: 1%; educational tech.: 0%; educational psych: 5%; elementary: 8%; higher education admin.: 5%; secondary: 20%; special: 18%; instructional media design: 1%; other: 18%

Seton Hall University[1]

400 S. Orange Avenue
South Orange, NJ 07079
http://www.shu.edu/academics/education/
Private
Admissions: (973) 761-9668
E-mail: educate@shu.edu
Financial aid: (973) 761-9350
Tuition: N/A
Room/board expenses: N/A
Enrollment: N/A

NEW MEXICO

New Mexico State University

PO Box 30001, MSC 3AC
Las Cruces, NM 88003-8001
http://education.nmsu.edu
Public
Admissions: (505) 646-2736
E-mail: gradinfo@nmsu.edu
Financial aid: (505) 646-4105
Application deadline: N/A
In-state tuition: full time: $6,513; part time: $218/credit hour
Out-of-state tuition: full time: $19,540
Room/board/expenses: $13,064
Full-time enrollment: 328
doctoral students: 27%; master's students: 69%; education specialists: 4%; men: 19%; women: 81%; minorities: 47%; international: 10%
Part-time enrollment: 534
doctoral students: 28%; master's students: 69%; education specialists: 3%; men: 24%; women: 76%; minorities: 57%; international: 2%
Acceptance rate (master's): 48%
Acceptance rate (doctoral): 36%
Entrance test required: GRE
Avg. GRE (of all entering students with scores): quantitative: N/A; verbal: N/A
Research assistantships: 18
Students reporting specialty: 100%
Students specializing in: admin.: 18%; counseling: 8%; curriculum/instr.: 14%; special: 8%; other: 52%

University of New Mexico

MSC05 3040
Albuquerque, NM 87131-0001
http://www.unm.edu
Public
Admissions: (505) 277-2447
Financial aid: (505) 277-8900
Application deadline: rolling
In-state tuition: full time: $5,031; part time: $277/credit hour
Out-of-state tuition: full time: $15,993
Room/board/expenses: $14,808
Full-time enrollment: 412
doctoral students: 26%; master's students: 71%; education specialists: 3%; men: 30%; women: 70%; minorities: 46%; international: 7%
Part-time enrollment: 732
doctoral students: 29%; master's students: 68%; education specialists: 2%; men: 23%; women: 77%; minorities: 45%; international: 4%
Acceptance rate (master's): 43%
Acceptance rate (doctoral): 33%
Entrance test required: GRE
Avg. GRE (of all entering students with scores): quantitative: N/A; verbal: N/A
Research assistantships: 32
Students reporting specialty: 100%
Students specializing in: admin.: 11%; counseling: 8%; curriculum/instr.: 2%; social/philosophical foundations: 15%; educational psych: 3%; elementary: 15%; secondary: 8%; special: 14%; other: 24%

NEW YORK

Binghamton University–SUNY

PO Box 6000
Binghamton, NY 13902-6000
http://www2.binghamton.edu/soe/index.html
Public
Admissions: (607) 777-2151
E-mail: gradad@binghamton.edu
Financial aid: (607) 777-2428
Application deadline: 02/01
In-state tuition: full time: $12,260; part time: $390/credit hour
Out-of-state tuition: full time: $19,570
Room/board/expenses: N/A
Full-time enrollment: 117
doctoral students: 8%; master's students: 92%; education specialists: N/A; men: 29%; women: 71%; minorities: 9%; international: 3%
Part-time enrollment: 102
doctoral students: 39%; master's students: 61%; education specialists: N/A; men: 17%; women: 83%; minorities: 9%; international: 2%
Acceptance rate (master's): N/A
Acceptance rate (doctoral): N/A
Entrance test required: GRE
Avg. GRE (of all entering students with scores): quantitative: N/A; verbal: N/A
Students reporting specialty: 0%
Students specializing in: N/A

CUNY–Graduate Center

365 Fifth Avenue
New York, NY 10016
http://www.gc.cuny.edu
Public
Admissions: (212) 817-7470
E-mail: admissions@gc.cuny.edu
Financial aid: (212) 817-7460
Application deadline: 01/15
In-state tuition: full time: $8,083; part time: $440/credit hour
Out-of-state tuition: full time: $755/credit hour
Room/board/expenses: $25,046
Full-time enrollment: 86
doctoral students: 100%; master's students: N/A; education specialists: N/A; men: 20%; women: 80%; minorities: 10%; international: 2%
Part-time enrollment: 6
doctoral students: 100%; master's students: N/A; education specialists: N/A; men: 17%; women: 83%; minorities: 33%; international: N/A
Acceptance rate (master's): N/A
Acceptance rate (doctoral): 12%
Entrance test required: GRE
Avg. GRE (of all entering students with scores): quantitative: 150; verbal: 159
Research assistantships: 11
Students reporting specialty: 0%
Students specializing in: N/A

D'Youville College[1]

1 D'Youville Square
320 Porter Avenue
Buffalo, NY 14201-1084
http://www.dyc.edu/academics/education/index.asp
Private
Admissions: (716) 829-7676
E-mail: graduateadmissions@dyc.edu
Financial aid: (716) 829-7500
Tuition: N/A
Room/board expenses: N/A
Enrollment: N/A

Fordham University

113 W. 60th Street
New York, NY 10023
http://www.fordham.edu/gse
Private
Admissions: (212) 636-6400
E-mail: gse_admiss@fordham.edu
Financial aid: (212) 636-6400
Application deadline: rolling
Tuition: full time: $1,136/credit hour; part time: $1,136/credit hour
Room/board/expenses: $23,500
Full-time enrollment: 819
doctoral students: 31%; master's students: 58%; education specialists: 11%; men: 22%; women: 78%; minorities: 10%; international: 6%
Part-time enrollment: 346
doctoral students: 29%; master's students: 71%; education specialists: 0%; men: 42%; women: 58%; minorities: 27%; international: 1%
Acceptance rate (master's): 86%
Acceptance rate (doctoral): 36%
Entrance test required: GRE
Avg. GRE (of all entering students with scores): quantitative: N/A; verbal: N/A
Research assistantships: 95
Students reporting specialty: 100%
Students specializing in: admin.: 25%; counseling: 27%; curriculum/instr.: 1%; educational psych: 2%; elementary: 7%; secondary: 16%; special: 13%; other: 9%

Hofstra University

Hagedorn Hall
Hempstead, NY 11549
http://www.hofstra.edu/graduate
Private
Admissions: (800) 463-7872
E-mail: gradstudent@hofstra.edu
Financial aid: (516) 463-6680
Application deadline: rolling
Tuition: full time: $1,055/credit hour; part time: $1,055/credit hour
Room/board/expenses: $20,435
Full-time enrollment: 380
doctoral students: 11%; master's students: 89%; education specialists: N/A; men: 21%; women: 79%; minorities: 17%; international: 6%
Part-time enrollment: 368
doctoral students: 34%; master's students: 66%; education specialists: N/A; men: 28%; women: 72%; minorities: 24%; international: 1%
Acceptance rate (master's): 87%
Acceptance rate (doctoral): 51%

Entrance test required: GRE
Avg. GRE (of all entering students with scores): quantitative: N/A; verbal: N/A
Research assistantships: 40
Students reporting specialty: 100%
Students specializing in: admin.: 13%; curriculum/instr.: 0%; social/philosophical foundations: 0%; elementary: 6%; junior high: 0%; secondary: 1%; special: 22%; other: 57%

New York University (Steinhardt)

82 Washington Square E
Fourth Floor
New York, NY 10003
http://www.steinhardt.nyu.edu/
Private
Admissions: (212) 998-5030
E-mail: steinhardt.gradadmission@nyu.edu
Financial aid: (212) 998-4444
Application deadline: rolling
Tuition: full time $35,080; part time: $1,367/credit hour
Room/board/expenses: $30,852
Full-time enrollment: 2,224
doctoral students: 15%; master's students: 85%; education specialists: N/A; men: 23%; women: 77%; minorities: 26%; international: 21%
Part-time enrollment: 1,227
doctoral students: 17%; master's students: 83%; education specialists: N/A; men: 21%; women: 79%; minorities: 28%; international: 12%
Acceptance rate (master's): 48%
Acceptance rate (doctoral): 8%
Entrance test required: GRE
Avg. GRE (of all entering students with scores): quantitative: 153; verbal: 157
Research assistantships: 53
Students reporting specialty: 100%
Students specializing in: admin.: 3%; counseling: 6%; curriculum/instr.: 12%; social/philosophical foundations: 1%; policy: 5%; educational tech.: 1%; educational psych: 0%; elementary: 1%; higher education admin.: 4%; secondary: 5%; special: 3%; instructional media design: 1%; other: 58%

St. John's University

8000 Utopia Parkway
Queens, NY 11439
http://www.stjohns.edu/academics/graduate/education
Private
Admissions: (718) 990-2304
E-mail: graded@stjohns.edu
Financial aid: (718) 990-2000
Application deadline: 08/17
Tuition: full time $1,050/credit hour; part time: $1,050/credit hour
Room/board/expenses: $3,865
Full-time enrollment: 395
doctoral students: 5%; master's students: 92%; education specialists: 3%; men: 19%; women: 81%; minorities: 34%; international: 18%
Part-time enrollment: 1,174
doctoral students: 17%; master's students: 65%; education specialists: 18%; men: 23%; women: 77%; minorities: 34%; international: 1%
Acceptance rate (master's): 90%
Acceptance rate (doctoral): 78%
Entrance test required: GRE
Avg. GRE (of all entering students with scores): quantitative: N/A; verbal: N/A
Research assistantships: 0
Students reporting specialty: 100%

Students specializing in: admin.: 16%; counseling: 4%; curriculum/instr.: 7%; elementary: 5%; secondary: 11%; special: 12%; other: 45%

Syracuse University

230 Huntington Hall
Syracuse, NY 13244-2340
http://soe.syr.edu
Private
Admissions: (315) 443-2505
E-mail: gradrcrt@gwmail.syr.edu
Financial aid: (315) 443-1513
Application deadline: rolling
Tuition: full time $1,249/credit hour; part time: $1,249/credit hour
Room/board/expenses: $18,192
Full-time enrollment: 387
doctoral students: 33%; master's students: 67%; education specialists: N/A; men: 30%; women: 70%; minorities: 17%; international: 13%
Part-time enrollment: 196
doctoral students: 51%; master's students: 49%; education specialists: N/A; men: 26%; women: 74%; minorities: 11%; international: 4%
Acceptance rate (master's): 74%
Acceptance rate (doctoral): 44%
Entrance test required: GRE
Avg. GRE (of all entering students with scores): quantitative: 153; verbal: 157
Research assistantships: 24
Students reporting specialty: 98%
Students specializing in: admin.: 13%; counseling: 12%; curriculum/instr.: 6%; social/philosophical foundations: 12%; educational tech.: 1%; elementary: 3%; higher education admin.: 9%; secondary: 13%; special: 14%; instructional media design 9%; other: 12%

Teachers College, Columbia University

525 W. 120th Street
New York, NY 10027
http://www.tc.columbia.edu/
Private
Admissions: (212) 678-3710
E-mail: tcinfo@tc.columbia.edu
Financial aid: (212) 678-3714
Application deadline: rolling
Tuition: full time $1,286/credit hour; part time: $1,286/credit hour
Room/board/expenses: $25,750
Full-time enrollment: 1,746
doctoral students: 26%; master's students: 74%; education specialists: N/A; men: 21%; women: 79%; minorities: 31%; international: 20%
Part-time enrollment: 3,288
doctoral students: 30%; master's students: 70%; education specialists: N/A; men: 25%; women: 75%; minorities: 33%; international: 13%
Acceptance rate (master's): 56%
Acceptance rate (doctoral): 19%
Entrance test required: GRE
Avg. GRE (of all entering students with scores): quantitative: 153; verbal: 156
Research assistantships: 110
Students reporting specialty: 97%
Students specializing in: admin.: 5%; counseling: 17%; curriculum/instr.: 11%; evaluation/research/statistics: 1%; social/philosophical foundations: 11%; policy: 2%; educational tech.: 2%; educational psych: 6%; elementary: 10%; higher education admin.: 5%; secondary: 15%; special: 4%; instructional media design: 2%; other: 12%

University at Albany–SUNY

1400 Washington Avenue, ED 212
Albany, NY 12222
http://www.albany.edu/education
Public
Admissions: (518) 442-3980
E-mail: graduate@uamail.albany.edu
Financial aid: (518) 442-5757
Application deadline: N/A
In-state tuition: full time $10,579; part time $390/credit hour
Out-of-state tuition: full time: $17,889
Room/board/expenses: $13,108
Full-time enrollment: 429
doctoral students: 26%; master's students: 68%; education specialists: 6%; men: 22%; women: 78%; minorities: 15%; international: 12%
Part-time enrollment: 572
doctoral students: 37%; master's students: 57%; education specialists: 6%; men: 22%; women: 78%; minorities: 10%; international: 6%
Acceptance rate (master's): 63%
Acceptance rate (doctoral): 26%
Entrance test required: GRE
Avg. GRE (of all entering students with scores): quantitative: N/A; verbal: N/A
Research assistantships: 85
Students reporting specialty: 100%
Students specializing in: admin.: 6%; counseling: 15%; curriculum/instr.: 11%; evaluation/research/statistics: 2%; policy: 3%; educational tech.: 4%; educational psych: 4%; elementary: 12%; higher education admin.: 7%; secondary: 7%; special: 8%; instructional media design: 2%; other: 17%

University at Buffalo–SUNY

367 Baldy Hall
Buffalo, NY 14260-1000
http://www.gse.buffalo.edu
Public
Admissions: (716) 645-2110
E-mail: gseinfo@buffalo.edu
Financial aid: (716) 645-8232
Application deadline: rolling
In-state tuition: full time $11,231; part time $390/credit hour
Out-of-state tuition: full time: $18,541
Room/board/expenses: $17,149
Full-time enrollment: 482
doctoral students: 32%; master's students: 68%; education specialists: N/A; men: 23%; women: 77%; minorities: 27%; international: 22%
Part-time enrollment: 485
doctoral students: 34%; master's students: 66%; education specialists: N/A; men: 28%; women: 72%; minorities: 13%; international: 2%
Acceptance rate (master's): 63%
Acceptance rate (doctoral): 40%
Entrance test required: GRE
Avg. GRE (of all entering students with scores): quantitative: 150; verbal: 151
Research assistantships: 83
Students reporting specialty: 100%
Students specializing in: admin.: 9%; counseling: 10%; curriculum/instr.: 10%; social/philosophical foundations: 2%; educational tech.: 0%; educational psych: 2%; elementary: 9%; higher education admin.: 9%; secondary: 12%; special: 1%; other: 37%

University of Rochester (Warner)[1]

2-147 Dewey Hall
Rochester, NY 14627
http://www.rochester.edu/warner/
Private
Admissions: (716) 275-3950
E-mail: tmug@dbl.cc.rochester.edu
Financial aid: (716) 275-3226
Tuition: N/A
Room/board expenses: N/A
Enrollment: N/A

Yeshiva University (Azrieli)[1]

245 Lexington Avenue
New York, NY 10016
http://www.yu.edu/azrieli
Private
Admissions: (212) 340-7705
Financial aid: (212) 960-5269
Tuition: N/A
Room/board expenses: N/A
Enrollment: N/A

NORTH CAROLINA

Appalachian State University

College of Education Building
Boone, NC 28608-2068
http://www.graduate.appstate.edu
Public
Admissions: (828) 262-2130
E-mail: KrauseSL@appstate.edu
Financial aid: (828) 262-2190
Application deadline: rolling
In-state tuition: full time $6,557; part time $198/credit hour
Out-of-state tuition: full time: $18,369
Room/board/expenses: N/A
Full-time enrollment: 297
doctoral students: 3%; master's students: 92%; education specialists: 5%; men: 18%; women: 82%; minorities: 5%; international: 1%
Part-time enrollment: 708
doctoral students: 11%; master's students: 81%; education specialists: 8%; men: 19%; women: 81%; minorities: 6%; international: 0%
Acceptance rate (master's): 62%
Acceptance rate (doctoral): 54%
Entrance test required: GRE
Avg. GRE (of all entering students with scores): quantitative: 148; verbal: 152
Research assistantships: 25
Students reporting specialty: 100%
Students specializing in: admin.: 19%; counseling: 15%; curriculum/instr.: 2%; educational tech.: 12%; educational psych: 2%; elementary: 3%; higher education admin.: 11%; junior high: 2%; secondary: 4%; special: 2%; instructional media design: 4%; other: 24%

East Carolina University

E. Fifth Street
Greenville, NC 27858
http://www.ecu.edu/gradschool/
Public
Admissions: (252) 328-6012
E-mail: gradschool@ecu.edu
Financial aid: (252) 737-6610
Application deadline: N/A
In-state tuition: full time $5,592; part time $4,590
Out-of-state tuition: full time: $17,423
Room/board/expenses: $6,868

Full-time enrollment: 272
doctoral students: 20%; master's students: 80%; education specialists: 0%; men: 22%; women: 78%; minorities: 18%; international: N/A
Part-time enrollment: 832
doctoral students: 8%; master's students: 88%; education specialists: 4%; men: 20%; women: 80%; minorities: 16%; international: N/A
Acceptance rate (master's): 52%
Acceptance rate (doctoral): 50%
Entrance test required: GRE
Avg. GRE (of all entering students with scores): quantitative: N/A; verbal: N/A
Students reporting specialty: 0%
Students specializing in: N/A

Gardner-Webb University

110 S. Main Street
Boiling Springs, NC 28017
http://www.gardner-webb.edu
Private
Admissions: (800) 492-4723
E-mail: gradschool@gardner-webb.edu
Financial aid: (704) 406-3271
Application deadline: rolling
Tuition: full time: N/A; part time: N/A
Room/board/expenses: N/A
Full-time enrollment: 5
doctoral students: 20%; master's students: 80%; education specialists: N/A; men: 40%; women: 60%; minorities: 60%; international: N/A
Part-time enrollment: 1,302
doctoral students: 15%; master's students: 85%; education specialists: N/A; men: 22%; women: 78%; minorities: 31%; international: N/A
Acceptance rate (master's): 66%
Acceptance rate (doctoral): 39%
Entrance test required: GRE
Avg. GRE (of all entering students with scores): quantitative: N/A; verbal: N/A
Students reporting specialty: 100%
Students specializing in: admin.: 62%; curriculum/instr.: 7%; elementary: 23%; junior high: 8%

North Carolina State University–Raleigh

Campus Box 7801
Raleigh, NC 27695-7801
http://ced.ncsu.edu/
Public
Admissions: (919) 515-2872
E-mail: graduate_admissions@ncsu.edu
Financial aid: (919) 515-3325
Application deadline: N/A
In-state tuition: full time $10,620; part time: $6,152
Out-of-state tuition: full time: $22,668
Room/board/expenses: $17,412
Full-time enrollment: 475
doctoral students: 26%; master's students: 74%; education specialists: N/A; men: 27%; women: 73%; minorities: 23%; international: 4%
Part-time enrollment: 742
doctoral students: 44%; master's students: 56%; education specialists: N/A; men: 26%; women: 74%; minorities: 22%; international: 1%
Acceptance rate (master's): 50%
Acceptance rate (doctoral): 40%
Entrance test required: GRE
Avg. GRE (of all entering students with scores): quantitative: N/A; verbal: N/A

Research assistantships: 51
Students reporting specialty: 69%
Students specializing in: admin.: 36%; counseling: 10%; curriculum/instr.: 14%; evaluation/research/statistics: 9%; policy: 9%; educational psych: 2%; elementary: 2%; higher education admin.: 6%; junior high: 2%; secondary: 3%; special: 1%; technical (vocational): 2%; instructional media design: 4%

University of North Carolina–Chapel Hill

CB#3500, 101 Peabody Hall
Chapel Hill, NC 27599-3500
http://soe.unc.edu
Public
Admissions: (919) 966-1346
E-mail: ed@unc.edu
Financial aid: (919) 966-1346
Application deadline: rolling
In-state tuition: full time: $10,690; part time: $8,481
Out-of-state tuition: full time: $26,780
Room/board/expenses: $23,314
Full-time enrollment: 367
doctoral students: 52%; master's students: 48%; education specialists: N/A; men: 27%; women: 73%; minorities: 32%; international: 9%
Part-time enrollment: 138
doctoral students: 27%; master's students: 73%; education specialists: N/A; men: 16%; women: 84%; minorities: 22%; international: 1%
Acceptance rate (master's): 54%
Acceptance rate (doctoral): 46%
Entrance test required: GRE
Avg. GRE (of all entering students with scores): quantitative: N/A; verbal: N/A
Research assistantships: 45
Students reporting specialty: 100%
Students specializing in: admin.: 27%; counseling: 5%; curriculum/instr.: 4%; evaluation/research/statistics: 8%; social/philosophical foundations: 12%; educational psych: 6%; elementary: 6%; junior high: 1%; secondary: 8%; special: 2%; other: 22%

University of North Carolina–Charlotte

9201 University City Boulevard
Charlotte, NC 28223
http://education.uncc.edu/coe/
Public
Admissions: (704) 687-3366
E-mail: gradadm@email.uncc.edu
Financial aid: (704) 687-2461
Application deadline: N/A
In-state tuition: full time: $6,349; part time: $5,367
Out-of-state tuition: full time: $18,636
Room/board/expenses: $10,888
Full-time enrollment: 229
doctoral students: 29%; master's students: 71%; education specialists: N/A; men: 20%; women: 80%; minorities: 25%; international: 1%
Part-time enrollment: 636
doctoral students: 26%; master's students: 74%; education specialists: N/A; men: 24%; women: 76%; minorities: 24%; international: 1%
Acceptance rate (master's): 72%
Acceptance rate (doctoral): 57%
Entrance test required: GRE
Avg. GRE (of all entering students with scores): quantitative: N/A; verbal: N/A

Research assistantships: 25
Students reporting specialty: 100%
Students specializing in: N/A

University of North Carolina–Greensboro

School of Education Building
P.O. Box 26170
Greensboro, NC 27402-6170
http://www.uncg.edu/grs
Public
Admissions: (336) 334-5596
E-mail: inquiries@uncg.edu
Financial aid: (336) 334-5702
Application deadline: rolling
In-state tuition: full time: $6,723; part time: $4,540
Out-of-state tuition: full time: $20,172
Room/board/expenses: $9,848
Full-time enrollment: 278
doctoral students: 28%; master's students: 63%; education specialists: 9%; men: 21%; women: 79%; minorities: 28%; international: 5%
Part-time enrollment: 559
doctoral students: 44%; master's students: 51%; education specialists: 5%; men: 25%; women: 75%; minorities: 28%; international: 1%
Acceptance rate (master's): 35%
Acceptance rate (doctoral): 41%
Entrance test required: GRE
Avg. GRE (of all entering students with scores): quantitative: 147; verbal: 154
Research assistantships: 23
Students reporting specialty: 100%
Students specializing in: admin.: 18%; counseling: 7%; curriculum/instr.: 21%; evaluation/research/statistics: 5%; social/philosophical foundations: 8%; educational tech.: 0%; elementary: 3%; higher education admin.: 7%; junior high: 3%; secondary: 5%; special: 10%; other: 31%

Western Carolina University

Killian Building, Room 204
Cullowhee, NC 28723
http://www.wcu.edu/
Public
Admissions: (828) 227-7398
E-mail: grad@wcu.edu
Financial aid: (828) 227-7290
Application deadline: rolling
In-state tuition: full time: $11,034; part time: $565/credit hour
Out-of-state tuition: full time: $20,619
Room/board/expenses: $11,672
Full-time enrollment: 223
doctoral students: 0%; master's students: 92%; education specialists: 8%; men: 36%; women: 64%; minorities: 2%; international: 1%
Part-time enrollment: 303
doctoral students: 9%; master's students: 90%; education specialists: 0%; men: 11%; women: 89%; minorities: 2%; international: 23%
Acceptance rate (master's): 81%
Acceptance rate (doctoral): 0%
Entrance test required: GRE
Avg. GRE (of all entering students with scores): quantitative: N/A; verbal: N/A
Research assistantships: 26
Students reporting specialty: 100%
Students specializing in: admin.: 34%; counseling: 5%; junior high: 3%; other: 58%

NORTH DAKOTA

North Dakota State University

Box 6050, Department 2600
Fargo, ND 58108-6050
http://www.ndsu.edu/gradschool/
Public
Admissions: (702) 231-7033
E-mail: ndsu.grad.school@ndsu.edu
Financial aid: (701) 231-6200
Application deadline: rolling
In-state tuition: full time: $7,233; part time: $316/credit hour
Out-of-state tuition: full time: $10,301
Room/board/expenses: N/A
Full-time enrollment: 36
doctoral students: 19%; master's students: 81%; education specialists: 0%; men: 17%; women: 83%; minorities: N/A; international: N/A
Part-time enrollment: 180
doctoral students: 43%; master's students: 56%; education specialists: 2%; men: 32%; women: 68%; minorities: 6%; international: 2%
Acceptance rate (master's): 61%
Acceptance rate (doctoral): 74%
Entrance test required: N/A
Avg. GRE (of all entering students with scores): quantitative: N/A; verbal: N/A
Research assistantships: 0
Students reporting specialty: 100%
Students specializing in: admin.: 19%; counseling: 12%; curriculum/instr.: 25%; evaluation/research/statistics: 16%; higher education admin.: 5%; secondary: 8%; other: 15%

University of North Dakota

Box 7189
Grand Forks, ND 58202-7189
http://www.und.edu/dept/ehd/
Public
Admissions: (701) 777-2945
E-mail: education.und.edu/graduate-degrees.cfm
Financial aid: (701) 777-3121
Application deadline: rolling
In-state tuition: full time: $266/credit hour; part time: $266/credit hour
Out-of-state tuition: full time: $710/credit hour
Room/board/expenses: N/A
Full-time enrollment: 189
doctoral students: 38%; master's students: 62%; education specialists: 0%; men: 25%; women: 75%; minorities: 16%; international: 15%
Part-time enrollment: 511
doctoral students: 32%; master's students: 67%; education specialists: 1%; men: 24%; women: 76%; minorities: 15%; international: 3%
Acceptance rate (master's): 89%
Acceptance rate (doctoral): 88%
Entrance test required: N/A
Avg. GRE (of all entering students with scores): quantitative: N/A; verbal: N/A
Research assistantships: 14
Students reporting specialty: 70%
Students specializing in: admin.: 32%; counseling: 12%; elementary: 5%; special: 45%; instructional media design: 6%

OHIO

Ashland University (Schar)[1]

401 College Avenue
Ashland, OH 44805
http://www.ashland.edu
Private
Admissions: (419) 289-5657
E-mail: ggerick@ashland.edu
Financial aid: (419) 289-5002
Tuition: N/A
Room/board expenses: N/A
Enrollment: N/A

Bowling Green State University

444 Education Building
Bowling Green, OH 43403
http://www.bgsu.edu/colleges/edhd/
Public
Admissions: (419) 372-BGSU
E-mail: prospct@bgsu.edu
Financial aid: (419) 372-2651
Application deadline: rolling
In-state tuition: full time: $17,448; part time: $424/credit hour
Out-of-state tuition: full time: $28,410
Room/board/expenses: $13,896
Full-time enrollment: 169
doctoral students: 9%; master's students: 89%; education specialists: 1%; men: 18%; women: 82%; minorities: 6%; international: 7%
Part-time enrollment: 345
doctoral students: 23%; master's students: 72%; education specialists: 4%; men: 28%; women: 72%; minorities: 9%; international: 2%
Acceptance rate (master's): 33%
Acceptance rate (doctoral): 38%
Entrance test required: GRE
Avg. GRE (of all entering students with scores): quantitative: N/A; verbal: N/A
Research assistantships: 88
Students reporting specialty: 77%
Students specializing in: admin.: 22%; counseling: 6%; curriculum/instr.: 18%; educational tech.: 15%; higher education admin.: 7%; special: 11%; other: 22%

Cleveland State University

2121 Euclid Avenue, JH 210
Cleveland, OH 44115
http://www.csuohio.edu/cehs/
Public
Admissions: (216) 687-5599
E-mail: graduate.admissions@csuohio.edu
Financial aid: (216) 687-5411
Application deadline: rolling
In-state tuition: full time: $6,640; part time: $511/credit hour
Out-of-state tuition: full time: $12,490
Room/board/expenses: $12,648
Full-time enrollment: 1,286
doctoral students: 10%; master's students: 88%; education specialists: 2%; men: 26%; women: 74%; minorities: 31%; international: 4%
Part-time enrollment: N/A
doctoral students: N/A; master's students: N/A; education specialists: N/A; men: N/A; women: N/A; minorities: N/A; international: N/A
Acceptance rate (master's): 88%
Acceptance rate (doctoral): 52%
Entrance test required: GRE
Avg. GRE (of all entering students with scores): quantitative: 145; verbal: 153

Research assistantships: 25
Students reporting specialty: 71%
Students specializing in: admin.: 28%; counseling: 6%; curriculum/instr.: 53%; evaluation/research/statistics: 1%; policy: 2%; educational tech.: 6%; elementary: 13%; higher education admin.: 5%; junior high: 0%; secondary: 3%; special: 29%; other: 21%

Kent State University

PO Box 5190
Kent, OH 44242-0001
http://www.ehhs.kent.edu
Public
Admissions: (330) 672-2576
E-mail: ogs@kent.edu
Financial aid: (330) 672-2972
Application deadline: rolling
In-state tuition: full time: $8,424; part time: $468/credit hour
Out-of-state tuition: full time: $14,580
Room/board/expenses: $15,268
Full-time enrollment: 961
doctoral students: 33%; master's students: 64%; education specialists: 3%; men: 24%; women: 76%; minorities: 12%; international: 11%
Part-time enrollment: 598
doctoral students: 20%; master's students: 77%; education specialists: 4%; men: 25%; women: 75%; minorities: 11%; international: 2%
Acceptance rate (master's): 38%
Acceptance rate (doctoral): 28%
Entrance test required: GRE
Avg. GRE (of all entering students with scores): quantitative: 148; verbal: 151
Research assistantships: 56
Students reporting specialty: 100%
Students specializing in: admin.: 3%; counseling: 9%; curriculum/instr.: 7%; evaluation/research/statistics: 1%; social/philosophical foundations: 2%; educational psych: 3%; higher education admin.: 7%; junior high: 0%; secondary: 1%; special: 5%; instructional media design: 3%; other: 57%

Miami University

207 McGuffey Hall
Oxford, OH 45056
http://www.miami.muohio.edu/graduate-studies/index.html
Public
Admissions: (513) 529-3734
E-mail: gradschool@muohio.edu
Financial aid: (513) 529-8734
Application deadline: N/A
In-state tuition: full time: $12,972; part time: $538/credit hour
Out-of-state tuition: full time: $28,011
Room/board/expenses: $17,264
Full-time enrollment: 272
doctoral students: 8%; master's students: 81%; education specialists: 11%; men: 32%; women: 68%; minorities: 15%; international: 14%
Part-time enrollment: 377
doctoral students: 7%; master's students: 93%; education specialists: 0%; men: 19%; women: 81%; minorities: 9%; international: 3%
Acceptance rate (master's): 61%
Acceptance rate (doctoral): 0%
Entrance test required: GRE
Avg. GRE (of all entering students with scores): quantitative: N/A; verbal: N/A
Research assistantships: 2
Students reporting specialty: 59%

Students specializing in: admin.: 26%; counseling: 7%; curriculum/instr.: 11%; educational psych: 9%; elementary: 2%; higher education admin.: 16%; secondary: 9%; special: 8%; instructional media design: 0%; other: 12%

Ohio State University

1945 N. High Street
Columbus, OH 43210-1172
http://ehe.osu.edu/
Public
Admissions: (614) 292-9444
E-mail: domestic.grad@osu.edu
Financial aid: (614) 292-0300
Application deadline: rolling
In-state tuition: full time: $12,579; part time: $354/credit hour
Out-of-state tuition: full time: $29,891
Room/board/expenses: $18,194
Full-time enrollment: 718
doctoral students: 26%; master's students: 72%; education specialists: 2%; men: 27%; women: 73%; minorities: 12%; international: 11%
Part-time enrollment: 356
doctoral students: 55%; master's students: 44%; education specialists: 2%; men: 24%; women: 76%; minorities: 11%; international: 13%
Acceptance rate (master's): 49%
Acceptance rate (doctoral): 34%
Entrance test required: GRE
Avg. GRE (of all entering students with scores): quantitative: 151; verbal: 153
Research assistantships: 72
Students reporting specialty: 100%
Students specializing in: admin.: 8%; counseling: 9%; curriculum/instr.: 18%; evaluation/research/statistics: 1%; social/philosophical foundations: 2%; policy: 0%; educational tech.: 2%; educational psych: 2%; elementary: 12%; higher education admin.: 6%; junior high: 19%; secondary: 11%; special: 4%; technical (vocational): 3%; other: 20%

Ohio University

133 McCracken Hall
Athens, OH 45701-2979
http://www.cehs.ohio.edu
Public
Admissions: (740) 593-2800
E-mail: graduate@ohio.edu
Financial aid: (740) 593-4141
Application deadline: rolling
In-state tuition: full time: $9,444; part time: $583/credit hour
Out-of-state tuition: full time: $17,436
Room/board/expenses: $13,303
Full-time enrollment: 392
doctoral students: 23%; master's students: 77%; education specialists: N/A; men: 35%; women: 65%; minorities: 11%; international: 15%
Part-time enrollment: 542
doctoral students: 27%; master's students: 73%; education specialists: N/A; men: 51%; women: 49%; minorities: 14%; international: 3%
Acceptance rate (master's): 61%
Acceptance rate (doctoral): 56%
Entrance test required: GRE
Avg. GRE (of all entering students with scores): quantitative: 152; verbal: 147
Research assistantships: 28
Students reporting specialty: 40%
Students specializing in: N/A

University of Akron

302 Buchtel Common
Akron, OH 44325-4201
http://www.uakron.edu/admissions/graduate
Public
Admissions: (330) 972-7663
E-mail: gradschool@uakron.edu
Financial aid: (330) 972-5858
Application deadline: rolling
In-state tuition: full time: $405/credit hour; part time: $405/credit hour
Out-of-state tuition: full time: $693/credit hour
Room/board/expenses: $12,500
Full-time enrollment: 462
doctoral students: 10%; master's students: 90%; education specialists: N/A; men: 37%; women: 63%; minorities: 16%; international: 6%
Part-time enrollment: 584
doctoral students: 19%; master's students: 81%; education specialists: N/A; men: 28%; women: 72%; minorities: 17%; international: 1%
Acceptance rate (master's): 67%
Acceptance rate (doctoral): 31%
Entrance test required: GRE
Avg. GRE (of all entering students with scores): quantitative: N/A; verbal: N/A
Research assistantships: 17
Students reporting specialty: 69%
Students specializing in: admin.: 16%; counseling: 16%; evaluation/research/statistics: 3%; social/philosophical foundations: 2%; elementary: 5%; higher education admin.: 8%; junior high: 1%; secondary: 12%; special: 14%; technical (vocational): 5%; instructional media design: 9%; other: 63%

University of Cincinnati

PO Box 210002
Cincinnati, OH 45221-0002
http://www.cech.uc.edu
Public
Admissions: (513) 556-3817
E-mail: mary.boat@uc.edu
Financial aid: (513) 556-4170
Application deadline: rolling
In-state tuition: full time: $15,842; part time: $710/credit hour
Out-of-state tuition: full time: $27,356
Room/board/expenses: $15,280
Full-time enrollment: 452
doctoral students: 42%; master's students: 52%; education specialists: 5%; men: 29%; women: 71%; minorities: 12%; international: 10%
Part-time enrollment: 562
doctoral students: 17%; master's students: 81%; education specialists: 2%; men: 28%; women: 72%; minorities: 12%; international: 4%
Acceptance rate (master's): 54%
Acceptance rate (doctoral): 27%
Entrance test required: GRE
Avg. GRE (of all entering students with scores): quantitative: 150; verbal: 152
Research assistantships: 27
Students reporting specialty: 100%
Students specializing in: admin.: 12%; counseling: 2%; curriculum/instr.: 27%; social/philosophical foundations: 6%; junior high: 0%; secondary: 0%; special: 6%; other: 45%

University of Dayton

300 College Park
Dayton, OH 45469-0510
http://www.udayton.edu/education/
Private
Admissions: (937) 229-4411
E-mail: gradadmission@udayton.edu
Financial aid: (937) 229-4311
Application deadline: rolling
Tuition: full time: $541/credit hour; part time: $541/credit hour
Room/board/expenses: N/A
Full-time enrollment: 556
doctoral students: 31%; master's students: 67%; education specialists: 2%; men: 27%; women: 73%; minorities: 12%; international: 7%
Part-time enrollment: 441
doctoral students: 0%; master's students: 97%; education specialists: 3%; men: 25%; women: 75%; minorities: 13%; international: 12%
Acceptance rate (master's): 48%
Acceptance rate (doctoral): 39%
Entrance test required: GRE
Avg. GRE (of all entering students with scores): quantitative: 150; verbal: 149
Students reporting specialty: 100%
Students specializing in: admin.: 37%; counseling: 12%; curriculum/instr.: 1%; educational tech.: 2%; elementary: 5%; higher education admin.: 1%; junior high: 1%; secondary: 3%; special: 4%; other: 43%

University of Toledo

2801 W. Bancroft Street
Toledo, OH 43606
http://gradschool.utoledo.edu
Public
Admissions: (419) 530-4723
E-mail: grdsch@utnet.utoledo.edu
Financial aid: (419) 530-5812
Application deadline: rolling
In-state tuition: full time: $13,937; part time: $525/credit hour
Out-of-state tuition: full time: $24,171
Room/board/expenses: $16,824
Full-time enrollment: 237
doctoral students: 26%; master's students: 73%; education specialists: 0%; men: 29%; women: 71%; minorities: 13%; international: 6%
Part-time enrollment: 584
doctoral students: 36%; master's students: 57%; education specialists: 7%; men: 29%; women: 71%; minorities: 20%; international: 3%
Acceptance rate (master's): 51%
Acceptance rate (doctoral): 66%
Entrance test required: GRE
Avg. GRE (of all entering students with scores): quantitative: N/A; verbal: N/A
Research assistantships: 5
Students reporting specialty: 67%
Students specializing in: admin.: 10%; counseling: 5%; curriculum/instr.: 11%; evaluation/research/statistics: 2%; social/philosophical foundations: 2%; educational tech.: 2%; educational psych: 2%; elementary: 2%; higher education admin.: 22%; junior high: 4%; secondary: 10%; special: 17%; technical (vocational): 3%; instructional media design: 3%; other: 5%

Youngstown State University[1]

1 University Plaza
Youngstown, OH 44555
http://www.coe.ysu.edu/
Public
Admissions: (330) 742-3091
E-mail: graduateschool@cc.ysu.edu
Financial aid: (330) 941-3505
Tuition: N/A
Room/board expenses: N/A
Enrollment: N/A

OKLAHOMA

Oklahoma State University

325 Willard Hall
Stillwater, OK 74078-4033
http://www.okstate.edu/education/
Public
Admissions: (405) 744-6368
E-mail: grad-i@okstate.edu
Financial aid: (405) 744-6604
Application deadline: rolling
In-state tuition: full time: $178/credit hour; part time: $178/credit hour
Out-of-state tuition: full time: $709/credit hour
Room/board/expenses: $7,080
Full-time enrollment: 289
doctoral students: 38%; master's students: 60%; education specialists: 3%; men: 34%; women: 66%; minorities: 25%; international: 5%
Part-time enrollment: 543
doctoral students: 57%; master's students: 43%; education specialists: 0%; men: 33%; women: 67%; minorities: 15%; international: 2%
Acceptance rate (master's): 46%
Acceptance rate (doctoral): 30%
Entrance test required: GRE
Avg. GRE (of all entering students with scores): quantitative: N/A; verbal: N/A
Students reporting specialty: 69%
Students specializing in: admin.: 13%; counseling: 6%; curriculum/instr.: 8%; evaluation/research/statistics: 2%; social/philosophical foundations: 2%; policy: 14%; educational tech.: 3%; educational psych: 7%; elementary: 5%; higher education admin.: 14%; junior high: 5%; secondary: 3%; special: 4%; technical (vocational): 10%; instructional media design: 2%

Oral Roberts University

7777 S. Lewis Avenue
Tulsa, OK 74171
http://www.oru.edu/
Private
Admissions: (918) 495-6553
E-mail: gradedu@oru.edu
Financial aid: (918) 495-6602
Application deadline: rolling
Tuition: full time: $563/credit hour; part time: $563/credit hour
Room/board/expenses: N/A
Full-time enrollment: N/A
doctoral students: N/A; master's students: N/A; education specialists: N/A; men: N/A; women: N/A; minorities: N/A; international: N/A
Part-time enrollment: N/A
doctoral students: N/A; master's students: N/A; education specialists: N/A; men: N/A; women: N/A; minorities: N/A; international: N/A
Acceptance rate (master's): N/A
Acceptance rate (doctoral): N/A
Entrance test required: N/A
Avg. GRE (of all entering students with scores): quantitative: N/A; verbal: N/A
Students reporting specialty: 0%
Students specializing in: N/A

University of Oklahoma (Rainbolt)

820 Van Vleet Oval, No. 100
Norman, OK 73019-2041
http://www.ou.edu/education
Public
Admissions: (405) 325-2252
E-mail: admission@ou.edu
Financial aid: (405) 325-4521
Application deadline: rolling
In-state tuition: full time: $7,664; part time: $175/credit hour
Out-of-state tuition: full time: $19,126
Room/board/expenses: $14,704
Full-time enrollment: 509
doctoral students: 31%; master's students: 69%; education specialists: N/A; men: 33%; women: 67%; minorities: 25%; international: 5%
Part-time enrollment: 219
doctoral students: 66%; master's students: 34%; education specialists: N/A; men: 31%; women: 69%; minorities: 25%; international: 1%
Acceptance rate (master's): 71%
Acceptance rate (doctoral): 16%
Entrance test required: GRE
Avg. GRE (of all entering students with scores): quantitative: 151; verbal: 152
Research assistantships: 86
Students reporting specialty: 95%
Students specializing in: admin.: 26%; counseling: 10%; curriculum/instr.: 23%; evaluation/research/statistics: 6%; social/philosophical foundations: 4%; educational psych: 0%; higher education admin.: 26%; special: 5%

OREGON

Lewis & Clark College

0615 S.W. Palatine Hill Road
Portland, OR 97219-7899
http://graduate.lclark.edu
Private
Admissions: (503) 768-6200
E-mail: gseadmit@lclark.edu
Financial aid: (503) 768-7090
Application deadline: rolling
Tuition: full time: $773/credit hour; part time: $773/credit hour
Room/board/expenses: $7,275
Full-time enrollment: 199
doctoral students: 2%; master's students: 86%; education specialists: 12%; men: 26%; women: 74%; minorities: 12%; international: 2%
Part-time enrollment: 129
doctoral students: 21%; master's students: 56%; education specialists: 23%; men: 27%; women: 73%; minorities: 9%; international: 1%
Acceptance rate (master's): 88%
Acceptance rate (doctoral): 69%
Entrance test required: GRE
Avg. GRE (of all entering students with scores): quantitative: N/A; verbal: N/A
Research assistantships: 0
Students reporting specialty: 99%
Students specializing in: admin.: 35%; counseling: 14%; curriculum/instr.: 6%; educational psych: 9%; elementary: 12%; secondary: 15%; special: 5%; other: 5%

Oregon State University

104 Furman Hall
Corvallis, OR 97331-3502
http://oregonstate.edu/education/
Public
Admissions: (541) 737-4411
E-mail: osuadmit@oregonstate.edu
Financial aid: (541) 737-2241
Application deadline: 06/01
In-state tuition: full time: $12,845; part time: $421/credit hour
Out-of-state tuition: full time: $19,757
Room/board/expenses: $14,598
Full-time enrollment: 96
doctoral students: 41%; master's students: 59%; education specialists: N/A; men: 35%; women: 65%; minorities: 26%; international: 4%
Part-time enrollment: 238
doctoral students: 53%; master's students: 47%; education specialists: N/A; men: 28%; women: 72%; minorities: 26%; international: 1%
Acceptance rate (master's): 33%
Acceptance rate (doctoral): 46%
Entrance test required: N/A
Avg. GRE (of all entering students with scores): quantitative: N/A; verbal: N/A
Research assistantships: 9
Students reporting specialty: 32%
Students specializing in: N/A

Portland State University

PO Box 751
Portland, OR 97207-0751
http://www.ed.pdx.edu/admissions.shtml
Public
Admissions: (503) 725-3511
E-mail: adm@pdx.edu
Financial aid: (503) 725-3461
Application deadline: rolling
In-state tuition: full time: $10,362; part time: $337/credit hour
Out-of-state tuition: full time: $15,492
Room/board/expenses: $15,297
Full-time enrollment: 448
doctoral students: 7%; master's students: 93%; education specialists: N/A; men: 29%; women: 71%; minorities: 24%; international: 4%
Part-time enrollment: 633
doctoral students: 12%; master's students: 88%; education specialists: N/A; men: 22%; women: 78%; minorities: 15%; international: 1%
Acceptance rate (master's): 71%
Acceptance rate (doctoral): 84%
Entrance test required: N/A
Avg. GRE (of all entering students with scores): quantitative: N/A; verbal: N/A
Research assistantships: 1
Students reporting specialty: 100%
Students specializing in: admin.: 7%; counseling: 15%; curriculum/instr.: 22%; social/philosophical foundations: 20%; elementary: 1%; higher education admin.: 2%; junior high: 1%; special: 17%; instructional media design: 2%; other: 16%

University of Oregon

1215 University of Oregon
Eugene, OR 97403-1215
http://education.uoregon.edu/path.htm?setpath=19
Public
Admissions: (541) 346-3201
E-mail: uoadmit@oregon.uoregon.edu
Financial aid: (541) 346-3221
Application deadline: rolling
In-state tuition: full time: $14,877; part time: $490/credit hour
Out-of-state tuition: full time: $22,545
Room/board/expenses: $13,740
Full-time enrollment: 386
doctoral students: 36%; master's students: 64%; education specialists: N/A; men: 24%; women: 76%; minorities: 18%; international: 8%
Part-time enrollment: 115
doctoral students: 37%; master's students: 63%; education specialists: N/A; men: 33%; women: 67%; minorities: 12%; international: 24%
Acceptance rate (master's): 44%
Acceptance rate (doctoral): 17%
Entrance test required: GRE
Avg. GRE (of all entering students with scores): quantitative: 150; verbal: 154
Students reporting specialty: 74%
Students specializing in: admin.: 23%; social/philosophical foundations: 5%; elementary: 18%; secondary: 18%; special: 19%; other: 35%

PENNSYLVANIA

Arcadia University

450 S. Easton Road
Glenside, PA 19038-3295
http://www.arcadia.edu/
Private
Admissions: (877) 272-2342
E-mail: admiss@arcadia.edu
Financial aid: (215) 572-2980
Application deadline: rolling
Tuition: full time: $695/credit hour; part time: $695/credit hour
Room/board/expenses: $1,400
Full-time enrollment: 65
doctoral students: 2%; master's students: 77%; education specialists: 22%; men: 17%; women: 83%; minorities: 9%; international: 2%
Part-time enrollment: 523
doctoral students: 14%; master's students: 67%; education specialists: 19%; men: 21%; women: 79%; minorities: 19%; international: 1%
Acceptance rate (master's): 67%
Acceptance rate (doctoral): 83%
Entrance test required: N/A
Avg. GRE (of all entering students with scores): quantitative: N/A; verbal: N/A
Students reporting specialty: 100%
Students specializing in: admin.: 17%; elementary: 6%; secondary: 5%; special: 29%; instructional media design: 1%; other: 42%

Drexel University

3141 Chestnut Street
Philadelphia, PA 19104
http://goodwin.drexel.edu/soe
Private
Admissions: (215) 895-2400
E-mail: admissions@drexel.edu
Financial aid: (215) 895-1627
Application deadline: rolling
Tuition: full time: $1,045/credit hour; part time: $1,045/credit hour
Room/board/expenses: $17,895
Full-time enrollment: 56
doctoral students: 21%; master's students: 75%; education specialists: 4%; men: 34%; women: 66%; minorities: 34%; international: 2%
Part-time enrollment: 1,054
doctoral students: 17%; master's students: 66%; education specialists: 16%; men: 26%; women: 74%; minorities: 28%; international: 2%
Acceptance rate (master's): 89%
Acceptance rate (doctoral): 71%
Entrance test required: GRE
Avg. GRE (of all entering students with scores): quantitative: N/A; verbal: N/A
Research assistantships: 0
Students reporting specialty: 100%
Students specializing in: N/A

Duquesne University

600 Forbes Avenue
Pittsburgh, PA 15282
http://www.duq.edu/education/
Private
Admissions: (412) 396-6091
E-mail: black@duq.edu
Financial aid: (412) 396-6607
Application deadline: rolling
Tuition: full time: $966/credit hour; part time: $966/credit hour
Room/board/expenses: $12,748
Full-time enrollment: 571
doctoral students: 36%; master's students: 64%; education specialists: N/A; men: 26%; women: 74%; minorities: 7%; international: 5%
Part-time enrollment: 102
doctoral students: 3%; master's students: 97%; education specialists: N/A; men: 20%; women: 80%; minorities: 3%; international: 12%
Acceptance rate (master's): 57%
Acceptance rate (doctoral): 47%
Entrance test required: GRE
Avg. GRE (of all entering students with scores): quantitative: 147; verbal: 149
Research assistantships: 0
Students reporting specialty: 98%
Students specializing in: admin.: 13%; counseling: 28%; curriculum/instr.: 0%; evaluation/research/statistics: 1%; educational tech.: 11%; educational psych: 14%; elementary: 6%; junior high: 0%; secondary: 9%; special: 3%; other: 15%

East Stroudsburg University of Pennsylvania

200 Prospect Street
East Stroudsburg, PA 18301-2999
http://www.esu.edu
Public
Admissions: (570) 422-3536
E-mail: grad@po-box.esu.edu
Financial aid: N/A
Application deadline: 07/31
In-state tuition: full time: $429/credit hour; part time: $429/credit hour
Out-of-state tuition: full time: $670/credit hour
Room/board/expenses: $2,978
Full-time enrollment: 68
doctoral students: N/A; master's students: 100%; education specialists: 0%; men: 24%; women: 76%; minorities: 18%; international: 4%
Part-time enrollment: 113
doctoral students: N/A; master's students: 93%; education specialists: 7%; men: 23%; women: 77%; minorities: 17%; international: N/A
Acceptance rate (master's): 73%
Acceptance rate (doctoral): N/A
Entrance test required: GRE
Avg. GRE (of all entering students with scores): quantitative: N/A; verbal: N/A
Students reporting specialty: 100%
Students specializing in: admin.: 23%; elementary: 5%; secondary: 22%; special: 19%; instructional media design: 11%; other: 21%

Indiana University of Pennsylvania

104 Stouffer Hall
Indiana, PA 15705-1083
http://www.iup.edu/graduate
Public
Admissions: (724) 357-4511
E-mail: graduate-admissions@iup.edu
Financial aid: (724) 357-2218
Application deadline: rolling
In-state tuition: full time: $9,893; part time: $429/credit hour
Out-of-state tuition: full time: $13,763
Room/board/expenses: $14,409
Full-time enrollment: 276
doctoral students: 9%; master's students: 87%; education specialists: 4%; men: 20%; women: 80%; minorities: 8%; international: 4%
Part-time enrollment: 451
doctoral students: 52%; master's students: 39%; education specialists: 8%; men: 27%; women: 73%; minorities: 9%; international: 0%
Acceptance rate (master's): 31%
Acceptance rate (doctoral): 59%
Entrance test required: GRE
Avg. GRE (of all entering students with scores): quantitative: 145; verbal: 150
Students reporting specialty: 100%
Students specializing in: admin.: 14%; counseling: 19%; educational psych: 2%; elementary: 14%; special: 5%; other: 46%

Lehigh University

111 Research Drive
Bethlehem, PA 18015
http://coe.lehigh.edu/
Private
Admissions: (610) 758-3231
E-mail: ineduc@lehigh.edu
Financial aid: (610) 758-3181
Application deadline: rolling
Tuition: full time: $550/credit hour; part time: $550/credit hour
Room/board/expenses: $19,270
Full-time enrollment: 161
doctoral students: 40%; master's students: 53%; education specialists: 6%; men: 21%; women: 79%; minorities: 9%; international: 12%
Part-time enrollment: 313
doctoral students: 26%; master's students: 74%; education specialists: 0%; men: 30%; women: 70%; minorities: 8%; international: 8%
Acceptance rate (master's): 56%
Acceptance rate (doctoral): 16%
Entrance test required: GRE
Avg. GRE (of all entering students with scores): quantitative: 146; verbal: 154
Research assistantships: 39
Students reporting specialty: 100%
Students specializing in: admin.: 24%; counseling: 11%; educational psych: 14%; elementary: 4%; secondary: 6%; special: 16%; instructional media design: 7%; other: 18%

Pennsylvania State University–Harrisburg

777 W. Harrisburg Pike
Middletown, PA 17057
http://hbg.psu.edu/admissions/index.php
Public
Admissions: (717) 948-6250
E-mail: hbgadmit@psu.edu
Financial aid: (717) 948-6307
Application deadline: rolling
In-state tuition: full time: $18,552; part time: $9,714
Out-of-state tuition: full time: $24,648
Room/board/expenses: $18,098
Full-time enrollment: 22
doctoral students: 18%; master's students: 82%; education specialists: 0%; men: 36%; women: 64%; minorities: 18%; international: 14%
Part-time enrollment: 276
doctoral students: 12%; master's students: 75%; education specialists: 13%; men: 21%; women: 79%; minorities: 9%; international: 0%
Acceptance rate (master's): 83%
Acceptance rate (doctoral): 80%
Entrance test required: GRE
Avg. GRE (of all entering students with scores): quantitative: N/A; verbal: N/A
Research assistantships: 2
Students reporting specialty: 98%
Students specializing in: curriculum/instr.: 51%; secondary: 10%; other: 39%

Pennsylvania State University–University Park

274 Chambers Building
University Park, PA 16802-3206
http://www.ed.psu.edu
Public
Admissions: (814) 865-1795
E-mail: gadm@psu.edu
Financial aid: (814) 863-1489
Application deadline: rolling
In-state tuition: full time: $18,552; part time: $736/credit hour
Out-of-state tuition: full time: $31,256
Room/board/expenses: $16,019
Full-time enrollment: 552
doctoral students: 70%; master's students: 30%; education specialists: N/A; men: 31%; women: 69%; minorities: 18%; international: 30%
Part-time enrollment: 477
doctoral students: 43%; master's students: 57%; education specialists: N/A; men: 30%; women: 70%; minorities: 15%; international: 4%
Acceptance rate (master's): 32%
Acceptance rate (doctoral): 41%
Entrance test required: GRE
Avg. GRE (of all entering students with scores): quantitative: N/A; verbal: N/A
Research assistantships: 106
Students reporting specialty: 100%
Students specializing in: admin.: 10%; counseling: 12%; curriculum/instr.: 19%; social/philosophical foundations: 14%; policy: 26%; educational tech.: 4%; educational psych: 3%; elementary: 10%; higher education admin.: 7%; junior high: 0%; secondary: 8%; special: 10%; technical (vocational): 9%; instructional media design: 6%; other: 14%

Robert Morris University

6001 University Boulevard
Moon Township, PA 15108-1189
http://www.rmu.edu
Private
Admissions: (412) 397-5200
E-mail: admissions@rmu.edu
Financial aid: (412) 262-8212
Application deadline: rolling
Tuition: full time: N/A; part time: $750/credit hour
Room/board/expenses: N/A

Full-time enrollment: N/A
doctoral students: N/A; master's students: N/A; education specialists: N/A; men: N/A; women: N/A; minorities: N/A; international: N/A
Part-time enrollment: 226
doctoral students: 29%; master's students: 71%; education specialists: N/A; men: 36%; women: 64%; minorities: 10%; international: 3%
Acceptance rate (master's): 87%
Acceptance rate (doctoral): 72%
Entrance test required: N/A
Avg. GRE (of all entering students with scores): quantitative: N/A; verbal: N/A
Students reporting specialty: 100%
Students specializing in: curriculum/instr.: 90%; secondary: 2%; special: 8%

St. Joseph's University[1]

5600 City Avenue
Philadelphia, PA 19131
http://www.sju.edu
Private
Admissions: (610) 660-1101
E-mail: graduate@sju.edu
Financial aid: (610) 660-1555
Tuition: N/A
Room/board expenses: N/A
Enrollment: N/A

Temple University

OSS RA238
Philadelphia, PA 19122
http://www.temple.edu/
Public
Admissions: (215) 204-8011
E-mail: educate@blue.vm.temple.edu
Financial aid: (215) 204-1492
Application deadline: rolling
In-state tuition: full time: $687/credit hour; part time: $687/credit hour
Out-of-state tuition: full time: $961/credit hour
Room/board/expenses: $16,410
Full-time enrollment: 297
doctoral students: 63%; master's students: 34%; education specialists: 3%; men: 31%; women: 69%; minorities: 25%; international: 6%
Part-time enrollment: 525
doctoral students: 43%; master's students: 56%; education specialists: 1%; men: 41%; women: 59%; minorities: 16%; international: 28%
Acceptance rate (master's): 61%
Acceptance rate (doctoral): 62%
Entrance test required: GRE
Avg. GRE (of all entering students with scores): quantitative: 149; verbal: 154
Research assistantships: 34
Students reporting specialty: 100%
Students specializing in: admin.: 6%; counseling: 5%; curriculum/instr.: 1%; social/philosophical foundations: 6%; educational psych: 7%; elementary: 2%; higher education admin.: 5%; junior high: 1%; secondary: 3%; special: 4%; technical (vocational): 6%; other: 54%

University of Pennsylvania

3700 Walnut Street
Philadelphia, PA 19104-6216
http://www.gse.upenn.edu
Private
Admissions: (215) 898-6455
E-mail: admissions@gse.upenn.edu
Financial aid: (215) 898-6455

Application deadline: rolling
Tuition: full time: $44,632; part time: $5,580/credit hour
Room/board/expenses: $24,595
Full-time enrollment: 756
doctoral students: 9%; master's students: 91%; education specialists: N/A; men: 22%; women: 78%; minorities: 28%; international: 32%
Part-time enrollment: 409
doctoral students: 43%; master's students: 57%; education specialists: N/A; men: 31%; women: 69%; minorities: 22%; international: 10%
Acceptance rate (master's): 70%
Acceptance rate (doctoral): 6%
Entrance test required: GRE
Avg. GRE (of all entering students with scores): quantitative: 155; verbal: 157
Research assistantships: 91
Students reporting specialty: 100%
Students specializing in: admin.: 4%; counseling: 12%; curriculum/instr.: 34%; evaluation/research/statistics: 2%; social/philosophical foundations: 4%; policy: 6%; educational tech.: 0%; educational psych: 4%; elementary: 3%; higher education admin.: 15%; junior high: 0%; special: 3%; other: 20%

University of Pittsburgh

5601 Wesley W. Posvar Hall
Pittsburgh, PA 15260
http://www.education.pitt.edu
Public
Admissions: (412) 648-2230
E-mail: soeinfo@pitt.edu
Financial aid: (412) 648-2230
Application deadline: rolling
In-state tuition: full time: $20,076; part time: $782/credit hour
Out-of-state tuition: full time: $32,398
Room/board/expenses: $17,184
Full-time enrollment: 500
doctoral students: 38%; master's students: 62%; education specialists: N/A; men: 28%; women: 72%; minorities: 11%; international: 18%
Part-time enrollment: 410
doctoral students: 39%; master's students: 61%; education specialists: N/A; men: 28%; women: 72%; minorities: 9%; international: 1%
Acceptance rate (master's): 70%
Acceptance rate (doctoral): 47%
Entrance test required: GRE
Avg. GRE (of all entering students with scores): quantitative: N/A; verbal: N/A
Research assistantships: 37
Students reporting specialty: 100%
Students specializing in: admin.: 13%; curriculum/instr.: 1%; evaluation/research/statistics: 2%; social/philosophical foundations: 10%; policy: 2%; educational psych: 8%; elementary: 7%; higher education admin.: 10%; secondary: 20%; special: 12%; other: 16%

Widener University

1 University Place
Chester, PA 19013-5792
http://www.widener.edu
Private
Admissions: (610) 499-4490
E-mail: JcFlynn@widener.edu
Financial aid: (610) 499-4174
Application deadline: rolling
Tuition: full time: $704/credit hour; part time: $704/credit hour
Room/board/expenses: N/A
Full-time enrollment: 125
doctoral students: 82%; master's students: 18%; education

specialists: N/A; men: 25%; women: 75%; minorities: 18%; international: 2%
Part-time enrollment: 150
doctoral students: 70%; master's students: 30%; education specialists: N/A; men: 30%; women: 70%; minorities: 23%; international: 1%
Acceptance rate (master's): 57%
Acceptance rate (doctoral): 61%
Entrance test required: GRE
Avg. GRE (of all entering students with scores): quantitative: N/A; verbal: N/A
Research assistantships: 0
Students reporting specialty: 98%
Students specializing in: admin.: 46%; counseling: 5%; social/philosophical foundations: 6%; educational tech.: 2%; educational psych: 1%; elementary: 3%; higher education admin.: 15%; junior high: 0%; special: 3%; other: 20%

RHODE ISLAND

University of Rhode Island-Rhode Island College (Feinstein)

600 Mount Pleasant Avenue
Providence, RI 02908
http://www.uri.edu/hss/education/phd/
Public
Admissions: (401) 456-8594
E-mail: kcastagno@ric.edu
Financial aid: (401) 456-8033
Application deadline: 01/31
In-state tuition: full time: $641/credit hour; part time: $641/credit hour
Out-of-state tuition: full time: $1,311/credit hour
Room/board/expenses: $600
Full-time enrollment: 2
doctoral students: 100%; master's students: N/A; education specialists: N/A; men: 50%; women: 50%; minorities: N/A; international: 50%
Part-time enrollment: 81
doctoral students: 100%; master's students: N/A; education specialists: N/A; men: 21%; women: 79%; minorities: 7%; international: 1%
Acceptance rate (master's): N/A
Acceptance rate (doctoral): 55%
Entrance test required: GRE
Avg. GRE (of all entering students with scores): quantitative: N/A; verbal: N/A
Students reporting specialty: 0%
Students specializing in: N/A

SOUTH CAROLINA

Clemson University (Moore)

102 Tillman Hall
Clemson, SC 29634-0702
http://www.grad.clemson.edu
Public
Admissions: (864) 656-3195
E-mail: grdapp@clemson.edu
Financial aid: (864) 656-2280
Application deadline: rolling
In-state tuition: full time: $7,488; part time: $442/credit hour
Out-of-state tuition: full time: $14,909
Room/board/expenses: $0
Full-time enrollment: 249
doctoral students: 22%; master's students: 77%; education specialists: 1%; men: 33%; women: 67%; minorities: 20%; international: 4%
Part-time enrollment: 248
doctoral students: 38%; master's

students: 48%; education specialists: 15%; men: 29%; women: 71%; minorities: 13%; international: N/A
Acceptance rate (master's): 67%
Acceptance rate (doctoral): 56%
Entrance test required: GRE
Avg. GRE (of all entering students with scores): quantitative: 147; verbal: 150
Research assistantships: 31
Students reporting specialty: 100%
Students specializing in: admin.: 23%; counseling: 31%; curriculum/instr.: 9%; junior high: 8%; secondary: 2%; special: 1%; other: 25%

South Carolina State University

PO Box 7298
300 College Street NE
Orangeburg, SC 29117
http://www.scsu.edu/academics/collegeofeducationhumanities
socialsciences.aspx
Public
Admissions: (803) 536-7186
E-mail: admissions@scsu.edu
Financial aid: (803) 536-7067
Application deadline: N/A
In-state tuition: full time: $9,258; part time: $514/credit hour
Out-of-state tuition: full time: $18,170
Room/board/expenses: N/A
Full-time enrollment: 105
doctoral students: 2%; master's students: 88%; education specialists: 10%; men: 19%; women: 81%; minorities: 98%; international: N/A
Part-time enrollment: 220
doctoral students: 47%; master's students: 26%; education specialists: 26%; men: 25%; women: 75%; minorities: 92%; international: N/A
Acceptance rate (master's): N/A
Acceptance rate (doctoral): 80%
Entrance test required: N/A
Avg. GRE (of all entering students with scores): quantitative: N/A; verbal: N/A
Students reporting specialty: 0%
Students specializing in: N/A

University of South Carolina

Wardlaw Building
Columbia, SC 29208
http://www.ed.sc.edu
Public
Admissions: (803) 777-4243
E-mail: gradapp@mailbox.sc.edu
Financial aid: (803) 777-8134
Application deadline: rolling
In-state tuition: full time: $11,672; part time: $470/credit hour
Out-of-state tuition: full time: $24,596
Room/board/expenses: $15,774
Full-time enrollment: 396
doctoral students: 17%; master's students: 74%; education specialists: 9%; men: 27%; women: 73%; minorities: 17%; international: 4%
Part-time enrollment: 687
doctoral students: 41%; master's students: 54%; education specialists: 5%; men: 25%; women: 75%; minorities: 25%; international: 1%
Acceptance rate (master's): 77%
Acceptance rate (doctoral): 54%
Entrance test required: GRE
Avg. GRE (of all entering students with scores): quantitative: 150; verbal: 150
Research assistantships: 17
Students reporting specialty: 100%

Students specializing in: admin.: 28%; counseling: 7%; curriculum/instr.: 4%; evaluation/research/statistics: 3%; social/philosophical foundations: 1%; elementary: 2%; higher education admin.: 12%; secondary: 8%; special: 7%; instructional media design: 1%; other: 28%

SOUTH DAKOTA

University of South Dakota

414 E. Clark Street
Vermillion, SD 57069
http://www.usd.edu/grad
Public
Admissions: (605) 677-6240
E-mail: grad@usd.edu
Financial aid: (605) 677-5446
Application deadline: rolling
In-state tuition: full time: $197/credit hour; part time: $197/credit hour
Out-of-state tuition: full time: $417/credit hour
Room/board/expenses: $10,931
Full-time enrollment: 161
doctoral students: 35%; master's students: 50%; education specialists: 15%; men: 36%; women: 64%; minorities: 6%; international: 6%
Part-time enrollment: 401
doctoral students: 47%; master's students: 38%; education specialists: 16%; men: 34%; women: 66%; minorities: 7%; international: 0%
Acceptance rate (master's): 82%
Acceptance rate (doctoral): 86%
Entrance test required: GRE
Avg. GRE (of all entering students with scores): quantitative: 148; verbal: 151
Research assistantships: 9
Students reporting specialty: 100%
Students specializing in: admin.: 33%; counseling: 12%; curriculum/instr.: 8%; educational psych: 12%; elementary: 3%; higher education admin.: 20%; secondary: 2%; special: 4%; instructional media design: 3%; other: 4%

TENNESSEE

East Tennessee State University (Clemmer)[1]

PO Box 70720
Johnson City, TN 37614-0720
http://www.etsu.edu/coe/
Public
Admissions: (423) 439-4221
E-mail: gradsch@etsu.edu
Financial aid: (423) 439-4300
Tuition: N/A
Room/board expenses: N/A
Enrollment: N/A

Tennessee State University[1]

3500 John A. Merritt Boulevard
Nashville, TN 37209-1561
http://www.tnstate.edu
Public
Admissions: (615) 963-5901
E-mail: gradschool@tnstate.edu
Financial aid: (615) 963-5701
Tuition: N/A
Room/board expenses: N/A
Enrollment: N/A

Tennessee Technological University

Box 5012
Cookeville, TN 38505-0001
http://www.tntech.edu/
Public
Admissions: (931) 372-3866
E-mail: gradstudies@tntech.edu
Financial aid: (931) 372-3073
Application deadline: 08/01
In-state tuition: full time: $12,666; part time: $441/credit hour
Out-of-state tuition: full time: $32,106
Room/board/expenses: $15,450
Full-time enrollment: 150
doctoral students: 4%; master's students: 85%; education specialists: 11%; men: 26%; women: 74%; minorities: 14%; international: 3%
Part-time enrollment: 388
doctoral students: 8%; master's students: 66%; education specialists: 27%; men: 26%; women: 74%; minorities: 6%; international: 1%
Acceptance rate (master's): 69%
Acceptance rate (doctoral): 57%
Entrance test required: GRE
Avg. GRE (of all entering students with scores): quantitative: N/A; verbal: N/A
Students reporting specialty: 56%
Students specializing in: admin.: 12%; counseling: 17%; curriculum/instr.: 24%; evaluation/research/statistics: 7%; educational tech.: 1%; educational psych: 4%; elementary: 5%; secondary: 12%; special: 7%; other: 11%

Trevecca Nazarene University[1]

333 Murfreesboro Road
Nashville, TN 37210
http://www.trevecca.edu
Private
Admissions: (800) 284-1594
E-mail: admissions_ged.@trevecca.edu
Financial aid: (615) 248-1242
Tuition: N/A
Room/board expenses: N/A
Enrollment: N/A

Union University

1050 Union University Drive
Jackson, TN 38305
http://www.uu.edu/
Private
Admissions: (731) 661-5374
E-mail: hfowler@uu.edu
Financial aid: (731) 661-5015
Application deadline: rolling
Tuition: full time: $425/credit hour; part time: $425/credit hour
Room/board/expenses: N/A
Full-time enrollment: N/A
doctoral students: N/A; master's students: N/A; education specialists: N/A; men: N/A; women: N/A; minorities: N/A; international: N/A
Part-time enrollment: N/A
doctoral students: N/A; master's students: N/A; education specialists: N/A; men: N/A; women: N/A; minorities: N/A; international: N/A
Acceptance rate (master's): N/A
Acceptance rate (doctoral): N/A
Entrance test required: GRE
Avg. GRE (of all entering students with scores): quantitative: N/A; verbal: N/A
Research assistantships: 2
Students reporting specialty: 90%
Students specializing in: admin.: 20%; curriculum/instr.: 26%; higher education admin.: 8%; other: 45%

University of Memphis

215 Ball Hall
Memphis, TN 38152-6015
http://www.memphis.edu/admissions.htm
Public
Admissions: (901) 678-2911
E-mail: admissions@memphis.edu
Financial aid: (901) 678-4825
Application deadline: rolling
In-state tuition: full time: $377/credit hour; part time: $540/credit hour
Out-of-state tuition: full time: $968/credit hour
Room/board/expenses: N/A
Full-time enrollment: 298
doctoral students: 23%; master's students: 76%; education specialists: 1%; men: 26%; women: 74%; minorities: 27%; international: 4%
Part-time enrollment: 661
doctoral students: 37%; master's students: 61%; education specialists: 2%; men: 26%; women: 74%; minorities: 43%; international: 1%
Acceptance rate (master's): 70%
Acceptance rate (doctoral): 42%
Entrance test required: GRE
Avg. GRE (of all entering students with scores): quantitative: 145; verbal: 150
Students reporting specialty: 92%
Students specializing in: admin.: 11%; counseling: 14%; curriculum/instr.: 48%; educational psych: 4%; higher education admin.: 6%; instructional media design: 2%; other: 18%

University of Tennessee–Knoxville

335 Claxton Complex
Knoxville, TN 37996-3400
http://cehhs.utk.edu
Public
Admissions: (865) 974-3251
E-mail: nfox@utk.edu
Financial aid: (865) 974-3131
Application deadline: rolling
In-state tuition: full time: $11,560; part time: $501/credit hour
Out-of-state tuition: full time: $30,048
Room/board/expenses: $17,534
Full-time enrollment: 344
doctoral students: 26%; master's students: 70%; education specialists: 4%; men: 20%; women: 80%; minorities: 13%; international: 3%
Part-time enrollment: 288
doctoral students: 45%; master's students: 39%; education specialists: 15%; men: 26%; women: 74%; minorities: 14%; international: 2%
Acceptance rate (master's): 78%
Acceptance rate (doctoral): 53%
Entrance test required: GRE
Avg. GRE (of all entering students with scores): quantitative: 148; verbal: 151
Research assistantships: 75
Students reporting specialty: 100%
Students specializing in: admin.: 6%; counseling: 8%; evaluation/research/statistics: 2%; social/philosophical foundations: 2%; policy: 5%; educational tech.: 4%; educational psych: 12%; elementary: 13%; higher education admin.: 6%; junior high: 3%; secondary: 10%; special: 6%; other: 22%

Vanderbilt University (Peabody)

PO Box 327
Nashville, TN 37203-9418
http://peabody.vanderbilt.edu
Private
Admissions: (615) 322-8410
E-mail: peabody.admissions@vanderbilt.edu
Financial aid: (615) 322-8400
Application deadline: 12/31
Tuition: full time: $1,712/credit hour; part time: $1,712/credit hour
Room/board/expenses: $22,610
Full-time enrollment: 648
doctoral students: 32%; master's students: 68%; education specialists: N/A; men: 22%; women: 78%; minorities: 15%; international: 11%
Part-time enrollment: 160
doctoral students: 39%; master's students: 61%; education specialists: N/A; men: 38%; women: 63%; minorities: 19%; international: 8%
Acceptance rate (master's): 58%
Acceptance rate (doctoral): 5%
Entrance test required: GRE
Avg. GRE (of all entering students with scores): quantitative: 154; verbal: 158
Research assistantships: 242
Students reporting specialty: 100%
Students specializing in: admin.: 4%; counseling: 7%; curriculum/instr.: 9%; evaluation/research/statistics: 16%; policy: 16%; elementary: 4%; higher education admin.: 10%; secondary: 5%; special: 16%; other: 13%

TEXAS

Baylor University

1 Bear Place #97304
Waco, TX 76798-7304
http://www.baylor.edu/SOE/
Private
Admissions: (254) 710-3584
E-mail: graduate_school@baylor.edu
Financial aid: (254) 710-2611
Application deadline: rolling
Tuition: full time: $1,274/credit hour; part time: $1,274/credit hour
Room/board/expenses: $10,498
Full-time enrollment: 174
doctoral students: 22%; master's students: 66%; education specialists: 12%; men: 34%; women: 66%; minorities: 25%; international: 7%
Part-time enrollment: 55
doctoral students: 31%; master's students: 69%; education specialists: 0%; men: 47%; women: 53%; minorities: 20%; international: 2%
Acceptance rate (master's): 53%
Acceptance rate (doctoral): 33%
Entrance test required: GRE
Avg. GRE (of all entering students with scores): quantitative: N/A; verbal: N/A
Research assistantships: 89
Students reporting specialty: 100%
Students specializing in: admin.: 16%; curriculum/instr.: 20%; educational psych: 10%; other: 55%

Lamar University

PO Box 10034
Lamar University Station
Beaumont, TX 77710
http://dept.lamar.edu/education/
Public
Admissions: (409) 880-8356
E-mail: gradmissions@hal.lamar.edu
Financial aid: (409) 880-8450
Application deadline: rolling
In-state tuition: full time: $7,208; part time: $298/credit hour
Out-of-state tuition: full time: $14,426
Room/board/expenses: $13,842
Full-time enrollment: 47
doctoral students: 30%; master's students: 70%; education specialists: N/A; men: 30%; women: 70%; minorities: 43%; international: 21%
Part-time enrollment: 2,963
doctoral students: 7%; master's students: 93%; education specialists: N/A; men: 25%; women: 75%; minorities: 33%; international: 0%
Acceptance rate (master's): N/A
Acceptance rate (doctoral): N/A
Entrance test required: GRE
Avg. GRE (of all entering students with scores): quantitative: N/A; verbal: N/A
Students reporting specialty: 87%
Students specializing in: admin.: 48%; curriculum/instr.: 4%; educational psych: 37%; elementary: 0%; secondary: 0%; special: 1%; instructional media design: 10%

Our Lady of the Lake University

411 S.W. 24th Street
San Antonio, TX 78207
http://www.ollusa.edu
Private
Admissions: (210) 431-3961
E-mail: gradadm@lake.ollusa.edu
Financial aid: (210) 431-3960
Application deadline: rolling
Tuition: full time: $23,613; part time: $735/credit hour
Room/board/expenses: $10,484
Full-time enrollment: 6
doctoral students: N/A; master's students: 100%; education specialists: N/A; men: N/A; women: 100%; minorities: 67%; international: N/A
Part-time enrollment: 38
doctoral students: N/A; master's students: 100%; education specialists: N/A; men: N/A; women: 100%; minorities: 47%; international: N/A
Acceptance rate (master's): N/A
Acceptance rate (doctoral): N/A
Entrance test required: GRE
Avg. GRE (of all entering students with scores): quantitative: N/A; verbal: N/A
Research assistantships: 1
Students reporting specialty: 94%
Students specializing in: counseling: 86%; educational tech.: 2%; elementary: 7%; other: 5%

Sam Houston State University

PO Box 2119
Huntsville, TX 77341
http://www.shsu.edu/~grs_www
Public
Admissions: (936) 294-1971
E-mail: graduate@shsu.edu
Financial aid: (936) 294-1724
Application deadline: 08/01
In-state tuition: full time: $237/credit hour; part time: $237/credit hour
Out-of-state tuition: full time: $588/credit hour
Room/board/expenses: $11,062
Full-time enrollment: 172
doctoral students: 15%; master's students: 69%; education specialists: 16%; men: 12%; women: 88%; minorities: 32%; international: 2%
Part-time enrollment: 1,021
doctoral students: 18%; master's students: 82%; education specialists: 0%; men: 16%; women: 84%; minorities: 41%; international: 1%
Acceptance rate (master's): 60%
Acceptance rate (doctoral): 42%
Entrance test required: GRE
Avg. GRE (of all entering students with scores): quantitative: 144; verbal: 148
Research assistantships: 15
Students reporting specialty: 100%
Students specializing in: admin.: 18%; counseling: 23%; curriculum/instr.: 20%; educational tech.: 3%; educational psych: 2%; higher education admin.: 6%; special: 8%; other: 20%

Stephen F. Austin State University

PO Box 13024, SFA Station
Nacogdoches, TX 75962
http://www.sfasu.edu/graduate
Public
Admissions: (936) 468-2807
E-mail: gschool@sfasu.edu
Financial aid: (936) 468-2403
Application deadline: rolling
In-state tuition: full time: $222/credit hour; part time: $222/credit hour
Out-of-state tuition: full time: $573/credit hour
Room/board/expenses: $11,412
Full-time enrollment: 269
doctoral students: 16%; master's students: 84%; education specialists: N/A; men: 21%; women: 79%; minorities: 23%; international: 3%
Part-time enrollment: 637
doctoral students: 6%; master's students: 94%; education specialists: N/A; men: 23%; women: 77%; minorities: 30%; international: 0%
Acceptance rate (master's): N/A
Acceptance rate (doctoral): N/A
Entrance test required: GRE
Avg. GRE (of all entering students with scores): quantitative: N/A; verbal: N/A
Students reporting specialty: 100%
Students specializing in: admin.: 30%; counseling: 0%; elementary: 10%; secondary: 6%; special: 10%; other: 44%

Tarleton State University

Box T-0350
Stephenville, TX 76402
http://www.tarleton.edu/~graduate
Public
Admissions: (254) 968-9104
E-mail: ljones@tarleton.edu
Financial aid: (254) 968-9070
Application deadline: rolling
In-state tuition: full time: $184/credit hour; part time: $184/credit hour
Out-of-state tuition: full time: $505/credit hour
Room/board/expenses: $12,187
Full-time enrollment: 242
doctoral students: 19%; master's students: 81%; education specialists: N/A; men: 23%; women: 77%; minorities: 32%; international: N/A
Part-time enrollment: 727
doctoral students: 4%; master's students: 96%; education specialists: N/A; men: 21%; women: 79%; minorities: 29%; international: N/A
Acceptance rate (master's): 98%
Acceptance rate (doctoral): 100%
Entrance test required: GRE
Avg. GRE (of all entering students with scores): quantitative: N/A; verbal: N/A

Research assistantships: 4
Students reporting specialty: 98%
Students specializing in: admin.: 19%; counseling: 16%; curriculum/instr.: 19%; educational psych: 2%; other: 44%

Texas A&M University– College Station

4222 TAMUS
College Station, TX 77843-4222
http://www.cehd.tamu.edu/
Public
Admissions: (979) 845-1071
E-mail: admissions@tamu.edu
Financial aid: (979) 845-3236
Application deadline: rolling
In-state tuition: full time: $227/credit hour; part time: $227/credit hour
Out-of-state tuition: full time: $778/credit hour
Room/board/expenses: $13,474
Full-time enrollment: 594
doctoral students: 47%; master's students: 53%; education specialists: N/A; men: 32%; women: 68%; minorities: 30%; international: 26%
Part-time enrollment: 685
doctoral students: 53%; master's students: 47%; education specialists: N/A; men: 31%; women: 69%; minorities: 39%; international: 2%
Acceptance rate (master's): 73%
Acceptance rate (doctoral): 58%
Entrance test required: GRE
Avg. GRE (of all entering students with scores): quantitative: 150; verbal: 151
Research assistantships: 69
Students reporting specialty: 100%
Students specializing in: admin.: 17%; counseling: 5%; curriculum/instr.: 30%; educational tech.: 0%; educational psych: 10%; special: 2%; other: 35%

Texas A&M University– Commerce[1]

PO Box 3011
Commerce, TX 75429-3011
http://www.tamu-commerce.edu
Public
Admissions: (903) 886-5167
E-mail: graduate_school@tamu-commerce.edu
Financial aid: (903) 886-5096
Tuition: N/A
Room/board expenses: N/A
Enrollment: N/A

Texas A&M University– Corpus Christi

6300 Ocean Drive
Corpus Christi, TX 78412
http://gradschool.tamucc.edu
Public
Admissions: (361) 825-2177
E-mail: gradweb@tamucc.edu
Financial aid: (361) 825-2332
Application deadline: rolling
In-state tuition: full time: $196/credit hour; part time: $196/credit hour
Out-of-state tuition: full time: $547/credit hour
Room/board/expenses: $10,891
Full-time enrollment: 208
doctoral students: 14%; master's students: 86%; education specialists: N/A; men: 22%; women: 78%; minorities: 40%; international: 8%
Part-time enrollment: 492
doctoral students: 27%; master's

students: 73%; education specialists: N/A; men: 19%; women: 81%; minorities: 54%; international: 1%
Acceptance rate (master's): 65%
Acceptance rate (doctoral): 34%
Entrance test required: GRE
Avg. GRE (of all entering students with scores): quantitative: N/A; verbal: N/A
Research assistantships: 12
Students reporting specialty: 100%
Students specializing in: admin.: 17%; counseling: 30%; curriculum/instr.: 13%; educational tech.: 4%; elementary: 5%; secondary: 8%; special: 6%; other: 16%

Texas A&M University–Kingsville

700 University Boulevard
Kingsville, TX 78363
http://www.tamuk.edu
Public
Admissions: (361) 593-2811
E-mail: admissions@tamuk.edu
Financial aid: (361) 593-3911
Application deadline: 01/07
In-state tuition: full time: $3,380; part time: $239/credit hour
Out-of-state tuition: full time: $2,729/credit hour
Room/board/expenses: $12,996
Full-time enrollment: N/A
doctoral students: N/A; master's students: N/A; education specialists: N/A; men: N/A; women: N/A; minorities: N/A; international: N/A
Part-time enrollment: N/A
doctoral students: N/A; master's students: N/A; education specialists: N/A; men: N/A; women: N/A; minorities: N/A; international: N/A
Acceptance rate (master's): N/A
Acceptance rate (doctoral): N/A
Entrance test required: GRE
Avg. GRE (of all entering students with scores): quantitative: N/A; verbal: N/A
Research assistantships: 9
Students reporting specialty: 0%
Students specializing in: N/A

Texas Christian University

3000 Bellaire Drive N
Fort Worth, TX 76129
http://www.coe.tcu.edu
Private
Admissions: (817) 257-7661
Financial aid: (817) 257-7872
Application deadline: N/A
Tuition: full time: $1,200/credit hour; part time: $1,200/credit hour
Room/board/expenses: $15,670
Full-time enrollment: 69
doctoral students: 25%; master's students: 75%; education specialists: N/A; men: 7%; women: 93%; minorities: 19%; international: 7%
Part-time enrollment: 113
doctoral students: 29%; master's students: 71%; education specialists: N/A; men: 31%; women: 69%; minorities: 27%; international: 1%
Acceptance rate (master's): 76%
Acceptance rate (doctoral): 49%
Entrance test required: GRE
Avg. GRE (of all entering students with scores): quantitative: N/A; verbal: N/A
Students reporting specialty: 100%
Students specializing in: admin.: 34%; counseling: 31%; curriculum/instr.: 5%; social/philosophical foundations: 1%; elementary:

6%; higher education admin.: 3%; junior high: 2%; secondary: 1%; special: 5%; other: 12%

Texas Southern University

3100 Cleburne Street
Houston, TX 77004
http://www.tsu.edu/academics/colleges__schools/The_Graduate_School/admissions.php
Public
Admissions: (713) 313-7435
E-mail: graduateadmissions@tsu.edu
Financial aid: (713) 313-7071
Application deadline: N/A
In-state tuition: full time: $6,383; part time: $100/credit hour
Out-of-state tuition: full time: $11,063
Room/board/expenses: $16,659
Full-time enrollment: 146
doctoral students: 43%; master's students: 57%; education specialists: N/A; men: 18%; women: 82%; minorities: 95%; international: 1%
Part-time enrollment: 160
doctoral students: 41%; master's students: 59%; education specialists: N/A; men: 19%; women: 81%; minorities: 96%; international: 1%
Acceptance rate (master's): 42%
Acceptance rate (doctoral): 48%
Entrance test required: GRE
Avg. GRE (of all entering students with scores): quantitative: N/A; verbal: N/A
Research assistantships: 0
Students reporting specialty: 0%
Students specializing in: N/A

Texas State University– San Marcos

601 University Drive
San Marcos, TX 78666
http://www.txstate.edu
Public
Admissions: (512) 245-2581
E-mail: gradcollege@txstate.edu
Financial aid: (512) 245-2315
Application deadline: rolling
In-state tuition: full time: $6,354; part time: $267/credit hour
Out-of-state tuition: full time: $12,672
Room/board/expenses: $12,182
Full-time enrollment: 546
doctoral students: 7%; master's students: 86%; education specialists: 8%; men: 25%; women: 75%; minorities: 36%; international: 3%
Part-time enrollment: 718
doctoral students: 15%; master's students: 82%; education specialists: 3%; men: 21%; women: 79%; minorities: 34%; international: 0%
Acceptance rate (master's): 66%
Acceptance rate (doctoral): 32%
Entrance test required: GRE
Avg. GRE (of all entering students with scores): quantitative: N/A; verbal: N/A
Research assistantships: 52
Students reporting specialty: 100%
Students specializing in: admin.: 21%; counseling: 0%; educational psych: 19%; elementary: 18%; higher education admin.: 3%; secondary: 11%; special: 8%; instructional media design: 3%; other: 20%

Texas Tech University

Box 41071
Lubbock, TX 79409-1071
http://www.educ.ttu.edu/
Public
Admissions: (806) 742-1998
E-mail: gradschool@ttu.edu
Financial aid: (806) 742-3681
Application deadline: 06/01
In-state tuition: full time: $253/credit hour; part time: $253/credit hour
Out-of-state tuition: full time: $604/credit hour
Room/board/expenses: $15,102
Full-time enrollment: 237
doctoral students: 51%; master's students: 49%; education specialists: N/A; men: 26%; women: 74%; minorities: 22%; international: 19%
Part-time enrollment: 582
doctoral students: 47%; master's students: 53%; education specialists: N/A; men: 27%; women: 73%; minorities: 26%; international: 3%
Acceptance rate (master's): 45%
Acceptance rate (doctoral): 45%
Entrance test required: GRE
Avg. GRE (of all entering students with scores): quantitative: 144; verbal: 150
Research assistantships: 64
Students reporting specialty: 100%
Students specializing in: admin.: 7%; counseling: 10%; curriculum/instr.: 12%; evaluation/research/statistics: 12%; educational psych: 4%; elementary: 1%; secondary: 2%; special: 19%; instructional media design: 7%; other: 25%

Texas Woman's University[1]

PO Box 425769
Denton, TX 76204-5769
http://www.twu.edu/admissions/
Public
Admissions: (940) 898-3188
E-mail: admissions@twu.edu
Financial aid: (940) 898-3050
Tuition: N/A
Room/board expenses: N/A
Enrollment: N/A

University of Houston

4800 Calhoun Road, Farish Hall
Houston, TX 77204-5023
http://www.coe.uh.edu/
Public
Admissions: (713) 743-4997
E-mail: coegradadmissions@mail.coe.uh.edu
Financial aid: (713) 743-9090
Application deadline: rolling
In-state tuition: full time: $9,522; part time: $478/credit hour
Out-of-state tuition: full time: $15,840
Room/board/expenses: $15,453
Full-time enrollment: 304
doctoral students: 59%; master's students: 41%; education specialists: N/A; men: 22%; women: 78%; minorities: 37%; international: 14%
Part-time enrollment: 387
doctoral students: 34%; master's students: 66%; education specialists: N/A; men: 23%; women: 77%; minorities: 41%; international: 3%
Acceptance rate (master's): 64%
Acceptance rate (doctoral): 32%
Entrance test required: GRE
Avg. GRE (of all entering students with scores): quantitative: 150; verbal: 152
Research assistantships: 15

Students reporting specialty: 94%
Students specializing in: admin.: 15%; curriculum/instr.: 44%; educational psych: 8%; higher education admin.: 5%; special: 1%; other: 30%

University of North Texas

1155 Union Circle #311337
Denton, TX 76203-1337
http://tsgs.unt.edu/overview
Public
Admissions: (940) 565-2383
E-mail: gradsch@unt.edu
Financial aid: (940) 565-2302
Application deadline: rolling
In-state tuition: full time: $291/credit hour; part time: $291/credit hour
Out-of-state tuition: full time: $642/credit hour
Room/board/expenses: $11,766
Full-time enrollment: 334
doctoral students: 36%; master's students: 64%; education specialists: N/A; men: 27%; women: 73%; minorities: 16%; international: 7%
Part-time enrollment: 692
doctoral students: 43%; master's students: 57%; education specialists: N/A; men: 24%; women: 76%; minorities: 14%; international: 2%
Acceptance rate (master's): 41%
Acceptance rate (doctoral): 41%
Entrance test required: GRE
Avg. GRE (of all entering students with scores): quantitative: 147; verbal: 151
Research assistantships: 39
Students reporting specialty: 77%
Students specializing in: admin.: 10%; counseling: 29%; curriculum/instr.: 14%; evaluation/research/statistics: 5%; educational psych: 4%; higher education admin.: 15%; secondary: 6%; special: 16%

University of Texas–Austin

1 University Station, D5000
Sanchez Building Room 210
Austin, TX 78712
http://www.edb.utexas.edu/education/
Public
Admissions: (512) 475-7398
E-mail: adgrd@utxdp.dp.utexas.edu
Financial aid: (512) 475-6282
Application deadline: rolling
In-state tuition: full time: $8,402; part time: $8,066
Out-of-state tuition: full time: $16,338
Room/board/expenses: $16,412
Full-time enrollment: 771
doctoral students: 55%; master's students: 45%; education specialists: N/A; men: 30%; women: 70%; minorities: 27%; international: 16%
Part-time enrollment: 443
doctoral students: 57%; master's students: 43%; education specialists: N/A; men: 35%; women: 65%; minorities: 39%; international: 6%
Acceptance rate (master's): 48%
Acceptance rate (doctoral): 19%
Entrance test required: GRE
Avg. GRE (of all entering students with scores): quantitative: 151; verbal: 155
Research assistantships: 263
Students reporting specialty: 100%
Students specializing in: admin.: 9%; counseling: 3%; curriculum/instr.: 27%; evaluation/research/

statistics: 3%; policy: 4%; educational tech.: 3%; educational psych: 14%; higher education admin.: 9%; special: 10%; other: 18%

University of Texas–El Paso

500 W. University Avenue
El Paso, TX 79968
http://academics.utep.edu/education
Public
Admissions: (915) 747-5572
E-mail: gradschool@utep.edu
Financial aid: (915) 747-5204
Application deadline: N/A
In-state tuition: full time: N/A; part time: N/A
Out-of-state tuition: full time: N/A
Room/board/expenses: N/A
Full-time enrollment: 189
doctoral students: 19%; master's students: 46%; education specialists: 35%; men: 25%; women: 75%; minorities: 72%; international: 16%
Part-time enrollment: 677
doctoral students: 11%; master's students: 52%; education specialists: 38%; men: 24%; women: 76%; minorities: 85%; international: 2%
Acceptance rate (master's): 94%
Acceptance rate (doctoral): 63%
Entrance test required: GRE
Avg. GRE (of all entering students with scores): quantitative: 143; verbal: 146
Students reporting specialty: 100%
Students specializing in: admin.: 21%; counseling: 18%; curriculum/instr.: 40%; special: 12%; other: 9%

University of Texas–Pan American

1201 W. University Drive
Edinburg, TX 78541-2999
http://www.utpa.edu/colleges/coe/
Public
Admissions: (956) 665-3661
E-mail: admissions@utpa.edu
Financial aid: (956) 665-2501
Application deadline: N/A
In-state tuition: full time: $5,489; part time: $224/credit hour
Out-of-state tuition: full-time: $12,509
Room/board/expenses: $10,660
Full-time enrollment: 93
doctoral students: 13%; master's students: 87%; education specialists: N/A; men: 37%; women: 63%; minorities: 78%; international: 6%
Part-time enrollment: 565
doctoral students: 8%; master's students: 92%; education specialists: N/A; men: 31%; women: 69%; minorities: 91%; international: N/A
Acceptance rate (master's): N/A
Acceptance rate (doctoral): N/A
Entrance test required: GRE
Avg. GRE (of all entering students with scores): quantitative: N/A; verbal: N/A
Research assistantships: 8
Students reporting specialty: 100%
Students specializing in: admin.: 36%; counseling: 20%; elementary: 3%; secondary: 3%; special: 9%; other: 28%

University of Texas–San Antonio

1 UTSA Circle
San Antonio, TX 78249-0617
http://www.graduateschool.utsa.edu
Public
Admissions: (210) 458-4331
E-mail: graduatestudies@usta.edu
Financial aid: (210) 458-8000
Application deadline: 07/01
In-state tuition: full time: $259/credit hour; part time: $259/credit hour
Out-of-state tuition: full time: $961/credit hour
Room/board/expenses: $13,695
Full-time enrollment: 545
doctoral students: 10%; master's students: 90%; education specialists: N/A; men: 24%; women: 76%; minorities: 51%; international: 17%
Part-time enrollment: 1,052
doctoral students: 14%; master's students: 86%; education specialists: N/A; men: 22%; women: 78%; minorities: 61%; international: 2%
Acceptance rate (master's): 89%
Acceptance rate (doctoral): 53%
Entrance test required: GRE
Avg. GRE (of all entering students with scores): quantitative: 145; verbal: 149
Research assistantships: 20
Students reporting specialty: 100%
Students specializing in: N/A

University of the Incarnate Word

4301 Broadway
San Antonio, TX 78209
http://www.uiw.edu
Private
Admissions: (210) 829-6005
E-mail: admis@universe.uiwtx.edu
Financial aid: (210) 829-6008
Application deadline: rolling
Tuition: full time: $755/credit hour; part time: $755/credit hour
Room/board/expenses: $8,556
Full-time enrollment: 11
doctoral students: 45%; master's students: 55%; education specialists: N/A; men: 45%; women: 55%; minorities: 36%; international: 27%
Part-time enrollment: 266
doctoral students: 67%; master's students: 33%; education specialists: N/A; men: 32%; women: 68%; minorities: 60%; international: 14%
Acceptance rate (master's): 86%
Acceptance rate (doctoral): 67%
Entrance test required: GRE
Avg. GRE (of all entering students with scores): quantitative: N/A; verbal: N/A
Research assistantships: 20
Students reporting specialty: 100%
Students specializing in: elementary: 10%; secondary: 2%; other: 87%

UTAH

Brigham Young University–Provo (McKay)

301 MCKB
Provo, UT 84602
http://www.byu.edu/gradstudies
Private
Admissions: (801) 422-4091
E-mail: admissions@byu.edu
Financial aid: (801) 422-4104
Application deadline: N/A
Tuition: full time: $6,397; part time: $331/credit hour
Room/board/expenses: $15,712

Full-time enrollment: 76
doctoral students: 39%; master's students: 34%; education specialists: 26%; men: N/A; women: N/A; minorities: N/A; international: N/A
Part-time enrollment: 226
doctoral students: 42%; master's students: 52%; education specialists: 6%; men: N/A; women: N/A; minorities: N/A; international: N/A
Acceptance rate (master's): 50%
Acceptance rate (doctoral): 22%
Entrance test required: GRE
Avg. GRE (of all entering students with scores): quantitative: 154; verbal: 158
Research assistantships: 119
Students reporting specialty: 90%
Students specializing in: admin.: 13%; curriculum/instr.: 8%; evaluation/research/statistics: 5%; educational tech.: 4%; educational psych: 12%; higher education admin.: 7%; special: 7%; instructional media design: 19%; other: 26%

University of Utah

1705 Campus Center Drive
Room 225
Salt Lake City, UT 84112-9251
http://admissions.utah.edu
Public
Admissions: (801) 581-7281
E-mail: admissions@utah.edu
Financial aid: (801) 581-6211
Application deadline: 04/01
In-state tuition: full time: $5,840; part time: $315/credit hour
Out-of-state tuition: full time: $18,516
Room/board/expenses: $15,516
Full-time enrollment: 389
doctoral students: 37%; master's students: 63%; education specialists: N/A; men: 28%; women: 72%; minorities: 19%; international: 5%
Part-time enrollment: 150
doctoral students: 56%; master's students: 44%; education specialists: N/A; men: 42%; women: 58%; minorities: 29%; international: 3%
Acceptance rate (master's): 54%
Acceptance rate (doctoral): 24%
Entrance test required: GRE
Avg. GRE (of all entering students with scores): quantitative: 158; verbal: 152
Research assistantships: 18
Students reporting specialty: 100%
Students specializing in: admin.: 8%; counseling: 15%; social/philosophical foundations: 17%; policy: 1%; educational psych: 23%; elementary: 5%; higher education admin.: 15%; secondary: 5%; special: 13%; instructional media design: 7%

Utah State University

2800 Old Main Hill
Logan, UT 84322-2800
http://www.rgs.usu.edu/graduateschool
Public
Admissions: (435) 797-1189
E-mail: graduateschool@usu.edu
Financial aid: (435) 797-0173
Application deadline: rolling
In-state tuition: full time: $5,100; part time: $4,694
Out-of-state tuition: full time: $15,836
Room/board/expenses: $10,300
Full-time enrollment: 302
doctoral students: 25%; master's students: 70%; education specialists: 5%; men: 36%; women: 64%; minorities: 6%; international: 6%

Part-time enrollment: 604
doctoral students: 26%; master's students: 72%; education specialists: 1%; men: 39%; women: 61%; minorities: 6%; international: 2%
Acceptance rate (master's): 53%
Acceptance rate (doctoral): 25%
Entrance test required: GRE
Avg. GRE (of all entering students with scores): quantitative: 161; verbal: 159
Research assistantships: 43
Students reporting specialty: 52%
Students specializing in: admin.: 11%; curriculum/instr.: 19%; elementary: 12%; secondary: 14%; special: 16%; instructional media design: 27%

VERMONT

University of Vermont

309 Waterman Building
Burlington, VT 05405-0160
http://www.uvm.edu/~gradcoll
Public
Admissions: (802) 656-2699
E-mail: graduate.admissions@uvm.edu
Financial aid: (802) 656-3156
Application deadline: 01/15
In-state tuition: full time: $15,052; part time: $556/credit hour
Out-of-state tuition: full time: $35,380
Room/board/expenses: $14,424
Full-time enrollment: 124
doctoral students: 10%; master's students: 41%; education specialists: 48%; men: 31%; women: 69%; minorities: 25%; international: 2%
Part-time enrollment: 226
doctoral students: 19%; master's students: 54%; education specialists: 27%; men: 23%; women: 77%; minorities: 8%; international: 0%
Acceptance rate (master's): 49%
Acceptance rate (doctoral): 55%
Entrance test required: GRE
Avg. GRE (of all entering students with scores): quantitative: 148; verbal: 154
Research assistantships: 3
Students reporting specialty: 100%
Students specializing in: admin.: 22%; counseling: 13%; curriculum/instr.: 29%; higher education admin.: 9%; junior high: 2%; secondary: 5%; special: 14%; other: 7%

VIRGINIA

College of William and Mary

PO Box 8795
Williamsburg, VA 23187-8795
http://education.wm.edu/
Public
Admissions: (757) 221-2317
E-mail: GradEd@wm.edu
Financial aid: (757) 221-2317
Application deadline: 01/15
In-state tuition: full time: $11,404; part time: $5,010
Out-of-state tuition: full time: $25,233
Room/board/expenses: $15,400
Full-time enrollment: 225
doctoral students: 21%; master's students: 73%; education specialists: 5%; men: 18%; women: 82%; minorities: 16%; international: 5%
Part-time enrollment: 173
doctoral students: 71%; master's students: 23%; education specialists: 6%; men: 29%; women: 71%; minorities: 23%; international: N/A

Acceptance rate (master's): 53%
Acceptance rate (doctoral): 48%
Entrance test required: GRE
Avg. GRE (of all entering students with scores): quantitative: 154; verbal: 158
Students reporting specialty: 100%
Students specializing in: admin.: 49%; counseling: 20%; curriculum/instr.: 23%; other: 9%

George Mason University

4400 University Drive, MSN 2F1
Fairfax, VA 22030-4444
http://cehd.gmu.edu
Public
Admissions: (703) 993-2892
E-mail: cehdgrad@gmu.edu
Financial aid: (703) 993-2349
Application deadline: rolling
In-state tuition: full time: $378/credit hour; part time: $378/credit hour
Out-of-state tuition: full time: $1,042/credit hour
Room/board/expenses: $25,144
Full-time enrollment: 414
doctoral students: 16%; master's students: 84%; education specialists: N/A; men: 18%; women: 82%; minorities: 25%; international: 4%
Part-time enrollment: 1,903
doctoral students: 14%; master's students: 86%; education specialists: N/A; men: 20%; women: 80%; minorities: 19%; international: 1%
Acceptance rate (master's): 75%
Acceptance rate (doctoral): 54%
Entrance test required: GRE
Avg. GRE (of all entering students with scores): quantitative: 149; verbal: 155
Research assistantships: 78
Students reporting specialty: 100%
Students specializing in: admin.: 15%; counseling: 3%; curriculum/instr.: 42%; educational psych: 2%; special: 23%; other: 16%

Liberty University

1971 University Boulevard
Lynchburg, VA 24502
http://www.liberty.edu/academics/graduate
Private
Admissions: (800) 424-9596
E-mail: gradadmissions@liberty.edu
Financial aid: (434) 582-2270
Application deadline: rolling
Tuition: full time: $465/credit hour; part time: $505/credit hour
Room/board/expenses: N/A
Full-time enrollment: 2,074
doctoral students: 18%; master's students: 46%; education specialists: 35%; men: 26%; women: 74%; minorities: 12%; international: 1%
Part-time enrollment: 4,010
doctoral students: 17%; master's students: 70%; education specialists: 13%; men: 25%; women: 75%; minorities: 13%; international: 1%
Acceptance rate (master's): 45%
Acceptance rate (doctoral): 14%
Entrance test required: N/A
Avg. GRE (of all entering students with scores): quantitative: N/A; verbal: N/A
Students reporting specialty: 62%
Students specializing in: admin.: 9%; counseling: 22%; curriculum/instr.: 24%; elementary: 16%; secondary: 10%; special: 13%; instructional media design: 7%

Old Dominion University (Darden)
Education Building, Room 218
Norfolk, VA 23529
http://education.odu.edu
Public
Admissions: (757) 683-3685
E-mail: admit@odu.edu
Financial aid: (757) 683-3683
Application deadline: 06/01
In-state tuition: full time: $393/credit hour; part time: $393/credit hour
Out-of-state tuition: full time: $997/credit hour
Room/board/expenses: $14,126
Full-time enrollment: 533
doctoral students: 16%; master's students: 83%; education specialists: 1%; men: 18%; women: 82%; minorities: 26%; international: 2%
Part-time enrollment: 587
doctoral students: 38%; master's students: 53%; education specialists: 9%; men: 24%; women: 76%; minorities: 22%; international: 1%
Acceptance rate (master's): 50%
Acceptance rate (doctoral): 40%
Entrance test required: GRE
Avg. GRE (of all entering students with scores): quantitative: 147; verbal: 151
Research assistantships: 55
Students reporting specialty: 0%
Students specializing in: N/A

Regent University
1000 Regent University Drive
Virginia Beach, VA 23464
http://www.regent.edu/acad/schedu
Private
Admissions: (888) 713-1595
E-mail: education@regent.edu
Financial aid: (757) 352-4125
Application deadline: rolling
Tuition: full time: $675/credit hour; part time: $675/credit hour
Room/board/expenses: N/A
Full-time enrollment: 123
doctoral students: 2%; master's students: 98%; education specialists: 0%; men: 19%; women: 81%; minorities: 34%; international: N/A
Part-time enrollment: 628
doctoral students: 28%; master's students: 68%; education specialists: 4%; men: 20%; women: 80%; minorities: 33%; international: 2%
Acceptance rate (master's): 67%
Acceptance rate (doctoral): 13%
Entrance test required: GRE
Avg. GRE (of all entering students with scores): quantitative: N/A; verbal: N/A
Students reporting specialty: 100%
Students specializing in: admin.: 21%; curriculum/instr.: 7%; educational psych: 2%; elementary: 1%; higher education admin.: 5%; special: 12%; other: 52%

Shenandoah University
1460 University Drive
Winchester, VA 22601
http://www.su.edu
Private
Admissions: (540) 665-4581
E-mail: admit@su.edu
Financial aid: (540) 665-4538
Application deadline: rolling
Tuition: full time: $28,800; part time: $800/credit hour
Room/board/expenses: $13,340
Full-time enrollment: 17
doctoral students: 0%; master's students: 100%; education specialists: N/A; men: 35%; women: 65%; minorities: 12%; international: 24%
Part-time enrollment: 282
doctoral students: 29%; master's students: 71%; education specialists: N/A; men: 28%; women: 72%; minorities: 11%; international: 2%
Acceptance rate (master's): 98%
Acceptance rate (doctoral): 70%
Entrance test required: N/A
Avg. GRE (of all entering students with scores): quantitative: N/A; verbal: N/A
Research assistantships: 0
Students reporting specialty: 32%
Students specializing in: N/A

University of Virginia (Curry)
405 Emmet Street S
Charlottesville, VA 22903-2495
http://curry.edschool.virginia.edu/
Public
Admissions: (434) 924-3334
E-mail: curry@virginia.edu
Financial aid: (434) 982-6000
Application deadline: N/A
In-state tuition: full time: $15,682; part time: $717/credit hour
Out-of-state tuition: full time: $25,006
Room/board/expenses: $20,211
Full-time enrollment: 542
doctoral students: 35%; master's students: 65%; education specialists: 0%; men: 25%; women: 75%; minorities: 15%; international: 5%
Part-time enrollment: 407
doctoral students: 25%; master's students: 61%; education specialists: 14%; men: 26%; women: 74%; minorities: 10%; international: 0%
Acceptance rate (master's): 45%
Acceptance rate (doctoral): 22%
Entrance test required: GRE
Avg. GRE (of all entering students with scores): quantitative: 152; verbal: 156
Research assistantships: 28
Students reporting specialty: 100%
Students specializing in: admin.: 10%; counseling: 2%; curriculum/instr.: 17%; evaluation/research/statistics: 1%; social/philosophical foundations: 9%; policy: 1%; educational tech.: 3%; educational psych: 3%; elementary: 6%; higher education admin.: 7%; secondary: 13%; special: 7%; other: 21%

Virginia Commonwealth University
1015 W. Main Street
PO Box 842020
Richmond, VA 23284-2020
http://www.soe.vcu.edu
Public
Admissions: (804) 828-3382
E-mail: htclark@vcu.edu
Financial aid: (804) 828-6181
Application deadline: 02/15
In-state tuition: full time: $11,522; part time: $530/credit hour
Out-of-state tuition: full time: $21,586
Room/board/expenses: $13,018
Full-time enrollment: 363
doctoral students: 6%; master's students: 94%; education specialists: 0%; men: 22%; women: 78%; minorities: 18%; international: 2%
Part-time enrollment: 405
doctoral students: 37%; master's students: 51%; education specialists: 12%; men: 26%; women: 74%; minorities: 23%; international: 1%
Acceptance rate (master's): 64%
Acceptance rate (doctoral): 40%
Entrance test required: GRE
Avg. GRE (of all entering students with scores): quantitative: 150; verbal: 153
Research assistantships: 28
Students reporting specialty: 100%
Students specializing in: admin.: 7%; counseling: 11%; curriculum/instr.: 1%; evaluation/research/statistics: 1%; policy: 4%; educational psych: 1%; elementary: 13%; secondary: 8%; special: 9%; other: 45%

Virginia State University
1 Hayden Street
Petersburg, VA 23806
http://www.vsu.edu/
Public
Admissions: (804) 524-5985
E-mail: admiss@vsu.edu
Financial aid: (804) 524-5990
Application deadline: N/A
In-state tuition: full time: $9,044; part time: $410/credit hour
Out-of-state tuition: full time: $17,012
Room/board/expenses: $10,580
Full-time enrollment: 38
doctoral students: 74%; master's students: 26%; education specialists: N/A; men: 26%; women: 74%; minorities: 89%; international: N/A
Part-time enrollment: 305
doctoral students: 7%; master's students: 93%; education specialists: N/A; men: 19%; women: 81%; minorities: 95%; international: N/A
Acceptance rate (master's): 43%
Acceptance rate (doctoral): 36%
Entrance test required: GRE
Avg. GRE (of all entering students with scores): quantitative: N/A; verbal: N/A
Students reporting specialty: 94%
Students specializing in: admin.: 23%; counseling: 65%; elementary: 5%; special: 8%

Virginia Tech
226 War Memorial Hall (0313)
Blacksburg, VA 24061
http://www.graduateschool.vt.edu/
Public
Admissions: (540) 231-8636
E-mail: gradappl@vt.edu
Financial aid: (540) 231-4558
Application deadline: rolling
In-state tuition: full time: $12,413; part time: $593/credit hour
Out-of-state tuition: full time: $22,662
Room/board/expenses: $12,488
Full-time enrollment: 363
doctoral students: 37%; master's students: 59%; education specialists: 4%; men: 33%; women: 67%; minorities: 15%; international: 12%
Part-time enrollment: 470
doctoral students: 47%; master's students: 47%; education specialists: 6%; men: 31%; women: 69%; minorities: 22%; international: 1%
Acceptance rate (master's): 65%
Acceptance rate (doctoral): 79%
Entrance test required: GRE
Avg. GRE (of all entering students with scores): quantitative: N/A; verbal: N/A
Research assistantships: 53
Students reporting specialty: 100%
Students specializing in: admin.: 35%; counseling: 12%; curriculum/instr.: 46%; evaluation/research/statistics: 2%; other: 5%

WASHINGTON

Gonzaga University[1]
502 E. Boone Avenue
Spokane, WA 99258-0025
http://www.gonzaga.edu/Academics/Graduate/default.htm
Private
Admissions: (509) 323-6572
E-mail: soriet@soe.gonzaga.edu
Financial aid: (509) 323-6582
Tuition: N/A
Room/board expenses: N/A
Enrollment: N/A

Seattle Pacific University
3307 Third Avenue W
Seattle, WA 98119-1997
http://www.spu.edu
Private
Admissions: (206) 378-5478
E-mail: hiemstra@spu.edu
Financial aid: (206) 281-2061
Application deadline: rolling
Tuition: full time: $697/credit hour; part time: N/A
Room/board/expenses: N/A
Full-time enrollment: 94
doctoral students: 9%; master's students: 91%; education specialists: N/A; men: 23%; women: 77%; minorities: 4%; international: 2%
Part-time enrollment: 236
doctoral students: 22%; master's students: 78%; education specialists: N/A; men: 26%; women: 74%; minorities: 8%; international: 4%
Acceptance rate (master's): N/A
Acceptance rate (doctoral): N/A
Entrance test required: N/A
Avg. GRE (of all entering students with scores): quantitative: N/A; verbal: N/A
Students reporting specialty: 0%
Students specializing in: N/A

Seattle University
900 Broadway
Seattle, WA 98122
http://www.seattleu.edu/soe/
Private
Admissions: (206) 296-2000
E-mail: grad-admissions@seattleu.edu
Financial aid: (206) 296-2000
Application deadline: rolling
Tuition: full time: $598/credit hour; part time: $598/credit hour
Room/board/expenses: N/A
Full-time enrollment: 158
doctoral students: 6%; master's students: 78%; education specialists: 16%; men: 22%; women: 78%; minorities: 27%; international: 3%
Part-time enrollment: 334
doctoral students: 16%; master's students: 74%; education specialists: 10%; men: 25%; women: 75%; minorities: 31%; international: 2%
Acceptance rate (master's): N/A
Acceptance rate (doctoral): N/A
Entrance test required: GRE
Avg. GRE (of all entering students with scores): quantitative: N/A; verbal: N/A
Research assistantships: 0
Students reporting specialty: 100%
Students specializing in: admin.: 11%; counseling: 11%; curriculum/instr.: 3%; educational psych: 10%; elementary: 6%; higher education admin.: 13%; secondary: 7%; special: 2%; other: 36%

University of Washington
PO Box 353600, 206 Miller
Seattle, WA 98195-3600
http://education.washington.edu
Public
Admissions: (206) 543-7834
E-mail: edinfo@u.washington.edu
Financial aid: (206) 543-7834
Application deadline: N/A
In-state tuition: full time: $14,451; part time: $649/credit hour
Out-of-state tuition: full time: $27,069
Room/board/expenses: $18,579
Full-time enrollment: 667
doctoral students: 36%; master's students: 58%; education specialists: 6%; men: 25%; women: 75%; minorities: 26%; international: 8%
Part-time enrollment: 189
doctoral students: 44%; master's students: 56%; education specialists: 1%; men: 31%; women: 69%; minorities: 27%; international: 1%
Acceptance rate (master's): 71%
Acceptance rate (doctoral): 38%
Entrance test required: GRE
Avg. GRE (of all entering students with scores): quantitative: 150; verbal: 155
Research assistantships: 73
Students reporting specialty: 100%
Students specializing in: N/A

Washington State University
PO Box 642114
Pullman, WA 99164-2114
http://education.wsu.edu
Public
Admissions: (509) 335-7718
E-mail: gradsch@wsu.edu
Financial aid: (509) 335-9711
Application deadline: 01/10
In-state tuition: full time: $12,600; part time: $587/credit hour
Out-of-state tuition: full time: $26,032
Room/board/expenses: $14,102
Full-time enrollment: 259
doctoral students: 44%; master's students: 56%; education specialists: N/A; men: 36%; women: 64%; minorities: 23%; international: 18%
Part-time enrollment: 259
doctoral students: 39%; master's students: 61%; education specialists: N/A; men: 30%; women: 70%; minorities: 14%; international: 7%
Acceptance rate (master's): 54%
Acceptance rate (doctoral): 36%
Entrance test required: GRE
Avg. GRE (of all entering students with scores): quantitative: 147; verbal: 151
Research assistantships: 45
Students reporting specialty: 76%
Students specializing in: admin.: 19%; curriculum/instr.: 9%; educational psych: 3%; elementary: 6%; higher education admin.: 3%; secondary: 8%; special: 7%; other: 48%

WEST VIRGINIA

Marshall University[1]
100 Angus E. Peyton Drive
South Charleston, WV 25303
http://www.marshall.edu/gsepd/
Public
Admissions: (800) 642-9842
E-mail: services@marshall.edu

Financial aid: (800) 438-5390
Tuition: N/A
Room/board expenses: N/A
Enrollment: N/A

West Virginia University

802 Allen Hall, PO Box 6122
Morgantown, WV 26506-6122
http://www.wvu.edu
Public
Admissions: (304) 293-2124
Financial aid: (304) 293-5242
Application deadline: rolling
In-state tuition: full time: $6,810;
part time: $378/credit hour
Out-of-state tuition: full time:
$19,508
Room/board/expenses: $11,022
Full-time enrollment: 557
doctoral students: 16%; master's
students: 84%; education
specialists: N/A; men: 23%;
women: 77%; minorities: 6%;
international: 6%
Part-time enrollment: 555
doctoral students: 26%; master's
students: 74%; education
specialists: N/A; men: 22%;
women: 78%; minorities: 7%;
international: 1%
Acceptance rate (master's): 60%
Acceptance rate (doctoral): 53%
Entrance test required: GRE
**Avg. GRE (of all entering students
with scores):** quantitative: 143;
verbal: 150
Research assistantships: 35
Students reporting specialty: 61%
Students specializing in: admin.:
5%; counseling: 7%; educational
psych: 3%; elementary: 20%;
secondary: 21%; special: 37%;
instructional media design: 6%

WISCONSIN

Cardinal Stritch University

6801 N. Yates Road
Milwaukee, WI 53217
http://www.stritch.edu/
Private
Admissions: N/A
Financial aid: N/A

Application deadline: rolling
Tuition: full time: N/A; part time:
N/A
Room/board/expenses: N/A
Full-time enrollment: 1,297
doctoral students: 10%; master's
students: 90%; education
specialists: N/A; men: 34%;
women: 66%; minorities: 27%;
international: 1%
Part-time enrollment: 446
doctoral students: 11%; master's
students: 89%; education
specialists: N/A; men: 37%;
women: 63%; minorities: 25%;
international: 2%
Acceptance rate (master's): N/A
Acceptance rate (doctoral): N/A
Entrance test required: N/A
**Avg. GRE (of all entering students
with scores):** quantitative: N/A;
verbal: N/A
Students reporting specialty: 0%
Students specializing in: N/A

Edgewood College

1000 Edgewood College Drive
Madison, WI 53711
http://www.edgewood.edu
Private
Admissions: (608) 663-3297
E-mail: gps@edgewood.edu
Financial aid: (608) 663-4300
Application deadline: rolling
Tuition: full time: $776/credit hour;
part time: $776/credit hour
Room/board/expenses: N/A
Full-time enrollment: 154
doctoral students: 72%; master's
students: 28%; education
specialists: N/A; men: 45%;
women: 55%; minorities: 16%;
international: 9%
Part-time enrollment: 129
doctoral students: 5%; master's
students: 95%; education
specialists: N/A; men: 26%;
women: 74%; minorities: 13%;
international: 2%
Acceptance rate (master's): 100%
Acceptance rate (doctoral): 73%
Entrance test required: N/A
**Avg. GRE (of all entering students
with scores):** quantitative: N/A;
verbal: N/A

Students reporting specialty: 56%
Students specializing in: admin.:
9%; special: 12%; other: 81%

Marquette University

Schroeder Complex Box 1881
Milwaukee, WI 53201
http://www.grad.marquette.edu
Private
Admissions: (414) 288-7137
E-mail: mugs@marquette.edu
Financial aid: (414) 288-5325
Application deadline: rolling
Tuition: full time: $735/credit hour;
part time: $735/credit hour
Room/board/expenses: $16,206
Full-time enrollment: 99
doctoral students: 19%; master's
students: 81%; education
specialists: N/A; men: 80%;
women: 20%; minorities: 14%;
international: 3%
Part-time enrollment: 120
doctoral students: 24%; master's
students: 76%; education
specialists: N/A; men: 69%;
women: 31%; minorities: 14%;
international: 1%
Acceptance rate (master's): 49%
Acceptance rate (doctoral): 14%
Entrance test required: GRE
**Avg. GRE (of all entering students
with scores):** quantitative: 150;
verbal: 155
Research assistantships: 18
Students reporting specialty: 100%
Students specializing in: admin.:
7%; counseling: 5%; curriculum/
instr.: 2%; social/philosophical
foundations: 17%; policy: 11%;
educational psych: 0%; elementary: 11%; higher education admin.:
13%; junior high: 25%; secondary:
14%; other: 31%

University of Wisconsin–Madison

1000 Bascom Mall; Suite 377
Madison, WI 53706-1326
http://www.education.wisc.edu
Public
Admissions: (608) 262-2433
E-mail: gradamiss@grad.wisc.edu
Financial aid: (608) 262-2087

Application deadline: rolling
In-state tuition: full time: $11,839;
part time: $743/credit hour
Out-of-state tuition: full time:
$25,166
Room/board/expenses: $12,610
Full-time enrollment: 690
doctoral students: 64%; master's
students: 36%; education
specialists: N/A; men: 27%;
women: 73%; minorities: 21%;
international: 18%
Part-time enrollment: 320
doctoral students: 41%; master's
students: 59%; education
specialists: N/A; men: 36%;
women: 64%; minorities: 19%;
international: 10%
Acceptance rate (master's): 29%
Acceptance rate (doctoral): 29%
Entrance test required: GRE
**Avg. GRE (of all entering students
with scores):** quantitative: 150;
verbal: 153
Research assistantships: 36
Students reporting specialty: 100%
Students specializing in: admin.:
24%; counseling: 8%; curriculum/
instr.: 29%; policy: 6%; educational psych: 11%; special: 4%;
other: 18%

University of Wisconsin–Milwaukee

PO Box 413
Milwaukee, WI 53201
http://www.
graduateschool.uwm.edu
Public
Admissions: (414) 229-4495
E-mail: haensgen@uwm.edu
Financial aid: (414) 229-4541
Application deadline: rolling
In-state tuition: full time: $12,578;
part time: $978/credit hour
Out-of-state tuition: full time:
$25,044
Room/board/expenses: $14,004
Full-time enrollment: 281
doctoral students: 32%; master's
students: 64%; education
specialists: 3%; men: 23%;
women: 77%; minorities: 28%;
international: 6%

Part-time enrollment: 345
doctoral students: 18%; master's
students: 80%; education
specialists: 3%; men: 27%;
women: 73%; minorities: 28%;
international: 1%
Acceptance rate (master's): 64%
Acceptance rate (doctoral): 25%
Entrance test required: GRE
**Avg. GRE (of all entering students
with scores):** quantitative: 150;
verbal: 153
Research assistantships: 0
Students reporting specialty: 100%
Students specializing in: admin.:
41%; curriculum/instr.: 12%;
social/philosophical foundations:
7%; educational psych: 32%;
special: 7%; other: 1%

WYOMING

University of Wyoming[1]

Department 3374
1000 E. University Avenue
Laramie, WY 82071
http://ed.uwyo.edu/
Public
Admissions: (307) 766-2287
E-mail: uwgrad@uwyo.edu
Financial aid: (307) 766-2118
Tuition: N/A
Room/board expenses: N/A
Enrollment: N/A

ENGINEERING

The engineering directory lists the country's 199 schools offering doctoral programs. One hundred ninety-three schools responded to the *U.S. News* survey conducted in the fall of 2012 and early 2013. Information about entrance requirements, enrollment, and costs is reported. Institutions that did not respond to the survey have abbreviated entries.

KEY TO THE TERMINOLOGY

1. A school footnoted with the numeral 1 did not return the *U.S. News* statistical survey; limited data appear in its entry.

N/A. Not available from the school or not applicable.

Admissions. The admissions office phone number.

E-mail. The address of the admissions office. If instead of an E-mail address a website is listed, the website will automatically present an E-mail screen programmed to reach the admissions office.

Financial aid. The financial aid office phone number.

Application deadline. For fall 2014 enrollment. "Rolling" means there is no deadline; the school acts on applications as they are received. "Varies" means deadlines vary according to department or whether applicants are U.S. citizens or foreign nationals.

Tuition. For the 2012-13 academic year. Includes fees.

Credit hour. The cost per credit hour for the 2012-13 academic year.

Room/board/expenses. For the 2012-13 academic year.

Enrollment. Full and part time for fall 2012. The total is the combination of master's and doctoral students, if the school offers both degrees. Where available, the breakdown for men, women, minorities, and international students is provided. Percentages for men and women may not add up to 100 because of rounding.

Minorities. For fall 2012, the percentage of students who are black or African-American, Asian, American Indian or Alaskan Native, Native Hawaiian or other Pacific Islander, Hispanic/Latino, or two or more races. The minority percentage was reported by each school.

Acceptance rate. Percentage of applicants who were accepted for fall 2012, including both master's and doctoral degree programs.

GRE requirement. "Yes" means Graduate Record Examination scores are required by some or all departments.

Average GRE scores. Combined for both master's and doctoral degree students who entered in fall 2012. GRE scores displayed are for fall 2012 entering master's and Ph.D. students and are only for those GRE exams taken during or after August 2011 using the new 130-170 score scale.

TOEFL requirement. "Yes" means that students from non-English-speaking countries must submit scores for the Test of English as a Foreign Language.

Minimum TOEFL score. The score listed is the minimum acceptable score for the paper TOEFL. (The computer-administered TOEFL is graded on a different scale.)

Total fellowships, teaching assistantships, and research assistantships. The number of student appointments for the 2012-13 academic year. Students may hold multiple appointments and would therefore be counted more than once.

Student specialties. Proportion of master's and doctoral students, both full and part time, in the specialty-reporting population (not necessarily the entire student body) who were enrolled in a particular specialty in fall 2012. Specialty fields listed are aerospace/aeronautical/astronautical; agriculture; architectural engineering; bioengineering/biomedical; chemical; civil; computer engineering; computer science; electrical/electronic/communications; engineering management; engineering science and physics; environmental/environmental health; industrial/manufacturing/systems; materials; mechanical; mining; nuclear; petroleum; and other. Numbers may not add up to 100 percent from rounding or because students are enrolled in multiple specialties.

ALABAMA

Auburn University (Ginn)
1301 Shelby Center
Auburn University, AL 36849
http://www.grad.auburn.edu
Public
Admissions: (334) 844-4700
E-mail: gradadm@auburn.edu
Financial aid: (334) 844-4367
Application deadline: rolling
In-state tuition: full time: $9,440; part time: $437/credit hour
Out-of-state tuition: full time: $25,172
Room/board/expenses: $17,102
Full-time enrollment: 428
men: 77%; women: 23%; minorities: 5%; international: 68%
Part-time enrollment: 423
men: 78%; women: 22%; minorities: 10%; international: 38%
Acceptance rate: 55%
GRE requirement: Yes
Avg. GRE: quantitative: 159
TOEFL requirement: Yes
Minimum TOEFL score: 550
Teaching assistantships: 209
Research assistantships: 382
Students specializing in: aerospace: 6%; chemical: 10%; civil: 13%; computer science: 15%; electrical: 20%; industrial: 15%; mechanical: 17%; other: 5%

Tuskegee University
202 Engineering Building
Tuskegee, AL 36088-1920
http://www.tuskegee.edu
Private
Admissions: (334) 727-8500
E-mail: adm@tuskegee.edu
Financial aid: (334) 727-8206
Application deadline: rolling
Tuition: full time: $18,900; part time: $750/credit hour
Room/board/expenses: $13,953
Full-time enrollment: 56
men: 63%; women: 38%; minorities: 66%; international: 34%
Part-time enrollment: 4
men: 100%; women: 0%; minorities: 100%; international: 75%
Acceptance rate: 65%
GRE requirement: Yes
Avg. GRE: quantitative: N/A
TOEFL requirement: Yes
Minimum TOEFL score: 500
Fellowships: 13
Teaching assistantships: 16
Research assistantships: 33
Students specializing in: electrical: 47%; materials: 33%; mechanical: 20%

University of Alabama
Box 870200
Tuscaloosa, AL 35487-0200
http://www.coeweb.eng.ua.edu/
Public
Admissions: (205) 348-5921
E-mail: usgradapply@aalan.ua.edu
Financial aid: (205) 348-2976
Application deadline: 07/01
In-state tuition: full time: $9,200; part time: N/A
Out-of-state tuition: full time: $22,950
Room/board/expenses: $12,758
Full-time enrollment: 293
men: 86%; women: 14%; minorities: 8%; international: 47%
Part-time enrollment: 92
men: 86%; women: 14%; minorities: 13%; international: 15%
Acceptance rate: 38%
GRE requirement: Yes
Avg. GRE: quantitative: 159
TOEFL requirement: Yes
Minimum TOEFL score: 550
Fellowships: 0
Teaching assistantships: 66
Research assistantships: 126
Students specializing in: aerospace: 17%; chemical: 8%; civil: 16%; computer science: 16%; electrical: 15%; materials: 9%; mechanical: 19%; other: 2%

University of Alabama–Birmingham
1720 2nd Ave S, HOEN 100
Birmingham, AL 35294-4440
http://www.uab.edu/engineering
Public
Admissions: (205) 934-8232
E-mail: gradschool@uab.edu
Financial aid: (205) 934-8132
Application deadline: 07/01
In-state tuition: full time: $7,188; part time: $335/credit hour
Out-of-state tuition: full time: $15,852
Room/board/expenses: $20,454
Full-time enrollment: 126
men: 75%; women: 25%; minorities: 21%; international: 35%
Part-time enrollment: 278
men: 78%; women: 22%; minorities: 30%; international: 5%
Acceptance rate: 65%
GRE requirement: Yes
Avg. GRE: quantitative: 155
TOEFL requirement: Yes
Minimum TOEFL score: 550
Fellowships: 35
Teaching assistantships: 2
Research assistantships: 48
Students specializing in: biomedical: 10%; civil: 11%; computer: 3%; electrical: 4%; management: 54%; environmental: 0%; materials: 5%; mechanical: 5%; other: 7%

University of Alabama–Huntsville
301 Sparkman Drive EB 102
Huntsville, AL 35899
http://www.uah.edu
Public
Admissions: (256) 824-6198
E-mail: Kimberly.Gray@uah.edu
Financial aid: (256) 824-6241
Application deadline: 07/16
In-state tuition: full time: $8,516; part time: $6,182
Out-of-state tuition: full time: $20,384
Room/board/expenses: $10,852
Full-time enrollment: 233
men: 71%; women: 29%; minorities: 9%; international: 57%
Part-time enrollment: 530
men: 80%; women: 20%; minorities: 13%; international: 3%
Acceptance rate: 63%
GRE requirement: Yes
Avg. GRE: quantitative: 157
TOEFL requirement: Yes
Minimum TOEFL score: N/A
Fellowships: 5
Teaching assistantships: 83
Research assistantships: 69
Students specializing in: aerospace: 10%; biomedical: 4%; chemical: 1%; civil: 4%; computer: 7%; computer science: 16%; electrical: 19%; management: 6%; industrial: 18%; materials: 1%; mechanical: 14%; other: 7%

ALASKA

University of Alaska–Fairbanks

PO Box 755960
Fairbanks, AK 99775-5960
http://www.uaf.edu/cem
Public
Admissions: (800) 478-1823
E-mail: admissions@uaf.edu
Financial aid: (888) 474-7256
Application deadline: 06/01
In-state tuition: full time: $383/credit hour; part time: $383/credit hour
Out-of-state tuition: full time: $783/credit hour
Room/board/expenses: $11,310
Full-time enrollment: 76
men: 71%; women: 29%;
minorities: 8%; international: 49%
Part-time enrollment: 41
men: 73%; women: 27%;
minorities: 10%; international: 17%
Acceptance rate: 25%
GRE requirement: Yes
Avg. GRE: quantitative: 157
TOEFL requirement: Yes
Minimum TOEFL score: 550
Fellowships: 0
Teaching assistantships: 33
Research assistantships: 37
Students specializing in: civil: 15%;
computer: 1%; computer science:
2%; electrical: 13%; management:
3%; environmental: 7%; mechanical: 7%; mining: 2%; petroleum:
15%; other: 36%

ARIZONA

Arizona State University (Fulton)

Box 879309
Tempe, AZ 85287-9309
http://engineering.asu.edu
Public
Admissions: (480) 965-6113
Financial aid: (480) 965-3355
Application deadline: rolling
In-state tuition: full time: $11,317;
part time: $918/credit hour
Out-of-state tuition: full time:
$25,865
Room/board/expenses: $11,872
Full-time enrollment: 1,904
men: 79%; women: 21%;
minorities: 7%; international: 76%
Part-time enrollment: 788
men: 81%; women: 19%;
minorities: 22%; international:
24%
Acceptance rate: 55%
GRE requirement: Yes
Avg. GRE: quantitative: 161
TOEFL requirement: Yes
Minimum TOEFL score: 550
Fellowships: 217
Teaching assistantships: 224
Research assistantships: 516
Students specializing in: aerospace: 2%; biomedical: 4%;
chemical: 2%; civil: 4%; computer:
2%; computer science: 20%;
electrical: 36%; environmental:
3%; industrial: 6%; materials: 5%;
mechanical: 9%; other: 7%

University of Arizona

Civil Engineering Building
Room 100
Tucson, AZ 85721-0072
http://grad.arizona.edu
Public
Admissions: (520) 621-3471
E-mail: gradadmission@grad.arizona.edu
Financial aid: (520) 621-1858
Application deadline: rolling
In-state tuition: full time: $11,137;
part time: $729/credit hour
Out-of-state tuition: full time:
$26,547
Room/board/expenses: $16,240

Full-time enrollment: 800
men: 76%; women: 24%;
minorities: 10%; international:
56%
Part-time enrollment: 193
men: 83%; women: 17%;
minorities: 18%; international: 12%
Acceptance rate: 31%
GRE requirement: Yes
Avg. GRE: quantitative: 166
TOEFL requirement: Yes
Minimum TOEFL score: 550
Fellowships: 48
Teaching assistantships: 78
Research assistantships: 302
Students specializing in: aerospace: 4%; agriculture: 2%;
biomedical: 4%; chemical: 4%;
civil: 7%; computer: 17%; computer science: 9%; electrical: 17%;
management: 2%; environmental:
5%; industrial: 6%; materials:
5%; mechanical: 6%; mining: 3%;
other: 32%

ARKANSAS

University of Arkansas–Fayetteville

Bell Engineering Center
Room 4183
Fayetteville, AR 72701
http://www.engr.uark.edu
Public
Admissions: (479) 575-4401
E-mail: gradinfo@uark.edu
Financial aid: (479) 575-3806
Application deadline: 08/01
In-state tuition: full time: $350/credit hour; part time: $350/credit hour
Out-of-state tuition: full time: $827/credit hour
Room/board/expenses: $11,467
Full-time enrollment: 290
men: 79%; women: 21%;
minorities: 7%; international: 64%
Part-time enrollment: 111
men: 86%; women: 14%;
minorities: 20%; international:
27%
Acceptance rate: 35%
GRE requirement: Yes
Avg. GRE: quantitative: 161
TOEFL requirement: Yes
Minimum TOEFL score: 550
Fellowships: 41
Teaching assistantships: 70
Research assistantships: 147
Students specializing in: biomedical: 8%; chemical: 9%; civil:
10%; computer: 7%; computer
science: 7%; electrical: 29%;
environmental: 1%; industrial:
12%; mechanical: 7%; other: 11%

CALIFORNIA

California Institute of Technology

1200 E. California Boulevard
Pasadena, CA 91125-4400
http://www.gradoffice.caltech.edu
Private
Admissions: (626) 395-6346
E-mail: gradofc@its.caltech.edu
Financial aid: (626) 395-6346
Application deadline: 12/15
Tuition: full time: $39,480; part
time: N/A
Room/board/expenses: $28,003
Full-time enrollment: 587
men: 76%; women: 24%;
minorities: 14%; international: 47%
Part-time enrollment: N/A
men: N/A; women: N/A;
minorities: N/A; international: N/A
Acceptance rate: 8%
GRE requirement: Yes
Avg. GRE: quantitative: 164
TOEFL requirement: Yes
Minimum TOEFL score: N/A
Fellowships: 181
Teaching assistantships: 87
Research assistantships: 366

Students specializing in: aerospace: 12%; biomedical: 6%;
chemical: 11%; civil: 3%; computer
science: 11%; electrical: 23%;
science and physics: 9%; environmental: 4%; materials: 11%;
mechanical: 11%

California State University–Long Beach

1250 Bellflower Boulevard
Long Beach, CA 90840-8306
http://www.csulb.edu/colleges/coe/
Public
Admissions: N/A
Financial aid: N/A
Application deadline: 04/15
In-state tuition: full time: $7,506;
part time: $4,674
Out-of-state tuition: full time:
$14,202
Room/board/expenses: $12,966
Full-time enrollment: 739
men: 82%; women: 18%;
minorities: 79%; international:
29%
Part-time enrollment: 35
men: 83%; women: 17%;
minorities: 23%; international:
23%
Acceptance rate: 56%
GRE requirement: Yes
Avg. GRE: quantitative: 158
TOEFL requirement: Yes
Minimum TOEFL score: 550
Fellowships: 4
Teaching assistantships: 12
Research assistantships: 8
Students specializing in: aerospace: 7%; chemical: 7%; civil:
17%; computer: 7%; computer
science: 26%; electrical: 28%;
mechanical: 7%

Naval Postgraduate School[1]

1 University Circle
Monterey, CA 93943-5001
http://www.nps.navy.mil/inps/GSEAS.htm
Public
Admissions: (831) 656-3093
E-mail: grad-ed@nps.navy.mil
Financial aid: N/A
Tuition: N/A
Room/board expenses: N/A
Enrollment: N/A

San Diego State University

5500 Campanile Drive
San Diego, CA 92182
http://engineering.sdsu.edu
Public
Admissions: (619) 594-6061
Financial aid: (619) 594-6323
Application deadline: N/A
In-state tuition: full time: $7,844;
part time: $5,012
Out-of-state tuition: full time: $372/credit hour
Room/board/expenses: $16,714
Full-time enrollment: 85
men: 69%; women: 31%;
minorities: 39%; international:
32%
Part-time enrollment: 179
men: 73%; women: 27%;
minorities: 45%; international:
20%
Acceptance rate: 46%
GRE requirement: Yes
Avg. GRE: quantitative: 156
TOEFL requirement: Yes
Minimum TOEFL score: 550
Fellowships: 0
Teaching assistantships: 20
Research assistantships: 0
Students specializing in: aerospace: 8%; biomedical: 6%; civil:
19%; electrical: 29%; science and
physics: 8%; environmental: 7%;
industrial: 6%; mechanical: 17%

Santa Clara University

500 El Camino Real
Santa Clara, CA 95053-0583
http://www.scu.edu/engineering/graduate
Private
Admissions: (408) 554-4313
E-mail: gradengineer@scu.edu
Financial aid: (408) 554-4505
Application deadline: rolling
Tuition: full time: $805/credit hour;
part time: $805/credit hour
Room/board/expenses: $17,118
Full-time enrollment: 307
men: 68%; women: 32%;
minorities: 71%; international:
56%
Part-time enrollment: 366
men: 77%; women: 23%;
minorities: 60%; international:
22%
Acceptance rate: 56%
GRE requirement: Yes
Avg. GRE: quantitative: 158
TOEFL requirement: Yes
Minimum TOEFL score: 550
Teaching assistantships: 26
Research assistantships: 15
Students specializing in: biomedical: 1%; civil: 19%; computer: 34%;
electrical: 19%; management:
25%; mechanical: 14%; other: 5%

Stanford University

Huang Engineering Center
Suite 226
Stanford, CA 94305-4121
http://engineering.stanford.edu
Private
Admissions: (650) 723-4291
E-mail: gradadmissions@stanford.edu
Financial aid: (650) 723-3058
Application deadline: N/A
Tuition: full time: $44,577; part
time: N/A
Room/board/expenses: $25,545
Full-time enrollment: 3,249
men: 74%; women: 26%;
minorities: 23%; international:
45%
Part-time enrollment: 299
men: 82%; women: 18%;
minorities: 37%; international:
23%
Acceptance rate: 19%
GRE requirement: Yes
Avg. GRE: quantitative: 165
TOEFL requirement: Yes
Minimum TOEFL score: 575
Fellowships: 1,047
Teaching assistantships: 483
Research assistantships: 1,026
Students specializing in: aerospace: 5%; biomedical: 3%;
chemical: 4%; civil: 12%; computer science: 14%; electrical: 25%;
management: 10%; materials: 5%;
mechanical: 14%; petroleum: 4%;
other: 4%

University of California–Berkeley

320 McLaughlin Hall, #1700
Berkeley, CA 94720-1700
http://www.grad.berkeley.edu/
Public
Admissions: (510) 642-7405
E-mail: gradadm@berkeley.edu
Financial aid: (510) 642-6442
Application deadline: N/A
In-state tuition: full time: $15,340;
part time: N/A
Out-of-state tuition: full time:
$30,442
Room/board/expenses: $18,760
Full-time enrollment: 1,797
men: 74%; women: 26%;
minorities: 22%; international:
39%
Part-time enrollment: 40
men: 70%; women: 30%;
minorities: 35%; international:
13%
Acceptance rate: 12%
GRE requirement: Yes

Avg. GRE: quantitative: 163
TOEFL requirement: Yes
Minimum TOEFL score: 570
Fellowships: 700
Teaching assistantships: 345
Research assistantships: 859
Students specializing in: biomedical: 10%; chemical: 7%; civil: 18%;
computer: 13%; electrical: 17%;
industrial: 5%; materials: 5%;
mechanical: 18%; nuclear: 5%;
other: 2%

University of California–Davis

1050 Kemper Hall
1 Shields Avenue
Davis, CA 95616-5294
http://engineering.ucdavis.edu
Public
Admissions: (530) 752-1473
Financial aid: (530) 752-9246
Application deadline: N/A
In-state tuition: full time: $15,387;
part time: $9,777
Out-of-state tuition: full time:
$30,489
Room/board/expenses: $17,177
Full-time enrollment: 1,122
men: 71%; women: 29%;
minorities: 21%; international:
38%
Part-time enrollment: 47
men: 77%; women: 23%;
minorities: 30%; international: 4%
Acceptance rate: 22%
GRE requirement: Yes
Avg. GRE: quantitative: 161
TOEFL requirement: Yes
Minimum TOEFL score: 550
Fellowships: 250
Teaching assistantships: 204
Research assistantships: 490
Students specializing in: aerospace: 14%; agriculture: 4%; biomedical: 12%; chemical: 6%; civil:
21%; computer: 15%; computer
science: 18%; electrical: 15%;
science and physics: 3%; environmental: 21%; materials: 4%;
mechanical: 14%; other: 4%

University of California–Irvine (Samueli)

305 REC
Irvine, CA 92697-2700
http://www.eng.uci.edu
Public
Admissions: (949) 824-4334
E-mail: gradengr@uci.edu
Financial aid: (949) 824-4889
Application deadline: 01/15
In-state tuition: full time: $15,145;
part time: $9,535
Out-of-state tuition: full time:
$30,247
Room/board/expenses: $17,709
Full-time enrollment: 1,136
men: 75%; women: 25%;
minorities: 19%; international:
57%
Part-time enrollment: 140
men: 81%; women: 19%;
minorities: 31%; international:
43%
Acceptance rate: 17%
GRE requirement: Yes
Avg. GRE: quantitative: 161
TOEFL requirement: Yes
Minimum TOEFL score: 550
Fellowships: 556
Teaching assistantships: 279
Research assistantships: 645
Students specializing in: aerospace: 4%; biomedical: 11%;
chemical: 5%; civil: 8%; computer:
11%; computer science: 31%;
electrical: 11%; management: 1%;
environmental: 3%; materials: 6%;
mechanical: 8%

University of California–Los Angeles (Samueli)

6426 Boelter Hall, Box 951601
Los Angeles, CA 90095-1601
http://www.engineer.ucla.edu
Public
Admissions: (310) 825-2514
E-mail: gradadm@ea.ucla.edu
Financial aid: (310) 206-0400
Application deadline: 12/01
In-state tuition: full time: $12,562; part time: N/A
Out-of-state tuition: full time: $27,664
Room/board/expenses: $20,424
Full-time enrollment: 1,776
men: 81%; women: 19%;
minorities: 29%; international: 47%
Part-time enrollment: N/A
men: N/A; women: N/A;
minorities: N/A; international: N/A
Acceptance rate: 26%
GRE requirement: Yes
Avg. GRE: quantitative: 163
TOEFL requirement: Yes
Minimum TOEFL score: 560
Fellowships: 608
Teaching assistantships: 541
Research assistantships: 1,577
Students specializing in: aerospace: 3%; biomedical: 10%; chemical: 4%; civil: 8%; computer science: 17%; electrical: 28%; materials: 7%; mechanical: 12%; other: 11%

University of California–Riverside (Bourns)

University Office Building
Riverside, CA 92521-0208
http://www.graddiv.ucr.edu
Public
Admissions: (951) 827-3313
E-mail: grdadmis@ucr.edu
Financial aid: (951) 827-3387
Application deadline: 01/05
In-state tuition: full time: $29,292; part time: $21,969
Out-of-state tuition: full time: $29,748
Room/board/expenses: $17,600
Full-time enrollment: 493
men: 72%; women: 28%;
minorities: 22%; international: 60%
Part-time enrollment: 41
men: 66%; women: 34%;
minorities: 24%; international: 93%
Acceptance rate: 21%
GRE requirement: Yes
Avg. GRE: quantitative: 161
TOEFL requirement: Yes
Minimum TOEFL score: 550
Fellowships: 123
Teaching assistantships: 162
Research assistantships: 270
Students specializing in: biomedical: 15%; chemical: 12%; computer science: 33%; electrical: 21%; materials: 8%; mechanical: 10%

University of California–San Diego (Jacobs)

9500 Gilman Drive
La Jolla, CA 92093-0403
http://www.jacobsschool.ucsd.edu
Public
Admissions: (858) 534-3555
E-mail: gradadmissions@ucsd.edu
Financial aid: (858) 534-4480
Application deadline: N/A
In-state tuition: full time: $12,734; part time: $7,124
Out-of-state tuition: full time: $27,836
Room/board/expenses: $17,740

Full-time enrollment: 1,548
men: 79%; women: 21%;
minorities: 22%; international: 48%
Part-time enrollment: 66
men: 89%; women: 11%;
minorities: 36%; international: 17%
Acceptance rate: 23%
GRE requirement: Yes
Avg. GRE: quantitative: 163
TOEFL requirement: Yes
Minimum TOEFL score: 550
Fellowships: 360
Teaching assistantships: 450
Research assistantships: 880
Students specializing in: aerospace: 2%; biomedical: 15%; chemical: 1%; civil: 9%; computer: 6%; computer science: 20%; electrical: 24%; science and physics: 3%; materials: 8%; mechanical: 11%; other: 2%

University of California–Santa Barbara

Harold Frank Hall 1038
Santa Barbara, CA 93106-5130
http://www.engineering.ucsb.edu
Public
Admissions: (805) 893-2277
E-mail: admissions@graddiv.ucsb.edu
Financial aid: (805) 893-2277
Application deadline: 12/15
In-state tuition: full time: $12,957; part time: N/A
Out-of-state tuition: full time: $28,059
Room/board/expenses: $13,225
Full-time enrollment: 760
men: 80%; women: 20%;
minorities: 9%; international: 46%
Part-time enrollment: N/A
men: N/A; women: N/A;
minorities: N/A; international: N/A
Acceptance rate: 17%
GRE requirement: Yes
Avg. GRE: quantitative: 164
TOEFL requirement: Yes
Minimum TOEFL score: 600
Fellowships: 156
Teaching assistantships: 109
Research assistantships: 390
Students specializing in: chemical: 11%; computer science: 21%; electrical: 39%; materials: 19%; mechanical: 11%

University of California–Santa Cruz (Baskin)

1156 High Street
Santa Cruz, CA 95064
http://ga.soe.ucsc.edu/
Public
Admissions: (831) 459-5905
E-mail: soegradadm@soe.ucsc.edu
Financial aid: (831) 459-2963
Application deadline: 01/03
In-state tuition: full time: $16,174; part time: $10,564
Out-of-state tuition: full time: $31,276
Room/board/expenses: $22,140
Full-time enrollment: 300
men: 69%; women: 31%;
minorities: 19%; international: 29%
Part-time enrollment: 34
men: 97%; women: 3%;
minorities: 32%; international: 18%
Acceptance rate: 27%
GRE requirement: Yes
Avg. GRE: quantitative: 162
TOEFL requirement: Yes
Minimum TOEFL score: 570
Fellowships: 84
Teaching assistantships: 238
Research assistantships: 408

Students specializing in: biomedical: 13%; computer: 17%; computer science: 35%; electrical: 17%; management: 4%; other: 13%

University of Southern California (Viterbi)

University Park, Olin Hall 200
Los Angeles, CA 90089-1450
http://viterbi.usc.edu
Private
Admissions: (213) 740-4530
E-mail: viterbi.gradadmission@usc.edu
Financial aid: (213) 740-0119
Application deadline: 12/01
Tuition: full time: $30,152; part time: $1,569/credit hour
Room/board/expenses: $21,547
Full-time enrollment: 2,962
men: 74%; women: 26%;
minorities: 9%; international: 80%
Part-time enrollment: 1,436
men: 77%; women: 23%;
minorities: 23%; international: 46%
Acceptance rate: 31%
GRE requirement: Yes
Avg. GRE: quantitative: 161
TOEFL requirement: Yes
Minimum TOEFL score: N/A
Fellowships: 257
Teaching assistantships: 580
Research assistantships: 1,136
Students specializing in: aerospace: 5%; biomedical: 6%; chemical: 4%; civil: 6%; computer: 2%; computer science: 24%; electrical: 30%; management: 3%; environmental: 2%; industrial: 7%; materials: 2%; mechanical: 7%; nuclear: 0%; petroleum: 4%

COLORADO

Colorado School of Mines

1500 Illinois Street
Golden, CO 80401-1887
http://gradschool.mines.edu
Public
Admissions: (303) 384-2221
E-mail: grad-school@mines.edu
Financial aid: (303) 273-3207
Application deadline: 03/01
In-state tuition: full time: $15,654; part time: $755/credit hour
Out-of-state tuition: full time: $30,684
Room/board/expenses: $24,232
Full-time enrollment: 1,164
men: 74%; women: 26%;
minorities: 10%; international: 32%
Part-time enrollment: 179
men: 79%; women: 21%;
minorities: 12%; international: 7%
Acceptance rate: 41%
GRE requirement: Yes
Avg. GRE: quantitative: 158
TOEFL requirement: Yes
Minimum TOEFL score: 550
Fellowships: 73
Teaching assistantships: 171
Research assistantships: 513
Students specializing in: chemical: 6%; civil: 6%; electrical: 8%; science and physics: 5%; environmental: 8%; materials: 5%; mechanical: 8%; mining: 3%; nuclear: 3%; petroleum: 8%; other: 48%

Colorado State University

Campus Delivery 1301
Fort Collins, CO 80523-1301
http://www.engr.colostate.edu
Public
Admissions: (970) 491-6817
E-mail: gschool@grad.colostate.edu
Financial aid: (970) 491-6321
Application deadline: 02/15

In-state tuition: full time: $12,445; part time: $576/credit hour
Out-of-state tuition: full time: $24,625
Room/board/expenses: $14,106
Full-time enrollment: 312
men: 74%; women: 26%;
minorities: 8%; international: 30%
Part-time enrollment: 348
men: 72%; women: 28%;
minorities: 8%; international: 39%
Acceptance rate: 42%
GRE requirement: Yes
Avg. GRE: quantitative: 159
TOEFL requirement: Yes
Minimum TOEFL score: 550
Fellowships: 41
Teaching assistantships: 59
Research assistantships: 210
Students specializing in: biomedical: 8%; chemical: 3%; civil: 32%; electrical: 26%; industrial: 2%; mechanical: 15%; other: 14%

University of Colorado–Boulder

422 UCB
Boulder, CO 80309-0422
http://www.colorado.edu/engineering
Public
Admissions: (303) 492-5071
Financial aid: (303) 492-5091
Application deadline: 12/15
In-state tuition: full time: $14,161; part time: $9,919
Out-of-state tuition: full time: $30,037
Room/board/expenses: $21,074
Full-time enrollment: 1,373
men: 75%; women: 25%;
minorities: 9%; international: 34%
Part-time enrollment: 240
men: 80%; women: 20%;
minorities: 13%; international: 15%
Acceptance rate: 33%
GRE requirement: Yes
Avg. GRE: quantitative: 160
TOEFL requirement: Yes
Minimum TOEFL score: 560
Fellowships: 142
Teaching assistantships: 92
Research assistantships: 469
Students specializing in: aerospace: 14%; chemical: 7%; civil: 17%; computer science: 15%; electrical: 18%; management: 9%; mechanical: 12%; other: 8%

University of Colorado–Colorado Springs

1420 Austin Bluffs Parkway
Colorado Springs, CO 80918
http://www.uccs.edu
Public
Admissions: (719) 255-3383
E-mail: admrec@uccs.edu
Financial aid: (719) 255-3460
Application deadline: rolling
In-state tuition: full time: $7,404; part time: $4,425
Out-of-state tuition: full time: $13,008
Room/board/expenses: N/A
Full-time enrollment: 155
men: 88%; women: 12%;
minorities: 11%; international: 32%
Part-time enrollment: 118
men: 84%; women: 16%;
minorities: 14%; international: 6%
Acceptance rate: 66%
GRE requirement: Yes
Avg. GRE: quantitative: N/A
TOEFL requirement: Yes
Minimum TOEFL score: 550
Students specializing in: N/A

University of Colorado–Denver

PO Box 173364, Campus Box 104
Denver, CO 80217-3364
http://www.ucdenver.edu/
Public
Admissions: (303) 556-2704
E-mail: admissions@ucdenver.edu
Financial aid: (303) 556-2886
Application deadline: rolling
In-state tuition: full time: $5,440; part time: $433/credit hour
Out-of-state tuition: full time: $12,710
Room/board/expenses: $15,852
Full-time enrollment: 278
men: 70%; women: 30%;
minorities: 13%; international: 39%
Part-time enrollment: 139
men: 77%; women: 23%;
minorities: 19%; international: 17%
Acceptance rate: 63%
GRE requirement: No
Avg. GRE: quantitative: N/A
TOEFL requirement: Yes
Minimum TOEFL score: 500
Fellowships: 0
Teaching assistantships: 4
Research assistantships: 31
Students specializing in: biomedical: 13%; civil: 27%; computer: 3%; computer science: 20%; electrical: 14%; science and physics: 13%; mechanical: 10%

University of Denver

2390 York Street
Denver, CO 80208
http://www.du.edu/secs/
Private
Admissions: (303) 871-2831
E-mail: grad-info@du.edu
Financial aid: (303) 871-4020
Application deadline: 02/01
Tuition: full time: $38,976; part time: N/A
Room/board/expenses: $13,779
Full-time enrollment: 7
men: 71%; women: 29%;
minorities: 0%; international: 100%
Part-time enrollment: 186
men: 82%; women: 18%;
minorities: 12%; international: 26%
Acceptance rate: 79%
GRE requirement: Yes
Avg. GRE: quantitative: 160
TOEFL requirement: Yes
Minimum TOEFL score: 550
Fellowships: 0
Teaching assistantships: 26
Research assistantships: 27
Students specializing in: computer: 9%; computer science: 24%; electrical: 34%; materials: 2%; mechanical: 32%

CONNECTICUT

University of Bridgeport

221 University Avenue
Bridgeport, CT 06604
http://www.bridgeport.edu/sed
Private
Admissions: (203) 576-4552
E-mail: admit@bridgeport.edu
Financial aid: (203) 576-4568
Application deadline: rolling
Tuition: full time: $720/credit hour; part time: $720/credit hour
Room/board/expenses: $15,120
Full-time enrollment: 303
men: 76%; women: 24%;
minorities: 4%; international: 94%
Part-time enrollment: 247
men: 80%; women: 20%;
minorities: 9%; international: 80%
Acceptance rate: 42%
GRE requirement: No
Avg. GRE: quantitative: N/A
TOEFL requirement: Yes
Minimum TOEFL score: 550

Teaching assistantships: 32
Research assistantships: 25
Students specializing in: biomedical: 15%; computer: 3%; computer science: 30%; electrical: 23%; management: 21%; mechanical: 8%

University of Connecticut

261 Glenbrook Road, Unit 2237
Storrs, CT 06269-2237
http://www.uconn.edu
Public
Admissions: (860) 486-0974
E-mail: gradadmissions@uconn.edu
Financial aid: (860) 486-2819
Application deadline: 02/15
In-state tuition: full time: $10,782; part time: $599/credit hour
Out-of-state tuition: full time: $27,990
Room/board/expenses: $19,778
Full-time enrollment: 568
men: 73%; women: 27%; minorities: 8%; international: 62%
Part-time enrollment: 206
men: 78%; women: 22%; minorities: 17%; international: 16%
Acceptance rate: 30%
GRE requirement: Yes
Avg. GRE: quantitative: 161
TOEFL requirement: Yes
Minimum TOEFL score: 550
Fellowships: 118
Teaching assistantships: 45
Research assistantships: 336
Students specializing in: biomedical: 17%; chemical: 10%; civil: 14%; electrical: 24%; environmental: 7%; materials: 22%; mechanical: 26%

Yale University

226 Dunham Lab
10 Hillhouse Avenue
New Haven, CT 06520
http://www.seas.yale.edu
Private
Admissions: (203) 432-2771
E-mail: graduate.admissions@yale.edu
Financial aid: (203) 432-2739
Application deadline: 01/02
Tuition: full time: $35,500; part time: $4,438/credit hour
Room/board/expenses: $26,720
Full-time enrollment: 209
men: 68%; women: 32%; minorities: 13%; international: 54%
Part-time enrollment: 8
men: 75%; women: 25%; minorities: 0%; international: 25%
Acceptance rate: 12%
GRE requirement: Yes
Avg. GRE: quantitative: 164
TOEFL requirement: Yes
Minimum TOEFL score: 590
Fellowships: 71
Teaching assistantships: 114
Research assistantships: 113
Students specializing in: biomedical: 32%; chemical: 29%; electrical: 23%; mechanical: 14%; other: 2%

DELAWARE

University of Delaware

102 DuPont Hall
Newark, DE 19716-3101
http://www.engr.udel.edu
Public
Admissions: (302) 831-2129
E-mail: gradadmissions@udel.edu
Financial aid: (302) 831-8189
Application deadline: rolling
In-state tuition: full time: $27,982; part time: $1,513/credit hour
Out-of-state tuition: full time: $27,982
Room/board/expenses: $13,258

Full-time enrollment: 744
men: 74%; women: 26%; minorities: 9%; international: 58%
Part-time enrollment: 118
men: 84%; women: 16%; minorities: 23%; international: 10%
Acceptance rate: 25%
GRE requirement: Yes
Avg. GRE: quantitative: 160
TOEFL requirement: Yes
Minimum TOEFL score: 570
Fellowships: 47
Teaching assistantships: 70
Research assistantships: 444
Students specializing in: biomedical: 3%; chemical: 17%; civil: 13%; computer science: 14%; electrical: 19%; environmental: 7%; materials: 9%; mechanical: 11%; other: 6%

DISTRICT OF COLUMBIA

Catholic University of America

620 Michigan Avenue NE
Washington, DC 20064
http://admissions.cua.edu/graduate/
Private
Admissions: (800) 673-2772
E-mail: cua-admissions@cua.edu
Financial aid: (202) 319-5307
Application deadline: 07/15
Tuition: full time: $37,030; part time: $1,420/credit hour
Room/board/expenses: $20,210
Full-time enrollment: 88
men: 76%; women: 24%; minorities: 11%; international: 59%
Part-time enrollment: 108
men: 68%; women: 32%; minorities: 21%; international: 27%
Acceptance rate: 69%
GRE requirement: No
Avg. GRE: quantitative: N/A
TOEFL requirement: Yes
Minimum TOEFL score: 580
Fellowships: 4
Teaching assistantships: 15
Research assistantships: 15
Students specializing in: biomedical: 15%; civil: 15%; computer science: 15%; electrical: 19%; management: 22%; materials: 3%; mechanical: 11%

George Washington University

725 23rd Street NW
Tompkins Hall
Washington, DC 20052
http://www.seas.gwu.edu/
Private
Admissions: (202) 994-8675
E-mail: engineering@gwu.edu
Financial aid: (202) 994-6822
Application deadline: N/A
Tuition: full time: $1,340/credit hour; part time: $1,340/credit hour
Room/board/expenses: $22,680
Full-time enrollment: 630
men: 72%; women: 28%; minorities: 5%; international: 83%
Part-time enrollment: 912
men: 77%; women: 23%; minorities: 29%; international: 13%
Acceptance rate: 37%
GRE requirement: Yes
Avg. GRE: quantitative: 160
TOEFL requirement: Yes
Minimum TOEFL score: 550
Fellowships: 83
Teaching assistantships: 63
Research assistantships: 55
Students specializing in: biomedical: 1%; civil: 3%; computer: 3%; computer science: 27%; electrical: 13%; management: 47%; mechanical: 6%

Howard University

2366 Sixth Street NW, Suite 100
Washington, DC 20059
http://www.gs.howard.edu
Private
Admissions: (202) 806-7469
E-mail: hugsadmissions@howard.edu
Financial aid: (202) 806-2820
Application deadline: 01/01
Tuition: full time: $27,327; part time: $1,405/credit hour
Room/board/expenses: $21,312
Full-time enrollment: 41
men: 80%; women: 20%; minorities: 54%; international: 46%
Part-time enrollment: 37
men: 59%; women: 41%; minorities: 49%; international: 51%
Acceptance rate: 54%
GRE requirement: Yes
Avg. GRE: quantitative: N/A
TOEFL requirement: Yes
Minimum TOEFL score: 550
Fellowships: 5
Teaching assistantships: 13
Research assistantships: 20
Students specializing in: chemical: 13%; civil: 8%; computer science: 19%; electrical: 35%; mechanical: 26%

FLORIDA

Florida A&M University-Florida State University

2525 Pottsdamer Street
Tallahassee, FL 32310
http://www.eng.fsu.edu
Public
Admissions: (850) 410-6423
E-mail: perry@eng.fsu.edu
Financial aid: (850) 410-6423
Application deadline: 03/31
In-state tuition: full time: $428/credit hour; part time: $428/credit hour
Out-of-state tuition: full time: $1,059/credit hour
Room/board/expenses: $10,700
Full-time enrollment: 268
men: 81%; women: 19%; minorities: 22%; international: 44%
Part-time enrollment: N/A
men: N/A; women: N/A; minorities: N/A; international: N/A
Acceptance rate: 46%
GRE requirement: Yes
Avg. GRE: quantitative: 157
TOEFL requirement: Yes
Minimum TOEFL score: 550
Fellowships: 9
Teaching assistantships: 34
Research assistantships: 112
Students specializing in: chemical: 12%; civil: 22%; electrical: 29%; industrial: 12%; mechanical: 26%

Florida Atlantic University

777 Glades Road
Boca Raton, FL 33431-0991
http://www.eng.fau.edu
Public
Admissions: (561) 297-3642
E-mail: graduatecollege@fau.edu
Financial aid: (561) 297-3530
Application deadline: rolling
In-state tuition: full time: $370/credit hour; part time: $370/credit hour
Out-of-state tuition: full time: $1,025/credit hour
Room/board/expenses: $14,378
Full-time enrollment: 125
men: 78%; women: 22%; minorities: 26%; international: 37%

Part-time enrollment: 152
men: 80%; women: 20%; minorities: 39%; international: 16%
Acceptance rate: 47%
GRE requirement: Yes
Avg. GRE: quantitative: N/A
TOEFL requirement: Yes
Minimum TOEFL score: 550
Fellowships: 9
Teaching assistantships: 88
Research assistantships: 115
Students specializing in: biomedical: 5%; civil: 8%; computer: 14%; computer science: 28%; electrical: 17%; mechanical: 9%; other: 18%

Florida Institute of Technology

150 W. University Boulevard
Melbourne, FL 32901-6975
http://www.fit.edu
Private
Admissions: (800) 944-4348
E-mail: grad-admissions@fit.edu
Financial aid: (321) 674-8070
Application deadline: rolling
Tuition: full time: $1,123/credit hour; part time: $1,123/credit hour
Room/board/expenses: $16,470
Full-time enrollment: 389
men: 80%; women: 20%; minorities: 5%; international: 67%
Part-time enrollment: 297
men: 81%; women: 19%; minorities: 19%; international: 23%
Acceptance rate: 52%
GRE requirement: Yes
Avg. GRE: quantitative: 157
TOEFL requirement: Yes
Minimum TOEFL score: 550
Fellowships: 0
Teaching assistantships: 62
Research assistantships: 31
Students specializing in: aerospace: 7%; biomedical: 1%; chemical: 2%; civil: 4%; computer: 3%; computer science: 34%; electrical: 16%; management: 14%; environmental: 10%; mechanical: 7%; other: 1%

Florida International University

10555 W. Flagler Street
Miami, FL 33174
http://www.eng.fiu.edu/
Public
Admissions: (305) 348-7442
E-mail: gradadm@fiu.edu
Financial aid: (305) 348-7272
Application deadline: 06/01
In-state tuition: full time: $10,684; part time: $422/credit hour
Out-of-state tuition: full time: $22,784
Room/board/expenses: $20,233
Full-time enrollment: 530
men: 76%; women: 24%; minorities: 28%; international: 64%
Part-time enrollment: 359
men: 78%; women: 22%; minorities: 65%; international: 19%
Acceptance rate: 56%
GRE requirement: Yes
Avg. GRE: quantitative: 156
TOEFL requirement: Yes
Minimum TOEFL score: 550
Fellowships: 22
Teaching assistantships: 121
Research assistantships: 101
Students specializing in: biomedical: 6%; civil: 13%; computer: 3%; computer science: 14%; electrical: 14%; management: 19%; environmental: 2%; materials: 3%; mechanical: 5%; other: 21%

University of Central Florida

4000 Central Florida Boulevard
Orlando, FL 32816-2993
http://www.cecs.ucf.edu/academics/graduateprograms
Public
Admissions: (407) 823-2455
E-mail: gradengr@ucf.edu
Financial aid: (407) 823-2827
Application deadline: 07/15
In-state tuition: full time: $357/credit hour; part time: $357/credit hour
Out-of-state tuition: full time: $1,182/credit hour
Room/board/expenses: $14,522
Full-time enrollment: 735
men: 78%; women: 22%; minorities: 14%; international: 58%
Part-time enrollment: 558
men: 79%; women: 21%; minorities: 32%; international: 0%
Acceptance rate: 41%
GRE requirement: Yes
Avg. GRE: quantitative: N/A
TOEFL requirement: Yes
Minimum TOEFL score: 560
Fellowships: 25
Teaching assistantships: 121
Research assistantships: 373
Students specializing in: aerospace: 3%; civil: 11%; computer: 6%; computer science: 23%; electrical: 14%; management: 4%; environmental: 3%; industrial: 18%; materials: 4%; mechanical: 13%

University of Florida

300 Weil Hall
Gainesville, FL 32611-6550
http://www.eng.ufl.edu
Public
Admissions: (352) 392-0943
E-mail: admissions@eng.ufl.edu
Financial aid: (352) 392-0943
Application deadline: 06/01
In-state tuition: full time: $12,589; part time: $525/credit hour
Out-of-state tuition: full time: $29,983
Room/board/expenses: $15,690
Full-time enrollment: 2,636
men: 78%; women: 22%; minorities: 10%; international: 65%
Part-time enrollment: 331
men: 77%; women: 23%; minorities: 20%; international: 28%
Acceptance rate: 43%
GRE requirement: Yes
Avg. GRE: quantitative: 161
TOEFL requirement: Yes
Minimum TOEFL score: 550
Fellowships: 155
Teaching assistantships: 117
Research assistantships: 693
Students specializing in: aerospace: 3%; agriculture: 2%; biomedical: 5%; chemical: 7%; civil: 10%; computer: 15%; computer science: 1%; electrical: 20%; management: 4%; environmental: 4%; industrial: 5%; materials: 8%; mechanical: 15%; nuclear: 1%

University of Miami

1251 Memorial Drive
Coral Gables, FL 33146
http://www.miami.edu/engineering
Private
Admissions: (305) 284-2942
E-mail: gradadm.eng@miami.edu
Financial aid: (305) 284-5212
Application deadline: 12/01
Tuition: full time: $1,660/credit hour; part time: $1,660/credit hour
Room/board/expenses: $18,020
Full-time enrollment: 232
men: 72%; women: 28%; minorities: 21%; international: 56%

Part-time enrollment: 25
men: 60%; women: 40%;
minorities: 60%; international:
24%
Acceptance rate: 54%
GRE requirement: Yes
Avg. GRE: quantitative: 159
TOEFL requirement: Yes
Minimum TOEFL score: 550
Fellowships: 10
Teaching assistantships: 38
Research assistantships: 72
Students specializing in: biomedical: 30%; civil: 9%; computer science: 7%; electrical: 18%; industrial: 24%; mechanical: 11%

University of South Florida

4202 E. Fowler Avenue, ENB118
Tampa, FL 33620
http://admissions.grad.usf.edu/
Public
Admissions: (813) 974-8800
E-mail: admissions@grad.usf.edu
Financial aid: (813) 974-4700
Application deadline: 02/15
In-state tuition: full time: $10,484;
part time: $431/credit hour
Out-of-state tuition: full time:
$20,674
Room/board/expenses: $15,500
Full-time enrollment: 611
men: 75%; women: 25%;
minorities: 19%; international:
54%
Part-time enrollment: 211
men: 79%; women: 21%;
minorities: 29%; international: 0%
Acceptance rate: 48%
GRE requirement: Yes
Avg. GRE: quantitative: 156
TOEFL requirement: Yes
Minimum TOEFL score: 550
Fellowships: 77
Teaching assistantships: 159
Research assistantships: 209
Students specializing in: biomedical: 4%; chemical: 5%; civil: 19%; computer: 6%; computer science: 8%; electrical: 22%; management: 12%; science and physics: 2%; environmental: 5%; industrial: 6%; materials: 0%; mechanical: 10%

GEORGIA

Georgia Institute of Technology

225 North Avenue
Atlanta, GA 30332-0360
http://www.gradadmiss.gatech.edu/
Public
Admissions: (404) 894-1610
E-mail: gradstudies@gatech.edu
Financial aid: (404) 894-4160
Application deadline: rolling
In-state tuition: full time: $12,964;
part time: $441/credit hour
Out-of-state tuition: full time:
$29,240
Room/board/expenses: $14,360
Full-time enrollment: 3,690
men: 80%; women: 20%;
minorities: 14%; international:
54%
Part-time enrollment: 961
men: 81%; women: 19%;
minorities: 19%; international:
24%
Acceptance rate: 26%
GRE requirement: Yes
Avg. GRE: quantitative: 162
TOEFL requirement: Yes
Minimum TOEFL score: 550
Fellowships: 810
Teaching assistantships: 308
Research assistantships: 2,133
Students specializing in: aerospace: 12%; biomedical: 4%; chemical: 5%; civil: 6%; computer science: 15%; electrical: 24%; science and physics: 0%;

environmental: 2%; industrial: 10%; materials: 3%; mechanical: 16%; nuclear: 1%; other: 2%

University of Georgia

Driftmier Engineering Center
Athens, GA 30602
http://www.engr.uga.edu
Public
Admissions: (706) 542-1739
E-mail: gradadm@uga.edu
Financial aid: (706) 542-6147
Application deadline: 07/01
In-state tuition: full time: $309/
credit hour; part time: $309/
credit hour
Out-of-state tuition: full time: $934/
credit hour
Room/board/expenses: $12,070
Full-time enrollment: 63
men: 70%; women: 30%;
minorities: 17%; international:
59%
Part-time enrollment: 5
men: 100%; women: 0%;
minorities: 20%; international: 0%
Acceptance rate: 29%
GRE requirement: Yes
Avg. GRE: quantitative: N/A
TOEFL requirement: Yes
Minimum TOEFL score: N/A
Fellowships: 0
Teaching assistantships: 8
Research assistantships: 49
Students specializing in: N/A

HAWAII

University of Hawaii–Manoa[1]

2540 Dole Street, Holmes Hall 240
Honolulu, HI 96822
http://www.eng.hawaii.edu/current-students/graduate-students
Public
Admissions: (808) 956-8544
E-mail: gradadm@hawaii.edu
Financial aid: (808) 956-7251
Tuition: N/A
Room/board expenses: N/A
Enrollment: N/A

IDAHO

Idaho State University[1]

921 S. Eighth Street, MS 8060
Pocatello, ID 83209-8060
http://www.isu.edu/engineer/
Public
Admissions: (208) 282-2150
E-mail: graddean@isu.edu
Financial aid: (208) 282-2756
Tuition: N/A
Room/board expenses: N/A
Enrollment: N/A

University of Idaho

PO Box 441011
Moscow, ID 83844-1011
http://www.engr.uidaho.edu/
Public
Admissions: (208) 885-4001
E-mail: gadms@uidaho.edu
Financial aid: (208) 885-6312
Application deadline: rolling
In-state tuition: full time: $7,162;
part time: $253/credit hour
Out-of-state tuition: full time:
$19,950
Room/board/expenses: $14,644
Full-time enrollment: 157
men: 85%; women: 15%;
minorities: 5%; international: 39%
Part-time enrollment: 264
men: 87%; women: 13%;
minorities: 8%; international: 9%
Acceptance rate: 30%
GRE requirement: Yes
Avg. GRE: quantitative: N/A
TOEFL requirement: Yes
Minimum TOEFL score: 550
Fellowships: 21
Teaching assistantships: 30

Research assistantships: 55
Students specializing in: agriculture: 3%; chemical: 3%; civil: 10%; computer: 1%; computer science: 13%; electrical: 26%; management: 7%; environmental: 1%; industrial: 5%; materials: 4%; mechanical: 16%; nuclear: 10%; other: 2%

Boise State University[1]

1910 University Drive
Boise, ID 83725
http://coen.boisestate.edu
Public
Admissions: N/A
Financial aid: N/A
Tuition: N/A
Room/board expenses: N/A
Enrollment: N/A

ILLINOIS

Illinois Institute of Technology (Armour)

10 West 33rd Street
Perlstein Hall, Suite 224
Chicago, IL 60616
http://www.iit.edu/engineering
Private
Admissions: (312) 567-3020
E-mail: gradstu@iit.edu
Financial aid: (312) 567-7219
Application deadline: rolling
Tuition: full time: $1,119/credit
hour; part time: $1,119/credit hour
Room/board/expenses: $14,449
Full-time enrollment: 1,059
men: 74%; women: 26%;
minorities: 1%; international: 87%
Part-time enrollment: 391
men: 77%; women: 23%;
minorities: 4%; international: 52%
Acceptance rate: 60%
GRE requirement: Yes
Avg. GRE: quantitative: 159
TOEFL requirement: Yes
Minimum TOEFL score: 523
Fellowships: 23
Teaching assistantships: 134
Research assistantships: 295
Students specializing in: aerospace: 11%; agriculture: 1%; architectural: 1%; biomedical: 2%; chemical: 11%; civil: 11%; computer: 8%; computer science: 29%; electrical: 22%; environmental: 4%; industrial: 0%; materials: 3%; mechanical: 11%

Northwestern University (McCormick)

2145 Sheridan Road
Evanston, IL 60208
http://www.tgs.northwestern.edu/
Private
Admissions: (847) 491-5279
E-mail: gradapp@northwestern.edu
Financial aid: (847) 491-8495
Application deadline: 12/31
Tuition: full time: $43,614; part
time: $5,146/credit hour
Room/board/expenses: $22,590
Full-time enrollment: 1,403
men: 72%; women: 28%;
minorities: 16%; international:
48%
Part-time enrollment: 266
men: 73%; women: 27%;
minorities: 23%; international:
19%
Acceptance rate: 22%
GRE requirement: Yes
Avg. GRE: quantitative: 163
TOEFL requirement: Yes
Minimum TOEFL score: 577
Fellowships: 200
Teaching assistantships: 80
Research assistantships: 531
Students specializing in: biomedical: 9%; chemical: 11%; civil: 9%;

computer: 2%; computer science: 10%; electrical: 8%; management: 12%; science and physics: 4%; environmental: 2%; industrial: 6%; materials: 13%; mechanical: 8%; other: 8%

Southern Illinois University–Carbondale

900 S. Normal Avenue
Mailcode 4716
Carbondale, IL 62901-6603
http://gradschool.siuc.edu/
Public
Admissions: (618) 536-7791
E-mail: gradschl@siu.edu
Financial aid: (618) 453-4334
Application deadline: rolling
In-state tuition: full time: $375/
credit hour; part time: $375/
credit hour
Out-of-state tuition: full time: $938/
credit hour
Room/board/expenses: $15,939
Full-time enrollment: 203
men: 84%; women: 16%;
minorities: 4%; international: 75%
Part-time enrollment: 101
men: 76%; women: 24%;
minorities: 9%; international: 60%
Acceptance rate: 44%
GRE requirement: Yes
Avg. GRE: quantitative: 149
TOEFL requirement: Yes
Minimum TOEFL score: 550
Fellowships: 8
Teaching assistantships: 264
Research assistantships: 30
Students specializing in: biomedical: 7%; civil: 12%; computer: 53%; electrical: 53%; science and physics: 14%; environmental: 12%; mechanical: 11%; mining: 4%

University of Illinois–Chicago

851 S. Morgan Street
Chicago, IL 60607-7043
http://www.uic.edu/
Public
Admissions: (312) 996-5133
E-mail: uicgrad@uic.edu
Financial aid: (312) 996-3126
Application deadline: N/A
In-state tuition: full time: $15,852;
part time: $11,530
Out-of-state tuition: full time:
$27,850
Room/board/expenses: $17,075
Full-time enrollment: 813
men: 74%; women: 26%;
minorities: 10%; international:
73%
Part-time enrollment: 265
men: 82%; women: 18%;
minorities: 22%; international:
24%
Acceptance rate: 31%
GRE requirement: Yes
Avg. GRE: quantitative: 159
TOEFL requirement: Yes
Minimum TOEFL score: 570
Fellowships: 21
Teaching assistantships: 165
Research assistantships: 220
Students specializing in: biomedical: 14%; chemical: 4%; civil: 10%; computer science: 29%; electrical: 17%; mechanical: 14%; other: 11%

University of Illinois–Urbana-Champaign

1308 W. Green
Urbana, IL 61801
http://engineering.illinois.edu
Public
Admissions: (217) 333-0035
Financial aid: (217) 333-0100
Application deadline: rolling
In-state tuition: full time: $19,858;
part time: $14,408

Out-of-state tuition: full time:
$33,124
Room/board/expenses: $16,926
Full-time enrollment: 2,810
men: 78%; women: 22%;
minorities: 11%; international: 61%
Part-time enrollment: 165
men: 85%; women: 15%;
minorities: 18%; international:
25%
Acceptance rate: 27%
GRE requirement: Yes
Avg. GRE: quantitative: 163
TOEFL requirement: Yes
Minimum TOEFL score: 550
Fellowships: 251
Teaching assistantships: 676
Research assistantships: 1,684
Students specializing in: aerospace: 4%; agriculture: 2%; biomedical: 3%; chemical: 4%; civil: 15%; computer: 16%; computer science: 17%; electrical: 16%; science and physics: 9%; environmental: 3%; industrial: 6%; materials: 6%; mechanical: 13%; nuclear: 2%

INDIANA

Indiana University-Purdue University-Indianapolis

799 W. Michigan Street, ET 219
Indianapolis, IN 46202-5160
http://engr.iupui.edu
Public
Admissions: (317) 278-4960
E-mail: gradengr@iupui.edu
Financial aid: N/A
Application deadline: 06/01
In-state tuition: full time: $352/
credit hour; part time: $352/
credit hour
Out-of-state tuition: full time:
$1,007/credit hour
Room/board/expenses: $2,500
Full-time enrollment: 171
men: 71%; women: 29%;
minorities: 6%; international: 75%
Part-time enrollment: 58
men: 90%; women: 10%;
minorities: 10%; international: 9%
Acceptance rate: 49%
GRE requirement: Yes
Avg. GRE: quantitative: 159
TOEFL requirement: Yes
Minimum TOEFL score: 550
Fellowships: 3
Teaching assistantships: 9
Research assistantships: 38
Students specializing in:
biomedical: 12%; computer: 18%; electrical: 37%; mechanical: 33%

Purdue University–West Lafayette

701 W. Stadium Avenue
Suite 3000 ARMS
West Lafayette, IN 47907-2045
http://engineering.purdue.edu
Public
Admissions: (765) 494-2598
E-mail: gradinfo@purdue.edu
Financial aid: (765) 494-2598
Application deadline: rolling
In-state tuition: full time: $11,024;
part time: $329/credit hour
Out-of-state tuition: full time:
$29,826
Room/board/expenses: $13,778
Full-time enrollment: 2,513
men: 80%; women: 20%;
minorities: 9%; international: 65%
Part-time enrollment: 557
men: 79%; women: 21%;
minorities: 16%; international: 13%
Acceptance rate: 27%
GRE requirement: Yes
Avg. GRE: quantitative: 162
TOEFL requirement: Yes
Minimum TOEFL score: 550
Fellowships: 323
Teaching assistantships: 501
Research assistantships: 1,512

Students specializing in: aerospace: 12%; agriculture: 4%; biomedical: 3%; chemical: 5%; civil: 12%; computer: 5%; computer science: 8%; electrical: 21%; environmental: 1%; industrial: 4%; materials: 3%; mechanical: 17%; nuclear: 2%; other: 11%

University of Notre Dame

257 Fitzpatrick Hall of Engineering
Notre Dame, IN 46556
http://www.nd.edu
Private
Admissions: (574) 631-7706
E-mail: gradad@nd.edu
Financial aid: (574) 631-7706
Application deadline: rolling
Tuition: full time: $42,815; part time: $2,353/credit hour
Room/board/expenses: $18,100
Full-time enrollment: 499
men: 77%; women: 23%;
minorities: 10%; international: 48%
Part-time enrollment: 2
men: 100%; women: 0%;
minorities: 0%; international: 0%
Acceptance rate: 17%
GRE requirement: Yes
Avg. GRE: quantitative: 162
TOEFL requirement: Yes
Minimum TOEFL score: N/A
Fellowships: 46
Teaching assistantships: 35
Research assistantships: 365
Students specializing in: biomedical: 3%; chemical: 17%; civil: 18%; computer science: 18%; electrical: 25%; mechanical: 19%

IOWA

Iowa State University

104 Marston Hall
Ames, IA 50011-2151
http://www.engineering.iastate.edu/
Public
Admissions: (800) 262-3810
E-mail: grad_admissions@iastate.edu
Financial aid: (515) 294-2223
Application deadline: rolling
In-state tuition: full time: $10,234; part time: $497/credit hour
Out-of-state tuition: full time: $22,108
Room/board/expenses: $12,192
Full-time enrollment: 1,013
men: 79%; women: 21%;
minorities: 6%; international: 52%
Part-time enrollment: N/A
men: N/A; women: N/A;
minorities: N/A; international: N/A
Acceptance rate: 17%
GRE requirement: Yes
Avg. GRE: quantitative: 159
TOEFL requirement: Yes
Minimum TOEFL score: 550
Fellowships: 35
Teaching assistantships: 178
Research assistantships: 499
Students specializing in: aerospace: 6%; agriculture: 5%; chemical: 6%; civil: 14%; computer: 15%; electrical: 16%; industrial: 7%; materials: 8%; mechanical: 17%; other: 7%

University of Iowa

3100 Seamans Center
Iowa City, IA 52242-1527
http://www.uiowa.edu/admissions/graduate/index.html
Public
Admissions: (319) 335-1525
E-mail: admissions@uiowa.edu
Financial aid: (319) 335-1450
Application deadline: rolling
In-state tuition: full time: $9,524; part time: N/A

Out-of-state tuition: full time: $25,688
Room/board/expenses: $16,125
Full-time enrollment: 418
men: 74%; women: 26%;
minorities: 8%; international: 52%
Part-time enrollment: N/A
men: N/A; women: N/A;
minorities: N/A; international: N/A
Acceptance rate: 25%
GRE requirement: Yes
Avg. GRE: quantitative: 160
TOEFL requirement: Yes
Minimum TOEFL score: 550
Fellowships: 28
Teaching assistantships: 81
Research assistantships: 225
Students specializing in: biomedical: 17%; chemical: 8%; civil: 22%; computer science: 16%; electrical: 16%; industrial: 5%; mechanical: 14%

KANSAS

Kansas State University

1046 Rathbone Hall
Manhattan, KS 66506-5201
http://www.engg.ksu.edu/
Public
Admissions: (785) 532-6191
E-mail: grad@ksu.edu
Financial aid: (785) 532-6420
Application deadline: rolling
In-state tuition: full time: $327/credit hour; part time: $327/credit hour
Out-of-state tuition: full time: $738/credit hour
Room/board/expenses: $10,546
Full-time enrollment: 248
men: 77%; women: 23%;
minorities: 20%; international: 48%
Part-time enrollment: 248
men: 79%; women: 21%;
minorities: 30%; international: 23%
Acceptance rate: 30%
GRE requirement: Yes
Avg. GRE: quantitative: 158
TOEFL requirement: Yes
Minimum TOEFL score: 550
Fellowships: 9
Teaching assistantships: 52
Research assistantships: 154
Students specializing in: agriculture: 1%; architectural: 3%; biomedical: 3%; chemical: 6%; civil: 19%; computer science: 22%; electrical: 22%; management: 7%; environmental: 3%; industrial: 7%; mechanical: 13%; nuclear: 3%

University of Kansas

1 Eaton Hall, 1520 W. 15th Street
Lawrence, KS 66045-7621
http://www.engr.ku.edu
Public
Admissions: (785) 864-3881
E-mail: kuengr@ku.edu
Financial aid: (785) 864-5491
Application deadline: rolling
In-state tuition: full time: $330/credit hour; part time: $330/credit hour
Out-of-state tuition: full time: $772/credit hour
Room/board/expenses: $16,658
Full-time enrollment: 342
men: 72%; women: 28%;
minorities: 6%; international: 47%
Part-time enrollment: 251
men: 83%; women: 17%;
minorities: 17%; international: 14%
Acceptance rate: 48%
GRE requirement: Yes
Avg. GRE: quantitative: 160
TOEFL requirement: Yes
Minimum TOEFL score: 530
Fellowships: 138
Teaching assistantships: 85
Research assistantships: 151

Students specializing in: aerospace: 7%; architectural: 3%; biomedical: 9%; chemical: 5%; civil: 17%; computer: 1%; computer science: 11%; electrical: 11%; management: 22%; environmental: 4%; mechanical: 8%; petroleum: 0%; other: 2%

Wichita State University

1845 N. Fairmount
Wichita, KS 67260-0044
http://www.wichita.edu/engineering
Public
Admissions: (316) 978-3095
E-mail: jordan.oleson@wichita.edu
Financial aid: (316) 978-3430
Application deadline: 07/15
In-state tuition: full time: $234/credit hour; part time: $234/credit hour
Out-of-state tuition: full time: $619/credit hour
Room/board/expenses: $10,350
Full-time enrollment: 283
men: 81%; women: 19%;
minorities: 6%; international: 85%
Part-time enrollment: 308
men: 83%; women: 17%;
minorities: 19%; international: 46%
Acceptance rate: 80%
GRE requirement: Yes
Avg. GRE: quantitative: N/A
TOEFL requirement: Yes
Minimum TOEFL score: 550
Teaching assistantships: 66
Research assistantships: 157
Students specializing in: aerospace: 17%; computer science: 6%; electrical: 28%; management: 3%; industrial: 19%; mechanical: 14%; other: 13%

KENTUCKY

University of Kentucky

351 Ralph G. Anderson Building
Lexington, KY 40506-0503
http://www.engr.uky.edu
Public
Admissions: (859) 257-4905
E-mail: grad.admit@uky.edu
Financial aid: (859) 257-3172
Application deadline: 07/27
In-state tuition: full time: $10,458; part time: $552/credit hour
Out-of-state tuition: full time: $21,546
Room/board/expenses: $11,847
Full-time enrollment: 449
men: 79%; women: 21%;
minorities: 5%; international: 59%
Part-time enrollment: 71
men: 82%; women: 18%;
minorities: 7%; international: 23%
Acceptance rate: 40%
GRE requirement: Yes
Avg. GRE: quantitative: 158
TOEFL requirement: Yes
Minimum TOEFL score: 550
Fellowships: 30
Teaching assistantships: 90
Research assistantships: 185
Students specializing in: agriculture: 6%; biomedical: 9%; chemical: 7%; civil: 14%; computer science: 17%; electrical: 18%; industrial: 2%; materials: 5%; mechanical: 19%; mining: 5%

University of Louisville (Speed)

2301 S. Third Street
Louisville, KY 40292
http://louisville.edu/speed/
Public
Admissions: (502) 852-3101
E-mail: gradadm@louisville.edu
Financial aid: (502) 852-5511
Application deadline: rolling
In-state tuition: full time: $10,728; part time: $571/credit hour

Out-of-state tuition: full time: $21,832
Room/board/expenses: $13,500
Full-time enrollment: 415
men: 80%; women: 20%;
minorities: 8%; international: 41%
Part-time enrollment: 187
men: 86%; women: 14%;
minorities: 12%; international: 46%
Acceptance rate: 54%
GRE requirement: Yes
Avg. GRE: quantitative: 160
TOEFL requirement: Yes
Minimum TOEFL score: 550
Fellowships: 29
Teaching assistantships: 43
Research assistantships: 82
Students specializing in: biomedical: 6%; chemical: 7%; civil: 10%; computer: 11%; computer science: 4%; electrical: 14%; management: 12%; industrial: 16%; mechanical: 20%

LOUISIANA

Louisiana State University– Baton Rouge

3304 Patrick F. Taylor Building
Baton Rouge, LA 70803
http://www.eng.lsu.edu
Public
Admissions: (225) 578-1641
E-mail: graddeanoffice@lsu.edu
Financial aid: (225) 578-3103
Application deadline: rolling
In-state tuition: full time: $7,560; part time: $4,402
Out-of-state tuition: full time: $22,948
Room/board/expenses: $13,898
Full-time enrollment: 531
men: 79%; women: 21%;
minorities: 6%; international: 74%
Part-time enrollment: 105
men: 83%; women: 17%;
minorities: 15%; international: 45%
Acceptance rate: 41%
GRE requirement: Yes
Avg. GRE: quantitative: 159
TOEFL requirement: Yes
Minimum TOEFL score: 550
Fellowships: 28
Teaching assistantships: 73
Research assistantships: 275
Students specializing in: agriculture: 2%; chemical: 8%; civil: 18%; computer science: 17%; electrical: 16%; science and physics: 11%; industrial: 2%; mechanical: 17%; petroleum: 10%; other: 0%

Louisiana Tech University

PO Box 10348
Ruston, LA 71272
http://www.latech.edu/tech/engr
Public
Admissions: (318) 257-2924
E-mail: gschool@latech.edu
Financial aid: (318) 257-2641
Application deadline: 08/01
In-state tuition: full time: $7,442; part time: $6,126
Out-of-state tuition: full time: $13,734
Room/board/expenses: $12,380
Full-time enrollment: 283
men: 80%; women: 20%;
minorities: 4%; international: 73%
Part-time enrollment: 84
men: 81%; women: 19%;
minorities: 6%; international: 48%
Acceptance rate: 79%
GRE requirement: Yes
Avg. GRE: quantitative: 157
TOEFL requirement: Yes
Minimum TOEFL score: 550
Fellowships: 15
Teaching assistantships: 67
Research assistantships: 129

Students specializing in: biomedical: 13%; chemical: 6%; civil: 7%; computer science: 14%; electrical: 19%; management: 20%; science and physics: 7%; industrial: 4%; mechanical: 7%; other: 3%

Tulane University

201 Lindy Boggs Building
New Orleans, LA 70118
http://tulane.edu/sse/academics/graduate/index.cfm
Private
Admissions: (504) 865-5764
E-mail: segrad@tulane.edu
Financial aid: (504) 865-5764
Application deadline: rolling
Tuition: full time: $45,240; part time: $2,450/credit hour
Room/board/expenses: $17,800
Full-time enrollment: 83
men: 64%; women: 36%;
minorities: 11%; international: 57%
Part-time enrollment: N/A
men: N/A; women: N/A;
minorities: N/A; international: N/A
Acceptance rate: 22%
GRE requirement: Yes
Avg. GRE: quantitative: 159
TOEFL requirement: Yes
Minimum TOEFL score: 600
Fellowships: 8
Teaching assistantships: 17
Research assistantships: 40
Students specializing in: biomedical: 52%; chemical: 48%

University of Louisiana–Lafayette

PO Box 42251
Lafayette, LA 70504
http://engineering.louisiana.edu/
Public
Admissions: (337) 482-6467
E-mail: gradschool@louisiana.edu
Financial aid: (337) 482-6506
Application deadline: rolling
In-state tuition: full time: $5,810; part time: $323/credit hour
Out-of-state tuition: full time: $14,780
Room/board/expenses: $13,657
Full-time enrollment: 208
men: 85%; women: 15%;
minorities: 5%; international: 69%
Part-time enrollment: 58
men: 79%; women: 21%;
minorities: 12%; international: 45%
Acceptance rate: 49%
GRE requirement: Yes
Avg. GRE: quantitative: N/A
TOEFL requirement: Yes
Minimum TOEFL score: 550
Fellowships: 7
Teaching assistantships: 14
Research assistantships: 56
Students specializing in: chemical: 5%; civil: 9%; computer: 17%; computer science: 37%; electrical: 2%; management: 9%; mechanical: 8%; petroleum: 14%

University of New Orleans

2000 Lakeshore Drive
New Orleans, LA 70148
http://www.uno.edu
Public
Admissions: (504) 280-6595
E-mail: admissions@uno.edu
Financial aid: (504) 280-6603
Application deadline: rolling
In-state tuition: full time: $6,312; part time: $287/credit hour
Out-of-state tuition: full time: $18,324
Room/board/expenses: $12,854
Full-time enrollment: 110
men: 79%; women: 21%;
minorities: 11%; international: 55%
Part-time enrollment: 55
men: 71%; women: 29%;
minorities: 16%; international: 20%

Acceptance rate: 41%
GRE requirement: Yes
Avg. GRE: quantitative: 156
TOEFL requirement: Yes
Minimum TOEFL score: 550
Fellowships: 0
Teaching assistantships: 0
Research assistantships: 35
Students specializing in: civil:
20%; computer science: 8%;
electrical: 10%; management:
12%; mechanical: 12%; other: 39%

MAINE

University of Maine
Advanced Manufacturing Center
Orono, ME 04469
http://www.
engineering.umaine.edu/
Public
Admissions: (207) 581-3291
E-mail: graduate@maine.edu
Financial aid: (207) 581-1324
Application deadline: rolling
In-state tuition: full time: $418/
credit hour; part time: $418/
credit hour
Out-of-state tuition: full time:
$1,259/credit hour
Room/board/expenses: $15,560
Full-time enrollment: 81
men: 80%; women: 20%;
minorities: 4%; international: 37%
Part-time enrollment: 40
men: 83%; women: 18%;
minorities: 15%; international:
25%
Acceptance rate: 34%
GRE requirement: Yes
Avg. GRE: quantitative: N/A
TOEFL requirement: Yes
Minimum TOEFL score: 550
Fellowships: 3
Teaching assistantships: 8
Research assistantships: 69
Students specializing in: biomedi-
cal: 7%; chemical: 13%; civil: 32%;
computer: 3%; electrical: 21%;
science and physics: 2%;
mechanical: 22%

MARYLAND

Johns Hopkins University (Whiting)
3400 N. Charles Street
Baltimore, MD 21218
http://engineering.jhu.edu
Private
Admissions: (410) 516-8174
E-mail:
graduateadmissions@jhu.edu
Financial aid: (410) 516-8028
Application deadline: N/A
Tuition: full time: $44,430; part
time: $1,058/credit hour
Room/board/expenses: $16,930
Full-time enrollment: 1,158
men: 70%; women: 30%;
minorities: 16%; international:
54%
Part-time enrollment: 2,276
men: 78%; women: 22%;
minorities: 28%; international: 2%
Acceptance rate: 28%
GRE requirement: Yes
Avg. GRE: quantitative: 162
TOEFL requirement: Yes
Minimum TOEFL score: 600
Fellowships: 169
Teaching assistantships: 80
Research assistantships: 502
Students specializing in: biomedi-
cal: 7%; chemical: 3%; civil: 2%;
computer science: 18%; electri-
cal: 14%; management: 1%;
environmental: 3%; materials: 2%;
mechanical: 6%; other: 44%

Morgan State University (Mitchell)
1700 E. Coldspring Lane
Baltimore, MD 21251
http://www.morgan.edu/
Prospective_Grad_Students.html
Public
Admissions: (443) 885-3185
E-mail:
mark.garrison@morgan.edu
Financial aid: (443) 885-3170
Application deadline: rolling
In-state tuition: full time: $212/
credit hour; part time: $212/
credit hour
Out-of-state tuition: full time: $552/
credit hour
Room/board/expenses: $14,278
Full-time enrollment: 29
men: 76%; women: 24%;
minorities: 59%; international:
38%
Part-time enrollment: 78
men: 69%; women: 31%;
minorities: 79%; international: 9%
Acceptance rate: 93%
GRE requirement: Yes
Avg. GRE: quantitative: N/A
TOEFL requirement: Yes
Minimum TOEFL score: 550
Students specializing in: N/A

University of Maryland–Baltimore County
1000 Hilltop Circle
Baltimore, MD 21250
http://www.
umbc.edu/gradschool/
Public
Admissions: (410) 455-2537
E-mail: umbcgrad@umbc.edu
Financial aid: (410) 455-2387
Application deadline: 06/01
In-state tuition: full time: $510/
credit hour; part time: $510/
credit hour
Out-of-state tuition: full time: $844/
credit hour
Room/board/expenses: $15,021
Full-time enrollment: 291
men: 74%; women: 26%;
minorities: 16%; international:
56%
Part-time enrollment: 296
men: 79%; women: 21%;
minorities: 32%; international: 7%
Acceptance rate: 63%
GRE requirement: Yes
Avg. GRE: quantitative: N/A
TOEFL requirement: Yes
Minimum TOEFL score: 550
Fellowships: 8
Teaching assistantships: 63
Research assistantships: 70
Students specializing in: chemical:
5%; civil: 3%; computer: 5%;
computer science: 29%; electri-
cal: 9%; management: 13%;
mechanical: 12%; other: 25%

University of Maryland–College Park (Clark)
3110 Jeong H. Kim
Engineering Building
College Park, MD 20742-2831
http://www.eng.umd.edu
Public
Admissions: (301) 405-0376
E-mail: gradschool@umd.edu
Financial aid: (301) 314-9000
Application deadline: N/A
In-state tuition: full time: $12,433;
part time: $551/credit hour
Out-of-state tuition: full time:
$25,173
Room/board/expenses: $17,249
Full-time enrollment: 1,570
men: 79%; women: 21%;
minorities: 11%; international: 62%
Part-time enrollment: 684
men: 82%; women: 18%;
minorities: 32%; international: 6%

Acceptance rate: 24%
GRE requirement: Yes
Avg. GRE: quantitative: 162
TOEFL requirement: Yes
Minimum TOEFL score: 574
Fellowships: 264
Teaching assistantships: 262
Research assistantships: 978
Students specializing in: aero-
space: 8%; agriculture: 0%; bio-
medical: 3%; chemical: 3%; civil:
10%; computer science: 10%;
electrical: 25%; materials: 3%;
mechanical: 12%; nuclear: 0%;
other: 26%

MASSACHUSETTS

Boston University
44 Cummington Street
Boston, MA 02215
http://www.bu.edu/eng
Private
Admissions: (617) 353-9760
E-mail: enggrad@bu.edu
Financial aid: (617) 353-9760
Application deadline: 01/15
Tuition: full time: $42,857; part
time: $1,325/credit hour
Room/board/expenses: $19,140
Full-time enrollment: 770
men: 75%; women: 25%;
minorities: 17%; international:
55%
Part-time enrollment: 87
men: 79%; women: 21%;
minorities: 36%; international:
15%
Acceptance rate: 26%
GRE requirement: Yes
Avg. GRE: quantitative: 162
TOEFL requirement: Yes
Minimum TOEFL score: 550
Fellowships: 87
Teaching assistantships: 93
Research assistantships: 380
Students specializing in: biomedi-
cal: 29%; computer: 8%; comput-
er science: 8%; electrical: 26%;
industrial: 1%; materials: 6%;
mechanical: 16%; other: 6%

Harvard University
29 Oxford Street, Room 217A
Pierce Hall
Cambridge, MA 02138
http://www.gsas.harvard.edu
Private
Admissions: (617) 495-5315
E-mail: admiss@fas.harvard.edu
Financial aid: (617) 495-5396
Application deadline: 12/15
Tuition: full time: $40,644; part
time: $1,174/credit hour
Room/board/expenses: $25,190
Full-time enrollment: 400
men: 70%; women: 30%;
minorities: 20%; international:
48%
Part-time enrollment: 4
men: 100%; women: 0%;
minorities: 25%; international: 0%
Acceptance rate: 10%
GRE requirement: Yes
Avg. GRE: quantitative: 160
TOEFL requirement: Yes
Minimum TOEFL score: N/A
Fellowships: 201
Teaching assistantships: 89
Research assistantships: 249
Students specializing in: biomedi-
cal: 14%; computer science: 16%;
electrical: 12%; environmental:
7%; materials: 2%; mechanical:
8%; other: 41%

Massachusetts Institute of Technology
77 Massachusetts Avenue
Room 1-206
Cambridge, MA 02139-4307
http://web.mit.edu/admissions/
graduate/
Private
Admissions: (617) 253-3400

E-mail: mitgrad@mit.edu
Financial aid: (617) 253-4971
Application deadline: N/A
Tuition: full time: $42,050; part
time: N/A
Room/board/expenses: $28,749
Full-time enrollment: 3,147
men: 73%; women: 27%;
minorities: 20%; international:
42%
Part-time enrollment: 16
men: 63%; women: 38%;
minorities: 19%; international: 13%
Acceptance rate: 16%
GRE requirement: Yes
Avg. GRE: quantitative: 164
Minimum TOEFL score: N/A
Fellowships: 658
Teaching assistantships: 261
Research assistantships: 1,644
Students specializing in: aero-
space: 8%; biomedical: 8%;
chemical: 7%; civil: 5%; computer
science: 12%; electrical: 13%;
management: 9%; environmental:
2%; materials: 7%; mechanical:
18%; nuclear: 4%; other: 7%

Northeastern University
130 Snell Engineering Center
Boston, MA 02115-5000
http://www.coe.neu.edu/gse
Private
Admissions: (617) 373-2711
E-mail: grad-eng@coe.neu.edu
Financial aid: (617) 373-3190
Application deadline: rolling
Tuition: full time: $1,270/credit
hour; part time: $1,270/credit hour
Room/board/expenses: $14,000
Full-time enrollment: 2,034
men: 72%; women: 28%;
minorities: 3%; international: 84%
Part-time enrollment: 261
men: 85%; women: 15%;
minorities: 16%; international: 6%
Acceptance rate: 45%
GRE requirement: Yes
Avg. GRE: quantitative: 160
TOEFL requirement: Yes
Minimum TOEFL score: 550
Fellowships: 36
Teaching assistantships: 142
Research assistantships: 302
Students specializing in: biomedi-
cal: 1%; chemical: 3%; civil: 7%;
computer: 3%; computer science:
28%; electrical: 17%; manage-
ment: 5%; industrial: 10%;
mechanical: 9%; other: 17%

Tufts University
Anderson Hall
Medford, MA 02155
http://engineering.tufts.edu
Private
Admissions: (617) 627-3395
E-mail: gradschool@ase.tufts.edu
Financial aid: (617) 627-2000
Application deadline: 01/15
Tuition: full time: $27,158; part
time: $4,286/credit hour
Room/board/expenses: $21,951
Full-time enrollment: 487
men: 69%; women: 31%;
minorities: 12%; international:
30%
Part-time enrollment: 135
men: 72%; women: 28%;
minorities: 15%; international: 6%
Acceptance rate: 38%
GRE requirement: Yes
Avg. GRE: quantitative: 161
TOEFL requirement: Yes
Minimum TOEFL score: 550
Fellowships: 18
Teaching assistantships: 57
Research assistantships: 152
Students specializing in: biomedi-
cal: 18%; chemical: 6%; civil: 6%;
computer science: 11%; electrical:
13%; management: 29%; envi-
ronmental: 9%; mechanical: 11%;
other: 1%

University of Massachusetts–Amherst
Room 125, Marston Hall
Amherst, MA 01003
http://www.
umass.edu/gradschool
Public
Admissions: (413) 545-0722
E-mail: gradadm@grad.umass.edu
Financial aid: (413) 577-0555
Application deadline: 01/15
In-state tuition: full time: $14,451;
part time: $110/credit hour
Out-of-state tuition: full time:
$21,748
Room/board/expenses: $12,937
Full-time enrollment: 862
men: 74%; women: 26%;
minorities: 5%; international: 60%
Part-time enrollment: 28
men: N/A; women: N/A;
minorities: N/A; international: N/A
Acceptance rate: 26%
GRE requirement: Yes
Avg. GRE: quantitative: 162
TOEFL requirement: Yes
Minimum TOEFL score: 550
Fellowships: 38
Teaching assistantships: 60
Research assistantships: 517
Students specializing in: chemical:
7%; civil: 11%; computer science:
27%; electrical: 29%; environmen-
tal: 0%; industrial: 3%; materials:
13%; mechanical: 10%

University of Massachusetts–Dartmouth
285 Old Westport Road
North Dartmouth, MA 02747-2300
http://www.umassd.edu/graduate
Public
Admissions: (508) 999-8604
E-mail: graduate@umassd.edu
Financial aid: (508) 999-8632
Application deadline: 02/15
In-state tuition: full time: $12,988;
part time: $550/credit hour
Out-of-state tuition: full time:
$23,028
Room/board/expenses: $13,885
Full-time enrollment: 94
men: 84%; women: 16%;
minorities: 5%; international: 61%
Part-time enrollment: 101
men: 80%; women: 20%;
minorities: 9%; international: 42%
Acceptance rate: 73%
GRE requirement: Yes
Avg. GRE: quantitative: N/A
TOEFL requirement: Yes
Minimum TOEFL score: 550
Fellowships: 0
Teaching assistantships: 43
Research assistantships: 27
Students specializing in: biomedi-
cal: 14%; civil: 9%; computer: 11%;
computer science: 24%; electri-
cal: 24%; science and physics:
5%; materials: 2%; mechanical:
11%

University of Massachusetts–Lowell (Francis)
1 University Avenue
Lowell, MA 01854
http://www.uml.edu/grad
Public
Admissions: (978) 934-2390
E-mail: graduate_school@uml.edu
Financial aid: (978) 934-4226
Application deadline: rolling
In-state tuition: full time: $11,229;
part time: $624/credit hour
Out-of-state tuition: full time:
$20,774
Room/board/expenses: $11,882
Full-time enrollment: 453
men: 75%; women: 25%;
minorities: 9%; international: 59%

Part-time enrollment: 399
men: 79%; women: 21%;
minorities: 22%; international:
10%
Acceptance rate: 79%
GRE requirement: Yes
Avg. GRE: quantitative: N/A
TOEFL requirement: Yes
Minimum TOEFL score: 550
Teaching assistantships: 114
Research assistantships: 206
Students specializing in: biomedical: 13%; chemical: 4%; civil: 12%;
computer: 6%; computer science:
19%; electrical: 17%; materials:
15%; mechanical: 14%; nuclear:
1%

Worcester Polytechnic Institute
100 Institute Road
Worcester, MA 01609-2280
http://grad.wpi.edu/
Private
Admissions: (508) 831-5301
E-mail: grad@wpi.edu
Financial aid: (508) 831-5469
Application deadline: rolling
Tuition: full time: $22,357; part
time: $1,239/credit hour
Room/board/expenses: $22,256
Full-time enrollment: 407
men: 76%; women: 24%;
minorities: 6%; international: 64%
Part-time enrollment: 650
men: 80%; women: 20%;
minorities: 11%; international: 19%
Acceptance rate: 43%
GRE requirement: Yes
Avg. GRE: quantitative: 160
TOEFL requirement: Yes
Minimum TOEFL score: 563
Fellowships: 13
Teaching assistantships: 81
Research assistantships: 102
Students specializing in: biomedi-
cal: 5%; chemical: 2%; civil: 5%;
computer science: 12%; electrical:
21%; environmental: 3%; industri-
al: 2%; materials: 8%; mechanical:
16%; other: 26%

MICHIGAN

Lawrence Technological University
21000 W. Ten Mile Road
Southfield, MI 48075
http://www.ltu.edu
Private
Admissions: (248) 204-3160
E-mail: admissions@ltu.edu
Financial aid: (248) 204-2126
Application deadline: rolling
Tuition: full time: $14,230; part
time: $8,290
Room/board/expenses: $14,333
Full-time enrollment: 78
men: 56%; women: 44%;
minorities: 10%; international: 10%
Part-time enrollment: 299
men: 85%; women: 15%;
minorities: 11%; international: 29%
Acceptance rate: 43%
GRE requirement: No
Avg. GRE: quantitative: N/A
TOEFL requirement: Yes
Minimum TOEFL score: 550
Fellowships: 4
Teaching assistantships: 0
Research assistantships: 3
Students specializing in: architec-
tural: 22%; civil: 11%; computer:
6%; management: 15%; industrial:
11%; mechanical: 16%; other: 24%

Michigan State University
3410 Engineering Building
East Lansing, MI 48824
http://www.egr.msu.edu
Public
Admissions: (517) 353-5221

E-mail: egrgrad@egr.msu.edu
Financial aid: (517) 353-3220
Application deadline: 12/31
In-state tuition: full time: $597/
credit hour; part time: $597/
credit hour
Out-of-state tuition: full time:
$1,173/credit hour
Room/board/expenses: $12,632
Full-time enrollment: 858
men: 75%; women: 25%;
minorities: 10%; international:
63%
Part-time enrollment: N/A
men: N/A; women: N/A;
minorities: N/A; international: N/A
Acceptance rate: 12%
GRE requirement: Yes
Avg. GRE: quantitative: N/A
TOEFL requirement: Yes
Minimum TOEFL score: 550
Fellowships: 183
Teaching assistantships: 120
Research assistantships: 351
Students specializing in: agricul-
ture: 6%; chemical: 8%; civil:
9%; computer science: 17%; elec-
trical: 26%; environmental: 11%;
materials: 5%; mechanical: 18%

Michigan Technological University
1400 Townsend Drive
Houghton, MI 49931-1295
http://www.mtu.edu/gradschool/
Public
Admissions: (906) 487-2327
E-mail: gradadms@mtu.edu
Financial aid: (906) 487-2622
Application deadline: rolling
In-state tuition: full time: $13,630;
part time: $744/credit hour
Out-of-state tuition: full time:
$13,630
Room/board/expenses: $12,863
Full-time enrollment: 641
men: 80%; women: 20%;
minorities: 4%; international: 69%
Part-time enrollment: 182
men: 79%; women: 21%;
minorities: 11%; international: 31%
Acceptance rate: 40%
GRE requirement: Yes
Avg. GRE: quantitative: N/A
TOEFL requirement: Yes
Minimum TOEFL score: 550
Fellowships: 46
Teaching assistantships: 91
Research assistantships: 166
Students specializing in: biomedi-
cal: 2%; chemical: 7%; civil: 7%;
computer: 3%; computer
science: 5%; electrical: 23%;
environmental: 8%; materials:
4%; mechanical: 35%; mining: 0%;
other: 7%

Oakland University
2200 Squirrel Road
Rochester, MI 48309
http://www2.oakland.edu/secs/
Public
Admissions: (248) 370-3167
E-mail: applygrad@oakland.edu
Financial aid: (248) 370-2550
Application deadline: 08/01
In-state tuition: full time: $595/
credit hour; part time: $595/
credit hour
Out-of-state tuition: full time:
$1,027/credit hour
Room/board/expenses: $11,486
Full-time enrollment: 197
men: 76%; women: 24%;
minorities: 11%; international: 41%
Part-time enrollment: 289
men: 85%; women: 15%;
minorities: 12%; international: 13%
Acceptance rate: 32%
GRE requirement: Yes
Avg. GRE: quantitative: N/A
TOEFL requirement: Yes
Minimum TOEFL score: 550
Teaching assistantships: 39
Research assistantships: 35

Students specializing in: computer
science: 11%; electrical: 28%;
management: 12%; industrial: 2%;
mechanical: 25%; other: 22%

University of Detroit Mercy[1]
4001 W. McNichols
Detroit, MI 48221-3038
http://www.udmercy.edu
Private
Admissions: (313) 993-1592
E-mail: coddinsm@udmercy.edu
Financial aid: (313) 993-3350
Tuition: N/A
Room/board expenses: N/A
Enrollment: N/A

University of Michigan–Ann Arbor
Robert H. Lurie
Engineering Center
Ann Arbor, MI 48109-2102
http://www.engin.umich.edu/
academics/gradprograms
Public
Admissions: (734) 647-7090
E-mail: grad-ed@engin.umich.edu
Financial aid: (734) 647-7090
Application deadline: rolling
In-state tuition: full time: $22,707;
part time: $1,178/credit hour
Out-of-state tuition: full time:
$42,103
Room/board/expenses: $18,186
Full-time enrollment: 2,921
men: 77%; women: 23%;
minorities: 9%; international: 57%
Part-time enrollment: 263
men: 89%; women: 11%;
minorities: 14%; international:
32%
Acceptance rate: 25%
GRE requirement: Yes
Avg. GRE: quantitative: 164
TOEFL requirement: Yes
Minimum TOEFL score: 560
Teaching assistantships: 257
Research assistantships: 948
Students specializing in: aerospace: 7%; biomedical: 6%;
chemical: 4%; civil: 4%; computer:
4%; computer science: 5%; electrical: 21%; environmental: 2%;
industrial: 6%; materials: 4%;
mechanical: 14%; nuclear: 4%;
other: 23%

Wayne State University
5050 Anthony Wayne Drive
Detroit, MI 48202
http://www.eng.wayne.edu
Public
Admissions: (313) 577-2170
E-mail: admissions@wayne.edu
Financial aid: (313) 577-3378
Application deadline: 06/01
In-state tuition: full time: $618/
credit hour; part time: $618/
credit hour
Out-of-state tuition: full time:
$1,262/credit hour
Room/board/expenses: $16,257
Full-time enrollment: 552
men: 75%; women: 25%;
minorities: 13%; international:
66%
Part-time enrollment: 336
men: 79%; women: 21%;
minorities: 28%; international: 17%
Acceptance rate: 44%
GRE requirement: Yes
Avg. GRE: quantitative: 157
TOEFL requirement: Yes
Minimum TOEFL score: 550
Fellowships: 21
Teaching assistantships: 78
Research assistantships: 107
Students specializing in: biomedi-
cal: 16%; chemical: 5%; civil: 8%;
computer: 4%; computer science:
18%; electrical: 9%; management:
6%; industrial: 10%; materials: 1%;
mechanical: 14%; other: 9%

Western Michigan University
1903 W. Michigan Avenue
Kalamazoo, MI 49008-5314
http://www.wmich.edu/engineer/
Public
Admissions: (269) 387-2000
E-mail: ask-wmu@wmich.edu
Financial aid: (269) 387-6000
Application deadline: rolling
In-state tuition: full time: $480/
credit hour; part time: $480/
credit hour
Out-of-state tuition: full time:
$1,016/credit hour
Room/board/expenses: $13,341
Full-time enrollment: 304
men: 82%; women: 18%;
minorities: 5%; international: 73%
Part-time enrollment: 97
men: 84%; women: 16%;
minorities: 6%; international: 26%
Acceptance rate: 69%
GRE requirement: Yes
Avg. GRE: quantitative: N/A
TOEFL requirement: Yes
Minimum TOEFL score: 550
Fellowships: 0
Teaching assistantships: 60
Research assistantships: 45
Students specializing in: chemical:
1%; civil: 13%; computer: 3%;
computer science: 19%; electri-
cal: 23%; management: 12%;
industrial: 12%; mechanical: 10%;
other: 6%

MINNESOTA

University of Minnesota–Twin Cities
117 Pleasant Street SE
Minneapolis, MN 55455
http://www.cse.umn.edu
Public
Admissions: (612) 625-3014
E-mail: gsquest@umn.edu
Financial aid: (612) 624-1111
Application deadline: 12/01
In-state tuition: full time: $16,142;
part time: $1,214/credit hour
Out-of-state tuition: full time:
$23,892
Room/board/expenses: $13,938
Full-time enrollment: 1,449
men: 78%; women: 22%;
minorities: 8%; international: 55%
Part-time enrollment: 471
men: 84%; women: 16%;
minorities: 16%; international: 27%
Acceptance rate: 22%
GRE requirement: Yes
Avg. GRE: quantitative: N/A
TOEFL requirement: Yes
Minimum TOEFL score: 550
Fellowships: 179
Teaching assistantships: 287
Research assistantships: 648
Students specializing in: aero-
space: 5%; biomedical: 7%;
chemical: 7%; civil: 8%; computer
science: 20%; electrical: 23%;
management: 3%; industrial: 3%;
materials: 4%; mechanical: 14%;
other: 7%

MISSISSIPPI

Mississippi State University (Bagley)
PO Box 9544
Mississippi State, MS 39762
http://www.bagley.msstate.edu/
Public
Admissions: (662) 325-7403
E-mail:
gradapps@grad.msstate.edu
Financial aid: (662) 325-2450
Application deadline: 07/01
In-state tuition: full time: $6,264;
part time: $348/credit hour
Out-of-state tuition: full time:
$15,828
Room/board/expenses: $17,158

Full-time enrollment: 344
men: 80%; women: 20%;
minorities: 11%; international: 51%
Part-time enrollment: 278
men: 81%; women: 19%;
minorities: 22%; international: 7%
Acceptance rate: 25%
GRE requirement: Yes
Avg. GRE: quantitative: 159
TOEFL requirement: Yes
Minimum TOEFL score: 550
Fellowships: 27
Teaching assistantships: 56
Research assistantships: 222
Students specializing in: aerospace: 6%; agriculture: 2%; biomedical: 3%; chemical: 3%; civil:
15%; computer: 2%; computer
science: 14%; electrical: 14%;
industrial: 14%; mechanical: 12%;
other: 14%

University of Mississippi
Brevard Hall, Room 227
University, MS 38677-1848
http://www.
engineering.olemiss.edu/
Public
Admissions: (662) 915-7474
E-mail: gschool@olemiss.edu
Financial aid: (800) 891-4596
Application deadline: 04/01
In-state tuition: full time: $6,282;
part time: $349/credit hour
Out-of-state tuition: full time:
$16,263
Room/board/expenses: $19,098
Full-time enrollment: 114
men: 75%; women: 25%;
minorities: 12%; international:
54%
Part-time enrollment: 32
men: 75%; women: 25%;
minorities: 25%; international:
22%
Acceptance rate: 34%
GRE requirement: Yes
Avg. GRE: quantitative: 154
TOEFL requirement: Yes
Minimum TOEFL score: 550
Teaching assistantships: 49
Research assistantships: 42
Students specializing in: chemical:
3%; civil: 15%; computer science:
33%; electrical: 18%; mechanical:
16%; other: 15%

MISSOURI

Missouri University of Science & Technology
500 W. 16th Street, 110 ERL
Rolla, MO 65409-0840
http://www.mst.edu
Public
Admissions: (800) 522-0938
E-mail: admissions@mst.edu
Financial aid: (800) 522-0938
Application deadline: 07/01
In-state tuition: full time: $7,428;
part time: $355/credit hour
Out-of-state tuition: full time:
$17,508
Room/board/expenses: $10,328
Full-time enrollment: 672
men: 81%; women: 19%;
minorities: 3%; international: 68%
Part-time enrollment: 378
men: 82%; women: 18%;
minorities: 14%; international:
25%
Acceptance rate: 61%
GRE requirement: Yes
Avg. GRE: quantitative: 158
TOEFL requirement: Yes
Minimum TOEFL score: 550
Fellowships: 46
Teaching assistantships: 103
Research assistantships: 352
Students specializing in: aero-
space: 4%; chemical: 4%; civil:
12%; computer: 4%; computer
science: 7%; electrical: 18%;
management: 28%; environmental: 2%; industrial: 3%; materials:

6%; mechanical: 11%; mining: 6%; nuclear: 3%; petroleum: 7%; other: 11%

St. Louis University (Parks)

3450 Lindell Boulevard
St. Louis, MO 63103
http://parks.slu.edu
Private
Admissions: (314) 977-8355
E-mail: pligrani@slu.edu
Financial aid: (314) 977-2350
Application deadline: rolling
Tuition: full time: $990/credit hour; part time: $990/credit hour
Room/board/expenses: $16,188
Full-time enrollment: 29
men: 76%; women: 24%; minorities: 14%; international: 31%
Part-time enrollment: 29
men: 83%; women: 17%; minorities: 7%; international: 3%
Acceptance rate: 67%
GRE requirement: Yes
Avg. GRE: quantitative: N/A
TOEFL requirement: Yes
Minimum TOEFL score: 550
Fellowships: 0
Teaching assistantships: 0
Research assistantships: 19
Students specializing in: biomedical: 12%; civil: 10%; computer: 2%; mechanical: 45%; other: 31%

University of Missouri

W1025 Thomas and Nell Lafferre Hall
Columbia, MO 65211
http://www.missouri.edu/
Public
Admissions: (573) 882-7786
E-mail: gradadmin@missouri.edu
Financial aid: (573) 882-2751
Application deadline: rolling
In-state tuition: full time: $6,338; part time: $396/credit hour
Out-of-state tuition: full time: $14,856
Room/board/expenses: $16,812
Full-time enrollment: 618
men: 78%; women: 22%; minorities: 5%; international: 63%
Part-time enrollment: N/A
men: N/A; women: N/A; minorities: N/A; international: N/A
Acceptance rate: 35%
GRE requirement: Yes
Avg. GRE: quantitative: 159
TOEFL requirement: Yes
Minimum TOEFL score: 550
Fellowships: 50
Teaching assistantships: 138
Research assistantships: 302
Students specializing in: biomedical: 10%; chemical: 5%; civil: 13%; computer: 1%; computer science: 16%; electrical: 23%; industrial: 6%; mechanical: 15%; nuclear: 9%; other: 2%

University of Missouri–Kansas City

534 R. H. Flarsheim Hall
5100 Rockhill Road
Kansas City, MO 64110-2499
http://www.umkc.edu/sce
Public
Admissions: (816) 235-1111
E-mail: graduate@umkc.edu
Financial aid: (816) 235-1154
Application deadline: rolling
In-state tuition: full time: $332/credit hour; part time: $332/credit hour
Out-of-state tuition: full time: $857/credit hour
Room/board/expenses: $19,068
Full-time enrollment: 123
men: 79%; women: 21%; minorities: 3%; international: 89%
Part-time enrollment: 175
men: 75%; women: 25%; minorities: 7%; international: 55%
Acceptance rate: 37%
GRE requirement: Yes
Avg. GRE: quantitative: 159
TOEFL requirement: Yes
Minimum TOEFL score: 550
Fellowships: 0
Teaching assistantships: 4
Research assistantships: 18
Students specializing in: N/A

Washington University in St. Louis

1 Brookings Drive
Campus Box 1100
St. Louis, MO 63130
http://www.engineering.wustl.edu/
Private
Admissions: (314) 935-7974
E-mail: gradengineering@seas.wustl.edu
Financial aid: (314) 935-5900
Application deadline: 01/15
Tuition: full time: $43,300; part time: $1,771/credit hour
Room/board/expenses: $27,650
Full-time enrollment: 523
men: 75%; women: 25%; minorities: 11%; international: 57%
Part-time enrollment: 252
men: 76%; women: 24%; minorities: 19%; international: 4%
Acceptance rate: 31%
GRE requirement: Yes
Avg. GRE: quantitative: 163
TOEFL requirement: Yes
Minimum TOEFL score: 550
Fellowships: 41
Teaching assistantships: 7
Research assistantships: 273
Students specializing in: aerospace: 2%; biomedical: 16%; computer: 4%; computer science: 18%; electrical: 14%; management: 2%; environmental: 13%; materials: 2%; mechanical: 9%; other: 20%

MONTANA

Montana State University

212 Roberts Hall, PO Box 173820
Bozeman, MT 59717-3820
http://www.montana.edu/wwwdg
Public
Admissions: (406) 994-4145
E-mail: gradstudy@montana.edu
Financial aid: (406) 994-2845
Application deadline: rolling
In-state tuition: full time: $6,100; part time: $266/credit hour
Out-of-state tuition: full time: $16,051
Room/board/expenses: $12,480
Full-time enrollment: 82
men: 89%; women: 11%; minorities: 2%; international: 52%
Part-time enrollment: 105
men: 75%; women: 25%; minorities: 14%; international: 30%
Acceptance rate: 42%
GRE requirement: Yes
Avg. GRE: quantitative: N/A
TOEFL requirement: Yes
Minimum TOEFL score: 550
Fellowships: 13
Teaching assistantships: 54
Research assistantships: 74
Students specializing in: chemical: 6%; civil: 19%; computer science: 32%; electrical: 11%; management: 3%; environmental: 7%; industrial: 7%; mechanical: 15%

NEBRASKA

University of Nebraska–Lincoln

114 Othmer Hall
Lincoln, NE 68588-0642
http://www.engineering.unl.edu/
Public
Admissions: (402) 472-2878
E-mail: graduate@unl.edu
Financial aid: (402) 472-2030
Application deadline: 03/01
In-state tuition: full time: $394/credit hour; part time: $394/credit hour
Out-of-state tuition: full time: $992/credit hour
Room/board/expenses: $11,846
Full-time enrollment: 496
men: 79%; women: 21%; minorities: 4%; international: 63%
Part-time enrollment: 103
men: 76%; women: 24%; minorities: 8%; international: 20%
Acceptance rate: 42%
GRE requirement: Yes
Avg. GRE: quantitative: 161
TOEFL requirement: Yes
Minimum TOEFL score: 550
Fellowships: 6
Teaching assistantships: 114
Research assistantships: 293
Students specializing in: agriculture: 4%; architectural: 11%; biomedical: 2%; chemical: 4%; civil: 15%; computer: 3%; computer science: 17%; electrical: 13%; science and physics: 13%; environmental: 2%; industrial: 1%; materials: 4%; mechanical: 7%; other: 5%

NEVADA

University of Nevada–Las Vegas (Hughes)

4505 Maryland Parkway
Box 544005
Las Vegas, NV 89154-4005
http://go.unlv.edu/
Public
Admissions: (702) 895-3320
E-mail: gradcollege@unlv.edu
Financial aid: (702) 895-3697
Application deadline: 02/01
In-state tuition: full time: $5,915; part time: $264/credit hour
Out-of-state tuition: full time: $19,510
Room/board/expenses: $16,088
Full-time enrollment: 69
men: 78%; women: 22%; minorities: 23%; international: 57%
Part-time enrollment: 166
men: 81%; women: 19%; minorities: 22%; international: 36%
Acceptance rate: 66%
GRE requirement: Yes
Avg. GRE: quantitative: N/A
TOEFL requirement: Yes
Minimum TOEFL score: 550
Fellowships: 3
Teaching assistantships: 65
Research assistantships: 27
Students specializing in: aerospace: 2%; biomedical: 1%; civil: 34%; computer science: 20%; electrical: 23%; mechanical: 16%; nuclear: 1%; other: 3%

University of Nevada–Reno

Mail Stop 0256
Reno, NV 89557-0256
http://www.unr.edu
Public
Admissions: (775) 784-4700
E-mail: asknevada@unr.edu
Financial aid: (775) 682-8097
Application deadline: 02/01
In-state tuition: full time: $321/credit hour; part time: $321/credit hour
Out-of-state tuition: full time: $1,044/credit hour
Room/board/expenses: $19,900
Full-time enrollment: 182
men: 79%; women: 21%; minorities: 20%; international: 52%
Part-time enrollment: 81
men: 78%; women: 22%; minorities: 26%; international: 12%
Acceptance rate: 57%
GRE requirement: Yes
Avg. GRE: quantitative: N/A
TOEFL requirement: Yes
Minimum TOEFL score: 500
Fellowships: 0
Teaching assistantships: 53
Research assistantships: 120
Students specializing in: N/A

NEW HAMPSHIRE

Dartmouth College (Thayer)

14 Engineering Drive
Hanover, NH 03755
http://engineering.dartmouth.edu
Private
Admissions: (603) 646-2606
E-mail: engineering.admissions@dartmouth.edu
Financial aid: (603) 646-3844
Application deadline: 01/01
Tuition: full time: $44,132; part time: N/A
Room/board/expenses: $23,349
Full-time enrollment: 288
men: 69%; women: 31%; minorities: 9%; international: 61%
Part-time enrollment: 1
men: 100%; women: 0%; minorities: 0%; international: 0%
Acceptance rate: 21%
GRE requirement: Yes
Avg. GRE: quantitative: 163
TOEFL requirement: Yes
Minimum TOEFL score: 600
Fellowships: 24
Teaching assistantships: 68
Research assistantships: 101
Students specializing in: computer science: 28%; science and physics: 72%

University of New Hampshire

Kingsbury Hall, 33 College Road
Durham, NH 03824
http://www.gradschool.unh.edu/
Public
Admissions: (603) 862-3000
E-mail: grad.school@unh.edu
Financial aid: (603) 862-3600
Application deadline: rolling
In-state tuition: full time: $16,164; part time: $804/credit hour
Out-of-state tuition: full time: $28,604
Room/board/expenses: $21,300
Full-time enrollment: 156
men: 78%; women: 22%; minorities: 7%; international: 38%
Part-time enrollment: 106
men: 75%; women: 25%; minorities: 7%; international: 21%
Acceptance rate: 64%
GRE requirement: Yes
Avg. GRE: quantitative: N/A
TOEFL requirement: Yes
Minimum TOEFL score: 550
Fellowships: 5
Teaching assistantships: 63
Research assistantships: 60
Students specializing in: chemical: 6%; civil: 26%; computer science: 21%; electrical: 13%; materials: 4%; mechanical: 23%; other: 7%

NEW JERSEY

New Jersey Institute of Technology

University Heights
Newark, NJ 07102-1982
http://www.njit.edu/
Public
Admissions: (973) 596-3300
E-mail: admissions@njit.edu
Financial aid: (973) 596-3479
Application deadline: 06/01
In-state tuition: full time: $19,154; part time: $915/credit hour
Out-of-state tuition: full time: $26,688
Room/board/expenses: $15,250
Full-time enrollment: 799
men: 71%; women: 29%; minorities: 18%; international: 70%
Part-time enrollment: 541
men: 73%; women: 27%; minorities: 47%; international: 15%
Acceptance rate: 68%
GRE requirement: Yes
Avg. GRE: quantitative: N/A
TOEFL requirement: Yes
Minimum TOEFL score: 550
Fellowships: 5
Teaching assistantships: 66
Research assistantships: 90
Students specializing in: biomedical: 13%; chemical: 12%; civil: 18%; electrical: 24%; mechanical: 31%; other: 3%

Princeton University

C230 Engineering Quadrangle
Princeton, NJ 08544-5263
http://engineering.princeton.edu
Private
Admissions: (609) 258-3034
E-mail: gsadmit@princeton.edu
Financial aid: (609) 258-3037
Application deadline: 12/15
Tuition: full time: $40,500; part time: N/A
Room/board/expenses: $19,827
Full-time enrollment: 574
men: 75%; women: 25%; minorities: 12%; international: 55%
Part-time enrollment: N/A
men: N/A; women: N/A; minorities: N/A; international: N/A
Acceptance rate: 10%
GRE requirement: Yes
Avg. GRE: quantitative: 163
TOEFL requirement: Yes
Minimum TOEFL score: N/A
Fellowships: 176
Teaching assistantships: 104
Research assistantships: 294
Students specializing in: chemical: 17%; civil: 11%; computer science: 18%; electrical: 30%; mechanical: 16%; other: 8%

Rutgers, the State University of New Jersey–New Brunswick

98 Brett Road
Piscataway, NJ 08854-8058
http://gradstudy.rutgers.edu
Public
Admissions: (732) 932-7711
E-mail: gradadm@rci.rutgers.edu
Financial aid: (732) 932-7057
Application deadline: rolling
In-state tuition: full time: $16,939; part time: $626/credit hour
Out-of-state tuition: full time: $26,515
Room/board/expenses: $17,578
Full-time enrollment: 654
men: 76%; women: 24%; minorities: 12%; international: 69%
Part-time enrollment: 350
men: 74%; women: 26%; minorities: 19%; international: 47%
Acceptance rate: 22%
GRE requirement: Yes
Avg. GRE: quantitative: 161
TOEFL requirement: Yes
Minimum TOEFL score: 550
Fellowships: 120
Teaching assistantships: 149
Research assistantships: 179
Students specializing in: biomedical: 8%; chemical: 12%; civil: 12%; computer science: 18%; electrical: 22%; industrial: 7%; materials: 6%; mechanical: 13%

More at www.usnews.com/grad

Stevens Institute of Technology (Schaefer)

Castle Point on Hudson
Hoboken, NJ 07030
http://www.
stevens.edu/ses/index.php
Private
Admissions: (201) 216-5197
E-mail:
gradadmissions@stevens.edu
Financial aid: (201) 216-8143
Application deadline: rolling
Tuition: full time: $29,506; part
time: $1,280/credit hour
Room/board/expenses: $13,800
Full-time enrollment: 1,061
men: 73%; women: 27%;
minorities: 71%; international:
80%
Part-time enrollment: 667
men: 76%; women: 24%;
minorities: 22%; international: 1%
Acceptance rate: 70%
GRE requirement: Yes
Avg. GRE: quantitative: N/A
TOEFL requirement: Yes
Minimum TOEFL score: 550
Fellowships: 40
Teaching assistantships: 120
Research assistantships: 130
Students specializing in: N/A

NEW MEXICO

New Mexico Institute of Mining and Technology

801 Leroy Place
Socorro, NM 87801
http://www.nmt.edu
Public
Admissions: (505) 835-5513
E-mail: graduate@nmt.edu
Financial aid: (505) 835-5333
Application deadline: 02/15
In-state tuition: full time: $5,692;
part time: $280/credit hour
Out-of-state tuition: full time:
$17,330
Room/board/expenses: $12,134
Full-time enrollment: 132
men: 80%; women: 20%;
minorities: 19%; international:
39%
Part-time enrollment: 62
men: 79%; women: 21%;
minorities: 24%; international:
13%
Acceptance rate: 34%
GRE requirement: Yes
Avg. GRE: quantitative: 154
TOEFL requirement: Yes
Minimum TOEFL score: 540
Fellowships: 2
Teaching assistantships: 94
Research assistantships: 102
Students specializing in: computer
science: 14%; electrical: 7%; man-
agement: 8%; environmental: 3%;
materials: 15%; mechanical: 26%;
mining: 10%; petroleum: 16%

New Mexico State University

PO Box 30001, Department 3449
Las Cruces, NM 88003
http://www.nmsu.edu
Public
Admissions: (575) 646-2340
E-mail: vpickett@nmsu.edu
Financial aid: (505) 646-4490
Application deadline: rolling
In-state tuition: full time: $7,788;
part time: $271/credit hour
Out-of-state tuition: full time:
$19,540
Room/board/expenses: $13,064
Full-time enrollment: 264
men: 81%; women: 19%;
minorities: 17%; international: 61%
Part-time enrollment: 192
men: 80%; women: 20%;
minorities: 38%; international: 9%
GRE requirement: Yes

Avg. GRE: quantitative: N/A
TOEFL requirement: Yes
Minimum TOEFL score: 550
Students specializing in: N/A

University of New Mexico

MSC 01 1140
1 University of New Mexico
Albuquerque, NM 87131
http://www.soe.unm.edu
Public
Admissions: (505) 277-2447
E-mail: grad@unm.edu
Financial aid: (505) 277-8900
Application deadline: 05/01
In-state tuition: full time: $7,848;
part time: $277/credit hour
Out-of-state tuition: full time:
$22,464
Room/board/expenses: $13,922
Full-time enrollment: 712
men: 79%; women: 21%;
minorities: 23%; international:
31%
Part-time enrollment: N/A
men: N/A; women: N/A;
minorities: N/A; international: N/A
Acceptance rate: 62%
GRE requirement: Yes
Avg. GRE: quantitative: 164
TOEFL requirement: Yes
Minimum TOEFL score: 520
Fellowships: 32
Teaching assistantships: 33
Research assistantships: 286
Students specializing in: biomedi-
cal: 3%; chemical: 4%; civil: 10%;
computer: 9%; computer science:
18%; electrical: 24%; industrial:
1%; mechanical: 11%; nuclear: 8%;
other: 12%

NEW YORK

Alfred University–New York State College of Ceramics (Inamori)

2 Pine Street
Alfred, NY 14802-1296
http://nyscc.alfred.edu
Public
Admissions: (800) 541-9229
E-mail: admwww@alfred.edu
Financial aid: (607) 871-2159
Application deadline: rolling
In-state tuition: full time: $22,668;
part time: $782/credit hour
Out-of-state tuition: full time:
$22,668
Room/board/expenses: $14,398
Full-time enrollment: 29
men: 59%; women: 41%;
minorities: 0%; international: 38%
Part-time enrollment: 19
men: 74%; women: 26%;
minorities: 0%; international: 26%
Acceptance rate: 60%
GRE requirement: No
Avg. GRE: quantitative: N/A
TOEFL requirement: Yes
Minimum TOEFL score: 590
Fellowships: 2
Teaching assistantships: 10
Research assistantships: 9
Students specializing in: N/A

Binghamton University–SUNY (Watson)

PO Box 6000
Binghamton, NY 13902-6000
http://watson.binghamton.edu
Public
Admissions: (607) 777-2151
E-mail: gradsch@binghamton.edu
Financial aid: (607) 777-2428
Application deadline: rolling
In-state tuition: full time: $11,009;
part time: $390/credit hour
Out-of-state tuition: full time:
$18,319

Room/board/expenses: $17,116
Full-time enrollment: 358
men: 78%; women: 22%;
minorities: 11%; international: 68%
Part-time enrollment: 306
men: 82%; women: 18%;
minorities: 9%; international: 56%
Acceptance rate: 65%
GRE requirement: Yes
Avg. GRE: quantitative: 159
TOEFL requirement: Yes
Minimum TOEFL score: 550
Fellowships: 12
Teaching assistantships: 80
Research assistantships: 124
Students specializing in: biomedi-
cal: 4%; computer: 1%; computer
science: 35%; electrical: 22%;
industrial: 25%; materials: 3%;
mechanical: 10%

Clarkson University

8 Clarkson Ave, Box 5700
Potsdam, NY 13699
http://www.clarkson.edu/
engineering/graduate/index.html
Private
Admissions: (315) 268-7929
E-mail: enggrad@clarkson.edu
Financial aid: (315) 268-7929
Application deadline: 01/30
Tuition: full time: $1,259/credit
hour; part time: $1,259/credit hour
Room/board/expenses: $16,680
Full-time enrollment: 206
men: 78%; women: 22%;
minorities: 7%; international: 53%
Part-time enrollment: 4
men: 75%; women: 25%;
minorities: 0%; international: 0%
Acceptance rate: 66%
GRE requirement: Yes
Avg. GRE: quantitative: 161
TOEFL requirement: Yes
Minimum TOEFL score: 550
Fellowships: 8
Teaching assistantships: 56
Research assistantships: 75
Students specializing in: chemical:
14%; civil: 16%; electrical: 21%;
science and physics: 4%; envi-
ronmental: 13%; materials: 4%;
mechanical: 27%

Columbia University (Fu Foundation)

500 W. 120th Street
Room 510 Mudd
New York, NY 10027
http://www.
engineering.columbia.edu
Private
Admissions: (212) 854-6438
E-mail:
seasgradmit@columbia.edu
Financial aid: (212) 854-6438
Application deadline: 12/15
Tuition: full time: $51,520; part
time: $1,578/credit hour
Room/board/expenses: $25,250
Full-time enrollment: 1,679
men: 71%; women: 29%;
minorities: 10%; international:
73%
Part-time enrollment: 846
men: 75%; women: 25%;
minorities: 9%; international: 66%
Acceptance rate: 23%
GRE requirement: Yes
Avg. GRE: quantitative: 164
TOEFL requirement: Yes
Minimum TOEFL score: 590
Fellowships: 108
Teaching assistantships: 171
Research assistantships: 435
Students specializing in: biomedical: 6%; chemical: 4%; civil: 9%;
computer: 2%; computer science:
18%; electrical: 20%; management: 5%; science and physics:
3%; environmental: 3%; industrial:
19%; materials: 1%; mechanical:
8%; other: 3%

Cornell University

242 Carpenter Hall
Ithaca, NY 14853
http://www.
engineering.cornell.edu
Private
Admissions: (607) 255-5820
E-mail: engr_grad@cornell.edu
Financial aid: (607) 255-5820
Application deadline: N/A
Tuition: full time: $29,581; part
time: $1,800/credit hour
Room/board/expenses: $22,900
Full-time enrollment: 1,690
men: 70%; women: 30%;
minorities: 18%; international:
52%
Part-time enrollment: 78
men: 82%; women: 18%;
minorities: 23%; international: 3%
Acceptance rate: 28%
GRE requirement: Yes
Avg. GRE: quantitative: 164
TOEFL requirement: Yes
Minimum TOEFL score: N/A
Fellowships: 412
Teaching assistantships: 210
Research assistantships: 770
Students specializing in: aerospace: 2%; agriculture: 4%; biomedical: 11%; chemical: 7%; civil:
6%; computer: 16%; computer
science: 14%; management:
2%; science and physics: 6%;
industrial: 9%; materials: 5%;
mechanical: 9%; other: 10%

CUNY–City College (Grove)

Convent Avenue at 138th Street
New York, NY 10031
http://www.ccny.cuny.edu/
Admissions/index.cfm
Public
Admissions: (212) 650-6853
E-mail: graduateadmissions@
ccny.cuny.edu
Financial aid: (212) 650-6656
Application deadline: 01/15
In-state tuition: full time: $10,441;
part time: $430/credit hour
Out-of-state tuition: full time: $750/
credit hour
Room/board/expenses: $25,050
Full-time enrollment: 374
men: 71%; women: 29%;
minorities: 29%; international:
49%
Part-time enrollment: 280
men: 76%; women: 24%;
minorities: 54%; international:
16%
Acceptance rate: 55%
GRE requirement: Yes
Avg. GRE: quantitative: 153
TOEFL requirement: Yes
Minimum TOEFL score: 550
Fellowships: 46
Teaching assistantships: 33
Research assistantships: 118
Students specializing in: biomedi-
cal: 10%; chemical: 8%; civil: 25%;
computer science: 19%; electrical:
22%; mechanical: 14%; other: 3%

Polytechnic Institute of New York University

6 MetroTech Center
Brooklyn, NY 11201
http://www.poly.edu
Private
Admissions: (718) 260-3200
E-mail: gradinfo@poly.edu
Financial aid: (718) 260-3300
Application deadline: 06/30
Tuition: full time: $1,304/credit
hour; part time: $1,304/credit hour
Room/board/expenses: $14,360
Full-time enrollment: 1,253
men: 74%; women: 26%;
minorities: 9%; international: 83%

Part-time enrollment: 861
men: 83%; women: 17%;
minorities: 31%; international:
22%
Acceptance rate: 40%
GRE requirement: Yes
Avg. GRE: quantitative: 160
TOEFL requirement: Yes
Minimum TOEFL score: 550
Fellowships: 37
Teaching assistantships: 17
Research assistantships: 152
Students specializing in: biomedi-
cal: 2%; chemical: 2%; civil: 11%;
computer: 3%; computer science:
28%; electrical: 31%; manage-
ment: 14%; environmental: 1%;
industrial: 4%; mechanical: 4%

Rensselaer Polytechnic Institute

Jonsson Engineering Center 3004
Troy, NY 12180-3590
http://www.rpi.edu
Private
Admissions: (518) 276-6216
E-mail: admissions@rpi.edu
Financial aid: (518) 276-6813
Application deadline: rolling
Tuition: full time: $45,299; part
time: $1,805/credit hour
Room/board/expenses: $14,340
Full-time enrollment: 566
men: 79%; women: 21%;
minorities: 9%; international: 53%
Part-time enrollment: 265
men: 84%; women: 16%;
minorities: 14%; international: 6%
Acceptance rate: 24%
GRE requirement: Yes
Avg. GRE: quantitative: 163
TOEFL requirement: Yes
Minimum TOEFL score: 570
Fellowships: 43
Teaching assistantships: 188
Research assistantships: 310
Students specializing in: aerospace: 2%; biomedical: 6%;
chemical: 10%; civil: 4%; computer: 2%; computer science:
13%; electrical: 17%; science and
physics: 2%; environmental: 1%;
industrial: 2%; materials: 8%;
mechanical: 29%; nuclear: 3%

Rochester Institute of Technology (Gleason)

77 Lomb Memorial Drive
Rochester, NY 14623
http://www.rit.edu
Private
Admissions: (585) 475-2229
E-mail: gradinfo@rit.edu
Financial aid: (585) 475-5520
Application deadline: rolling
Tuition: full time: $36,216; part
time: $999/credit hour
Room/board/expenses: $12,725
Full-time enrollment: 350
men: 80%; women: 20%;
minorities: 3%; international: 71%
Part-time enrollment: 262
men: 86%; women: 14%;
minorities: 6%; international: 40%
Acceptance rate: 55%
GRE requirement: No
Avg. GRE: quantitative: N/A
TOEFL requirement: Yes
Minimum TOEFL score: 550
Fellowships: 17
Teaching assistantships: 41
Research assistantships: 65
Students specializing in: computer:
5%; electrical: 33%; management:
4%; industrial: 8%; mechanical:
17%; other: 34%

Stony Brook University–SUNY

Engineering Room 100
Stony Brook, NY 11794-2200
https://www.grad.stonybrook.edu
Public
Admissions: (631) 632-7035
E-mail: gradadmissions@stonybrook.edu
Financial aid: (631) 632-6840
Application deadline: 01/15
In-state tuition: full time: $10,584; part time: $390/credit hour
Out-of-state tuition: full time: $17,894
Room/board/expenses: $18,302
Full-time enrollment: 1,312
men: 72%; women: 28%; minorities: 7%; international: 82%
Part-time enrollment: 121
men: 77%; women: 23%; minorities: 23%; international: 17%
Acceptance rate: 37%
GRE requirement: Yes
Avg. GRE: quantitative: N/A
TOEFL requirement: Yes
Minimum TOEFL score: N/A
Fellowships: 22
Teaching assistantships: 171
Research assistantships: 250
Students specializing in: biomedical: 5%; computer: 4%; computer science: 29%; electrical: 13%; materials: 10%; mechanical: 11%; other: 27%

SUNY College of Environmental Science and Forestry

227 Bray Hall
Syracuse, NY 13210
http://www.esf.edu
Public
Admissions: (315) 470-6599
E-mail: esfgrad@esf.edu
Financial aid: (315) 470-6706
Application deadline: 01/15
In-state tuition: full time: $10,251; part time: $390/credit hour
Out-of-state tuition: full time: $17,561
Room/board/expenses: $16,650
Full-time enrollment: 49
men: 73%; women: 27%; minorities: 6%; international: 53%
Part-time enrollment: 48
men: 73%; women: 27%; minorities: 2%; international: 42%
Acceptance rate: 49%
GRE requirement: Yes
Avg. GRE: quantitative: 159
TOEFL requirement: Yes
Minimum TOEFL score: 550
Fellowships: 6
Teaching assistantships: 31
Research assistantships: 9
Students specializing in: environmental: 100%

Syracuse University

223 Link Hall
Syracuse, NY 13244-1240
http://www.lcs.syr.edu/
Private
Admissions: (315) 443-4492
Financial aid: (315) 443-2545
Application deadline: rolling
Tuition: full time: $1,249/credit hour; part time: $1,249/credit hour
Room/board/expenses: $16,692
Full-time enrollment: 753
men: 75%; women: 25%; minorities: 4%; international: 87%
Part-time enrollment: 109
men: 86%; women: 14%; minorities: 17%; international: 25%
Acceptance rate: 39%
GRE requirement: Yes
Avg. GRE: quantitative: 162
TOEFL requirement: Yes
Minimum TOEFL score: 550
Fellowships: 16
Teaching assistantships: 84
Research assistantships: 90
Students specializing in: aerospace: 18%; biomedical: 7%; chemical: 5%; civil: 9%; computer: 23%; computer science: 12%; electrical: 14%; management: 8%; environmental: 4%; mechanical: 18%

University at Buffalo–SUNY

412 Bonner Hall
Buffalo, NY 14260-1900
http://www.eng.buffalo.edu
Public
Admissions: (716) 645-2771
E-mail: seasgrad@buffalo.edu
Financial aid: (716) 645-2450
Application deadline: rolling
In-state tuition: full time: $11,232; part time: $531/credit hour
Out-of-state tuition: full time: $18,542
Room/board/expenses: $15,630
Full-time enrollment: 1,232
men: 79%; women: 21%; minorities: 3%; international: 83%
Part-time enrollment: 92
men: 87%; women: 13%; minorities: 10%; international: 0%
Acceptance rate: 24%
GRE requirement: Yes
Avg. GRE: quantitative: 161
TOEFL requirement: Yes
Minimum TOEFL score: 550
Fellowships: 35
Teaching assistantships: 206
Research assistantships: 209
Students specializing in: aerospace: 3%; biomedical: 0%; chemical: 8%; civil: 11%; computer science: 32%; electrical: 19%; environmental: 0%; industrial: 13%; mechanical: 13%

University of Rochester

Lattimore Hall, Box 270076
Rochester, NY 14627-0076
http://www.Hajim.rochester.edu
Private
Admissions: (585) 275-2059
E-mail: graduate.admissions@rochester.edu
Financial aid: (585) 275-3226
Application deadline: 01/01
Tuition: full time: $1,340/credit hour; part time: $1,340/credit hour
Room/board/expenses: $16,410
Full-time enrollment: 508
men: 74%; women: 26%; minorities: 9%; international: 56%
Part-time enrollment: 39
men: 72%; women: 28%; minorities: 15%; international: 26%
Acceptance rate: 31%
GRE requirement: Yes
Avg. GRE: quantitative: 160
TOEFL requirement: Yes
Minimum TOEFL score: 600
Fellowships: 124
Teaching assistantships: 70
Research assistantships: 207
Students specializing in: biomedical: 13%; chemical: 9%; computer science: 12%; electrical: 24%; materials: 8%; mechanical: 6%; other: 29%

NORTH CAROLINA

Duke University (Pratt)

305 Teer Building
Durham, NC 27708-0271
http://www.pratt.duke.edu
Private
Admissions: (919) 684-3913
E-mail: grad-admissions@duke.edu
Financial aid: (919) 681-1552
Application deadline: 12/08
Tuition: full time: $43,150; part time: $2,660/credit hour
Room/board/expenses: $20,149
Full-time enrollment: 888
men: 69%; women: 31%; minorities: 14%; international: 57%
Part-time enrollment: 56
men: 73%; women: 27%; minorities: 16%; international: 11%
Acceptance rate: 19%
GRE requirement: Yes
Avg. GRE: quantitative: 162
TOEFL requirement: Yes
Minimum TOEFL score: 550
Fellowships: 300
Teaching assistantships: 9
Research assistantships: 196
Students specializing in: biomedical: 24%; civil: 6%; computer science: 8%; electrical: 23%; management: 25%; mechanical: 7%; other: 7%

North Carolina A&T State University

1601 E. Market Street
651 McNair Hall
Greensboro, NC 27411
http://www.eng.ncat.edu
Public
Admissions: (336) 334-7920
E-mail: gradsch@ncat.edu
Financial aid: (336) 334-7973
Application deadline: rolling
In-state tuition: full time: $7,212; part time: N/A
Out-of-state tuition: full time: $18,645
Room/board/expenses: $11,391
Full-time enrollment: 215
men: 70%; women: 30%; minorities: 54%; international: 34%
Part-time enrollment: 105
men: 78%; women: 22%; minorities: 50%; international: 34%
Acceptance rate: 66%
GRE requirement: Yes
Avg. GRE: quantitative: 145
TOEFL requirement: Yes
Minimum TOEFL score: 550
Fellowships: 16
Teaching assistantships: 106
Research assistantships: 114
Students specializing in: biomedical: 5%; chemical: 6%; civil: 9%; computer science: 10%; electrical: 18%; industrial: 21%; mechanical: 19%; other: 13%

North Carolina State University

PO Box 7901
Raleigh, NC 27695
http://www.engr.ncsu.edu/
Public
Admissions: (919) 515-2872
Financial aid: (919) 515-2421
Application deadline: 06/25
In-state tuition: full time: $9,068; part time: $7,347
Out-of-state tuition: full time: $21,116
Room/board/expenses: $17,997
Full-time enrollment: 2,104
men: 76%; women: 24%; minorities: 6%; international: 66%
Part-time enrollment: 814
men: 81%; women: 19%; minorities: 12%; international: 27%
Acceptance rate: 17%
GRE requirement: Yes
Avg. GRE: quantitative: 163
TOEFL requirement: Yes
Minimum TOEFL score: 550
Fellowships: 211
Teaching assistantships: 302
Research assistantships: 848
Students specializing in: aerospace: 3%; agriculture: 3%; biomedical: 3%; chemical: 6%; civil: 11%; computer: 5%; computer science: 20%; electrical: 16%; environmental: 1%; industrial: 8%; materials: 5%; mechanical: 10%; nuclear: 4%; other: 5%

University of North Carolina–Chapel Hill

CB #7431, 166 Rosenau Hall
Chapel Hill, NC 27599-7431
http://www.sph.unc.edu/envr
Public
Admissions: (919) 966-3844
E-mail: jack_whaley@unc.edu
Financial aid: (919) 966-3844
Application deadline: 04/10
In-state tuition: full time: $10,550; part time: $725/credit hour
Out-of-state tuition: full time: $25,883
Room/board/expenses: $23,314
Full-time enrollment: 125
men: 42%; women: 58%; minorities: 0%; international: 18%
Part-time enrollment: 4
men: 75%; women: 25%; minorities: 0%; international: 0%
Acceptance rate: 28%
GRE requirement: Yes
Avg. GRE: quantitative: 157
TOEFL requirement: Yes
Minimum TOEFL score: 550
Fellowships: 29
Teaching assistantships: 12
Research assistantships: 49
Students specializing in: environmental: 100%

University of North Carolina–Charlotte (Lee)

Duke Centennial Hall
9201 University City Boulevard
Charlotte, NC 28223-0001
http://graduateschool.uncc.edu
Public
Admissions: (704) 687-5503
E-mail: gradadm@uncc.edu
Financial aid: (704) 687-5504
Application deadline: 05/01
In-state tuition: full time: $8,149; part time: $5,285
Out-of-state tuition: full time: $20,436
Room/board/expenses: $12,277
Full-time enrollment: 263
men: 81%; women: 19%; minorities: 9%; international: 63%
Part-time enrollment: 189
men: 80%; women: 20%; minorities: 18%; international: 32%
Acceptance rate: 67%
GRE requirement: Yes
Avg. GRE: quantitative: 156
TOEFL requirement: Yes
Minimum TOEFL score: 557
Teaching assistantships: 69
Research assistantships: 114
Students specializing in: civil: 10%; computer: 0%; electrical: 42%; management: 8%; environmental: 9%; mechanical: 22%; other: 8%

NORTH DAKOTA

North Dakota State University

NDSU Dept. 2450, P.O. Box 6050
Fargo, ND 58108-6050
http://www.ndsu.nodak.edu/ndsu/cea/
Public
Admissions: (701) 231-7033
E-mail: ndsu.grad.school@ndsu.edu
Financial aid: (701) 231-7533
Application deadline: rolling
In-state tuition: full time: $300/credit hour; part time: $300/credit hour
Out-of-state tuition: full time: $801/credit hour
Room/board/expenses: $11,840
Full-time enrollment: 62
men: 89%; women: 11%; minorities: 73%; international: 73%
Part-time enrollment: 168
men: 82%; women: 18%; minorities: 65%; international: 60%
Acceptance rate: 39%
GRE requirement: Yes
Avg. GRE: quantitative: 158
TOEFL requirement: Yes
Minimum TOEFL score: 525
Fellowships: 5
Teaching assistantships: 45
Research assistantships: 54
Students specializing in: N/A

University of North Dakota

243 Centennial Drive Stop 8155
Grand Forks, ND 58202-8155
http://engineering.und.edu/sem/graduate.cfm
Public
Admissions: (701) 777-2945
E-mail: questions@gradschool.und.edu
Financial aid: (701) 777-3121
Application deadline: rolling
In-state tuition: full time: $266/credit hour; part time: $266/credit hour
Out-of-state tuition: full time: $710/credit hour
Room/board/expenses: N/A
Full-time enrollment: 106
men: 86%; women: 14%; minorities: 5%; international: 62%
Part-time enrollment: 42
men: 83%; women: 17%; minorities: 5%; international: 36%
GRE requirement: Yes
Avg. GRE: quantitative: N/A
TOEFL requirement: Yes
Minimum TOEFL score: 550
Students specializing in: chemical: 15%; civil: 10%; computer science: 29%; electrical: 14%; science and physics: 14%; environmental: 2%; mechanical: 14%; other: 1%

OHIO

Air Force Institute of Technology[1]

AFIT/RRA, 2950 P Street
Wright Patterson AFB, OH 45433
http://www.afit.edu
Public
Admissions: (800) 211-5097
E-mail: counselors@afit.edu
Financial aid: N/A
Tuition: N/A
Room/board expenses: N/A
Enrollment: N/A

Case Western Reserve University

500 Nord Hall
10900 Euclid Avenue
Cleveland, OH 44106-7220
http://gradstudies.case.edu
Private
Admissions: (216) 368-4390
E-mail: gradstudies@case.edu
Financial aid: (216) 368-4530
Application deadline: rolling
Tuition: full time: $37,146; part time: $1,546/credit hour
Room/board/expenses: $14,800
Full-time enrollment: 543
men: 75%; women: 25%; minorities: 11%; international: 56%
Part-time enrollment: 90
men: 79%; women: 21%; minorities: 14%; international: 11%
Acceptance rate: 19%
GRE requirement: Yes
Avg. GRE: quantitative: 162
TOEFL requirement: Yes
Minimum TOEFL score: 577
Fellowships: 61
Teaching assistantships: 27
Research assistantships: 250

Students specializing in: aerospace: 2%; biomedical: 22%; chemical: 16%; civil: 4%; computer: 5%; computer science: 10%; electrical: 16%; management: 6%; materials: 6%; mechanical: 11%; other: 1%

Cleveland State University (Fenn)

2121 Euclid Avenue, SH 104
Cleveland, OH 44115-2425
http://www.csuohio.edu/engineering/
Public
Admissions: (216) 687-5599
E-mail: graduate.admissions@csuohio.edu
Financial aid: (216) 687-3764
Application deadline: 07/01
In-state tuition: full time: $511/credit hour; part time: $511/credit hour
Out-of-state tuition: full time: $961/credit hour
Room/board/expenses: $15,622
Full-time enrollment: 232
men: 77%; women: 23%; minorities: 12%; international: 62%
Part-time enrollment: 171
men: 82%; women: 18%; minorities: 20%; international: 29%
Acceptance rate: 49%
GRE requirement: Yes
Avg. GRE: quantitative: 157
TOEFL requirement: Yes
Minimum TOEFL score: 525
Fellowships: 0
Teaching assistantships: 40
Research assistantships: 48
Students specializing in: biomedical: 16%; chemical: 7%; civil: 9%; electrical: 36%; environmental: 2%; industrial: 4%; mechanical: 13%; other: 13%

Ohio State University

2070 Neil Avenue
Columbus, OH 43210-1278
http://engineering.osu.edu/
Public
Admissions: (614) 292-9444
E-mail: gradadmissions@osu.edu
Financial aid: (614) 292-0300
Application deadline: rolling
In-state tuition: full time: $12,711; part time: $732/credit hour
Out-of-state tuition: full time: $30,023
Room/board/expenses: $15,246
Full-time enrollment: 1,570
men: 78%; women: 22%; minorities: 7%; international: 60%
Part-time enrollment: 168
men: 76%; women: 24%; minorities: 3%; international: 44%
Acceptance rate: 18%
GRE requirement: Yes
Avg. GRE: quantitative: 163
TOEFL requirement: Yes
Minimum TOEFL score: 550
Fellowships: 243
Teaching assistantships: 151
Research assistantships: 680
Students specializing in: aerospace: 3%; agriculture: 3%; biomedical: 4%; chemical: 5%; civil: 6%; computer science: 18%; electrical: 23%; environmental: 1%; industrial: 10%; materials: 9%; mechanical: 17%; nuclear: 2%

Ohio University (Russ)

150 Stocker Center
Athens, OH 45701
http://www.ohio.edu/engineering
Public
Admissions: (740) 593-2800
E-mail: graduate@ohio.edu
Financial aid: (740) 593-4141
Application deadline: 01/13
In-state tuition: full time: $9,810; part time: $334/credit hour
Out-of-state tuition: full time: $17,802
Room/board/expenses: $14,794
Full-time enrollment: 210
men: 76%; women: 24%; minorities: 2%; international: 60%
Part-time enrollment: 178
men: 81%; women: 19%; minorities: 16%; international: 25%
Acceptance rate: 33%
GRE requirement: Yes
Avg. GRE: quantitative: 159
TOEFL requirement: Yes
Minimum TOEFL score: 550
Fellowships: 22
Teaching assistantships: 127
Research assistantships: 240
Students specializing in: biomedical: 3%; chemical: 13%; civil: 12%; computer science: 13%; electrical: 13%; management: 26%; industrial: 9%; mechanical: 10%; other: 2%

University of Akron

201 ASEC
Akron, OH 44325-3901
http://www.uakron.edu/gradsch/
Public
Admissions: (330) 972-7663
E-mail: gradschool@uakron.edu
Financial aid: (330) 972-7663
Application deadline: rolling
In-state tuition: full time: $8,938; part time: $405/credit hour
Out-of-state tuition: full time: $14,126
Room/board/expenses: $14,878
Full-time enrollment: 291
men: 80%; women: 20%; minorities: 3%; international: 75%
Part-time enrollment: 97
men: 78%; women: 22%; minorities: 6%; international: 28%
Acceptance rate: 57%
GRE requirement: Yes
Avg. GRE: quantitative: 159
TOEFL requirement: Yes
Minimum TOEFL score: 550
Fellowships: 0
Teaching assistantships: 137
Research assistantships: 118
Students specializing in: biomedical: 8%; chemical: 21%; civil: 25%; computer: 1%; electrical: 19%; management: 3%; mechanical: 24%; other: 1%

University of Cincinnati

PO Box 210077
Cincinnati, OH 45221-0077
http://www.eng.uc.edu
Public
Admissions: (513) 556-6347
E-mail: engrgrad@uc.edu
Financial aid: (513) 556-3647
Application deadline: 03/15
In-state tuition: full time: $16,994; part time: $627/credit hour
Out-of-state tuition: full time: $28,508
Room/board/expenses: $12,819
Full-time enrollment: 818
men: 79%; women: 21%; minorities: 4%; international: 67%
Part-time enrollment: 41
men: 95%; women: 5%; minorities: 17%; international: 5%
Acceptance rate: 25%
GRE requirement: Yes
Avg. GRE: quantitative: 161
TOEFL requirement: Yes
Minimum TOEFL score: 550
Fellowships: 44
Teaching assistantships: 156
Research assistantships: 483
Students specializing in: aerospace: 12%; biomedical: 4%; chemical: 4%; civil: 5%; computer: 8%; computer science: 13%; electrical: 13%; environmental: 10%; materials: 6%; mechanical: 23%; nuclear: 1%

University of Dayton

300 College Park
Dayton, OH 45469-0228
http://www.udayton.edu/apply
Private
Admissions: (937) 229-4411
E-mail: gradadmission@udayton.edu
Financial aid: (937) 229-4311
Application deadline: rolling
Tuition: full time: $788/credit hour; part time: $788/credit hour
Room/board/expenses: $17,625
Full-time enrollment: 526
men: 82%; women: 18%; minorities: 5%; international: 67%
Part-time enrollment: 163
men: 79%; women: 21%; minorities: 11%; international: 27%
Acceptance rate: 48%
GRE requirement: No
Avg. GRE: quantitative: N/A
TOEFL requirement: Yes
Minimum TOEFL score: 550
Fellowships: 4
Teaching assistantships: 18
Research assistantships: 85
Students specializing in: aerospace: 4%; biomedical: 1%; chemical: 8%; civil: 4%; electrical: 23%; management: 12%; materials: 13%; mechanical: 14%; other: 19%

University of Toledo

2801 W. Bancroft
Toledo, OH 43606
http://www.eng.utoledo.edu/coe/grad_studies/
Public
Admissions: (419) 530-4723
E-mail: gradoff@eng.utoledo.edu
Financial aid: (419) 530-8700
Application deadline: rolling
In-state tuition: full time: $12,594; part time: $525/credit hour
Out-of-state tuition: full time: $22,829
Room/board/expenses: $14,700
Full-time enrollment: 158
men: 77%; women: 23%; minorities: 1%; international: 70%
Part-time enrollment: 192
men: 82%; women: 18%; minorities: 3%; international: 63%
Acceptance rate: 83%
GRE requirement: Yes
Avg. GRE: quantitative: 157
TOEFL requirement: Yes
Minimum TOEFL score: 550
Fellowships: 2
Teaching assistantships: 75
Research assistantships: 84
Students specializing in: biomedical: 11%; chemical: 9%; civil: 12%; computer science: 10%; electrical: 24%; industrial: 3%; mechanical: 24%; other: 7%

Wright State University

3640 Colonel Glenn Highway
Dayton, OH 45435
http://www.wright.edu/sogs/
Public
Admissions: (937) 775-2976
E-mail: wsugrad@wright.edu
Financial aid: (937) 775-5721
Application deadline: rolling
In-state tuition: full time: $12,240; part time: $564/credit hour
Out-of-state tuition: full time: $20,792
Room/board/expenses: $13,412
Full-time enrollment: 362
men: 78%; women: 22%; minorities: 8%; international: 51%
Part-time enrollment: 128
men: 78%; women: 22%; minorities: 10%; international: 20%
Acceptance rate: 60%
GRE requirement: Yes
Avg. GRE: quantitative: 157
TOEFL requirement: No
Minimum TOEFL score: 550
Fellowships: 7
Teaching assistantships: 35
Research assistantships: 147
Students specializing in: biomedical: 11%; computer: 4%; computer science: 31%; electrical: 37%; industrial: 15%; materials: 3%; mechanical: 16%; other: 8%

OKLAHOMA

Oklahoma State University

201 ATRC
Stillwater, OK 74078-0535
http://gradcollege.okstate.edu
Public
Admissions: (405) 744-6368
E-mail: grad-i@okstate.edu
Financial aid: (405) 744-6604
Application deadline: rolling
In-state tuition: full time: $178/credit hour; part time: $178/credit hour
Out-of-state tuition: full time: $709/credit hour
Room/board/expenses: $13,910
Full-time enrollment: 366
men: 73%; women: 27%; minorities: 5%; international: 79%
Part-time enrollment: 515
men: 84%; women: 16%; minorities: 15%; international: 43%
Acceptance rate: 43%
GRE requirement: Yes
Avg. GRE: quantitative: N/A
TOEFL requirement: Yes
Minimum TOEFL score: 550
Fellowships: 39
Teaching assistantships: 149
Research assistantships: 252
Students specializing in: agriculture: 6%; chemical: 6%; civil: 8%; computer: 11%; electrical: 22%; industrial: 29%; mechanical: 19%

University of Oklahoma

202 W. Boyd, CEC 107
Norman, OK 73019
http://www.ou.edu/coe
Public
Admissions: (405) 325-2252
E-mail: admrec@ou.edu
Financial aid: (405) 325-5505
Application deadline: rolling
In-state tuition: full time: $175/credit hour; part time: $175/credit hour
Out-of-state tuition: full time: $654/credit hour
Room/board/expenses: $14,704
Full-time enrollment: 371
men: 78%; women: 22%; minorities: 6%; international: 69%
Part-time enrollment: 226
men: 81%; women: 19%; minorities: 11%; international: 44%
Acceptance rate: 45%
GRE requirement: Yes
Avg. GRE: quantitative: 159
TOEFL requirement: Yes
Minimum TOEFL score: 550
Fellowships: 33
Teaching assistantships: 106
Research assistantships: 255
Students specializing in: aerospace: 7%; biomedical: 4%; chemical: 10%; civil: 12%; computer science: 17%; electrical: 6%; environmental: 4%; industrial: 13%; mechanical: 9%; petroleum: 14%; other: 5%

University of Tulsa

800 S. Tucker Drive
Tulsa, OK 74104-3189
http://www.utulsa.edu
Private
Admissions: (918) 631-2336
E-mail: grad@utulsa.edu
Financial aid: (918) 631-2526
Application deadline: rolling
Tuition: full time: $1,035/credit hour; part time: $1,035/credit hour
Room/board/expenses: $13,964
Full-time enrollment: 187
men: 78%; women: 22%; minorities: 4%; international: 70%
Part-time enrollment: 13
men: 62%; women: 38%; minorities: 15%; international: 0%
Acceptance rate: 27%
GRE requirement: Yes
Avg. GRE: quantitative: 160
TOEFL requirement: Yes
Minimum TOEFL score: 550
Fellowships: 7
Teaching assistantships: 43
Research assistantships: 91
Students specializing in: chemical: 14%; computer science: 27%; electrical: 5%; science and physics: 1%; mechanical: 19%; petroleum: 36%

OREGON

Oregon Health and Science University[1]

3181 SW Sam Jackson Park Rd
MC: CH13B
Portland, OR 97239
http://www.ohsu.edu/som/graduate
Public
Admissions: (503) 494-6222
E-mail: somgrad@ohsu.edu
Financial aid: (503) 494-5117
Tuition: N/A
Room/board expenses: N/A
Enrollment: N/A

Oregon State University

101 Covell Hall
Corvallis, OR 97331-2409
http://engr.oregonstate.edu/
Public
Admissions: (541) 737-4411
E-mail: osuadmit@orst.edu
Financial aid: (541) 737-2241
Application deadline: 01/15
In-state tuition: full time: $14,825; part time: $476/credit hour
Out-of-state tuition: full time: $21,737
Room/board/expenses: $14,598
Full-time enrollment: 680
men: 82%; women: 18%; minorities: 7%; international: 47%
Part-time enrollment: 154
men: 79%; women: 21%; minorities: 14%; international: 22%
Acceptance rate: 23%
GRE requirement: Yes
Avg. GRE: quantitative: 158
TOEFL requirement: Yes
Minimum TOEFL score: 550
Fellowships: 52
Teaching assistantships: 131
Research assistantships: 286
Students specializing in: agriculture: 1%; chemical: 10%; civil: 17%; computer science: 15%; electrical: 21%; industrial: 6%; materials: 4%; mechanical: 11%; nuclear: 5%; other: 10%

Portland State University (Maseeh)

PO Box 751
Portland, OR 97207
http://www.cecs.pdx.edu
Public
Admissions: (503) 725-4289
E-mail: fischerm@cecs.pdx.edu
Financial aid: (503) 725-3461
Application deadline: rolling
In-state tuition: full time: $11,712; part time: $387/credit hour
Out-of-state tuition: full time: $16,842
Room/board/expenses: $15,297

Full-time enrollment: 346
men: 70%; women: 30%;
minorities: 7%; international: 67%
Part-time enrollment: 329
men: 75%; women: 25%;
minorities: 22%; international:
21%
Acceptance rate: 61%
GRE requirement: Yes
Avg. GRE: quantitative: N/A
TOEFL requirement: Yes
Minimum TOEFL score: 550
Teaching assistantships: 62
Research assistantships: 90
Students specializing in: civil: 19%;
computer science: 16%; electrical:
36%; management: 18%; science
and physics: 2%; mechanical: 8%;
other: 1%

PENNSYLVANIA

Carnegie Mellon University
5000 Forbes Avenue
Pittsburgh, PA 15213
http://www.cit.cmu.edu/
Private
Admissions: (412) 268-2478
Financial aid: (412) 268-2482
Application deadline: rolling
Tuition: full time: $39,564; part
time: $1,620/credit hour
Room/board/expenses: $26,840
Full-time enrollment: 2,604
men: 73%; women: 27%;
minorities: 9%; international: 66%
Part-time enrollment: 253
men: 81%; women: 19%;
minorities: 19%; international:
47%
Acceptance rate: 29%
GRE requirement: Yes
Avg. GRE: quantitative: 161
TOEFL requirement: Yes
Minimum TOEFL score: N/A
Fellowships: 410
Teaching assistantships: 32
Research assistantships: 919
Students specializing in:
biomedical: 4%; chemical: 5%;
civil: 7%; computer science: 35%;
electrical: 23%; materials: 5%;
mechanical: 10%; other: 13%

Drexel University
3141 Chestnut Street
Philadelphia, PA 19104
http://www.drexel.edu/coe
Private
Admissions: (215) 895-6700
E-mail: enroll@drexel.edu
Financial aid: (215) 895-2964
Application deadline: rolling
Tuition: full time: $29,025; part
time: $1,045/credit hour
Room/board/expenses: $20,750
Full-time enrollment: 671
men: 70%; women: 30%;
minorities: 5%; international: 54%
Part-time enrollment: 457
men: 83%; women: 17%;
minorities: 11%; international: 4%
Acceptance rate: 46%
GRE requirement: Yes
Avg. GRE: quantitative: 159
TOEFL requirement: Yes
Minimum TOEFL score: 600
Fellowships: 177
Teaching assistantships: 65
Research assistantships: 62
Students specializing in: biomedical: 16%; chemical: 4%; civil: 4%;
computer: 1%; computer science:
10%; electrical: 25%; management: 13%; environmental: 3%;
materials: 6%; mechanical: 13%;
other: 4%

Lehigh University (Rossin)
19 Memorial Drive W
Bethlehem, PA 18015
http://www.lehigh.edu/engineering/
Private
Admissions: (610) 758-6310
E-mail: ineas@lehigh.edu
Financial aid: (610) 758-3181
Application deadline: 01/15
Tuition: full time: $1,260/credit
hour; part time: $1,260/credit hour
Room/board/expenses: $14,100
Full-time enrollment: 686
men: 70%; women: 30%;
minorities: 6%; international: 66%
Part-time enrollment: 101
men: 68%; women: 32%;
minorities: 17%; international: 2%
Acceptance rate: 18%
GRE requirement: Yes
Avg. GRE: quantitative: 163
TOEFL requirement: Yes
Minimum TOEFL score: 550
Fellowships: 36
Teaching assistantships: 70
Research assistantships: 189
Students specializing in: biomedical: 2%; chemical: 12%; civil: 12%;
computer: 2%; computer science:
5%; electrical: 8%; management:
2%; environmental: 4%; industrial:
25%; materials: 5%; mechanical:
20%; other: 4%

Pennsylvania State University– University Park
101 Hammond Building
University Park, PA 16802
http://www.gradsch.psu.edu
Public
Admissions: (814) 865-1795
E-mail: gswww@psu.edu
Financial aid: N/A
Application deadline: 12/02
In-state tuition: full time: $19,554;
part time: $778/credit hour
Out-of-state tuition: full time:
$32,394
Room/board/expenses: $13,266
Full-time enrollment: 1,612
men: 77%; women: 23%;
minorities: 7%; international: 60%
Part-time enrollment: 251
men: 85%; women: 15%;
minorities: 10%; international:
24%
Acceptance rate: 24%
GRE requirement: Yes
Avg. GRE: quantitative: 162
TOEFL requirement: Yes
Minimum TOEFL score: 550
Fellowships: 55
Teaching assistantships: 313
Research assistantships: 654
Students specializing in: aerospace: 6%; agriculture: 2%;
architectural: 6%; biomedical: 2%;
chemical: 5%; civil: 5%; computer:
11%; electrical: 12%; science and
physics: 5%; environmental: 2%;
industrial: 9%; materials: 7%;
mechanical: 10%; nuclear: 5%;
other: 14%

Temple University
1947 N. 12th Street
Philadelphia, PA 19122
http://www.temple.edu/engineering/academic-programs/graduate-programs/
Public
Admissions: (215) 204-7800
E-mail: gradengr@temple.edu
Financial aid: (215) 204-2244
Application deadline: 01/15
In-state tuition: full time: $795/
credit hour; part time: $795/
credit hour
Out-of-state tuition: full time:
$1,068/credit hour

Room/board/expenses: N/A
Full-time enrollment: 173
men: 74%; women: 26%;
minorities: 8%; international: 71%
Part-time enrollment: 37
men: 81%; women: 19%;
minorities: 16%; international:
35%
Acceptance rate: 68%
GRE requirement: Yes
Avg. GRE: quantitative: 158
TOEFL requirement: Yes
Minimum TOEFL score: 550
Fellowships: 2
Teaching assistantships: 68
Research assistantships: 53
Students specializing in: biomedical: 5%; civil: 5%; computer
science: 44%; electrical: 12%;
environmental: 1%; mechanical:
4%; other: 28%

University of Pennsylvania
107 Towne Building
Philadelphia, PA 19104
http://www.seas.upenn.edu/grad
Private
Admissions: (215) 898-4542
E-mail: engstats@seas.upenn.edu
Financial aid: (215) 898-1988
Application deadline: 05/15
Tuition: full time: $30,800; part
time: $5,574/credit hour
Room/board/expenses: $20,569
Full-time enrollment: 1,419
men: 70%; women: 30%;
minorities: 12%; international:
63%
Part-time enrollment: 285
men: 68%; women: 32%;
minorities: 25%; international:
36%
Acceptance rate: 23%
GRE requirement: Yes
Avg. GRE: quantitative: 167
TOEFL requirement: Yes
Minimum TOEFL score: 600
Fellowships: 143
Teaching assistantships: 0
Research assistantships: 316
Students specializing in: biomedical: 19%; chemical: 8%; computer
science: 25%; electrical: 14%;
management: 2%; industrial: 2%;
materials: 9%; mechanical: 11%;
other: 12%

University of Pittsburgh (Swanson)
109 Benedum Hall
Pittsburgh, PA 15261
http://www.engineering.pitt.edu
Public
Admissions: (412) 624-9800
E-mail: ssoeadm@pitt.edu
Financial aid: (412) 624-7488
Application deadline: 03/01
In-state tuition: full time: $22,936;
part time: $1,054/credit hour
Out-of-state tuition: full time:
$37,088
Room/board/expenses: $19,578
Full-time enrollment: 705
men: 75%; women: 25%;
minorities: 8%; international: 59%
Part-time enrollment: 327
men: 81%; women: 19%;
minorities: 8%; international: 5%
Acceptance rate: 30%
GRE requirement: Yes
Avg. GRE: quantitative: 161
TOEFL requirement: Yes
Minimum TOEFL score: 550
Fellowships: 59
Teaching assistantships: 114
Research assistantships: 274
Students specializing in: biomedical: 15%; chemical: 5%; civil: 16%;
computer: 1%; computer science:
9%; electrical: 15%; industrial:
11%; materials: 6%; mechanical:
21%; petroleum: 1%

RHODE ISLAND

Brown University
Box D
Providence, RI 02912
http://www.brown.edu/academics/gradschool
Private
Admissions: (401) 863-2600
E-mail: Admission_Graduate@brown.edu
Financial aid: (401) 863-2721
Application deadline: rolling
Tuition: full time: $43,532; part
time: $11,426
Room/board/expenses: $15,280
Full-time enrollment: 299
men: 72%; women: 28%;
minorities: 7%; international: 64%
Part-time enrollment: 24
men: 83%; women: 17%;
minorities: 8%; international: 54%
Acceptance rate: 21%
GRE requirement: Yes
Avg. GRE: quantitative: 160
TOEFL requirement: Yes
Minimum TOEFL score: 577
Fellowships: 62
Teaching assistantships: 32
Research assistantships: 160
Students specializing in: computer
science: 45%; other: 55%

University of Rhode Island
102 Bliss Hall
Kingston, RI 02881
http://www.uri.edu/gsadmis/
Public
Admissions: (401) 874-2872
E-mail: gradadm@etal.uri.edu
Financial aid: (401) 874-2314
Application deadline: 02/01
In-state tuition: full time: $14,596;
part time: $641/credit hour
Out-of-state tuition: full time:
$26,670
Room/board/expenses: $19,750
Full-time enrollment: 137
men: 82%; women: 18%;
minorities: 18%; international:
43%
Part-time enrollment: 93
men: 76%; women: 24%;
minorities: 25%; international: 8%
Acceptance rate: 63%
GRE requirement: Yes
Avg. GRE: quantitative: N/A
TOEFL requirement: Yes
Minimum TOEFL score: 550
Fellowships: 2
Teaching assistantships: 28
Research assistantships: 33
Students specializing in: chemical:
10%; civil: 15%; electrical: 22%;
industrial: 7%; mechanical: 26%;
other: 21%

SOUTH CAROLINA

Clemson University
Room 109, Riggs Hall
Clemson, SC 29634-0901
http://www.grad.clemson.edu/
Public
Admissions: (864) 656-4172
E-mail: grdapp@clemson.edu
Financial aid: (864) 656-2280
Application deadline: rolling
In-state tuition: full time: $9,128;
part time: $604/credit hour
Out-of-state tuition: full time:
$17,430
Room/board/expenses: $14,654
Full-time enrollment: 1,072
men: 78%; women: 22%;
minorities: 6%; international: 65%
Part-time enrollment: 245
men: 76%; women: 24%;
minorities: 10%; international:
28%
Acceptance rate: 38%
GRE requirement: Yes
Avg. GRE: quantitative: N/A
TOEFL requirement: Yes
Minimum TOEFL score: N/A

Fellowships: 55
Teaching assistantships: 239
Research assistantships: 399
Students specializing in: biomedical: 11%; chemical: 3%; civil: 11%;
computer: 4%; computer science:
14%; electrical: 11%; environmental: 9%; industrial: 17%; materials:
5%; mechanical: 13%; other: 17%

University of South Carolina
Swearingen Engineering Center
Columbia, SC 29208
http://www.cec.sc.edu
Public
Admissions: (803) 777-4243
E-mail: gradapp@mailbox.sc.edu
Financial aid: (803) 777-8134
Application deadline: 07/01
In-state tuition: full time: $13,340;
part time: $470/credit hour
Out-of-state tuition: full time:
$25,864
Room/board/expenses: $15,277
Full-time enrollment: 327
men: 79%; women: 21%;
minorities: 9%; international: 67%
Part-time enrollment: 207
men: 84%; women: 16%;
minorities: 20%; international:
29%
Acceptance rate: 34%
GRE requirement: Yes
Avg. GRE: quantitative: 159
TOEFL requirement: Yes
Minimum TOEFL score: 570
Fellowships: 14
Teaching assistantships: 27
Research assistantships: 282
Students specializing in: aerospace: 0%; biomedical: 4%;
chemical: 16%; civil: 16%; computer: 20%; computer science:
20%; electrical: 20%; mechanical:
16%; nuclear: 7%

SOUTH DAKOTA

South Dakota School of Mines and Technology
501 E. St. Joseph Street
Rapid City, SD 57701-3995
http://www.sdsmt.edu/
Public
Admissions: (605) 394-2341
E-mail: graduate.admissions@sdsmt.edu
Financial aid: (605) 394-2400
Application deadline: rolling
In-state tuition: full time: $197/
credit hour; part time: $197/
credit hour
Out-of-state tuition: full time: $417/
credit hour
Room/board/expenses: $10,790
Full-time enrollment: 158
men: 75%; women: 25%;
minorities: 4%; international: 44%
Part-time enrollment: 85
men: 81%; women: 19%;
minorities: 1%; international: 7%
Acceptance rate: 66%
GRE requirement: Yes
Avg. GRE: quantitative: 156
TOEFL requirement: Yes
Minimum TOEFL score: 520
Fellowships: 7
Teaching assistantships: 61
Research assistantships: 103
Students specializing in: biomedical: 5%; chemical: 5%; civil: 9%;
computer science: 3%; electrical:
7%; management: 15%; materials:
12%; mechanical: 6%; mining: 1%;
other: 38%

South Dakota State University

CEH 201, Box 2219
Brookings, SD 57007-0096
http://www3.sdstate.edu/
Public
Admissions: (605) 688-4181
E-mail:
gradschl@adm.sdstate.edu
Financial aid: (605) 688-4695
Application deadline: 04/04
In-state tuition: full time: $196/
credit hour; part time: $196/
credit hour
Out-of-state tuition: full time: $368/
credit hour
Room/board/expenses: $7,280
Full-time enrollment: 217
men: 76%; women: 24%;
minorities: 5%; international: 53%
Part-time enrollment: N/A
men: N/A; women: N/A;
minorities: N/A; international: N/A
Acceptance rate: 48%
GRE requirement: No
Avg. GRE: quantitative: N/A
TOEFL requirement: Yes
Minimum TOEFL score: 550
Fellowships: 9
Teaching assistantships: 58
Research assistantships: 67
Students specializing in: agriculture: 7%; civil: 17%; computer science: 12%; electrical: 23%; industrial: 12%; mechanical: 10%; other: 22%

TENNESSEE

Tennessee State University

3500 John Merritt Boulevard
Nashville, TN 37209-1651
http://www.tnstate.edu/
interior.asp?ptid=1&mid=284
Public
Admissions: (615) 963-5107
E-mail: jcade@tnstate.edu
Financial aid: (615) 963-5772
Application deadline: N/A
In-state tuition: full time: $6,426;
part time: $229/credit hour
Out-of-state tuition: full time:
$18,954
Room/board/expenses: N/A
Full-time enrollment: 44
men: 70%; women: 30%;
minorities: 75%; international:
55%
Part-time enrollment: 29
men: 76%; women: 24%;
minorities: 48%; international:
34%
Acceptance rate: 24%
GRE requirement: No
Avg. GRE: quantitative: N/A
TOEFL requirement: Yes
Minimum TOEFL score: 500
Students specializing in: computer:
52%; management: 42%; other:
5%

Tennessee Technological University

N. Dixie Avenue
Cookeville, TN 38505
http://www.
tntech.edu/engineering
Public
Admissions: (931) 372-3233
E-mail: g_admissions@tntech.edu
Financial aid: (931) 372-3073
Application deadline: 08/05
In-state tuition: full time: $9,026;
part time: $441/credit hour
Out-of-state tuition: full time:
$20,626
Room/board/expenses: $14,460
Full-time enrollment: 81
men: 83%; women: 17%;
minorities: 41%; international:
58%

Part-time enrollment: 69
men: 87%; women: 13%;
minorities: 54%; international:
43%
Acceptance rate: 48%
GRE requirement: Yes
Avg. GRE: quantitative: 159
TOEFL requirement: Yes
Minimum TOEFL score: 550
Fellowships: 2
Teaching assistantships: 33
Research assistantships: 51
Students specializing in: chemical: 13%; civil: 22%; computer science: 11%; electrical: 38%; mechanical: 15%

University of Memphis (Herff)

201 Engineering Administration
Building
Memphis, TN 38152
http://www.
memphis.edu/herff/index.php
Public
Admissions: (901) 678-2111
E-mail: recruitment@memphis.edu
Financial aid: (901) 678-4825
Application deadline: N/A
In-state tuition: full time: $8,670;
part time: $470/credit hour
Out-of-state tuition: full time:
$19,848
Room/board/expenses: $14,909
Full-time enrollment: 162
men: 75%; women: 25%;
minorities: 10%; international:
69%
Part-time enrollment: 66
men: 79%; women: 21%;
minorities: 17%; international:
35%
Acceptance rate: 71%
GRE requirement: Yes
Avg. GRE: quantitative: 158
TOEFL requirement: Yes
Minimum TOEFL score: 550
Fellowships: 23
Teaching assistantships: 17
Research assistantships: 69
Students specializing in: biomedical: 16%; civil: 16%; computer: 7%; computer science: 32%; electrical: 20%; mechanical: 7%; other: 3%

University of Tennessee–Knoxville

124 Perkins Hall
Knoxville, TN 37996-2000
http://graduateadmissions.
utk.edu/
Public
Admissions: (865) 974-3251
E-mail: graduateadmissions@
utk.edu
Financial aid: (865) 974-3131
Application deadline: 02/01
In-state tuition: full time: $10,280;
part time: $501/credit hour
Out-of-state tuition: full time:
$28,768
Room/board/expenses: $19,172
Full-time enrollment: 698
men: 81%; women: 19%;
minorities: 7%; international: 43%
Part-time enrollment: 302
men: 83%; women: 17%;
minorities: 12%; international: 7%
Acceptance rate: 28%
GRE requirement: Yes
Avg. GRE: quantitative: 159
TOEFL requirement: Yes
Minimum TOEFL score: 550
Fellowships: 52
Teaching assistantships: 213
Research assistantships: 508
Students specializing in: aerospace: 4%; agriculture: 1%; biomedical: 5%; chemical: 6%; civil: 12%; computer: 4%; computer science: 6%; electrical: 13%; management: 0%; science and physics: 1%; environmental: 2%;

industrial: 16%; materials: 9%;
mechanical: 8%; nuclear: 12%;
other: 2%

Vanderbilt University

VU Station B 351826
2301 Vanderbilt Place
Nashville, TN 37235
http://www.vuse.vanderbilt.edu
Private
Admissions: (615) 322-3825
E-mail: vandygrad@vanderbilt.edu
Financial aid: (615) 343-5931
Application deadline: 01/15
Tuition: full time: $1,712/credit
hour; part time: $1,712/credit hour
Room/board/expenses: $22,641
Full-time enrollment: 436
men: 72%; women: 28%;
minorities: 13%; international:
40%
Part-time enrollment: 21
men: 71%; women: 29%;
minorities: 5%; international: 19%
Acceptance rate: 13%
GRE requirement: Yes
Avg. GRE: quantitative: N/A
TOEFL requirement: Yes
Minimum TOEFL score: 570
Fellowships: 26
Teaching assistantships: 108
Research assistantships: 243
Students specializing in: biomedical: 13%; chemical: 11%; civil: 10%; computer science: 17%; electrical: 21%; environmental: 9%; materials: 7%; mechanical: 11%

TEXAS

Lamar University

4400 Martin Luther King
Boulevard
Beaumont, TX 77710
http://dept.lamar.edu/
engineering/coe/
Public
Admissions: (409) 880-8888
E-mail: admissions@hal.lamar.edu
Financial aid: (409) 880-8450
Application deadline: N/A
In-state tuition: full time: $7,208;
part time: $298/credit hour
Out-of-state tuition: full time:
$14,426
Room/board/expenses: $13,842
Full-time enrollment: 159
men: 78%; women: 22%;
minorities: 8%; international: 87%
Part-time enrollment: 69
men: 81%; women: 19%;
minorities: 10%; international:
78%
Acceptance rate: 72%
GRE requirement: Yes
Avg. GRE: quantitative: N/A
TOEFL requirement: Yes
Minimum TOEFL score: 525
Fellowships: 49
Teaching assistantships: 9
Research assistantships: 22
Students specializing in: chemical: 28%; civil: 16%; electrical: 26%; industrial: 12%; mechanical: 17%; other: 1%

Prairie View A&M University

PO Box 519, MS 2500
Prairie View, TX 77446
http://www.pvamu.edu
Public
Admissions: (936) 261-3518
E-mail: gradadmissions@
pvamu.edu
Financial aid: (936) 261-1000
Application deadline: 07/01
In-state tuition: full time: $210/
credit hour; part time: $210/
credit hour
Out-of-state tuition: full time: $563/
credit hour
Room/board/expenses: $11,826

Full-time enrollment: 88
men: 76%; women: 24%;
minorities: 51%; international:
35%
Part-time enrollment: 37
men: 59%; women: 41%;
minorities: 62%; international:
22%
Acceptance rate: 84%
GRE requirement: Yes
Avg. GRE: quantitative: N/A
TOEFL requirement: Yes
Minimum TOEFL score: 500
Students specializing in: computer science: 12%; electrical: 33%; other: 55%

Rice University (Brown)

PO Box 1892, MS 364
Houston, TX 77251-1892
http://engr.rice.edu
Private
Admissions: (713) 348-4002
E-mail: graduate@rice.edu
Financial aid: (713) 348-4958
Application deadline: 12/31
Tuition: full time: $37,138; part
time: $2,034/credit hour
Room/board/expenses: $15,200
Full-time enrollment: 683
men: 71%; women: 29%;
minorities: 17%; international:
58%
Part-time enrollment: 33
men: 82%; women: 18%;
minorities: 15%; international:
39%
Acceptance rate: 17%
GRE requirement: Yes
Avg. GRE: quantitative: 164
TOEFL requirement: Yes
Minimum TOEFL score: 600
Fellowships: 226
Teaching assistantships: 11
Research assistantships: 287
Students specializing in: biomedical: 17%; chemical: 10%; civil: 4%; computer science: 14%; electrical: 20%; environmental: 5%; materials: 4%; mechanical: 9%; other: 17%

Southern Methodist University

3145 Dyer Street
Dallas, TX 75275-0335
http://www.engr.smu.edu
Private
Admissions: (214) 768-3484
E-mail: valerin@engr.smu.edu
Financial aid: (214) 768-3484
Application deadline: 07/01
Tuition: full time: $1,095/credit
hour; part time: $1,095/credit
hour
Room/board/expenses: $25,465
Full-time enrollment: 275
men: 73%; women: 27%;
minorities: 9%; international: 71%
Part-time enrollment: 600
men: 79%; women: 21%;
minorities: 33%; international:
13%
Acceptance rate: 67%
GRE requirement: Yes
Avg. GRE: quantitative: N/A
TOEFL requirement: Yes
Minimum TOEFL score: 550
Fellowships: 0
Teaching assistantships: 48
Research assistantships: 59
Students specializing in: civil: 2%; computer: 2%; computer science: 20%; electrical: 19%; management: 44%; environmental: 4%; mechanical: 8%

Texas A&M University– College Station (Look)

204 Zachry Engineering Center
College Station, TX 77843-3126
http://engineering.tamu.edu/
graduate
Public
Admissions: (979) 845-7200
E-mail: gradengineer@tamu.edu
Financial aid: (979) 845-3236
Application deadline: rolling
In-state tuition: full time: $277/
credit hour; part time: $277/
credit hour
Out-of-state tuition: full time: $577/
credit hour
Room/board/expenses: $12,406
Full-time enrollment: 2,421
men: 79%; women: 21%;
minorities: 9%; international: 69%
Part-time enrollment: 497
men: 81%; women: 19%;
minorities: 24%; international:
33%
Acceptance rate: 26%
GRE requirement: Yes
Avg. GRE: quantitative: 161
TOEFL requirement: Yes
Minimum TOEFL score: 550
Fellowships: 442
Teaching assistantships: 302
Research assistantships: 1,200
Students specializing in: aerospace: 4%; agriculture: 3%; biomedical: 4%; chemical: 4%; civil: 14%; computer science: 9%; electrical: 19%; industrial: 7%; materials: 3%; mechanical: 14%; nuclear: 4%; petroleum: 13%; other: 1%

Texas A&M University–Kingsville (Dotterweich)

MSC 188
Kingsville, TX 78363
http://www.engineer.tamuk.edu
Public
Admissions: (361) 593-2315
Financial aid: (361) 593-3911
Application deadline: 06/01
In-state tuition: full time: $3,228;
part time: $653/credit hour
Out-of-state tuition: full time:
$7,704
Room/board/expenses: $13,158
Full-time enrollment: 294
men: 81%; women: 19%;
minorities: 12%; international:
82%
Part-time enrollment: 143
men: 80%; women: 20%;
minorities: 34%; international:
59%
Acceptance rate: 85%
GRE requirement: Yes
Avg. GRE: quantitative: 154
TOEFL requirement: Yes
Minimum TOEFL score: 550
Teaching assistantships: 48
Research assistantships: 56
Students specializing in: chemical: 6%; civil: 9%; computer science: 26%; electrical: 23%; environmental: 13%; industrial: 5%; mechanical: 8%; petroleum: 7%; other: 3%

Texas Tech University (Whitacre)

Box 43103
Lubbock, TX 79409-3103
http://www.depts.ttu.edu/coe/
Public
Admissions: (806) 742-2787
E-mail: gradschool@ttu.edu
Financial aid: (806) 742-3681
Application deadline: 06/01
In-state tuition: full time: $253/
credit hour; part time: $253/
credit hour
Out-of-state tuition: full time: $604/
credit hour

Room/board/expenses: $15,102
Full-time enrollment: 543
men: 79%; women: 21%; minorities: 9%; international: 67%
Part-time enrollment: 182
men: 83%; women: 17%; minorities: 22%; international: 27%
Acceptance rate: 33%
GRE requirement: Yes
Avg. GRE: quantitative: 158
TOEFL requirement: Yes
Minimum TOEFL score: 550
Fellowships: 13
Teaching assistantships: 116
Research assistantships: 171
Students specializing in: biomedical: 1%; chemical: 8%; civil: 10%; computer science: 13%; electrical: 23%; environmental: 1%; industrial: 5%; mechanical: 17%; petroleum: 10%; other: 13%

University of Houston (Cullen)

E421 Engineering Building 2
Houston, TX 77204-4007
http://www.egr.uh.edu
Public
Admissions: (713) 743-4200
E-mail: grad-admit@egr.uh.edu
Financial aid: (713) 743-9090
Application deadline: 02/01
In-state tuition: full time: $478/credit hour; part time: $478/credit hour
Out-of-state tuition: full time: $829/credit hour
Room/board/expenses: $14,856
Full-time enrollment: 845
men: 71%; women: 29%; minorities: 8%; international: 83%
Part-time enrollment: 225
men: 73%; women: 27%; minorities: 41%; international: 25%
Acceptance rate: 44%
GRE requirement: Yes
Avg. GRE: quantitative: 161
TOEFL requirement: Yes
Minimum TOEFL score: 550
Fellowships: 532
Teaching assistantships: 31
Research assistantships: 311
Students specializing in: aerospace: 0%; biomedical: 2%; chemical: 11%; civil: 11%; computer: 0%; computer science: 24%; electrical: 20%; environmental: 3%; industrial: 5%; materials: 2%; mechanical: 11%; petroleum: 9%

University of North Texas

1155 Union Circle, #310440
Denton, TX 76203-5017
http://tsgs.unt.edu/overview
Public
Admissions: (940) 565-2383
E-mail: gradsch@unt.edu
Financial aid: (940) 565-2302
Application deadline: 07/15
In-state tuition: full time: $217/credit hour; part time: $217/credit hour
Out-of-state tuition: full time: $568/credit hour
Room/board/expenses: $12,124
Full-time enrollment: 316
men: 76%; women: 24%; minorities: 7%; international: 84%
Part-time enrollment: 128
men: 83%; women: 17%; minorities: 25%; international: 49%
Acceptance rate: 48%
GRE requirement: Yes
Avg. GRE: quantitative: 157
TOEFL requirement: Yes
Minimum TOEFL score: 550
Fellowships: 10
Teaching assistantships: 45
Research assistantships: 97
Students specializing in: computer: 6%; computer science: 51%; electrical: 15%; materials: 22%; mechanical: 9%; other: 19%

University of Texas–Arlington

UTA Box 19019
Arlington, TX 76019
http://www.uta.edu/engineering/
Public
Admissions: (817) 272-2380
E-mail: graduate.school@uta.edu
Financial aid: (817) 272-3561
Application deadline: 06/15
In-state tuition: full time: $8,558; part time: N/A
Out-of-state tuition: full time: $14,876
Room/board/expenses: $13,106
Full-time enrollment: 927
men: 76%; women: 24%; minorities: 8%; international: 82%
Part-time enrollment: 549
men: 80%; women: 20%; minorities: 18%; international: 46%
Acceptance rate: 61%
GRE requirement: Yes
Avg. GRE: quantitative: N/A
TOEFL requirement: Yes
Minimum TOEFL score: 550
Fellowships: 93
Teaching assistantships: 118
Research assistantships: 170
Students specializing in: aerospace: 7%; biomedical: 10%; civil: 14%; computer: 3%; computer science: 19%; electrical: 19%; management: 2%; industrial: 9%; materials: 4%; mechanical: 13%

University of Texas–Austin (Cockrell)

301 E. Dean Keeton Street
Stop C2100
Austin, TX 78712-2100
http://www.engr.utexas.edu/
Public
Admissions: (512) 475-7391
E-mail: adgrd@utxdp.its.utexas.edu
Financial aid: (512) 475-6282
Application deadline: rolling
In-state tuition: full time: $9,564; part time: N/A
Out-of-state tuition: full time: $17,506
Room/board/expenses: $16,325
Full-time enrollment: 2,033
men: 80%; women: 20%; minorities: 12%; international: 54%
Part-time enrollment: 392
men: 84%; women: 16%; minorities: 25%; international: 24%
Acceptance rate: 19%
GRE requirement: Yes
Avg. GRE: quantitative: 162
TOEFL requirement: Yes
Minimum TOEFL score: 550
Fellowships: 633
Teaching assistantships: 470
Research assistantships: 994
Students specializing in: aerospace: 6%; architectural: 0%; biomedical: 4%; chemical: 8%; civil: 16%; computer: 14%; computer science: 10%; electrical: 15%; management: 3%; environmental: 2%; industrial: 3%; materials: 3%; mechanical: 10%; petroleum: 7%

University of Texas–Dallas (Jonsson)

800 W. Campbell Road
Mail Station EC32
Richardson, TX 75080-3021
http://www.utdallas.edu
Public
Admissions: (972) 883-2270
E-mail: interest@utdallas.edu
Financial aid: (972) 883-2941
Application deadline: 07/01
In-state tuition: full time: $11,940; part time: N/A
Out-of-state tuition: full time: $21,606
Room/board/expenses: $13,900
Full-time enrollment: 1,350
men: 77%; women: 23%; minorities: 5%; international: 86%
Part-time enrollment: 459
men: 78%; women: 22%; minorities: 19%; international: 56%
Acceptance rate: 51%
GRE requirement: Yes
Avg. GRE: quantitative: N/A
TOEFL requirement: Yes
Minimum TOEFL score: 550
Fellowships: 23
Teaching assistantships: 110
Research assistantships: 248
Students specializing in: biomedical: 2%; computer: 3%; computer science: 40%; electrical: 39%; management: 3%; materials: 4%; mechanical: 2%; other: 5%

University of Texas–El Paso

500 W. University Avenue
El Paso, TX 79968
http://www.utep.edu/graduate
Public
Admissions: (915) 747-5491
E-mail: gradschool@utep.edu
Financial aid: (915) 747-5204
Application deadline: rolling
In-state tuition: full time: N/A; part time: N/A
Out-of-state tuition: full time: N/A
Room/board/expenses: N/A
Full-time enrollment: 306
men: 75%; women: 25%; minorities: 43%; international: 49%
Part-time enrollment: 242
men: 74%; women: 26%; minorities: 52%; international: 38%
Acceptance rate: 79%
GRE requirement: Yes
Avg. GRE: quantitative: 157
TOEFL requirement: Yes
Minimum TOEFL score: 550
Students specializing in: civil: 18%; computer: 1%; computer science: 13%; electrical: 17%; environmental: 11%; industrial: 19%; materials: 9%; mechanical: 9%; other: 4%

University of Texas–San Antonio

1 UTSA Circle
San Antonio, TX 78249-0665
http://www.graduateschool.utsa.edu
Public
Admissions: (210) 458-4330
E-mail: gradstudies@utsa.edu
Financial aid: (210) 458-8000
Application deadline: 02/01
In-state tuition: full time: $260/credit hour; part time: $260/credit hour
Out-of-state tuition: full time: $962/credit hour
Room/board/expenses: $13,695
Full-time enrollment: 314
men: 76%; women: 24%; minorities: 15%; international: 74%
Part-time enrollment: 248
men: 81%; women: 19%; minorities: 29%; international: 27%
Acceptance rate: 72%
GRE requirement: Yes
Avg. GRE: quantitative: 157
TOEFL requirement: Yes
Minimum TOEFL score: 550
Fellowships: 75
Teaching assistantships: 65
Research assistantships: 70
Students specializing in: biomedical: 10%; civil: 9%; computer: 4%; computer science: 30%; electrical: 29%; environmental: 5%; mechanical: 13%

UTAH

Brigham Young University (Fulton)

270 CB
Provo, UT 84602
http://www.byu.edu/gradstudies
Private
Admissions: (801) 422-4091
E-mail: gradstudies@byu.edu
Financial aid: (801) 422-4104
Application deadline: N/A
Tuition: full time: $8,925; part time: $331/credit hour
Room/board/expenses: $14,265
Full-time enrollment: 375
men: 91%; women: 9%; minorities: 6%; international: 19%
Part-time enrollment: N/A
men: N/A; women: N/A; minorities: N/A; international: N/A
Acceptance rate: 66%
GRE requirement: Yes
Avg. GRE: quantitative: 162
TOEFL requirement: Yes
Minimum TOEFL score: 580
Fellowships: 19
Teaching assistantships: 237
Research assistantships: 534
Students specializing in: chemical: 11%; civil: 19%; computer science: 23%; electrical: 20%; mechanical: 26%

University of Utah

72 S. Central Campus Drive
1650 WEB
Salt Lake City, UT 84112-9200
http://www.utah.edu
Public
Admissions: (801) 581-7281
E-mail: admissions@sa.utah.edu
Financial aid: (801) 581-6211
Application deadline: 04/01
In-state tuition: full time: $6,455; part time: $3,558
Out-of-state tuition: full time: $16,945
Room/board/expenses: $15,516
Full-time enrollment: 790
men: 82%; women: 18%; minorities: 6%; international: 48%
Part-time enrollment: 283
men: 87%; women: 13%; minorities: 9%; international: 22%
Acceptance rate: 37%
GRE requirement: Yes
Avg. GRE: quantitative: 161
TOEFL requirement: Yes
Minimum TOEFL score: 500
Fellowships: 75
Teaching assistantships: 138
Research assistantships: 491
Students specializing in: biomedical: 14%; chemical: 7%; civil: 11%; computer science: 24%; electrical: 14%; materials: 3%; mechanical: 19%; mining: 1%; nuclear: 2%; other: 5%

Utah State University

4100 Old Main Hill
Logan, UT 84322-4100
http://www.engineering.usu.edu/
Public
Admissions: (435) 797-1189
E-mail: grad.admissions@aggiemail.usu.edu
Financial aid: (435) 797-0173
Application deadline: rolling
In-state tuition: full time: $6,624; part time: $5,016
Out-of-state tuition: full time: $17,771
Room/board/expenses: $9,200
Full-time enrollment: 192
men: 86%; women: 14%; minorities: 5%; international: 47%
Part-time enrollment: 221
men: 84%; women: 16%; minorities: 3%; international: 48%
GRE requirement: Yes
Avg. GRE: quantitative: 156
TOEFL requirement: Yes
Minimum TOEFL score: 550
Students specializing in: aerospace: 3%; agriculture: 8%; civil: 29%; computer: 2%; computer science: 21%; electrical: 19%; mechanical: 15%; other: 2%

VERMONT

University of Vermont

109 Votey Hall
Burlington, VT 05405
http://www.cems.uvm.edu
Public
Admissions: (802) 656-2699
E-mail: graduate.admissions@uvm.edu
Financial aid: (802) 656-1194
Application deadline: N/A
In-state tuition: full time: $556/credit hour; part time: $556/credit hour
Out-of-state tuition: full time: $1,403/credit hour
Room/board/expenses: $12,786
Full-time enrollment: 87
men: 80%; women: 20%; minorities: 2%; international: 30%
Part-time enrollment: 46
men: 83%; women: 17%; minorities: 7%; international: 11%
Acceptance rate: 40%
GRE requirement: Yes
Avg. GRE: quantitative: 160
TOEFL requirement: Yes
Minimum TOEFL score: 550
Fellowships: 37
Research assistantships: 59
Students specializing in: biomedical: 6%; civil: 23%; computer science: 20%; electrical: 18%; materials: 6%; mechanical: 27%

VIRGINIA

George Mason University (Volgenau)

4400 University Drive, MS4A3
Fairfax, VA 22030-4444
http://volgenau.gmu.edu/
Public
Admissions: (703) 993-1512
E-mail: vsegadm@gmu.edu
Financial aid: (703) 993-2353
Application deadline: 01/15
In-state tuition: full time: $14,090; part time: $587/credit hour
Out-of-state tuition: full time: $27,620
Room/board/expenses: $23,344
Full-time enrollment: 588
men: 74%; women: 26%; minorities: 15%; international: 62%
Part-time enrollment: 1,009
men: 77%; women: 23%; minorities: 29%; international: 11%
Acceptance rate: 59%
GRE requirement: Yes
Avg. GRE: quantitative: 155
TOEFL requirement: Yes
Minimum TOEFL score: 575
Fellowships: 19
Teaching assistantships: 149
Research assistantships: 102
Students specializing in: civil: 5%; computer: 3%; computer science: 43%; electrical: 24%; industrial: 11%; other: 14%

Old Dominion University

102 Kaufman Hall
Norfolk, VA 23529
http://www.admissions.odu.edu
Public
Admissions: (757) 683-3685
E-mail: gradadmit@odu.edu

More at www.usnews.com/grad

Financial aid: (757) 683-3689
Application deadline: 06/01
In-state tuition: full time: $393/credit hour; part time: $393/credit hour
Out-of-state tuition: full time: $997/credit hour
Room/board/expenses: $12,456
Full-time enrollment: 211
men: 75%; women: 25%; minorities: 12%; international: 53%
Part-time enrollment: 586
men: 82%; women: 18%; minorities: 18%; international: 9%
Acceptance rate: 73%
GRE requirement: Yes
Avg. GRE: quantitative: 157
TOEFL requirement: Yes
Minimum TOEFL score: 550
Fellowships: 8
Teaching assistantships: 70
Research assistantships: 71
Students specializing in: aerospace: 8%; biomedical: 1%; civil: 9%; computer: 5%; electrical: 6%; management: 56%; environmental: 9%; mechanical: 8%; other: 9%

University of Virginia

Thornton Hall
Charlottesville, VA 22904-4246
http://www.seas.virginia.edu/
Public
Admissions: (434) 924-3897
E-mail: seas-grad-admission@virginia.edu
Financial aid: (434) 924-3897
Application deadline: 08/01
In-state tuition: full time: $16,892; part time: $717/credit hour
Out-of-state tuition: full time: $26,216
Room/board/expenses: $20,211
Full-time enrollment: 604
men: 77%; women: 23%; minorities: 10%; international: 42%
Part-time enrollment: 63
men: 81%; women: 19%; minorities: 17%; international: 3%
Acceptance rate: 17%
GRE requirement: Yes
Avg. GRE: quantitative: 162
TOEFL requirement: Yes
Minimum TOEFL score: 600
Fellowships: 431
Teaching assistantships: 90
Research assistantships: 419
Students specializing in: biomedical: 9%; chemical: 8%; civil: 8%; computer: 4%; computer science: 10%; electrical: 16%; science and physics: 3%; materials: 9%; mechanical: 14%; other: 18%

Virginia Commonwealth University

PO Box 843068
Richmond, VA 23284-3068
http://www.egr.vcu.edu/
Public
Admissions: (804) 828-1087
E-mail: josephl@vcu.edu
Financial aid: (804) 828-3925
Application deadline: 06/01
In-state tuition: full time: $10,466; part time: $437/credit hour
Out-of-state tuition: full time: $19,365

Room/board/expenses: $15,118
Full-time enrollment: 157
men: 73%; women: 27%; minorities: 20%; international: 47%
Part-time enrollment: 85
men: 79%; women: 21%; minorities: 25%; international: 25%
Acceptance rate: 63%
GRE requirement: Yes
Avg. GRE: quantitative: 156
TOEFL requirement: Yes
Minimum TOEFL score: 550
Fellowships: 5
Teaching assistantships: 44
Research assistantships: 69
Students specializing in: biomedical: 24%; chemical: 11%; computer science: 24%; electrical: 18%; mechanical: 21%; nuclear: 2%

Virginia Tech

3046 Torgersen Hall
Blacksburg, VA 24061-0217
http://www.grads.vt.edu
Public
Admissions: (540) 231-8636
E-mail: gradappl@vt.edu
Financial aid: (540) 231-5179
Application deadline: 08/01
In-state tuition: full time: $13,017; part time: $593/credit hour
Out-of-state tuition: full time: $23,266
Room/board/expenses: $15,490
Full-time enrollment: 1,941
men: 78%; women: 22%; minorities: 15%; international: 44%
Part-time enrollment: 337
men: 77%; women: 23%; minorities: 20%; international: 25%
Acceptance rate: 25%
GRE requirement: Yes
Avg. GRE: quantitative: 160
TOEFL requirement: Yes
Minimum TOEFL score: 565
Fellowships: 168
Teaching assistantships: 326
Research assistantships: 828
Students specializing in: aerospace: 5%; agriculture: 2%; biomedical: 5%; chemical: 2%; civil: 16%; computer: 7%; computer science: 12%; electrical: 17%; science and physics: 5%; industrial: 11%; materials: 3%; mechanical: 13%; mining: 1%; other: 1%

University of Washington

371 Loew Hall, Box 352180
Seattle, WA 98195-2180
http://www.engr.washington.edu
Public
Admissions: (206) 685-2630
E-mail: uwgrad@uw.edu
Financial aid: (206) 543-6101
Application deadline: 12/01
In-state tuition: full time: $14,986; part time: $664/credit hour
Out-of-state tuition: full time: $27,846
Room/board/expenses: $18,579
Full-time enrollment: 1,225
men: 71%; women: 29%; minorities: 15%; international: 38%

Part-time enrollment: 805
men: 75%; women: 25%; minorities: 27%; international: 11%
Acceptance rate: 18%
GRE requirement: Yes
Avg. GRE: quantitative: 162
TOEFL requirement: Yes
Minimum TOEFL score: 500
Fellowships: 182
Teaching assistantships: 194
Research assistantships: 630
Students specializing in: aerospace: 10%; biomedical: 9%; chemical: 4%; civil: 15%; computer: 16%; electrical: 17%; industrial: 3%; materials: 3%; mechanical: 13%; other: 11%

Washington State University

PO Box 642714
Pullman, WA 99164-2714
http://www.cea.wsu.edu
Public
Admissions: (509) 335-1446
E-mail: gradsch@wsu.edu
Financial aid: (509) 335-9711
Application deadline: 01/10
In-state tuition: full time: $12,600; part time: $587/credit hour
Out-of-state tuition: full time: $26,032
Room/board/expenses: $15,536
Full-time enrollment: 462
men: 71%; women: 29%; minorities: 5%; international: 63%
Part-time enrollment: 212
men: 74%; women: 26%; minorities: 18%; international: 18%
Acceptance rate: 30%
GRE requirement: Yes
Avg. GRE: quantitative: 159
TOEFL requirement: Yes
Minimum TOEFL score: 550
Fellowships: 36
Teaching assistantships: 96
Research assistantships: 229
Students specializing in: agriculture: 11%; chemical: 10%; civil: 12%; computer: 1%; computer science: 12%; electrical: 15%; management: 13%; environmental: 4%; materials: 9%; mechanical: 13%

West Virginia University

PO Box 6070
Morgantown, WV 26506-6070
http://www.cemr.wvu.edu
Public
Admissions: (304) 293-4821
E-mail: info@cemr.wvu.edu
Financial aid: (304) 293-5242
Application deadline: 08/01
In-state tuition: full time: $7,804; part time: $433/credit hour
Out-of-state tuition: full time: $21,054
Room/board/expenses: $11,022
Full-time enrollment: 526
men: 78%; women: 22%; minorities: 6%; international: 59%
Part-time enrollment: 178
men: 83%; women: 17%; minorities: 7%; international: 30%
Acceptance rate: 48%
GRE requirement: Yes
Avg. GRE: quantitative: N/A
TOEFL requirement: Yes

Minimum TOEFL score: 550
Fellowships: 9
Teaching assistantships: 99
Research assistantships: 292
Students specializing in: aerospace: 4%; chemical: 5%; civil: 10%; computer: 1%; computer science: 13%; electrical: 16%; industrial: 7%; mechanical: 18%; mining: 4%; petroleum: 5%; other: 17%

Marquette University

PO Box 1881
Milwaukee, WI 53201-1881
http://www.grad.marquette.edu
Private
Admissions: (414) 288-7137
E-mail: mugs@mu.edu
Financial aid: (414) 288-5325
Application deadline: rolling
Tuition: full time: $985/credit hour; part time: $985/credit hour
Room/board/expenses: $16,206
Full-time enrollment: 112
men: 81%; women: 19%; minorities: 9%; international: 46%
Part-time enrollment: 81
men: 85%; women: 15%; minorities: 12%; international: 20%
Acceptance rate: 45%
GRE requirement: Yes
Avg. GRE: quantitative: 158
TOEFL requirement: Yes
Minimum TOEFL score: 590
Students specializing in: biomedical: 24%; civil: 18%; electrical: 27%; management: 5%; mechanical: 21%; other: 4%

University of Wisconsin–Madison

2610 Engineering Hall
Madison, WI 53706
http://www.engr.wisc.edu/
Public
Admissions: (608) 262-2433
E-mail: gradadmiss@bascom.wisc.edu
Financial aid: (608) 262-3060
Application deadline: N/A
In-state tuition: full time: $12,950; part time: $743/credit hour
Out-of-state tuition: full time: $26,277
Room/board/expenses: $16,610
Full-time enrollment: 1,546
men: 79%; women: 21%; minorities: 9%; international: 52%
Part-time enrollment: 357
men: 86%; women: 14%; minorities: 9%; international: 26%
Acceptance rate: 16%
GRE requirement: Yes
Avg. GRE: quantitative: 162
TOEFL requirement: Yes
Minimum TOEFL score: 550
Fellowships: 57
Teaching assistantships: 220
Research assistantships: 880
Students specializing in: biomedical: 6%; chemical: 7%; civil: 8%; computer science: 16%; electrical: 21%; industrial: 9%; materials: 6%; mechanical: 11%; nuclear: 6%; other: 9%

University of Wisconsin–Milwaukee

PO Box 784
Milwaukee, WI 53201-0784
http://www.uwm.edu/CEAS
Public
Admissions: (414) 229-6169
E-mail: bwarras@uwm.edu
Financial aid: (414) 229-4541
Application deadline: rolling
In-state tuition: full time: $11,482; part time: $978/credit hour
Out-of-state tuition: full time: $23,948
Room/board/expenses: $12,404
Full-time enrollment: 308
men: 72%; women: 28%; minorities: 6%; international: 74%
Part-time enrollment: 85
men: 92%; women: 8%; minorities: 27%; international: 0%
Acceptance rate: 61%
GRE requirement: Yes
Avg. GRE: quantitative: N/A
TOEFL requirement: Yes
Minimum TOEFL score: 550
Fellowships: 150
Teaching assistantships: 96
Research assistantships: 63
Students specializing in: civil: 17%; computer science: 23%; electrical: 22%; industrial: 9%; materials: 5%; mechanical: 23%

University of Wyoming

1000 E. University Avenue
Department 3295
Laramie, WY 82071
http://wwweng.uwyo.edu
Public
Admissions: (307) 766-5160
E-mail: why-wyo@uwyo.edu
Financial aid: (307) 766-2116
Application deadline: rolling
In-state tuition: full time: $206/credit hour; part time: $206/credit hour
Out-of-state tuition: full time: $602/credit hour
Room/board/expenses: $15,250
Full-time enrollment: 170
men: 74%; women: 26%; minorities: 0%; international: 50%
Part-time enrollment: 58
men: 78%; women: 22%; minorities: 0%; international: 57%
Acceptance rate: 48%
GRE requirement: Yes
Avg. GRE: quantitative: 159
TOEFL requirement: Yes
Minimum TOEFL score: 550
Fellowships: 0
Teaching assistantships: 44
Research assistantships: 137
Students specializing in: chemical: 12%; civil: 14%; computer science: 14%; electrical: 14%; environmental: 3%; mechanical: 19%; petroleum: 13%; other: 11%

LAW

The law directory lists the 200 schools in the country offering the J.D. degree that were fully or provisionally accredited by the American Bar Association in August 2012. One hundred ninety-four schools responded to the *U.S. News* survey conducted in the fall of 2012 and early 2013, and their data are reported here. Nonresponders have abbreviated entries.

KEY TO THE TERMINOLOGY

1. A school whose name is footnoted with the numeral 1 did not return the *U.S. News* statistical survey; limited data appear in its entry.

N/A. Not available from the school or not applicable.

Admissions. The admissions office phone number.

E-mail. The address of the admissions office. If instead of an E-mail address a website is listed, the website will automatically present an E-mail screen programmed to reach the admissions office.

Financial aid. The financial aid office phone number.

Application deadline. For fall 2014 enrollment. "Rolling" means there is no deadline; the school acts on applications as they are received. "Varies" means deadlines vary according to department or whether applicants are U.S. citizens or foreign nationals.

Tuition. For the 2012-13 academic year. Includes fees.

Credit hour. The cost per credit hour for the 2012-13 academic year.

Room/board/expenses. For the 2012-13 academic year.

Median grant. The median value of grants to full-time students enrolled in 2012-13. This is calculated for all full-time students (not just those in the first year) who received grants and scholarships from internal sources.

Average law school indebtedness. For 2012 graduates, the average law school debt for those taking out at least one educational loan while in school.

Enrollment. Full and part time, fall 2012. Gender figure is for full and part time.

Minorities. For fall 2012, the percentage of full-time and part-time U.S. students who are black or African-American, Asian, American Indian or Alaskan Native, Native Hawaiian or other Pacific Islander, Hispanic/Latino, or two or more races.

Acceptance rate. Percentage of applicants who were accepted for the fall 2012 full-time J.D. program.

Midrange Law School Admission Test (LSAT) score. For full-time students who entered in fall 2012. The first number is the 25th percentile test score for the class; the second, the 75th percentile.

Midrange undergraduate grade point average. For full-time students who entered in fall 2012. The first number is the 25th percentile GPA for the class; the second is the 75th percentile.

Midrange of full-time private sector starting salaries. For the 2011 graduating class, the starting salary is for those employed full time in the private sector in law firms, business, industry, or other jobs. The first number is the starting salary at the 25th percentile of the graduating class; the second number is the starting salary at the 75th percentile. When a school has the same salary at the 25th and 75th percentiles, it means that the starting salaries for private sector jobs were the same for a large proportion of the class.

Job classifications. For the 2011 graduating class, represents the breakdown for the following types of employment: in law firms, business and industry (legal and nonlegal), government, public interest, judicial clerkship, academia, and unknown. Numbers may not add up to 100 percent because of rounding.

Employment locations. For the 2011 graduating class. Abbreviations: **Intl.**, international; **N.E.**, New England (Conn., Maine, Mass., N.H., R.I., Vt.); **M.A.**, Middle Atlantic (N.J., N.Y., Pa.); **S.A.**, South Atlantic (Del., D.C., Fla., Ga., Md., N.C., S.C., Va., W.Va.); **E.N.C.**, East North Central (Ill., Ind., Mich., Ohio, Wis.); **W.N.C.**, West North Central (Iowa, Kan., Minn., Mo., Neb., N.D., S.D.); **E.S.C.**, East South Central (Ala., Ky., Miss., Tenn.); **W.S.C.**, West South Central (Ark., La., Okla., Texas); **Mt.**, Mountain (Ariz., Colo., Idaho, Mont., Nev., N.M., Utah, Wyo.); **Pac.**, Pacific (Alaska, Calif., Hawaii, Ore., Wash.).

ALABAMA

Faulkner University (Jones)
5345 Atlanta Highway
Montgomery, AL 36109
http://www.faulkner.edu/law
Private
Admissions: (334) 386-7210
E-mail: law@faulkner.edu
Financial aid: (334) 386-7197
Application deadline: 06/15
Tuition: full time: N/A; part time: N/A
Room/board/expenses: N/A
Median grant: $16,500
Average student indebtedness at graduation: $107,330
Enrollment: full time: 314; part time: N/A
men: 55%; women: 45%; minorities: 18%
Acceptance rate (full time): 62%
Midrange LSAT (full time): 145-150
Midrange undergraduate GPA (full time): 2.69-3.34
Midrange of full-time private-sector salaries of 2011 grads: $37,500-$53,750
2011 grads employed in: law firms: 61%; business and industry: 18%; government: 17%; public interest: 1%; judicial clerk: 3%; academia: 0%; unknown: 0%
Employment location for 2011 class: Intl. 0%; N.E. 0%; M.A. 1%; E.N.C. 0%; W.N.C. 0%; S.A. 20%; E.S.C. 75%; W.S.C. 2%; Mt. 1%; Pac. N/A; unknown 0%

Samford University (Cumberland)
800 Lakeshore Drive
Birmingham, AL 35229
http://cumberland.samford.edu
Private
Admissions: (205) 726-2702
E-mail: law.admissions@samford.edu
Financial aid: (205) 726-2905
Application deadline: 03/15
Tuition: full time: $36,216; part time: $21,367
Room/board/expenses: $21,934
Median grant: $15,000
Average student indebtedness at graduation: $126,202
Enrollment: full time: 421; part time: N/A
men: 57%; women: 43%; minorities: 14%
Acceptance rate (full time): 41%
Midrange LSAT (full time): 151-158
Midrange undergraduate GPA (full time): 3.09-3.57
Midrange of full-time private-sector salaries of 2011 grads: $45,000-$85,000
2011 grads employed in: law firms: 71%; business and industry: 14%; government: 5%; public interest: 3%; judicial clerk: 6%; academia: 1%; unknown: 1%
Employment location for 2011 class: Intl. 0%; N.E. 0%; M.A. 0%; E.N.C. 0%; W.N.C. 0%; S.A. 19%; E.S.C. 76%; W.S.C. 3%; Mt. 2%; Pac. 1%; unknown 0%

University of Alabama
Box 870382
Tuscaloosa, AL 35487
http://www.law.ua.edu
Public
Admissions: (205) 348-5440
E-mail: admissions@law.ua.edu
Financial aid: (205) 348-6756
Application deadline: rolling
In-state tuition: full time: $19,660; part time: N/A
Out-of-state tuition: full time: $32,920
Room/board/expenses: $18,552
Median grant: $14,250
Average student indebtedness at graduation: $67,611
Enrollment: full time: 487; part time: N/A
men: 60%; women: 40%; minorities: 14%
Acceptance rate (full time): 25%
Midrange LSAT (full time): 158-167
Midrange undergraduate GPA (full time): 3.31-3.94
Midrange of full-time private-sector salaries of 2011 grads: $56,000-$105,000
2011 grads employed in: law firms: 49%; business and industry: 16%; government: 11%; public interest: 8%; judicial clerk: 14%; academia: 3%; unknown: 0%
Employment location for 2011 class: Intl. 1%; N.E. 1%; M.A. 1%; E.N.C. 2%; W.N.C. 1%; S.A. 20%; E.S.C. 70%; W.S.C. 3%; Mt. 1%; Pac. 1%; unknown 0%

ARIZONA

Arizona State University (O'Connor)
1100 S. McAllister Avenue
Tempe, AZ 85287-7906
http://www.law.asu.edu
Public
Admissions: (480) 965-1474
E-mail: law.admissions@asu.edu
Financial aid: (480) 965-1474
Application deadline: 02/01
In-state tuition: full time: $26,267; part time: N/A
Out-of-state tuition: full time: $40,815
Room/board/expenses: $21,388
Median grant: $10,000
Average student indebtedness at graduation: $101,560
Enrollment: full time: 577; part time: N/A
men: 59%; women: 41%; minorities: 23%
Acceptance rate (full time): 34%
Midrange LSAT (full time): 161-165
Midrange undergraduate GPA (full time): 3.30-3.82
Midrange of full-time private-sector salaries of 2011 grads: $125,000-$125,000
2011 grads employed in: law firms: 46%; business and industry: 16%; government: 22%; public interest: 6%; judicial clerk: 9%; academia: 1%; unknown: 0%
Employment location for 2011 class: Intl. 1%; N.E. 0%; M.A. 1%; E.N.C. 1%; W.N.C. 1%; S.A. 3%; E.S.C. 0%; W.S.C. 0%; Mt. 87%; Pac. 7%; unknown 1%

Phoenix School of Law

One North Central Avenue
Phoenix, AZ 85004
http://www.phoenixlaw.edu
Private
Admissions: (602) 682-6800
E-mail: admissions@
phoenixlaw.edu
Financial aid: (602) 682-6800
Application deadline: rolling
Tuition: full time: $39,533; part
time: $31,984
Room/board/expenses: $21,984
Median grant: $6,000
**Average student indebtedness at
graduation:** $162,627
Enrollment: full time: 745; part
time: 347
men: 51%; women: 49%;
minorities: 37%
Acceptance rate (full time): 86%
Midrange LSAT (full time): 142-150
**Midrange undergraduate GPA (full
time):** 2.53-3.30
**Midrange of full-time private-sector
salaries of 2011 grads:** $44,750-
$73,750
2011 grads employed in: law firms:
48%; business and industry: 15%;
government: 7%; public interest:
20%; judicial clerk: 1%; academia:
7%; unknown: 2%
Employment location for 2011 class:
Intl. 0%; N.E. 1%; M.A. 0%; E.N.C.
2%; W.N.C. 0%; S.A. 2%; E.S.C.
0%; W.S.C. 0%; Mt. 87%; Pac.
3%; unknown 5%

University of Arizona (Rogers)

PO Box 210176
Tucson, AZ 85721-0176
http://www.law.arizona.edu
Public
Admissions: (520) 621-9949
E-mail:
admissions@law.arizona.edu
Financial aid: (520) 621-9949
Application deadline: 02/15
In-state tuition: full time: $27,288;
part time: N/A
Out-of-state tuition: full time:
$42,298
Room/board/expenses: $23,023
Median grant: $12,000
**Average student indebtedness at
graduation:** $88,052
Enrollment: full time: 407; part
time: N/A
men: 57%; women: 43%;
minorities: 22%
Acceptance rate (full time): 40%
Midrange LSAT (full time): 159-162
**Midrange undergraduate GPA (full
time):** 3.28-3.79
**Midrange of full-time private-sector
salaries of 2011 grads:** $61,000-
$95,000
2011 grads employed in: law firms:
46%; business and industry: 10%;
government: 13%; public interest:
11%; judicial clerk: 18%; academia:
1%; unknown: 0%
Employment location for 2011 class:
Intl. 1%; N.E. 0%; M.A. 0%; E.N.C.
2%; W.N.C. 0%; S.A. 6%; E.S.C.
0%; W.S.C. 0%; Mt. 80%; Pac.
12%; unknown 0%

University of Arkansas–Fayetteville

Robert A. Leflar Law Center
Fayetteville, AR 72701
http://law.uark.edu/
Public
Admissions: (479) 575-3102
E-mail: jkmiller@uark.edu
Financial aid: (479) 575-3806

Application deadline: 04/01
In-state tuition: full time: $417/
credit hour; part time: N/A
Out-of-state tuition: full time: $855/
credit hour
Room/board/expenses: $17,492
Median grant: $6,125
**Average student indebtedness at
graduation:** $59,384
Enrollment: full time: 391; part
time: N/A
men: 61%; women: 39%;
minorities: 17%
Acceptance rate (full time): 37%
Midrange LSAT (full time): 153-158
**Midrange undergraduate GPA (full
time):** 3.25-3.74
**Midrange of full-time private-sector
salaries of 2011 grads:** $65,000-
$85,000
2011 grads employed in: law firms:
56%; business and industry: 21%;
government: 10%; public interest:
5%; judicial clerk: 7%; academia:
1%; unknown: 0%
Employment location for 2011 class:
Intl. 0%; N.E. 0%; M.A. 2%; E.N.C.
1%; W.N.C. 6%; S.A. 6%; E.S.C.
4%; W.S.C. 77%; Mt. 4%; Pac. 0%;
unknown 0%

University of Arkansas–Little Rock (Bowen)

1201 McMath Avenue
Little Rock, AR 72202-5142
http://www.law.ualr.edu/
Public
Admissions: (501) 324-9439
E-mail: lawadm@ualr.edu
Financial aid: (501) 569-3035
Application deadline: 04/15
In-state tuition: full time: $12,701;
part time: $8,867
Out-of-state tuition: full time:
$25,838
Room/board/expenses: $15,585
Median grant: $7,050
**Average student indebtedness at
graduation:** $64,207
Enrollment: full time: 296; part
time: 155
men: 57%; women: 43%;
minorities: 18%
Acceptance rate (full time): 32%
Midrange LSAT (full time): 150-157
**Midrange undergraduate GPA (full
time):** 2.95-3.54
**Midrange of full-time private-sector
salaries of 2011 grads:** $45,000-
$65,000
2011 grads employed in: law firms:
57%; business and industry: 27%;
government: 7%; public interest:
5%; judicial clerk: 3%; academia:
1%; unknown: 1%
Employment location for 2011 class:
Intl. 1%; N.E. 0%; M.A. 1%; E.N.C.
2%; W.N.C. 2%; S.A. 6%; E.S.C.
2%; W.S.C. 83%; Mt. 2%; Pac. 1%;
unknown 0%

California Western School of Law

225 Cedar Street
San Diego, CA 92101-3090
http://www.cwsl.edu
Private
Admissions: (619) 525-1401
E-mail: admissions@cwsl.edu
Financial aid: (619) 525-7060
Application deadline: 04/01
Tuition: full time: $43,700; part
time: $30,700
Room/board/expenses: $24,042
Median grant: $15,975

**Average student indebtedness at
graduation:** $167,867
Enrollment: full time: 629; part
time: 150
men: 46%; women: 54%;
minorities: 35%
Acceptance rate (full time): 69%
Midrange LSAT (full time): 148-155
**Midrange undergraduate GPA (full
time):** 2.89-3.45
**Midrange of full-time private-sector
salaries of 2011 grads:** $48,000-
$75,000
2011 grads employed in: law firms:
71%; business and industry: 10%;
government: 6%; public interest:
6%; judicial clerk: 3%; academia:
1%; unknown: 2%
Employment location for 2011 class:
Intl. 2%; N.E. 0%; M.A. 2%; E.N.C.
2%; W.N.C. 1%; S.A. 2%; E.S.C.
0%; W.S.C. 1%; Mt. 8%; Pac. 76%;
unknown 6%

Chapman University

1 University Drive
Orange, CA 92866
http://www.chapman.edu/law
Private
Admissions: (714) 628-2500
E-mail: lawadm@chapman.edu
Financial aid: (714) 628-2510
Application deadline: 04/15
Tuition: full time: $43,536; part
time: $34,586
Room/board/expenses: $31,235
Median grant: $37,314
**Average student indebtedness at
graduation:** $133,711
Enrollment: full time: 480; part
time: 28
men: 51%; women: 49%;
minorities: 31%
Acceptance rate (full time): 44%
Midrange LSAT (full time): 154-160
**Midrange undergraduate GPA (full
time):** 3.20-3.60
**Midrange of full-time private-sector
salaries of 2011 grads:** $52,000-
$75,000
2011 grads employed in: law firms:
57%; business and industry: 24%;
government: 8%; public interest:
1%; judicial clerk: 2%; academia:
7%; unknown: 1%
Employment location for 2011 class:
Intl. 2%; N.E. 0%; M.A. 1%; E.N.C.
1%; W.N.C. 1%; S.A. 1%; E.S.C.
0%; W.S.C. 1%; Mt. 1%; Pac. 92%;
unknown 0%

Golden Gate University

536 Mission Street
San Francisco, CA 94105
http://www.law.ggu.edu
Private
Admissions: (415) 442-6630
E-mail: lawadmit@ggu.edu
Financial aid: (415) 442-6635
Application deadline: 04/01
Tuition: full time: $42,010; part
time: $32,280
Room/board/expenses: $27,350
Median grant: $12,020
**Average student indebtedness at
graduation:** $137,484
Enrollment: full time: 543; part
time: 127
men: 46%; women: 54%;
minorities: 35%
Acceptance rate (full time): 73%
Midrange LSAT (full time): 149-154
**Midrange undergraduate GPA (full
time):** 2.79-3.37
**Midrange of full-time private-sector
salaries of 2011 grads:** $42,500-
$76,500

2011 grads employed in: law firms:
45%; business and industry: 21%;
government: 14%; public interest:
11%; judicial clerk: 2%; academia:
8%; unknown: 0%
Employment location for 2011 class:
Intl. 0%; N.E. 1%; M.A. 2%; E.N.C.
1%; W.N.C. 1%; S.A. 2%; E.S.C.
1%; W.S.C. 1%; Mt. 2%; Pac. 90%;
unknown 1%

Loyola Marymount University

919 Albany Street
Los Angeles, CA 90015-1211
http://www.lls.edu
Private
Admissions: (213) 736-1074
E-mail: Admissions@lls.edu
Financial aid: (213) 736-1140
Application deadline: 02/03
Tuition: full time: $44,230; part
time: $29,625
Room/board/expenses: $27,472
Median grant: $23,000
**Average student indebtedness at
graduation:** $141,936
Enrollment: full time: 1,011; part
time: 227
men: 48%; women: 52%;
minorities: 39%
Acceptance rate (full time): 39%
Midrange LSAT (full time): 158-162
**Midrange undergraduate GPA (full
time):** 3.32-3.65
**Midrange of full-time private-sector
salaries of 2011 grads:** $62,000-
$100,000
2011 grads employed in: law firms:
58%; business and industry: 20%;
government: 8%; public interest:
9%; judicial clerk: 3%; academia:
3%; unknown: 0%
Employment location for 2011 class:
Intl. 2%; N.E. 0%; M.A. 2%; E.N.C.
0%; W.N.C. 0%; S.A. 1%; E.S.C.
0%; W.S.C. 1%; Mt. 1%; Pac. 92%;
unknown 0%

Pepperdine University

24255 Pacific Coast Highway
Malibu, CA 90263
http://law.pepperdine.edu
Private
Admissions: (310) 506-4631
E-mail: soladmis@pepperdine.edu
Financial aid: (310) 506-4633
Application deadline: 01/02
Tuition: full time: $44,980; part
time: N/A
Room/board/expenses: $27,410
Median grant: $7,000
**Average student indebtedness at
graduation:** $128,669
Enrollment: full time: 618; part
time: N/A
men: 51%; women: 49%;
minorities: 26%
Acceptance rate (full time): 43%
Midrange LSAT (full time): 156-164
**Midrange undergraduate GPA (full
time):** 3.34-3.74
**Midrange of full-time private-sector
salaries of 2011 grads:** $60,000-
$95,000
2011 grads employed in: law firms:
58%; business and industry: 21%;
government: 5%; public interest:
2%; judicial clerk: 7%; academia:
7%; unknown: 1%
Employment location for 2011 class:
Intl. 1%; N.E. 1%; M.A. 2%; E.N.C.
1%; W.N.C. 1%; S.A. 2%; E.S.C.
2%; W.S.C. 6%; Mt. 4%; Pac. 81%;
unknown 0%

Santa Clara University

500 El Camino Real
Santa Clara, CA 95053-0421
http://www.scu.edu/law
Private
Admissions: (408) 554-4800
E-mail: lawadmissions@scu.edu
Financial aid: (408) 554-4447
Application deadline: 02/01
Tuition: full time: $1,456/credit
hour; part time: $1,456/credit hour
Room/board/expenses: $22,580
Median grant: $10,000
**Average student indebtedness at
graduation:** $129,621
Enrollment: full time: 693; part
time: 187
men: 53%; women: 47%;
minorities: 42%
Acceptance rate (full time): 53%
Midrange LSAT (full time): 156-160
**Midrange undergraduate GPA (full
time):** 3.00-3.45
**Midrange of full-time private-sector
salaries of 2011 grads:** $72,000-
$160,000
2011 grads employed in: law firms:
53%; business and industry: 30%;
government: 6%; public interest:
5%; judicial clerk: 1%; academia:
1%; unknown: 4%
Employment location for 2011 class:
Intl. 2%; N.E. 0%; M.A. 2%; E.N.C.
1%; W.N.C. 1%; S.A. 2%; E.S.C.
0%; W.S.C. 1%; Mt. 2%; Pac. 82%;
unknown 10%

Southwestern Law School

3050 Wilshire Boulevard
Los Angeles, CA 90010-1106
http://www.swlaw.edu
Private
Admissions: (213) 738-6717
E-mail: admissions@swlaw.edu
Financial aid: (213) 738-6719
Application deadline: 04/01
Tuition: full time: $43,850; part
time: $29,300
Room/board/expenses: $28,620
Median grant: $20,000
**Average student indebtedness at
graduation:** $147,976
Enrollment: full time: 691; part
time: 395
men: 47%; women: 53%;
minorities: 45%
Acceptance rate (full time): 44%
Midrange LSAT (full time): 152-156
**Midrange undergraduate GPA (full
time):** 3.09-3.52
**Midrange of full-time private-sector
salaries of 2011 grads:** $50,000-
$90,000
2011 grads employed in: law firms:
50%; business and industry: 36%;
government: 5%; public interest:
4%; judicial clerk: 1%; academia:
1%; unknown: 1%
Employment location for 2011 class:
Intl. 1%; N.E. 0%; M.A. 2%; E.N.C.
1%; W.N.C. 1%; S.A. 2%; E.S.C.
0%; W.S.C. 0%; Mt. 2%; Pac.
92%; unknown 0%

Stanford University

Crown Quadrangle
559 Nathan Abbott Way
Stanford, CA 94305-8610
http://www.law.stanford.edu/
Private
Admissions: (650) 723-4985
E-mail:
admissions@law.stanford.edu
Financial aid: (650) 723-9247
Application deadline: 02/03
Tuition: full time: $50,802; part
time: N/A
Room/board/expenses: $26,727

Median grant: $23,369
Average student indebtedness at graduation: $110,275
Enrollment: full time: 575; part time: N/A
men: 57%; women: 43%; minorities: 38%
Acceptance rate (full time): 10%
Midrange LSAT (full time): 168-173
Midrange undergraduate GPA (full time): 3.76-3.96
Midrange of full-time private-sector salaries of 2011 grads: $160,000-$160,000
2011 grads employed in: law firms: 53%; business and industry: 5%; government: 4%; public interest: 10%; judicial clerk: 26%; academia: 2%; unknown: 0%
Employment location for 2011 class: Intl. 1%; N.E. 2%; M.A. 17%; E.N.C. 8%; W.N.C. 1%; S.A. 18%; E.S.C. 1%; W.S.C. 2%; Mt. 6%; Pac. 45%; unknown 0%

Thomas Jefferson School of Law

1155 Island Avenue
San Diego, CA 92101
http://www.tjsl.edu
Private
Admissions: (619) 297-9700
E-mail: info@tjsl.edu
Financial aid: (619) 297-9700
Application deadline: rolling
Tuition: full time: $42,000; part time: $31,500
Room/board/expenses: $23,700
Median grant: $16,000
Average student indebtedness at graduation: $168,800
Enrollment: full time: 722; part time: 310
men: 55%; women: 45%; minorities: 37%
Acceptance rate (full time): 73%
Midrange LSAT (full time): 147-153
Midrange undergraduate GPA (full time): 2.71-3.20
Midrange of full-time private-sector salaries of 2011 grads: $49,000-$94,000
2011 grads employed in: law firms: 54%; business and industry: 27%; government: 9%; public interest: 2%; judicial clerk: 7%; academia: 1%; unknown: 1%
Employment location for 2011 class: Intl. 3%; N.E. 0%; M.A. 1%; E.N.C. 2%; W.N.C. 1%; S.A. 8%; E.S.C. 1%; W.S.C. 1%; Mt. 9%; Pac. 71%; unknown 1%

University of California–Berkeley

Boalt Hall
Berkeley, CA 94720-7200
http://www.law.berkeley.edu
Public
Admissions: (510) 642-2274
E-mail: admissions@law.berkeley.edu
Financial aid: (510) 642-1563
Application deadline: 02/01
In-state tuition: full time: $48,068; part time: N/A
Out-of-state tuition: full time: $52,019
Room/board/expenses: $24,844
Median grant: $18,118
Average student indebtedness at graduation: $115,349
Enrollment: full time: 856; part time: N/A
men: 43%; women: 57%; minorities: 43%
Acceptance rate (full time): 12%
Midrange LSAT (full time): 163-170

Midrange undergraduate GPA (full time): 3.68-3.91
Midrange of full-time private-sector salaries of 2011 grads: $145,000-$160,000
2011 grads employed in: law firms: 53%; business and industry: 6%; government: 10%; public interest: 16%; judicial clerk: 13%; academia: 2%; unknown: 0%
Employment location for 2011 class: Intl. 2%; N.E. 1%; M.A. 6%; E.N.C. 2%; W.N.C. 1%; S.A. 11%; E.S.C. 0%; W.S.C. 2%; Mt. 5%; Pac. 70%; unknown 0%

University of California–Davis

400 Mrak Hall Drive
Davis, CA 95616-5201
http://www.law.ucdavis.edu
Public
Admissions: (530) 752-6477
E-mail: admissions@law.ucdavis.edu
Financial aid: (530) 752-6573
Application deadline: 01/02
In-state tuition: full time: $49,564; part time: N/A
Out-of-state tuition: full time: $58,815
Room/board/expenses: $17,032
Median grant: $23,000
Average student indebtedness at graduation: $96,664
Enrollment: full time: 569; part time: N/A
men: 53%; women: 47%; minorities: 39%
Acceptance rate (full time): 36%
Midrange LSAT (full time): 160-165
Midrange undergraduate GPA (full time): 3.38-3.71
Midrange of full-time private-sector salaries of 2011 grads: $70,000-$110,000
2011 grads employed in: law firms: 52%; business and industry: 8%; government: 12%; public interest: 8%; judicial clerk: 6%; academia: 13%; unknown: 0%
Employment location for 2011 class: Intl. 2%; N.E. 0%; M.A. 4%; E.N.C. 1%; W.N.C. 0%; S.A. 6%; E.S.C. 1%; W.S.C. 1%; Mt. 3%; Pac. 82%; unknown 0%

University of California (Hastings)

200 McAllister Street
San Francisco, CA 94102
http://www.uchastings.edu
Public
Admissions: (415) 565-4623
E-mail: admiss@uchastings.edu
Financial aid: (415) 565-4624
Application deadline: 03/01
In-state tuition: full time: $46,806; part time: N/A
Out-of-state tuition: full time: $52,806
Room/board/expenses: $21,156
Median grant: $12,150
Average student indebtedness at graduation: $114,736
Enrollment: full time: 1,097; part time: 3
men: 47%; women: 53%; minorities: 42%
Acceptance rate (full time): 30%
Midrange LSAT (full time): 158-165
Midrange undergraduate GPA (full time): 3.29-3.75
Midrange of full-time private-sector salaries of 2011 grads: $65,000-$145,000
2011 grads employed in: law firms: 49%; business and industry: 18%; government: 16%; public interest: 8%; judicial clerk: 5%; academia: 4%; unknown: 0%

Employment location for 2011 class: Intl. 1%; N.E. 1%; M.A. 1%; E.N.C. 0%; W.N.C. 0%; S.A. 3%; E.S.C. 0%; W.S.C. 0%; Mt. 2%; Pac. 90%; unknown 1%

University of California–Irvine

401 East Peltason Drive
Suite 1000
Irvine, CA 92697-8000
http://www.law.uci.edu/prospective/index.html
Private
Admissions: (949) 824-4545
E-mail: lawadmit@law.uci.edu
Financial aid: (949) 824-8080
Application deadline: 03/01
Tuition: full time: $44,717; part time: N/A
Room/board/expenses: $24,057
Median grant: $22,173
Average student indebtedness at graduation: $49,602
Enrollment: full time: 297; part time: N/A
men: 51%; women: 49%; minorities: 44%
Acceptance rate (full time): 21%
Midrange LSAT (full time): 162-167
Midrange undergraduate GPA (full time): 3.29-3.68
Midrange of full-time private-sector salaries of 2011 grads: N/A-N/A
2011 grads employed in: law firms: N/A; business and industry: N/A; government: N/A; public interest: N/A; judicial clerk: N/A; academia: N/A; unknown: N/A
Employment location for 2011 class: Intl. N/A; N.E. N/A; M.A. N/A; E.N.C. N/A; W.N.C. N/A; S.A. N/A; E.S.C. N/A; W.S.C. N/A; Mt. N/A; Pac. N/A; unknown N/A

University of California– Los Angeles

71 Dodd Hall, PO Box 951445
Los Angeles, CA 90095-1445
http://www.law.ucla.edu
Public
Admissions: (310) 825-2260
E-mail: admissions@law.ucla.edu
Financial aid: (310) 825-2459
Application deadline: 02/01
In-state tuition: full time: $45,221; part time: N/A
Out-of-state tuition: full time: $51,715
Room/board/expenses: $22,667
Median grant: $15,439
Average student indebtedness at graduation: $109,539
Enrollment: full time: 994; part time: N/A
men: 55%; women: 45%; minorities: 33%
Acceptance rate (full time): 24%
Midrange LSAT (full time): 164-169
Midrange undergraduate GPA (full time): 3.58-3.89
Midrange of full-time private-sector salaries of 2011 grads: $80,000-$160,000
2011 grads employed in: law firms: 54%; business and industry: 9%; government: 11%; public interest: 16%; judicial clerk: 7%; academia: 3%; unknown: 0%
Employment location for 2011 class: Intl. 2%; N.E. 1%; M.A. 4%; E.N.C. 0%; W.N.C. 0%; S.A. 5%; E.S.C. 0%; W.S.C. 1%; Mt. 3%; Pac. 85%; unknown 0%

University of La Verne

320 E. D Street
Ontario, CA 91764
http://law.laverne.edu
Private
Admissions: (909) 460-2006
E-mail: lawadm@laverne.edu
Financial aid: (909) 593-3511
Application deadline: 07/14
Tuition: full time: $40,732; part time: $32,102
Room/board/expenses: $22,734
Median grant: $16,750
Average student indebtedness at graduation: $112,628
Enrollment: full time: 122; part time: 66
men: 53%; women: 47%; minorities: 42%
Acceptance rate (full time): 48%
Midrange LSAT (full time): 147-154
Midrange undergraduate GPA (full time): 2.46-3.17
Midrange of full-time private-sector salaries of 2011 grads: $45,000-$84,000
2011 grads employed in: law firms: 63%; business and industry: 29%; government: 0%; public interest: 3%; judicial clerk: 1%; academia: 4%; unknown: 0%
Employment location for 2011 class: Intl. 0%; N.E. 1%; M.A. 0%; E.N.C. 0%; W.N.C. 0%; S.A. 0%; E.S.C. 0%; W.S.C. 0%; Mt. 4%; Pac. 94%; unknown 0%

University of San Diego

5998 Alcala Park
San Diego, CA 92110-2492
http://www.law.sandiego.edu
Private
Admissions: (619) 260-4528
E-mail: jdinfo@SanDiego.edu
Financial aid: (619) 260-4570
Application deadline: 02/03
Tuition: full time: $43,860; part time: $31,690
Room/board/expenses: $22,749
Median grant: $22,000
Average student indebtedness at graduation: $122,932
Enrollment: full time: 768; part time: 100
men: 50%; women: 50%; minorities: 34%
Acceptance rate (full time): 45%
Midrange LSAT (full time): 157-162
Midrange undergraduate GPA (full time): 3.28-3.63
Midrange of full-time private-sector salaries of 2011 grads: $56,160-$105,000
2011 grads employed in: law firms: 54%; business and industry: 26%; government: 8%; public interest: 4%; judicial clerk: 3%; academia: 4%; unknown: 1%
Employment location for 2011 class: Intl. 0%; N.E. 2%; M.A. 3%; E.N.C. 0%; W.N.C. 1%; S.A. 3%; E.S.C. 0%; W.S.C. 2%; Mt. 4%; Pac. 85%; unknown 1%

University of San Francisco

2130 Fulton Street
San Francisco, CA 94117-1080
http://www.usfca.edu/law
Private
Admissions: (415) 422-6586
E-mail: lawadmissions@usfca.edu
Financial aid: (415) 422-6210
Application deadline: 02/01
Tuition: full time: $42,364; part time: $31,757
Room/board/expenses: $22,760
Median grant: $11,330

Average student indebtedness at graduation: $133,118
Enrollment: full time: 538; part time: 118
men: 48%; women: 52%; minorities: 43%
Acceptance rate (full time): 46%
Midrange LSAT (full time): 154-159
Midrange undergraduate GPA (full time): 2.98-3.50
Midrange of full-time private-sector salaries of 2011 grads: $60,000-$92,250
2011 grads employed in: law firms: 49%; business and industry: 26%; government: 6%; public interest: 11%; judicial clerk: 1%; academia: 7%; unknown: 0%
Employment location for 2011 class: Intl. 0%; N.E. 1%; M.A. 2%; E.N.C. 2%; W.N.C. 0%; S.A. 2%; E.S.C. 1%; W.S.C. 2%; Mt. 1%; Pac. 90%; unknown 0%

University of Southern California (Gould)

699 Exposition Boulevard
Los Angeles, CA 90089-0071
http://lawweb.usc.edu
Private
Admissions: (213) 740-2523
E-mail: admissions@law.usc.edu
Financial aid: (213) 740-6314
Application deadline: 02/01
Tuition: full time: $52,598; part time: N/A
Room/board/expenses: $22,194
Median grant: $18,000
Average student indebtedness at graduation: $138,858
Enrollment: full time: 637; part time: N/A
men: 53%; women: 47%; minorities: 39%
Acceptance rate (full time): 29%
Midrange LSAT (full time): 165-168
Midrange undergraduate GPA (full time): 3.51-3.80
Midrange of full-time private-sector salaries of 2011 grads: $100,000-$160,000
2011 grads employed in: law firms: 70%; business and industry: 9%; government: 7%; public interest: 6%; judicial clerk: 5%; academia: 4%; unknown: 0%
Employment location for 2011 class: Intl. 1%; N.E. 1%; M.A. 5%; E.N.C. 1%; W.N.C. 1%; S.A. 3%; E.S.C. 1%; W.S.C. 0%; Mt. 4%; Pac. 83%; unknown 0%

University of the Pacific (McGeorge)

3200 Fifth Avenue
Sacramento, CA 95817
http://www.mcgeorge.edu
Private
Admissions: (916) 739-7105
E-mail: admissionsmcgeorge@pacific.edu
Financial aid: (916) 739-7158
Application deadline: rolling
Tuition: full time: $43,045; part time: $28,631
Room/board/expenses: $22,433
Median grant: $13,000
Average student indebtedness at graduation: $140,566
Enrollment: full time: 594; part time: 227
men: 55%; women: 45%; minorities: 29%
Acceptance rate (full time): 50%
Midrange LSAT (full time): 154-159
Midrange undergraduate GPA (full time): 2.98-3.57
Midrange of full-time private-sector salaries of 2011 grads: $55,000-$80,000

2011 grads employed in: law firms: 45%; business and industry: 13%; government: 20%; public interest: 10%; judicial clerk: 6%; academia: 4%; unknown: 0%
Employment location for 2011 class: Intl. 2%; N.E. 0%; M.A. 0%; E.N.C. 1%; W.N.C. 0%; S.A. 2%; E.S.C. 0%; W.S.C. 1%; Mt. 6%; Pac. 87%; unknown 0%

Western State College of Law at Argosy University

1111 N. State College Boulevard
Fullerton, CA 92831
http://www.wsulaw.edu
Private
Admissions: (714) 459-1101
E-mail: adm@wsulaw.edu
Financial aid: (714) 459-1120
Application deadline: 06/01
Tuition: full time: $39,600; part time: $26,620
Room/board/expenses: $22,839
Median grant: $14,000
Average student indebtedness at graduation: $98,968
Enrollment: full time: 101; part time: 43
men: 50%; women: 50%; minorities: 35%
Acceptance rate (full time): 56%
Midrange LSAT (full time): 149-155
Midrange undergraduate GPA (full time): 2.79-3.36
Midrange of full-time private-sector salaries of 2011 grads: $30,000-$65,000
2011 grads employed in: law firms: 61%; business and industry: 22%; government: 4%; public interest: 3%; judicial clerk: 1%; academia: 6%; unknown: 1%
Employment location for 2011 class: Intl. 0%; N.E. 2%; M.A. 3%; E.N.C. 0%; W.N.C. 2%; S.A. 0%; E.S.C. 0%; W.S.C. 0%; Mt. 2%; Pac. 92%; unknown 1%

Whittier College

3333 Harbor Boulevard
Costa Mesa, CA 92626-1501
http://www.law.whittier.edu
Private
Admissions: (800) 808-8188
E-mail: info@law.whittier.edu
Financial aid: (714) 444-4141
Application deadline: 08/01
Tuition: full time: $40,310; part time: $26,890
Room/board/expenses: $26,924
Median grant: $9,772
Average student indebtedness at graduation: $143,536
Enrollment: full time: 490; part time: 171
men: 51%; women: 49%; minorities: 47%
Acceptance rate (full time): 70%
Midrange LSAT (full time): 148-153
Midrange undergraduate GPA (full time): 2.73-3.22
Midrange of full-time private-sector salaries of 2011 grads: $40,000-$75,000
2011 grads employed in: law firms: 48%; business and industry: 41%; government: 2%; public interest: 6%; judicial clerk: 0%; academia: 2%; unknown: 2%
Employment location for 2011 class: Intl. 0%; N.E. 3%; M.A. 3%; E.N.C. 0%; W.N.C. 0%; S.A. 0%; E.S.C. 0%; W.S.C. 0%; Mt. 3%; Pac. 82%; unknown 9%

COLORADO

University of Colorado–Boulder

Box 401
Boulder, CO 80309-0401
http://www.colorado.edu/law/
Public
Admissions: (303) 492-7203
E-mail: lawadmin@colorado.edu
Financial aid: (303) 492-0647
Application deadline: 03/15
In-state tuition: full time: $31,495; part time: N/A
Out-of-state tuition: full time: $38,281
Room/board/expenses: $18,692
Median grant: $8,000
Average student indebtedness at graduation: $100,813
Enrollment: full time: 509; part time: N/A
men: 53%; women: 47%; minorities: 21%
Acceptance rate (full time): 34%
Midrange LSAT (full time): 159-166
Midrange undergraduate GPA (full time): 3.35-3.79
Midrange of full-time private-sector salaries of 2011 grads: $50,000-$100,000
2011 grads employed in: law firms: 41%; business and industry: 14%; government: 12%; public interest: 6%; judicial clerk: 24%; academia: 3%; unknown: 1%
Employment location for 2011 class: Intl. 1%; N.E. 2%; M.A. 2%; E.N.C. 1%; W.N.C. 2%; S.A. 4%; E.S.C. 0%; W.S.C. 1%; Mt. 81%; Pac. 4%; unknown 1%

University of Denver (Sturm)

2255 E. Evans Avenue
Denver, CO 80208
http://www.law.du.edu
Private
Admissions: (303) 871-6135
E-mail: admissions@law.du.edu
Financial aid: (303) 871-6362
Application deadline: 06/01
Tuition: full time: $39,840; part time: $29,368
Room/board/expenses: $17,423
Median grant: $20,000
Average student indebtedness at graduation: $127,420
Enrollment: full time: 746; part time: 148
men: 50%; women: 50%; minorities: 17%
Acceptance rate (full time): 47%
Midrange LSAT (full time): 156-161
Midrange undergraduate GPA (full time): 3.16-3.66
Midrange of full-time private-sector salaries of 2011 grads: $51,000-$105,000
2011 grads employed in: law firms: 34%; business and industry: 23%; government: 11%; public interest: 12%; judicial clerk: 9%; academia: 11%; unknown: 0%
Employment location for 2011 class: Intl. 0%; N.E. 1%; M.A. 1%; E.N.C. 1%; W.N.C. 0%; S.A. 4%; E.S.C. 0%; W.S.C. 1%; Mt. 1%; Pac. 2%; unknown 1%

CONNECTICUT

Quinnipiac University

275 Mount Carmel Avenue
Hamden, CT 06518
http://law.quinnipiac.edu
Private
Admissions: (203) 582-3400
E-mail: ladm@quinnipiac.edu
Financial aid: (203) 582-3405
Application deadline: 03/01
Tuition: full time: $47,076; part time: $33,216
Room/board/expenses: $19,724
Median grant: $20,000
Average student indebtedness at graduation: $111,952
Enrollment: full time: 328; part time: 78
men: 49%; women: 51%; minorities: 11%
Acceptance rate (full time): 52%
Midrange LSAT (full time): 153-159
Midrange undergraduate GPA (full time): 3.16-3.74
Midrange of full-time private-sector salaries of 2011 grads: $50,000-$83,000
2011 grads employed in: law firms: 44%; business and industry: 34%; government: 4%; public interest: 5%; judicial clerk: 5%; academia: 9%; unknown: 0%
Employment location for 2011 class: Intl. 0%; N.E. 85%; M.A. 5%; E.N.C. 1%; W.N.C. 0%; S.A. 5%; E.S.C. 0%; W.S.C. 0%; Mt. 3%; Pac. 0%; unknown 1%

University of Connecticut

55 Elizabeth Street
Hartford, CT 06105-2296
http://www.law.uconn.edu
Public
Admissions: (860) 570-5100
E-mail: admit@law.uconn.edu
Financial aid: (860) 570-5147
Application deadline: 04/01
In-state tuition: full time: $23,244; part time: $16,222
Out-of-state tuition: full time: $48,012
Room/board/expenses: $16,896
Median grant: $11,000
Average student indebtedness at graduation: $65,641
Enrollment: full time: 447; part time: 118
men: 54%; women: 46%; minorities: 24%
Acceptance rate (full time): 39%
Midrange LSAT (full time): 158-162
Midrange undergraduate GPA (full time): 3.24-3.69
Midrange of full-time private-sector salaries of 2011 grads: $65,000-$110,000
2011 grads employed in: law firms: 50%; business and industry: 18%; government: 12%; public interest: 4%; judicial clerk: 12%; academia: 4%; unknown: 0%
Employment location for 2011 class: Intl. 1%; N.E. 83%; M.A. 7%; E.N.C. 1%; W.N.C. 0%; S.A. 4%; E.S.C. 0%; W.S.C. 1%; Mt. 1%; Pac. 2%; unknown 0%

Yale University

PO Box 208215
New Haven, CT 06520-8215
http://www.law.yale.edu
Private
Admissions: (203) 432-4995
E-mail: admissions.law@yale.edu
Financial aid: (203) 432-1688
Application deadline: rolling
Tuition: full time: $53,600; part time: N/A

Room/board/expenses: $20,080
Median grant: $23,011
Average student indebtedness at graduation: $110,741
Enrollment: full time: 615; part time: N/A
men: 53%; women: 47%; minorities: 31%
Acceptance rate (full time): 8%
Midrange LSAT (full time): 170-176
Midrange undergraduate GPA (full time): 3.84-3.98
Midrange of full-time private-sector salaries of 2011 grads: $160,000-$160,000
2011 grads employed in: law firms: 36%; business and industry: 4%; government: 6%; public interest: 12%; judicial clerk: 39%; academia: 4%; unknown: 0%
Employment location for 2011 class: Intl. 6%; N.E. 9%; M.A. 32%; E.N.C. 3%; W.N.C. 3%; S.A. 22%; E.S.C. 3%; W.S.C. 6%; Mt. 4%; Pac. 12%; unknown 1%

DELAWARE

Widener University

PO Box 7474
Wilmington, DE 19803-0474
http://www.law.widener.edu
Private
Admissions: (302) 477-2162
E-mail: law.admissions@law.widener.edu
Financial aid: (302) 477-2272
Application deadline: 05/15
Tuition: full time: $1,272/credit hour; part time: $1,272/credit hour
Room/board/expenses: $19,433
Median grant: $5,000
Average student indebtedness at graduation: $123,071
Enrollment: full time: 813; part time: 362
men: 53%; women: 47%; minorities: 16%
Acceptance rate (full time): 60%
Midrange LSAT (full time): 148-153
Midrange undergraduate GPA (full time): 2.94-3.44
Midrange of full-time private-sector salaries of 2011 grads: $43,710-$67,500
2011 grads employed in: law firms: 48%; business and industry: 18%; government: 10%; public interest: 6%; judicial clerk: 15%; academia: 3%; unknown: 1%
Employment location for 2011 class: Intl. 0%; N.E. 1%; M.A. 79%; E.N.C. 0%; W.N.C. 0%; S.A. 19%; E.S.C. 0%; W.S.C. 0%; Mt. 1%; Pac. 0%; unknown 0%

DISTRICT OF COLUMBIA

American University (Washington)

4801 Massachusetts Avenue NW
Washington, DC 20016-8192
http://www.wcl.american.edu
Private
Admissions: (202) 274-4101
E-mail: wcladmit@wcl.american.edu
Financial aid: (202) 274-4040
Application deadline: 03/01
Tuition: full time: $46,794; part time: $32,812
Room/board/expenses: $23,410
Median grant: $10,000
Average student indebtedness at graduation: $152,659
Enrollment: full time: 1,215; part time: 307
men: 43%; women: 57%; minorities: 35%

Acceptance rate (full time): 33%
Midrange LSAT (full time): 156-162
Midrange undergraduate GPA (full time): 3.19-3.58
Midrange of full-time private-sector salaries of 2011 grads: $55,000-$152,500
2011 grads employed in: law firms: 30%; business and industry: 21%; government: 19%; public interest: 16%; judicial clerk: 10%; academia: 4%; unknown: 0%
Employment location for 2011 class: Intl. 3%; N.E. 2%; M.A. 10%; E.N.C. 1%; W.N.C. 2%; S.A. 74%; E.S.C. 0%; W.S.C. 1%; Mt. 3%; Pac. 3%; unknown 0%

Catholic University of America (Columbus)

3600 John McCormack Road NE
Washington, DC 20064
http://www.law.edu
Private
Admissions: (202) 319-5151
E-mail: admissions@law.edu
Financial aid: (202) 319-5143
Application deadline: 03/16
Tuition: full time: $43,080; part time: $1,560/credit hour
Room/board/expenses: $26,218
Median grant: $10,000
Average student indebtedness at graduation: $142,115
Enrollment: full time: 401; part time: 211
men: 48%; women: 52%; minorities: 23%
Acceptance rate (full time): 37%
Midrange LSAT (full time): 153-159
Midrange undergraduate GPA (full time): 3.08-3.56
Midrange of full-time private-sector salaries of 2011 grads: $60,000-$110,000
2011 grads employed in: law firms: 37%; business and industry: 26%; government: 26%; public interest: 3%; judicial clerk: 7%; academia: 1%; unknown: 0%
Employment location for 2011 class: Intl. 1%; N.E. 1%; M.A. 5%; E.N.C. 1%; W.N.C. 0%; S.A. 85%; E.S.C. 1%; W.S.C. 1%; Mt. 0%; Pac. 3%; unknown 1%

Georgetown University

600 New Jersey Avenue NW
Washington, DC 20001-2075
http://www.law.georgetown.edu
Private
Admissions: (202) 662-9015
E-mail: admis@law.georgetown.edu
Financial aid: (202) 662-9210
Application deadline: 03/01
Tuition: full time: $48,835; part time: $34,600
Room/board/expenses: $24,665
Median grant: $17,500
Average student indebtedness at graduation: $146,169
Enrollment: full time: 1,683; part time: 243
men: 54%; women: 46%; minorities: 17%
Acceptance rate (full time): 29%
Midrange LSAT (full time): 165-170
Midrange undergraduate GPA (full time): 3.43-3.82
Midrange of full-time private-sector salaries of 2011 grads: $160,000-$160,000
2011 grads employed in: law firms: 47%; business and industry: 11%; government: 15%; public interest: 17%; judicial clerk: 9%; academia: 2%; unknown: 1%

Employment location for 2011 class:
Intl. 2%; N.E. 3%; M.A. 24%;
E.N.C. 3%; W.N.C. 0%; S.A. 50%;
E.S.C. 1%; W.S.C. 2%; Mt. 2%;
Pac. 10%; unknown 3%

George Washington University

2000 H Street NW
Washington, DC 20052
http://www.law.gwu.edu
Private
Admissions: (202) 994-7230
E-mail: jdadmit@law.gwu.edu
Financial aid: (202) 994-6592
Application deadline: 03/31
Tuition: full time: $47,535; part time: $36,795
Room/board/expenses: $29,765
Median grant: $13,000
Average student indebtedness at graduation: $128,341
Enrollment: full time: 1,351; part time: 322
men: 55%; women: 45%;
minorities: 25%
Acceptance rate (full time): 31%
Midrange LSAT (full time): 162-168
Midrange undergraduate GPA (full time): 3.31-3.78
Midrange of full-time private-sector salaries of 2011 grads: $120,000-$160,000
2011 grads employed in: law firms: 43%; business and industry: 12%; government: 18%; public interest: 9%; judicial clerk: 9%; academia: 7%; unknown: 2%
Employment location for 2011 class: Intl. 2%; N.E. 1%; M.A. 13%; E.N.C. 2%; W.N.C. 1%; S.A. 68%; E.S.C. 0%; W.S.C. 1%; Mt. 4%; Pac. 5%; unknown 3%

Howard University

2900 Van Ness Street NW
Washington, DC 20008
http://www.law.howard.edu
Private
Admissions: (202) 806-8009
E-mail: admissions@law.howard.edu
Financial aid: (202) 806-8005
Application deadline: 03/15
Tuition: full time: $31,640; part time: N/A
Room/board/expenses: $25,221
Median grant: $16,000
Average student indebtedness at graduation: $123,068
Enrollment: full time: 393; part time: N/A
men: 40%; women: 60%;
minorities: 93%
Acceptance rate (full time): 33%
Midrange LSAT (full time): 150-155
Midrange undergraduate GPA (full time): 2.99-3.49
Midrange of full-time private-sector salaries of 2011 grads: $85,000-$160,000
2011 grads employed in: law firms: 26%; business and industry: 23%; government: 20%; public interest: 8%; judicial clerk: 17%; academia: 2%; unknown: 3%
Employment location for 2011 class: Intl. 4%; N.E. 0%; M.A. 20%; E.N.C. 3%; W.N.C. 1%; S.A. 58%; E.S.C. 1%; W.S.C. 2%; Mt. 3%; Pac. 5%; unknown 4%

University of the District of Columbia (Clarke)

4200 Connecticut Avenue NW
Building 38 & 52
Washington, DC 20008
http://www.law.udc.edu
Public
Admissions: (202) 274-7341
E-mail: vcanty@udc.edu
Financial aid: (202) 274-7337
Application deadline: 03/16
In-state tuition: full time: $11,265; part time: $360/credit hour
Out-of-state tuition: full time: $21,285
Room/board/expenses: $26,200
Median grant: $4,425
Enrollment: full time: 216; part time: 150
men: 46%; women: 54%;
minorities: 49%
Acceptance rate (full time): 27%
Midrange LSAT (full time): 148-153
Midrange undergraduate GPA (full time): 2.66-3.25
Midrange of full-time private-sector salaries of 2011 grads: $45,000-$85,000
2011 grads employed in: law firms: 26%; business and industry: 30%; government: 13%; public interest: 17%; judicial clerk: 9%; academia: 6%; unknown: 0%
Employment location for 2011 class: Intl. 2%; N.E. 0%; M.A. 13%; E.N.C. 2%; W.N.C. 0%; S.A. 80%; E.S.C. 0%; W.S.C. 0%; Mt. 0%; Pac. 2%; unknown 0%

FLORIDA

Ave Maria School of Law

1025 Commons Circle
Naples, FL 34119
http://www.avemarialaw.edu
Private
Admissions: (239) 687-5420
E-mail: info@avemarialaw.edu
Financial aid: (239) 687-5335
Application deadline: 07/01
Tuition: full time: $37,270; part time: N/A
Room/board/expenses: $20,999
Median grant: $15,000
Average student indebtedness at graduation: $126,485
Enrollment: full time: 382; part time: N/A
men: 53%; women: 47%;
minorities: 20%
Acceptance rate (full time): 57%
Midrange LSAT (full time): 144-153
Midrange undergraduate GPA (full time): 2.81-3.48
Midrange of full-time private-sector salaries of 2011 grads: $31,200-$55,000
2011 grads employed in: law firms: 49%; business and industry: 33%; government: 11%; public interest: 0%; judicial clerk: 4%; academia: 4%; unknown: 0%
Employment location for 2011 class: Intl. 4%; N.E. 0%; M.A. 13%; E.N.C. 11%; W.N.C. 2%; S.A. 29%; E.S.C. 4%; W.S.C. 15%; Mt. 20%; Pac. 4%; unknown 0%

Barry University[1]

6441 E. Colonial Drive
Orlando, FL 32807
http://www.barry.edu/law/
Private
Admissions: (866) 532-2779
E-mail: lawinfo@mail.barry.edu
Financial aid: (321) 206-5621
Tuition: N/A
Room/board/expenses: N/A
Enrollment: N/A

Florida A&M University[1]

201 Beggs Avenue
Orlando, FL 32801
http://www.famu.edu/index.cfm?a=law
Public
Admissions: (407) 254-3263
E-mail: famulaw.admissions@famu.edu
Financial aid: (850) 599-3730
Tuition: N/A
Room/board/expenses: N/A
Enrollment: N/A

Florida Coastal School of Law

8787 Baypine Road
Jacksonville, FL 32256
http://www.fcsl.edu
Private
Admissions: (904) 680-7710
E-mail: admissions@fcsl.edu
Financial aid: (904) 680-7717
Application deadline: rolling
Tuition: full time: $39,370; part time: $31,854
Room/board/expenses: $21,110
Median grant: $7,500
Average student indebtedness at graduation: $143,111
Enrollment: full time: 1,371; part time: 223
men: 47%; women: 53%;
minorities: 34%
Acceptance rate (full time): 76%
Midrange LSAT (full time): 143-151
Midrange undergraduate GPA (full time): 2.83-3.34
Midrange of full-time private-sector salaries of 2011 grads: $40,000-$55,000
2011 grads employed in: law firms: 39%; business and industry: 16%; government: 16%; public interest: 22%; judicial clerk: 2%; academia: 3%; unknown: 2%
Employment location for 2011 class: Intl. 1%; N.E. 1%; M.A. 3%; E.N.C. 2%; W.N.C. 0%; S.A. 80%; E.S.C. 2%; W.S.C. 1%; Mt. 3%; Pac. 1%; unknown 4%

Florida International University

Modesto A. Maidique Campus
RDB 2015
Miami, FL 33199
http://law.fiu.edu
Public
Admissions: (305) 348-8006
E-mail: lawadmit@fiu.edu
Financial aid: (305) 348-8006
Application deadline: 05/01
In-state tuition: full time: $18,841; part time: $12,886
Out-of-state tuition: full time: $33,086
Room/board/expenses: $26,024
Median grant: $5,000
Average student indebtedness at graduation: $94,937
Enrollment: full time: 346; part time: 162
men: 48%; women: 52%;
minorities: 60%

Acceptance rate (full time): 23%
Midrange LSAT (full time): 153-158
Midrange undergraduate GPA (full time): 3.13-3.75
Midrange of full-time private-sector salaries of 2011 grads: N/A-N/A
2011 grads employed in: law firms: 66%; business and industry: 8%; government: 11%; public interest: 5%; judicial clerk: 2%; academia: 7%; unknown: 0%
Employment location for 2011 class: Intl. N/A; N.E. N/A; M.A. N/A; E.N.C. N/A; W.N.C. N/A; S.A. N/A; E.S.C. N/A; W.S.C. N/A; Mt. N/A; Pac. N/A; unknown N/A

Florida State University

425 W. Jefferson Street
Tallahassee, FL 32306-1601
http://www.law.fsu.edu
Public
Admissions: (850) 644-3787
E-mail: admissions@law.fsu.edu
Financial aid: (850) 644-5716
Application deadline: 04/01
In-state tuition: full time: $19,731; part time: N/A
Out-of-state tuition: full time: $39,744
Room/board/expenses: $17,700
Median grant: $2,500
Average student indebtedness at graduation: $73,114
Enrollment: full time: 658; part time: 40
men: 59%; women: 41%;
minorities: 21%
Acceptance rate (full time): 33%
Midrange LSAT (full time): 157-162
Midrange undergraduate GPA (full time): 3.29-3.73
Midrange of full-time private-sector salaries of 2011 grads: $52,500-$91,725
2011 grads employed in: law firms: 47%; business and industry: 14%; government: 23%; public interest: 6%; judicial clerk: 7%; academia: 2%; unknown: 1%
Employment location for 2011 class: Intl. 1%; N.E. 0%; M.A. 5%; E.N.C. 2%; W.N.C. 0%; S.A. 88%; E.S.C. 1%; W.S.C. 1%; Mt. 1%; Pac. 2%; unknown 0%

Nova Southeastern University (Broad)

3305 College Avenue
Fort Lauderdale, FL 33314-7721
http://www.nsulaw.nova.edu/
Private
Admissions: (954) 262-6117
E-mail: admission@nsu.law.nova.edu
Financial aid: (954) 262-7412
Application deadline: 05/01
Tuition: full time: $34,330; part time: $25,895
Room/board/expenses: $26,494
Median grant: $10,000
Average student indebtedness at graduation: $135,548
Enrollment: full time: 829; part time: 200
men: 46%; women: 54%;
minorities: 36%
Acceptance rate (full time): 54%
Midrange LSAT (full time): 148-153
Midrange undergraduate GPA (full time): 2.93-3.40
Midrange of full-time private-sector salaries of 2011 grads: $48,000-$70,000
2011 grads employed in: law firms: 67%; business and industry: 18%;

government: 8%; public interest: 4%; judicial clerk: 2%; academia: 2%; unknown: 0%
Employment location for 2011 class: Intl. 3%; N.E. 1%; M.A. 4%; E.N.C. 0%; W.N.C. 0%; S.A. 91%; E.S.C. 0%; W.S.C. 0%; Mt. 1%; Pac. 0%; unknown 0%

Stetson University

1401 61st Street S
Gulfport, FL 33707
http://www.law.stetson.edu
Private
Admissions: (727) 562-7802
E-mail: lawadmit@law.stetson.edu
Financial aid: (727) 562-7813
Application deadline: 05/15
Tuition: full time: $36,168; part time: $25,068
Room/board/expenses: $17,652
Median grant: $17,574
Average student indebtedness at graduation: $131,178
Enrollment: full time: 778; part time: 226
men: 51%; women: 49%;
minorities: 24%
Acceptance rate (full time): 44%
Midrange LSAT (full time): 152-158
Midrange undergraduate GPA (full time): 3.07-3.55
Midrange of full-time private-sector salaries of 2011 grads: $48,500-$75,000
2011 grads employed in: law firms: 51%; business and industry: 11%; government: 17%; public interest: 8%; judicial clerk: 5%; academia: 2%; unknown: 5%
Employment location for 2011 class: Intl. 0%; N.E. 0%; M.A. 1%; E.N.C. 1%; W.N.C. 0%; S.A. 90%; E.S.C. 1%; W.S.C. 0%; Mt. 0%; Pac. 1%; unknown 5%

St. Thomas University

16401 N.W. 37th Avenue
Miami Gardens, FL 33054
http://www.stu.edu
Private
Admissions: (305) 623-2310
E-mail: admitme@stu.edu
Financial aid: (305) 474-2409
Application deadline: 06/01
Tuition: full time: $36,226; part time: N/A
Room/board/expenses: $23,461
Median grant: $15,000
Average student indebtedness at graduation: $122,913
Enrollment: full time: 678; part time: N/A
men: 49%; women: 51%;
minorities: 56%
Acceptance rate (full time): 63%
Midrange LSAT (full time): 146-150
Midrange undergraduate GPA (full time): 2.77-3.26
Midrange of full-time private-sector salaries of 2011 grads: $42,000-$60,000
2011 grads employed in: law firms: 70%; business and industry: 10%; government: 12%; public interest: 4%; judicial clerk: 1%; academia: 1%; unknown: 1%
Employment location for 2011 class: Intl. 1%; N.E. 0%; M.A. 3%; E.N.C. 3%; W.N.C. 0%; S.A. 88%; E.S.C. 0%; W.S.C. 1%; Mt. 1%; Pac. 3%; unknown 1%

University of Florida (Levin)

PO Box 117620
Gainesville, FL 32611-7620
http://www.law.ufl.edu
Public
Admissions: (352) 273-0890
E-mail: admissions@law.ufl.edu
Financial aid: (352) 273-0628
Application deadline: 03/15
In-state tuition: full time: $21,421;
part time: N/A
Out-of-state tuition: full time:
$40,786
Room/board/expenses: $15,740
Median grant: $5,200
**Average student indebtedness at
graduation:** $72,974
Enrollment: full time: 960; part
time: N/A
men: 58%; women: 42%;
minorities: 24%
Acceptance rate (full time): 33%
Midrange LSAT (full time): 160-164
**Midrange undergraduate GPA (full
time):** 3.33-3.73
**Midrange of full-time private-sector
salaries of 2011 grads:** $54,000-
$100,000
2011 grads employed in: law firms:
55%; business and industry: 15%;
government: 12%; public interest:
9%; judicial clerk: 7%; academia:
3%; unknown: 0%
Employment location for 2011 class:
Intl. 1%; N.E. 1%; M.A. 1%; E.N.C.
3%; W.N.C. 2%; S.A. 1%; E.S.C.
88%; W.S.C. 1%; Mt. 1%; Pac. 2%;
unknown 0%

University of Miami

PO Box 248087
Coral Gables, FL 33124-8087
http://www.law.miami.edu
Private
Admissions: (305) 284-2795
E-mail:
admissions@law.miami.edu
Financial aid: (305) 284-3115
Application deadline: 07/31
Tuition: full time: $42,938; part
time: $1,500/credit hour
Room/board/expenses: $22,611
Median grant: $20,000
**Average student indebtedness at
graduation:** $140,032
Enrollment: full time: 1,282; part
time: 25
men: 58%; women: 42%;
minorities: 31%
Acceptance rate (full time): 55%
Midrange LSAT (full time): 155-159
**Midrange undergraduate GPA (full
time):** 3.14-3.57
**Midrange of full-time private-sector
salaries of 2011 grads:** $57,000-
$88,000
2011 grads employed in: law firms:
54%; business and industry: 17%;
government: 13%; public interest:
9%; judicial clerk: 5%; academia:
2%; unknown: 0%
Employment location for 2011 class:
Intl. 1%; N.E. 3%; M.A. 5%; E.N.C.
2%; W.N.C. 0%; S.A. 82%; E.S.C.
0%; W.S.C. 2%; Mt. 0%; Pac. 3%;
unknown 2%

Atlanta's John Marshall Law School

1422 W. Peachtree Street, NW
Atlanta, GA 30309
http://www.johnmarshall.edu
Private
Admissions: (404) 872-3593
E-mail:
admissions@johnmarshall.edu
Financial aid: (404) 872-3593
Application deadline: 08/23
Tuition: full time: $1,200/credit
hour; part time: $1,200/credit
hour
Room/board/expenses: $22,131
Median grant: $6,000
**Average student indebtedness at
graduation:** $142,515
Enrollment: full time: 480; part
time: 205
men: 49%; women: 51%;
minorities: 43%
Acceptance rate (full time): 52%
Midrange LSAT (full time): 148-153
**Midrange undergraduate GPA (full
time):** 2.57-3.23
**Midrange of full-time private-sector
salaries of 2011 grads:** $45,500-
$71,250
2011 grads employed in: law firms:
55%; business and industry: 27%;
government: 12%; public interest:
4%; judicial clerk: 2%; academia:
1%; unknown: 0%
Employment location for 2011 class:
Intl. 0%; N.E. 0%; M.A. 2%; E.N.C.
0%; W.N.C. 0%; S.A. 95%; E.S.C.
4%; W.S.C. 0%; Mt. 0%; Pac. 0%;
unknown 0%

Emory University

1301 Clifton Road
Atlanta, GA 30322-2770
http://www.law.emory.edu
Private
Admissions: (404) 727-6802
E-mail: lawinfo@law.emory.edu
Financial aid: (404) 727-6039
Application deadline: 03/01
Tuition: full time: $46,414; part
time: N/A
Room/board/expenses: $24,720
Median grant: $20,000
**Average student indebtedness at
graduation:** $105,838
Enrollment: full time: 813; part
time: N/A
men: 55%; women: 45%;
minorities: 27%
Acceptance rate (full time): 31%
Midrange LSAT (full time): 161-166
**Midrange undergraduate GPA (full
time):** 3.35-3.82
**Midrange of full-time private-sector
salaries of 2011 grads:** $70,000-
$135,000
2011 grads employed in: law firms:
47%; business and industry: 11%;
government: 12%; public interest:
12%; judicial clerk: 11%; academia:
4%; unknown: 3%
Employment location for 2011 class:
Intl. 0%; N.E. 1%; M.A. 13%; E.N.C.
3%; W.N.C. 1%; S.A. 67%; E.S.C.
2%; W.S.C. 5%; Mt. 2%; Pac. 2%;
unknown 5%

Georgia State University

PO Box 4049
Atlanta, GA 30302-4049
http://law.gsu.edu
Public
Admissions: (404) 651-2048
E-mail: admissions@
gsulaw.gsu.edu
Financial aid: (404) 651-2227
Application deadline: 03/01
In-state tuition: full time: $15,154;
part time: $11,940
Out-of-state tuition: full time:
$34,834
Room/board/expenses: $15,438
Median grant: $2,500
**Average student indebtedness at
graduation:** $68,283
Enrollment: full time: 461; part
time: 185
men: 54%; women: 46%;
minorities: 22%
Acceptance rate (full time): 27%
Midrange LSAT (full time): 158-161
**Midrange undergraduate GPA (full
time):** 3.21-3.60
**Midrange of full-time private-sector
salaries of 2011 grads:** $50,000-
$75,000
2011 grads employed in: law firms:
52%; business and industry: 26%;
government: 14%; public interest:
2%; judicial clerk: 5%; academia:
1%; unknown: 0%
Employment location for 2011 class:
Intl. 0%; N.E. 0%; M.A. 1%; E.N.C.
0%; W.N.C. 0%; S.A. 96%; E.S.C.
1%; W.S.C. 0%; Mt. 1%; Pac. 1%;
unknown 0%

Mercer University (George)

1021 Georgia Avenue
Macon, GA 31207-0001
http://www.law.mercer.edu
Private
Admissions: (478) 301-2605
E-mail:
admissions@law.mercer.edu
Financial aid: (478) 301-5902
Application deadline: 03/15
Tuition: full time: $37,260; part
time: N/A
Room/board/expenses: $18,437
Median grant: $25,000
**Average student indebtedness at
graduation:** $113,935
Enrollment: full time: 433; part
time: N/A
men: 55%; women: 45%;
minorities: 23%
Acceptance rate (full time): 53%
Midrange LSAT (full time): 149-156
**Midrange undergraduate GPA (full
time):** 3.18-3.60
**Midrange of full-time private-sector
salaries of 2011 grads:** $52,000-
$70,000
2011 grads employed in: law firms:
67%; business and industry: 6%;
government: 12%; public interest:
7%; judicial clerk: 7%; academia:
1%; unknown: 0%
Employment location for 2011 class:
Intl. 0%; N.E. 1%; M.A. 0%; E.N.C.
1%; W.N.C. 0%; S.A. 87%; E.S.C.
6%; W.S.C. 0%; Mt. 5%; Pac. 0%;
unknown 0%

University of Georgia

Herty Drive
Athens, GA 30602
http://www.law.uga.edu
Public
Admissions: (706) 542-7060
E-mail: ugajd@uga.edu
Financial aid: (706) 542-6147
Application deadline: 04/01
In-state tuition: full time: $18,058;
part time: N/A
Out-of-state tuition: full time:
$35,480
Room/board/expenses: $16,902
Median grant: $10,000
**Average student indebtedness at
graduation:** $80,775
Enrollment: full time: 663; part
time: N/A
men: 56%; women: 44%;
minorities: 19%
Acceptance rate (full time): 31%
Midrange LSAT (full time): 158-165
**Midrange undergraduate GPA (full
time):** 3.33-3.82
**Midrange of full-time private-sector
salaries of 2011 grads:** $55,000-
$90,000
2011 grads employed in: law firms:
53%; business and industry: 12%;
government: 10%; public interest:
8%; judicial clerk: 15%; academia:
2%; unknown: 0%
Employment location for 2011 class:
Intl. 1%; N.E. 1%; M.A. 4%; E.N.C.
1%; W.N.C. 1%; S.A. 91%; E.S.C.
2%; W.S.C. 1%; Mt. 1%; Pac. 1%;
unknown 0%

University of Hawaii–Manoa (Richardson)

2515 Dole Street
Honolulu, HI 96822-2328
http://www.law.hawaii.edu/
Public
Admissions: (808) 956-5557
E-mail: lawadm@hawaii.edu
Financial aid: (808) 956-7966
Application deadline: 02/01
In-state tuition: full time: $18,094;
part time: $726/credit hour
Out-of-state tuition: full time:
$34,486
Room/board/expenses: $15,925
Median grant: $5,000
**Average student indebtedness at
graduation:** $68,016
Enrollment: full time: 261; part
time: 82
men: 43%; women: 57%;
minorities: 72%
Acceptance rate (full time): 29%
Midrange LSAT (full time): 155-160
**Midrange undergraduate GPA (full
time):** 3.04-3.59
**Midrange of full-time private-sector
salaries of 2011 grads:** $40,800-
$70,000
2011 grads employed in: law firms:
27%; business and industry: 16%;
government: 13%; public interest:
2%; judicial clerk: 38%; academia:
2%; unknown: 1%
Employment location for 2011 class:
Intl. 0%; N.E. 1%; M.A. 0%; E.N.C.
1%; W.N.C. 0%; S.A. 1%; E.S.C.
0%; W.S.C. 0%; Mt. 1%; Pac. 95%;
unknown 0%

University of Idaho

PO Box 442321
Moscow, ID 83844-2321
http://www.
uidaho.edu/law/admissions
Public
Admissions: (208) 885-2300
E-mail: lawadmit@uidaho.edu
Financial aid: (208) 885-6312
Application deadline: 03/01
In-state tuition: full time: $15,036;
part time: N/A
Out-of-state tuition: full time:
$27,824
Room/board/expenses: $16,228
Median grant: $4,000
**Average student indebtedness at
graduation:** $96,406
Enrollment: full time: 340; part
time: 4
men: 60%; women: 40%;
minorities: 15%
Acceptance rate (full time): 65%
Midrange LSAT (full time): 149-156
**Midrange undergraduate GPA (full
time):** 2.94-3.52
**Midrange of full-time private-sector
salaries of 2011 grads:** $44,250-
$55,000
2011 grads employed in: law firms:
46%; business and industry: 14%;
government: 18%; public interest:
5%; judicial clerk: 17%; academia:
0%; unknown: 0%
Employment location for 2011 class:
Intl. 1%; N.E. 0%; M.A. 0%; E.N.C.
0%; W.N.C. 0%; S.A. 4%; E.S.C.
0%; W.S.C. 1%; Mt. 77%; Pac.
17%; unknown 0%

DePaul University

25 E. Jackson Boulevard
Chicago, IL 60604
http://www.law.depaul.edu
Private
Admissions: (312) 362-6831
E-mail: lawinfo@depaul.edu
Financial aid: (312) 362-8091
Application deadline: 03/01
Tuition: full time: $43,220; part
time: $28,085
Room/board/expenses: $20,343
Median grant: $15,000
**Average student indebtedness at
graduation:** $131,125
Enrollment: full time: 743; part
time: 142
men: 49%; women: 51%;
minorities: 21%
Acceptance rate (full time): 56%
Midrange LSAT (full time): 153-160
**Midrange undergraduate GPA (full
time):** 3.02-3.58
**Midrange of full-time private-sector
salaries of 2011 grads:** $41,500-
$67,500
2011 grads employed in: law firms:
57%; business and industry: 22%;
government: 9%; public interest:
4%; judicial clerk: 4%; academia:
2%; unknown: 0%
Employment location for 2011 class:
Intl. 0%; N.E. 0%; M.A. 1%; E.N.C.
85%; W.N.C. 2%; S.A. 6%; E.S.C.
0%; W.S.C. 1%; Mt. 2%; Pac. 3%;
unknown 0%

Illinois Institute of Technology (Chicago-Kent)

565 W. Adams Street
Chicago, IL 60661-3691
http://www.kentlaw.iit.edu/
Private
Admissions: (312) 906-5020
E-mail:
admissions@kentlaw.iit.edu
Financial aid: (312) 906-5180
Application deadline: 03/15
Tuition: full time: $43,260; part time: $31,620
Room/board/expenses: $18,666
Median grant: $20,000
Average student indebtedness at graduation: $112,750
Enrollment: full time: 738; part time: 161
men: 52%; women: 48%; minorities: 23%
Acceptance rate (full time): 52%
Midrange LSAT (full time): 155-161
Midrange undergraduate GPA (full time): 3.06-3.62
Midrange of full-time private-sector salaries of 2011 grads: $50,000-$100,000
2011 grads employed in: law firms: 55%; business and industry: 25%; government: 10%; public interest: 3%; judicial clerk: 4%; academia: 3%; unknown: 0%
Employment location for 2011 class: Intl. 2%; N.E. 1%; M.A. 2%; E.N.C. 89%; W.N.C. 0%; S.A. 3%; E.S.C. 0%; W.S.C. 1%; Mt. 0%; Pac. 3%; unknown 0%

John Marshall Law School

315 S. Plymouth Court
Chicago, IL 60604
http://www.jmls.edu
Private
Admissions: (800) 537-4280
E-mail: admission@jmls.edu
Financial aid: (800) 537-4280
Application deadline: 03/01
Tuition: full time: $41,304; part time: $28,524
Room/board/expenses: $26,004
Median grant: $12,000
Average student indebtedness at graduation: $142,587
Enrollment: full time: 1,138; part time: 328
men: 53%; women: 47%; minorities: 23%
Acceptance rate (full time): 66%
Midrange LSAT (full time): 149-155
Midrange undergraduate GPA (full time): 2.91-3.39
Midrange of full-time private-sector salaries of 2011 grads: $45,000-$71,000
2011 grads employed in: law firms: 53%; business and industry: 25%; government: 15%; public interest: 3%; judicial clerk: 1%; academia: 4%; unknown: 0%
Employment location for 2011 class: Intl. 1%; N.E. 0%; M.A. 2%; E.N.C. 90%; W.N.C. 0%; S.A. 4%; E.S.C. 0%; W.S.C. 1%; Mt. 1%; Pac. 1%; unknown 0%

Loyola University Chicago

25 E. Pearson Street
Chicago, IL 60611
http://www.luc.edu/law/
Private
Admissions: (312) 915-7170
E-mail: law-admissions@luc.edu
Financial aid: (312) 915-7170
Application deadline: 03/01

Tuition: full time: $40,582; part time: $30,642
Room/board/expenses: $19,888
Median grant: $12,000
Average student indebtedness at graduation: $117,688
Enrollment: full time: 747; part time: 107
men: 48%; women: 52%; minorities: 27%
Acceptance rate (full time): 44%
Midrange LSAT (full time): 157-160
Midrange undergraduate GPA (full time): 3.15-3.58
Midrange of full-time private-sector salaries of 2011 grads: $47,789-$85,314
2011 grads employed in: law firms: 50%; business and industry: 22%; government: 14%; public interest: 3%; judicial clerk: 6%; academia: 5%; unknown: 0%
Employment location for 2011 class: Intl. 1%; N.E. 2%; M.A. 1%; E.N.C. 87%; W.N.C. 3%; S.A. 4%; E.S.C. 1%; W.S.C. 1%; Mt. 1%; Pac. 1%; unknown 0%

Northern Illinois University

Swen Parson Hall, Room 276
De Kalb, IL 60115
http://niu.edu/law
Public
Admissions: (815) 753-8595
E-mail: lawadm@niu.edu
Financial aid: (815) 753-8595
Application deadline: 04/01
In-state tuition: full time: $19,811; part time: $638/credit hour
Out-of-state tuition: full time: $35,129
Room/board/expenses: $18,189
Median grant: $7,500
Average student indebtedness at graduation: $72,479
Enrollment: full time: 322; part time: 9
men: 56%; women: 44%; minorities: 21%
Acceptance rate (full time): 60%
Midrange LSAT (full time): 147-153
Midrange undergraduate GPA (full time): 2.81-3.39
Midrange of full-time private-sector salaries of 2011 grads: $40,000-$60,000
2011 grads employed in: law firms: 50%; business and industry: 19%; government: 15%; public interest: 8%; judicial clerk: 4%; academia: 4%; unknown: 0%
Employment location for 2011 class: Intl. 0%; N.E. 0%; M.A. 0%; E.N.C. 91%; W.N.C. 1%; S.A. 5%; E.S.C. 0%; W.S.C. 0%; Mt. 3%; Pac. 0%; unknown 0%

Northwestern University

375 E. Chicago Avenue
Chicago, IL 60611
http://www.law.northwestern.edu
Private
Admissions: (312) 503-8465
E-mail: admissions@law.northwestern.edu
Financial aid: (312) 503-8465
Application deadline: 03/01
Tuition: full time: $53,468; part time: N/A
Room/board/expenses: $22,494
Median grant: $20,000
Average student indebtedness at graduation: $156,791

Enrollment: full time: 811; part time: N/A
men: 53%; women: 47%; minorities: 30%
Acceptance rate (full time): 24%
Midrange LSAT (full time): 164-171
Midrange undergraduate GPA (full time): 3.38-3.84
Midrange of full-time private-sector salaries of 2011 grads: $145,000-$160,000
2011 grads employed in: law firms: 70%; business and industry: 11%; government: 4%; public interest: 4%; judicial clerk: 10%; academia: 2%; unknown: 0%
Employment location for 2011 class: Intl. 3%; N.E. 4%; M.A. 19%; E.N.C. 45%; W.N.C. 1%; S.A. 9%; E.S.C. 0%; W.S.C. 3%; Mt. 2%; Pac. 14%; unknown 0%

Southern Illinois University-Carbondale

Lesar Law Building
Carbondale, IL 62901
http://www.law.siu.edu
Public
Admissions: (800) 739-9187
E-mail: lawadmit@siu.edu
Financial aid: (618) 453-4334
Application deadline: 04/01
In-state tuition: full time: $16,995; part time: N/A
Out-of-state tuition: full time: $38,567
Room/board/expenses: $15,989
Median grant: $5,000
Average student indebtedness at graduation: $67,072
Enrollment: full time: 345; part time: N/A
men: 63%; women: 37%; minorities: 11%
Acceptance rate (full time): 57%
Midrange LSAT (full time): 149-155
Midrange undergraduate GPA (full time): 2.65-3.43
Midrange of full-time private-sector salaries of 2011 grads: $40,000-$60,000
2011 grads employed in: law firms: 70%; business and industry: 11%; government: 12%; public interest: 2%; judicial clerk: 2%; academia: 1%; unknown: 0%
Employment location for 2011 class: Intl. 1%; N.E. 0%; M.A. 0%; E.N.C. 69%; W.N.C. 12%; S.A. 7%; E.S.C. 9%; W.S.C. 1%; Mt. 0%; Pac. 0%; unknown 0%

University of Chicago

1111 E. 60th Street
Chicago, IL 60637
http://www.law.uchicago.edu
Private
Admissions: (773) 702-9484
E-mail: admissions@law.uchicago.edu
Financial aid: (773) 702-9484
Application deadline: 02/01
Tuition: full time: $50,727; part time: N/A
Room/board/expenses: $24,291
Median grant: $11,334
Average student indebtedness at graduation: $135,307
Enrollment: full time: 610; part time: N/A
men: 57%; women: 43%; minorities: 27%
Acceptance rate (full time): 20%
Midrange LSAT (full time): 167-173
Midrange undergraduate GPA (full time): 3.65-3.96

Midrange of full-time private-sector salaries of 2011 grads: $160,000-$160,000
2011 grads employed in: law firms: 58%; business and industry: 9%; government: 5%; public interest: 16%; judicial clerk: 10%; academia: 3%; unknown: 0%
Employment location for 2011 class: Intl. 4%; N.E. 4%; M.A. 13%; E.N.C. 42%; W.N.C. 3%; S.A. 10%; E.S.C. 1%; W.S.C. 7%; Mt. 4%; Pac. 14%; unknown 0%

University of Illinois-Urbana-Champaign

504 E. Pennsylvania Avenue
Champaign, IL 61820
http://www.law.illinois.edu
Public
Admissions: (217) 244-6415
E-mail: law.admissions@illinois.edu
Financial aid: (217) 244-6415
Application deadline: 03/15
In-state tuition: full time: $38,497; part time: N/A
Out-of-state tuition: full time: $45,917
Room/board/expenses: $16,926
Median grant: $20,000
Average student indebtedness at graduation: $95,830
Enrollment: full time: 627; part time: N/A
men: 57%; women: 43%; minorities: 31%
Acceptance rate (full time): 43%
Midrange LSAT (full time): 158-165
Midrange undergraduate GPA (full time): 3.23-3.73
Midrange of full-time private-sector salaries of 2011 grads: $55,000-$145,000
2011 grads employed in: law firms: 45%; business and industry: 20%; government: 17%; public interest: 7%; judicial clerk: 6%; academia: 6%; unknown: 0%
Employment location for 2011 class: Intl. 1%; N.E. 0%; M.A. 5%; E.N.C. 62%; W.N.C. 5%; S.A. 8%; E.S.C. 1%; W.S.C. 5%; Mt. 6%; Pac. 9%; unknown 0%

INDIANA

Indiana University-Bloomington (Maurer)

211 S. Indiana Avenue
Bloomington, IN 47405-1001
http://www.law.indiana.edu
Public
Admissions: (812) 855-4765
E-mail: lawadmis@indiana.edu
Financial aid: (812) 855-7746
Application deadline: 05/01
In-state tuition: full time: $29,946; part time: N/A
Out-of-state tuition: full time: $48,021
Room/board/expenses: $19,784
Median grant: $18,970
Average student indebtedness at graduation: $113,011
Enrollment: full time: 665; part time: N/A
men: 60%; women: 40%; minorities: 18%
Acceptance rate (full time): 46%
Midrange LSAT (full time): 156-166
Midrange undergraduate GPA (full time): 3.39-3.88
Midrange of full-time private-sector salaries of 2011 grads: $76,000-$105,000

2011 grads employed in: law firms: 44%; business and industry: 16%; government: 16%; public interest: 7%; judicial clerk: 10%; academia: 7%; unknown: 0%
Employment location for 2011 class: Intl. 1%; N.E. 0%; M.A. 5%; E.N.C. 63%; W.N.C. 1%; S.A. 11%; E.S.C. 7%; W.S.C. 3%; Mt. 3%; Pac. 7%; unknown 0%

Indiana University-Indianapolis[1]

530 W. New York Street
Indianapolis, IN 46202-3225
http://www.indylaw.indiana.edu
Public
Admissions: (317) 274-2459
E-mail: pkkinney@iupui.edu
Financial aid: (317) 278-2862
Tuition: N/A
Room/board/expenses: N/A
Enrollment: N/A

University of Notre Dame

PO Box 780
Notre Dame, IN 46556-0780
http://law.nd.edu
Private
Admissions: (574) 631-6626
E-mail: lawadmit@nd.edu
Financial aid: (574) 631-6626
Application deadline: 03/15
Tuition: full time: $45,980; part time: N/A
Room/board/expenses: $18,100
Median grant: $18,000
Average student indebtedness at graduation: $101,512
Enrollment: full time: 545; part time: N/A
men: 56%; women: 44%; minorities: 28%
Acceptance rate (full time): 24%
Midrange LSAT (full time): 161-167
Midrange undergraduate GPA (full time): 3.43-3.80
Midrange of full-time private-sector salaries of 2011 grads: $70,000-$117,500
2011 grads employed in: law firms: 37%; business and industry: 9%; government: 17%; public interest: 12%; judicial clerk: 22%; academia: 2%; unknown: 1%
Employment location for 2011 class: Intl. 1%; N.E. 1%; M.A. 16%; E.N.C. 31%; W.N.C. 6%; S.A. 21%; E.S.C. 2%; W.S.C. 9%; Mt. 5%; Pac. 8%; unknown 1%

Valparaiso University

656 S. Greenwich Street
Wesemann Hall
Valparaiso, IN 46383
http://www.valpo.edu/law
Private
Admissions: (888) 825-7652
E-mail: valpolaw@valpo.edu
Financial aid: (219) 465-7818
Application deadline: 06/01
Tuition: full time: $38,852; part time: $1,490/credit hour
Room/board/expenses: $12,350
Median grant: $18,620
Average student indebtedness at graduation: $125,495
Enrollment: full time: 488; part time: 20
men: 53%; women: 47%; minorities: 28%
Acceptance rate (full time): 78%
Midrange LSAT (full time): 145-152
Midrange undergraduate GPA (full time): 2.95-3.49

Midrange of full-time private-sector salaries of 2011 grads: $45,000–$65,000
2011 grads employed in: law firms: 51%; business and industry: 23%; government: 12%; public interest: 2%; judicial clerk: 9%; academia: 2%; unknown: 2%
Employment location for 2011 class: Intl. 0%; N.E. 1%; M.A. 1%; E.N.C. 78%; W.N.C. 4%; S.A. 4%; E.S.C. 5%; W.S.C. 4%; Mt. 2%; Pac. 2%; unknown 0%

IOWA

Drake University
2507 University Avenue
Des Moines, IA 50311
http://www.law.drake.edu/
Private
Admissions: (515) 271-2782
E-mail: lawadmit@drake.edu
Financial aid: (515) 271-2782
Application deadline: 04/01
Tuition: full time: $35,282; part time: $1,210/credit hour
Room/board/expenses: $19,265
Median grant: $15,500
Average student indebtedness at graduation: $106,368
Enrollment: full time: 403; part time: 8
men: 55%; women: 45%; minorities: 11%
Acceptance rate (full time): 66%
Midrange LSAT (full time): 152–159
Midrange undergraduate GPA (full time): 3.06–3.58
Midrange of full-time private-sector salaries of 2011 grads: $40,000–$55,000
2011 grads employed in: law firms: 58%; business and industry: 19%; government: 9%; public interest: 6%; judicial clerk: 8%; academia: 0%; unknown: 0%
Employment location for 2011 class: Intl. 0%; N.E. 0%; M.A. 2%; E.N.C. 8%; W.N.C. 83%; S.A. 1%; E.S.C. 1%; W.S.C. 2%; Mt. 2%; Pac. 3%; unknown 0%

University of Iowa
320 Melrose Avenue
Iowa City, IA 52242
http://www.law.uiowa.edu
Public
Admissions: (319) 335-9095
E-mail: law-admissions@uiowa.edu
Financial aid: (319) 335-9142
Application deadline: 03/01
In-state tuition: full time: $27,344; part time: N/A
Out-of-state tuition: full time: $47,792
Room/board/expenses: $17,245
Median grant: $19,708
Average student indebtedness at graduation: $95,574
Enrollment: full time: 517; part time: N/A
men: 58%; women: 42%; minorities: 17%
Acceptance rate (full time): 49%
Midrange LSAT (full time): 158–164
Midrange undergraduate GPA (full time): 3.46–3.80
Midrange of full-time private-sector salaries of 2011 grads: $46,000–$80,500
2011 grads employed in: law firms: 49%; business and industry: 15%; government: 18%; public interest: 7%; judicial clerk: 8%; academia: 2%; unknown: 1%

Employment location for 2011 class: Intl. 4%; N.E. 1%; M.A. 5%; E.N.C. 16%; W.N.C. 49%; S.A. 14%; E.S.C. 0%; W.S.C. 3%; Mt. 4%; Pac. 7%; unknown 0%

KANSAS

University of Kansas
Green Hall, 1535 W. 15th Street
Lawrence, KS 66045-7608
http://www.law.ku.edu
Public
Admissions: (866) 220-3654
E-mail: admitlaw@ku.edu
Financial aid: (785) 864-4700
Application deadline: 05/01
In-state tuition: full time: $18,664; part time: N/A
Out-of-state tuition: full time: $31,474
Room/board/expenses: $17,058
Median grant: $2,325
Average student indebtedness at graduation: $74,454
Enrollment: full time: 441; part time: N/A
men: 61%; women: 39%; minorities: 16%
Acceptance rate (full time): 54%
Midrange LSAT (full time): 154–159
Midrange undergraduate GPA (full time): 3.22–3.71
Midrange of full-time private-sector salaries of 2011 grads: $45,000–$70,000
2011 grads employed in: law firms: 51%; business and industry: 22%; government: 14%; public interest: 4%; judicial clerk: 6%; academia: 3%; unknown: 0%
Employment location for 2011 class: Intl. 2%; N.E. 0%; M.A. 2%; E.N.C. 2%; W.N.C. 76%; S.A. 5%; E.S.C. 0%; W.S.C. 4%; Mt. 5%; Pac. 5%; unknown 0%

Washburn University
1700 S.W. College Avenue
Topeka, KS 66621
http://washburnlaw.edu
Public
Admissions: (785) 670-1185
E-mail: admissions@washburnlaw.edu
Financial aid: (785) 670-1151
Application deadline: 04/01
In-state tuition: full time: $597/credit hour; part time: N/A
Out-of-state tuition: full time: $932/credit hour
Room/board/expenses: $15,299
Median grant: $13,125
Average student indebtedness at graduation: $86,135
Enrollment: full time: 385; part time: N/A
men: 61%; women: 39%; minorities: 15%
Acceptance rate (full time): 59%
Midrange LSAT (full time): 150–156
Midrange undergraduate GPA (full time): 2.93–3.51
Midrange of full-time private-sector salaries of 2011 grads: $40,000–$55,000
2011 grads employed in: law firms: 51%; business and industry: 19%; government: 21%; public interest: 2%; judicial clerk: 4%; academia: 1%; unknown: 2%
Employment location for 2011 class: Intl. 0%; N.E. 0%; M.A. 1%; E.N.C. 1%; W.N.C. 77%; S.A. 2%; E.S.C. 0%; W.S.C. 4%; Mt. 12%; Pac. 3%; unknown 2%

KENTUCKY

Northern Kentucky University (Chase)
Nunn Hall
Highland Heights, KY 41099-6031
http://chaselaw.nku.edu
Public
Admissions: (859) 572-5841
E-mail: chaseadmissions@nku.edu
Financial aid: (859) 572-6437
Application deadline: 04/01
In-state tuition: full time: $16,562; part time: $14,014
Out-of-state tuition: full time: $35,204
Room/board/expenses: $14,920
Median grant: $6,500
Average student indebtedness at graduation: $79,898
Enrollment: full time: 364; part time: 182
men: 62%; women: 38%; minorities: 7%
Acceptance rate (full time): 73%
Midrange LSAT (full time): 149–155
Midrange undergraduate GPA (full time): 2.97–3.41
Midrange of full-time private-sector salaries of 2011 grads: $38,000–$62,000
2011 grads employed in: law firms: 40%; business and industry: 26%; government: 12%; public interest: 6%; judicial clerk: 9%; academia: 5%; unknown: 2%
Employment location for 2011 class: Intl. 0%; N.E. 0%; M.A. 2%; E.N.C. 38%; W.N.C. 0%; S.A. 3%; E.S.C. 54%; W.S.C. 1%; Mt. 1%; Pac. 1%; unknown 0%

University of Kentucky
209 Law Building
Lexington, KY 40506-0048
http://www.law.uky.edu
Public
Admissions: (859) 257-6770
E-mail: lawadmissions@email.uky.edu
Financial aid: (859) 257-3172
Application deadline: 03/14
In-state tuition: full time: $19,404; part time: N/A
Out-of-state tuition: full time: $33,618
Room/board/expenses: $15,996
Median grant: $6,000
Average student indebtedness at graduation: $75,738
Enrollment: full time: 402; part time: N/A
men: 57%; women: 43%; minorities: 12%
Acceptance rate (full time): 51%
Midrange LSAT (full time): 155–161
Midrange undergraduate GPA (full time): 3.25–3.73
Midrange of full-time private-sector salaries of 2011 grads: $45,000–$65,000
2011 grads employed in: law firms: 49%; business and industry: 19%; government: 8%; public interest: 4%; judicial clerk: 18%; academia: 2%; unknown: 0%
Employment location for 2011 class: Intl. 0%; N.E. 2%; M.A. 1%; E.N.C. 6%; W.N.C. 0%; S.A. 12%; E.S.C. 76%; W.S.C. 2%; Mt. 1%; Pac. 0%; unknown 0%

University of Louisville (Brandeis)
2301 S. Third Street
Louisville, KY 40292
http://www.law.louisville.edu
Public
Admissions: (502) 852-6365
E-mail: lawadmissions@louisville.edu
Financial aid: (502) 852-6391
Application deadline: 03/15
In-state tuition: full time: $17,854; part time: $16,090
Out-of-state tuition: full time: $34,026
Room/board/expenses: $18,802
Median grant: $6,000
Average student indebtedness at graduation: $85,634
Enrollment: full time: 363; part time: 28
men: 54%; women: 46%; minorities: 10%
Acceptance rate (full time): 47%
Midrange LSAT (full time): 155–159
Midrange undergraduate GPA (full time): 3.16–3.65
Midrange of full-time private-sector salaries of 2011 grads: $45,700–$75,000
2011 grads employed in: law firms: 40%; business and industry: 19%; government: 21%; public interest: 8%; judicial clerk: 9%; academia: 3%; unknown: 0%
Employment location for 2011 class: Intl. 0%; N.E. 1%; M.A. 1%; E.N.C. 8%; W.N.C. 0%; S.A. 8%; E.S.C. 81%; W.S.C. 2%; Mt. 1%; Pac. 0%; unknown 0%

LOUISIANA

Louisiana State University–Baton Rouge (Hebert)
400 Paul M. Hebert Law Center
Baton Rouge, LA 70803
http://www.law.lsu.edu
Public
Admissions: (225) 578-8646
E-mail: admissions@law.lsu.edu
Financial aid: (225) 578-3103
Application deadline: 03/01
In-state tuition: full time: $18,618; part time: N/A
Out-of-state tuition: full time: $36,006
Room/board/expenses: $20,020
Median grant: $3,956
Average student indebtedness at graduation: $78,762
Enrollment: full time: 634; part time: 16
men: 56%; women: 44%; minorities: 24%
Acceptance rate (full time): 45%
Midrange LSAT (full time): 153–160
Midrange undergraduate GPA (full time): 3.09–3.60
Midrange of full-time private-sector salaries of 2011 grads: $47,500–$71,720
2011 grads employed in: law firms: 58%; business and industry: 10%; government: 10%; public interest: 3%; judicial clerk: 20%; academia: 0%; unknown: 0%
Employment location for 2011 class: Intl. 1%; N.E. 0%; M.A. 1%; E.N.C. 0%; W.N.C. 0%; S.A. 1%; E.S.C. 1%; W.S.C. 96%; Mt. 0%; Pac. 1%; unknown 0%

Loyola University New Orleans
7214 St. Charles Avenue
PO Box 901
New Orleans, LA 70118
http://law.loyno.edu/
Private
Admissions: (504) 861-5575
E-mail: ladmit@loyno.edu
Financial aid: (504) 865-3231
Application deadline: rolling
Tuition: full time: $41,448; part time: $28,428
Room/board/expenses: $20,700
Median grant: $20,000
Average student indebtedness at graduation: $124,355
Enrollment: full time: 635; part time: 118
men: 52%; women: 48%; minorities: 24%
Acceptance rate (full time): 69%
Midrange LSAT (full time): 150–155
Midrange undergraduate GPA (full time): 2.98–3.46
Midrange of full-time private-sector salaries of 2011 grads: N/A–N/A
2011 grads employed in: law firms: 54%; business and industry: 15%; government: 12%; public interest: 6%; judicial clerk: 9%; academia: 3%; unknown: 0%
Employment location for 2011 class: Intl. 0%; N.E. 0%; M.A. 3%; E.N.C. 2%; W.N.C. 0%; S.A. 6%; E.S.C. 2%; W.S.C. 84%; Mt. 1%; Pac. 2%; unknown 0%

Southern University Law Center
PO Box 9294
Baton Rouge, LA 70813
http://www.sulc.edu/index_v3.htm
Public
Admissions: (225) 771-5340
E-mail: Admission@sulc.edu
Financial aid: (225) 771-2141
Application deadline: 12/31
In-state tuition: full time: $10,990; part time: $9,370
Out-of-state tuition: full time: $18,590
Room/board/expenses: $18,922
Average student indebtedness at graduation: $21,911
Enrollment: full time: 565; part time: 193
men: 47%; women: 53%; minorities: 65%
Acceptance rate (full time): 58%
Midrange LSAT (full time): 143–149
Midrange undergraduate GPA (full time): 2.64–3.27
Midrange of full-time private-sector salaries of 2011 grads: $36,101–$63,750
2011 grads employed in: law firms: 35%; business and industry: 21%; government: 20%; public interest: 6%; judicial clerk: 11%; academia: 7%; unknown: 0%
Employment location for 2011 class: Intl. 0%; N.E. 1%; M.A. 3%; E.N.C. 3%; W.N.C. 2%; S.A. 5%; E.S.C. 6%; W.S.C. 81%; Mt. 0%; Pac. 1%; unknown 0%

Tulane University
6329 Freret Street
John Giffen Weinmann Hall
New Orleans, LA 70118-6231
http://www.law.tulane.edu
Private
Admissions: (504) 865-5930
E-mail: admissions@law.tulane.edu
Financial aid: (504) 865-5931
Application deadline: 03/15

Tuition: full time: $45,240; part time: N/A
Room/board/expenses: $20,990
Median grant: $20,000
Average student indebtedness at graduation: $115,029
Enrollment: full time: 743; part time: N/A
men: 50%; women: 50%; minorities: 18%
Acceptance rate (full time): 48%
Midrange LSAT (full time): 156-163
Midrange undergraduate GPA (full time): 3.23-3.63
Midrange of full-time private-sector salaries of 2011 grads: $70,000-$103,000
2011 grads employed in: law firms: 49%; business and industry: 20%; government: 11%; public interest: 7%; judicial clerk: 11%; academia: 1%; unknown: 2%
Employment location for 2011 class: Intl. 2%; N.E. 4%; M.A. 14%; E.N.C. 3%; W.N.C. 2%; S.A. 15%; E.S.C. 1%; W.S.C. 54%; Mt. 1%; Pac. 4%; unknown 3%

MAINE

University of Maine

246 Deering Avenue
Portland, ME 04102
http://mainelaw.maine.edu
Public
Admissions: (207) 780-4341
E-mail: lawadmissions@maine.edu
Financial aid: (207) 780-5250
Application deadline: 04/15
In-state tuition: full time: $23,610; part time: N/A
Out-of-state tuition: full time: $34,680
Room/board/expenses: $15,794
Median grant: $5,000
Average student indebtedness at graduation: $97,805
Enrollment: full time: 266; part time: 10
men: 52%; women: 48%; minorities: 8%
Acceptance rate (full time): 56%
Midrange LSAT (full time): 152-157
Midrange undergraduate GPA (full time): 3.10-3.53
Midrange of full-time private-sector salaries of 2011 grads: $40,000-$65,000
2011 grads employed in: law firms: 44%; business and industry: 25%; government: 11%; public interest: 5%; judicial clerk: 13%; academia: 2%; unknown: 0%
Employment location for 2011 class: Intl. 0%; N.E. 87%; M.A. 0%; E.N.C. 2%; W.N.C. 0%; S.A. 6%; E.S.C. 0%; W.S.C. 2%; Mt. 0%; Pac. 3%; unknown 0%

MARYLAND

University of Baltimore

1420 N. Charles Street
Baltimore, MD 21201-5779
http://law.ubalt.edu
Public
Admissions: (410) 837-4459
E-mail: lawadmiss@ubalt.edu
Financial aid: (410) 837-4763
Application deadline: 03/15
In-state tuition: full time: $26,156; part time: $20,613
Out-of-state tuition: full time: $38,440
Room/board/expenses: $22,200
Median grant: $1,000
Average student indebtedness at graduation: $110,431

Enrollment: full time: 726; part time: 360
men: 52%; women: 48%; minorities: 25%
Acceptance rate (full time): 64%
Midrange LSAT (full time): 150-156
Midrange undergraduate GPA (full time): 2.91-3.46
Midrange of full-time private-sector salaries of 2011 grads: $45,000-$77,000
2011 grads employed in: law firms: 38%; business and industry: 18%; government: 16%; public interest: 4%; judicial clerk: 20%; academia: 3%; unknown: 0%
Employment location for 2011 class: Intl. 0%; N.E. 0%; M.A. 1%; E.N.C. 1%; W.N.C. 0%; S.A. 93%; E.S.C. 0%; W.S.C. 0%; Mt. 0%; Pac. 0%; unknown 3%

University of Maryland (Carey)

500 W. Baltimore Street
Baltimore, MD 21201-1786
http://www.law.umaryland.edu
Public
Admissions: (410) 706-3492
E-mail: admissions@law.umaryland.edu
Financial aid: (410) 706-0873
Application deadline: 04/01
In-state tuition: full time: $26,093; part time: $19,958
Out-of-state tuition: full time: $37,710
Room/board/expenses: $28,953
Median grant: $3,900
Average student indebtedness at graduation: $122,349
Enrollment: full time: 711; part time: 195
men: 50%; women: 50%; minorities: 35%
Acceptance rate (full time): 27%
Midrange LSAT (full time): 152-164
Midrange undergraduate GPA (full time): 3.33-3.76
Midrange of full-time private-sector salaries of 2011 grads: $50,000-$110,000
2011 grads employed in: law firms: 29%; business and industry: 13%; government: 16%; public interest: 11%; judicial clerk: 22%; academia: 9%; unknown: 0%
Employment location for 2011 class: Intl. 0%; N.E. 1%; M.A. 5%; E.N.C. 2%; W.N.C. 0%; S.A. 88%; E.S.C. 0%; W.S.C. 1%; Mt. 1%; Pac. 2%; unknown 0%

MASSACHUSETTS

Boston College

885 Centre Street
Newton, MA 02459-1154
http://www.bc.edu/lawschool
Private
Admissions: (617) 552-4351
E-mail: bclawadm@bc.edu
Financial aid: (617) 552-4243
Application deadline: 03/31
Tuition: full time: $43,170; part time: N/A
Room/board/expenses: $19,360
Median grant: $20,000
Average student indebtedness at graduation: $106,550
Enrollment: full time: 759; part time: N/A
men: 53%; women: 47%; minorities: 20%
Acceptance rate (full time): 29%
Midrange LSAT (full time): 161-166
Midrange undergraduate GPA (full time): 3.40-3.71

Midrange of full-time private-sector salaries of 2011 grads: $105,000-$160,000
2011 grads employed in: law firms: 49%; business and industry: 7%; government: 13%; public interest: 7%; judicial clerk: 16%; academia: 7%; unknown: 0%
Employment location for 2011 class: Intl. 3%; N.E. 60%; M.A. 12%; E.N.C. 5%; W.N.C. 0%; S.A. 11%; E.S.C. 1%; W.S.C. 2%; Mt. 0%; Pac. 6%; unknown 0%

Boston University

765 Commonwealth Avenue
Boston, MA 02215
http://www.bu.edu/law/
Private
Admissions: (617) 353-3100
E-mail: bulawadm@bu.edu
Financial aid: (617) 353-3160
Application deadline: 03/31
Tuition: full time: $44,168; part time: N/A
Room/board/expenses: $17,842
Median grant: $15,000
Average student indebtedness at graduation: $110,437
Enrollment: full time: 740; part time: N/A
men: 49%; women: 51%; minorities: 25%
Acceptance rate (full time): 30%
Midrange LSAT (full time): 162-167
Midrange undergraduate GPA (full time): 3.52-3.83
Midrange of full-time private-sector salaries of 2011 grads: $70,750-$160,000
2011 grads employed in: law firms: 39%; business and industry: 12%; government: 15%; public interest: 15%; judicial clerk: 11%; academia: 7%; unknown: 0%
Employment location for 2011 class: Intl. 2%; N.E. 53%; M.A. 21%; E.N.C. 4%; W.N.C. 0%; S.A. 7%; E.S.C. 0%; W.S.C. 3%; Mt. 3%; Pac. 8%; unknown 0%

Harvard University

1563 Massachusetts Avenue
Cambridge, MA 02138
http://www.law.harvard.edu
Private
Admissions: (617) 495-3109
E-mail: jdadmiss@law.harvard.edu
Financial aid: (617) 495-4606
Application deadline: 02/01
Tuition: full time: $50,880; part time: N/A
Room/board/expenses: $24,920
Median grant: $19,800
Average student indebtedness at graduation: $124,312
Enrollment: full time: 1,727; part time: N/A
men: 53%; women: 47%; minorities: 32%
Acceptance rate (full time): 16%
Midrange of full-time private-sector salaries of 2011 grads: $160,000-$160,000
2011 grads employed in: law firms: 57%; business and industry: 5%; government: 6%; public interest: 10%; judicial clerk: 22%; academia: 0%; unknown: 0%
Employment location for 2011 class: Intl. 3%; N.E. 11%; M.A. 33%; E.N.C. 7%; W.N.C. 2%; S.A. 19%; E.S.C. 2%; W.S.C. 7%; Mt. 2%; Pac. 14%; unknown 0%

New England Law Boston

154 Stuart Street
Boston, MA 02116
http://www.nesl.edu
Private
Admissions: (617) 422-7210
E-mail: admit@nesl.edu
Financial aid: (617) 422-7298
Application deadline: 03/15
Tuition: full time: $42,570; part time: $31,948
Room/board/expenses: $19,930
Median grant: $15,000
Average student indebtedness at graduation: $132,632
Enrollment: full time: 835; part time: 332
men: 43%; women: 57%; minorities: 19%
Acceptance rate (full time): 88%
Midrange LSAT (full time): 145-153
Midrange undergraduate GPA (full time): 2.76-3.43
Midrange of full-time private-sector salaries of 2011 grads: $45,000-$69,000
2011 grads employed in: law firms: 40%; business and industry: 32%; government: 12%; public interest: 6%; judicial clerk: 7%; academia: 1%; unknown: 2%
Employment location for 2011 class: Intl. 1%; N.E. 78%; M.A. 7%; E.N.C. 2%; W.N.C. 1%; S.A. 6%; E.S.C. 1%; W.S.C. 1%; Mt. 1%; Pac. 2%; unknown 0%

Northeastern University

400 Huntington Avenue
Boston, MA 02115
http://northeastern.edu/law
Private
Admissions: (617) 373-2395
E-mail: lawadmissions@neu.edu
Financial aid: (617) 373-4620
Application deadline: 03/01
Tuition: full time: $43,048; part time: N/A
Room/board/expenses: $22,648
Median grant: $8,500
Average student indebtedness at graduation: $129,467
Enrollment: full time: 604; part time: N/A
men: 40%; women: 60%; minorities: 35%
Acceptance rate (full time): 39%
Midrange LSAT (full time): 154-163
Midrange undergraduate GPA (full time): 3.27-3.67
Midrange of full-time private-sector salaries of 2011 grads: $47,750-$80,000
2011 grads employed in: law firms: 34%; business and industry: 13%; government: 11%; public interest: 24%; judicial clerk: 9%; academia: 8%; unknown: 1%
Employment location for 2011 class: Intl. 2%; N.E. 65%; M.A. 9%; E.N.C. 1%; W.N.C. 1%; S.A. 10%; E.S.C. 0%; W.S.C. 2%; Mt. 2%; Pac. 9%; unknown 0%

Suffolk University

120 Tremont Street
Boston, MA 02108
http://www.law.suffolk.edu/
Private
Admissions: (617) 573-8144
E-mail: lawadm@admin.suffolk.edu
Financial aid: (617) 573-8147
Application deadline: 03/01
Tuition: full time: $44,064; part time: $33,048

Room/board/expenses: $16,484
Median grant: $15,000
Average student indebtedness at graduation: $126,280
Enrollment: full time: 1,073; part time: 559
men: 49%; women: 51%; minorities: 22%
Acceptance rate (full time): 75%
Midrange LSAT (full time): 148-156
Midrange undergraduate GPA (full time): 3.06-3.50
Midrange of full-time private-sector salaries of 2011 grads: $50,000-$120,000
2011 grads employed in: law firms: 45%; business and industry: 27%; government: 16%; public interest: 4%; judicial clerk: 5%; academia: 3%; unknown: 0%
Employment location for 2011 class: Intl. 1%; N.E. 90%; M.A. 3%; E.N.C. 1%; W.N.C. 0%; S.A. 2%; E.S.C. 0%; W.S.C. 1%; Mt. 0%; Pac. 1%; unknown 1%

University of Massachusetts-Dartmouth

333 Faunce Corner Road
North Dartmouth, MA 02747
http://www.umass.edu/law/admissions
Public
Admissions: (508) 985-1110
E-mail: lawadmissions@umass.edu
Financial aid: (508) 985-1187
Application deadline: 06/15
In-state tuition: full time: $24,178; part time: $18,252
Out-of-state tuition: full time: $31,870
Room/board/expenses: $15,742
Median grant: $5,764
Average student indebtedness at graduation: $96,105
Enrollment: full time: 189; part time: 125
men: 50%; women: 50%; minorities: 26%
Acceptance rate (full time): 66%
Midrange LSAT (full time): 144-150
Midrange undergraduate GPA (full time): 2.78-3.28
Midrange of full-time private-sector salaries of 2011 grads: $39,750-$55,250
2011 grads employed in: law firms: 33%; business and industry: 33%; government: 11%; public interest: 3%; judicial clerk: 11%; academia: 8%; unknown: 0%
Employment location for 2011 class: Intl. 0%; N.E. 89%; M.A. 3%; E.N.C. 0%; W.N.C. 3%; S.A. 6%; E.S.C. 0%; W.S.C. 0%; Mt. 0%; Pac. 0%; unknown 0%

Western New England University

1215 Wilbraham Road
Springfield, MA 01119-2684
http://www.law.wne.edu
Private
Admissions: (413) 782-1406
E-mail: admissions@law.wne.edu
Financial aid: (413) 796-2080
Application deadline: rolling
Tuition: full time: $39,574; part time: $29,280
Room/board/expenses: $23,203
Median grant: $16,000
Average student indebtedness at graduation: $118,900

Enrollment: full time: 259; part time: 106
men: 49%; **women:** 51%; **minorities:** 18%
Acceptance rate (full time): 76%
Midrange LSAT (full time): 148–152
Midrange undergraduate GPA (full time): 2.91–3.41
Midrange of full-time private-sector salaries of 2011 grads: $40,000–$70,000
2011 grads employed in: law firms: 35%; business and industry: 27%; government: 11%; public interest: 15%; judicial clerk: 7%; academia: 6%; unknown: 0%
Employment location for 2011 class: Intl. 4%; N.E. 64%; M.A. 17%; E.N.C. 1%; W.N.C. 1%; S.A. 7%; E.S.C. 0%; W.S.C. 3%; Mt. 2%; Pac. 1%; unknown 0%

MICHIGAN

Michigan State University

648 N. Shaw Lane, Room 368
East Lansing, MI 48824-1300
http://www.law.msu.edu
Private
Admissions: (517) 432-0222
E-mail: law@msu.edu
Financial aid: (517) 432-6810
Application deadline: 04/30
Tuition: full time: $35,377; part time: $26,893
Room/board/expenses: $13,580
Median grant: $27,621
Average student indebtedness at graduation: $114,438
Enrollment: full time: 765; part time: 176
men: 55%; **women:** 45%; **minorities:** 22%
Acceptance rate (full time): 32%
Midrange LSAT (full time): 153–160
Midrange undergraduate GPA (full time): 3.25–3.75
Midrange of full-time private-sector salaries of 2011 grads: $42,000–$68,250
2011 grads employed in: law firms: 41%; business and industry: 26%; government: 11%; public interest: 10%; judicial clerk: 3%; academia: 5%; unknown: 4%
Employment location for 2011 class: Intl. 7%; N.E. 0%; M.A. 7%; E.N.C. 66%; W.N.C. 2%; S.A. 6%; E.S.C. 0%; W.S.C. 4%; Mt. 5%; Pac. 4%; unknown 0%

Thomas M. Cooley Law School

300 S. Capitol Avenue
PO Box 13038
Lansing, MI 48901
http://www.cooley.edu
Private
Admissions: (517) 371-5140
E-mail: admissions@cooley.edu
Financial aid: (517) 371-5140
Application deadline: 09/01
Tuition: full time: $37,140; part time: $23,890
Room/board/expenses: $14,686
Median grant: $13,218
Average student indebtedness at graduation: $122,395
Enrollment: full time: 604; part time: 2,491
men: 49%; **women:** 51%; **minorities:** 30%
Midrange LSAT (full time): 147–155
Midrange undergraduate GPA (full time): 2.65–3.37
Midrange of full-time private-sector salaries of 2011 grads: N/A–N/A

2011 grads employed in: law firms: 57%; business and industry: 22%; government: 10%; public interest: 4%; judicial clerk: 5%; academia: 2%; unknown: 0%
Employment location for 2011 class: Intl. 2%; N.E. 0%; M.A. 9%; E.N.C. 61%; W.N.C. 3%; S.A. 11%; E.S.C. 2%; W.S.C. 4%; Mt. 4%; Pac. 4%; unknown 0%

University of Detroit Mercy

651 E. Jefferson Avenue
Detroit, MI 48226
http://www.law.udmercy.edu
Private
Admissions: (313) 596-0264
E-mail: udmlawao@udmercy.edu
Financial aid: (313) 596-0214
Application deadline: 04/15
Tuition: full time: $38,180; part time: $30,560
Room/board/expenses: $22,537
Median grant: $10,000
Average student indebtedness at graduation: $130,166
Enrollment: full time: 502; part time: 113
men: 54%; **women:** 46%; **minorities:** 18%
Acceptance rate (full time): 48%
Midrange LSAT (full time): 147–158
Midrange undergraduate GPA (full time): 2.85–3.33
Midrange of full-time private-sector salaries of 2011 grads: $40,000–$75,000
2011 grads employed in: law firms: 56%; business and industry: 26%; government: 7%; public interest: 5%; judicial clerk: 4%; academia: 2%; unknown: 0%
Employment location for 2011 class: Intl. 22%; N.E. 0%; M.A. 4%; E.N.C. 65%; W.N.C. 0%; S.A. 5%; E.S.C. 0%; W.S.C. 1%; Mt. 1%; Pac. 2%; unknown 0%

University of Michigan–Ann Arbor

625 S. State Street
Ann Arbor, MI 48109-1215
http://www.law.umich.edu/
Public
Admissions: (734) 764-0537
E-mail: law.jd.admissions@umich.edu
Financial aid: (734) 764-5289
Application deadline: 02/15
In-state tuition: full time: $48,250; part time: N/A
Out-of-state tuition: full time: $51,250
Room/board/expenses: $18,700
Median grant: $15,000
Average student indebtedness at graduation: $120,136
Enrollment: full time: 1,124; part time: N/A
men: 55%; **women:** 45%; **minorities:** 22%
Acceptance rate (full time): 24%
Midrange LSAT (full time): 166–170
Midrange undergraduate GPA (full time): 3.57–3.83
Midrange of full-time private-sector salaries of 2011 grads: $140,000–$160,000
2011 grads employed in: law firms: 47%; business and industry: 11%; government: 9%; public interest: 13%; judicial clerk: 16%; academia: 3%; unknown: 1%
Employment location for 2011 class: Intl. 3%; N.E. 3%; M.A. 22%; E.N.C. 30%; W.N.C. 3%; S.A. 20%; E.S.C. 0%; W.S.C. 3%; Mt. 3%; Pac. 14%; unknown 0%

Wayne State University

471 W. Palmer Street
Detroit, MI 48202
http://www.law.wayne.edu
Public
Admissions: (313) 577-3937
E-mail: lawinquire@wayne.edu
Financial aid: (313) 577-7731
Application deadline: 05/15
In-state tuition: full time: $27,135; part time: $14,665
Out-of-state tuition: full time: $29,660
Room/board/expenses: $23,025
Median grant: $20,317
Average student indebtedness at graduation: $80,482
Enrollment: full time: 382; part time: 156
men: 58%; **women:** 42%; **minorities:** 18%
Acceptance rate (full time): 54%
Midrange LSAT (full time): 153–159
Midrange undergraduate GPA (full time): 3.07–3.59
Midrange of full-time private-sector salaries of 2011 grads: $52,500–$100,000
2011 grads employed in: law firms: 53%; business and industry: 23%; government: 5%; public interest: 10%; judicial clerk: 5%; academia: 4%; unknown: 1%
Employment location for 2011 class: Intl. 1%; N.E. 0%; M.A. 3%; E.N.C. 87%; W.N.C. 0%; S.A. 5%; E.S.C. 0%; W.S.C. 0%; Mt. 1%; Pac. 1%; unknown 2%

MINNESOTA

Hamline University

1536 Hewitt Avenue
St. Paul, MN 55104-1284
http://www.hamline.edu/law
Private
Admissions: (651) 523-2461
E-mail: lawadm@hamline.edu
Financial aid: (651) 523-3000
Application deadline: 05/01
Tuition: full time: $36,396; part time: $26,240
Room/board/expenses: $19,883
Median grant: $26,010
Average student indebtedness at graduation: $104,647
Enrollment: full time: 378; part time: 158
men: 45%; **women:** 55%; **minorities:** 18%
Acceptance rate (full time): 61%
Midrange LSAT (full time): 149–157
Midrange undergraduate GPA (full time): 3.14–3.65
Midrange of full-time private-sector salaries of 2011 grads: $45,000–$62,000
2011 grads employed in: law firms: 38%; business and industry: 35%; government: 9%; public interest: 4%; judicial clerk: 8%; academia: 2%; unknown: 4%
Employment location for 2011 class: Intl. 1%; N.E. 1%; M.A. 2%; E.N.C. 10%; W.N.C. 77%; S.A. 3%; E.S.C. 0%; W.S.C. 0%; Mt. 3%; Pac. 3%; unknown 1%

University of Minnesota–Twin Cities

229 19th Avenue S
Minneapolis, MN 55455
http://www.law.umn.edu
Public
Admissions: (612) 625-3487
E-mail: umnlsadm@umn.edu
Financial aid: (612) 625-3487
Application deadline: 04/01

In-state tuition: full time: $36,820; part time: N/A
Out-of-state tuition: full time: $45,484
Room/board/expenses: $14,604
Median grant: $18,000
Average student indebtedness at graduation: $100,699
Enrollment: full time: 740; part time: 19
men: 57%; **women:** 43%; **minorities:** 22%
Acceptance rate (full time): 23%
Midrange LSAT (full time): 158–168
Midrange undergraduate GPA (full time): 3.36–3.89
Midrange of full-time private-sector salaries of 2011 grads: $85,000–$120,000
2011 grads employed in: law firms: 40%; business and industry: 18%; government: 8%; public interest: 9%; judicial clerk: 16%; academia: 3%; unknown: 6%
Employment location for 2011 class: Intl. 0%; N.E. 0%; M.A. 6%; E.N.C. 8%; W.N.C. 66%; S.A. 3%; E.S.C. 0%; W.S.C. 2%; Mt. 4%; Pac. 7%; unknown 5%

University of St. Thomas

MSL 411, 1000 LaSalle Avenue
Minneapolis, MN 55403-2015
http://www.stthomas.edu/law
Private
Admissions: (651) 962-4895
E-mail: lawschool@stthomas.edu
Financial aid: (651) 962-4895
Application deadline: 07/01
Tuition: full time: $1,256/credit hour; part time: N/A
Room/board/expenses: $19,745
Median grant: $25,000
Average student indebtedness at graduation: $96,659
Enrollment: full time: 445; part time: 3
men: 56%; **women:** 44%; **minorities:** 13%
Acceptance rate (full time): 67%
Midrange LSAT (full time): 152–160
Midrange undergraduate GPA (full time): 3.13–3.67
Midrange of full-time private-sector salaries of 2011 grads: $41,600–$85,000
2011 grads employed in: law firms: 44%; business and industry: 32%; government: 8%; public interest: 6%; judicial clerk: 7%; academia: 1%; unknown: 1%
Employment location for 2011 class: Intl. 2%; N.E. 0%; M.A. 1%; E.N.C. 4%; W.N.C. 79%; S.A. 2%; E.S.C. 2%; W.S.C. 3%; Mt. 4%; Pac. 4%; unknown 0%

William Mitchell College of Law

875 Summit Avenue
St. Paul, MN 55105-3076
http://www.wmitchell.edu
Private
Admissions: (651) 290-6476
E-mail: admissions@wmitchell.edu
Financial aid: (651) 290-6403
Application deadline: 08/01
Tuition: full time: $36,020; part time: $26,050
Room/board/expenses: $19,570
Median grant: $17,830
Average student indebtedness at graduation: $116,575
Enrollment: full time: 624; part time: 300
men: 51%; **women:** 49%; **minorities:** 14%

Acceptance rate (full time): 72%
Midrange LSAT (full time): 151–158
Midrange undergraduate GPA (full time): 3.16–3.59
Midrange of full-time private-sector salaries of 2011 grads: $45,000–$72,000
2011 grads employed in: law firms: 47%; business and industry: 25%; government: 8%; public interest: 4%; judicial clerk: 11%; academia: 1%; unknown: 4%
Employment location for 2011 class: Intl. 0%; N.E. 1%; M.A. 0%; E.N.C. 2%; W.N.C. 83%; S.A. 2%; E.S.C. 0%; W.S.C. 0%; Mt. 2%; Pac. 2%; unknown 7%

MISSISSIPPI

Mississippi College

151 E. Griffith Street
Jackson, MS 39201
http://www.law.mc.edu
Private
Admissions: (601) 925-7151
E-mail: hweaver@mc.edu
Financial aid: (601) 925-7110
Application deadline: 07/01
Tuition: full time: $29,450; part time: $965/credit hour
Room/board/expenses: $21,225
Median grant: $12,075
Average student indebtedness at graduation: $119,180
Enrollment: full time: 520; part time: 22
men: 59%; **women:** 41%; **minorities:** 16%
Acceptance rate (full time): 67%
Midrange LSAT (full time): 146–152
Midrange undergraduate GPA (full time): 3.06–3.57
Midrange of full-time private-sector salaries of 2011 grads: $45,000–$96,000
2011 grads employed in: law firms: 58%; business and industry: 13%; government: 7%; public interest: 4%; judicial clerk: 16%; academia: 1%; unknown: 0%
Employment location for 2011 class: Intl. 0%; N.E. 0%; M.A. 3%; E.N.C. 2%; W.N.C. 1%; S.A. 7%; E.S.C. 71%; W.S.C. 12%; Mt. 3%; Pac. 1%; unknown 0%

University of Mississippi

PO Box 1848
University, MS 38677
http://law.olemiss.edu
Public
Admissions: (662) 915-6910
E-mail: lawmiss@olemiss.edu
Financial aid: (800) 891-4569
Application deadline: 03/01
In-state tuition: full time: $12,388; part time: N/A
Out-of-state tuition: full time: $27,087
Room/board/expenses: $19,198
Median grant: $2,000
Average student indebtedness at graduation: $55,992
Enrollment: full time: 520; part time: N/A
men: 58%; **women:** 42%; **minorities:** 18%
Acceptance rate (full time): 36%
Midrange LSAT (full time): 151–157
Midrange undergraduate GPA (full time): 3.07–3.67
Midrange of full-time private-sector salaries of 2011 grads: $43,500–$75,000

2011 grads employed in: law firms: 58%; business and industry: 14%; government: 14%; public interest: 4%; judicial clerk: 8%; academia: 2%; unknown: 0%
Employment location for 2011 class: Intl. 0%; N.E. 1%; M.A. 1%; E.N.C. 1%; W.N.C. 1%; S.A. 22%; E.S.C. 72%; W.S.C. 3%; Mt. 0%; Pac. 0%; unknown 0%

MISSOURI

St. Louis University
3700 Lindell Boulevard
St. Louis, MO 63108
http://law.slu.edu
Private
Admissions: (314) 977-2800
E-mail: admissions@law.slu.edu
Financial aid: (314) 977-3369
Application deadline: 05/01
Tuition: full time: $36,885; part time: $26,845
Room/board/expenses: $18,216
Median grant: $18,000
Average student indebtedness at graduation: $121,742
Enrollment: full time: 709; part time: 105
men: 54%; women: 46%;
minorities: 14%
Acceptance rate (full time): 61%
Midrange LSAT (full time): 152-159
Midrange undergraduate GPA (full time): 3.23-3.73
Midrange of full-time private-sector salaries of 2011 grads: $45,000-$75,000
2011 grads employed in: law firms: 45%; business and industry: 26%; government: 16%; public interest: 9%; judicial clerk: 3%; academia: 2%; unknown: 0%
Employment location for 2011 class: Intl. 0%; N.E. 0%; M.A. 2%; E.N.C. 19%; W.N.C. 66%; S.A. 5%; E.S.C. 1%; W.S.C. 3%; Mt. 2%; Pac. 2%; unknown 0%

University of Missouri
203 Hulston Hall
Columbia, MO 65211-4300
http://www.law.missouri.edu
Public
Admissions: (573) 882-6042
E-mail: mulawadmissions@missouri.edu
Financial aid: (573) 882-1383
Application deadline: 03/01
In-state tuition: full time: $18,649; part time: N/A
Out-of-state tuition: full time: $35,677
Room/board/expenses: $17,836
Median grant: $6,000
Average student indebtedness at graduation: $78,110
Enrollment: full time: 402; part time: 10
men: 61%; women: 39%;
minorities: 19%
Acceptance rate (full time): 56%
Midrange LSAT (full time): 152-159
Midrange undergraduate GPA (full time): 3.10-3.74
Midrange of full-time private-sector salaries of 2011 grads: $52,000-$85,000
2011 grads employed in: law firms: 48%; business and industry: 12%; government: 15%; public interest: 6%; judicial clerk: 11%; academia: 6%; unknown: 2%
Employment location for 2011 class: Intl. 1%; N.E. 0%; M.A. 1%; E.N.C.

2%; W.N.C. 84%; S.A. 3%; E.S.C. 0%; W.S.C. 3%; Mt. 3%; Pac. 3%; unknown 0%

University of Missouri-Kansas City
5100 Rockhill Road
Kansas City, MO 64110
http://www.law.umkc.edu
Public
Admissions: (816) 235-1644
E-mail: law@umkc.edu
Financial aid: (816) 235-1154
Application deadline: 03/04
In-state tuition: full time: $17,058; part time: $10,416
Out-of-state tuition: full time: $32,853
Room/board/expenses: $18,250
Median grant: $7,521
Average student indebtedness at graduation: $100,887
Enrollment: full time: 434; part time: 29
men: 62%; women: 38%;
minorities: 11%
Acceptance rate (full time): 59%
Midrange LSAT (full time): 150-156
Midrange undergraduate GPA (full time): 3.00-3.53
Midrange of full-time private-sector salaries of 2011 grads: $45,000-$68,000
2011 grads employed in: law firms: 52%; business and industry: 21%; government: 11%; public interest: 4%; judicial clerk: 9%; academia: 3%; unknown: 0%
Employment location for 2011 class: Intl. 1%; N.E. 0%; M.A. 1%; E.N.C. 1%; W.N.C. 90%; S.A. 1%; E.S.C. 0%; W.S.C. 2%; Mt. 4%; Pac. 0%; unknown 0%

Washington University in St. Louis
1 Brookings Drive, Box 1120
St. Louis, MO 63130
http://www.law.wustl.edu
Private
Admissions: (314) 935-4525
E-mail: admiss@wulaw.wustl.edu
Financial aid: (314) 935-4605
Application deadline: 03/01
Tuition: full time: $47,490; part time: N/A
Room/board/expenses: $21,925
Median grant: $20,000
Average student indebtedness at graduation: $117,964
Enrollment: full time: 768; part time: 5
men: 57%; women: 43%;
minorities: 25%
Acceptance rate (full time): 29%
Midrange LSAT (full time): 160-168
Midrange undergraduate GPA (full time): 3.34-3.78
Midrange of full-time private-sector salaries of 2011 grads: $66,250-$160,000
2011 grads employed in: law firms: 49%; business and industry: 19%; government: 14%; public interest: 10%; judicial clerk: 7%; academia: 1%; unknown: 0%
Employment location for 2011 class: Intl. 8%; N.E. 2%; M.A. 10%; E.N.C. 13%; W.N.C. 30%; S.A. 18%; E.S.C. 2%; W.S.C. 6%; Mt. 3%; Pac. 10% unknown 0%

MONTANA

University of Montana
32 Campus Drive
Missoula, MT 59812
http://www.umt.edu/law
Public
Admissions: (406) 243-2698
E-mail: lori.freeman@umontana.edu
Financial aid: (406) 243-5524
Application deadline: 03/15
In-state tuition: full time: $11,250; part time: N/A
Out-of-state tuition: full time: $27,917
Room/board/expenses: $14,790
Median grant: $2,500
Average student indebtedness at graduation: $64,539
Enrollment: full time: 247; part time: N/A
men: 57%; women: 43%;
minorities: 9%
Acceptance rate (full time): 58%
Midrange LSAT (full time): 152-158
Midrange undergraduate GPA (full time): 3.01-3.66
Midrange of full-time private-sector salaries of 2011 grads: $45,000-$55,000
2011 grads employed in: law firms: 62%; business and industry: 1%; government: 12%; public interest: 3%; judicial clerk: 21%; academia: 0%; unknown: 1%
Employment location for 2011 class: Intl. 0%; N.E. 3%; M.A. 0%; E.N.C. 0%; W.N.C. 6%; S.A. 3%; E.S.C. 2%; W.S.C. 2%; Mt. 79%; Pac. 6%; unknown 0%

NEBRASKA

Creighton University
2500 California Plaza
Omaha, NE 68178
http://www.creighton.edu/law
Private
Admissions: (800) 282-5835
E-mail: lawadmit@creighton.edu
Financial aid: (402) 280-2352
Application deadline: 05/01
Tuition: full time: $33,490; part time: $1,050/credit hour
Room/board/expenses: $16,955
Median grant: $10,000
Average student indebtedness at graduation: $116,817
Enrollment: full time: 385; part time: 10
men: 67%; women: 33%;
minorities: 13%
Acceptance rate (full time): 69%
Midrange LSAT (full time): 150-156
Midrange undergraduate GPA (full time): 2.92-3.52
Midrange of full-time private-sector salaries of 2011 grads: $52,000-$72,000
2011 grads employed in: law firms: 49%; business and industry: 22%; government: 11%; public interest: 5%; judicial clerk: 8%; academia: 4%; unknown: 1%
Employment location for 2011 class: Intl. 0%; N.E. 1%; M.A. 3%; E.N.C. 2%; W.N.C. 74%; S.A. 3%; E.S.C. 0%; W.S.C. 2%; Mt. 13%; Pac. 2%; unknown 0%

University of Nebraska-Lincoln
PO Box 830902
Lincoln, NE 68583-0902
http://law.unl.edu
Public
Admissions: (402) 472-8333
E-mail: lawadm@unl.edu
Financial aid: (402) 472-8333
Application deadline: 03/01

In-state tuition: full time: $14,363; part time: N/A
Out-of-state tuition: full time: $31,044
Room/board/expenses: $14,480
Median grant: $10,000
Average student indebtedness at graduation: $54,989
Enrollment: full time: 387; part time: 2
men: 59%; women: 41%;
minorities: 6%
Acceptance rate (full time): 51%
Midrange LSAT (full time): 155-161
Midrange undergraduate GPA (full time): 3.31-3.83
Midrange of full-time private-sector salaries of 2011 grads: $42,500-$62,500
2011 grads employed in: law firms: 48%; business and industry: 25%; government: 15%; public interest: 6%; judicial clerk: 3%; academia: 2%; unknown: 1%
Employment location for 2011 class: Intl. 0%; N.E. 1%; M.A. 0%; E.N.C. 0%; W.N.C. 82%; S.A. 6%; E.S.C. 0%; W.S.C. 3%; Mt. 6%; Pac. 2%; unknown 0%

NEVADA

University of Nevada-Las Vegas
4505 S. Maryland Parkway
Box 451003
Las Vegas, NV 89154-1003
http://www.law.unlv.edu/
Public
Admissions: (702) 895-2440
E-mail: elizabeth.karl@unlv.edu
Financial aid: (702) 895-4107
Application deadline: 03/15
In-state tuition: full time: $24,749; part time: $18,713
Out-of-state tuition: full time: $35,749
Room/board/expenses: $21,010
Median grant: $17,925
Average student indebtedness at graduation: $92,191
Enrollment: full time: 315; part time: 130
men: 57%; women: 43%;
minorities: 32%
Acceptance rate (full time): 28%
Midrange LSAT (full time): 157-162
Midrange undergraduate GPA (full time): 3.26-3.74
Midrange of full-time private-sector salaries of 2011 grads: $60,000-$80,400
2011 grads employed in: law firms: 48%; business and industry: 18%; government: 9%; public interest: 3%; judicial clerk: 22%; academia: 1%; unknown: 0%
Employment location for 2011 class: Intl. 3%; N.E. 0%; M.A. 0%; E.N.C. 2%; W.N.C. 1%; S.A. 1%; E.S.C. 0%; W.S.C. 0%; Mt. 88%; Pac. 6%; unknown 0%

NEW HAMPSHIRE

University of New Hampshire School of Law
2 White Street
Concord, NH 03301
http://www.law.unh.edu
Private
Admissions: (603) 228-9217
E-mail: admissions@law.unh.edu
Financial aid: (603) 228-1541
Application deadline: 04/01
Tuition: full time: $41,190; part time: N/A

Room/board/expenses: $20,105
Median grant: $8,000
Average student indebtedness at graduation: $123,171
Enrollment: full time: 304; part time: 1
men: 61%; women: 39%;
minorities: 13%
Acceptance rate (full time): 59%
Midrange LSAT (full time): 151-159
Midrange undergraduate GPA (full time): 2.92-3.59
Midrange of full-time private-sector salaries of 2011 grads: $60,000-$130,000
2011 grads employed in: law firms: 41%; business and industry: 20%; government: 10%; public interest: 5%; judicial clerk: 4%; academia: 20%; unknown: 0%
Employment location for 2011 class: Intl. 2%; N.E. 56%; M.A. 11%; E.N.C. 4%; W.N.C. 2%; S.A. 17%; E.S.C. 2%; W.S.C. 2%; Mt. 4%; Pac. 1%; unknown 0%

NEW JERSEY

Rutgers, the State University of New Jersey-Camden
217 N. Fifth Street
Camden, NJ 08102-1203
http://camlaw.rutgers.edu
Public
Admissions: (800) 466-7561
E-mail: admissions@camlaw.rutgers.edu
Financial aid: (856) 225-6039
Application deadline: rolling
In-state tuition: full time: $25,475; part time: $20,454
Out-of-state tuition: full time: $37,207
Room/board/expenses: $16,514
Median grant: $5,000
Average student indebtedness at graduation: $93,990
Enrollment: full time: 562; part time: 149
men: 65%; women: 35%;
minorities: 22%
Midrange LSAT (full time): 157-162
Midrange undergraduate GPA (full time): 2.94-3.64
Midrange of full-time private-sector salaries of 2011 grads: $55,000-$110,000
2011 grads employed in: law firms: 29%; business and industry: 16%; government: 9%; public interest: 3%; judicial clerk: 42%; academia: 2%; unknown: 0%
Employment location for 2011 class: Intl. 0%; N.E. 1%; M.A. 88%; E.N.C. 1%; W.N.C. 1%; S.A. 6%; E.S.C. N/A; W.S.C. N/A; Mt. 1%; Pac. 3%; unknown 0%

Rutgers, the State University of New Jersey-Newark
123 Washington Street
Newark, NJ 07102
http://law.newark.rutgers.edu
Public
Admissions: (973) 353-5554
E-mail: lawinfo@andromeda.rutgers.edu
Financial aid: (973) 353-1702
Application deadline: 03/15
In-state tuition: full time: $25,424; part time: $16,577
Out-of-state tuition: full time: $37,156
Room/board/expenses: $17,156
Median grant: $6,000

Average student indebtedness at graduation: $87,272
Enrollment: full time: 579; part time: 205
men: 56%; women: 44%; minorities: 40%
Acceptance rate (full time): 41%
Midrange LSAT (full time): 155-161
Midrange undergraduate GPA (full time): 3.03-3.45
Midrange of full-time private-sector salaries of 2011 grads: $75,000-$145,000
2011 grads employed in: law firms: 25%; business and industry: 17%; government: 12%; public interest: 3%; judicial clerk: 39%; academia: 3%; unknown: 0%
Employment location for 2011 class: Intl. 1%; N.E. N/A; M.A. 94%; E.N.C. N/A; W.N.C. N/A; S.A. 3%; E.S.C. 1%; W.S.C. 1%; Mt. 1%; Pac. 1%; unknown 1%

Seton Hall University

1 Newark Center
Newark, NJ 07102-5210
http://law.shu.edu
Private
Admissions: (888) 415-7271
E-mail: admitme@shu.edu
Financial aid: (973) 642-8850
Application deadline: 04/01
Tuition: full time: $48,170; part time: $36,330
Room/board/expenses: $21,846
Median grant: $25,000
Average student indebtedness at graduation: $125,745
Enrollment: full time: 604; part time: 246
men: 51%; women: 49%; minorities: 21%
Acceptance rate (full time): 57%
Midrange LSAT (full time): 156-162
Midrange undergraduate GPA (full time): 3.32-3.75
Midrange of full-time private-sector salaries of 2011 grads: $115,000-$140,000
2011 grads employed in: law firms: 38%; business and industry: 13%; government: 6%; public interest: 1%; judicial clerk: 41%; academia: 1%; unknown: 1%
Employment location for 2011 class: Intl. 0%; N.E. 1%; M.A. 90%; E.N.C. 0%; W.N.C. 0%; S.A. 2%; E.S.C. 0%; W.S.C. 0%; Mt. 0%; Pac. 1%; unknown 4%

NEW MEXICO

University of New Mexico

1117 Stanford Drive NE
MSC11 6070
Albuquerque, NM 87131-0001
http://lawschool.unm.edu
Public
Admissions: (505) 277-0958
E-mail: admissions@law.unm.edu
Financial aid: (505) 277-0958
Application deadline: 02/15
In-state tuition: full time: $15,098; part time: N/A
Out-of-state tuition: full time: $33,908
Room/board/expenses: $15,354
Median grant: $5,400
Average student indebtedness at graduation: $68,131
Enrollment: full time: 342; part time: 4
men: 53%; women: 47%; minorities: 42%
Acceptance rate (full time): 32%
Midrange LSAT (full time): 152-158

Midrange undergraduate GPA (full time): 3.09-3.70
Midrange of full-time private-sector salaries of 2011 grads: $45,000-$65,000
2011 grads employed in: law firms: 53%; business and industry: 7%; government: 18%; public interest: 9%; judicial clerk: 9%; academia: 3%; unknown: 0%
Employment location for 2011 class: Intl. 1%; N.E. 1%; M.A. 95%; E.N.C. 0%; W.N.C. 0%; S.A. 3%; E.S.C. 0%; W.S.C. 1%; Mt. 0%; Pac. 0%; unknown 0%

NEW YORK

Albany Law School

80 New Scotland Avenue
Albany, NY 12208-3494
http://www.albanylaw.edu
Private
Admissions: (518) 445-2326
E-mail: admissions@albanylaw.edu
Financial aid: (518) 445-2357
Application deadline: 03/15
Tuition: full time: $42,675; part time: $32,075
Room/board/expenses: $18,000
Median grant: $20,000
Average student indebtedness at graduation: $113,674
Enrollment: full time: 567; part time: 41
men: 52%; women: 48%; minorities: 19%
Acceptance rate (full time): 69%
Midrange LSAT (full time): 149-155
Midrange undergraduate GPA (full time): 3.02-3.55
Midrange of full-time private-sector salaries of 2011 grads: $49,250-$78,000
2011 grads employed in: law firms: 53%; business and industry: 24%; government: 9%; public interest: 5%; judicial clerk: 5%; academia: 3%; unknown: 1%
Employment location for 2011 class: Intl. 1%; N.E. 4%; M.A. 90%; E.N.C. 1%; W.N.C. 1%; S.A. 2%; E.S.C. 0%; W.S.C. 1%; Mt. 2%; Pac. 1%; unknown 1%

Brooklyn Law School

250 Joralemon Street
Brooklyn, NY 11201
http://www.brooklaw.edu
Private
Admissions: (718) 780-7906
E-mail: admitq@brooklaw.edu
Financial aid: (718) 780-7915
Application deadline: rolling
Tuition: full time: $49,976; part time: $37,568
Room/board/expenses: $25,535
Median grant: $25,400
Average student indebtedness at graduation: $105,916
Enrollment: full time: 998; part time: 262
men: 55%; women: 45%; minorities: 25%
Acceptance rate (full time): 40%
Midrange LSAT (full time): 159-164
Midrange undergraduate GPA (full time): 3.10-3.51
Midrange of full-time private-sector salaries of 2011 grads: $60,000-$160,000
2011 grads employed in: law firms: 44%; business and industry: 22%; government: 18%; public interest: 9%; judicial clerk: 7%; academia: 1%; unknown: 0%

Employment location for 2011 class: Intl. 1%; N.E. 1%; M.A. 95%; E.N.C. 0%; W.N.C. 0%; S.A. 3%; E.S.C. 0%; W.S.C. 1%; Mt. 0%; Pac. 0%; unknown 0%

Columbia University

435 W. 116th Street
New York, NY 10027
http://www.law.columbia.edu
Private
Admissions: (212) 854-2670
E-mail: admissions@law.columbia.edu
Financial aid: (212) 854-7730
Application deadline: 02/15
Tuition: full time: $55,488; part time: N/A
Room/board/expenses: $22,200
Median grant: $12,000
Average student indebtedness at graduation: $141,607
Enrollment: full time: 1,290; part time: 4
men: 54%; women: 46%; minorities: 32%
Acceptance rate (full time): 18%
Midrange LSAT (full time): 170-174
Midrange undergraduate GPA (full time): 3.58-3.82
Midrange of full-time private-sector salaries of 2011 grads: $160,000-$160,000
2011 grads employed in: law firms: 69%; business and industry: 5%; government: 9%; public interest: 6%; judicial clerk: 10%; academia: 1%; unknown: 0%
Employment location for 2011 class: Intl. 5%; N.E. 4%; M.A. 63%; E.N.C. 2%; W.N.C. 0%; S.A. 11%; E.S.C. 1%; W.S.C. 2%; Mt. 0%; Pac. 11%; unknown 0%

Cornell University

Myron Taylor Hall
Ithaca, NY 14853-4901
http://www.lawschool.cornell.edu
Private
Admissions: (607) 255-5141
E-mail: lawadmit@lawschool.cornell.edu
Financial aid: (607) 255-5141
Application deadline: 02/01
Tuition: full time: $55,220; part time: N/A
Room/board/expenses: $19,460
Median grant: $15,000
Average student indebtedness at graduation: $140,000
Enrollment: full time: 596; part time: N/A
men: 53%; women: 47%; minorities: 37%
Acceptance rate (full time): 29%
Midrange LSAT (full time): 166-169
Midrange undergraduate GPA (full time): 3.54-3.77
Midrange of full-time private-sector salaries of 2011 grads: $160,000-$160,000
2011 grads employed in: law firms: 54%; business and industry: 2%; government: 18%; public interest: 9%; judicial clerk: 14%; academia: 1%; unknown: 3%
Employment location for 2011 class: Intl. 6%; N.E. 5%; M.A. 47%; E.N.C. 2%; W.N.C. 1%; S.A. 16%; E.S.C. 2%; W.S.C. 6%; Mt. 2%; Pac. 12%; unknown 3%

CUNY

2 Court Square
Long Island City, NY 11101-4356
http://www.law.cuny.edu/
Public
Admissions: (718) 340-4210
E-mail: admissions@law.cuny.edu
Financial aid: (718) 340-4284
Application deadline: 04/15
In-state tuition: full time: $13,802; part time: N/A
Out-of-state tuition: full time: $21,802
Room/board/expenses: $18,090
Median grant: $11,420
Average student indebtedness at graduation: $79,680
Enrollment: full time: 424; part time: 4
men: 36%; women: 64%; minorities: 42%
Acceptance rate (full time): 25%
Midrange LSAT (full time): 154-159
Midrange undergraduate GPA (full time): 2.97-3.56
Midrange of full-time private-sector salaries of 2011 grads: $37,000-$60,000
2011 grads employed in: law firms: 25%; business and industry: 16%; government: 5%; public interest: 41%; judicial clerk: 7%; academia: 5%; unknown: 1%
Employment location for 2011 class: Intl. 0%; N.E. 0%; M.A. 78%; E.N.C. 5%; W.N.C. 1%; S.A. 11%; E.S.C. 0%; W.S.C. 1%; Mt. 1%; Pac. 2%; unknown 0%

Fordham University

140 W. 62nd Street
New York, NY 10023-7485
http://law.fordham.edu
Private
Admissions: (212) 636-6810
E-mail: lawadmissions@law.fordham.edu
Financial aid: (212) 636-6815
Application deadline: 03/01
Tuition: full time: $49,526; part time: $37,216
Room/board/expenses: $26,396
Median grant: $10,000
Average student indebtedness at graduation: $134,319
Enrollment: full time: 1,206; part time: 221
men: 54%; women: 46%; minorities: 26%
Acceptance rate (full time): 34%
Midrange LSAT (full time): 162-166
Midrange undergraduate GPA (full time): 3.36-3.68
Midrange of full-time private-sector salaries of 2011 grads: $74,450-$160,000
2011 grads employed in: law firms: 50%; business and industry: 14%; government: 13%; public interest: 10%; judicial clerk: 9%; academia: 4%; unknown: 0%
Employment location for 2011 class: Intl. 1%; N.E. 3%; M.A. 85%; E.N.C. 1%; W.N.C. 0%; S.A. 6%; E.S.C. 0%; W.S.C. 0%; Mt. 1%; Pac. 3%; unknown 0%

Hofstra University (Deane)

121 Hofstra University
Hempstead, NY 11549
http://law.hofstra.edu
Private
Admissions: (516) 463-5916
E-mail: lawadmissions@hofstra.edu
Financial aid: (516) 463-5929
Application deadline: 04/15

Tuition: full time: $47,660; part time: $35,670
Room/board/expenses: $23,607
Median grant: $25,000
Average student indebtedness at graduation: $129,461
Enrollment: full time: 945; part time: 34
men: 55%; women: 45%; minorities: 30%
Acceptance rate (full time): 53%
Midrange LSAT (full time): 153-159
Midrange undergraduate GPA (full time): 2.96-3.59
Midrange of full-time private-sector salaries of 2011 grads: $50,000-$80,000
2011 grads employed in: law firms: 56%; business and industry: 24%; government: 7%; public interest: 5%; judicial clerk: 2%; academia: 5%; unknown: 1%
Employment location for 2011 class: Intl. 0%; N.E. 2%; M.A. 88%; E.N.C. 1%; W.N.C. 0%; S.A. 5%; E.S.C. 0%; W.S.C. 0%; Mt. 1%; Pac. 1%; unknown 1%

New York Law School

185 W. Broadway
New York, NY 10013-2960
http://www.nyls.edu
Private
Admissions: (212) 431-2888
E-mail: admissions@nyls.edu
Financial aid: (212) 431-2828
Application deadline: 06/01
Tuition: full time: $49,225; part time: $38,300
Room/board/expenses: $23,591
Median grant: $10,000
Average student indebtedness at graduation: $154,647
Enrollment: full time: 1,092; part time: 411
men: 48%; women: 52%; minorities: 27%
Acceptance rate (full time): 57%
Midrange LSAT (full time): 150-155
Midrange undergraduate GPA (full time): 2.86-3.41
Midrange of full-time private-sector salaries of 2011 grads: $50,000-$82,000
2011 grads employed in: law firms: 41%; business and industry: 33%; government: 12%; public interest: 7%; judicial clerk: 4%; academia: 3%; unknown: 1%
Employment location for 2011 class: Intl. 0%; N.E. 2%; M.A. 88%; E.N.C. 0%; W.N.C. 0%; S.A. 4%; E.S.C. 0%; W.S.C. 1%; Mt. 0%; Pac. 3%; unknown 2%

New York University

40 Washington Square S
New York, NY 10012
http://www.law.nyu.edu
Private
Admissions: (212) 998-6060
E-mail: law.moreinfo@nyu.edu
Financial aid: (212) 998-6050
Application deadline: 02/15
Tuition: full time: $51,150; part time: N/A
Median grant: $15,000
Average student indebtedness at graduation: $149,336
Enrollment: full time: 1,471; part time: N/A
men: 58%; women: 42%; minorities: 26%
Acceptance rate (full time): 28%
Midrange LSAT (full time): 169-173
Midrange undergraduate GPA (full time): 3.54-3.84

Midrange of full-time private-sector salaries of 2011 grads: $160,000-$160,000

2011 grads employed in: law firms: 54%; business and industry: 5%; government: 8%; public interest: 18%; judicial clerk: 14%; academia: 0%; unknown: 0%
Employment location for 2011 class: Intl. 3%; N.E. 2%; M.A. 68%; E.N.C. 1%; W.N.C. 1%; S.A. 8%; E.S.C. 3%; W.S.C. 2%; Mt. 1%; Pac. 12%; unknown 0%

Pace University

78 N. Broadway
White Plains, NY 10603
http://www.law.pace.edu
Private
Admissions: (914) 422-4210
E-mail: admissions@law.pace.edu
Financial aid: (914) 422-4050
Application deadline: 03/01
Tuition: full time: $42,198; part time: $31,662
Room/board/expenses: $17,908
Median grant: $14,000
Average student indebtedness at graduation: $120,315
Enrollment: full time: 565; part time: 115
men: 43%; women: 57%; minorities: 20%
Acceptance rate (full time): 47%
Midrange LSAT (full time): 149-155
Midrange undergraduate GPA (full time): 3.11-3.58
Midrange of full-time private-sector salaries of 2011 grads: $55,000-$85,000
2011 grads employed in: law firms: 39%; business and industry: 28%; government: 10%; public interest: 8%; judicial clerk: 2%; academia: 8%; unknown: 4%
Employment location for 2011 class: Intl. 3%; N.E. 7%; M.A. 77%; E.N.C. 1%; W.N.C. 0%; S.A. 9%; E.S.C. 0%; W.S.C. 0%; Mt. 1%; Pac. 1%; unknown 7%

St. John's University

8000 Utopia Parkway
Jamaica, NY 11439
http://www.law.stjohns.edu/
Private
Admissions: (718) 990-6474
E-mail: lawinfo@stjohns.edu
Financial aid: (718) 990-1485
Application deadline: 04/01
Tuition: full time: $48,070; part time: $36,060
Room/board/expenses: $25,540
Median grant: $30,000
Average student indebtedness at graduation: $119,203
Enrollment: full time: 742; part time: 147
men: 58%; women: 42%; minorities: 24%
Acceptance rate (full time): 52%
Midrange LSAT (full time): 154-161
Midrange undergraduate GPA (full time): 3.13-3.64
Midrange of full-time private-sector salaries of 2011 grads: $60,000-$145,000
2011 grads employed in: law firms: 49%; business and industry: 18%; government: 14%; public interest: 10%; judicial clerk: 4%; academia: 4%; unknown: 1%
Employment location for 2011 class: Intl. 0%; N.E. 1%; M.A. 93%; E.N.C. 0%; W.N.C. 0%; S.A. 3%; E.S.C. 0%; W.S.C. 1%; Mt. 0%; Pac. 1%; unknown 1%

SUNY Buffalo Law School

John Lord O'Brian Hall
Buffalo, NY 14260
http://www.law.buffalo.edu
Public
Admissions: (716) 645-2907
E-mail: law-admissions@buffalo.edu
Financial aid: (716) 645-7324
Application deadline: 03/01
In-state tuition: full time: $22,624; part time: N/A
Out-of-state tuition: full time: $37,114
Room/board/expenses: $18,758
Median grant: $5,000
Average student indebtedness at graduation: $72,680
Enrollment: full time: 598; part time: 52
men: 54%; women: 46%; minorities: 14%
Acceptance rate (full time): 44%
Midrange of full-time private-sector salaries of 2011 grads: $45,000-$70,000
2011 grads employed in: law firms: 54%; business and industry: 20%; government: 12%; public interest: 6%; judicial clerk: 4%; academia: 3%; unknown: 3%
Employment location for 2011 class: Intl. 3%; N.E. 1%; M.A. 81%; E.N.C. 1%; W.N.C. 1%; S.A. 7%; E.S.C. 0%; W.S.C. 1%; Mt. 1%; Pac. 1%; unknown 3%

Syracuse University

Suite 440
Syracuse, NY 13244-1030
http://www.law.syr.edu
Private
Admissions: (315) 443-1962
E-mail: admissions@law.syr.edu
Financial aid: (315) 443-1963
Application deadline: 04/01
Tuition: full time: $45,690; part time: N/A
Room/board/expenses: $16,310
Median grant: $8,900
Average student indebtedness at graduation: $138,073
Enrollment: full time: 661; part time: 4
men: 57%; women: 43%; minorities: 18%
Acceptance rate (full time): 47%
Midrange LSAT (full time): 152-156
Midrange undergraduate GPA (full time): 3.12-3.46
Midrange of full-time private-sector salaries of 2011 grads: $50,000-$85,000
2011 grads employed in: law firms: 42%; business and industry: 31%; government: 12%; public interest: 8%; judicial clerk: 6%; academia: 1%; unknown: 0%
Employment location for 2011 class: Intl. 2%; N.E. 3%; M.A. 83%; E.N.C. 3%; W.N.C. 0%; S.A. 5%; E.S.C. 0%; W.S.C. 1%; Mt. 0%; Pac. 3%; unknown 0%

Touro College (Fuchsberg)

225 Eastview Drive
Central Islip, NY 11722
http://www.tourolaw.edu
Private
Admissions: (631) 761-7010
E-mail: admissions@tourolaw.edu
Financial aid: (631) 761-7020
Application deadline: 07/31
Tuition: full time: $42,930; part time: $32,040

Room/board/expenses: $27,210
Median grant: $8,000
Average student indebtedness at graduation: $137,781
Enrollment: full time: 531; part time: 210
men: 52%; women: 48%; minorities: 29%
Acceptance rate (full time): 66%
Midrange LSAT (full time): 146-151
Midrange undergraduate GPA (full time): 2.88-3.37
Midrange of full-time private-sector salaries of 2011 grads: $45,000-$60,000
2011 grads employed in: law firms: 63%; business and industry: 15%; government: 15%; public interest: 4%; judicial clerk: 3%; academia: 1%; unknown: 0%
Employment location for 2011 class: Intl. 1%; N.E. N/A; M.A. 98%; E.N.C. N/A; W.N.C. N/A; S.A. 1%; E.S.C. N/A; W.S.C. N/A; Mt. N/A; Pac. 1%; unknown 0%

Yeshiva University (Cardozo)

55 Fifth Avenue, 10th Floor
New York, NY 10003
http://www.cardozo.yu.edu
Private
Admissions: (212) 790-0274
E-mail: lawinfo@yu.edu
Financial aid: (212) 790-0392
Application deadline: 04/01
Tuition: full time: $50,046; part time: $50,046
Room/board/expenses: $24,778
Median grant: $25,000
Average student indebtedness at graduation: $120,008
Enrollment: full time: 1,032; part time: 107
men: 47%; women: 53%; minorities: 26%
Acceptance rate (full time): 34%
Midrange LSAT (full time): 160-166
Midrange undergraduate GPA (full time): 3.35-3.68
Midrange of full-time private-sector salaries of 2011 grads: $60,000-$145,000
2011 grads employed in: law firms: 47%; business and industry: 19%; government: 12%; public interest: 11%; judicial clerk: 8%; academia: 2%; unknown: 1%
Employment location for 2011 class: Intl. 2%; N.E. 3%; M.A. 83%; E.N.C. 3%; W.N.C. 0%; S.A. 5%; E.S.C. 0%; W.S.C. 1%; Mt. 0%; Pac. 3%; unknown 0%

NORTH CAROLINA

Campbell University

225 Hillsborough Street, Suite 401
Raleigh, NC 27603
http://www.law.campbell.edu
Private
Admissions: (919) 865-5989
E-mail: admissions@law.campbell.edu
Financial aid: (910) 893-1310
Application deadline: 05/01
Tuition: full time: $35,340; part time: N/A
Room/board/expenses: $27,000
Median grant: $13,100
Average student indebtedness at graduation: $130,428
Enrollment: full time: 453; part time: N/A
men: 50%; women: 50%; minorities: 11%
Acceptance rate (full time): 53%
Midrange LSAT (full time): 152-157
Midrange undergraduate GPA (full time): 2.98-3.55

Midrange of full-time private-sector salaries of 2011 grads: $41,000-$65,000
2011 grads employed in: law firms: 61%; business and industry: 20%; government: 8%; public interest: 4%; judicial clerk: 6%; academia: 1%; unknown: 0%
Employment location for 2011 class: Intl. 1%; N.E. 0%; M.A. 0%; E.N.C. 0%; W.N.C. 0%; S.A. 97%; E.S.C. 2%; W.S.C. 0%; Mt. 0%; Pac. 1%; unknown 0%

Charlotte School of Law

2145 Suttle Avenue
Charlotte, NC 28208
http://www.charlottelaw.edu/
Private
Admissions: (704) 971-8500
E-mail: admissions@charlottelaw.edu
Financial aid: (704) 971-8386
Application deadline: 12/31
Tuition: full time: $38,600; part time: $31,232
Room/board/expenses: $18,015
Median grant: $11,750
Average student indebtedness at graduation: $115,747
Enrollment: full time: 1,168; part time: 224
men: 45%; women: 55%; minorities: 32%
Acceptance rate (full time): 77%
Midrange LSAT (full time): 143-150
Midrange undergraduate GPA (full time): 2.68-3.35
Midrange of full-time private-sector salaries of 2011 grads: $48,380-$66,250
2011 grads employed in: law firms: 34%; business and industry: 34%; government: 9%; public interest: 10%; judicial clerk: 1%; academia: 4%; unknown: 9%
Employment location for 2011 class: Intl. 0%; N.E. 0%; M.A. 0%; E.N.C. 0%; W.N.C. 1%; S.A. 89%; E.S.C. 3%; W.S.C. 0%; Mt. 1%; Pac. 0%; unknown 6%

Duke University

210 Science Drive, Box 90362
Durham, NC 27708-0362
http://www.law.duke.edu
Private
Admissions: (919) 613-7020
E-mail: admissions@law.duke.edu
Financial aid: (919) 613-7026
Application deadline: 02/15
Tuition: full time: $50,750; part time: N/A
Room/board/expenses: $18,120
Median grant: $18,000
Average student indebtedness at graduation: $131,092
Enrollment: full time: 660; part time: N/A
men: 59%; women: 41%; minorities: 27%
Acceptance rate (full time): 19%
Midrange LSAT (full time): 166-170
Midrange undergraduate GPA (full time): 3.58-3.85
Midrange of full-time private-sector salaries of 2011 grads: $110,000-$160,000
2011 grads employed in: law firms: 62%; business and industry: 6%; government: 7%; public interest: 6%; judicial clerk: 17%; academia: 3%; unknown: 0%

Employment location for 2011 class: Intl. 4%; N.E. 3%; M.A. 21%; E.N.C. 5%; W.N.C. 1%; S.A. 42%; E.S.C. 3%; W.S.C. 10%; Mt. 1%; Pac. 12%; unknown 0%

Elon University

201 N. Greene Street
Greensboro, NC 27401
http://law.elon.edu
Private
Admissions: (336) 279-9200
E-mail: law@elon.edu
Financial aid: (336) 278-2000
Application deadline: 08/08
Tuition: full time: $36,100; part time: N/A
Room/board/expenses: $24,225
Median grant: $10,000
Average student indebtedness at graduation: $115,289
Enrollment: full time: 327; part time: N/A
men: 57%; women: 43%; minorities: 13%
Acceptance rate (full time): 56%
Midrange LSAT (full time): 150-158
Midrange undergraduate GPA (full time): 2.80-3.48
Midrange of full-time private-sector salaries of 2011 grads: $45,000-$65,000
2011 grads employed in: law firms: 68%; business and industry: 15%; government: 8%; public interest: 3%; judicial clerk: 5%; academia: 0%; unknown: 0%
Employment location for 2011 class: Intl. 0%; N.E. 0%; M.A. 4%; E.N.C. 0%; W.N.C. 0%; S.A. 90%; E.S.C. 1%; W.S.C. 4%; Mt. 0%; Pac. 0%; unknown 0%

North Carolina Central University

640 Nelson Street
Durham, NC 27707
http://law.nccu.edu
Public
Admissions: (919) 530-5243
E-mail: recruiter@nccu.edu
Financial aid: (919) 530-6365
Application deadline: 03/31
In-state tuition: full time: $11,375; part time: $11,375
Out-of-state tuition: full time: $25,303
Room/board/expenses: $22,312
Median grant: $6,400
Average student indebtedness at graduation: $87,671
Enrollment: full time: 481; part time: 102
men: 40%; women: 60%; minorities: 56%
Acceptance rate (full time): 34%
Midrange LSAT (full time): 143-149
Midrange undergraduate GPA (full time): 2.91-3.47
Midrange of full-time private-sector salaries of 2011 grads: $36,000-$65,000
2011 grads employed in: law firms: 40%; business and industry: 24%; government: 20%; public interest: 6%; judicial clerk: 2%; academia: 6%; unknown: 2%
Employment location for 2011 class: Intl. 1%; N.E. 2%; M.A. 5%; E.N.C. 2%; W.N.C. 2%; S.A. 87%; E.S.C. 0%; W.S.C. 2%; Mt. 0%; Pac. 0%; unknown 0%

University of North Carolina–Chapel Hill

Van Hecke-Wettach Hall
CB No. 3380
Chapel Hill, NC 27599-3380
http://www.law.unc.edu
Public
Admissions: (919) 962-5109
E-mail: law_admission@unc.edu
Financial aid: (919) 962-8396
Application deadline: 03/01
In-state tuition: full time: $21,556; part time: N/A
Out-of-state tuition: full time: $37,066
Room/board/expenses: $22,338
Median grant: $5,000
Average student indebtedness at graduation: $74,485
Enrollment: full time: 741; part time: N/A
men: 51%; women: 49%; minorities: 26%
Acceptance rate (full time): 29%
Midrange LSAT (full time): 160-164
Midrange undergraduate GPA (full time): 3.33-3.69
Midrange of full-time private-sector salaries of 2011 grads: $70,000-$145,000
2011 grads employed in: law firms: 49%; business and industry: 18%; government: 10%; public interest: 11%; judicial clerk: 11%; academia: 1%; unknown: 0%
Employment location for 2011 class: Intl. 1%; N.E. 1%; M.A. 7%; E.N.C. 2%; W.N.C. 1%; S.A. 79%; E.S.C. 1%; W.S.C. 5%; Mt. 1%; Pac. 1%; unknown 1%

Wake Forest University

Reynolda Station, PO Box 7206
Winston-Salem, NC 27109
http://www.law.wfu.edu
Private
Admissions: (336) 758-5437
E-mail: lawadmissions@wfu.edu
Financial aid: (336) 758-5437
Application deadline: 03/15
Tuition: full time: $39,920; part time: N/A
Room/board/expenses: $19,550
Median grant: $20,000
Average student indebtedness at graduation: $112,563
Enrollment: full time: 465; part time: N/A
men: 58%; women: 42%; minorities: 22%
Acceptance rate (full time): 42%
Midrange LSAT (full time): 159-165
Midrange undergraduate GPA (full time): 3.40-3.75
Midrange of full-time private-sector salaries of 2011 grads: $61,500-$130,000
2011 grads employed in: law firms: 48%; business and industry: 19%; government: 16%; public interest: 6%; judicial clerk: 7%; academia: 2%; unknown: 1%
Employment location for 2011 class: Intl. 2%; N.E. 0%; M.A. 10%; E.N.C. 3%; W.N.C. 1%; S.A. 73%; E.S.C. 2%; W.S.C. 8%; Mt. 0%; Pac. 2%; unknown 0%

University of North Dakota

215 Centennial Drive, Stop 9003
Grand Forks, ND 58202
http://www.law.und.edu
Public
Admissions: (701) 777-2260
E-mail: benjamin.hoffman@law.und.edu
Financial aid: (701) 777-3121
Application deadline: 07/15
In-state tuition: full time: $10,417; part time: N/A
Out-of-state tuition: full time: $22,394
Room/board/expenses: $19,653
Median grant: $3,400
Average student indebtedness at graduation: $64,100
Enrollment: full time: 241; part time: N/A
men: 53%; women: 47%; minorities: 12%
Acceptance rate (full time): 44%
Midrange LSAT (full time): 145-153
Midrange undergraduate GPA (full time): 3.04-3.58
Midrange of full-time private-sector salaries of 2011 grads: $43,500-$52,000
2011 grads employed in: law firms: 41%; business and industry: 24%; government: 11%; public interest: 4%; judicial clerk: 11%; academia: 7%; unknown: 0%
Employment location for 2011 class: Intl. 6%; N.E. 1%; M.A. 0%; E.N.C. 0%; W.N.C. 81%; S.A. 1%; E.S.C. 0%; W.S.C. 4%; Mt. 1%; Pac. 4%; unknown 0%

Capital University

303 E. Broad Street
Columbus, OH 43215-3200
http://www.law.capital.edu
Private
Admissions: (614) 236-6310
E-mail: admissions@law.capital.edu
Financial aid: (614) 236-6350
Application deadline: rolling
Tuition: full time: $1,147/credit hour; part time: $1,147/credit hour
Room/board/expenses: $15,495
Median grant: $12,000
Average student indebtedness at graduation: $120,471
Enrollment: full time: 401; part time: 176
men: 52%; women: 48%; minorities: 14%
Acceptance rate (full time): 72%
Midrange LSAT (full time): 147-154
Midrange undergraduate GPA (full time): 3.02-3.51
Midrange of full-time private-sector salaries of 2011 grads: $38,000-$75,000
2011 grads employed in: law firms: 59%; business and industry: 15%; government: 23%; public interest: 1%; judicial clerk: 0%; academia: 3%; unknown: 0%
Employment location for 2011 class: Intl. 0%; N.E. 1%; M.A. 2%; E.N.C. 90%; W.N.C. 0%; S.A. 4%; E.S.C. 1%; W.S.C. 2%; Mt. 0%; Pac. 1%; unknown 0%

Ohio Northern University (Pettit)

525 S. Main Street
Ada, OH 45810-1599
http://www.law.onu.edu
Private
Admissions: (877) 452-9668
E-mail: lawadmissions@onu.edu
Financial aid: (419) 772-2272

Case Western Reserve University

11075 E. Boulevard
Cleveland, OH 44106-7148
http://www.law.case.edu
Private
Admissions: (800) 756-0036
E-mail: lawadmissions@case.edu
Financial aid: (877) 889-4279
Application deadline: 04/01
Tuition: full time: $44,620; part time: N/A
Room/board/expenses: $21,340
Median grant: $15,333
Average student indebtedness at graduation: $118,806
Enrollment: full time: 567; part time: 6
men: 53%; women: 47%; minorities: 18%
Acceptance rate (full time): 54%
Midrange LSAT (full time): 156-161
Midrange undergraduate GPA (full time): 3.10-3.60
Midrange of full-time private-sector salaries of 2011 grads: $60,000-$104,000
2011 grads employed in: law firms: 47%; business and industry: 20%; government: 15%; public interest: 12%; judicial clerk: 4%; academia: 3%; unknown: 0%
Employment location for 2011 class: Intl. 4%; N.E. 3%; M.A. 12%; E.N.C. 58%; W.N.C. 2%; S.A. 12%; E.S.C. 2%; W.S.C. 3%; Mt. 1%; Pac. 6%; unknown 0%

Cleveland State University (Cleveland-Marshall)

2121 Euclid Avenue, LB 138
Cleveland, OH 44115-2214
https://www.law.csuohio.edu
Public
Admissions: (216) 687-2304
E-mail: admissions@law.csuohio.edu
Financial aid: (216) 687-2304
Application deadline: 05/01
In-state tuition: full time: $21,749; part time: $17,567
Out-of-state tuition: full time: $29,816
Room/board/expenses: $18,142
Median grant: $9,957
Average student indebtedness at graduation: $82,269
Enrollment: full time: 375; part time: 120
men: 58%; women: 42%; minorities: 17%
Acceptance rate (full time): 46%
Midrange LSAT (full time): 152-158
Midrange undergraduate GPA (full time): 3.03-3.63
Midrange of full-time private-sector salaries of 2011 grads: $60,000-$83,500
2011 grads employed in: law firms: 57%; business and industry: 24%; government: 13%; public interest: 3%; judicial clerk: 1%; academia: 1%; unknown: 3%
Employment location for 2011 class: Intl. 1%; N.E. 0%; M.A. 3%; E.N.C. 93%; W.N.C. 0%; S.A. 3%; E.S.C. 1%; W.S.C. 0%; Mt. 0%; Pac. 0%; unknown 0%

University of Akron

C. Blake McDowell Law Center
Akron, OH 44325-2901
http://www.uakron.edu/law
Public
Admissions: (800) 425-7668
E-mail: lawadmissions@uakron.edu
Financial aid: (800) 621-3847
Application deadline: 03/01
In-state tuition: full time: $23,085; part time: $14,842
Out-of-state tuition: full time: $36,268
Room/board/expenses: $16,134
Median grant: $10,000
Average student indebtedness at graduation: $66,283

Application deadline: 08/15
Tuition: full time: $33,684; part time: N/A
Room/board/expenses: $16,748
Median grant: $17,000
Average student indebtedness at graduation: $97,968
Enrollment: full time: 274; part time: N/A
men: 59%; women: 41%; minorities: 11%
Acceptance rate (full time): 51%
Midrange LSAT (full time): 145-154
Midrange undergraduate GPA (full time): 2.81-3.45
Midrange of full-time private-sector salaries of 2011 grads: $35,000-$55,000
2011 grads employed in: law firms: 47%; business and industry: 25%; government: 15%; public interest: 3%; judicial clerk: 6%; academia: 4%; unknown: 0%
Employment location for 2011 class: Intl. 3%; N.E. 4%; M.A. 8%; E.N.C. 62%; W.N.C. 4%; S.A. 10%; E.S.C. 3%; W.S.C. 3%; Mt. 4%; Pac. 1%; unknown 0%

Ohio State University (Moritz)

55 W. 12th Avenue
Columbus, OH 43210
http://www.moritzlaw.osu.edu
Public
Admissions: (614) 292-8810
E-mail: lawadmit@osu.edu
Financial aid: (614) 292-8807
Application deadline: 03/31
In-state tuition: full time: $27,497; part time: N/A
Out-of-state tuition: full time: $42,449
Room/board/expenses: $21,788
Median grant: $9,975
Average student indebtedness at graduation: $98,674
Enrollment: full time: 605; part time: 9
men: 56%; women: 44%; minorities: 22%
Acceptance rate (full time): 47%
Midrange LSAT (full time): 158-164
Midrange undergraduate GPA (full time): 3.43-3.79
Midrange of full-time private-sector salaries of 2011 grads: $52,000-$98,000
2011 grads employed in: law firms: 44%; business and industry: 26%; government: 16%; public interest: 5%; judicial clerk: 6%; academia: 3%; unknown: 0%
Employment location for 2011 class: Intl. 1%; N.E. 1%; M.A. 4%; E.N.C. 74%; W.N.C. 1%; S.A. 10%; E.S.C. 2%; W.S.C. 2%; Mt. 2%; Pac. 3%; unknown 0%

University of Cincinnati

PO Box 210040
Cincinnati, OH 45221-0040
http://www.law.uc.edu
Public
Admissions: (513) 556-6805
E-mail: admissions@law.uc.edu
Financial aid: (513) 556-0078
Application deadline: 03/01
In-state tuition: full time: $23,536; part time: N/A
Out-of-state tuition: full time: $41,044
Room/board/expenses: $18,336
Median grant: $6,500
Average student indebtedness at graduation: $84,140
Enrollment: full time: 386; part time: 2
men: 60%; women: 40%; minorities: 14%
Acceptance rate (full time): 59%
Midrange LSAT (full time): 156-161
Midrange undergraduate GPA (full time): 3.20-3.73
Midrange of full-time private-sector salaries of 2011 grads: $62,500-$103,750
2011 grads employed in: law firms: 42%; business and industry: 22%; government: 15%; public interest: 7%; judicial clerk: 3%; academia: 10%; unknown: 1%
Employment location for 2011 class: Intl. 1%; N.E. 1%; M.A. 0%; E.N.C. 74%; W.N.C. 1%; S.A. 9%; E.S.C. 6%; W.S.C. 1%; Mt. 3%; Pac. 3%; unknown 2%

University of Dayton

300 College Park
Dayton, OH 45469-2772
http://www.udayton.edu/law
Private
Admissions: (937) 229-3555
E-mail: lawinfo@udayton.edu
Financial aid: (937) 229-3555
Application deadline: 05/01
Tuition: full time: $33,630; part time: N/A
Room/board/expenses: $17,500
Median grant: $9,000
Average student indebtedness at graduation: $118,333
Enrollment: full time: 407; part time: N/A
men: 58%; women: 42%; minorities: 14%
Acceptance rate (full time): 69%
Midrange LSAT (full time): 146-152
Midrange undergraduate GPA (full time): 2.84-3.37
Midrange of full-time private-sector salaries of 2011 grads: $37,750-$67,500

Enrollment: full time: 299; part time: 216
men: 58%; women: 42%; minorities: 13%
Acceptance rate (full time): 45%
Midrange LSAT (full time): 153-157
Midrange undergraduate GPA (full time): 3.14-3.69
Midrange of full-time private-sector salaries of 2011 grads: $40,000-$66,000
2011 grads employed in: law firms: 37%; business and industry: 32%; government: 19%; public interest: 2%; judicial clerk: 7%; academia: 3%; unknown: 0%
Employment location for 2011 class: Intl. 2%; N.E. 0%; M.A. 8%; E.N.C. 78%; W.N.C. 1%; S.A. 5%; E.S.C. 1%; W.S.C. 1%; Mt. 2%; Pac. 3%; unknown 0%

2011 grads employed in: law firms; 53%; business and industry: 25%; government: 12%; public interest: 5%; judicial clerk: 2%; academia: 2%; unknown: 0%
Employment location for 2011 class: Intl. 0%; N.E. 1%; M.A. 8%; E.N.C. 66%; W.N.C. 2%; S.A. 9%; E.S.C. 5%; W.S.C. 4%; Mt. 2%; Pac. 5%; unknown 0%

University of Toledo

2801 W. Bancroft
Toledo, OH 43606
http://law.utoledo.edu/
Public
Admissions: (419) 530-4131
E-mail: law.admissions@utoledo.edu
Financial aid: (419) 530-7929
Application deadline: 08/01
In-state tuition: full time: $21,507; part time: $16,104
Out-of-state tuition: full time: $33,056
Room/board/expenses: $19,596
Median grant: $12,104
Average student indebtedness at graduation: $95,375
Enrollment: full time: 309; part time: 79
men: 61%; women: 39%; minorities: 13%
Acceptance rate (full time): 47%
Midrange LSAT (full time): 150-155
Midrange undergraduate GPA (full time): 3.02-3.53
Midrange of full-time private-sector salaries of 2011 grads: $46,000-$70,000
2011 grads employed in: law firms: 38%; business and industry: 33%; government: 10%; public interest: 5%; judicial clerk: 8%; academia: 5%; unknown: 1%
Employment location for 2011 class: Intl. 1%; N.E. 1%; M.A. 8%; E.N.C. 75%; W.N.C. 0%; S.A. 7%; E.S.C. 1%; W.S.C. 1%; Mt. 4%; Pac. 1%; unknown 1%

OKLAHOMA

Oklahoma City University

2501 N. Blackwelder Avenue
Oklahoma City, OK 73106-1493
http://www.law.okcu.edu
Private
Admissions: (866) 529-6281
E-mail: lawquestions@okcu.edu
Financial aid: (800) 633-7242
Application deadline: 08/01
Tuition: full time: $1,065/credit hour; part time: $1,065/credit hour
Room/board/expenses: $18,692
Median grant: $16,000
Average student indebtedness at graduation: $120,318
Enrollment: full time: 474; part time: 65
men: 58%; women: 42%; minorities: 22%
Acceptance rate (full time): 69%
Midrange LSAT (full time): 147-153
Midrange undergraduate GPA (full time): 2.87-3.49
Midrange of full-time private-sector salaries of 2011 grads: $48,000-$80,000
2011 grads employed in: law firms: 58%; business and industry: 28%; government: 8%; public interest: 5%; judicial clerk: 1%; academia: 1%; unknown: 0%

Employment location for 2011 class: Intl. 0%; N.E. 0%; M.A. 1%; E.N.C. 1%; W.N.C. 3%; S.A. 0%; E.S.C. 1%; W.S.C. 76%; Mt. 16%; Pac. 1%; unknown 0%

University of Oklahoma

Andrew M. Coats Hall
300 Timberdell Road
Norman, OK 73019-5081
http://www.law.ou.edu
Public
Admissions: (405) 325-4728
E-mail: admissions@law.ou.edu
Financial aid: (405) 325-4521
Application deadline: 03/15
In-state tuition: full time: $19,763; part time: N/A
Out-of-state tuition: full time: $30,188
Room/board/expenses: $18,208
Median grant: $4,000
Average student indebtedness at graduation: $77,146
Enrollment: full time: 505; part time: N/A
men: 55%; women: 45%; minorities: 20%
Acceptance rate (full time): 38%
Midrange LSAT (full time): 155-161
Midrange undergraduate GPA (full time): 3.10-3.58
Midrange of full-time private-sector salaries of 2011 grads: $40,456-$70,000
2011 grads employed in: law firms: 59%; business and industry: 20%; government: 17%; public interest: 1%; judicial clerk: 2%; academia: 1%; unknown: 0%
Employment location for 2011 class: Intl. 1%; N.E. 0%; M.A. 1%; E.N.C. 0%; W.N.C. 2%; S.A. 6%; E.S.C. 0%; W.S.C. 86%; Mt. 2%; Pac. 1%; unknown 0%

University of Tulsa

3120 E. Fourth Place
Tulsa, OK 74104
http://www.utulsa.edu/law
Private
Admissions: (918) 631-2709
E-mail: lawadmissions@utulsa.edu
Financial aid: (918) 631-2526
Application deadline: 07/31
Tuition: full time: $31,836; part time: $22,287
Room/board/expenses: $19,200
Median grant: $16,000
Average student indebtedness at graduation: $104,785
Enrollment: full time: 300; part time: 30
men: 57%; women: 43%; minorities: 22%
Acceptance rate (full time): 36%
Midrange LSAT (full time): 153-158
Midrange undergraduate GPA (full time): 3.07-3.61
Midrange of full-time private-sector salaries of 2011 grads: $50,000-$60,000
2011 grads employed in: law firms: 56%; business and industry: 19%; government: 14%; public interest: 6%; judicial clerk: 4%; academia: 1%; unknown: 0%
Employment location for 2011 class: Intl. 0%; N.E. 2%; M.A. 0%; E.N.C. 2%; W.N.C. 9%; S.A. 2%; E.S.C. 0%; W.S.C. 76%; Mt. 6%; Pac. 4%; unknown 0%

OREGON

Lewis & Clark College (Northwestern)

10015 S.W. Terwilliger Boulevard
Portland, OR 97219
http://law.lclark.edu
Private
Admissions: (503) 768-6613
E-mail: lawadmss@lclark.edu
Financial aid: (503) 768-7090
Application deadline: 03/15
Tuition: full time: $38,180; part time: $28,636
Room/board/expenses: $21,400
Median grant: $15,000
Average student indebtedness at graduation: $109,419
Enrollment: full time: 483; part time: 267
men: 49%; women: 51%; minorities: 24%
Acceptance rate (full time): 56%
Midrange LSAT (full time): 157-163
Midrange undergraduate GPA (full time): 3.28-3.65
Midrange of full-time private-sector salaries of 2011 grads: $50,000-$86,750
2011 grads employed in: law firms: 40%; business and industry: 17%; government: 17%; public interest: 12%; judicial clerk: 8%; academia: 4%; unknown: 2%
Employment location for 2011 class: Intl. 1%; N.E. 1%; M.A. 2%; E.N.C. 3%; W.N.C. 0%; S.A. 7%; E.S.C. 0%; W.S.C. 2%; Mt. 8%; Pac. 77%; unknown 1%

University of Oregon

1221 University of Oregon
Eugene, OR 97403-1221
http://www.law.uoregon.edu
Public
Admissions: (541) 346-3846
E-mail: admissions@law.uoregon.edu
Financial aid: (800) 760-6953
Application deadline: 03/01
In-state tuition: full time: $28,354; part time: N/A
Out-of-state tuition: full time: $35,374
Room/board/expenses: $15,044
Median grant: $5,000
Average student indebtedness at graduation: $100,169
Enrollment: full time: 480; part time: N/A
men: 58%; women: 42%; minorities: 17%
Acceptance rate (full time): 53%
Midrange LSAT (full time): 155-160
Midrange undergraduate GPA (full time): 3.09-3.63
Midrange of full-time private-sector salaries of 2011 grads: $46,500-$60,000
2011 grads employed in: law firms: 46%; business and industry: 8%; government: 17%; public interest: 10%; judicial clerk: 17%; academia: 1%; unknown: 1%
Employment location for 2011 class: Intl. 0%; N.E. 0%; M.A. 1%; E.N.C. 1%; W.N.C. 0%; S.A. 6%; E.S.C. 0%; W.S.C. 1%; Mt. 6%; Pac. 84%; unknown 2%

Willamette University (Collins)

245 Winter Street SE
Salem, OR 97301
http://www.willamette.edu/wucl
Private
Admissions: (503) 370-6282
E-mail: law-admission@willamette.edu
Financial aid: (503) 370-6273

Application deadline: 03/03
Tuition: full time: $34,690; part time: $26,047
Room/board/expenses: $16,480
Median grant: $8,000
Average student indebtedness at graduation: $119,468
Enrollment: full time: 378; part time: 8
men: 60%; women: 40%; minorities: 18%
Acceptance rate (full time): 62%
Midrange LSAT (full time): 151-156
Midrange undergraduate GPA (full time): 2.81-3.42
Midrange of full-time private-sector salaries of 2011 grads: $50,000-$70,000
2011 grads employed in: law firms: 56%; business and industry: 17%; government: 15%; public interest: 6%; judicial clerk: 4%; academia: 1%; unknown: 0%
Employment location for 2011 class: Intl. 0%; N.E. 0%; M.A. 1%; E.N.C. 1%; W.N.C. 1%; S.A. 0%; E.S.C. 0%; W.S.C. 0%; Mt. 9%; Pac. 88%; unknown 0%

PENNSYLVANIA

Drexel University (Mack)

3320 Market Street, Suite 400
Philadelphia, PA 19104
http://www.earlemacklaw.drexel.edu/admissions
Private
Admissions: (215) 895-1529
E-mail: lawadmissions@drexel.edu
Financial aid: (215) 895-1044
Application deadline: rolling
Tuition: full time: $38,078; part time: N/A
Room/board/expenses: $22,200
Median grant: $20,000
Average student indebtedness at graduation: $98,820
Enrollment: full time: 411; part time: 11
men: 56%; women: 44%; minorities: 19%
Acceptance rate (full time): 39%
Midrange LSAT (full time): 154-159
Midrange undergraduate GPA (full time): 3.02-3.60
Midrange of full-time private-sector salaries of 2011 grads: $50,000-$70,000
2011 grads employed in: law firms: 38%; business and industry: 23%; government: 7%; public interest: 10%; judicial clerk: 17%; academia: 5%; unknown: 1%
Employment location for 2011 class: Intl. 0%; N.E. 1%; M.A. 82%; E.N.C. 1%; W.N.C. 0%; S.A. 10%; E.S.C. 1%; W.S.C. 1%; Mt. 1%; Pac. 1%; unknown 2%

Duquesne University

600 Forbes Avenue
Pittsburgh, PA 15282
http://www.duq.edu/law
Private
Admissions: (412) 396-6296
E-mail: lawadmissions@duq.edu
Financial aid: (412) 396-6607
Application deadline: 03/01
Tuition: full time: $35,354; part time: $27,336
Room/board/expenses: $13,980
Median grant: $15,000
Average student indebtedness at graduation: $100,081

Enrollment: full time: 392; part time: 165
men: 58%; women: 42%; minorities: 6%
Acceptance rate (full time): 63%
Midrange LSAT (full time): 150-154
Midrange undergraduate GPA (full time): 3.15-3.54
Midrange of full-time private-sector salaries of 2011 grads: $45,000-$90,000
2011 grads employed in: law firms: 48%; business and industry: 29%; government: 7%; public interest: 4%; judicial clerk: 10%; academia: 2%; unknown: 0%
Employment location for 2011 class: Intl. 0%; N.E. 1%; M.A. 88%; E.N.C. 2%; W.N.C. 0%; S.A. 8%; E.S.C. 0%; W.S.C. 0%; Mt. 1%; Pac. 1%; unknown 0%

Pennsylvania State University (Dickinson)

Lewis Katz Building
University Park, PA 16802
http://www.law.psu.edu
Public
Admissions: (800) 840-1122
E-mail: admissions@law.psu.edu
Financial aid: (800) 840-1122
Application deadline: 04/30
In-state tuition: full time: $40,532; part time: N/A
Out-of-state tuition: full time: $40,532
Room/board/expenses: $23,680
Median grant: $11,000
Average student indebtedness at graduation: $121,134
Enrollment: full time: 541; part time: N/A
men: 56%; women: 44%; minorities: 14%
Acceptance rate (full time): 42%
Midrange LSAT (full time): 156-160
Midrange undergraduate GPA (full time): 3.23-3.73
Midrange of full-time private-sector salaries of 2011 grads: $48,288-$100,000
2011 grads employed in: law firms: 40%; business and industry: 18%; government: 9%; public interest: 3%; judicial clerk: 20%; academia: 6%; unknown: 3%
Employment location for 2011 class: Intl. 1%; N.E. 1%; M.A. 59%; E.N.C. 0%; W.N.C. 0%; S.A. 19%; E.S.C. 0%; W.S.C. 1%; Mt. 4%; Pac. 1%; unknown 14%

Temple University (Beasley)

1719 N. Broad Street
Philadelphia, PA 19122
http://www.law.temple.edu
Public
Admissions: (800) 560-1428
E-mail: lawadmis@temple.edu
Financial aid: (800) 560-1428
Application deadline: 03/01
In-state tuition: full time: $19,788; part time: $15,958
Out-of-state tuition: full time: $32,718
Room/board/expenses: $21,752
Median grant: $7,500
Average student indebtedness at graduation: $87,794
Enrollment: full time: 688; part time: 173
men: 58%; women: 42%; minorities: 27%
Acceptance rate (full time): 43%
Midrange LSAT (full time): 159-163
Midrange undergraduate GPA (full time): 3.20-3.62

Midrange of full-time private-sector salaries of 2011 grads: $58,750-$121,000
2011 grads employed in: law firms: 41%; business and industry: 15%; government: 12%; public interest: 13%; judicial clerk: 12%; academia: 6%; unknown: 2%
Employment location for 2011 class: Intl. 2%; N.E. 1%; M.A. 84%; E.N.C. 1%; W.N.C. 0%; S.A. 9%; E.S.C. 0%; W.S.C. 0%; Mt. 0%; Pac. 1%; unknown 1%

University of Pennsylvania
3501 Sansom Street
Philadelphia, PA 19104-6204
http://www.law.upenn.edu
Private
Admissions: (215) 898-7400
E-mail: contactadmissions@law.upenn.edu
Financial aid: (215) 898-7400
Application deadline: 03/01
Tuition: full time: $53,138; part time: N/A
Room/board/expenses: $21,392
Median grant: $15,000
Average student indebtedness at graduation: $118,278
Enrollment: full time: 776; part time: N/A
men: 54%; women: 46%; minorities: 30%
Acceptance rate (full time): 16%
Midrange LSAT (full time): 164-171
Midrange undergraduate GPA (full time): 3.55-3.94
Midrange of full-time private-sector salaries of 2011 grads: $130,000-$160,000
2011 grads employed in: law firms: 68%; business and industry: 7%; government: 4%; public interest: 4%; judicial clerk: 16%; academia: 1%; unknown: 0%
Employment location for 2011 class: Intl. 1%; N.E. 3%; M.A. 66%; E.N.C. 3%; W.N.C. 1%; S.A. 15%; E.S.C. 0%; W.S.C. 3%; Mt. 0%; Pac. 7%; unknown 0%

University of Pittsburgh
3900 Forbes Avenue
Pittsburgh, PA 15260
http://www.law.pitt.edu
Public
Admissions: (412) 648-1415
E-mail: admissions@law.pitt.edu
Financial aid: (412) 648-1415
Application deadline: 03/01
In-state tuition: full time: $29,468; part time: N/A
Out-of-state tuition: full time: $36,444
Room/board/expenses: $17,714
Median grant: $12,000
Average student indebtedness at graduation: $94,879
Enrollment: full time: 677; part time: N/A
men: 60%; women: 40%; minorities: 18%
Acceptance rate (full time): 50%
Midrange LSAT (full time): 155-160
Midrange undergraduate GPA (full time): 3.09-3.60
Midrange of full-time private-sector salaries of 2011 grads: $45,600-$86,000
2011 grads employed in: law firms: 43%; business and industry: 30%; government: 12%; public interest: 6%; judicial clerk: 9%; academia: 1%; unknown: 0%

Employment location for 2011 class: Intl. 3%; N.E. 1%; M.A. 78%; E.N.C. 4%; W.N.C. 1%; S.A. 11%; E.S.C. 0%; W.S.C. 2%; Mt. 1%; Pac. 0%; unknown 0%

Villanova University
299 N. Spring Mill Road
Villanova, PA 19085
http://www.law.villanova.edu/
Private
Admissions: (610) 519-7010
E-mail: admissions@law.villanova.edu
Financial aid: (610) 519-7015
Application deadline: 04/01
Tuition: full time: $38,910; part time: N/A
Room/board/expenses: $22,816
Median grant: $20,000
Average student indebtedness at graduation: $113,283
Enrollment: full time: 684; part time: N/A
men: 54%; women: 46%; minorities: 17%
Acceptance rate (full time): 62%
Midrange LSAT (full time): 155-161
Midrange undergraduate GPA (full time): 3.29-3.69
Midrange of full-time private-sector salaries of 2011 grads: $51,000-$100,000
2011 grads employed in: law firms: 52%; business and industry: 20%; government: 11%; public interest: 2%; judicial clerk: 13%; academia: 1%; unknown: 0%
Employment location for 2011 class: Intl. 1%; N.E. 2%; M.A. 79%; E.N.C. 1%; W.N.C. 0%; S.A. 14%; E.S.C. 1%; W.S.C. 1%; Mt. 1%; Pac. 1%; unknown 0%

PUERTO RICO

Catholic University[1]
2250 Avenida Las Americas
Suite 584
Ponce, PR 00717-0777
http://www.pucpr.edu
Private
Admissions: (787) 841-2000
E-mail: admisiones@pucpr.edu
Financial aid: (787) 841-2000
Tuition: N/A
Room/board/expenses: N/A
Enrollment: N/A

Inter-American University[1]
PO Box 70351
San Juan, PR 00936-8351
http://www.metro.inter.edu
Private
Admissions: (787) 765-1270
E-mail: edmendez@inter.edu
Financial aid: (787) 250-1912
Tuition: N/A
Room/board/expenses: N/A
Enrollment: N/A

University of Puerto Rico[1]
PO Box 23303
Estacion Universidad
Rio Piedras, PR 00931-3302
http://www.upr.edu
Public
Admissions: (787) 764-0000
E-mail: admisiones@upr.edu
Financial aid: (787) 764-0000
Tuition: N/A
Room/board/expenses: N/A
Enrollment: N/A

RHODE ISLAND

Roger Williams University
10 Metacom Avenue
Bristol, RI 02809-5171
http://law.rwu.edu
Private
Admissions: (401) 254-4555
E-mail: Admissions@rwu.edu
Financial aid: (401) 254-4510
Application deadline: 04/01
Tuition: full time: $40,930; part time: N/A
Room/board/expenses: $19,625
Median grant: $16,500
Average student indebtedness at graduation: $132,699
Enrollment: full time: 506; part time: N/A
men: 48%; women: 52%; minorities: 16%
Acceptance rate (full time): 79%
Midrange LSAT (full time): 147-156
Midrange undergraduate GPA (full time): 2.96-3.57
Midrange of full-time private-sector salaries of 2011 grads: $42,000-$60,000
2011 grads employed in: law firms: 39%; business and industry: 24%; government: 10%; public interest: 11%; judicial clerk: 13%; academia: 3%; unknown: 0%
Employment location for 2011 class: Intl. 0%; N.E. 69%; M.A. 14%; E.N.C. 0%; W.N.C. 0%; S.A. 13%; E.S.C. 0%; W.S.C. 1%; Mt. 3%; Pac. 0%; unknown 0%

SOUTH CAROLINA

Charleston School of Law
PO Box 535
Charleston, SC 29402
http://www.charlestonlaw.edu
Private
Admissions: (843) 377-2143
E-mail: info@charlestonlaw.edu
Financial aid: (843) 377-4901
Application deadline: 03/01
Tuition: full time: $37,874; part time: $30,450
Room/board/expenses: $19,250
Median grant: $6,000
Average student indebtedness at graduation: $141,457
Enrollment: full time: 447; part time: 184
men: 55%; women: 45%; minorities: 12%
Acceptance rate (full time): 57%
Midrange LSAT (full time): 149-155
Midrange undergraduate GPA (full time): 2.96-3.43
Midrange of full-time private-sector salaries of 2011 grads: $38,000-$60,000
2011 grads employed in: law firms: 48%; business and industry: 17%; government: 11%; public interest: 6%; judicial clerk: 16%; academia: 1%; unknown: 1%
Employment location for 2011 class: Intl. 0%; N.E. 1%; M.A. 0%; E.N.C. 1%; W.N.C. 0%; S.A. 93%; E.S.C. 1%; W.S.C. 1%; Mt. 0%; Pac. 1%; unknown 2%

University of South Carolina
701 S. Main Street
Columbia, SC 29208
http://www.law.sc.edu/admissions
Public
Admissions: (803) 777-6605
E-mail: usclaw@law.sc.edu

Financial aid: (803) 777-6605
Application deadline: 03/01
In-state tuition: full time: $21,688; part time: N/A
Out-of-state tuition: full time: $43,398
Room/board/expenses: $17,304
Median grant: $19,384
Average student indebtedness at graduation: $85,602
Enrollment: full time: 632; part time: 1
men: 60%; women: 40%; minorities: 15%
Acceptance rate (full time): 50%
Midrange LSAT (full time): 154-159
Midrange undergraduate GPA (full time): 3.01-3.58
Midrange of full-time private-sector salaries of 2011 grads: $50,000-$75,000
2011 grads employed in: law firms: 39%; business and industry: 25%; government: 9%; public interest: 3%; judicial clerk: 22%; academia: 2%; unknown: 0%
Employment location for 2011 class: Intl. 1%; N.E. 1%; M.A. 1%; E.N.C. 2%; W.N.C. 0%; S.A. 91%; E.S.C. 2%; W.S.C. 1%; Mt. 2%; Pac. 0%; unknown 0%

SOUTH DAKOTA

University of South Dakota
414 E. Clark Street
Vermillion, SD 57069-2390
http://www.usd.edu/law/
Public
Admissions: (605) 677-5444
E-mail: law@usd.edu
Financial aid: (605) 677-5446
Application deadline: 03/15
In-state tuition: full time: $13,288; part time: $7,162
Out-of-state tuition: full time: $26,880
Room/board/expenses: $11,639
Median grant: $0
Average student indebtedness at graduation: $54,352
Enrollment: full time: 217; part time: N/A
men: 60%; women: 40%; minorities: 8%
Acceptance rate (full time): 66%
Midrange LSAT (full time): 146-153
Midrange undergraduate GPA (full time): 3.01-3.67
Midrange of full-time private-sector salaries of 2011 grads: N/A-N/A
2011 grads employed in: law firms: 27%; business and industry: 17%; government: 20%; public interest: 2%; judicial clerk: 32%; academia: 0%; unknown: 2%
Employment location for 2011 class: Intl. 0%; N.E. 0%; M.A. 0%; E.N.C. 2%; W.N.C. 80%; S.A. 2%; E.S.C. 0%; W.S.C. 2%; Mt. 12%; Pac. 0%; unknown 2%

TENNESSEE

University of Memphis (Humphreys)
1 North Front Street
Memphis, TN 38103-2189
http://www.memphis.edu/law
Public
Admissions: (901) 678-5403
E-mail: lawadmissions@memphis.edu
Financial aid: (901) 678-3737
Application deadline: 03/01
In-state tuition: full time: $16,834; part time: $775/credit hour

Out-of-state tuition: full time: $38,706
Room/board/expenses: $16,213
Median grant: $7,770
Average student indebtedness at graduation: $72,993
Enrollment: full time: 359; part time: 21
men: 62%; women: 38%; minorities: 15%
Acceptance rate (full time): 34%
Midrange LSAT (full time): 152-157
Midrange undergraduate GPA (full time): 3.03-3.54
Midrange of full-time private-sector salaries of 2011 grads: $45,000-$72,000
2011 grads employed in: law firms: 58%; business and industry: 11%; government: 12%; public interest: 4%; judicial clerk: 13%; academia: 1%; unknown: 0%
Employment location for 2011 class: Intl. 0%; N.E. 0%; M.A. 0%; E.N.C. 0%; W.N.C. 1%; S.A. 4%; E.S.C. 91%; W.S.C. 3%; Mt. 0%; Pac. 0%; unknown 1%

University of Tennessee–Knoxville
1505 W. Cumberland Avenue
Knoxville, TN 37996-1810
http://www.law.utk.edu
Public
Admissions: (865) 974-4131
E-mail: lawadmit@utk.edu
Financial aid: (865) 974-4131
Application deadline: 02/01
In-state tuition: full time: $17,678; part time: N/A
Out-of-state tuition: full time: $36,422
Room/board/expenses: $17,680
Median grant: $5,000
Average student indebtedness at graduation: $76,381
Enrollment: full time: 443; part time: N/A
men: 60%; women: 40%; minorities: 24%
Acceptance rate (full time): 37%
Midrange LSAT (full time): 156-161
Midrange undergraduate GPA (full time): 3.30-3.75
Midrange of full-time private-sector salaries of 2011 grads: $47,500-$75,000
2011 grads employed in: law firms: 50%; business and industry: 20%; government: 9%; public interest: 5%; judicial clerk: 13%; academia: 2%; unknown: 0%
Employment location for 2011 class: Intl. 2%; N.E. 0%; M.A. 0%; E.N.C. 1%; W.N.C. 1%; S.A. 12%; E.S.C. 80%; W.S.C. 2%; Mt. 2%; Pac. 0%; unknown 0%

Vanderbilt University
131 21st Avenue S
Nashville, TN 37203-1181
http://www.vanderbilt.edu/law/
Private
Admissions: (615) 322-6452
E-mail: admissions@law.vanderbilt.edu
Financial aid: (615) 322-6452
Application deadline: 04/01
Tuition: full time: $46,804; part time: N/A
Room/board/expenses: $23,342
Median grant: $20,000
Average student indebtedness at graduation: $124,493
Enrollment: full time: 580; part time: N/A
men: 56%; women: 44%; minorities: 21%

Acceptance rate (full time): 30%
Midrange LSAT (full time): 163-170
Midrange undergraduate GPA (full time): 3.43-3.85
Midrange of full-time private-sector salaries of 2011 grads: $105,000-$169,000
2011 grads employed in: law firms: 48%; business and industry: 10%; government: 12%; public interest: 13%; judicial clerk: 16%; academia: 2%; unknown: 1%
Employment location for 2011 class: Intl. 1%; N.E. 2%; M.A. 10%; E.N.C. 9%; W.N.C. 3%; S.A. 29%; E.S.C. 29%; W.S.C. 8%; Mt. 4%; Pac. 6%; unknown 1%

TEXAS

Baylor University
1114 S. University Parks Drive
1 Bear Place # 97288
Waco, TX 76798-7288
http://www.baylor.edu/law/
Private
Admissions: (254) 710-3239
E-mail: nicole_neeley@baylor.edu
Financial aid: (254) 710-2611
Application deadline: 01/03
Tuition: full time: $46,420; part time: N/A
Room/board/expenses: $15,888
Median grant: $28,714
Average student indebtedness at graduation: $99,852
Enrollment: full time: 401; part time: 4
men: 51%; women: 49%; minorities: 14%
Acceptance rate (full time): 21%
Midrange LSAT (full time): 158-163
Midrange undergraduate GPA (full time): 3.23-3.72
Midrange of full-time private-sector salaries of 2011 grads: $50,000-$85,500
2011 grads employed in: law firms: 65%; business and industry: 15%; government: 15%; public interest: 0%; judicial clerk: 4%; academia: 1%; unknown: 1%
Employment location for 2011 class: Intl. 0%; N.E. 0%; M.A. 2%; E.N.C. 0%; W.N.C. 2%; S.A. 3%; E.S.C. 1%; W.S.C. 89%; Mt. 2%; Pac. 2%; unknown N/A

Southern Methodist University (Dedman)
PO Box 750116
Dallas, TX 75275-0116
http://www.law.smu.edu
Private
Admissions: (214) 768-2540
E-mail: lawadmit@mail.smu.edu
Financial aid: (214) 768-4119
Application deadline: 02/15
Tuition: full time: $44,017; part time: $33,013
Room/board/expenses: $20,238
Median grant: $22,000
Average student indebtedness at graduation: $113,266
Enrollment: full time: 527; part time: 295
men: 58%; women: 42%; minorities: 25%
Acceptance rate (full time): 31%
Midrange LSAT (full time): 157-165
Midrange undergraduate GPA (full time): 3.34-3.84
Midrange of full-time private-sector salaries of 2011 grads: $62,500-$135,000

South Texas College of Law
1303 San Jacinto Street
Houston, TX 77002-7006
http://www.stcl.edu
Private
Admissions: (713) 646-1810
E-mail: admissions@stcl.edu
Financial aid: (713) 646-1820
Application deadline: 02/15
Tuition: full time: $27,600; part time: $18,600
Room/board/expenses: $21,900
Median grant: $4,776
Average student indebtedness at graduation: $113,551
Enrollment: full time: 964; part time: 261
men: 56%; women: 44%; minorities: 31%
Acceptance rate (full time): 55%
Midrange LSAT (full time): 151-156
Midrange undergraduate GPA (full time): 2.89-3.40
Midrange of full-time private-sector salaries of 2011 grads: $50,000-$80,000
2011 grads employed in: law firms: 59%; business and industry: 27%; government: 8%; public interest: 2%; judicial clerk: 1%; academia: 2%; unknown: 0%
Employment location for 2011 class: Intl. 0%; N.E. 0%; M.A. 1%; E.N.C. 0%; W.N.C. 1%; S.A. 1%; E.S.C. 0%; W.S.C. 95%; Mt. 1%; Pac. 1%; unknown 0%

St. Mary's University
1 Camino Santa Maria
San Antonio, TX 78228-8602
http://www.stmarytx.edu/law
Private
Admissions: (210) 436-3523
E-mail: lawadmissions@stmarytx.edu
Financial aid: (210) 431-6743
Application deadline: 03/01
Tuition: full time: $30,566; part time: $18,278
Room/board/expenses: $18,686
Median grant: $2,240
Average student indebtedness at graduation: $111,758
Enrollment: full time: 642; part time: 173
men: 56%; women: 44%; minorities: 38%
Acceptance rate (full time): 56%
Midrange LSAT (full time): 151-155
Midrange undergraduate GPA (full time): 2.79-3.40
Midrange of full-time private-sector salaries of 2011 grads: $46,500-$80,625
2011 grads employed in: law firms: 70%; business and industry: 10%; government: 11%; public interest: 2%; judicial clerk: 4%; academia: 3%; unknown: 0%
Employment location for 2011 class: Intl. 0%; N.E. 0%; M.A. 0%; E.N.C. 0%; W.N.C. 1%; S.A. 1%; E.S.C. 0%; W.S.C. 95%; Mt. 1%; Pac. 2%; unknown 0%

Texas Southern University (Marshall)
3100 Cleburne Street
Houston, TX 77004
http://www.tsulaw.edu
Public
Admissions: (713) 313-7114
E-mail: lawadmit@tsulaw.edu
Financial aid: (713) 313-7243
Application deadline: 04/01
In-state tuition: full time: $16,262; part time: N/A
Out-of-state tuition: full time: $21,212
Room/board/expenses: $19,588
Median grant: $7,495
Average student indebtedness at graduation: $99,992
Enrollment: full time: 540; part time: N/A
men: 44%; women: 56%; minorities: 83%
Acceptance rate (full time): 35%
Midrange LSAT (full time): 144-148
Midrange undergraduate GPA (full time): 2.84-3.40
Midrange of full-time private-sector salaries of 2011 grads: $45,000-$60,000
2011 grads employed in: law firms: 60%; business and industry: 24%; government: 9%; public interest: 1%; judicial clerk: 2%; academia: 2%; unknown: 1%
Employment location for 2011 class: Intl. 0%; N.E. 1%; M.A. 3%; E.N.C. 2%; W.N.C. 0%; S.A. 7%; E.S.C. 0%; W.S.C. 83%; Mt. 2%; Pac. 0%; unknown 2%

Texas Tech University
1802 Hartford Avenue
Lubbock, TX 79409-0004
http://www.law.ttu.edu
Public
Admissions: (806) 742-3990
E-mail: donna.williams@ttu.edu
Financial aid: (806) 742-3990
Application deadline: 02/15
In-state tuition: full time: $22,518; part time: N/A
Out-of-state tuition: full time: $32,148
Room/board/expenses: $15,102
Median grant: $4,921
Average student indebtedness at graduation: $69,596
Enrollment: full time: 688; part time: N/A
men: 54%; women: 46%; minorities: 28%
Acceptance rate (full time): 48%
Midrange LSAT (full time): 152-158
Midrange undergraduate GPA (full time): 3.24-3.68
Midrange of full-time private-sector salaries of 2011 grads: $48,000-$79,000
2011 grads employed in: law firms: 56%; business and industry: 16%; government: 15%; public interest: 7%; judicial clerk: 3%; academia: 2%; unknown: 0%
Employment location for 2011 class: Intl. 0%; N.E. 0%; M.A. 1%; E.N.C. 1%; W.N.C. 1%; S.A. 4%; E.S.C. 1%; W.S.C. 84%; Mt. 8%; Pac. 1%; unknown 0%

Texas Wesleyan University
1515 Commerce Street
Fort Worth, TX 76102
http://www.law.txwes.edu/
Private
Admissions: (817) 212-4040
E-mail: lawadmissions@law.txwes.edu
Financial aid: (817) 212-4090

Application deadline: 03/31
Tuition: full time: $30,580; part time: $21,800
Room/board/expenses: $15,450
Median grant: $8,750
Average student indebtedness at graduation: $107,571
Enrollment: full time: 471; part time: 268
men: 51%; women: 49%; minorities: 25%
Acceptance rate (full time): 55%
Midrange LSAT (full time): 150-155
Midrange undergraduate GPA (full time): 2.86-3.34
Midrange of full-time private-sector salaries of 2011 grads: $50,000-$75,000
2011 grads employed in: law firms: 60%; business and industry: 30%; government: 6%; public interest: 0%; judicial clerk: 1%; academia: 2%; unknown: 1%
Employment location for 2011 class: Intl. 0%; N.E. 1%; M.A. 1%; E.N.C. 1%; W.N.C. 0%; S.A. 2%; E.S.C. 0%; W.S.C. 94%; Mt. 1%; Pac. 0%; unknown 0%

University of Houston
100 Law Center
Houston, TX 77204-6060
http://www.law.uh.edu
Public
Admissions: (713) 743-2280
E-mail: lawadmissions@uh.edu
Financial aid: (713) 743-2269
Application deadline: 11/15
In-state tuition: full time: $29,748; part time: $20,448
Out-of-state tuition: full time: $39,699
Room/board/expenses: $18,600
Median grant: $2,000
Average student indebtedness at graduation: $81,721
Enrollment: full time: 632; part time: 143
men: 56%; women: 44%; minorities: 32%
Acceptance rate (full time): 33%
Midrange LSAT (full time): 159-163
Midrange undergraduate GPA (full time): 3.23-3.71
Midrange of full-time private-sector salaries of 2011 grads: $60,000-$120,000
2011 grads employed in: law firms: 56%; business and industry: 26%; government: 8%; public interest: 5%; judicial clerk: 3%; academia: 2%; unknown: 0%
Employment location for 2011 class: Intl. 1%; N.E. 0%; M.A. 1%; E.N.C. 1%; W.N.C. 0%; S.A. 2%; E.S.C. 0%; W.S.C. 91%; Mt. 2%; Pac. 2%; unknown 0%

University of Texas–Austin
727 E. Dean Keeton Street
Austin, TX 78705-3299
http://www.utexas.edu/law
Public
Admissions: (512) 232-1200
E-mail: admissions@law.utexas.edu
Financial aid: (512) 232-1130
Application deadline: 03/01
In-state tuition: full time: $32,376; part time: N/A
Out-of-state tuition: full time: $48,075
Room/board/expenses: $16,412
Median grant: $7,644
Average student indebtedness at graduation: $86,312

Enrollment: full time: 1,065; part time: N/A
men: 54%; women: 46%; minorities: 30%
Acceptance rate (full time): 27%
Midrange LSAT (full time): 163-169
Midrange undergraduate GPA (full time): 3.52-3.82
Midrange of full-time private-sector salaries of 2011 grads: $90,000-$160,000
2011 grads employed in: law firms: 55%; business and industry: 15%; government: 11%; public interest: 6%; judicial clerk: 13%; academia: 0%; unknown: 0%
Employment location for 2011 class: Intl. 1%; N.E. 0%; M.A. 5%; E.N.C. 1%; W.N.C. 0%; S.A. 9%; E.S.C. 2%; W.S.C. 72%; Mt. 4%; Pac. 6%; unknown 0%

UTAH

Brigham Young University (Clark)
340 JRCB
Provo, UT 84602-8000
http://www.law.byu.edu
Private
Admissions: (801) 422-4277
E-mail: kucharg@lawgate.byu.edu
Financial aid: (801) 422-6386
Application deadline: 03/01
Tuition: full time: $10,950; part time: N/A
Room/board/expenses: $19,876
Median grant: $5,300
Average student indebtedness at graduation: $56,112
Enrollment: full time: 420; part time: 6
men: 63%; women: 37%; minorities: 20%
Acceptance rate (full time): 29%
Midrange LSAT (full time): 158-165
Midrange undergraduate GPA (full time): 3.40-3.81
Midrange of full-time private-sector salaries of 2011 grads: $64,000-$107,500
2011 grads employed in: law firms: 47%; business and industry: 15%; government: 13%; public interest: 6%; judicial clerk: 14%; academia: 4%; unknown: 1%
Employment location for 2011 class: Intl. 1%; N.E. 0%; M.A. 3%; E.N.C. 1%; W.N.C. 1%; S.A. 6%; E.S.C. 1%; W.S.C. 1%; Mt. 71%; Pac. 15%; unknown 0%

University of Utah (Quinney)
332 S. 1400 E, Room 101
Salt Lake City, UT 84112
http://www.law.utah.edu
Public
Admissions: (801) 581-7479
E-mail: admissions@law.utah.edu
Financial aid: (801) 581-6211
Application deadline: 02/15
In-state tuition: full time: $21,113; part time: N/A
Out-of-state tuition: full time: $40,142
Room/board/expenses: $19,495
Median grant: $6,416
Average student indebtedness at graduation: $80,608
Enrollment: full time: 381; part time: N/A
men: 59%; women: 41%; minorities: 10%
Acceptance rate (full time): 35%
Midrange LSAT (full time): 156-162
Midrange undergraduate GPA (full time): 3.32-3.80

Midrange of full-time private-sector salaries of 2011 grads: $55,000–$100,000
2011 grads employed in: law firms: 56%; business and industry: 14%; government: 14%; public interest: 4%; judicial clerk: 9%; academia: 2%; unknown: 0%
Employment location for 2011 class: Intl. 0%; N.E. 0%; M.A. 1%; E.N.C. 0%; W.N.C. 1%; S.A. 1%; E.S.C. 1%; W.S.C. 0%; Mt. 90%; Pac. 7%; unknown 0%

VERMONT

Vermont Law School
Chelsea Street
South Royalton, VT 05068-0096
http://www.vermontlaw.edu
Private
Admissions: (888) 277-5985
E-mail: admiss@vermontlaw.edu
Financial aid: (888) 277-5985
Application deadline: 03/01
Tuition: full time: $45,207; part time: N/A
Room/board/expenses: $23,752
Median grant: $20,000
Average student indebtedness at graduation: $132,337
Enrollment: full time: 512; part time: N/A
men: 50%; women: 50%; minorities: 12%
Acceptance rate (full time): 83%
Midrange LSAT (full time): 149-158
Midrange undergraduate GPA (full time): 3.00-3.51
Midrange of full-time private-sector salaries of 2011 grads: $48,000–$62,000
2011 grads employed in: law firms: 35%; business and industry: 19%; government: 18%; public interest: 12%; judicial clerk: 16%; academia: 0%; unknown: 0%
Employment location for 2011 class: Intl. 1%; N.E. 37%; M.A. 9%; E.N.C. 4%; W.N.C. 1%; S.A. 17%; E.S.C. 1%; W.S.C. 4%; Mt. 16%; Pac. 11%; unknown 0%

VIRGINIA

Appalachian School of Law
1169 Edgewater Drive
Grundy, VA 24614-2825
http://www.asl.edu
Private
Admissions: (800) 895-7411
E-mail: aslinfo@asl.edu
Financial aid: (800) 895-7411
Application deadline: rolling
Tuition: full time: $31,525; part time: N/A
Room/board/expenses: N/A
Median grant: $14,906
Average student indebtedness at graduation: $114,740
Enrollment: full time: 860; part time: N/A
men: 57%; women: 43%; minorities: 33%
Acceptance rate (full time): 71%
Midrange LSAT (full time): 143-149
Midrange undergraduate GPA (full time): 2.73-3.51
Midrange of full-time private-sector salaries of 2011 grads: $29,900–$48,380
2011 grads employed in: law firms: 62%; business and industry: 23%; government: 8%; public interest: 4%; judicial clerk: 2%; academia: 2%; unknown: 0%

Employment location for 2011 class: Intl. 0%; N.E. 4%; M.A. 2%; E.N.C. 6%; W.N.C. 0%; S.A. 44%; E.S.C. 35%; W.S.C. 0%; Mt. 8%; Pac. 0%; unknown 2%

College of William and Mary (Marshall-Wythe)
PO Box 8795
Williamsburg, VA 23187-8795
http://law.wm.edu/
Public
Admissions: (757) 221-3785
E-mail: lawadm@wm.edu
Financial aid: (757) 221-2420
Application deadline: 03/01
In-state tuition: full time: $27,800; part time: N/A
Out-of-state tuition: full time: $37,800
Room/board/expenses: $16,300
Median grant: $8,000
Average student indebtedness at graduation: $94,852
Enrollment: full time: 618; part time: 1
men: 51%; women: 49%; minorities: 20%
Acceptance rate (full time): 32%
Midrange LSAT (full time): 161-166
Midrange undergraduate GPA (full time): 3.45-3.84
Midrange of full-time private-sector salaries of 2011 grads: $60,000–$95,000
2011 grads employed in: law firms: 31%; business and industry: 16%; government: 23%; public interest: 5%; judicial clerk: 20%; academia: 4%; unknown: 0%
Employment location for 2011 class: Intl. 2%; N.E. 2%; M.A. 10%; E.N.C. 3%; W.N.C. 1%; S.A. 72%; E.S.C. 1%; W.S.C. 3%; Mt. 4%; Pac. 3%; unknown 1%

George Mason University
3301 Fairfax Drive
Arlington, VA 22201-4426
http://www.law.gmu.edu
Public
Admissions: (703) 993-8010
E-mail: lawadmit@gmu.edu
Financial aid: (703) 993-2353
Application deadline: 04/01
In-state tuition: full time: $24,623; part time: $879/credit hour
Out-of-state tuition: full time: $39,561
Room/board/expenses: $23,344
Median grant: $8,000
Average student indebtedness at graduation: $115,381
Enrollment: full time: 442; part time: 194
men: 58%; women: 42%; minorities: 14%
Acceptance rate (full time): 29%
Midrange LSAT (full time): 156-164
Midrange undergraduate GPA (full time): 3.31-3.79
Midrange of full-time private-sector salaries of 2011 grads: $60,000–$140,000
2011 grads employed in: law firms: 41%; business and industry: 15%; government: 25%; public interest: 7%; judicial clerk: 9%; academia: 3%; unknown: 0%
Employment location for 2011 class: Intl. 0%; N.E. 1%; M.A. 3%; E.N.C. 1%; W.N.C. 0%; S.A. 90%; E.S.C. 1%; W.S.C. 1%; Mt. 1%; Pac. 3%; unknown 0%

Liberty University
1971 University Boulevard
Lynchburg, VA 24502
http://law.liberty.edu
Private
Admissions: (434) 592-5300
E-mail: lawadmissions@liberty.edu
Financial aid: (434) 592-5300
Application deadline: 06/01
Tuition: full time: $32,002; part time: N/A
Room/board/expenses: $16,800
Median grant: $14,544
Average student indebtedness at graduation: $76,730
Enrollment: full time: 258; part time: N/A
men: 63%; women: 37%; minorities: 17%
Acceptance rate (full time): 48%
Midrange LSAT (full time): 148-155
Midrange undergraduate GPA (full time): 2.78-3.63
Midrange of full-time private-sector salaries of 2011 grads: $35,700–$53,250
2011 grads employed in: law firms: 46%; business and industry: 21%; government: 20%; public interest: 5%; judicial clerk: 3%; academia: 2%; unknown: 3%
Employment location for 2011 class: Intl. 2%; N.E. 0%; M.A. 2%; E.N.C. 8%; W.N.C. 3%; S.A. 48%; E.S.C. 2%; W.S.C. 7%; Mt. 0%; Pac. 8%; unknown 21%

Regent University
1000 Regent University Drive
Virginia Beach, VA 23464-9880
http://www.regent.edu/law/admissions
Private
Admissions: (757) 226-4584
E-mail: lawschool@regent.edu
Financial aid: (757) 352-4559
Application deadline: 06/01
Tuition: full time: $1,095/credit hour; part time: $1,095/credit hour
Room/board/expenses: $20,490
Median grant: $7,000
Average student indebtedness at graduation: $116,061
Enrollment: full time: 395; part time: 22
men: 51%; women: 49%; minorities: 15%
Acceptance rate (full time): 49%
Midrange LSAT (full time): 151-159
Midrange undergraduate GPA (full time): 2.97-3.61
Midrange of full-time private-sector salaries of 2011 grads: $40,000–$51,500
2011 grads employed in: law firms: 45%; business and industry: 24%; government: 11%; public interest: 7%; judicial clerk: 4%; academia: 4%; unknown: 4%
Employment location for 2011 class: Intl. 0%; N.E. 0%; M.A. 2%; E.N.C. 3%; W.N.C. 0%; S.A. 58%; E.S.C. 4%; W.S.C. 10%; Mt. 4%; Pac. 6%; unknown 12%

University of Richmond (Williams)
28 Westhampton Way
Richmond, VA 23173
http://law.richmond.edu
Private
Admissions: (804) 289-8189
E-mail: mrahman@richmond.edu
Financial aid: (804) 289-8438
Application deadline: 03/15
Tuition: full time: $36,850; part time: $1,843/credit hour

Room/board/expenses: $15,950
Median grant: $15,000
Average student indebtedness at graduation: $110,830
Enrollment: full time: 460; part time: N/A
men: 55%; women: 45%; minorities: 24%
Acceptance rate (full time): 21%
Midrange LSAT (full time): 158-163
Midrange undergraduate GPA (full time): 3.21-3.60
Midrange of full-time private-sector salaries of 2011 grads: $53,000–$85,000
2011 grads employed in: law firms: 38%; business and industry: 32%; government: 9%; public interest: 4%; judicial clerk: 16%; academia: 1%; unknown: 1%
Employment location for 2011 class: Intl. 0%; N.E. 1%; M.A. 5%; E.N.C. 1%; W.N.C. 1%; S.A. 87%; E.S.C. 1%; W.S.C. 3%; Mt. 3%; Pac. 0%; unknown 0%

University of Virginia
580 Massie Road
Charlottesville, VA 22903-1738
http://www.law.virginia.edu
Public
Admissions: (434) 924-7351
E-mail: lawadmit@virginia.edu
Financial aid: (434) 924-7805
Application deadline: 03/01
In-state tuition: full time: $46,400; part time: N/A
Out-of-state tuition: full time: $51,400
Room/board/expenses: $20,400
Median grant: $25,000
Average student indebtedness at graduation: $122,721
Enrollment: full time: 1,078; part time: N/A
men: 55%; women: 45%; minorities: 24%
Acceptance rate (full time): 15%
Midrange LSAT (full time): 164-171
Midrange undergraduate GPA (full time): 3.53-3.93
Midrange of full-time private-sector salaries of 2011 grads: $125,000–$160,000
2011 grads employed in: law firms: 53%; business and industry: 4%; government: 14%; public interest: 11%; judicial clerk: 17%; academia: 1%; unknown: 0%
Employment location for 2011 class: Intl. 1%; N.E. 3%; M.A. 17%; E.N.C. 4%; W.N.C. 2%; S.A. 55%; E.S.C. 4%; W.S.C. 5%; Mt. 2%; Pac. 7%; unknown 0%

Washington and Lee University
Sydney Lewis Hall
Lexington, VA 24450-0303
http://law.wlu.edu
Private
Admissions: (540) 458-8504
E-mail: lawadm@wlu.edu
Financial aid: (540) 458-8729
Application deadline: 03/01
Tuition: full time: $43,462; part time: N/A
Room/board/expenses: $18,623
Median grant: $20,000
Average student indebtedness at graduation: $111,825
Enrollment: full time: 457; part time: N/A
men: 55%; women: 45%; minorities: 15%
Acceptance rate (full time): 30%
Midrange LSAT (full time): 159-165

Midrange undergraduate GPA (full time): 3.40-3.73
Midrange of full-time private-sector salaries of 2011 grads: $59,000–$110,000
2011 grads employed in: law firms: 46%; business and industry: 17%; government: 10%; public interest: 5%; judicial clerk: 20%; academia: 2%; unknown: 0%
Employment location for 2011 class: Intl. 0%; N.E. 2%; M.A. 13%; E.N.C. 5%; W.N.C. 1%; S.A. 62%; E.S.C. 2%; W.S.C. 5%; Mt. 2%; Pac. 8%; unknown 0%

WASHINGTON

Gonzaga University
PO Box 3528
Spokane, WA 99220-3528
http://www.law.gonzaga.edu
Private
Admissions: (800) 793-1710
E-mail: admissions@lawschool.gonzaga.edu
Financial aid: (800) 448-2138
Application deadline: 04/15
Tuition: full time: $35,460; part time: N/A
Room/board/expenses: $16,609
Median grant: $13,500
Average student indebtedness at graduation: $102,316
Enrollment: full time: 460; part time: N/A
men: 54%; women: 46%; minorities: 11%
Acceptance rate (full time): 63%
Midrange LSAT (full time): 152-157
Midrange undergraduate GPA (full time): 3.00-3.58
Midrange of full-time private-sector salaries of 2011 grads: $47,500–$64,500
2011 grads employed in: law firms: 50%; business and industry: 18%; government: 15%; public interest: 6%; judicial clerk: 11%; academia: 1%; unknown: 0%
Employment location for 2011 class: Intl. 0%; N.E. 1%; M.A. 1%; E.N.C. 3%; W.N.C. 0%; S.A. 3%; E.S.C. 1%; W.S.C. 1%; Mt. 30%; Pac. 62%; unknown 0%

Seattle University
901 12th Avenue
Seattle, WA 98122-1090
http://www.law.seattleu.edu
Private
Admissions: (206) 398-4200
E-mail: lawadmis@seattleu.edu
Financial aid: (206) 398-4250
Application deadline: rolling
Tuition: full time: $39,884; part time: $33,225
Room/board/expenses: $20,958
Median grant: $10,000
Average student indebtedness at graduation: $119,918
Enrollment: full time: 762; part time: 199
men: 49%; women: 51%; minorities: 28%
Acceptance rate (full time): 50%
Midrange LSAT (full time): 154-159
Midrange undergraduate GPA (full time): 3.07-3.54
Midrange of full-time private-sector salaries of 2011 grads: $60,000–$102,500
2011 grads employed in: law firms: 38%; business and industry: 26%; government: 15%; public interest: 11%; judicial clerk: 9%; academia: 2%; unknown: 0%

Employment location for 2011 class: Intl. 2%; N.E. 1%; M.A. 1%; E.N.C. 0%; W.N.C. 1%; S.A. 3%; E.S.C. 0%; W.S.C. 2%; Mt. 4%; Pac. 86%; unknown 0%

University of Washington

Campus Box 353020
Seattle, WA 98195-3020
http://www.law.washington.edu
Public
Admissions: (206) 543-4078
E-mail: lawadm@u.washington.edu
Financial aid: (206) 543-4078
Application deadline: 02/15
In-state tuition: full time: $29,948; part time: N/A
Out-of-state tuition: full time: $42,918
Room/board/expenses: $18,807
Median grant: $8,000
Average student indebtedness at graduation: $90,348
Enrollment: full time: 557; part time: N/A
men: 54%; women: 46%; minorities: 25%
Acceptance rate (full time): 22%
Midrange LSAT (full time): 162-166
Midrange undergraduate GPA (full time): 3.50-3.82
Midrange of full-time private-sector salaries of 2011 grads: $68,875-$120,000
2011 grads employed in: law firms: 44%; business and industry: 14%; government: 17%; public interest: 11%; judicial clerk: 12%; academia: 3%; unknown: 0%
Employment location for 2011 class: Intl. 5%; N.E. 0%; M.A. 3%; E.N.C. 0%; W.N.C. 2%; S.A. 3%; E.S.C. 1%; W.S.C. 1%; Mt. 3%; Pac. 85%; unknown 0%

WEST VIRGINIA

West Virginia University

PO Box 6130
Morgantown, WV 26506-6130
http://law.wvu.edu/
Public
Admissions: (304) 293-5304
E-mail: wvulaw.admissions@mail.wvu.edu
Financial aid: (304) 293-5302
Application deadline: 03/01
In-state tuition: full time: $17,240; part time: $957/credit hour
Out-of-state tuition: full time: $32,924
Room/board/expenses: $14,616
Median grant: $3,738
Average student indebtedness at graduation: $72,068
Enrollment: full time: 394; part time: 8
men: 64%; women: 36%; minorities: 12%
Acceptance rate (full time): 54%
Midrange LSAT (full time): 152-158
Midrange undergraduate GPA (full time): 3.14-3.66
Midrange of full-time private-sector salaries of 2011 grads: $60,000-$75,000
2011 grads employed in: law firms: 61%; business and industry: 20%; government: 0%; public interest: 3%; judicial clerk: 13%; academia: 3%; unknown: 0%
Employment location for 2011 class: Intl. 1%; N.E. 1%; M.A. 6%; E.N.C. 1%; W.N.C. 1%; S.A. 89%; E.S.C. 1%; W.S.C. 0%; Mt. 0%; Pac. 0%; unknown 0%

WISCONSIN

Marquette University

Eckstein Hall, PO Box 1881
Milwaukee, WI 53201-1881
http://law.marquette.edu
Private
Admissions: (414) 288-6767
E-mail: law.admission@marquette.edu
Financial aid: (414) 288-7390
Application deadline: 04/01
Tuition: full time: $38,690; part time: $23,175
Room/board/expenses: $19,490
Median grant: $9,300
Average student indebtedness at graduation: $118,782
Enrollment: full time: 599; part time: 131
men: 57%; women: 43%; minorities: 19%
Acceptance rate (full time): 66%
Midrange LSAT (full time): 153-158
Midrange undergraduate GPA (full time): 3.15-3.57
Midrange of full-time private-sector salaries of 2011 grads: $50,000-$87,125
2011 grads employed in: law firms: 52%; business and industry: 28%; government: 7%; public interest: 5%; judicial clerk: 3%; academia: 3%; unknown: 0%
Employment location for 2011 class: Intl. 0%; N.E. 1%; M.A. 1%; E.N.C. 88%; W.N.C. 3%; S.A. 3%; E.S.C. 0%; W.S.C. 2%; Mt. 1%; Pac. 2%; unknown 0%

University of Wisconsin–Madison

975 Bascom Mall
Madison, WI 53706-1399
http://www.law.wisc.edu
Public
Admissions: (608) 262-5914
E-mail: admissions@law.wisc.edu
Financial aid: (608) 262-5914
Application deadline: 04/01
In-state tuition: full time: $21,347; part time: $1,784/credit hour
Out-of-state tuition: full time: $40,043
Room/board/expenses: $18,810
Median grant: $9,000
Average student indebtedness at graduation: $77,077
Enrollment: full time: 690; part time: 42
men: 59%; women: 41%; minorities: 21%
Acceptance rate (full time): 37%
Midrange LSAT (full time): 157-164
Midrange undergraduate GPA (full time): 3.33-3.72
Midrange of full-time private-sector salaries of 2011 grads: $52,500-$110,000
2011 grads employed in: law firms: 46%; business and industry: 19%; government: 17%; public interest: 14%; judicial clerk: 3%; academia: 2%; unknown: 0%
Employment location for 2011 class: Intl. 0%; N.E. 0%; M.A. 2%; E.N.C. 78%; W.N.C. 7%; S.A. 9%; E.S.C. 0%; W.S.C. 0%; Mt. 2%; Pac. 2%; unknown 0%

WYOMING

University of Wyoming

Department 3035
1000 E. University Avenue
Laramie, WY 82071
http://www.uwyo.edu/law
Public
Admissions: (307) 766-6416
E-mail: lawadmis@uwyo.edu
Financial aid: (307) 766-2116
Application deadline: 03/01
In-state tuition: full time: $13,428; part time: N/A
Out-of-state tuition: full time: $26,628
Room/board/expenses: $15,548
Median grant: $4,500
Average student indebtedness at graduation: $61,837
Enrollment: full time: 229; part time: N/A
men: 57%; women: 43%; minorities: 15%
Acceptance rate (full time): 46%
Midrange LSAT (full time): 149-156
Midrange undergraduate GPA (full time): 3.15-3.58
Midrange of full-time private-sector salaries of 2011 grads: $45,840-$77,500
2011 grads employed in: law firms: 50%; business and industry: 7%; government: 15%; public interest: 7%; judicial clerk: 20%; academia: 0%; unknown: 0%
Employment location for 2011 class: Intl. 0%; N.E. 0%; M.A. 2%; E.N.C. 0%; W.N.C. 2%; S.A. 4%; E.S.C. 0%; W.S.C. 11%; Mt. 80%; Pac. 2%; unknown 0%

MEDICINE

This directory lists the 126 schools offering M.D. degrees that were accredited by the Liaison Committee on Medical Education in 2012, plus the 23 schools that offer D.O. degrees and were accredited by the American Osteopathic Association in 2012. Of those, 99 M.D.-granting schools and 15 D.O.-granting schools responded to the *U.S. News* survey, conducted in the fall of 2012 and early 2013. Their data are reported below. Schools that did not respond have abbreviated entries.

KEY TO THE TERMINOLOGY

1. A school whose name is footnoted with the numeral 1 did not return the *U.S. News* statistical survey; limited data appear in its entry.
N/A. Not available from the school or not applicable.
Admissions. The admissions office phone number.
E-mail. The address of the admissions office. If instead of an E-mail address a website is listed, the website will automatically present an E-mail screen programmed to reach the admissions office.
Financial aid. The financial aid office phone number.
Application deadline. For fall 2014 enrollment.
Tuition. For the 2012-13 academic year. Includes fees.
Room/board/expenses. For the 2012-13 academic year.
Students receiving grants. The percentage of the entire student body during the 2012-13 academic year that received grants or scholarships.
Average indebtedness. For 2011 graduates who incurred medical school-related debt.
Enrollment. Total doctor of medicine (M.D.) or doctor of osteopathy (D.O.) degree program enrollment for fall 2012.
Minorities. For fall 2012, percentage of U.S. students who fall in one of these groups: black or African-American, Asian, American Indian or Alaskan Native, Native Hawaiian or other Pacific Islander, Hispanic/Latino, or two or more races. The minority percentage was reported by the school.

Underrepresented minorities. For fall 2012, percentage of U.S. students who are black or African-American, American Indian or Alaskan Native, Native Hawaiian or other Pacific Islander, Hispanic/Latino, or two or more races. (This category is used only for medical schools. The underrepresented minority percentage was reported by the school.)
Acceptance rate. Percentage of applicants who were accepted for fall 2012 to an M.D. or D.O. degree program.
Average Medical College Admission Test (MCAT) score. For M.D. or D.O. students who entered the medical or osteopathic program in the fall of 2012. The average of verbal and physical and biological sciences MCAT scores. (These MCAT scores are reported to test-takers on a scale of 1 to 15.)
Average undergraduate grade point average (GPA). For M.D. or D.O. students who entered in the fall of 2012.
Most popular undergraduate majors. For students who entered in the fall of 2012. The main areas are biological sciences, including microbiology; physical sciences, including chemistry; nonsciences, including the humanities; and other, including double majors, mixed disciplines, and other health professions like nursing and pharmacy.
Graduates entering primary care specialties. This is the three-year average percentage of all medical or osteopathic school graduates entering primary care residencies in the fields of family practice, general pediatrics, or general internal medicine during 2010, 2011, and 2012.

ALABAMA

University of Alabama–Birmingham
Medical Student Services
VH Suite 100
Birmingham, AL 35294-0019
http://www.uab.edu/medicine/admissions
Public
Admissions: (205) 934-2433
E-mail: medschool@uab.edu
Financial aid: (205) 934-8223
Application deadline: 11/01
In-state tuition: $26,618
Out-of-state tuition: $62,194
Room/board/expenses: $18,981
Percent receiving grants: 31%
Average student indebtedness at graduation: $124,970
Enrollment: 747
men: 56%; women: 44%; minorities: 26%; underrepresented minorities: 7%; in state: 92%
Acceptance rate: 9%
Average MCAT: 10.0
Average GPA: 3.76
Most popular undergraduate majors: biological sciences: 61%; physical sciences: 18%; nonsciences: 7%; other: 14%
Percent of graduates entering primary-care specialties: 47.0%

University of South Alabama[1]
307 University Boulevard
170 CSAB
Mobile, AL 36688
http://southmed.usouthal.edu/
Public
Admissions: (251) 460-7176
E-mail: mscott@usouthal.edu
Financial aid: (251) 460-7918
Tuition: N/A
Room/board/expenses: N/A
Enrollment: N/A

ARIZONA

University of Arizona
1501 N. Campbell Avenue
Tucson, AZ 85724
http://www.medicine.arizona.edu/
Public
Admissions: (520) 626-6214
E-mail: admissions@medicine.arizona.edu
Financial aid: (520) 626-7145
Application deadline: 11/01
In-state tuition: $28,771
Out-of-state tuition: $47,388
Room/board/expenses: $12,760
Percent receiving grants: 79%
Average student indebtedness at graduation: $144,709
Enrollment: 475
men: 48%; women: 52%; minorities: 31%; underrepresented minorities: 14%; in state: 91%
Acceptance rate: 6%
Average GPA: 3.70
Most popular undergraduate majors: biological sciences: 49%; physical sciences: 30%; nonsciences: 11%; other: 10%
Percent of graduates entering primary-care specialties: 43.7%

ARKANSAS

University of Arkansas for Medical Sciences[1]
4301 W. Markham Street, Slot 551
Little Rock, AR 72205
http://www.uams.edu
Public
Admissions: (501) 686-5354
E-mail: southtomg@uams.edu
Financial aid: (501) 686-5451
Tuition: N/A
Room/board/expenses: N/A
Enrollment: N/A

CALIFORNIA

Loma Linda University[1]
Loma Linda, CA 92350
http://www.llu.edu/
Private
Admissions: (909) 558-4467
E-mail: ledwards@som.llu.edu
Financial aid: (909) 558-4509
Tuition: N/A
Room/board/expenses: N/A
Enrollment: N/A

Stanford University
300 Pasteur Drive, Suite M121
Stanford, CA 94305
http://med.stanford.edu
Private
Admissions: (650) 723-6861
E-mail: mdadmissions@stanford.edu
Financial aid: (650) 723-6958
Application deadline: 10/15
Tuition: $48,030
Room/board/expenses: $25,005
Percent receiving grants: 82%
Average student indebtedness at graduation: $101,462
Enrollment: 461
men: 51%; women: 49%; minorities: 58%; underrepresented minorities: 16%; in state: 43%
Acceptance rate: 3%
Average MCAT: 11.8
Average GPA: 3.79
Most popular undergraduate majors: biological sciences: 35%; physical sciences: 27%; nonsciences: 14%; other: 24%
Percent of graduates entering primary-care specialties: 30.0%

University of California–Davis
4610 X Street
Sacramento, CA 95817
http://www.ucdmc.ucdavis.edu
Public
Admissions: (916) 734-4800
E-mail: medadmsinfo@ucdavis.edu
Financial aid: (916) 734-4120
Application deadline: 10/01
In-state tuition: $39,651
Out-of-state tuition: $51,896
Room/board/expenses: $15,011
Percent receiving grants: 93%
Average student indebtedness at graduation: $131,314
Enrollment: 413
men: 46%; women: 54%; minorities: 55%; underrepresented minorities: 22%; in state: 100%
Acceptance rate: 5%

Average MCAT: 10.3
Average GPA: 3.60
Most popular undergraduate majors: biological sciences: 49%; physical sciences: 17%; nonsciences: 15%; other: 19%
Percent of graduates entering primary-care specialties: 44.8%

University of California–Irvine

252 Irvine Hall
Irvine, CA 92697-3950
http://www.som.uci.edu
Public
Admissions: (949) 824-5388
E-mail: medadmit@uci.edu
Financial aid: (949) 824-6476
Application deadline: 01/11
In-state tuition: $35,334
Out-of-state tuition: $47,579
Room/board/expenses: $15,245
Percent receiving grants: 55%
Average student indebtedness at graduation: $141,174
Enrollment: 423
men: 49%; women: 51%; minorities: 53%; underrepresented minorities: 20%; in state: 96%
Acceptance rate: 5%
Average MCAT: 10.7
Average GPA: 3.68
Most popular undergraduate majors: biological sciences: 53%; physical sciences: 20%; nonsciences: 16%; other: 11%
Percent of graduates entering primary-care specialties: 38.0%

University of California– Los Angeles (Geffen)

12-138 CHS
10833 Le Conte Avenue
Los Angeles, CA 90095-1720
http://www.medsch.ucla.edu
Public
Admissions: (310) 825-6081
E-mail: somadmiss@mednet.ucla.edu
Financial aid: (310) 825-4181
Application deadline: 11/01
In-state tuition: $34,784
Out-of-state tuition: $47,029
Room/board/expenses: $16,010
Percent receiving grants: 94%
Average student indebtedness at graduation: $114,955
Enrollment: 767
men: 53%; women: 47%; minorities: 61%; underrepresented minorities: 24%; in state: 96%
Acceptance rate: 4%
Average MCAT: 11.3
Average GPA: 3.73
Most popular undergraduate majors: biological sciences: 45%; physical sciences: 26%; nonsciences: 13%; other: 16%
Percent of graduates entering primary-care specialties: 45.0%

University of California–San Diego

9500 Gilman Drive
La Jolla, CA 92093-0602
http://meded.ucsd.edu/
Public
Admissions: (858) 534-3880
E-mail: somadmissions@ucsd.edu
Financial aid: (858) 534-4664
Application deadline: 11/01
In-state tuition: $34,491
Out-of-state tuition: $46,736
Room/board/expenses: $10,980
Percent receiving grants: 50%
Average student indebtedness at graduation: $93,862

Enrollment: 520
men: 51%; women: 49%; minorities: 46%; underrepresented minorities: 13%; in state: 89%
Acceptance rate: 5%
Average MCAT: 11.0
Average GPA: 3.73
Most popular undergraduate majors: biological sciences: 66%; physical sciences: 14%; nonsciences: 10%; other: 10%
Percent of graduates entering primary-care specialties: 36.1%

University of California– San Francisco

513 Parnassus Avenue
Room S224
San Francisco, CA 94143-0410
http://medschool.ucsf.edu/
Public
Admissions: (415) 476-4044
E-mail: admissions@medsch.ucsf.edu
Financial aid: (415) 476-4181
Application deadline: 10/15
In-state tuition: $35,134
Out-of-state tuition: $47,379
Room/board/expenses: $20,280
Percent receiving grants: 82%
Average student indebtedness at graduation: $111,664
Enrollment: 648
men: 46%; women: 54%; minorities: 52%; underrepresented minorities: 27%; in state: 95%
Acceptance rate: 4%
Average MCAT: 11.5
Average GPA: 3.77
Most popular undergraduate majors: biological sciences: 52%; physical sciences: 20%; nonsciences: 13%; other: 15%
Percent of graduates entering primary-care specialties: 44.7%

University of Southern California (Keck)

1975 Zonal Avenue
KAM 500
Los Angeles, CA 90033
http://www.usc.edu/keck
Private
Admissions: (323) 442-2552
E-mail: medadmit@usc.edu
Financial aid: (213) 740-5462
Application deadline: 11/01
Tuition: $52,242
Room/board/expenses: $17,667
Percent receiving grants: 38%
Average student indebtedness at graduation: $204,996
Enrollment: 700
men: 52%; women: 48%; minorities: 46%; underrepresented minorities: 17%; in state: 73%
Acceptance rate: 5%
Average MCAT: 11.4
Average GPA: 3.64
Most popular undergraduate majors: biological sciences: 49%; physical sciences: 14%; nonsciences: 17%; other: 20%
Percent of graduates entering primary-care specialties: 31.0%

University of Colorado–Denver

13001 E. 17th Place, MS C290
Aurora, CO 80045
http://www.ucdenver.edu/academics/colleges/medicalschool/education/Admissions/Pages/Admissions.aspx
Public
Admissions: (303) 724-8025
E-mail: somadmin@ucdenver.edu
Financial aid: (303) 556-2886
Application deadline: 11/01
In-state tuition: $34,728
Out-of-state tuition: $60,682
Room/board/expenses: $16,810
Percent receiving grants: 58%
Average student indebtedness at graduation: $154,570
Enrollment: 644
men: 52%; women: 48%; minorities: 21%; underrepresented minorities: 11%; in state: 76%
Acceptance rate: 5%
Average MCAT: 10.7
Average GPA: 3.74
Most popular undergraduate majors: biological sciences: 37%; physical sciences: 27%; nonsciences: 20%; other: 17%
Percent of graduates entering primary-care specialties: 46.6%

University of Connecticut

263 Farmington Avenue
Farmington, CT 06030-1905
http://medicine.uchc.edu
Public
Admissions: (860) 679-4713
E-mail: admissions@uchc.edu
Financial aid: (860) 679-3574
Application deadline: 11/15
In-state tuition: $30,879
Out-of-state tuition: $57,051
Room/board/expenses: $20,950
Percent receiving grants: 55%
Average student indebtedness at graduation: $140,249
Enrollment: 359
men: 48%; women: 52%; minorities: 36%; underrepresented minorities: 18%; in state: 93%
Acceptance rate: 7%
Average MCAT: 10.6
Average GPA: 3.70
Most popular undergraduate majors: biological sciences: 27%; physical sciences: 13%; nonsciences: 19%; other: 41%
Percent of graduates entering primary-care specialties: 40.0%

Yale University

333 Cedar Street, PO Box 208055
New Haven, CT 06520-8055
http://medicine.yale.edu
Private
Admissions: (203) 785-2643
E-mail: medical.admissions@yale.edu
Financial aid: (203) 785-2645
Application deadline: 10/15
Tuition: $50,080
Room/board/expenses: $12,240
Percent receiving grants: 56%
Average student indebtedness at graduation: $110,060
Enrollment: 397
men: 53%; women: 47%; minorities: 42%; underrepresented minorities: 15%; in state: 10%
Acceptance rate: 6%

Average MCAT: 12.1
Average GPA: 3.79
Most popular undergraduate majors: biological sciences: 51%; physical sciences: 33%; nonsciences: 14%; other: 2%
Percent of graduates entering primary-care specialties: 29.9%

Georgetown University

3900 Reservoir Road NW
Med-Dent Building
Washington, DC 20007
http://som.georgetown.edu/
Private
Admissions: (202) 687-1154
E-mail: medicaladmissions@georgetown.edu
Financial aid: (202) 687-1693
Application deadline: 10/31
Tuition: $50,901
Room/board/expenses: $19,250
Percent receiving grants: 45%
Average student indebtedness at graduation: $205,322
Enrollment: 805
men: 51%; women: 49%; minorities: 31%; underrepresented minorities: 11%; in state: 0%
Acceptance rate: 3%
Average MCAT: 10.3
Average GPA: 3.60
Most popular undergraduate majors: biological sciences: 47%; physical sciences: 19%; nonsciences: 15%; other: 19%
Percent of graduates entering primary-care specialties: 42.6%

George Washington University

2300 Eye Street NW, Room 713W
Washington, DC 20037
http://www.gwumc.edu/
Private
Admissions: (202) 994-3506
E-mail: medadmit@gwu.edu
Financial aid: (202) 994-2960
Application deadline: N/A
Tuition: $51,278
Room/board/expenses: $17,937
Average student indebtedness at graduation: $197,208
Enrollment: 716
men: 47%; women: 53%; minorities: 40%; underrepresented minorities: 15%; in state: 0%
Acceptance rate: 2%
Average MCAT: 10.2
Average GPA: 3.70
Most popular undergraduate majors: biological sciences: 49%; physical sciences: 9%; nonsciences: 24%; other: 19%
Percent of graduates entering primary-care specialties: 40.0%

Howard University[1]

520 W. Street NW
Washington, DC 20059
http://medicine.howard.edu
Private
Admissions: (202) 806-6279
E-mail: jwalk@howard.edu
Financial aid: (202) 806-6388
Tuition: N/A
Room/board/expenses: N/A
Enrollment: N/A

Florida State University

1115 W. Call Street
Tallahassee, FL 32306-4300
http://www.med.fsu.edu/
Public
Admissions: (850) 644-7904
E-mail: medadmissions@med.fsu.edu
Financial aid: (850) 645-7270
Application deadline: 12/01
In-state tuition: $23,464
Out-of-state tuition: $58,015
Room/board/expenses: $15,104
Percent receiving grants: 69%
Average student indebtedness at graduation: $143,687
Enrollment: 478
men: 53%; women: 47%; minorities: 37%; underrepresented minorities: 23%; in state: 100%
Acceptance rate: 5%
Average MCAT: 9.1
Average GPA: 3.64
Most popular undergraduate majors: biological sciences: 47%; physical sciences: 18%; nonsciences: 8%; other: 27%
Percent of graduates entering primary-care specialties: 42.7%

University of Florida

Box 100216 UFHSC
Gainesville, FL 32610-0216
http://www.med.ufl.edu
Public
Admissions: (352) 273-7990
E-mail: med-admissions@ufl.edu
Financial aid: (352) 273-7939
Application deadline: 12/02
In-state tuition: $35,487
Out-of-state tuition: $48,697
Room/board/expenses: $12,240
Percent receiving grants: 72%
Average student indebtedness at graduation: $135,000
Enrollment: 534
men: 55%; women: 45%; minorities: 31%; underrepresented minorities: 19%; in state: 99%
Acceptance rate: 7%
Average MCAT: 10.7
Average GPA: 3.78
Most popular undergraduate majors: biological sciences: 50%; physical sciences: 19%; nonsciences: 9%; other: 22%
Percent of graduates entering primary-care specialties: 32.0%

University of Miami (Miller)

1600 N.W. 10th Avenue
Miami, FL 33136
http://www.med.miami.edu
Private
Admissions: (305) 243-3234
E-mail: med.admissions@miami.edu
Financial aid: (305) 243-6211
Application deadline: 12/01
Tuition: $32,672
Room/board/expenses: $26,315
Percent receiving grants: 34%
Average student indebtedness at graduation: $165,250
Enrollment: 753
men: 52%; women: 48%; minorities: 42%; underrepresented minorities: 19%; in state: 67%
Acceptance rate: 5%
Average MCAT: 10.7
Average GPA: 3.72

Most popular undergraduate majors: biological sciences: 41%; physical sciences: 12%; nonsciences: 2%; other: 45%
Percent of graduates entering primary-care specialties: 35.0%

University of South Florida
12901 Bruce B. Downs Boulevard
MDC 2
Tampa, FL 33612
http://www.health.usf.edu/medicine/home.html
Public
Admissions: (813) 974-2229
E-mail: md-admissions@health.usf.edu
Financial aid: (813) 974-2068
Application deadline: 11/15
In-state tuition: $33,708
Out-of-state tuition: $54,897
Room/board/expenses: $12,250
Percent receiving grants: 45%
Average student indebtedness at graduation: $138,360
Enrollment: 554
men: 55%; women: 45%; minorities: 43%; underrepresented minorities: 19%; in state: 86%
Acceptance rate: 10%
Average MCAT: 10.1
Average GPA: 3.70
Most popular undergraduate majors: biological sciences: 46%; physical sciences: 33%; nonsciences: 8%; other: 13%
Percent of graduates entering primary-care specialties: 43.1%

GEORGIA

Emory University
1648 Pierce Drive
Atlanta, GA 30322-1053
http://www.med.emory.edu
Private
Admissions: (404) 727-5660
E-mail: medadmiss@emory.edu
Financial aid: (404) 727-6039
Application deadline: 10/15
Tuition: $47,764
Room/board/expenses: $24,172
Percent receiving grants: 61%
Average student indebtedness at graduation: $138,088
Enrollment: 564
men: 48%; women: 52%; minorities: 31%; underrepresented minorities: 13%; in state: 31%
Acceptance rate: 6%
Average MCAT: 11.5
Average GPA: 3.69
Most popular undergraduate majors: biological sciences: 44%; physical sciences: 19%; nonsciences: 16%; other: 22%
Percent of graduates entering primary-care specialties: 36.6%

Georgia Regents University
1120 15th Street
Augusta, GA 30912-4750
http://www.georgiahealth.edu/medicine/admit/
Public
Admissions: (706) 721-3186
E-mail: stdadmin@georgiahealth.edu
Financial aid: (706) 721-4901
Application deadline: 11/01
In-state tuition: $28,239
Out-of-state tuition: $49,469
Room/board/expenses: $20,515
Percent receiving grants: 24%
Average student indebtedness at graduation: $104,867

Enrollment: 884
men: 58%; women: 42%; minorities: 37%; underrepresented minorities: 13%; in state: 99%
Acceptance rate: 15%
Average MCAT: 10.2
Average GPA: 3.70
Most popular undergraduate majors: biological sciences: 54%; physical sciences: 17%; nonsciences: 11%; other: 18%
Percent of graduates entering primary-care specialties: 37.0%

Mercer University
1550 College Street
Macon, GA 31207
http://medicine.mercer.edu
Private
Admissions: (478) 301-2542
E-mail: admissions@med.mercer.edu
Financial aid: (478) 301-2853
Application deadline: 11/01
Tuition: $41,757
Room/board/expenses: $14,290
Percent receiving grants: 45%
Average student indebtedness at graduation: $192,332
Enrollment: 399
men: 53%; women: 47%; minorities: 22%; underrepresented minorities: 9%; in state: 100%
Acceptance rate: 17%
Average MCAT: 9.3
Average GPA: 3.57
Most popular undergraduate majors: biological sciences: 42%; physical sciences: 26%; nonsciences: 11%; other: 21%
Percent of graduates entering primary-care specialties: 37.0%

Morehouse School of Medicine[1]
720 Westview Drive SW
Atlanta, GA 30310
http://www.msm.edu
Private
Admissions: (404) 752-1650
E-mail: mdadmissions@msm.edu
Financial aid: (404) 752-1655
Tuition: N/A
Room/board/expenses: N/A
Enrollment: N/A

HAWAII

University of Hawaii–Manoa (Burns)
651 Ilalo Street
Honolulu, HI 96813
http://jabsom.hawaii.edu
Public
Admissions: (808) 692-1000
E-mail: medadmin@hawaii.edu
Financial aid: (808) 956-7251
Application deadline: 11/01
In-state tuition: $30,742
Out-of-state tuition: $63,982
Room/board/expenses: $15,682
Average student indebtedness at graduation: $104,586
Enrollment: 258
men: 48%; women: 52%; minorities: 73%; underrepresented minorities: 10%; in state: 82%
Acceptance rate: 6%
Average MCAT: 10.0
Average GPA: 3.64
Most popular undergraduate majors: biological sciences: 59%; physical sciences: 18%; nonsciences: 12%; other: 11%
Percent of graduates entering primary-care specialties: 46.3%

ILLINOIS

Loyola University Chicago (Stritch)[1]
2160 S. First Avenue, Building 120
Maywood, IL 60153
http://www.meddean.lumc.edu
Private
Admissions: (708) 216-3229
Financial aid: (708) 216-3227
Tuition: N/A
Room/board/expenses: N/A
Enrollment: N/A

Northwestern University (Feinberg)
420 E. Superior Street
(Rubloff Building), 12th Floor
Chicago, IL 60611
http://www.feinberg.northwestern.edu
Private
Admissions: (312) 503-8206
E-mail: med-admissions@northwestern.edu
Financial aid: (312) 503-8722
Application deadline: 10/15
Tuition: $51,490
Room/board/expenses: $14,958
Percent receiving grants: 52%
Average student indebtedness at graduation: $156,232
Enrollment: 712
men: 55%; women: 45%; minorities: 44%; underrepresented minorities: 16%; in state: 24%
Acceptance rate: 7%
Average MCAT: 11.4
Average GPA: 3.77
Most popular undergraduate majors: biological sciences: 43%; physical sciences: 17%; nonsciences: 23%; other: 17%
Percent of graduates entering primary-care specialties: 41.7%

Rosalind Franklin University of Medicine and Science[1]
3333 Green Bay Road
North Chicago, IL 60064
http://www.rosalindfranklin.edu
Private
Admissions: (847) 578-3204
E-mail: cms.admissions@rosalindfranklin.edu
Financial aid: (847) 578-3217
Tuition: N/A
Room/board/expenses: N/A
Enrollment: N/A

Rush University
600 S. Paulina Street
Chicago, IL 60612
http://www.rushu.rush.edu/medcol/
Private
Admissions: N/A
E-mail: RMC_Admissions@rush.edu
Financial aid: (312) 942-6256
Application deadline: 11/01
Tuition: $48,088
Room/board/expenses: $9,360
Percent receiving grants: 58%
Average student indebtedness at graduation: $187,805
Enrollment: 550
men: 50%; women: 50%; minorities: 35%; underrepresented minorities: 18%; in state: 67%
Acceptance rate: 6%
Average MCAT: 10.3
Average GPA: 3.64

Most popular undergraduate majors: biological sciences: 63%; physical sciences: 5%; nonsciences: 23%; other: 9%
Percent of graduates entering primary-care specialties: 40.0%

Southern Illinois University–Springfield[1]
801 N. Rutledge, PO Box 19620
Springfield, IL 62794-9620
http://www.siumed.edu/
Public
Admissions: (217) 545-6013
E-mail: admissions@siumed.edu
Financial aid: (217) 545-2224
Tuition: N/A
Room/board/expenses: N/A
Enrollment: N/A

University of Chicago (Pritzker)
5841 S. Maryland Avenue
MC 1000
Chicago, IL 60637-5416
http://pritzker.bsd.uchicago.edu
Private
Admissions: (773) 702-1937
E-mail: pritzkeradmissions@bsd.uchicago.edu
Financial aid: (773) 702-1938
Application deadline: 10/15
Tuition: $48,293
Room/board/expenses: $17,000
Percent receiving grants: 90%
Average student indebtedness at graduation: $113,007
Enrollment: 377
men: 51%; women: 49%; minorities: 35%; underrepresented minorities: 15%; in state: 28%
Acceptance rate: 4%
Average MCAT: 12.1
Average GPA: 3.83
Most popular undergraduate majors: biological sciences: 24%; physical sciences: 25%; nonsciences: 13%; other: 39%
Percent of graduates entering primary-care specialties: 41.0%

University of Illinois
1853 W. Polk Street, M/C 784
Chicago, IL 60612
http://www.medicine.uic.edu
Public
Admissions: (312) 996-5635
E-mail: medadmit@uic.edu
Financial aid: (312) 413-0127
Application deadline: 11/01
In-state tuition: $37,764
Out-of-state tuition: $74,764
Room/board/expenses: $14,464
Percent receiving grants: 51%
Average student indebtedness at graduation: $187,529
Enrollment: 1,305
men: 52%; women: 48%; minorities: 41%; underrepresented minorities: 29%; in state: 78%
Acceptance rate: 13%
Average MCAT: 10.2
Average GPA: 3.59
Most popular undergraduate majors: biological sciences: 61%; physical sciences: 4%; nonsciences: 15%; other: 20%
Percent of graduates entering primary-care specialties: 36.0%

INDIANA

Indiana University–Indianapolis
340 W. 10th Street, Suite 6200
Indianapolis, IN 46202
http://www.medicine.iu.edu
Public
Admissions: (317) 274-3772
E-mail: inmedadm@iupui.edu
Financial aid: (317) 274-1967
Application deadline: 12/15
In-state tuition: $33,146
Out-of-state tuition: $50,587
Room/board/expenses: $15,168
Percent receiving grants: 34%
Average student indebtedness at graduation: $157,076
Enrollment: 1,332
men: 56%; women: 44%; minorities: 26%; underrepresented minorities: 12%; in state: 83%
Acceptance rate: 14%
Average MCAT: 10.2
Average GPA: 3.70
Most popular undergraduate majors: biological sciences: 47%; physical sciences: 27%; nonsciences: 1%; other: 25%
Percent of graduates entering primary-care specialties: 39.3%

IOWA

University of Iowa (Carver)
200 CMAB
Iowa City, IA 52242-1101
http://www.medicine.uiowa.edu
Public
Admissions: (319) 335-8052
E-mail: medical-admissions@uiowa.edu
Financial aid: (319) 335-8059
Application deadline: 11/01
In-state tuition: $33,345
Out-of-state tuition: $49,409
Room/board/expenses: $10,350
Percent receiving grants: 60%
Average student indebtedness at graduation: $142,788
Enrollment: 588
men: 57%; women: 43%; minorities: 23%; underrepresented minorities: 11%; in state: 68%
Acceptance rate: 8%
Average MCAT: 10.8
Average GPA: 3.74
Most popular undergraduate majors: biological sciences: 55%; physical sciences: 9%; nonsciences: 18%; other: 18%
Percent of graduates entering primary-care specialties: 38.4%

KANSAS

University of Kansas Medical Center
3901 Rainbow Boulevard
Kansas City, KS 66160
http://medicine.kumc.edu
Public
Admissions: (913) 588-5245
E-mail: premedinfo@kumc.edu
Financial aid: (913) 588-5170
Application deadline: 10/15
In-state tuition: $32,528
Out-of-state tuition: $55,257
Room/board/expenses: $12,402
Percent receiving grants: 92%
Average student indebtedness at graduation: $132,987
Enrollment: 765
men: 56%; women: 44%; minorities: 20%; underrepresented minorities: 11%; in state: 90%
Acceptance rate: 10%

Average MCAT: 9.5
Average GPA: 3.65
Most popular undergraduate majors: biological sciences: 51%; physical sciences: 22%; nonsciences: 7%; other: 20%
Percent of graduates entering primary-care specialties: 48.4%

KENTUCKY

University of Kentucky

138 Leader Avenue
Lexington, KY 40506-9983
http://www.mc.uky.edu/medicine/
Public
Admissions: (859) 323-6161
E-mail: kymedap@uky.edu
Financial aid: (859) 257-1652
Application deadline: 11/01
In-state tuition: $32,889
Out-of-state tuition: $60,334
Room/board/expenses: $13,500
Percent receiving grants: 49%
Average student indebtedness at graduation: $145,758
Enrollment: 479
men: 59%; women: 41%; minorities: 18%; underrepresented minorities: 8%; in state: 77%
Acceptance rate: 9%
Average MCAT: 10.6
Average GPA: 3.67
Most popular undergraduate majors: biological sciences: 63%; physical sciences: 19%; nonsciences: 4%; other: 14%
Percent of graduates entering primary-care specialties: 42.5%

University of Louisville

Abell Administration Center H.S.C.
Louisville, KY 40202
http://www.louisville.edu
Public
Admissions: (502) 852-5193
E-mail: medadm@louisville.edu
Financial aid: (502) 852-5187
Application deadline: 10/15
In-state tuition: $32,313
Out-of-state tuition: $48,253
Room/board/expenses: $8,370
Percent receiving grants: 45%
Average student indebtedness at graduation: $158,439
Enrollment: 654
men: 55%; women: 45%; minorities: 17%; underrepresented minorities: 8%; in state: 75%
Acceptance rate: 9%
Average MCAT: 10.0
Average GPA: 3.65
Most popular undergraduate majors: biological sciences: 51%; physical sciences: 21%; nonsciences: 10%; other: 18%
Percent of graduates entering primary-care specialties: 38.6%

LOUISIANA

Louisiana State University Health Sciences Center–New Orleans[1]

Admissions Office
1901 Perdido Street
New Orleans, LA 70112-1393
http://www.medschool.lsumc.edu
Public
Admissions: (504) 568-6262
E-mail: ms-admissions@lsumc.edu
Financial aid: (504) 568-4820
Tuition: N/A
Room/board/expenses: N/A
Enrollment: N/A

Louisiana State University Health Sciences Center–Shreveport[1]

PO Box 33932
1501 Kings Highway
Shreveport, LA 71130-3932
http://www.lsuhscshreveport.edu
Public
Admissions: (318) 675-5190
E-mail: shvadm@lsuhsc.edu
Financial aid: (318) 675-5561
Tuition: N/A
Room/board/expenses: N/A
Enrollment: N/A

Tulane University[1]

1430 Tulane Avenue, SL67
New Orleans, LA 70112-2699
http://www.mcl.tulane.edu
Private
Admissions: (504) 988-5331
E-mail: medsch@tulane.edu
Financial aid: (504) 988-6135
Tuition: N/A
Room/board/expenses: N/A
Enrollment: N/A

MARYLAND

Johns Hopkins University

733 N. Broadway
Baltimore, MD 21205
http://www.hopkinsmedicine.org
Private
Admissions: (410) 955-3182
E-mail: somadmiss@jhmi.edu
Financial aid: (410) 955-1324
Application deadline: 10/15
Tuition: $45,434
Room/board/expenses: $24,452
Percent receiving grants: 60%
Average student indebtedness at graduation: $112,080
Enrollment: 479
men: 53%; women: 47%; minorities: 45%; underrepresented minorities: 15%; in state: 24%
Acceptance rate: 6%
Average MCAT: 11.8
Average GPA: 3.87
Most popular undergraduate majors: biological sciences: 52%; physical sciences: 24%; nonsciences: 18%; other: 6%
Percent of graduates entering primary-care specialties: 34.8%

Uniformed Services University of the Health Sciences (Hebert)

4301 Jones Bridge Road
Bethesda, MD 20814
http://www.usuhs.edu
Public
Admissions: (800) 772-1743
E-mail: admissions@usuhs.edu
Financial aid: N/A
Application deadline: 11/15
In-state tuition: N/A
Out-of-state tuition: N/A
Room/board/expenses: $0
Percent receiving grants: 0%
Average student indebtedness at graduation: $0
Enrollment: 685
men: 70%; women: 30%; minorities: 22%; underrepresented minorities: 6%; in state: 9%
Acceptance rate: 11%
Average MCAT: 10.4
Average GPA: 3.54

Most popular undergraduate majors: biological sciences: 48%; physical sciences: 20%; nonsciences: 15%; other: 17%
Percent of graduates entering primary-care specialties: 43.0%

University of Maryland

655 W. Baltimore Street
Room 14-029
Baltimore, MD 21201-1559
http://medschool.umaryland.edu
Public
Admissions: (410) 706-7478
E-mail: admissions@som.umaryland.edu
Financial aid: (410) 706-7347
Application deadline: 11/01
In-state tuition: $29,883
Out-of-state tuition: $53,532
Room/board/expenses: $21,500
Percent receiving grants: 82%
Average student indebtedness at graduation: $155,219
Enrollment: 663
men: 43%; women: 57%; minorities: 35%; underrepresented minorities: 10%; in state: 84%
Acceptance rate: 7%
Average MCAT: 10.5
Average GPA: 3.74
Most popular undergraduate majors: biological sciences: 50%; physical sciences: 19%; nonsciences: 17%; other: 14%
Percent of graduates entering primary-care specialties: 35.4%

MASSACHUSETTS

Boston University

72 E. Concord Street, L-103
Boston, MA 02118
http://www.bumc.bu.edu
Private
Admissions: (617) 638-4630
E-mail: medadms@bu.edu
Financial aid: (617) 638-5130
Application deadline: 11/01
Tuition: $51,548
Room/board/expenses: $9,975
Percent receiving grants: 44%
Average student indebtedness at graduation: $170,217
Enrollment: 730
men: 49%; women: 51%; minorities: 51%; underrepresented minorities: 21%; in state: 18%
Acceptance rate: 5%
Average MCAT: 11.2
Average GPA: 3.66
Most popular undergraduate majors: biological sciences: 37%; physical sciences: 23%; nonsciences: 17%; other: 23%
Percent of graduates entering primary-care specialties: 41.7%

Harvard University

25 Shattuck Street
Boston, MA 02115-6092
http://hms.harvard.edu
Private
Admissions: (617) 432-1550
E-mail: admissions_office@hms.harvard.edu
Financial aid: (617) 432-0449
Application deadline: 10/15
Tuition: $53,496
Room/board/expenses: $13,640
Percent receiving grants: 69%
Average student indebtedness at graduation: $104,890
Enrollment: 700
men: 51%; women: 49%; minorities: 48%; underrepresented minorities: 21%; in state: N/A
Acceptance rate: 4%
Average MCAT: 12.1
Average GPA: 3.88

Most popular undergraduate majors: biological sciences: 46%; physical sciences: 21%; nonsciences: 21%; other: 12%
Percent of graduates entering primary-care specialties: 44.0%

Tufts University

136 Harrison Avenue
Boston, MA 02111
http://www.tufts.edu/med
Private
Admissions: (617) 636-6571
E-mail: med-admissions@tufts.edu
Financial aid: (617) 636-6574
Application deadline: 11/01
Tuition: $55,667
Room/board/expenses: $14,620
Percent receiving grants: 41%
Average student indebtedness at graduation: $195,813
Enrollment: 810
men: 53%; women: 47%; minorities: 31%; underrepresented minorities: 12%; in state: 27%
Acceptance rate: 7%
Average MCAT: 10.7
Average GPA: 3.62
Most popular undergraduate majors: biological sciences: 56%; physical sciences: 9%; nonsciences: 27%; other: 8%
Percent of graduates entering primary-care specialties: 45.6%

University of Massachusetts–Worcester

55 Lake Avenue N
Worcester, MA 01655
http://www.umassmed.edu
Public
Admissions: (508) 856-2323
E-mail: admissions@umassmed.edu
Financial aid: (508) 856-2265
Application deadline: 11/01
In-state tuition: $20,662
Out-of-state tuition: N/A
Room/board/expenses: $13,704
Percent receiving grants: 43%
Average student indebtedness at graduation: $108,811
Enrollment: 519
men: 47%; women: 53%; minorities: 25%; underrepresented minorities: 7%; in state: 97%
Acceptance rate: 19%
Average MCAT: 10.7
Average GPA: 3.72
Most popular undergraduate majors: biological sciences: 38%; physical sciences: 14%; nonsciences: 14%; other: 34%
Percent of graduates entering primary-care specialties: 54.4%

MICHIGAN

Michigan State University (College of Human Medicine)

15 Michigan St. NE
Grand Rapids, MI 49503
http://humanmedicine.msu.edu
Public
Admissions: (517) 353-9620
E-mail: MDadmissions@msu.edu
Financial aid: (517) 353-5940
Application deadline: 11/01
In-state tuition: $28,988
Out-of-state tuition: $60,408
Room/board/expenses: $14,616
Percent receiving grants: 40%
Average student indebtedness at graduation: $204,659

Enrollment: 796
men: 50%; women: 50%; minorities: 28%; underrepresented minorities: 8%; in state: 77%
Acceptance rate: 6%
Average MCAT: 9.3
Average GPA: 3.56
Most popular undergraduate majors: biological sciences: 72%; physical sciences: 13%; nonsciences: 10%; other: 5%
Percent of graduates entering primary-care specialties: 45.2%

University of Michigan–Ann Arbor

1301 Catherine Road
Ann Arbor, MI 48109-0624
http://www.umich.edu/medschool/
Public
Admissions: (734) 764-6317
E-mail: umichmedadmiss@umich.edu
Financial aid: (734) 763-4147
Application deadline: N/A
In-state tuition: $29,546
Out-of-state tuition: $47,138
Room/board/expenses: $22,175
Percent receiving grants: 57%
Average student indebtedness at graduation: $121,087
Enrollment: 679
men: 52%; women: 48%; minorities: 35%; underrepresented minorities: 11%; in state: 51%
Acceptance rate: 8%
Average MCAT: 11.6
Average GPA: 3.78
Most popular undergraduate majors: biological sciences: 45%; physical sciences: 19%; nonsciences: 6%; other: 30%
Percent of graduates entering primary-care specialties: 43.5%

Wayne State University

540 E. Canfield
Detroit, MI 48201
http://www.med.wayne.edu/Admissions
Public
Admissions: (313) 577-1466
E-mail: admissions@med.wayne.edu
Financial aid: (313) 577-1039
Application deadline: 12/15
In-state tuition: $31,790
Out-of-state tuition: $64,065
Room/board/expenses: $12,750
Percent receiving grants: 38%
Average student indebtedness at graduation: $163,738
Enrollment: 1,218
men: 54%; women: 46%; minorities: 28%; underrepresented minorities: 9%; in state: 80%
Acceptance rate: 11%
Average MCAT: 10.1
Average GPA: 3.72
Most popular undergraduate majors: biological sciences: 53%; physical sciences: 20%; nonsciences: 5%; other: 22%
Percent of graduates entering primary-care specialties: 31.0%

MINNESOTA

Mayo Medical School

200 First Street SW
Rochester, MN 55905
http://www.mayo.edu/mms/
Private
Admissions: (507) 284-3671
E-mail: medschooladmissions@mayo.edu

Financial aid: (507) 284-4839
Application deadline: 09/01
Tuition: $35,960
Room/board/expenses: $18,048
Percent receiving grants: 100%
Average student indebtedness at graduation: $75,217
Enrollment: 194
men: 51%; women: 49%; minorities: 40%; underrepresented minorities: 18%; in state: 16%
Acceptance rate: 2%
Average MCAT: 10.8
Average GPA: 3.87
Most popular undergraduate majors: biological sciences: 48%; physical sciences: 26%; nonsciences: 14%; other: 12%
Percent of graduates entering primary-care specialties: 39.0%

University of Minnesota

420 Delaware Street SE
MMC 293
Minneapolis, MN 55455
http://www.med.umn.edu
Public
Admissions: (612) 625-7977
E-mail: meded@umn.edu
Financial aid: (612) 625-4998
Application deadline: 11/15
In-state tuition: $41,782
Out-of-state tuition: $53,443
Room/board/expenses: $12,735
Percent receiving grants: 66%
Average student indebtedness at graduation: $174,703
Enrollment: 984
men: 51%; women: 49%; minorities: 22%; underrepresented minorities: 10%; in state: 87%
Acceptance rate: 7%
Average MCAT: 10.5
Average GPA: 3.72
Most popular undergraduate majors: biological sciences: 42%; physical sciences: 18%; nonsciences: 7%; other: 33%
Percent of graduates entering primary-care specialties: 48.5%

MISSISSIPPI

University of Mississippi[1]

2500 N. State Street
Jackson, MS 39216-4505
http://www.umc.edu
Public
Admissions: (601) 984-5010
Financial aid: (601) 984-1117
Tuition: N/A
Room/board/expenses: N/A
Enrollment: N/A

MISSOURI

St. Louis University

1402 S. Grand Boulevard
St. Louis, MO 63104
http://medschool.slu.edu
Private
Admissions: (314) 977-9870
E-mail: slumd@slu.edu
Financial aid: (314) 977-9840
Application deadline: 12/15
Tuition: $48,130
Room/board/expenses: $10,380
Percent receiving grants: 65%
Average student indebtedness at graduation: $188,190
Enrollment: 725
men: 58%; women: 42%; minorities: 38%; underrepresented minorities: 9%; in state: 40%

Acceptance rate: 10%
Average MCAT: 10.9
Average GPA: 3.71
Most popular undergraduate majors: biological sciences: 47%; physical sciences: 17%; nonsciences: 11%; other: 25%
Percent of graduates entering primary-care specialties: 40.4%

University of Missouri

1 Hospital Drive
Columbia, MO 65212
http://medicine.missouri.edu
Public
Admissions: (573) 882-9219
E-mail: MizzouMed@missouri.edu
Financial aid: (573) 882-2923
Application deadline: 10/15
In-state tuition: $28,380
Out-of-state tuition: $54,170
Room/board/expenses: $11,790
Percent receiving grants: 62%
Average student indebtedness at graduation: $134,867
Enrollment: 401
men: 51%; women: 49%; minorities: 20%; underrepresented minorities: 10%; in state: 97%
Acceptance rate: 9%
Average MCAT: 10.1
Average GPA: 3.77
Most popular undergraduate majors: biological sciences: 31%; physical sciences: 25%; nonsciences: 14%; other: 30%
Percent of graduates entering primary-care specialties: 44.3%

University of Missouri–Kansas City[1]

2411 Holmes
Kansas City, MO 64108
http://www.med.umkc.edu
Public
Admissions: (816) 235-1208
E-mail: dehaemersj@umkc.edu
Financial aid: (816) 235-1242
Tuition: N/A
Room/board/expenses: N/A
Enrollment: N/A

Washington University in St. Louis

660 S. Euclid Avenue
St. Louis, MO 63110
http://medadmissions.wustl.edu
Private
Admissions: (314) 362-6858
E-mail: wumscoa@wustl.edu
Financial aid: (314) 362-6671
Application deadline: 12/01
Tuition: $52,020
Room/board/expenses: $11,385
Percent receiving grants: 79%
Average student indebtedness at graduation: $101,040
Enrollment: 478
men: 51%; women: 49%; minorities: 42%; underrepresented minorities: 11%; in state: 8%
Acceptance rate: 10%
Average MCAT: 12.3
Average GPA: 3.87
Most popular undergraduate majors: biological sciences: 27%; physical sciences: 31%; nonsciences: 8%; other: 34%
Percent of graduates entering primary-care specialties: 30.2%

NEBRASKA

Creighton University

2500 California Plaza
Omaha, NE 68178
http://medicine.creighton.edu
Private
Admissions: (402) 280-2799
E-mail: medadmissions@creighton.edu
Financial aid: (402) 280-2666
Application deadline: 11/01
Tuition: $50,774
Room/board/expenses: $14,400
Percent receiving grants: 60%
Average student indebtedness at graduation: $206,112
Enrollment: 582
men: 51%; women: 49%; minorities: 12%; underrepresented minorities: 8%; in state: 11%
Acceptance rate: 7%
Average MCAT: 9.9
Average GPA: 3.68
Most popular undergraduate majors: biological sciences: 53%; physical sciences: 17%; nonsciences: 19%; other: 12%
Percent of graduates entering primary-care specialties: 38.3%

University of Nebraska Medical Center

985527 Nebraska Medical Center
Omaha, NE 68198-5527
http://www.unmc.edu/com/admissions.htm
Public
Admissions: (402) 559-2259
E-mail: grrogers@unmc.edu
Financial aid: (402) 559-4199
Application deadline: 11/01
In-state tuition: $30,937
Out-of-state tuition: $68,579
Room/board/expenses: $15,300
Percent receiving grants: 58%
Average student indebtedness at graduation: $141,378
Enrollment: 514
men: 57%; women: 43%; minorities: 11%; underrepresented minorities: 3%; in state: 84%
Acceptance rate: 11%
Average MCAT: 10.2
Average GPA: 3.77
Most popular undergraduate majors: biological sciences: 49%; physical sciences: 24%; nonsciences: 11%; other: 16%
Percent of graduates entering primary-care specialties: 65.0%

NEVADA

University of Nevada

Pennington Building, Mailstop 357
Reno, NV 89557-0357
http://www.medicine.nevada.edu
Public
Admissions: (775) 784-6063
E-mail: asa@medicine.nevada.edu
Financial aid: (775) 682-8358
Application deadline: 11/01
In-state tuition: $26,072
Out-of-state tuition: $57,248
Room/board/expenses: $13,806
Percent receiving grants: 84%
Average student indebtedness at graduation: $137,683
Enrollment: 250
men: 56%; women: 44%; minorities: 34%; underrepresented minorities: 16%; in state: 92%
Acceptance rate: 11%
Average MCAT: 10.0
Average GPA: 3.72

Most popular undergraduate majors: biological sciences: 60%; physical sciences: 15%; nonsciences: 6%; other: 19%
Percent of graduates entering primary-care specialties: 44.0%

NEW HAMPSHIRE

Dartmouth College (Geisel)

1 Rope Ferry Road
Hanover, NH 03755-1404
http://dms.dartmouth.edu
Private
Admissions: (603) 650-1505
E-mail: dms.admissions@dartmouth.edu
Financial aid: (603) 650-1919
Application deadline: 11/01
Tuition: $52,406
Room/board/expenses: $10,750
Percent receiving grants: 58%
Average student indebtedness at graduation: $139,053
Enrollment: 395
men: 49%; women: 51%; minorities: 28%; underrepresented minorities: 9%; in state: 7%
Acceptance rate: 6%
Average MCAT: 10.9
Average GPA: 3.65
Most popular undergraduate majors: biological sciences: 48%; physical sciences: 20%; nonsciences: 18%; other: 13%
Percent of graduates entering primary-care specialties: 41.3%

NEW JERSEY

University of Medicine and Dentistry of New Jersey–Newark[1]

185 S. Orange Avenue
PO Box 1709
Newark, NJ 07101-1709
http://www.njms.umdnj.edu
Public
Admissions: (973) 972-4631
E-mail: njmsadmiss@umdnj.edu
Financial aid: (973) 972-7030
Tuition: N/A
Room/board/expenses: N/A
Enrollment: N/A

University of Medicine and Dentistry of New Jersey–New Brunswick (Johnson)

125 Paterson Street
New Brunswick, NJ 08903-0019
http://rwjms.umdnj.edu
Public
Admissions: (732) 235-4576
E-mail: rwjapadm@umdnj.edu
Financial aid: (732) 235-4689
Application deadline: 12/01
In-state tuition: $38,742
Out-of-state tuition: $59,565
Room/board/expenses: $14,160
Percent receiving grants: 28%
Average student indebtedness at graduation: $145,547
Enrollment: 608
men: 44%; women: 56%; minorities: 45%; underrepresented minorities: 14%; in state: 97%
Acceptance rate: 7%
Average MCAT: 10.3
Average GPA: 3.63
Most popular undergraduate majors: biological sciences: 56%; physical sciences: 15%; nonsciences: 15%; other: 14%
Percent of graduates entering primary-care specialties: 37.0%

NEW MEXICO

University of New Mexico

Basic Medical Sciences Building
Room 107
Albuquerque, NM 87131
http://hsc.unm.edu/som/
Public
Admissions: (505) 272-4766
E-mail: somadmissions@salud.unm.edu
Financial aid: (505) 272-8008
Application deadline: 11/15
In-state tuition: $19,294
Out-of-state tuition: $49,471
Room/board/expenses: $16,193
Percent receiving grants: 70%
Average student indebtedness at graduation: $118,674
Enrollment: 374
men: 45%; women: 55%; minorities: 44%; underrepresented minorities: 38%; in state: 99%
Acceptance rate: 13%
Average MCAT: 9.4
Average GPA: 3.65
Most popular undergraduate majors: biological sciences: 53%; physical sciences: 20%; nonsciences: 12%; other: 16%
Percent of graduates entering primary-care specialties: 40.7%

NEW YORK

Albany Medical College[1]

47 New Scotland Avenue
Albany, NY 12208
http://www.amc.edu
Private
Admissions: (518) 262-5521
E-mail: admissions@mail.amc.edu
Financial aid: (518) 262-5435
Tuition: N/A
Room/board/expenses: N/A
Enrollment: N/A

Columbia University

630 W. 168th Street
New York, NY 10032
http://ps.columbia.edu
Private
Admissions: (212) 305-3595
E-mail: psadmissions@columbia.edu
Financial aid: (212) 305-4100
Application deadline: 10/15
Tuition: $54,855
Room/board/expenses: $16,339
Percent receiving grants: 65%
Average student indebtedness at graduation: $130,043
Enrollment: 662
men: 50%; women: 50%; minorities: 37%; underrepresented minorities: 21%; in state: 35%
Acceptance rate: 4%
Average MCAT: 11.9
Average GPA: 3.78
Most popular undergraduate majors: biological sciences: 26%; physical sciences: 23%; nonsciences: 26%; other: 25%
Percent of graduates entering primary-care specialties: 35.6%

Cornell University (Weill)

525 E. 68th Street
New York, NY 10065
http://www.weill.cornell.edu
Private
Admissions: (212) 746-1067
E-mail: wcmc-admissions@med.cornell.edu
Financial aid: (212) 746-1066

Application deadline: 10/15
Tuition: $50,765
Room/board/expenses: $12,053
Percent receiving grants: 56%
Average student indebtedness at graduation: $131,017
Enrollment: 409
men: 54%; women: 46%; minorities: 44%; underrepresented minorities: 20%; in state: 36%
Acceptance rate: 5%
Average MCAT: 11.5
Average GPA: 3.78
Most popular undergraduate majors: biological sciences: 39%; physical sciences: 13%; nonsciences: 20%; other: 28%
Percent of graduates entering primary-care specialties: 35.0%

Mount Sinai School of Medicine

1 Gustave L. Levy Place
PO Box 1217
New York, NY 10029
http://www.mssm.edu
Private
Admissions: (212) 241-6696
E-mail: admissions@mssm.edu
Financial aid: (212) 241-5245
Application deadline: 10/15
Tuition: $46,618
Room/board/expenses: $12,462
Percent receiving grants: 38%
Average student indebtedness at graduation: $138,183
Enrollment: 568
men: 53%; women: 47%; minorities: 43%; underrepresented minorities: 18%; in state: 32%
Acceptance rate: 7%
Average MCAT: 11.9
Average GPA: 3.75
Most popular undergraduate majors: biological sciences: 31%; physical sciences: 13%; nonsciences: 42%; other: 14%
Percent of graduates entering primary-care specialties: 36.4%

New York Medical College

40 Sunshine Cottage Road
Valhalla, NY 10595
http://www.nymc.edu
Private
Admissions: (914) 594-4507
E-mail: mdadmit@nymc.edu
Financial aid: (914) 594-4491
Application deadline: 12/15
Tuition: $49,156
Room/board/expenses: $20,612
Percent receiving grants: 42%
Average student indebtedness at graduation: $189,000
Enrollment: 817
men: 51%; women: 49%; minorities: 38%; underrepresented minorities: 14%; in state: 32%
Acceptance rate: 8%
Average MCAT: 10.4
Average GPA: 3.60
Most popular undergraduate majors: biological sciences: 39%; physical sciences: 11%; nonsciences: 18%; other: 32%
Percent of graduates entering primary-care specialties: 36.0%

New York University

550 First Avenue
New York, NY 10016
http://school.med.nyu.edu
Private
Admissions: (212) 263-5290
E-mail: admissions@nyumc.org
Financial aid: (212) 263-5286
Application deadline: 11/01

Tuition: $49,560
Room/board/expenses: $13,620
Percent receiving grants: 31%
Average student indebtedness at graduation: $147,104
Enrollment: 651
men: 51%; women: 49%; minorities: 42%; underrepresented minorities: 11%; in state: 38%
Acceptance rate: 6%
Average MCAT: 11.4
Average GPA: 3.81
Most popular undergraduate majors: biological sciences: 37%; physical sciences: 30%; nonsciences: 15%; other: 18%
Percent of graduates entering primary-care specialties: 34.0%

Stony Brook University–SUNY

Office of Admissions
Health Science Center, L4
Stony Brook, NY 11794-8434
http://www.stonybrookmedicalcenter.org/som/
Public
Admissions: (631) 444-2113
E-mail: admissions@stonybrook.edu
Financial aid: (631) 444-2341
Application deadline: 12/01
In-state tuition: $31,144
Out-of-state tuition: $56,264
Room/board/expenses: $11,413
Percent receiving grants: 27%
Average student indebtedness at graduation: $141,165
Enrollment: 512
men: 56%; women: 44%; minorities: 38%; underrepresented minorities: 11%; in state: 82%
Acceptance rate: 7%
Average MCAT: 10.7
Average GPA: 3.70
Most popular undergraduate majors: biological sciences: 55%; physical sciences: 25%; nonsciences: 20%; other: N/A
Percent of graduates entering primary-care specialties: 35.8%

SUNY Downstate Medical Center[1]

450 Clarkson Avenue, Box 60
Brooklyn, NY 11203
http://www.hscbklyn.edu
Public
Admissions: (718) 270-2446
E-mail: admissions@downstate.edu
Financial aid: (718) 270-2488
Tuition: N/A
Room/board/expenses: N/A
Enrollment: N/A

SUNY–Syracuse[1]

766 Irving Avenue
Syracuse, NY 13210
http://www.upstate.edu/
Public
Admissions: (315) 464-4570
E-mail: admiss@upstate.edu
Financial aid: (315) 464-4329
Tuition: N/A
Room/board/expenses: N/A
Enrollment: N/A

University at Buffalo–SUNY

155 Biomedical Education Building
Buffalo, NY 14214
http://medicine.buffalo.edu
Public
Admissions: (716) 829-3466
E-mail: jjrosso@buffalo.edu
Financial aid: (716) 645-2450
Application deadline: 11/15
In-state tuition: $31,514
Out-of-state tuition: $61,004
Room/board/expenses: $13,008
Percent receiving grants: 17%
Average student indebtedness at graduation: $152,500
Enrollment: 581
men: 59%; women: 41%; minorities: 31%; underrepresented minorities: 6%; in state: N/A
Acceptance rate: 10%
Average MCAT: 10.5
Average GPA: 3.75
Most popular undergraduate majors: biological sciences: 29%; physical sciences: 24%; nonsciences: 33%; other: 14%
Percent of graduates entering primary-care specialties: 38.5%

University of Rochester

601 Elmwood Avenue, Box 706
Rochester, NY 14642
http://www.urmc.rochester.edu/education/md/admissions
Private
Admissions: (585) 275-4542
E-mail: mdadmish@urmc.rochester.edu
Financial aid: (585) 275-4523
Application deadline: 10/15
Tuition: $47,116
Room/board/expenses: $16,500
Percent receiving grants: 64%
Average student indebtedness at graduation: $139,899
Enrollment: 435
men: 51%; women: 49%; minorities: 34%; underrepresented minorities: 15%; in state: 58%
Acceptance rate: 6%
Average MCAT: 11.0
Average GPA: 3.74
Most popular undergraduate majors: biological sciences: 46%; physical sciences: 14%; nonsciences: 20%; other: 20%
Percent of graduates entering primary-care specialties: 39.6%

Yeshiva University (Einstein)

1300 Morris Park Avenue
Bronx, NY 10461
http://www.einstein.yu.edu
Private
Admissions: (718) 430-2106
E-mail: admissions@einstein.yu.edu
Financial aid: (718) 862-1813
Application deadline: 11/01
Tuition: $49,435
Room/board/expenses: $15,000
Percent receiving grants: 48%
Average student indebtedness at graduation: $142,235
Enrollment: 803
men: 51%; women: 49%; minorities: 36%; underrepresented minorities: 12%; in state: 58%
Acceptance rate: 6%
Average MCAT: 11.0
Average GPA: 3.75
Most popular undergraduate majors: biological sciences: 44%; physical sciences: 16%; nonsciences: 18%; other: 22%
Percent of graduates entering primary-care specialties: 42.0%

Duke University

Durham, NC 27710
http://dukemed.duke.edu
Private
Admissions: (919) 684-2985
E-mail: medadm@mc.duke.edu
Financial aid: (919) 684-6649
Application deadline: 11/01
Tuition: $51,366
Room/board/expenses: $15,888
Percent receiving grants: 63%
Average student indebtedness at graduation: $111,641
Enrollment: 425
men: 51%; women: 49%; minorities: 52%; underrepresented minorities: 23%; in state: 14%
Acceptance rate: 5%
Average MCAT: 11.7
Average GPA: 3.79
Most popular undergraduate majors: biological sciences: 37%; physical sciences: 37%; nonsciences: 10%; other: 16%
Percent of graduates entering primary-care specialties: 27.0%

East Carolina University (Brody)

600 Moye Boulevard
Greenville, NC 27834
http://www.ecu.edu/bsomadmissions
Public
Admissions: (252) 744-2202
E-mail: somadmissions@ecu.edu
Financial aid: (252) 744-2278
Application deadline: 11/15
In-state tuition: $14,695
Out-of-state tuition: $41,380
Room/board/expenses: $13,493
Percent receiving grants: 87%
Average student indebtedness at graduation: $107,532
Enrollment: 320
men: 50%; women: 50%; minorities: 33%; underrepresented minorities: 16%; in state: 100%
Acceptance rate: 15%
Average MCAT: 9.0
Average GPA: 3.60
Most popular undergraduate majors: biological sciences: 41%; physical sciences: 13%; nonsciences: 7%; other: 39%
Percent of graduates entering primary-care specialties: 54.4%

University of North Carolina–Chapel Hill

CB #7000, 4030 Bondurant Hall
Chapel Hill, NC 27599-7000
http://www.med.unc.edu/admit/
Public
Admissions: (919) 962-8331
E-mail: admissions@med.unc.edu
Financial aid: (919) 962-6117
Application deadline: 11/01
In-state tuition: $17,888
Out-of-state tuition: $43,646
Room/board/expenses: $30,768
Percent receiving grants: 85%
Average student indebtedness at graduation: $100,846
Enrollment: 782
men: 51%; women: 49%; minorities: 30%; underrepresented minorities: 18%; in state: 94%
Acceptance rate: 5%
Average MCAT: 10.9
Average GPA: 3.65
Most popular undergraduate majors: biological sciences: 47%;

physical sciences: 13%; nonsciences: 16%; other: 24%
Percent of graduates entering primary-care specialties: 60.3%

Wake Forest University

Medical Center Boulevard
Winston-Salem, NC 27157
http://www.wakehealth.edu
Private
Admissions: (336) 716-4264
E-mail: medadmit@wakehealth.edu
Financial aid: (336) 716-2889
Application deadline: 11/01
Tuition: $44,696
Room/board/expenses: $22,060
Percent receiving grants: 69%
Average student indebtedness at graduation: $156,340
Enrollment: 486
men: 54%; women: 46%; minorities: 29%; underrepresented minorities: 11%; in state: 40%
Acceptance rate: 3%
Average MCAT: 10.7
Average GPA: 3.57
Most popular undergraduate majors: biological sciences: 37%; physical sciences: 32%; nonsciences: 22%; other: 9%
Percent of graduates entering primary-care specialties: 48.0%

University of North Dakota[1]

501 N. Columbia Road, Stop 9037
Grand Forks, ND 58202-9037
http://www.med.und.nodak.edu
Public
Admissions: (701) 777-4221
E-mail: Judy.heit@med.und.edu
Financial aid: (701) 777-2849
Tuition: N/A
Room/board/expenses: N/A
Enrollment: N/A

Case Western Reserve University

10900 Euclid Avenue
Cleveland, OH 44106
http://casemed.case.edu/
Private
Admissions: (216) 368-3450
E-mail: casemed-admissions@case.edu
Financial aid: (216) 368-3666
Application deadline: 11/01
Tuition: $53,040
Room/board/expenses: $19,900
Percent receiving grants: 60%
Average student indebtedness at graduation: $154,835
Enrollment: 846
men: 54%; women: 46%; minorities: 40%; underrepresented minorities: 11%; in state: 21%
Acceptance rate: 9%
Average MCAT: 11.6
Average GPA: 3.70
Most popular undergraduate majors: biological sciences: 33%; physical sciences: 28%; nonsciences: 7%; other: 33%
Percent of graduates entering primary-care specialties: 34.0%

Northeast Ohio Medical University[1]

4209 State Route 44, PO Box 95
Rootstown, OH 44272-0095
http://www.neoucom.edu
Public
Admissions: (330) 325-6270
E-mail: admission@neoucom.edu
Financial aid: (330) 325-6481
Tuition: N/A
Room/board/expenses: N/A
Enrollment: N/A

Ohio State University

200 Meiling Hall
370 W. Ninth Avenue
Columbus, OH 43210-1238
http://medicine.osu.edu
Public
Admissions: (614) 292-7137
E-mail: medicine@osu.edu
Financial aid: (614) 688-4955
Application deadline: 11/01
In-state tuition: $29,953
Out-of-state tuition: $34,317
Room/board/expenses: $9,708
Percent receiving grants: 68%
Average student indebtedness at graduation: $152,510
Enrollment: 878
men: 54%; women: 46%; minorities: 39%; underrepresented minorities: 18%; in state: 86%
Acceptance rate: 7%
Average MCAT: 11.3
Average GPA: 3.68
Most popular undergraduate majors: biological sciences: 48%; physical sciences: 25%; nonsciences: 10%; other: 17%
Percent of graduates entering primary-care specialties: 42.0%

University of Cincinnati

231 Albert Sabin Way
Cincinnati, OH 45267-0552
http://www.MedOneStop.uc.edu
Public
Admissions: (513) 558-7314
E-mail: comadmis@ucmail.uc.edu
Financial aid: (513) 558-6797
Application deadline: 11/15
In-state tuition: $30,990
Out-of-state tuition: $48,720
Room/board/expenses: $19,015
Percent receiving grants: 36%
Average student indebtedness at graduation: $169,020
Enrollment: 663
men: 52%; women: 48%; minorities: 33%; underrepresented minorities: 9%; in state: 94%
Acceptance rate: 8%
Average MCAT: 10.7
Average GPA: 3.72
Most popular undergraduate majors: biological sciences: 51%; physical sciences: 36%; nonsciences: 4%; other: 9%
Percent of graduates entering primary-care specialties: 30.5%

University of Toledo

3000 Arlington Avenue
Toledo, OH 43614
http://hsc.utoledo.edu
Public
Admissions: (419) 383-4229
E-mail: medadmissions@utoledo.edu
Financial aid: (419) 383-4232
Application deadline: 11/01
In-state tuition: $31,992
Out-of-state tuition: $62,196
Room/board/expenses: $12,467
Percent receiving grants: 16%
Average student indebtedness at graduation: $166,480
Enrollment: 702
men: 55%; women: 45%; minorities: 19%; underrepresented minorities: 5%; in state: 92%
Acceptance rate: 9%
Average MCAT: 10.3
Average GPA: 3.70
Most popular undergraduate majors: biological sciences: 55%; physical sciences: 22%; nonsciences: 10%; other: 13%
Percent of graduates entering primary-care specialties: 34.4%

Wright State University (Boonshoft)

PO Box 1751
Dayton, OH 45401-1751
http://www.med.wright.edu
Public
Admissions: (937) 775-2934
E-mail: som_saa@wright.edu
Financial aid: (937) 775-2934
Application deadline: 11/01
In-state tuition: $32,834
Out-of-state tuition: $49,136
Room/board/expenses: $14,440
Percent receiving grants: 34%
Average student indebtedness at graduation: $169,964
Enrollment: 422
men: 51%; women: 49%; minorities: 29%; underrepresented minorities: 9%; in state: 98%
Acceptance rate: 7%
Average MCAT: 10.1
Average GPA: 3.68
Most popular undergraduate majors: biological sciences: N/A; physical sciences: N/A; nonsciences: N/A; other: N/A
Percent of graduates entering primary-care specialties: 46.3%

OKLAHOMA

University of Oklahoma

PO Box 26901, BMSB 357
Oklahoma City, OK 73126
http://www.medicine.ouhsc.edu
Public
Admissions: (405) 271-2331
E-mail: adminmed@ouhsc.edu
Financial aid: (405) 271-2118
Application deadline: 10/15
In-state tuition: $23,793
Out-of-state tuition: $50,263
Room/board/expenses: $20,926
Percent receiving grants: 37%
Average student indebtedness at graduation: $145,196
Enrollment: 658
men: 59%; women: 41%; minorities: 19%; underrepresented minorities: 6%; in state: 93%
Acceptance rate: 15%
Average MCAT: 10.0
Average GPA: 3.74
Most popular undergraduate majors: biological sciences: 37%; physical sciences: 26%; nonsciences: 20%; other: 17%
Percent of graduates entering primary-care specialties: 39.4%

OREGON

Oregon Health and Science University

3181 S.W. Sam Jackson Park Road, L102
Portland, OR 97239-3098
http://www.ohsu.edu/xd
Public
Admissions: (503) 494-2998
Financial aid: (503) 494-7800
Application deadline: 10/15
In-state tuition: $39,919
Out-of-state tuition: $54,859
Room/board/expenses: $19,500
Percent receiving grants: 67%
Average student indebtedness at graduation: $182,226
Enrollment: 522
men: 47%; women: 53%; minorities: 24%; underrepresented minorities: 11%; in state: 70%
Acceptance rate: 5%
Average MCAT: 10.5
Average GPA: 3.66
Most popular undergraduate majors: biological sciences: 30%; physical sciences: 18%; nonsciences: 24%; other: 28%
Percent of graduates entering primary-care specialties: 52.0%

PENNSYLVANIA

Drexel University

2900 Queen Lane
Philadelphia, PA 19129
http://www.drexelmed.edu
Private
Admissions: (215) 991-8202
E-mail: Medadmis@drexel.edu
Financial aid: (215) 991-8210
Application deadline: 12/01
Tuition: $49,506
Room/board/expenses: $15,500
Percent receiving grants: 27%
Average student indebtedness at graduation: $201,651
Enrollment: 1,080
men: 50%; women: 50%; minorities: 45%; underrepresented minorities: 11%; in state: 32%
Acceptance rate: 5%
Average MCAT: 10.1
Average GPA: 3.57
Most popular undergraduate majors: biological sciences: N/A; physical sciences: N/A; nonsciences: N/A; other: N/A
Percent of graduates entering primary-care specialties: 40.5%

Jefferson Medical College

1025 Walnut Street, Room 100
Philadelphia, PA 19107-5083
http://www.tju.edu
Private
Admissions: (215) 955-6983
E-mail: jmc.admissions@jefferson.edu
Financial aid: (215) 955-2867
Application deadline: 11/15
Tuition: $50,936
Room/board/expenses: $16,698
Percent receiving grants: 47%
Average student indebtedness at graduation: $170,179
Enrollment: 1,053
men: 49%; women: 51%; minorities: 34%; underrepresented minorities: 8%; in state: 47%
Acceptance rate: 5%
Average MCAT: 10.7
Average GPA: 3.69
Most popular undergraduate majors: biological sciences: 40%; physical sciences: 14%; nonsciences: 8%; other: 38%

Percent of graduates entering primary-care specialties: 38.3%

Pennsylvania State University College of Medicine[1]

500 University Drive
Hershey, PA 17033
http://www.hmc.psu.edu
Public
Admissions: (717) 531-8755
E-mail: StudentAffairs@hmc.psu.edu
Financial aid: (717) 531-4103
Tuition: N/A
Room/board/expenses: N/A
Enrollment: N/A

Temple University

3500 N. Broad Street
MERB 1140
Philadelphia, PA 19140
http://www.temple.edu/medicine
Private
Admissions: (215) 707-4010
E-mail: medadmissions@temple.edu
Financial aid: (215) 707-2667
Application deadline: 12/15
Tuition: $44,404
Room/board/expenses: $13,180
Percent receiving grants: 45%
Average student indebtedness at graduation: $208,122
Enrollment: 805
men: 54%; women: 46%; minorities: 35%; underrepresented minorities: 15%; in state: 51%
Acceptance rate: 5%
Average MCAT: 10.4
Average GPA: 3.68
Most popular undergraduate majors: biological sciences: 47%; physical sciences: 21%; nonsciences: 20%; other: 12%
Percent of graduates entering primary-care specialties: 41.0%

University of Pennsylvania (Perelman)

237 John Morgan Building
3620 Hamilton Walk
Philadelphia, PA 19104-6055
http://www.med.upenn.edu
Private
Admissions: (215) 898-8001
E-mail: admiss@mail.med.upenn.edu
Financial aid: (215) 573-3423
Application deadline: 10/15
Tuition: $50,746
Room/board/expenses: $19,510
Percent receiving grants: 67%
Average student indebtedness at graduation: $127,725
Enrollment: 646
men: 51%; women: 49%; minorities: 41%; underrepresented minorities: 23%; in state: 30%
Acceptance rate: 6%
Average MCAT: 12.3
Average GPA: 3.82
Most popular undergraduate majors: biological sciences: 46%; physical sciences: 10%; nonsciences: 20%; other: 24%
Percent of graduates entering primary-care specialties: 37.0%

University of Pittsburgh

401 Scaife Hall
Pittsburgh, PA 15261
http://www.medschool.pitt.edu
Public
Admissions: (412) 648-9891
E-mail: admissions@medschool.pitt.edu
Financial aid: (412) 648-9891
Application deadline: 10/15
In-state tuition: $45,509
Out-of-state tuition: $46,629
Room/board/expenses: $15,795
Percent receiving grants: 62%
Average student indebtedness at graduation: $136,947
Enrollment: 591
men: 53%; women: 47%; minorities: 54%; underrepresented minorities: 18%; in state: 25%
Acceptance rate: 8%
Average MCAT: 11.7
Average GPA: 3.74
Most popular undergraduate majors: biological sciences: 41%; physical sciences: 18%; nonsciences: 12%; other: 29%
Percent of graduates entering primary-care specialties: 38.0%

PUERTO RICO

Ponce School of Medicine[1]

PO Box 7004
Ponce, PR 00732
http://www.psm.edu
Private
Admissions: (787) 840-2575
E-mail: admissions@psm.edu
Financial aid: (787) 840-2575
Tuition: N/A
Room/board/expenses: N/A
Enrollment: N/A

San Juan Bautista School of Medicine[1]

PO Box 4968
Caguas, PR 00726-4968
http://www.sanjuanbautista.edu
Private
Admissions: (787) 743-3038
E-mail: admissions@sanjuanbautista.edu
Financial aid: (787) 743-3038
Tuition: N/A
Room/board/expenses: N/A
Enrollment: N/A

Universidad Central del Caribe[1]

PO Box 60-327
Bayamon, PR 00960-6032
http://www.uccaribe.edu
Private
Admissions: (787) 740-1611
E-mail: icordero@uccaribe.edu
Financial aid: (787) 740-1611
Tuition: N/A
Room/board/expenses: N/A
Enrollment: N/A

University of Puerto Rico School of Medicine[1]

PO Box 365067
San Juan, PR 00936-5067
http://medweb.rcm.upr.edu/
Public
Admissions: (787) 758-2525
E-mail: marrivera@rcm.upr.edu
Financial aid: (787) 758-2525
Tuition: N/A
Room/board/expenses: N/A
Enrollment: N/A

RHODE ISLAND

Brown University (Alpert)
222 Richmond Street, Box G-M
Providence, RI 02912-9706
http://med.brown.edu
Private
Admissions: (401) 863-2149
E-mail: medschool_admissions@
brown.edu
Financial aid: (401) 863-1142
Application deadline: 11/01
Tuition: $51,137
Room/board/expenses: $18,115
Percent receiving grants: 53%
Average student indebtedness at
graduation: $122,554
Enrollment: 452
men: 45%; women: 55%; minori-
ties: 50%; underrepresented
minorities: 26%; in state: 6%
Acceptance rate: 3%
Average MCAT: 10.9
Average GPA: 3.68
Most popular undergraduate
majors: biological sciences: 42%;
physical sciences: 10%;
nonsciences: 37%; other: 12%
Percent of graduates entering
primary-care specialties: 46.9%

SOUTH CAROLINA

Medical University of South Carolina
96 Jonathan Lucas St
Suite 601
Charleston, SC 29425
http://www.musc.edu/com1
Public
Admissions: (843) 792-2055
E-mail: taylorwl@musc.edu
Financial aid: (843) 792-2536
Application deadline: 12/01
In-state tuition: $37,911
Out-of-state tuition: $64,366
Room/board/expenses: $13,340
Percent receiving grants: 34%
Average student indebtedness at
graduation: $157,785
Enrollment: 706
men: 56%; women: 44%; minori-
ties: 28%; underrepresented
minorities: 18%; in state: 86%
Acceptance rate: 11%
Average MCAT: 9.9
Average GPA: 3.66
Most popular undergraduate
majors: biological sciences: 47%;
physical sciences: 13%;
nonsciences: 6%; other: 34%
Percent of graduates entering
primary-care specialties: 39.6%

University of South Carolina
6311 Garners Ferry Road
Columbia, SC 29208
http://www.med.sc.edu
Public
Admissions: (803) 216-3625
E-mail:
jeanette.ford@uscmed.sc.edu
Financial aid: (803) 216-3629
Application deadline: 12/01
In-state tuition: $34,888
Out-of-state tuition: $76,400
Room/board/expenses: $13,310
Percent receiving grants: 26%
Average student indebtedness at
graduation: $149,298
Enrollment: 358
men: 51%; women: 49%; minori-
ties: 18%; underrepresented
minorities: 7%; in state: 94%
Acceptance rate: 6%
Average MCAT: 9.3

Average GPA: 3.70
Most popular undergraduate
majors: biological sciences: 59%;
physical sciences: 28%;
nonsciences: 2%; other: 11%
Percent of graduates entering
primary-care specialties: 49.5%

SOUTH DAKOTA

University of South Dakota (Sanford)
1400 W. 22nd Street
Sioux Falls, SD 57105
http://www.usd.edu/med/md
Public
Admissions: (605) 677-6886
E-mail: md@usd.edu
Financial aid: (605) 677-5112
Application deadline: 11/15
In-state tuition: $28,646
Out-of-state tuition: $60,164
Room/board/expenses: $16,556
Percent receiving grants: 83%
Average student indebtedness at
graduation: $130,568
Enrollment: 220
men: 59%; women: 41%; minori-
ties: 5%; underrepresented
minorities: 4%; in state: 90%
Acceptance rate: 14%
Average MCAT: 9.8
Average GPA: 3.80
Most popular undergraduate
majors: biological sciences: 38%;
physical sciences: 14%;
nonsciences: 29%; other: 20%
Percent of graduates entering
primary-care specialties: 37.2%

TENNESSEE

East Tennessee State University (Quillen)
PO Box 70694
Johnson City, TN 37614
http://www.etsu.edu/com
Public
Admissions: (423) 439-2033
E-mail: sacom@etsu.edu
Financial aid: (423) 439-2035
Application deadline: 11/15
In-state tuition: $31,135
Out-of-state tuition: $59,677
Room/board/expenses: $10,821
Average student indebtedness at
graduation: $143,689
Enrollment: 278
men: 56%; women: 44%; minori-
ties: 17%; underrepresented
minorities: 6%; in state: 94%
Acceptance rate: 6%
Average MCAT: 9.4
Average GPA: 3.69
Most popular undergraduate
majors: biological sciences: 35%;
physical sciences: 38%;
nonsciences: 15%; other: 12%
Percent of graduates entering
primary-care specialties: 45.1%

Meharry Medical College[1]
1005 D. B. Todd Jr. Boulevard
Nashville, TN 37208
http://www.mmc.edu
Private
Admissions: (615) 327-6223
E-mail: amosley@mmc.edu
Financial aid: (615) 327-6826
Tuition: N/A
Room/board/expenses: N/A
Enrollment: N/A

University of Tennessee Health Science Center
910 Madison Avenue, Suite 1002
Memphis, TN 38163
http://www.uthsc.edu/Medicine/
Public
Admissions: (901) 448-5559
E-mail: diharris@uthsc.edu
Financial aid: (901) 448-5568
Application deadline: 11/15
In-state tuition: $35,347
Out-of-state tuition: $66,207
Room/board/expenses: $21,516
Percent receiving grants: 41%
Average student indebtedness at
graduation: $130,979
Enrollment: 658
men: 62%; women: 38%; minori-
ties: 24%; underrepresented
minorities: 14%; in state: 95%
Acceptance rate: 17%
Average MCAT: 10.0
Average GPA: 3.68
Most popular undergraduate
majors: biological sciences: 39%;
physical sciences: 20%;
nonsciences: 15%; other: 26%
Percent of graduates entering
primary-care specialties: 54.3%

Vanderbilt University
21st Avenue S
and Garland Avenue
Nashville, TN 37232-2104
http://www.
mc.vanderbilt.edu/medschool/
Private
Admissions: (615) 322-2145
E-mail:
vusmadmissions@vanderbilt.edu
Financial aid: (615) 343-6310
Application deadline: 11/01
Tuition: $46,316
Room/board/expenses: $17,787
Percent receiving grants: 83%
Average student indebtedness at
graduation: $127,674
Enrollment: 444
men: 48%; women: 52%; minori-
ties: 42%; underrepresented
minorities: 13%; in state: 12%
Acceptance rate: 5%
Average MCAT: 11.6
Average GPA: 3.78
Most popular undergraduate
majors: biological sciences: 48%;
physical sciences: 18%;
nonsciences: 3%; other: 31%
Percent of graduates entering
primary-care specialties: 36.3%

TEXAS

Baylor College of Medicine
1 Baylor Plaza
Houston, TX 77030
http://www.bcm.edu
Private
Admissions: (713) 798-4842
E-mail: admissions@bcm.tmc.edu
Financial aid: (713) 798-4612
Application deadline: 11/01
Tuition: $16,968
Room/board/expenses: $23,784
Percent receiving grants: 56%
Average student indebtedness at
graduation: $94,155
Enrollment: 751
men: 53%; women: 47%; minori-
ties: 58%; underrepresented
minorities: 20%; in state: 86%
Acceptance rate: 6%
Average MCAT: 11.5
Average GPA: 3.83

Most popular undergraduate
majors: biological sciences: 28%;
physical sciences: 34%;
nonsciences: 17%; other: 21%
Percent of graduates entering
primary-care specialties: 42.3%

Texas A&M Health Science Center
8447 State Highway 47
Bryan, TX 77807-3260
http://medicine.tamhsc.edu
Public
Admissions: (979) 436-0237
E-mail: admissions@
medicine.tamhsc.edu
Financial aid: (979) 436-0199
Application deadline: 10/01
In-state tuition: $16,404
Out-of-state tuition: $29,504
Room/board/expenses: $13,543
Percent receiving grants: 50%
Average student indebtedness at
graduation: $104,390
Enrollment: 706
men: 53%; women: 47%; minori-
ties: 43%; underrepresented
minorities: 14%; in state: 95%
Acceptance rate: 19%
Average MCAT: 9.6
Average GPA: 3.65
Most popular undergraduate
majors: biological sciences: 48%;
physical sciences: 16%;
nonsciences: 13%; other: 23%
Percent of graduates entering
primary-care specialties: 41.0%

Texas Tech University Health Sciences Center[1]
3601 Fourth Street
Lubbock, TX 79430
http://www.ttuhsc.edu/SOM/
Public
Admissions: (806) 743-2297
E-mail: somadm@ttuhsc.edu
Financial aid: (806) 743-3025
Tuition: N/A
Room/board/expenses: N/A
Enrollment: N/A

University of Texas Health Science Center–Houston
6431 Fannin Street, MSB G.400
Houston, TX 77030
https://med.uth.edu
Public
Admissions: (713) 500-5116
E-mail: ms.admissions@
uth.tmc.edu
Financial aid: (713) 500-3860
Application deadline: 10/01
In-state tuition: $16,200
Out-of-state tuition: $29,300
Room/board/expenses: $15,370
Percent receiving grants: 25%
Average student indebtedness at
graduation: $112,746
Enrollment: 965
men: 58%; women: 42%; minori-
ties: 36%; underrepresented
minorities: 20%; in state: 94%
Acceptance rate: 12%
Average MCAT: 10.4
Average GPA: 3.77
Most popular undergraduate
majors: biological sciences: 38%;
physical sciences: 28%;
nonsciences: 10%; other: 24%
Percent of graduates entering
primary-care specialties: 31.7%

University of Texas Health Science Center–San Antonio
7703 Floyd Curl Drive
San Antonio, TX 78229-3900
http://som.uthscsa.edu
Public
Admissions: (210) 567-6080
E-mail:
medadmissions@uthscsa.edu
Financial aid: (210) 567-2635
Application deadline: 10/01
In-state tuition: $18,281
Out-of-state tuition: $32,688
Room/board/expenses: N/A
Percent receiving grants: 79%
Average student indebtedness at
graduation: $103,178
Enrollment: 889
men: 52%; women: 48%; minori-
ties: 41%; underrepresented
minorities: 25%; in state: 93%
Acceptance rate: 14%
Average MCAT: 10.1
Average GPA: 3.57
Most popular undergraduate
majors: biological sciences: 48%;
physical sciences: 22%;
nonsciences: 11%; other: 19%
Percent of graduates entering
primary-care specialties: 42.0%

University of Texas Medical Branch–Galveston[1]
301 University Boulevard
Galveston, TX 77555-0133
http://www.
utmb.edu/somstudentaffairs
Public
Admissions: (409) 772-6958
E-mail: tsilva@utmb.edu
Financial aid: (409) 772-4955
Tuition: N/A
Room/board/expenses: N/A
Enrollment: N/A

University of Texas Southwestern Medical Center
5323 Harry Hines Boulevard
Dallas, TX 75390
http://www.utsouthwestern.edu/
Public
Admissions: (214) 648-5617
E-mail: admissions@
utsouthwestern.edu
Financial aid: (214) 648-3606
Application deadline: N/A
In-state tuition: $17,231
Out-of-state tuition: $30,331
Room/board/expenses: $21,184
Percent receiving grants: 61%
Average student indebtedness at
graduation: $107,000
Enrollment: 939
men: 51%; women: 49%; minori-
ties: 51%; underrepresented
minorities: 15%; in state: 87%
Acceptance rate: 10%
Average MCAT: 11.2
Average GPA: 3.84
Most popular undergraduate
majors: biological sciences: 42%;
physical sciences: 28%;
nonsciences: 13%; other: 17%
Percent of graduates entering
primary-care specialties: 41.4%

UTAH

University of Utah
30 N. 1900 E.
Salt Lake City, UT 84132-2101
http://medicine.utah.edu
Public
Admissions: (801) 581-7498
E-mail: deans.admissions@
hsc.utah.edu
Financial aid: (801) 581-6499
Application deadline: 11/01
In-state tuition: $31,404
Out-of-state tuition: $58,610
Room/board/expenses: $9,072
Percent receiving grants: 72%
**Average student indebtedness at
graduation:** $131,607
Enrollment: 326
men: 67%; women: 33%; minorities: 21%; underrepresented minorities: 11%; in state: 83%
Acceptance rate: 9%
Average MCAT: 9.8
Average GPA: 3.68
**Most popular undergraduate
majors:** biological sciences: 40%;
physical sciences: 22%;
nonsciences: 19%; other: 19%
**Percent of graduates entering
primary-care specialties:** 39.2%

VERMONT

University of Vermont
E-126 Given Building
89 Beaumont Avenue
Burlington, VT 05405
http://www.
uvm.edu/medicine/admissions/
Public
Admissions: (802) 656-2154
E-mail: medadmissions@uvm.edu
Financial aid: (802) 656-5700
Application deadline: 11/01
In-state tuition: $31,983
Out-of-state tuition: $54,543
Room/board/expenses: $9,912
Percent receiving grants: 47%
**Average student indebtedness at
graduation:** $154,332
Enrollment: 446
men: 50%; women: 50%; minorities: 25%; underrepresented minorities: 10%; in state: 29%
Acceptance rate: 5%
Average MCAT: 10.1
Average GPA: 3.68
**Most popular undergraduate
majors:** biological sciences: 47%;
physical sciences: 12%;
nonsciences: 26%; other: 15%
**Percent of graduates entering
primary-care specialties:** 39.0%

VIRGINIA

Eastern Virginia Medical School
721 Fairfax Avenue, PO Box 1980
Norfolk, VA 23501-1980
http://www.evms.edu
Public
Admissions: (757) 446-5812
E-mail: mclendm@evms.edu
Financial aid: (757) 446-5804
Application deadline: 11/15
In-state tuition: $30,842
Out-of-state tuition: $57,828
Room/board/expenses: $13,419
Percent receiving grants: 35%
**Average student indebtedness at
graduation:** $185,597
Enrollment: 529
men: 57%; women: 43%; minorities: 36%; underrepresented minorities: 11%; in state: 54%
Acceptance rate: 7%
Average MCAT: 10.2
Average GPA: 3.53
**Most popular undergraduate
majors:** biological sciences: 33%;
physical sciences: 30%;
nonsciences: 17%; other: 20%
**Percent of graduates entering
primary-care specialties:** 52.0%

University of Virginia
PO Box 800793, McKim Hall
Charlottesville, VA 22908-0793
http://www.
medicine.virginia.edu/education/
medical-students/admissions
Public
Admissions: (434) 924-5571
E-mail: medsch-adm@virginia.edu
Financial aid: (434) 924-0033
Application deadline: 11/01
In-state tuition: $43,378
Out-of-state tuition: $52,800
Room/board/expenses: $20,520
Percent receiving grants: 70%
**Average student indebtedness at
graduation:** $118,532
Enrollment: 614
men: 56%; women: 44%; minorities: 42%; underrepresented minorities: 21%; in state: 53%
Acceptance rate: 13%
Average MCAT: 11.5
Average GPA: 3.80
**Most popular undergraduate
majors:** biological sciences: 37%;
physical sciences: 20%;
nonsciences: 17%; other: 26%
**Percent of graduates entering
primary-care specialties:** 40.0%

Virginia Commonwealth University
PO Box 980565
Richmond, VA 23298-0565
http://www.medschool.vcu.edu
Public
Admissions: (804) 828-9629
E-mail: somume@hsc.vcu.edu
Financial aid: (804) 828-4006
Application deadline: 10/15
In-state tuition: $31,146
Out-of-state tuition: $45,492
Room/board/expenses: $14,000
Percent receiving grants: 55%
**Average student indebtedness at
graduation:** $156,849
Enrollment: 801
men: 54%; women: 46%; minorities: 43%; underrepresented minorities: 11%; in state: 57%
Acceptance rate: 6%
Average MCAT: 9.8
Average GPA: 3.63
**Most popular undergraduate
majors:** biological sciences: 41%;
physical sciences: 20%;
nonsciences: 13%; other: 26%
**Percent of graduates entering
primary-care specialties:** 40.3%

WASHINGTON

University of Washington
PO Box 356350
Seattle, WA 98195
http://www.
uwmedicine.org/admissions
Public
Admissions: (206) 543-7212
E-mail: askuwsom@uw.edu
Financial aid: (206) 685-9229
Application deadline: 10/15
In-state tuition: $28,388
Out-of-state tuition: $57,318
Room/board/expenses: $16,077
Percent receiving grants: 73%
**Average student indebtedness at
graduation:** $140,352
Enrollment: 908
men: 46%; women: 54%; minorities: 23%; underrepresented minorities: 8%; in state: 91%
Acceptance rate: 5%
Average MCAT: 10.4
Average GPA: 3.69
**Most popular undergraduate
majors:** biological sciences: 59%;
physical sciences: 8%;
nonsciences: 14%; other: 19%
**Percent of graduates entering
primary-care specialties:** 51.0%

WEST VIRGINIA

Marshall University (Edwards)
1600 Medical Center Drive
Huntington, WV 25701-3655
http://musom.marshall.edu
Public
Admissions: (800) 544-8514
E-mail: warren@marshall.edu
Financial aid: (304) 691-8739
Application deadline: 11/01
In-state tuition: $20,080
Out-of-state tuition: $47,670
Room/board/expenses: $14,500
Percent receiving grants: 65%
**Average student indebtedness at
graduation:** $166,214
Enrollment: 290
men: 62%; women: 38%; minorities: 13%; underrepresented minorities: 4%; in state: 66%
Acceptance rate: 9%
Average MCAT: 9.7
Average GPA: 3.50
**Most popular undergraduate
majors:** biological sciences: 42%;
physical sciences: 27%;
nonsciences: 17%; other: 14%
**Percent of graduates entering
primary-care specialties:** 49.7%

West Virginia University
1 Medical Center Drive
Morgantown, WV 26506-9111
http://medicine.hsc.wvu.edu/
students
Public
Admissions: (304) 293-2408
E-mail: medadmissions@
hsc.wvu.edu
Financial aid: (304) 293-3706
Application deadline: 11/01
In-state tuition: $24,633
Out-of-state tuition: $52,651
Room/board/expenses: $10,344
Percent receiving grants: 55%
**Average student indebtedness at
graduation:** $149,778
Enrollment: 422
men: 61%; women: 39%; minorities: 18%; underrepresented minorities: 4%; in state: 63%
Acceptance rate: 6%
Average MCAT: 9.4
Average GPA: 3.77
**Most popular undergraduate
majors:** biological sciences: 49%;
physical sciences: 22%;
nonsciences: 22%; other: 7%
**Percent of graduates entering
primary-care specialties:** 45.0%

WISCONSIN

Medical College of Wisconsin
8701 Watertown Plank Road
Milwaukee, WI 53226
http://www.mcw.edu/acad/
admission
Private
Admissions: (414) 955-8246
E-mail: medschool@mcw.edu
Financial aid: (414) 955-8208
Application deadline: 11/01
Tuition: $39,315
Room/board/expenses: $9,000
Percent receiving grants: 57%
**Average student indebtedness at
graduation:** $167,671
Enrollment: 810
men: 55%; women: 45%; minorities: 30%; underrepresented minorities: 11%; in state: 41%
Acceptance rate: 7%
Average MCAT: 10.6
Average GPA: 3.76
**Most popular undergraduate
majors:** biological sciences: 57%;
physical sciences: 16%;
nonsciences: 12%; other: 15%
**Percent of graduates entering
primary-care specialties:** 35.0%

University of Wisconsin–Madison
750 Highland Avenue
Madison, WI 53705-2221
http://www.
med.wisc.edu/education
Public
Admissions: (608) 263-4925
E-mail: medadmissions@
med.wisc.edu
Financial aid: (608) 262-3060
Application deadline: 11/01
In-state tuition: $24,918
Out-of-state tuition: $34,815
Room/board/expenses: $19,110
Percent receiving grants: 22%
**Average student indebtedness at
graduation:** $137,753
Enrollment: 701
men: 51%; women: 49%; minorities: 22%; underrepresented minorities: 12%; in state: 75%
Acceptance rate: 6%
Average MCAT: 10.4
Average GPA: 3.74
**Most popular undergraduate
majors:** biological sciences: 48%;
physical sciences: 22%;
nonsciences: 14%; other: 16%
**Percent of graduates entering
primary-care specialties:** 41.7%

NEXT PAGE: INSTITUTIONS THAT GRANT THE DOCTOR OF OSTEOPATHIC MEDICINE (D.O.) DEGREE

INSTITUTIONS THAT GRANT THE DOCTOR OF OSTEOPATHIC MEDICINE (D.O.) DEGREE

ARIZONA

A.T. Still University of Health Sciences–Mesa[1]
5850 E. Still Circle
Mesa, AZ 85206
http://www.atsu.edu
Private
Admissions: (480) 219-6000
Financial aid: N/A
Tuition: N/A
Room/board/expenses: N/A
Enrollment: N/A

Midwestern University[1]
19555 N. 59th Avenue
Glendale, AZ 85308
http://www.midwestern.edu
Private
Admissions: (623) 572-3275
E-mail: admissaz@midwestern.edu
Financial aid: (623) 572-3321
Tuition: N/A
Room/board/expenses: N/A
Enrollment: N/A

CALIFORNIA

Touro University California
1310 Club Drive
Vallejo, CA 94592
http://www.tu.edu
Private
Admissions: (707) 638-5270
E-mail: steven.davis@tu.edu
Financial aid: (707) 638-5280
Application deadline: 03/01
Tuition: $45,250
Room/board/expenses: $30,810
Percent receiving grants: 7%
Average student indebtedness at graduation: $210,000
Enrollment: 540
men: 52%; women: 48%; minorities: N/A; underrepresented minorities: N/A; in state: 71%
Acceptance rate: 7%
Average MCAT: 9.8
Average GPA: 3.44
Most popular undergraduate majors: biological sciences: 50%; physical sciences: 14%; nonsciences: 4%; other: 32%
Percent of graduates entering primary-care specialties: 55.2%

Western University of Health Sciences
309 E. Second Street
Pomona, CA 91766-1854
http://prospective.westernu.edu/index.html
Private
Admissions: (909) 469-5335
E-mail: admissions@westernu.edu
Financial aid: (909) 469-5350
Application deadline: 02/01
Tuition: $49,550
Room/board/expenses: $13,007
Percent receiving grants: 11%
Average student indebtedness at graduation: $218,461
Enrollment: 1,110
men: 55%; women: 45%; minorities: 42%; underrepresented minorities: 6%; in state: 70%
Acceptance rate: 22%
Average MCAT: 9.3
Average GPA: 3.47

Most popular undergraduate majors: biological sciences: 65%; physical sciences: 11%; nonsciences: 18%; other: 6%
Percent of graduates entering primary-care specialties: 50.9%

FLORIDA

Nova Southeastern University
3200 S. University Drive
Fort Lauderdale, FL 33328
http://medicine.nova.edu
Private
Admissions: (954) 262-1101
E-mail: comreply@nova.edu
Financial aid: (954) 262-3380
Application deadline: 01/15
Tuition: $43,520
Room/board/expenses: $22,704
Percent receiving grants: 11%
Average student indebtedness at graduation: $205,118
Enrollment: 968
men: 62%; women: 38%; minorities: 36%; underrepresented minorities: 16%; in state: 45%
Acceptance rate: 14%
Average MCAT: 9.0
Average GPA: 3.43
Most popular undergraduate majors: biological sciences: 58%; physical sciences: 8%; nonsciences: 12%; other: 22%
Percent of graduates entering primary-care specialties: 49.1%

ILLINOIS

Midwestern University[1]
555 31st Street
Downers Grove, IL 60515
http://www.midwestern.edu
Private
Admissions: (630) 515-7200
E-mail: admissil@midwestern.edu
Financial aid: (630) 515-6035
Tuition: N/A
Room/board/expenses: N/A
Enrollment: N/A

IOWA

Des Moines University[1]
3200 Grand Avenue
Des Moines, IA 50312
http://www.dmu.edu
Private
Admissions: (515) 271-1450
E-mail: doadmit@dmu.edu
Financial aid: (515) 271-1470
Tuition: N/A
Room/board/expenses: N/A
Enrollment: N/A

KENTUCKY

University of Pikeville
147 Sycamore Street
Pikeville, KY 41501
http://www.upike.edu
Private
Admissions: (606) 218-5409
E-mail: kycomadmissions@upike.edu
Financial aid: (606) 218-5407
Application deadline: 03/01
Tuition: $37,450
Room/board/expenses: N/A
Percent receiving grants: 35%
Average student indebtedness at graduation: $160,429

Enrollment: 373
men: 53%; women: 47%; minorities: 13%; underrepresented minorities: 5%; in state: 50%
Acceptance rate: 9%
Average MCAT: 7.8
Average GPA: 3.48
Most popular undergraduate majors: biological sciences: 70%; physical sciences: 7%; nonsciences: 7%; other: 16%
Percent of graduates entering primary-care specialties: 69.2%

MAINE

University of New England
11 Hills Beach Road
Biddeford, ME 04005
http://www.une.edu/com/
Private
Admissions: (800) 477-4863
E-mail: unecomadmissions@une.edu
Financial aid: (207) 283-0171
Application deadline: 02/01
Tuition: $49,515
Room/board/expenses: $12,500
Percent receiving grants: 24%
Average student indebtedness at graduation: $231,664
Enrollment: 499
men: 44%; women: 56%; minorities: 11%; underrepresented minorities: 4%; in state: 19%
Acceptance rate: 6%
Average MCAT: 9.4
Average GPA: 3.53
Most popular undergraduate majors: biological sciences: 69%; physical sciences: 9%; nonsciences: 21%; other: 1%
Percent of graduates entering primary-care specialties: 61.0%

MICHIGAN

Michigan State University (College of Osteopathic Medicine)
A308 E. Fee Hall
East Lansing, MI 48824
http://www.com.msu.edu
Public
Admissions: (517) 353-7740
E-mail: com.admissions@hc.msu.edu
Financial aid: (517) 353-5188
Application deadline: 12/01
In-state tuition: $38,647
Out-of-state tuition: $80,536
Room/board/expenses: $17,276
Percent receiving grants: 33%
Average student indebtedness at graduation: $196,379
Enrollment: 1,254
men: 54%; women: 46%; minorities: 22%; underrepresented minorities: 6%; in state: 89%
Acceptance rate: 13%
Average MCAT: 9.1
Average GPA: 3.56
Most popular undergraduate majors: biological sciences: 55%; physical sciences: 7%; nonsciences: 6%; other: 32%
Percent of graduates entering primary-care specialties: 79.4%

MISSOURI

A.T. Still University of Health Sciences–Kirksville[1]
800 W. Jefferson Street
Kirksville, MO 63501
http://www.atsu.edu
Private
Admissions: (866) 626-2878
E-mail: admissions@atsu.edu
Financial aid: (660) 626-2529
Tuition: N/A
Room/board/expenses: N/A
Enrollment: N/A

Kansas City University of Medicine and Biosciences[1]
1750 Independence Avenue
Kansas City, MO 64106-1453
http://www.kcumb.edu/
Private
Admissions: (800) 234-4847
E-mail: admissions@uhs.edu
Financial aid: (816) 283-2000
Tuition: N/A
Room/board/expenses: N/A
Enrollment: N/A

NEW JERSEY

University of Medicine and Dentistry of New Jersey–Stratford
1 Medical Center Drive
Stratford, NJ 08084-1501
http://som.umdnj.edu
Public
Admissions: (856) 566-7050
E-mail: somadm@umdnj.edu
Financial aid: (856) 566-6008
Application deadline: 01/02
In-state tuition: $38,240
Out-of-state tuition: $59,063
Room/board/expenses: $13,850
Average student indebtedness at graduation: $165,724
Enrollment: 597
men: 50%; women: 50%; minorities: 53%; underrepresented minorities: 19%; in state: 94%
Acceptance rate: 8%
Average MCAT: 9.2
Average GPA: 3.61
Most popular undergraduate majors: biological sciences: 48%; physical sciences: 33%; nonsciences: 5%; other: 14%
Percent of graduates entering primary-care specialties: 46.7%

NEW YORK

New York Institute of Technology
Old Westbury
Northern Boulevard
Long Island, NY 11568
http://www.nyit.edu
Private
Admissions: (516) 686-3747
E-mail: rzaika@nyit.edu
Financial aid: (516) 686-7960
Application deadline: 02/01
Tuition: $51,171
Room/board/expenses: N/A
Percent receiving grants: 17%
Average student indebtedness at graduation: $206,493

Enrollment: 1,190
men: 47%; women: 53%; minorities: 45%; underrepresented minorities: 10%; in state: 87%
Acceptance rate: 25%
Average MCAT: 9.4
Average GPA: 3.60
Most popular undergraduate majors: biological sciences: 47%; physical sciences: 23%; nonsciences: 13%; other: 17%
Percent of graduates entering primary-care specialties: 43.0%

Touro College of Osteopathic Medicine[1]
2090 Adam Clayton Powell Boulevard
New York, NY 10027
http://www.touro.edu/med
Private
Admissions: (212) 851-1199
Financial aid: N/A
Tuition: N/A
Room/board/expenses: N/A
Enrollment: N/A

OHIO

Ohio University
Grosvenor and Irvine Halls
Athens, OH 45701
http://www.oucom.ohiou.edu
Public
Admissions: (740) 593-4313
E-mail: ou-hcom@ohio.edu
Financial aid: (740) 593-2158
Application deadline: 02/01
In-state tuition: $29,878
Out-of-state tuition: $42,268
Room/board/expenses: $13,494
Percent receiving grants: 42%
Average student indebtedness at graduation: $174,697
Enrollment: 511
men: 49%; women: 51%; minorities: 23%; underrepresented minorities: 18%; in state: 96%
Acceptance rate: 5%
Average MCAT: 9.0
Average GPA: 3.64
Most popular undergraduate majors: biological sciences: 63%; physical sciences: 15%; nonsciences: 6%; other: 16%
Percent of graduates entering primary-care specialties: 54.0%

OKLAHOMA

Oklahoma State University
1111 W. 17th Street
Tulsa, OK 74107-1898
http://healthsciences.okstate.edu
Public
Admissions: (918) 561-8421
E-mail: sarah.quinten@okstate.edu
Financial aid: (918) 561-1228
Application deadline: 02/01
In-state tuition: $23,275
Out-of-state tuition: $44,719
Room/board/expenses: $11,700
Percent receiving grants: 12%
Average student indebtedness at graduation: $192,271
Enrollment: 385
men: 54%; women: 46%; minorities: 23%; underrepresented minorities: 16%; in state: 91%
Acceptance rate: 21%
Average MCAT: 8.7
Average GPA: 3.62

Most popular undergraduate **majors:** biological sciences: 51%; physical sciences: 20%; nonsciences: 12%; other: 17%
Percent of graduates entering primary-care specialties: 49.0%

PENNSYLVANIA

Lake Erie College of Osteopathic Medicine

1858 W. Grandview Boulevard
Erie, PA 16509
http://www.lecom.edu
Private
Admissions: (814) 866-6641
E-mail: admissions@lecom.edu
Financial aid: (814) 866-6641
Application deadline: 04/01
Tuition: $29,793
Room/board/expenses: $11,250
Percent receiving grants: 37%
Average student indebtedness at graduation: $163,156
Enrollment: 2,166
men: 58%; women: 42%; minorities: 25%; underrepresented minorities: 9%; in state: 35%
Acceptance rate: 7%
Average MCAT: 9.0
Average GPA: 3.47
Most popular undergraduate majors: biological sciences: 57%; physical sciences: 19%; nonsciences: 8%; other: 15%
Percent of graduates entering primary-care specialties: 65.5%

Philadelphia College of Osteopathic Medicine[1]

4170 City Avenue
Philadelphia, PA 19131
http://www.pcom.edu
Private
Admissions: (800) 999-6998
E-mail: admissions@pcom.edu
Financial aid: (215) 871-6170
Tuition: N/A
Room/board/expenses: N/A
Enrollment: N/A

TENNESSEE

Lincoln Memorial University (DeBusk)

6965 Cumberland Gap Parkway
Harrogate, TN 37752
http://www.lmunet.edu/dcom/admissions
Private
Admissions: (800) 325-0900
E-mail: dcomadmissions@lmunet.edu
Financial aid: (423) 869-7107
Application deadline: 03/01
Tuition: $39,245
Room/board/expenses: $13,050
Percent receiving grants: 2%
Average student indebtedness at graduation: $205,124
Enrollment: 697
men: 57%; women: 43%; minorities: 21%; underrepresented minorities: 9%; in state: 31%

Acceptance rate: 13%
Average MCAT: 8.2
Average GPA: 3.43
Most popular undergraduate majors: biological sciences: 50%; physical sciences: 10%; nonsciences: 15%; other: 25%
Percent of graduates entering primary-care specialties: N/A

TEXAS

University of North Texas Health Science Center

3500 Camp Bowie Boulevard
Fort Worth, TX 76107-2699
http://www.hsc.unt.edu
Public
Admissions: (800) 535-8266
E-mail: TCOMAdmissions@unthsc.edu
Financial aid: (800) 346-8266
Application deadline: 10/01
In-state tuition: $16,285
Out-of-state tuition: $31,384
Room/board/expenses: $16,026
Percent receiving grants: 59%
Average student indebtedness at graduation: $129,875
Enrollment: 857
men: 47%; women: 53%; minorities: 43%; underrepresented minorities: 12%; in state: 96%
Acceptance rate: 20%
Average MCAT: 9.2
Average GPA: 3.57

Most popular undergraduate **majors:** biological sciences: 67%; physical sciences: 6%; nonsciences: 9%; other: 18%
Percent of graduates entering primary-care specialties: 67.0%

VIRGINIA

Edward Via College of Osteopathic Medicine–Virginia and Carolinas

2265 Kraft Drive
Blacksburg, VA 24060
http://www.vcom.vt.edu
Private
Admissions: (540) 231-6138
E-mail: admissions@vcom.vt.edu
Financial aid: (540) 231-6021
Application deadline: 02/01
Tuition: $39,530
Room/board/expenses: N/A
Percent receiving grants: 32%
Enrollment: 1,067
men: 51%; women: 49%; minorities: 29%; underrepresented minorities: 20%; in state: 46%
Acceptance rate: 11%
Average MCAT: 8.2
Average GPA: 3.60
Most popular undergraduate majors: biological sciences: 60%; physical sciences: 12%; nonsciences: 8%; other: 20%
Percent of graduates entering primary-care specialties: 59.0%

WEST VIRGINIA

West Virginia School of Osteopathic Medicine

400 N. Lee Street
Lewisburg, WV 24901
http://www.wvsom.edu
Public
Admissions: (800) 356-7836
E-mail: admissions@wvsom.edu
Financial aid: (800) 356-7836
Application deadline: 02/15
In-state tuition: $20,950
Out-of-state tuition: $50,950
Room/board/expenses: $14,980
Percent receiving grants: 17%
Average student indebtedness at graduation: $242,742
Enrollment: 837
men: 54%; women: 46%; minorities: 23%; underrepresented minorities: 4%; in state: 30%
Acceptance rate: 10%
Average MCAT: 8.0
Average GPA: 3.40
Most popular undergraduate majors: biological sciences: 57%; physical sciences: 13%; nonsciences: 8%; other: 20%
Percent of graduates entering primary-care specialties: 67.6%

BUSINESS

ENGINEERING

OSTEOPATHIC MEDICINE